The Business Environment
Third Edition

PEARSON CUSTOM PUBLISHING

The Business Environment
Third Edition

Compiled from:

The Business Environment
Sixth Edition
by Ian Worthington and Chris Britton

Essentials of Economics
Fourth Edition
by John Sloman

The Business Environment
Fifth Edition
by Ian Worthington and Chris Britton

ALWAYS LEARNING   PEARSON

Harlow, England • London • New York • Boston • San Francisco • Toronto • Sydney • Auckland • Singapore • Hong Kong
Tokyo • Seoul • Taipei • New Delhi • Cape Town • Sao Paulo • Mexico City • Madrid • Amsterdam • Munich • Paris • Milan

Pearson Education Limited
Edinburgh Gate
Harlow
Essex CM20 2JE

And associated companies throughout the world

Visit us on the World Wide Web at:
www.pearsoned.co.uk

First published 2006
This Custom Book Edition © Pearson Education Limited 2012

Compiled from:

The Business Environment
Sixth Edition
Ian Worthington and Chris Britton
ISBN 978 0 27371 675 4
Copyright © Ian Worthington and Chris Britton 1994, 1997, 2000, 2003, 2006, 2009

Essentials of Economics
Fourth Edition
John Sloman
ISBN 978 0 273 70881 0
Copyright © John Sloman 1998
Copyright © Pearson Education 2001, 2004, 2007

The Business Environment
Fifth Edition
Ian Worthington and Chris Britton
ISBN 978 0 273 70424 9
Copyright © Ian Worthington and Chris Britton 1994, 1997, 2000, 2003, 2006

ISBN 978 1 78016 121 1

Printed and bound in Great Britain by Henry Ling Limited at the Dorset Press,
Dorchester, DT1 1HD.

Contents

Preface

This book provides a range of material, including study help, to assist in our understanding of business activity and its environment. Relevant business and economic concepts, with an emphasis on external influences and current issues, are categorised into the ten subject areas of:

- The Business Environment: A systems approach; the transformation system; internal and external environments; PESTLE analysis; monitoring change.

- The Macroeconomic Environment: Economic systems; how societies allocate (scarce) resources; the economic context of business; the circular flow of income; the business cycle; output; unemployment; inflation; macroeconomic policy.

- The Microeconomic Environment: The market mechanism; demand and supply; the notion of equilibrium.

- Market Structures & Analysis of the Business Environment: Market structures of perfect competition, monopoly, oligopoly and monopolistic competition; Porter's 5 forces; Structure-Conduct-Performance analysis; mergers and acquisitions; firm size.

- Demand, Elasticity & Revenue: Principles that influence business decision making.

- Costs & Revenues: The short and the long run; revenue and profit maximisation.

- Balance of Payments, Exchange Rates and EMU: The balance of payments; exchange rate regimes; fixed versus flexible exchange rates; European Monetary Union and arguments for/against joining the Euro Zone.

- Government Intervention and Business: Market failures; government intervention; privatisation policy; competition policy.

- Corporate Responsibility and the Environment: Stakeholder theory; social responsibility; ethical business.

- The Technological Environment: e-business; business models; benefits, opportunities and limitations.

Learning Outcomes

Upon reading and engaging with the material in this book students should be able to:

- Explain how business organisations function within, and are affected by, their internal and external environments;

- Compare and contrast the significance for business organisations of diverse factors within their environment;

- Demonstrate an understanding of the market mechanism and different market structures and exemplify their use in the study of business organisations;

- Outline and assess the role of government in market economies;

- Communicate information and concepts effectively through the production of written materials.

PART ONE
The Business Environment

Chapter 1
Business Organisations:
The External Environment

Business organisations: the external environment

Ian Worthington

Business organisations differ in many ways, but they also have a common feature: the transformation of inputs into output. This transformation process takes place against a background of external influences which affect the firm and its activities. This external environment is complex, volatile and interactive, but it cannot be ignored in any meaningful analysis of business activity.

Learning outcomes

Having read this chapter you should be able to:

- indicate the basic features of business activity
- portray the business organisation as a system interacting with its environment
- demonstrate the range and complexity of the external influences on business activity
- identify the central themes inherent in the study of the business environment

Key terms

Environmental change
External environment
General (or contextual)
  environment

Immediate (or operational)
  environment
Inputs
Open system

Outputs
PESTLE analysis
Transformation system

Introduction

Business activity is a fundamental and universal feature of human existence and yet the concept of 'business' is difficult to define with any degree of precision. Dictionary definitions tend to describe it as being concerned with buying and selling or with trade and commerce, or the concern of profit-making organisations, and clearly all of these would come within the accepted view of business. Such a restricted view, however, would exclude large parts of the work of government and its agencies and the activities of non-profit-making organisations – a perspective it would be hard to sustain in a climate in which business methods, skills, attitudes and objectives are being increasingly adopted by these organisations. It is this broader view of business and its activities which is adopted below and which forms the focus of an investigation into the business environment.

The business organisation and its environment

A model of business activity

Most business activity takes place within an organisational context and even a cursory investigation of the business world reveals the wide variety of organisations involved, ranging from the small local supplier of a single good or service to the multibillion dollar international or multinational corporation producing and trading on a global scale. Given this rich organisational diversity, most observers of the business scene tend to differentiate between organisations in terms of their size, type of product and/or market, methods of finance, scale of operations, legal status and so on. Nissan, for example, would be characterised as a major multinational car producer and distributor trading on world markets, while a local builder is likely to be seen as a small business operating at a local level with a limited market and relatively restricted turnover.

 Further information on Nissan is available at *www.nissan-global.com*
The Nissan UK website address is *www.nissan.co.uk*

While such distinctions are both legitimate and informative, they can conceal the fact that all business organisations are ultimately involved in the same basic activity, namely, the transformation of **inputs** (resources) into **outputs** (goods or services). This process is illustrated in Figure 1.1.

In essence, all organisations acquire resources – including labour, premises, technology, finance, materials – and transform these resources into the goods or services required by their customers. While the type, amount and combination of resources will vary according to the needs of each organisation and may also vary over time, the simple process described above is common to all types of business organisation and provides a useful starting-point for investigating business activity and the environment in which it takes place.

A more detailed analysis of business resources and those internal aspects of organisations which help to transform inputs into output can be found in Chapters 2 and 7 below. The need, here, is simply to appreciate the idea of the firm as a **transformation**

Figure 1.1   The business organisation as a transformation system

Inputs

Land, premises
Materials
Labour → BUSINESS
Technology → ORGANISATIONS
Finance →
Managerial skills, etc.

Outputs

Goods
Services
Ideas
Information, etc.

- - - - → Consumption - - - -

system and to recognise that in producing and selling output most organisations hope to earn sufficient revenue to allow them to maintain and replenish their resources, thus permitting them to produce further output which in turn produces further inputs. In short, inputs help to create output and output creates inputs. Moreover, the output of one organisation may represent an input for another, as in the case of the firm producing capital equipment or basic materials or information or ideas. This interrelationship between business organisations is just one example of the complex and integrated nature of business activity and it helps to highlight the fact that the fortunes of any single business organisation are invariably linked with those of another or others – a point clearly illustrated in many of the examples cited in the text.

The firm in its environment

The simple model of business activity described above is based on the systems approach to management (see Chapter 2). One of the benefits of this approach is that it stresses that organisations are entities made up of interrelated parts which are intertwined with the outside world – the **external environment** in systems language. This environment comprises a wide range of influences – economic, demographic, social, political, legal, technological, etc. – which affect business activity in a variety of ways and which can impinge not only on the transformation process itself, but also on the process of resource acquisition and on the creation and consumption of output. This idea of the firm in its environment is illustrated in Figure 1.2.

Figure 1.2   The firm in its environment

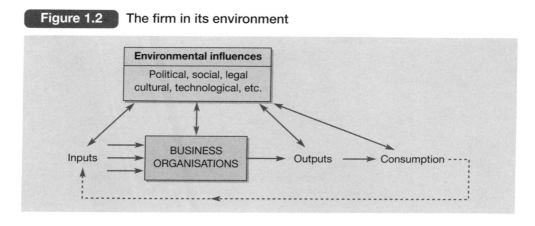

Figure 1.3 Two levels of environment

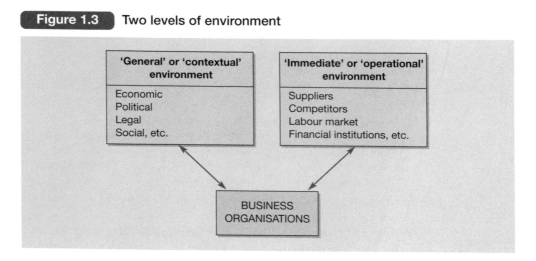

In examining the business environment, a useful distinction can be made between those external factors which tend to have a more immediate effect on the day-to-day operations of a firm and those which tend to have a more general influence. Figure 1.3 makes this distinction.

The **immediate** or **operational environment** for most firms includes suppliers, competitors, labour markets, financial institutions and customers, and may also include trading organisations, trade unions and possibly a parent company. In contrast the **general** or **contextual environment** comprises those macroenvironmental factors such as economic, political, socio-cultural, technological, legal and ethical influences on business which affect a wide variety of businesses and which can emanate not only from local and national sources but also from international and supranational developments.

This type of analysis can also be extended to the different functional areas of an organisation's activities such as marketing or personnel or production or finance, as illustrated in Figure 1.4. Such an analysis can be seen to be useful in at least two ways. First, it emphasises the influence of external factors on specific activities within the firm and in doing so underlines the importance of the interface between the internal and external environments. Second, by drawing attention to this interface, it highlights the fact that, while business organisations are often able to exercise some degree of control over their internal activities and processes, it is often very difficult, if not impossible, to control the external environment in which they operate.

Figure 1.4 Environmental influences on a firm's marketing system

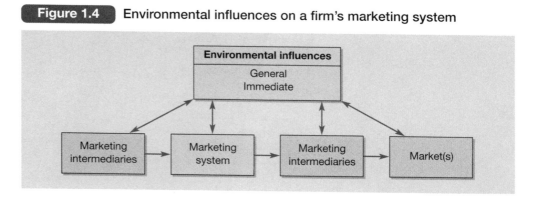

The general or contextual environment

While the external factors referred to above form the subject-matter of the rest of the book, it is useful at this point to gain an overview of the business environment by highlighting some of the key environmental influences on business activity. In keeping with the distinction made between general and more immediate influences, these are discussed separately below. In this section we examine what are frequently referred to as the 'PESTLE' factors (i.e. political, economic, socio-cultural, technological, legal and ethical influences). A **'PESTLE'** (or **'PEST'**) **analysis** can be used to analyse a firm's current and future environment as part of the strategic management process (see Chapter 18).

The political environment

A number of aspects of the political environment clearly impinge on business activity. These range from general questions concerning the nature of the political system and its institutions and processes (Chapter 4), to the more specific questions relating to government involvement in the working of the economy (Chapter 5) and its attempts to influence market structure and behaviour (Chapters 11, 15, 17). Government activities, both directly and indirectly, influence business activity and government can be seen as the biggest business enterprise at national or local level (Chapter 13). Given the trend towards the globalisation of markets (Chapters 3 and 16) and the existence of international trading organisations and blocs, international politico-economic influences on business activity represent one key feature of the business environment (Chapters 4, 7 and 16). Another is the influence of public, as well as political, opinion in areas such as environmental policy and corporate responsibility (Chapter 9).

The economic environment

The distinction made between the political and economic environment – and, for that matter, the legal environment – is somewhat arbitrary. Government, as indicated above, plays a major role in the economy at both national and local level (Chapters 5 and 13) and its activities help to influence both the demand and supply side (e.g. see Chapter 14). Nevertheless there are a number of other economic aspects related to business activity which are worthy of consideration. These include various structural aspects of both firms and markets (Chapters 10, 11, 12 and 15) and a comparison of economic theory and practice (e.g. Chapters 14, 15 and 16).

mini case   A healthy business?

Even the world's largest and most powerful business organisations are affected by a changing business environment, a point well illustrated by the problems faced by General Motors (GM), in recent years. In the first quarter of 2005, GM reported losses of over $1 billion in North America and subsequently announced its intention to close some of its plants and cut 25–30 000 jobs over the next three years from its North American operations. This plan followed in the wake of its job-cutting exercise in GM Europe which was ultimately expected to reduce its European workforce by around 12 000 jobs, most of them in Germany.

GM's decline in fortunes was attributed to a number of important developments: a falling market share, problems with its product mix, rising raw material prices and the soaring costs of providing healthcare for its US workers (see e.g. *Guardian*, 8 June 2005, p.19). According to the company's Chief Executive, the latter was the most challenging problem facing the business, with the cost of the healthcare programme estimated to account for around $1500 on the price of every vehicle sold.

By slimming down its operations and running its remaining plants at full capacity, GM hoped to address some of the demand (i.e. sales) and supply side (i.e. costs) problems it had been experiencing. The company has also taken steps to make its offering more attractive to customers by increasing its spending on new vehicles and by improving its marketing effort in the hope that this will arrest the decline in market share.

As far as the healthcare programme is concerned, this is likely to prove more of an intractable problem for the organisation's management, particularly as the unions have resisted any attempt to shift some of the burden on to the employees. It is worth noting that the burgeoning cost of healthcare provision is by no means unique to GM, but is one facing a large number of US corporations. Indeed, according to some observers, the healthcare burden faced by corporate America is so substantial that it threatens not only the future prospects of individual businesses but also the long-term strength of the American economy and its international competitiveness.

In the period since the last edition was published, GM's position does not appear to have changed significantly for the better. Talks with Nissan and Renault on forming a global manufacturing alliance – designed to drive down costs – were abandoned in late 2006. By early 2007 Toyota had overtaken GM as the world's leading supplier of cars. Like Ford, GM has continued to be affected by the switch in consumer tastes away from SUVs and pick-up trucks and towards smaller, cheaper, more environmentally friendly vehicles. Rising petrol prices, the slow-down in the US economy and unfavourable exchange rates have not helped GM and the company has found it necessary to invest in new fuel-efficient models (including hybrids) to meet the challenge from its rivals.

On the cost side, it also announced plans in mid-2008 to make savings of around $15 billion to cope with plummeting car sales which have been affected by the global financial crisis. Among the measures announced were a pay freeze for its workers, a programme of voluntary redundancies, scrapping of health insurance for many of its retired workers and a suspension of dividend payments to shareholders.

The social, cultural and demographic environment

Both demand and supply are influenced by social, cultural and demographic factors. Cultural factors, for example, may affect the type of products being produced or sold, the markets they are sold in, the price at which they are sold and a range of other variables. People are a key organisational resource and a fundamental part of the market for goods and services. Accordingly, socio-cultural influences and developments have an important effect on business operations, as do demographic changes (Chapters 6 and 7).

The technological environment

Technology is both an input and an output of business organisations as well as being an environmental influence on them. Investment in technology and innovation is frequently seen as a key to the success of an enterprise and has been used to explain differences in the relative competitiveness of different countries (Chapter 7). It has also been responsible for significant developments in the internal organisation of businesses in the markets for economic resources.

The legal environment

Businesses operate within a framework of law which has a significant impact on various aspects of their existence. Laws usually govern, among other things, the status of the organisation (Chapter 10), its relationship with its customers and suppliers and certain internal procedures and activities (Chapter 8). They may also influence market structures and behaviour (e.g. Chapters 15 and 17). Since laws emanate from government (including supranational governments) and from the judgments of the courts, some understanding of the relevant institutions and processes is desirable (e.g. Chapters 4 and 8).

The ethical and ecological environment

Ethical considerations have become an increasingly important influence on business behaviour, particularly among the larger, more high profile companies. One area where this has been manifest is in the demand for firms to act in a more socially responsible way and to consider the impact they might have on people, their communities and the natural environment (Chapter 9).

The immediate or operational environment

Resources and resource markets

An organisation's need for resources makes it dependent to a large degree on the suppliers of those resources, some of whom operate in markets which are structured to a considerable extent (e.g. Chapter 7). Some aspects of the operation of resource markets or indeed the activities of an individual supplier can have a fundamental impact on an organisation's success and upon the way in which it structures its internal procedures and processes. By the same token, the success of suppliers is often intimately connected with the decisions and/or fortunes of their customers. While some organisations may seek to gain an advantage in price, quality or delivery by purchasing resources from overseas, such a decision can engender a degree of uncertainty, particularly where exchange rates are free rather than fixed (Chapter 16). Equally, organisations may face uncertainty and change in the domestic markets for resources as a result of factors as varied as technological change, government intervention or public opinion (e.g. conservation issues).

Customers

Customers are vital to all organisations and the ability both to identify and to meet consumer needs is seen as one of the keys to organisational survival and prosperity – a point not overlooked by politicians, who are increasingly using business techniques to attract the support of the electorate. This idea of consumer sovereignty – where resources are allocated to produce output to satisfy customer demands – is a central tenet of the market economy (Chapter 5) and is part of an ideology whose influence has become all pervasive in recent years. Understanding the many factors affecting both individual and market demand, and the ways in which firms organise themselves to satisfy that demand is a vital component of a business environment that is increasingly market led.

Competitors

Competition – both direct and indirect – is an important part of the context in which many firms operate and is a factor equally applicable to the input as well as the output side of business. The effects of competition, whether from domestic organisations or from overseas firms (e.g. see Chapter 16), is significant at the macro as well as the micro level and its influence can be seen in the changing structures of many advanced industrial economies (Chapter 12). How firms respond to these competitive challenges (e.g. Chapter 11) and the attitudes of governments to anti-competitive practices (Chapter 17) is a legitimate area of concern for students of business.

Analysing the business environment

In a subject as all encompassing as the business environment it is possible to identify numerous approaches to the organisation of the material. One obvious solution would be to examine the various factors mentioned above, devoting separate chapters to each of the environmental influences and discussing their impact on business organisations. While this solution has much to recommend it – not least of which is its simplicity – the approach adopted below is based on the grouping of environmental influences into three main areas, in the belief that this helps to focus attention on key aspects of the business world, notably contexts, firms and their markets.

mini case   The people's car

Changing economic circumstances (e.g. oil price rises, growth or recession) provide 'opportunities' as well as 'threats' for business organisations, a point well illustrated by the Indian car manufacturer Tata Motors. While many of the world's leading car producers continue to face tough economic circumstances, Tata has been able to capitalise on the growth in the Indian economy and a potentially huge, untapped domestic market by producing the world's cheapest car, the Nano, which is scheduled to go on sale in 2008 with a price tag of 100,000 rupees (around £1260). The Nano is less than half the price of its rivals, making it affordable to the millions of Indian citizens who currently buy motorbikes and scooters. Its price has been kept low by replacing some of the steel parts with plastic and by swapping traditional welding technology with hi-tech glue.

Tata Motors is a subsidiary of one of India's largest conglomerates, which includes the Anglo-Dutch steelmaker Corus and Tetley Tea. In 2008, the group acquired the Land Rover and Jaguar marques from Ford as part of a longer-term plan to become an international car company. Tata also has plans to bring an upgraded version of the Nano to Europe in what some observers see as a reflection of the global shift in wealth from the developed world to the developing one.

All has not been plain sailing, however, for the Indian car producer. Violent protests by farmers in the state of West Bengal – whose land had been acquired for the Tata factory – looks likely to hold up production of the Nano. At the time of writing (September 2008), the company was threatening to move production to another state if the protests did not cease.

web link   The website for Tata Motors is *www.tatamotors.com*

Following a basic introduction to the idea of the 'business environment', in Part Two consideration is given to the political, economic, social, cultural, demographic, legal, ethical and ecological contexts within which businesses function. In addition to examining the influence of political and economic systems, institutions and processes on the conduct of business, this section focuses on the macroeconomic environment and on those broad social influences which affect both consumers and organisations alike. The legal system and the influence of law in a number of critical areas of business activity is also a primary concern and one which has links with Part Three.

In Part Three, attention is focused on three central structural aspects: legal structure, size structure and industrial structure. The chapter on legal structure examines the impact of different legal definitions on a firm's operations and considers possible variations in organisational goals based on legal and other influences. The focus then shifts to how differences in size can affect the organisation (e.g. access to capital, economies of scale) and to an examination of how changes in scale and/or direction can occur, including the role of government in assisting small-business development and growth. One of the consequences of changes in the component elements of the economy is its effect on the overall structure of industry and commerce – a subject which helps to highlight the impact of international competition on the economic structure of many advanced industrial economies. Since government is a key actor in the economy, the section concludes with an analysis of government involvement in business and in particular its influence on the supply as well as the demand side of the economy at both national and local level.

In Part Four, the aim is to compare theory with practice by examining issues such as pricing, market structure and foreign trade. The analysis of price theory illustrates the degree to which the theoretical models of economists shed light on the operation of business in the 'real' world. Similarly, by analysing basic models of market structure, it is possible to gain an understanding of the effects of competition on a firm's behaviour and to appreciate the significance of both price and non-price decisions in the operation of markets.

The analysis continues with an examination of external markets and the role of government in influencing both the structure and operation of the marketplace. The chapter on international markets looks at the theoretical basis of trade and the development of overseas markets in practice, particularly in the context of recent institutional, economic and financial developments (e.g. the Single Market, globalisation, the Euro). The section concludes with an investigation of the rationale for government intervention in markets and a review of government action in three areas, namely, privatisation and deregulation, competition policy and the operation of the labour market.

To emphasise the international dimension of the study of the business environment, each of the three main parts of the book conclude with a section entitled 'International business in action' which draws together some of the key themes discussed in the previous chapters. By examining specific issues and/or organisations, the aim is to highlight linkages between the material discussed in the text and to provide an appreciation of some of the ways in which business activity reaches well beyond national boundaries.

The concluding chapter in the book stresses the continuing need for organisations to monitor change in the business environment and examines a number of frameworks through which such an analysis can take place. In seeking to make sense of their environment, businesses need access to a wide range of information, much of which is available from published material, including government sources. Some of the major types of information available to students of business and to business organisations – including statistical and other forms of information – are considered in the final part of this chapter.

Central themes

A number of themes run through the text and it is useful to draw attention to these at this point.

Interaction with the environment

Viewed as an **open system**, the business organisation is in constant interaction with its environment. Changes in the environment can cause changes in inputs, in the transformation process and in outputs and these in turn may engender further changes in the organisation's environment. The internal and external environments should be seen as interrelated and interdependent, not as separate entities.

Interaction between environmental variables

In addition to the interaction between the internal and external environments, the various external influences affecting business organisations are also frequently interrelated. Changes in interest rates, for example, may affect consumer confidence and this can have an important bearing on business activity. Subsequent attempts by government to influence the level of demand could exacerbate the situation and this may lead to changes in general economic conditions, causing further problems for firms. The combined effect of these factors could be to create a turbulent environment which could result in uncertainty in the minds of managers. Failure to respond to the challenges (or opportunities) presented by such changes could signal the demise of the organisation or at best a significant decline in its potential performance.

The complexity of the environment

The environmental factors identified above are only some of the potential variables faced by all organisations. These external influences are almost infinite in number and variety and no study could hope to consider them all. For students of business and for managers alike, the requirement is to recognise the complexity of the external environment and to pay greater attention to those influences which appear the most pertinent and pressing for the organisation in question, rather than to attempt to consider all possible contingencies.

Environmental volatility and change

The organisation's external environment is further complicated by the tendency towards **environmental change**. This volatility may be particularly prevalent in some areas (e.g. technology) or in some markets or in some types of industry or organisation. As indicated above, a highly volatile environment causes uncertainty for the organisation (or for its sub-units) and this makes decision-making more difficult (see Case study: A shock to the system).

Environmental uniqueness

Implicit in the remarks above is the notion that each organisation has to some degree a unique environment in which it operates and which will affect it in a unique way. Thus, while it is possible to make generalisations about the impact of the external environment on the firm, it is necessary to recognise the existence of this uniqueness and where appropriate to take into account exceptions to the general rule.

Different spatial levels of analysis

External influences operate at different spatial levels – local, regional, national, supra-national, international/global. There are few businesses, if any, today which could justifiably claim to be unaffected by influences outside their immediate market(s).

Two-way flow of influence

As a final point, it is important to recognise that the flow of influence between the organisation and its environment operates in both directions. The external environment influences firms, but by the same token firms can influence their environment and this is an acceptable feature of business in a democratic society which is operating through a market-based economic system. This idea of democracy and its relationship with the market economy is considered in Chapters 4 and 5.

Synopsis

In the process of transforming inputs into output, business organisations operate in a multifaceted environment which affects and is affected by their activities. This environment tends to be complex and volatile and comprises influences which are of both a general and an immediate kind and which operate at different spatial levels. Understanding this environment and its effects on business operations is of vital importance to the study and practice of business.

Summary of key points

- Business activity is essentially concerned with transforming inputs into outputs for consumption purposes.

- All businesses operate within an external environment which shapes their operations and decisions.

- This environment comprises influences which are both operational and general.

- The operational environment of business is concerned with such factors as customers, suppliers, creditors and competitors.

- The general environment focuses on what are known as the PESTLE factors.

- In analysing a firm's external environment attention needs to be paid to the interaction between the different environmental variables, environmental complexity, volatility and change and to the spatial influences.

- While all firms are affected by the environment in which they exist and operate, at times they help to shape that environment by their activities and behaviour.

A shock to the system

For the most part changes in a firm's (or industry's or sector's) external environment tend to be relatively predictable and this can aid business planning. Economic indicators, for example, usually signal the onset of a recession (or recovery) well before it occurs and this provides businesses with time to consider not only how they are likely to be affected by economic change, but also what steps they can take to minimise any potential threat to the organisation (or maximise any opportunity). On occasions, however, the business environment can change dramatically and unexpectedly for the worse, leaving some firms to face rapidly deteriorating trading conditions often without any contingency plans in place.

Such a situation occurred on Tuesday 11 September 2001 when terrorist attacks on the World Trade Center and the US Department of Defense rapidly sent shock waves through the global economic system, engulfing a wide range of firms and industries in all countries. The most immediate and obvious manifestation of the crisis was seen in the airline industry where the major airline operators suddenly found people unwilling to fly, thereby significantly exacerbating the problems already being experienced as a result of increased competition and recession in some of their markets. In the United States carriers such as United, Delta and Continental announced tens of thousands of redundancies and further job losses were announced by British Airways, Virgin and Air Canada. Elsewhere in Europe both Swissair and Sabena went into receivership and other operators signalled a period of retrenchment.

The knock-on effect of the reduction in air travel also impacted on two allied industries: aircraft manufacturing and tourism. Again this found expression in falling demand and the inevitable loss of jobs. Companies such as Airbus Industrie, Boeing and Bombardier slimmed down their workforces and additional job losses occurred in supplier organisations including Rolls-Royce and in travel, tourism and allied industries such as hotels, catering and car hire. For a company such as Disney, for instance, the impact on visitor numbers at its theme parks in America and Europe was immediately felt and numerous other organisations and holiday destinations rapidly experienced the effect of the decline in overseas tourists in the immediate aftermath of the attack.

While it was suggested at the time by a number of observers that some businesses might have been taking advantage of the crisis to slim down their workforces, there seems little doubt that the attack had a significant economic as well as human and psychological impact. Mercifully such shocks to the system tend to be few and far between and even when they occur some enterprising firms will find they provide unexpected business opportunities.

Case study questions

1   Can you think of any other examples of major unanticipated events in your own country that have had a serious adverse effect on businesses?

2   Can you think of any businesses which may have benefited commercially from the events of September 11?

There is a great deal of commentary on September 11 and its aftermath. You should try typing 'September 11 and Business' in *Google*. There is also an archive of material at *September11.archive.org*

Review and discussion questions

1 In what senses could a college or university be described as a business organisation? How would you characterise its 'inputs' and 'outputs'?

2 Taking examples from a range of quality newspapers, illustrate ways in which business organisations are affected by their external environment.

3 Give examples of the ways in which business organisations can affect the external environment in which they operate.

Assignments

1 Assume you are a trainee in a firm of management consultants. As part of your induction process you have been asked to collect a file of information on an organisation of your choice. This file should contain information not only on the structure of the organisation and on its products, but also on the key external influences which have affected its operations in recent years.

2 For a firm or industry of your choice, undertake a 'PESTLE' analysis indicating the likely major environmental influences to be faced by the firm/industry in the next five to ten years.

Further reading

Brooks, I., Weatherston, J. and Wilkinson, G., *The International Business Environment*, FT/Prentice Hall, 2004.

Daniels, J. D., Radebough, L. H. and Sullivan, D. P., *International Business: Environments and Operations*, 10th edition, Prentice Hall, 2004.

Morris, H. and Willey, B., *The Corporate Environment*, Financial Times/Prentice Hall, 1996.

Steiner, G. A. and Steiner, J. F., *Business, Government and Society: A Managerial Perspective*, 7th edition, McGraw-Hill, 1994.

Wetherly, P. and Otter, D. (eds) *The Business Environment: Themes and Issues*, Oxford University Press, 2008.

Worthington, I., Britton, C. and Rees, A., *Economics for Business: Blending Theory and Practice*, 2nd edition, Financial Times/Prentice Hall, 2005, Chapter 1.

Web links and further questions are available on the website at:
www.pearsoned.co.uk/worthington

Chapter 2
Business Organisations:
The Internal Environment

Business organisations: the internal environment

Ian Worthington and Zena Cumberpatch

The systems approach to the study of business organisations stresses the interaction between a firm's internal and external environments. Key aspects of the internal context of business include the organisation's structure and functions and the way they are configured in pursuit of specified organisational objectives. If the enterprise is to remain successful, constant attention needs to be paid to balancing the different influences on the organisation and to the requirement to adapt to new external circumstances. This responsibility lies essentially with the organisation's management, which has the task of blending people, technologies, structures and environments.

Learning outcomes

Having read this chapter you should be able to:

- outline the broad approaches to organisational and management, paying particular attention to the systems approach
- identify alternative organisational structures used by business organisations
- discuss major aspects of the functional management of firms
- illustrate the interaction between a firm's internal and external environments

Key terms

Bureaucracy
Classical theories of organisation
Contingency approaches
Divisional structure
Downsizing
Formal structures
Functional organisation
Functional specialisation
Hierarchy of needs

Holding company
Human relations approach
Human resource management
Management
Marketing
Marketing concept
Marketing mix
Matrix structure
Organisation by product

Organisation chart
Profit centre
Project team
Re-engineering
Scientific management
Sub-systems
Systems approach
Theory X and Theory Y
Theory Z
Virtual organisation

Introduction

The internal features of business organisations have received considerable attention from scholars of organisation and management, and a large number of texts have been devoted to this aspect of business studies.[1] In the discussion below, the aim is to focus on three areas of the internal organisation that relate directly to a study of the business environment: approaches to understanding organisations, organisational structures, and key functions within the enterprise. Further insight into these aspects and into management and organisational behaviour generally can be gained by consulting the many specialist books in this field, a number of which are mentioned at the end of this chapter. Issues relating to a firm's legal structure are examined in Chapter 10.

A central theme running through any analysis of the internal environment is the idea of **management**, which has been subjected to a wide variety of definitions. As used in this context, management is seen both as a system of roles fulfilled by individuals who manage the organisation (e.g. entrepreneur, resource manager, co-ordinator, leader, motivator, organiser) and as a process which enables an organisation to achieve its objectives. The essential point is that management should be seen as a function of organisations, rather than as a controlling element, and its task is to enable the organisation to identify and achieve its objectives and to adapt to change. Managers need to integrate the various influences on the organisation – including people, technology, systems and the environment – in a manner best designed to meet the needs of the enterprise at the time in question and be prepared to institute change as and when circumstances dictate.

Approaches to organisation and management

An important insight into the principles which are felt to underlie the process of management can be gained by a brief examination of organisational theories. These theories or approaches – some of which date back to the late nineteenth century – represent the views of both practising managers and academics as to the factors that determine organisational effectiveness and the influences on individuals and groups within the work environment. Broadly speaking, these approaches can be broken down into three main categories: the classical approach, the human relations approach, and the systems approach.[2] Since the last of these encompasses the model presented in Chapter 1, particular attention is paid to this perspective.

The classical approach

Classical theories of organisation and management mostly date from the first half of the twentieth century and are associated with the work of writers such as Taylor, Fayol, Urwick and Brech. In essence, the classicists viewed organisations as **formal structures** established to achieve a particular number of objectives under the direction of management. By identifying a set of principles to guide managers in the design of the organisational structure, the proponents of the classical view believed that organisations would be able to achieve their objectives more effectively. Fayol, for example, identified fourteen principles which included the division of work, the scalar chain, centralisation and the unity of command – features which also found expression in Weber's notion of 'bureaucracy'. Urwick's rules or principles similarly emphasised aspects of organisation structure and operations – such as specialisation, co-ordination, authority, responsibility and the span of control – and were presented essentially as a code of good management practice.

Within the classical approach special attention is often given to two important sub-groupings, known as **scientific management** and **bureaucracy**. The former is associated with the pioneering work of F. W. Taylor (1856–1915) who believed that scientific methods could be attached to the design of work so that productivity could be increased. For Taylor, the systematic analysis of jobs (e.g. using some form of work study technique) was seen as the key to finding the best way to perform a particular task and thereby of achieving significant productivity gains from individuals which would earn them increased financial rewards. In Taylor's view, the responsibility for the institution of a scientific approach lay with management, under whose control and direction the workers would operate to the mutual benefit of all concerned.

The second sub-group, bureaucracy, draws heavily on the work of Max Weber (1864–1920) whose studies of authority structures highlighted the importance of 'office' and 'rules' in the operation of organisations. According to Weber, bureaucracy – with its system of rules and procedures, specified spheres of competence, hierarchical organisation of offices, appointment based on merit, high level of specialisation and impersonality – possessed a degree of technical superiority over other forms of organisation, and this explained why an increasing number of enterprises were becoming bureaucratic in structure. Over 50 years after Weber's studies were first published in English, bureaucratic organisation remains a key feature of many enterprises throughout the world and is clearly linked to increasing organisational size and complexity. Notwithstanding the many valid criticisms of Weber's work, it is difficult to imagine how it could be otherwise.

The human relations approach

Whereas the classical approach focuses largely on structure and on the formal organisation, the **human relations approach** to management emphasises the importance of people in the work situation and the influence of social and psychological factors in shaping organisational behaviour. Human relations theorists have primarily been concerned with issues such as individual motivation, leadership, communications and group dynamics and have stressed the significance of the informal pattern of relationships which exist within the formal structure. The factors influencing human behaviour have accordingly been portrayed as a key to achieving greater organisational effectiveness, thus elevating the 'management of people' to a prime position in the determination of managerial strategies.

The early work in this field is associated with Elton Mayo (1880–1949) and with the famous Hawthorne Experiments, conducted at the Western Electric Company (USA) between 1924 and 1932. What these experiments basically showed was that individuals at work were members of informal (i.e. unofficial) as well as formal groups

Figure 2.1   A hierarchy of needs

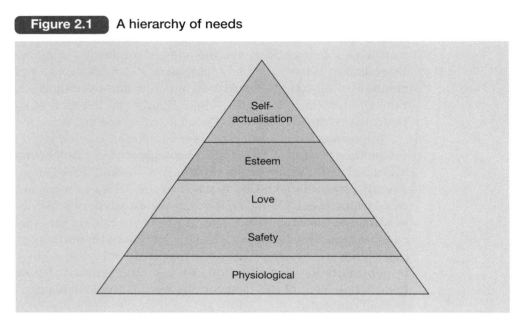

and that group influences were fundamental to explaining individual behaviour. Later work by writers such as Maslow, McGregor, Argyris, Likert and Herzberg continued to stress the importance of the human factor in determining organisational effectiveness, but tended to adopt a more psychological orientation, as exemplified by Maslow's '**hierarchy of needs**' and McGregor's '**Theory X and Theory Y**'. Maslow's central proposition was that individuals seek to satisfy specific groups of needs, ranging from basic physiological requirements (e.g. food, sleep, sex), through safety, love and esteem, to self-actualisation (i.e. self-fulfilment), progressing systematically up the hierarchy as each lower-level need is satisfied (see Figure 2.1). To McGregor individuals at work were seen by management as either inherently lazy (Theory X) or committed to the organisation's objectives and often actively seeking responsibility (Theory Y). These perceptions consequently provided the basis for different styles of management, which ranged from the coercive to the supportive.

McGregor's concern with management styles is reflected in later studies, including Ouichi's notion of **Theory Z**.[3] According to Ouichi one of the key factors in the success of Japanese manufacturing industries was their approach to the management of people. Theory Z organisations were those which offered workers long-term (often lifetime) employment, a share in decision making, opportunities for training, development and promotion, and a number of other advantages which gave them a positive orientation towards the organisation. For Ouichi, the key to organisational effectiveness lay in the development of a Japanese-style Theory Z environment, adapted to western requirements.

The systems approach

More recent approaches to organisation and management have helped to integrate previous work on structures, people and technology, by portraying organisations as socio-technical systems interacting with their environment. Under this approach –

which became popular in the 1960s – organisations were seen as complex systems of people, tasks and technologies that were part of and interacted with a larger environment, comprising a wide range of influences (see Chapter 1). This environment was frequently subject to fluctuations, which on occasions could become turbulent (i.e. involving rapid and often unpredictable change). For organisations to survive and prosper, adaptation to environmental demands was seen as a necessary requirement and one which was central to the process of management.

The essence of the **systems approach** has been described in Chapter 1, but is worth repeating here. Organisations, including those involved in business, are open systems, interacting with their environment as they convert inputs into output. Inputs include people, finance, materials and information, provided by the environment in which the organisation exists and operates. Output comprises such items as goods and services, information, ideas and waste, discharged into the environment for consumption by 'end' or 'intermediate' users and in some cases representing inputs used by other organisations.

Systems invariably comprise a number of **sub-systems** through which the process of conversion or transformation occurs. Business organisations, for example, usually have sub-systems which deal with activities such as production, marketing, accounting and human resource management and each of these in turn may involve smaller sub-systems (e.g. sales, quality control, training) which collectively constitute the whole. Just as the organisation as a system interacts with its environment, so do the sub-systems and their component elements, which also interact with each other. In the case of the latter, the boundary between sub-systems is usually known as an 'interface'.

While the obvious complexities of the systems approach need not be discussed, it is important to emphasise that most modern views of organisations draw heavily on the work in this area, paying particular attention to the interactions between people, technology, structure and environment and to the key role of management in directing the organisation's activities towards the achievement of its goals. Broadly speaking, management is seen as a critical sub-system within the total organisation, responsible for the co-ordination of the other sub-systems and for ensuring that internal and external relationships are managed effectively. As changes occur in one part of the system these will induce changes elsewhere and this will require a management response that will have implications for the organisation and for its sub-systems. Such changes may be either the cause or effect of changes in the relationship between the organisation and its environment, and the requirement for managers is to adapt to the new conditions without reducing the organisation's effectiveness.

Given the complex nature of organisations and the environments in which they operate, a number of writers have suggested a **contingency approach** to organisational design and management (e.g. Lawrence and Lorsch, Woodward, Perrow, Burns and Stalker).[4] In essence, this approach argues that there is no single form of organisation best suited to all situations and that the most appropriate organisational structure and system of management is dependent upon the contingencies of the situation (e.g. size, technology, environment) for each organisation. In some cases a bureaucratic structure might be the best way to operate, while in others much looser and more organic methods of organisation might be more effective. In short, issues of organisational design and management depend on choosing the best combination in the light of the relevant situational variables; this might mean different structures and styles coexisting within an organisation.

Organisational structures

Apart from the very simplest form of enterprise in which one individual carries out all tasks and responsibilities, business organisations are characterised by a division of labour which allows employees to specialise in particular roles and to occupy designated positions in pursuit of the organisation's objectives. The resulting pattern of relationships between individuals and roles constitutes what is known as the organisation's structure and represents the means by which the purpose and work of the enterprise is carried out. It also provides a framework through which communications can occur and within which the processes of management can be applied.

Responsibility for establishing the formal structure of the organisation lies with management and a variety of options is available. Whatever form is chosen, the basic need is to identify a structure which will best sustain the success of the enterprise and will permit the achievement of a number of important objectives. Through its structure an organisation should be able to:

- achieve efficiency in the utilisation of resources;
- provide opportunities for monitoring organisational performance;
- ensure the accountability of individuals;
- guarantee co-ordination between the different parts of the enterprise;
- provide an efficient and effective means of organisational communication;
- create job satisfaction, including opportunities for progression; and
- adapt to changing circumstances brought about by internal or external developments.

In short, structure is not an end in itself, but a means to an end and should ideally reflect the needs of the organisation within its existing context and taking into account its future requirements.

mini case 'Into the Dragon's Den'

As the chapter illustrates, the structure of an organisation is a means by which an enterprise can achieve its objectives. As the environment in which a business operates changes, firms should be willing to adapt the structure to meet the new circumstances. This might mean moving beyond the traditional models discussed below, in an effort to improve performance.

The global pharmaceutical giant GlaxoSmithKline (GSK) illustrates this idea of an evolving organisational structure. In July 2008, GSK announced that in future its scientists would have to pitch their ideas for new drugs to a development board, based essentially on the lines of the 'Dragon's Den', a popular UK television programme where would-be entrepreneurs seek to gain backing for their ideas from a group of financiers. The board will include two venture capitalists and will be a mixture of executives from inside the company and GSK outsiders. The plan is to stimulate innovation by requiring smaller teams of scientists to pitch three-year business plans to the new drug discovery investment board in an effort to secure funding for new drug treatments.

You can access the website for GSK at *www.gsk.com*

The essence of structure is the division of work between individuals and the formal organisational relationships that are created between them. These relationships will be reflected not only in individual job descriptions, but also in the overall **organisation chart** which designates the formal pattern of role relationships, and the interactions between roles and the individuals occupying those roles. Individual authority relationships can be classified as line, staff, functional and lateral and arise from the defined pattern of responsibilities, as follows:

● *Line relationships* occur when authority flows vertically downward through the structure from superior to subordinate (e.g. managers–section leader–staff).
● *Staff relationships* are created when senior personnel appoint assistants who normally have no authority over other staff but act as an extension of their superior.
● *Functional relationships* are those between specialists (or advisers) and line managers and their subordinates (e.g. when a specialist provides a common service throughout the organisation but has no authority over the users of the service). The personnel or computing function may be one such service that creates a functional relationship. (Note that specialists have line relationships with their own subordinates.)
● *Lateral relationships* exist across the organisation, particularly between individuals occupying equivalent positions within different departments or sections (e.g. committees, heads of departments, section leaders).

With regard to the division of work and the grouping of organisational activities, this can occur in a variety of ways. These include:

● *By function or major purpose*, associated particularly with departmental structures.
● *By product or service*, where individuals responsible for a particular product or service are grouped together.
● *By location*, based on geographical criteria.
● *By common processes* (e.g. particular skills or methods of operation).
● *By client group* (e.g. children, the disabled, the elderly).

In some organisations a particular method of grouping will predominate; in others there will tend to be a variety of types and each has its own particular advantages and disadvantages. In the discussion below, attention is focused on five main methods of grouping activities in business organisations. Students should attempt to discover what types of structure exist within their own educational institution and the logic (if any) which underlies the choices made.

Functional organisation

The functional approach to organisation is depicted in Figure 2.2. As its name indicates, in this type of structure activities are clustered together by common purpose or function. All marketing activities, for example, are grouped together as a

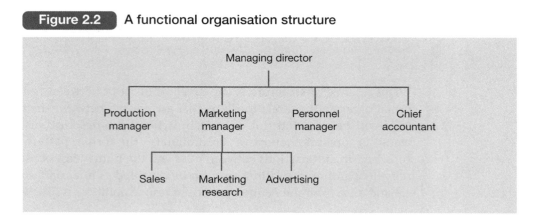

Figure 2.2   A functional organisation structure

common function, typically within a marketing department. Similarly, other areas of activity, such as production, finance, personnel and research and development, have their own specialised sections or departments, responsible for all the tasks required of that function.

Apart from its obvious simplicity, the functional organisation structure allows individuals to be grouped together on the basis of their specialisms and technical expertise, and this can facilitate the development of the function they offer as well as providing a recognised path for promotion and career development. On the downside, functional specialisation, particularly through departments, is likely to create sectional interests which may operate to the disadvantage of the organisation as a whole, particularly where inequalities in resource allocation between functions become a cause for interfunction rivalry. It could also be argued that this form of structure is most suited to single-product firms and that it becomes less appropriate as organisations diversify their products and/or markets. In such circumstances, the tendency will be for businesses to look for the benefits which can arise from specialisation by product or from the divisionalisation of the enterprise.

Organisation by product or service

In this case the division of work and the grouping of activities is dictated by the product or service provided (see Figure 2.3), such that each group responsible for a

Figure 2.3   A product-based structure

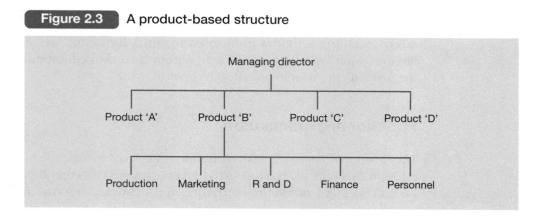

particular part of the output of the organisation may have its own specialist in the different functional areas (e.g. marketing, finance, personnel). One advantage of this type of structure is that it allows an organisation to offer a diversified range of products, as exemplified by the different services available in National Health Service hospitals (e.g. maternity, orthopaedic, geriatric, and so forth). Its main disadvantage is the danger that the separate units or divisions within the enterprise may attempt to become too autonomous, even at the expense of other parts of the organisation, and this can present management with problems of co-ordination and control.

The divisional structure

As firms diversify their products and/or markets – often as a result of merger or takeover – a structure is needed to co-ordinate and control the different parts of the organisation. This structure is likely to be the divisional (or multi-divisional) company.

A **divisionalised structure** is formed when an organisation is split up into a number of self-contained business units, each of which operates as a profit centre. Such a division may occur on the basis of product or market or a combination of the two, with each unit tending to operate along functional or product lines, but with certain key functions (e.g. finance, personnel, corporate planning) provided centrally, usually at company headquarters (see Figure 2.4).

The main benefit of the multi-divisional company is that it allows each part of what can be a very diverse organisation to operate semi-independently in producing and marketing its products, thus permitting each division to design its offering to suit local market conditions – a factor of prime importance where the firm operates on a multinational basis. The dual existence of divisional **profit centres** and a central unit responsible for establishing strategy at a global level can, however, be a source of considerable tension, particularly where the needs and aims of the centre appear to conflict with operations at the local level or to impose burdens seen to be unreasonable by divisional managers (e.g. the allocation of central overhead costs).

Figure 2.4   A divisional structure

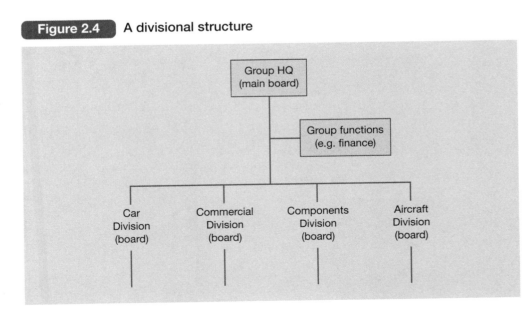

Much the same kind of arguments apply to the **holding company**, though this tends to be a much looser structure for managing diverse organisations, favoured by both UK and Japanese companies. Under this arrangement, the different elements of the organisation (usually companies) are co-ordinated and controlled by a parent body, which may be just a financial entity established to maintain or gain control of other trading companies. Holding companies are associated with the growth of firms by acquisition which gives rise to a high degree of product or market diversification. They are also a popular means of operating a multinational organisation.

Matrix structures

A **matrix** is an arrangement for combining functional specialisation (e.g. through departments) with structures built around products, projects or programmes (see Figure 2.5). The resulting grid (or matrix) has a two-way flow of authority and responsibility. Within the functional elements, the flow is vertically down the line from superior to subordinate and this creates a degree of stability and certainty for the individuals located within the department or unit. Simultaneously, as a member of a project group or product team, an individual is normally answerable horizontally to the project manager whose responsibility is to oversee the successful completion of the project, which in some cases may be of very limited duration.

Matrix structures offer various advantages, most notably flexibility, opportunities for staff development, an enhanced sense of ownership of a project or programme, customer orientation and the co-ordination of information and expertise. On the negative side, difficulties can include problems of co-ordination and control,

Figure 2.5 A matrix structure in a business school

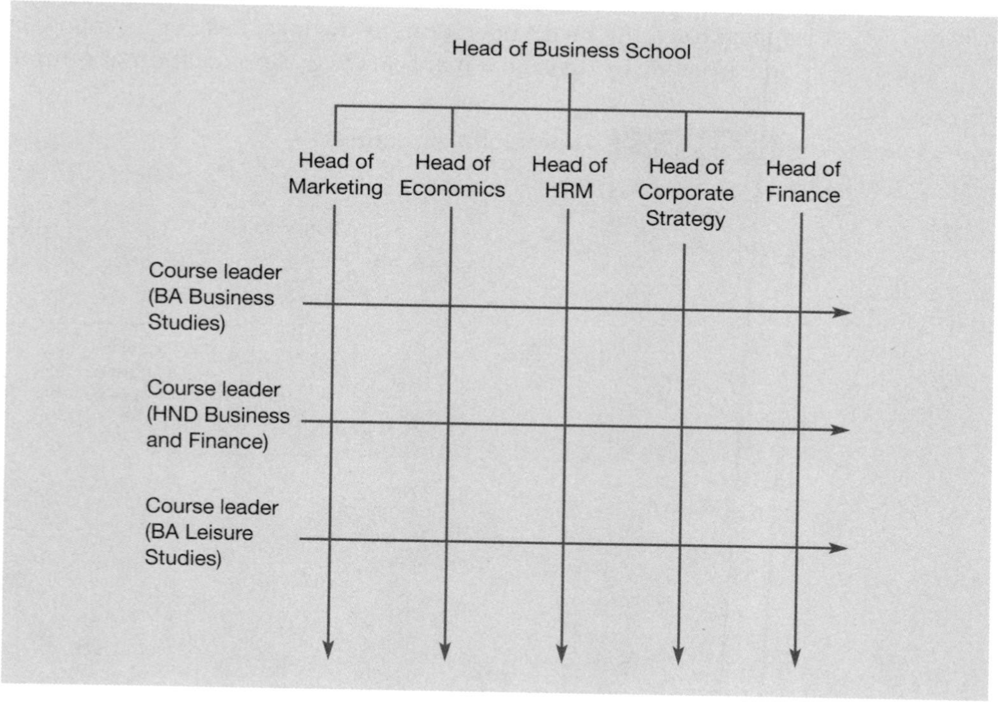

conflicting loyalties for staff and uncertain lines of authority. It is not uncommon in an organisation designed on matrix lines for project or programme leaders to be unsure of their authority over the staff from the contributing departments. Nor is it unknown for functional managers to withdraw their co-operation and/or support for projects located outside their immediate sphere of influence.

Project teams

Despite its flexibility, the matrix often has a degree of permanence; in contrast, the project team is essentially a temporary structure established as a means of carrying out a particular task, often in a highly unstable environment. Once the task is complete, the team is disbanded and individuals return to their usual departments or are assigned to a new project.

Fashioned around technical expertise rather than managerial rank and often operating closely with clients, project teams are increasingly common in high-technology firms, construction companies and in some types of service industry, especially management consultancies and advertising. Rather than being a replacement for the existing structure, they operate alongside it and utilise in-house staff (and in some cases, outside specialists) on a project-by-project basis. While this can present logistical and scheduling problems and may involve some duplication of resources, it can assist an organisation in adapting to change and uncertainty and in providing products to the customer's specifications. Project teams tend to be at their most effective when objectives and tasks are well defined, when the client is clear as to the desired outcome and when the team is chosen with care.

---

mini case   Royal Dutch Shell

In March 1995 the multinational Anglo-Dutch oil giant, Royal Dutch Shell, announced its intention to radically change its long-admired matrix organisation (see, for example, the *Financial Times*, 30 March 1995). For historical reasons, Shell had developed a structure based on geographically defined operating companies. These operating companies had executives representing national or regional units, business sectors (or divisions) and functions such as finance. Within this three-dimensional matrix, powerful individuals were able to influence the organisation's policies at regional level and a considerable bureaucracy was required to 'police' the matrix and to co-ordinate decisions between the different elements of the structure.

Faced with growing global competition and shareholder pressure for improved performance,

Shell decided to restructure the organisation by attacking problems of overstaffing and bureaucracy and by eliminating many of the regional fiefdoms through which the company had come to run its worldwide empire. Its plan involved shaping the group around five business organisations covering its main activities (e.g. exploration and production, refining and marketing, etc.), with each operating company reporting to and receiving its strategic targets from whichever of the five organisations were relevant to its activities. A new system of business committees was given responsibility for strategic and investment decisions within the different organisations, although executive authority rested with the operating companies. Through this arrangement Shell hoped to retain the sensitivity to local market needs that had traditionally been part of its organisational creed.

In a further effort to improve the company's performance, Shell indicated that more restructuring needed to take place (see, for example, the *Guardian*, 15 December 1998). Part of its blueprint for reshaping itself for the twenty-first century included additional streamlining of its management structure, away from committee-based decision making and towards a system based on American-style chief executives.

Subsequently in October 2004 the company announced the merger of its two elements – Royal Dutch and Shell Transport and Trading – into a single company, to be known as Royal Dutch Shell plc. The new entity comprises an Executive Board, a Supervisory Board, a Board of Management and a Board of Directors for Shell Transport. Members of the Executive Committee are also members of the latter two boards.

> **web link** The website address for Royal Dutch Shell is *www.shell.com*

The virtual organisation

As indicated above, traditional organisations have structures which are designed to facilitate the transformation of inputs into output. Increasingly as the business environment changes, relationships both within and between organisations have needed to become more flexible and this has given rise to such developments as the growth in teleworking and the establishment of dynamic broker/agent networks involving considerable outsourcing of sub-tasks to 'agents' (e.g. manufacturing, distribution) by the core organisation (the 'broker'). It is fair to say that this demand for greater flexibility has been driven partly by the market and partly by cost considerations and the process of change has been facilitated by relatively rapid developments in information technology. One area currently exciting the interest of writers on management and organisation is the concept of the **virtual organisation**, arguably the ultimate form of organisational flexibility.

In essence a virtual organisation or firm signifies an extremely loose web of essentially freelance individuals or businesses who organise themselves to produce a specific customer product (e.g. an individual holiday package with particular features unique to the customer). Without any permanent structure or hierarchy this so-called firm can constantly change its shape and, despite existing across space and time, tends to appear edgeless, with its inputs, outputs and employees increasingly dispersed across the linked world of information systems. Given modern forms of communication, the potential exists for a totally electronic-based organisation trading in expertise and information with no real-world physical identity. This stands in stark contrast to the traditional view of the firm as an arrangement which adds value by transforming basic economic inputs (e.g. land, labour, capital) into physical outputs or services.

> **web link** For a useful reading list on virtual organisations *see* *www–users.cs.york.ac.uk/~kimble/teaching/mis/Virtual_Organisations.html*

Structural change

Internal change is an important feature of the modern business organisation. In order to remain competitive and meet stakeholder needs, a firm may have to find ways to restructure its organisation as the environment in which it operates changes. Solutions can range from a partial or wholesale shift in the organisation's structural form to strategies for reducing the overall size and shape of the company (e.g. **downsizing**) or a radical redesign of business processes (e.g. **re-engineering**).

Whereas business re-engineering normally connotes a root-and-branch reform of the way in which the business operates, downsizing essentially involves shrinking the organisation to make it leaner and fitter and hopefully more flexible in its response to the marketplace. For some companies this means little more than reducing the size of the workforce through natural wastage and/or redundancies, as and when opportunities arise; for others it involves delayering the organisation by removing a tier, or tiers, of management, thus effectively flattening the organisation's hierarchy and helping it to reduce its unit costs of production.

In its most systematic and long-term form, downsizing can be used as a vehicle for cultural change through which an organisation's employees are encouraged to embrace notions of continuous improvement and innovation, and to accept that structural reform is a permanent and natural state of affairs. Under such an approach, retraining and reskilling become vital tools in implementing the chosen strategy and in shaping the organisation to meet the demands of its changing environment. The danger is, however, that a firm may become too concerned with restructuring as a cure for all its problems, when the real cause of its difficulties lies in its marketplace. Cutting the number of employees, in such a situation, is unlikely to make unattractive products attractive, nor is it likely to boost morale within the organisation.

Aspects of functional management

Most organisation structures reflect a degree of **functional specialisation**, with individuals occupying roles in departments, units or sections which have titles such as Production, Finance, Marketing, Personnel, and Research and Development. These functional areas of the internal organisation, and the individuals who are allocated to them, are central to the process of transforming organisational inputs into output. The management of these functions and of the relationships between them will be a key factor in the success of the enterprise and in its ability to respond to external demands for change.

The interdependence of the internal functions can be demonstrated by a simple example. Providing goods and services to meet the market's needs often involves research and development which necessitates a financial input, usually from the capital market or the organisation's own resources. It also requires, as do all the other functions, the recruitment of staff of the right quality, a task which is more often than not the responsibility of the Personnel department. If research and development activities lead to a good idea which the Marketing department is able to sell, then the Production department is required to produce it in the right quantities, to the right specifications and at the time the market needs it. This depends not only on internal scheduling procedures within the Production department, but also on having the right kind of materials supplied on time by the Purchasing department, an appropriate system of quality control and work monitoring, machinery that is working and regularly serviced, the finished items packed, despatched and delivered and a multitude of other activities, all operating towards the same end.

The extent to which all of these requirements can be met simultaneously depends not only on internal factors, many of which are controllable, but also on a host of external influences, the majority of which tend to be beyond the organisation's control. To demonstrate this interface between the internal and external environments, two key areas of functional management are discussed briefly below – marketing and human resource management. An examination of the other functions within the organisation would yield very similar findings.

Human resource management (HRM)

People are the key organisational resource; without them organisations would not exist or function. All businesses need to plan for and manage the people they employ if they are to use this resource effectively and efficiently in pursuit of their objectives. In modern and forward-looking organisations this implies a proactive approach to the management of people which goes beyond the bounds of traditional personnel management and involves the establishment of systems for planning, monitoring, appraisal and evaluation, training and development and for integrating the internal needs of the organisation with the external demands of the marketplace. Such an approach is associated with the idea of **human resource management**.

As in other areas of management, HRM involves a wide variety of activities related to the formulation and implementation of appropriate organisational policies, the provision of opportunities for monitoring, evaluation and change, and the application of resources to the fulfilment of organisational ends. Key aspects of 'people management' include:

- recruitment and selection;
- working conditions;
- training and career development;
- job evaluation;
- employee relations;
- manpower planning; and
- legal aspects of employment.

In most, if not all, cases these will be affected by both internal and external influences (e.g. size of the firm, management style, competition, economic and political developments), some of which will vary over time as well as between organisations.

The provision of these activities within an organisation can occur in a variety of ways and to different degrees of sophistication. Some very small firms may have little in the way of a recognisable HRM function, being concerned primarily with questions of hiring and firing, pay and other working conditions, but not with notions of career development, staff appraisal or job enrichment. In contrast, very large companies may have a specialist HRM or Personnel department, often organised on functional lines and responsible for the formulation and implementation of personnel policies throughout the organisation. Such centralisation provides not only some economies of scale, but also a degree of standardisation and consistency across departments. To allow for flexibility, centralised systems are often combined with an element of decentralisation which permits individual departments or sections to exercise some influence in matters such as the recruitment and selection of staff, working conditions, training and career development.

To illustrate how the different aspects of HRM are influenced by external factors, one part of this function – recruitment and selection of staff – has been chosen. This is the activity within the organisation which seeks to ensure that it has the right quantity and quality of labour in the right place and at the right time to meet its requirements at all levels. To achieve this aim, the organisation initially needs to consider a large number of factors, including possible changes in the demand for labour, the need for new skills and likely labour turnover, before the processes of recruitment and selection can begin. These aspects in turn will be conditioned by a variety of factors such as changes in the demand for the product, the introduction of new technology and social, economic and demographic changes, some of which may not be anticipated or expected by strategic planners.

Once recruitment and selection is ready to begin, a further raft of influences will impinge upon the process, some of which emanate from external sources. In drawing up a job specification, for example, attention will normally need to be paid to the state of the local labour market, including skill availability, competition from other employers, wage rates in comparable jobs and/or organisations, and socio-demographic trends. If the quality of labour required is in short supply, an organisation may find itself having to offer improved pay and working conditions simply to attract a sufficient number of applicants to fill the vacancies on offer. Equally, in fashioning its job advertisements and in drawing up the material it sends out to potential applicants, a firm will need to pay due attention to the needs of current legislation in areas such as equal opportunities, race discrimination and employment protection, if it is not to infringe the law.

Among the other external factors the enterprise may need to take into consideration in recruiting and selecting staff will be:

- the relative cost and effectiveness of the different advertising media;
- existing relationships with external sources of recruitment (e.g. job centres, schools, colleges, universities);
- commitments to the local community;
- relationships with employee organisations (e.g. trade unions, staff associations); and
- opportunities for staff training and development in local training and educational institutions.

Ideally, it should also pay some attention to possible future changes in the technology of the workplace, in order to recruit individuals either with appropriate skills or who can be retrained relatively easily with a minimum amount of disruption and expense to the organisation.

The marketing function

The processes of human resource management provide a good illustration of the interactions between a firm's internal and external environments. An even better example is provided by an examination of its marketing activities, which are directed primarily, though not exclusively, towards what is happening outside the organisation.

Like 'management', the term **marketing** has been defined in a wide variety of ways, ranging from Kotler's essentially economic notion of an activity directed at satisfying human needs and wants through exchange processes, to the more managerial definitions associated with bodies like the Chartered Institute of Marketing.[5] A common thread running through many of these definitions is the idea that marketing is concerned with meeting the needs of the consumer in a way which is profitable to the enterprise. Hence, strategic marketing management is normally characterised as the process of ensuring a good fit between the opportunities afforded by the marketplace and the abilities and resources of an organisation operating in it.

> **web link** Information about the Chartered Institute of Marketing is available at *www.cim.co.uk*

This notion of marketing as an integrative function within the organisation – linking the needs of the consumer with the various functional areas of the firm – is central to modern definitions of the term and lies at the heart of what is known as the **marketing concept**. This is the idea that the customer is of prime importance to the organisation and that the most significant managerial task in any enterprise is first to identify the needs and wants of the consumer and then to ensure that its operations are geared to meeting these requirements profitably. Though it would be true to say that not all organisations subscribe to this view, it is generally accepted that the successful businesses are predominantly those with a customer rather than a production or sales orientation. Equally, the evidence suggests that the need to adopt such a customer-centred approach applies not only to private sector trading organisations, but also increasingly to public sector enterprises and to bodies not established for the pursuit of profits but for other purposes (e.g. charities, political parties, trade unions).

When viewed from a customer perspective, marketing can be seen to comprise a range of activities that go beyond the simple production of an item for sale. These include:

- Identifying the needs of consumers (e.g. through marketing research).
- Designing different 'offerings' to meet the needs of different types of customers (e.g. through market segmentation).
- Choosing products, prices, promotional techniques and distribution channels that are appropriate to a particular market (i.e. designing a 'marketing mix' strategy).

- Undertaking market and product planning.
- Deciding on brand names, types of packages, and methods of communicating with the customer.
- Creating a marketing information system.

As already indicated, in carrying out these activities the firm is brought into contact with a range of external influences of both an immediate and indirect kind. This external marketing environment can have a fundamental impact on the degree to which the firm is able to develop and maintain successful transactions with its customers and hence on its profitability and chances of survival.

To illustrate how a firm's marketing effort can be influenced by external factors, the following brief discussion focuses on 'pricing', which is one of the key elements of the **marketing mix**, that is, the set of controllable variables which a business can use to influence the buyer's response, namely, product, price, promotion and place – the 4Ps. Of all the mix elements, price is the only one which generates revenue, while the others result in expenditure. It is therefore a prime determinant of a firm's turnover and profitability and can have a considerable influence on the demand for its products and frequently for those of its competitors (see Chapter 14).

web link

There are lots of useful websites discussing the idea of the 'marketing mix'. Try typing the term into Google.

Leaving aside the broader question of a firm's pricing goals and the fact that prices will tend to vary according to the stage a product has reached in its life cycle, price determination can be said to be influenced by a number of factors. Of these, the costs of production, the prices charged by one's competitors and the price sensitivity of consumers tend to be the most significant.

In the case of cost-based pricing, this occurs when a firm relates its price to the cost of buying or producing the product, adding a profit margin or 'mark-up' to arrive at the final selling price. Such an approach tends to be common amongst smaller enterprises (e.g. builders, corner shops) where costs are often easier to estimate and where likely consumer reactions are given less attention than the need to make an adequate return on the effort involved. The essential point about this form of price determination is that many of the firm's costs are influenced by external organisations – including the suppliers of materials, components and energy – and hence pricing will often vary according to changes in the prices of inputs. Only larger organisations, or a group of small businesses operating together, will generally be able to exercise some influence over input prices and even then not all costs will be controllable by the enterprise.

Organisations which take an essentially cost-based approach to pricing will sometimes be influenced by the prices charged by competitors – particularly in markets where considerable competition exists and where the products are largely homogeneous and a buyer's market is evident (e.g. builders during a recession). The competitive approach to pricing, however, is also found in markets where only a few large firms operate and where the need to increase or maintain market share can give rise to virtually identical prices and to fierce non-price competition between the market leaders (see Chapter 15). In Britain, for instance, a big cross-Channel ferry operator will normally provide the service to customers at the same price as its rivals, differentiating its offering in terms of additional benefits (e.g. on-board entertainment) rather than price. Where this is the case, the external demands of the market rather than costs constitute the primary influence on a firm's decisions, and changes in market conditions (e.g. the actual or potential entry of new firms; changes in a competitor's prices; economic recession) will tend to be reflected in price changes.

This idea of market factors influencing pricing decisions also applies to situations where firms fix their prices according to the actual or anticipated reactions of consumers to the price charged for a product – known in economics as the price elasticity of demand (see Chapter 14). In this case, the customer rather than a firm's competitors is the chief influence on price determination, although the two are often interrelated in that consumers are usually more price sensitive in markets where some choice exists. Differential levels of price sensitivity between consumers of a product normally arise when a market has distinct segments based on factors such as differences in income or age or location. In such cases a firm will often fix its prices according to the segment of the market it is serving, a process known as 'price discrimination' and one which is familiar to students claiming concessionary fares on public transport.

While the above discussion has been oversimplified and does not take into account factors such as the price of other products in an organisation's product portfolio (e.g. different models of car), it illustrates quite clearly how even one of the so-called controllable variables in a firm's marketing mix is subject to a range of external influences that are often beyond its ability to control. The same argument applies to the other elements of the marketing function and students could usefully add to their understanding of the internal/external interface by examining how the external environment impinges upon such marketing activities as promotion, distribution or market research.

Synopsis

The internal dimension of business organisations constitutes an extensive field of study and one to which students of business devote a considerable amount of time. In seeking to illustrate how a firm's internal organisation is influenced by its external environment, emphasis has been placed on a selected number of aspects of a firm's internal operations. Of these, its structure and functions were seen to provide a good illustration of the interface between the internal and external environments. Appreciating the existence of this interface is facilitated by adopting a systems approach to organisational analysis.

Summary of key points

- Management is a key aspect of the internal environment of the business organisation.

- Theories of organisation and management basically fall into three categories: classical theories; human relations approaches; systems approaches.

● The systems view of organisations depicts businesses as open systems interacting with their external environment as they convert inputs into outputs.

● The external environment of the organisation affects all aspects of the business including its structures, functions and processes.

● To carry out their tasks businesses can structure themselves in a variety of ways, including functionally, by product/service, by divisions, in a matrix format or via project teams. Each has its advantages and disadvantages.

● Structural change tends to be a feature of large modern organisations.

● Within the organisation the different business functions such as marketing, production, HRM, purchasing and so on are influenced by external factors of both a general and operational kind.

● An examination of the marketing and HRM functions reveals the importance of the wide range of external influences that can impinge upon the day-to-day areas of organisational work.

● Investigations of other functional areas within the organisation would produce a similar picture.

case study
Structuring global companies

As the chapter illustrates, to carry out their activities in pursuit of their objectives, virtually all organisations adopt some form of organisational structure. One traditional method of organisation is to group individuals by function or purpose, using a departmental structure to allocate individuals to their specialist areas (e.g. Marketing, HRM and so on). Another is to group activities by product or service, with each product group normally responsible for providing its own functional requirements. A third is to combine the two in the form of a matrix structure with its vertical and horizontal flows of responsibility and authority, a method of organisation much favoured in university Business Schools.

What of companies with a global reach: how do they usually organise themselves?

Writing in the *Financial Times* in November 2000 Julian Birkinshaw, Associate Professor of Strategic and International Management at London Business School, identifies four basic models of global company structure:

● *The International Division* – an arrangement in which the company establishes a separate division to deal with business outside its own country. The International Division would typically be concerned with tariff and trade issues, foreign agents/partners and other aspects involved in selling overseas. Normally the division does not make anything itself, it is simply responsible for international sales. This arrangement tends to be found in medium-sized companies with limited international sales.

● *The Global Product Division* – a product-based structure with managers responsible for their product line globally. The company is split into a number of global businesses arranged by product (or service) and usually overseen by their own president. It has been a favoured structure among large global companies such as BP, Siemens and 3M.

● *The Area Division* – a geographically based structure in which the major line of authority lies with the country (e.g. Germany) or regional (e.g. Europe) manager who is responsible for the different product offerings within her/his geographical area.

▶

- *The Global Matrix* – as the name suggests, a hybrid of the two previous structural types. In the global matrix each business manager reports to two bosses, one responsible for the global product and one for the country/region. As we indicated in the previous edition of this book, this type of structure tends to come into and go out of fashion. Ford, for example, adopted a matrix structure in the later 1990s, while a number of other global companies were either streamlining or dismantling theirs (e.g. Shell, BP, IBM).

As Professor Birkinshaw indicates, ultimately there is no perfect structure and organisations tend to change their approach over time according to changing circumstances, fads, the perceived needs of the senior executives or the predispositions of powerful individuals. This observation is no less true of universities than it is of traditional businesses.

Case study questions

1 Professor Birkinshaw's article identifies the advantages and disadvantages of being a global business. What are his major arguments?

2 In your opinion what are likely to be the key factors determining how a global company will organise itself?

Review and discussion questions

1 In the systems approach to organisations, reference is made to 'feedback'. What is meant by this term and how can feedback influence the process of transforming 'inputs' into 'output'?

2 Should a firm's internal structure be influenced by considerations of management or by the market it serves? Are the two incompatible?

3 Examine ways in which a firm's external environment can influence one of the following functional areas: finance or production or research and development.

4 Describe the structure of an organisation with which you are familiar (e.g. through employment or work experience), indicating why the organisation is structured in the way it is. Are there any alternative forms of structure the organisation could adopt?

Assignments

1 As a student on a business studies course, you have decided to get some practical experience of the business world by running a small venture with a number of colleagues which you hope will also earn you enough income to support you during your time at college or university. Your idea involves printing and selling customised T-shirts throughout the institution and possibly to a wider market. Design an appropriate organisational structure which you feel will help you achieve your objectives, indicating your rationale for choosing such a structure and the formal pattern of relationships between individuals.

2 In self-selecting groups of three or four, identify an organisation which you feel has a bureaucratic structure. Produce a report indicating:

(a) those features of the organisation's structure, management and operations which best fit the idea of bureaucracy; and

(b) the practical consequences of these features for the working of the organisation.

Give examples to support your comments.

Notes and references

1 See, for example, Mullins, L. J., *Management and Organisational Behaviour*, 8th edition, Financial Times/Prentice Hall, 2007; Cole, G. A., *Management: Theory and Practice*, 6th edition, Thomson, 2004.

2 For a more detailed account of the three approaches see, *inter alia*, the texts referred to in n. 1.

3 Ouichi, W. G., *Theory Z: How American Business can Meet the Japanese Challenge*, Addison-Wesley, 1981.

4 The contingency approach is discussed in Cole, *op. cit.*

5 See, for example, Kotler, P. and Armstrong, G., *Principles of Marketing*, 11th edition, Prentice Hall, 2005.

Further reading

Campbell, D. J., *Organizations and the Business Environment*, Butterworth-Heinemann, 1997.

Cole, G. A., *Management: Theory and Practice*, 6th edition, Thomson, 2004.

Handy, C., *The Age of Unreason*, Arrow Books, 2nd edition, 1995.

Kotler, P., *Principles of Marketing*, 4th European edition, Prentice Hall International, 2005.

Morrison, J., *The International Business Environment: Global and Local Marketplaces in a Changing World*, 2nd revised edition, Palgrave Macmillan, 2006.

Mullins, L. J., *Management and Organisational Behaviour*, 8th edition, Financial Times/Prentice Hall, 2007.

Mullins, L. J., *Essentials of Organisational Behaviour*, FT/Prentice Hall, 2008.

Pugh, D. S. and Hickson, D. J., *Great Writers on Organizations*, 2nd Omnibus edition, Ashgate, 2007.

Web links and further questions are available on the website at:
www.pearsoned.co.uk/worthington

Chapter 3
Monitoring Change

Monitoring change

David Orton and Ian Worthington

Business organisations operate within a changing and often uncertain environment. To ensure that corporate resources are used effectively in pursuit of organisational objectives, firms need ideally to examine the external influences upon them and, where possible, to anticipate the nature and extent of environmental change. The study and practice of strategic management and decision-making has provided a number of useful approaches in this area and has generated a variety of techniques for analysing the business environment. These techniques rely on the generation of data and information, much of which is in the public domain. Accessing this information has become significantly easier with improvements in computer technology and in collecting and collating material from both national and international sources.

Learning outcomes

Having read this chapter you should be able to:

- demonstrate the need to monitor the changing business environment
- explain broad approaches to environmental analysis
- analyse a range of qualitative and quantitative techniques used by business organisations as an aid to decision making
- access a variety of national and international sources of information and data useful to both students and practitioners of business

Key terms

Brainstorming
Cross-impact matrix
Environmental analysis
Environmental scanning
PESTLE analysis

Porter's five-forces model
   of competition
Scenario writing
Strategic fit
Strategic management

SWOT (or TOWS) analysis
The Delphi method
Trend extrapolation
Trend–impact analysis

Introduction

The purpose of strategy is to provide the future direction and objectives of the organisation and to identify and gather the resources necessary in order to achieve these objectives. A simplified and popular perspective of strategy views it as a series of chronological phases: strategic analysis, identification and selection of strategic choices and, finally, implementation. For many managers this begins with a consideration of the following questions;

- Where are we now?
- What is the situation we face?
- Where do we wish to be?
- Which factors in our environment may pose challenges or opportunities to us in the future?

Managers need to be keenly aware of their organisation's internal environment (where its strengths and weaknesses may lie), and also be able to diagnose their external environment. It can be argued that the successful strategies are those that best match the organisation's resources to the pressures and forces of the environment. In short, the organisation is seeking a **strategic fit** between the internal and external environments.

Kenneth Andrews, a Harvard Professor and acclaimed as one of the earliest and foremost thinkers in corporate strategy, believed that strategy could be prescribed and should adopt the following structure in its development and application within an organisation (see Figure 18.1).

Figure 18.1 Corporate strategy

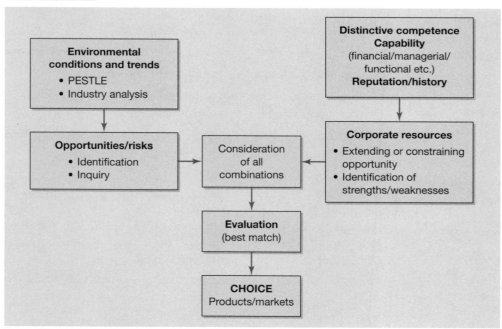

Source: Adapted from Andrews, K. (1980) *The Concept of Corporate Strategy.*

This structure emphasises the importance of assessing environmental conditions and trends as a necessary first stage in the generation of organisational strategies. The external environment is examined with the objective of identifying opportunities and risks (commonly termed threats). At the same time, the organisation should also identify its own strengths and weaknesses, which result from analysing its own internal resources. The organisation may then bring together these two forms of analysis, external and internal, and seek to identify an optimal 'fit' or 'best match' between the two. This process led to the development of the popular **SWOT** tool, which will be explored later in this chapter.

The need to monitor environmental change

Every organisation, from the smallest sole trader to the largest multinational firm, whether public or private sector, ought ideally to continually monitor its environment in order to identify potential changes or the development of long-term trends that could affect the enterprise. For some organisations, the environment is likely to be relatively stable during the mid-term, as in the case of civil service departments, the emergency services and heavy manufacturing. That said, there will always exist the possibility of environmental shocks that can destabilise the *status quo*, such as acts of terrorism, financial scandals and, more recently, the effects of the global financial crisis (see 'International business in action').

In other organisations and industries, the environment may prove to be far more turbulent. The retail sector, especially the fast moving consumer goods sector (FMCG) and consumer electronics, experiences continual innovation in product development that both shapes and reflects changing consumer demand patterns as well as increasing competition through the bewildering proliferation of product choices and condensing of product life cycles. The markets for mobile phones and portable MP3 players are just two such examples, and of course, technological developments and technology transfer now permit the boundaries of these previously distinct markets to become blurred.

The nature of the environment, or at least the way it may be perceived by each organisation in terms of stability versus dynamism, may then reflect the actions and efforts of organisations with regard to engaging in external analysis.

For organisations that perceive their environment as turbulent, the impetus for thorough and formal external analysis may be high and efforts towards such analysis might be afforded a prominent role in formulating strategies. This, however, is sometimes not sufficient. Some organisations may see their environment as so chaotic and complex that they simply do not know where to start or what to consider. With an absence of direction and clarity, organisations may inadvertently enter into a phase of soporific stupor or inertia. Alternatively, for many organisations undertaking external analysis may seem too resource intensive, in terms of money, time and people and hence may not be an attractive proposition. The act of external analysis *per se* will not confer a competitive advantage for the organisation and therefore it can sometime become difficult to justify the initial resource commitment when the returns or rewards for doing so may be unknown or uncertain.

Equally, for organisations that may perceive their environment as relatively stable, the act of continual monitoring may seem inappropriate or even illogical. If the organisation believes that the external environment in the future is likely to share the same or broadly similar characteristics as the environment it has operated within in the past, then there is little incentive to engage in external analysis.

This attitude can be likened to the simple parable of the 'boiled frog syndrome'. A frog that is placed into a pot of boiling water will immediately jump out. If the frog is placed into a tepid pot of water, it will sit there contentedly. If that pot is then slowly heated up, the frog will continue to stay in the water, until it becomes too late. The frog is unable to identify incremental changes in its environment, given that its internal apparatus is geared towards sensing sudden changes instead.

An example of this 'boiled frog syndrome' can be seen with the American giant car manufacturer General Motors (GM). In 1998, GM bought the Hummer brand name, and the off-road vehicle became an icon for GM during the early part of the millennium as it was favoured by the celebrity and Hollywood set, including high-publicity owners such as David Beckham and Governor of California and former movie star Arnold Schwarzenegger. However, in recent times, sales of the Hummer car have fallen dramatically, as rising fuel prices and concern over its impact on the natural environment have made the vehicle increasingly unpopular with consumers. GM is currently seeking to sell the Hummer brand but is finding it difficult to find another car manufacturer that is seriously interested in purchasing the brand and continuing production of the vehicle.

Analysing the environment is therefore important for all organisations. To do nothing is at best foolish and at worst, potentially disastrous.

Analysing the business environment: broad approaches

Environmental analysis is the process of scanning the environment to identify changes or trends that have the potential to generate opportunities and threats to the organisation's current or future intended strategies. The form and means by which this **environmental scanning** may be operationalised within an organisation will vary from firm to firm and can be undertaken informally or using quite sophisticated analytical tools and techniques that may require significant employment of an organisation's resources.

Informal scanning may take the form of getting information about, and from, the organisation's customers, suppliers, rivals, consultants and pressure groups. Such information from customers could, for instance, be gathered through questionnaires, sample interviewing or from feedback from the organisation's own sales and customer service staff. In retail, it is not uncommon for shop staff within a town or shopping centre to visit local rival stores and shops to get information about the prices being charged and promotional activities of their competitors. All such informal activities, whilst relatively low cost to implement and generally lacking structure, should not be undervalued. Whilst neither elaborate nor sophisticated, for smaller organisations especially, such informal techniques can provide necessary local market information.

An example of such informal scanning is where a local independent music store sends out a staff member of its small team at the beginning of each week to check up on the prices being charged by the large music chain retailers within the town for popular CD albums. This ensures that the small independent record shop is able to price its products competitively and react quickly to any price changes or promotional activities by its competitors.

For many larger organisations, however, they may prefer a more systematic and formal means for scanning and analysing the environment. In broad terms, these more deliberate approaches to environmental analysis tend to focus on the firm's societal and task environments.

As discussed in Chapter 1, the societal and general environment (often termed the macroenvironment) is typically analysed through the lens of **PESTLE** analysis, which focuses attention on political, economic, socio-cultural, technological, legal and environmental and/or ethical issues. At this point, for the organisation a distinction can be drawn between environmental scanning and environmental analysis. The process of scanning is the identification of trends and changes, whilst analysis is the consideration of which trends and environmental changes will, or are likely to, impact on the organisation in terms of presenting new challenges and also opportunities. For example, a period of relatively high or rising interest rates may be of general concern, but it is how increases in interest rates may directly affect a firm's borrowing capacity, expansion or plans for further investment that is really of relevance to the organisation.

mini case | Multinational inward investment: a PESTLE analysis

In highly competitive markets businesses must be constantly alert to the challenges they face and ideally should attempt to gain some form of advantage over their main rivals. For some organisations this might mean investing in production and/or service facilities in other countries, either as a means of reducing costs (e.g. by exploiting cheaper sources of labour) or as a strategy for boosting demand (e.g. by developing new markets). Given that many industries could be described as 'footloose' (i.e. relatively free to locate anywhere), one key question facing organisational decision makers is *where* to invest: what are the relative merits of one country over another? One way of beginning to answer this question is to undertake a PESTLE analysis in order to provide useful information about the broad macro-environmental context against which the final decision has to be taken.

To illustrate how this might occur the hypothetical example in this mini case looks at how a major car manufacturer considering investing in a new greenfield facility in Eastern Europe might identify some of the key influences on the locational decision. Given that there is no definitive way in which to undertake an analysis of this kind, the approach adopted here is to highlight some of the key questions that are likely to be considered by those charged with the final decision on where to invest. For convenience these questions are presented in tabular form (Table 18.1). You should note that the allocation of questions to categories can be a matter of personal choice (e.g. is a government tax law *political* or *legal* or *economic*?); the important point is that the questions are asked, not which category they go in.

As Table 18.1 illustrates, a PESTLE analysis can provide a valuable insight into some of the potential risks and uncertainties of a locational decision and can encourage corporate decision makers to examine future as well as current circumstances in each of the alternative locations. By adding weightings to reflect the relative importance of the different factors to the final decision and building in some allowance for the perceived degree of risk, the analysis can become more sophisticated and hence a more useful tool that can be used by the organisation. While it is likely that an approach of this kind will often be used negatively (i.e. to rule out certain locations), the fact that a particular country looks a less favourable location than the alternatives does not necessarily mean it will not be chosen. It could be, for example, that other factors weigh heavily in the final choice of location and that the PESTLE analysis has more influence on the level and nature of the investment undertaken (e.g. a joint venture might be seen as preferable to a direct commitment of funds) rather than where it occurs.

Table 18.1 Locating a car plant: a PESTLE approach

Political
- How stable is the government now and in the future?
- Is the political regime favourable to foreign investment?
- Is membership of the EU planned and likely in the near future?

Economic
- Is there a favourable economic framework within which to engage in business?
- Is the economy likely to remain stable over the longer term?
- Is there a favourable business infrastructure?

Social
- How will the structure of the population impact upon the demand for the product and/or the supply of labour?
- Are economic conditions likely to provide increased market opportunities?
- What skills currently exist within the labour force?
- Are the welfare and educational systems supportive of the planned investment?

Technological
- What is the current state of technological advance?
- Is technology transfer feasible?
- Will the current (or future) infrastructure help or hinder the investment process?
- What facilities exist for technological training?

Legal
- Is the current legal framework likely to support or hinder business operations?
- Do the current (or planned) employment laws provide an advantage or disadvantage to the business?
- Do the current tax laws favour the organisation?

Ethical
- Are the ethical standards in a chosen location likely to affect the operations of the business favourably or unfavourably and/or the company's image?
- How will the organisation be affected by current (or planned) environmental standards and regulations?

Organisations can also analyse their task or competitive environment (frequently termed the microenvironment). Analysis of this kind focuses attention on external factors that are most proximal to the organisation, typically residing at the industry level. A number of models and frameworks have been designed that explore how industry-level factors influence organisational performance, with the best known being Harvard Professor Michael **Porter's five-forces framework** (1980). Porter argued that average industry profitability and therefore organisational performance was predominantly determined by five key industry characteristics:

- The intensity of incumbent rivalry.
- The threat of new entrants.
- The threat of substitutes.

- The power of buyers.
- The power of suppliers.

In very broad terms, the greater the power of each of these forces, the lower the profitability for competing organisations within the industry. The influence or power of each force will vary from industry to industry and therefore explain why some industries (e.g. pharmaceuticals) are inherently more profitable than others (e.g. airlines). An important additional component of Porter's work was his application of 'barriers to entry'. Whilst barriers to entry was not a new concept, Porter used it to demonstrate how their existence would determine the extent to which the stability of average profitability could be maintained. With barriers to entry high, the threat of new entrants would remain low, whilst low barriers to entry would encourage new firms to enter the industry and increase the level of rivalry and therefore reduce profitability. These barriers to entry have already been described in Chapter 15, but what is of relevance here is to recognise that an organisation's external analysis should not just be restricted to the consideration of the five forces but also needs to incorporate environmental factors that might influence the height of these barriers to entry.

An example of this was in the United States during October 2001. During that month there had been a series of terrorist attacks using the US postal system to deliver letters to American citizens that contained anthrax spores. The American government, assuming the worst and unaware of the potential scale of the threat, wished to procure treatments for exposure to anthrax for up to 12 million people. Treatment against anthrax was a patented drug called ciprofloxacin, which was sold under the brand name Cipro by the German pharmaceutical firm Bayer. The American government had significant concerns as to Bayer's ability to supply such large volumes of Cipro in an extremely short period of time and at a relatively high cost. The US Congress indicated its intention to disregard Bayer's patent and buy ciprofloxacin cheaper elsewhere. After a series of talks between US officials and Bayer, the pharmaceutical firm eventually maintained its patent but had to agree to a reduction in the contracted price from $1.83 to less than $1 a tablet.

The five-forces framework remains perhaps the most influential method for analysing an industry and understanding a firm's performance. Underpinning the framework is an acceptance that value and, ultimately, profit are distributed between these five forces, and the extent to which the firm can capture an increasing share of the profit is determined by its ability to reduce the power of these forces. Inherent within the framework is the notion that relationships between the five forces are competitive, with all organisations competing in what may be considered a 'zero-sum' game.

Whilst the five-forces framework therefore provides a useful means of exploring industry characteristics, it has not been beyond criticism. Brandenburger and Nalebuff, for example, in 1995 introduced their 'value net' framework. In many ways it is similar to Porter's five forces, in that it also identifies competitors, suppliers and customers as key industry characteristics but it also introduced a further component, that of 'complementors' (see Figure 18.2).

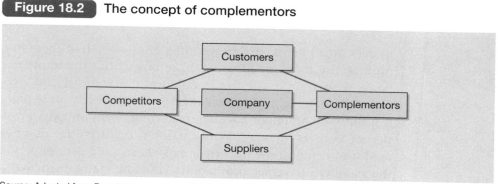

Figure 18.2 The concept of complementors

Source: Adapted from Brandenburger, A. and Nalebuff, B. (1995) 'The Right Game: Use Game Theory to Shape Strategy', *Harvard Business Review*, July–August, pp. 57–71.

For Brandenburger and Nalebuff, competing firms could also at times be complementors and in so doing could further add value (and, ultimately, profitability) to the industry. They argued that a complementor existed if the customer was to value an organisation's product more when they have another organisation's product.

This has led to a popular view that the five-forces framework should be extended to incorporate a sixth force, that of complementors; in short, in undertaking external analysis an organisation will need to consider both competition and cooperation, which has become known by the portmanteau term 'co-opetition' (see case study at the end of the chapter).

Techniques

Organisations may employ a range of techniques to assist them in analysing the external environment. Some of these techniques use statistical measures, such as the various forms of trend extrapolation and cross-impact matrices, whilst others, such as Delphi methods and scenario planning, use qualitative or narrative assessments. Some techniques for external analysis seek to predict likely future states or identify relationships between external variables, whilst others strive to illuminate possible future states. Furthermore, each tool presented below often focuses on different future time frames.

The value of the techniques will vary from organisation to organisation, and there is no hierarchy in terms of their quality. Each technique that will be explored within this chapter has both strengths and limitations. These methods of external analysis should not be considered as surrogates for each other, but rather whether the merits of a particular technique or techniques can help illuminate understanding of the external environment and aid the organisation in its identification of environmental opportunities and threats. The various techniques presented here also have differing resource requirements in terms of cost, labour and time, and therefore the organisation needs to find a balance between its desire for understanding and gaining insight into the environment and its willingness to commit resources to achieve such understanding. There is also the danger of paralysis – achieved through analysis. The organisation can never gain a complete appreciation of all external issues, and nor should it attempt to. Analysis by itself only has value once it is acted upon by the organisation in terms of designing new strategies to either take advantage of opportunities or mitigate environmental threats. A well thought through and considered strategy is desirable, but one that is well thought through, considered and implemented before those of the organisation's rivals is preferable.

If you would like more details of the various techniques referred to in this section (e.g. SWOT, the cross-impact matrix, the Delphi technique) try typing these terms into Yahoo.

Trend extrapolation

As its name suggests, **trend extrapolation** is essentially a technique for predicting the future based on an analysis of the past. Implicit in this is the assumption that, in the short run at least, most factors tend to remain fairly constant and critical changes in the key variables are unlikely to occur. Accordingly, extending present trends into the future is seen as a useful means of anticipating forthcoming events and tends to be one of the techniques most frequently used by business organisations seeking a relatively simple and inexpensive means of forecasting.

At its simplest level, trend analysis tends to be used to predict changes over time (e.g. in the likely demand for a product), a process which can sometimes prove relatively accurate where there are sufficient historical data to allow seasonal and cyclical fluctuations to be taken into consideration. The analysis can also be refined to examine an observed relationship between one factor (e.g. sales) and another (e.g. levels of disposable income) and can even be extended to the simultaneous consideration of several variables felt to influence the subject under consideration (e.g. by using multiple regression techniques). In addition, techniques also exist to investigate causal or explanatory factors that link two or more time series together (e.g. statistical modelling techniques) and to consider the likely impact on forecasted trends of a range of factors, identified by analysts as likely both to occur and to have an effect on the predicted outcome. The latter technique is generally known as **trend–impact analysis** and is sometimes used by large companies in conjunction with other methods of forecasting, including the Delphi approach and opinion canvassing (see below).

The fundamental drawback in the use of trend analysis as a forecasting tool is that there is no guarantee that the trends identified from historic patterns will continue in the future; sudden discontinuities – such as the United Kingdom's decision to leave the ERM – can invalidate or undermine the existing assumptions on which a trend was predicted. In a majority of cases, trends are based on a series of patterns or relationships among a wide range of variables, a change in any one of which can drastically alter the future course of events. These variables are not always easy to identify and the interactions between them are not necessarily fully understood. Attempts to link a simple cause with a simple effect run the danger of underestimating the complexities of the business environment.

Scenario planning

Scenario planning is about undertaking a disciplined method for imagining and examining possible futures. It is not an attempt to predict the future, and indeed it would be typical for an organisation to generate between two and four generically different possible futures as an outcome of the scenario planning process. This technique often focuses on 'best case' and 'worst case' scenarios, although Royal Dutch Shell – the company most renowned for the use of scenario planning as a core component of its environmental analysis activities for over thirty years – has in its most recent scenarios (published in 2008) expressed a preference for one particular scenario case.

Scenario planning as a strategic tool can be traced back to the Rand Corporation in the early 1960s, and is often associated with the work of one of its employees, physicist and mathematician Herman Kahn. At the time of his research, the Cold War between the United States and the Soviet Union was at its peak. In 1962, the Cuban Missile Crisis brought the two Cold War Superpowers perhaps within only a matter of days of nuclear war, when US air force reconnaissance planes took aerial photographs of Soviet installations of nuclear bases on the island of Cuba, which would provide a direct nuclear threat to American soil.

Herman Kahn, in conjunction with the Rand Corporation, presented his text entitled 'On Thermonuclear War' in 1962, which argued against common views at the time that 'mutually assured destruction' would happen in a nuclear war. Instead, Kahn presented the view that, as with any other form of warfare, a nuclear war could be ultimately winnable and his text identified a range of scenarios by which this might be possible.

In business organisations, scenario planning seeks to consider the possible effects of, and interactions between, various external environmental forces on the future and to test the resiliency of specific strategies that the organisation may be considering, in such a scenario. Typically, scenario planning is most relevant to large organisations, as it is a resource-intensive technique and is most commonly found in industries considered to have highly dynamic, complex and uncertain environments and/or those industries that require heavy forward investment (e.g. energy companies).

The process of scenario planning normally begins with the organisation considering which key environmental trends to consider, and over what time period. Royal Dutch Shell has historically published scenarios on a three- to four-year cycle that project 20–25 years ahead. Its most recent scenarios consider the nature of the energy markets by 2050. General consensus, however, suggests that scenarios should ideally be looking at least ten years ahead. Once the key trends have been identified, organisational focus then moves to considering what external forces or developments are likely to have the greatest ability to shape the future, which could include such factors as regulatory policy and corporate social responsibility.

The following case of Royal Dutch Shell presents its latest scenarios looking towards the global energy markets in 2050.

mini case | Scenario planning at Shell – the global energy market in 2050

Royal Dutch Shell has utilised scenario planning as an integral part of its range of techniques for undertaking external analysis since the early 1970s (see Figure 18.3). Its first scenarios were developed in 1972 and were narrow in scope, concentrating on forecasts for economic growth and the impacts of a discontinuity or shortage of supply of oil on prices. Until this point, both economic growth and oil supply had shown high levels of consistent and predictable growth, and Royal Dutch Shell was interested in exploring a 'what if' scenario should oil supply become destabilised. This scenario became realised in October 1974, following the Yom Kippur War and subsequent Arab oil embargo on supply of oil to the United States and supporting governments of the state of Israel.

The realisation of Shell's first scenarios acted as a powerful argument for the continued investment in scenario planning, and Shell has continued to produce scenarios, typically on a three-year cycle, to the present day.

Initially, Shell's scenarios tended to focus narrowly on economic perspectives of oil demand and supply over a relatively short time horizon (3–5 years). The scenarios were presented as 'in-house' publications only, having been produced by the organisation's own strategic analysts. As Shell's experience, willingness to invest increasing resources and scenario planning skills matured, the scenarios gradually became more complex and broader in scope, incorporating both geo-political and geo-societal trends. The decade of the 1980s was characterised by Shell as being driven by what it termed 'transition', trends that would see the end of the Cold War, the beginning of the collapse of the former Soviet Block and increasing market liberisation. The 1990s would be one of continuing liberalisation, underpinned by powerful

Figure 18.3 | Evolution of scenario planning at Royal Dutch Shell

1970s Methodology Development	1980s Integration into Corporate Strategy	1990s Focus on External Stakeholders	2000s Integration into Business Strategy
The rapids	**Transition**	**Tina: there is no alternative**	**People and Connections**
• Pioneering of scenarios to prepare the organization for uncertainty and change	• Broadly based global scenarios	• Scenarios involve external stakeholders & incorporate their views	• Global scenarios are used to develop focused scenarios on specific business initiatives
• Focus on energy markets (oil)	• Energy focus is combined with political and economic analysis	• Deeper analysis of social trends and environment change	• Scenarios are used systematically to test business strategy robustness
• Internal publication only	• Internal publication only	• Internal and external publication	• Internal and external publication
	• Workshop with business units	• Workshop with business units & externals	

Source: Copyright © 2005, by The Regents of the University of California. Reprinted from the California Management Review, Vol.48, No. 1. By permission of The Regents.

forces for globalisation and technological innovation. So pervasive and dominant were these trends considered to be that Shell coined the expression 'TINA' (there is no alternative) to describe them. The evolution of the scope of Shell's scenarios is presented in Figure 18.3.

In 2005, Shell introduced three new scenarios that were looking ahead to 2025. These scenarios questioned for the first time the assumptions of its 'TINA' trends. The scenarios published – named 'Open Doors', 'Low Trust Globalisation' and 'Flags' – suggested that there might be a break on globalisation and market liberalisation. Shell drew upon the events of 9/11 and the financial scandal of Enron as examples of geo-political crises of security and trust. These environmental shocks could foreshadow a period of slowing international trade, as governments became more protective in their policies towards their own domestic industries and, specifically, energy resources. Additionally, there would be increased pressure on all organisations to be far more transparent and accountable towards society in all their business activities and disclosure of performance.

In early 2008, Shell published its latest scenarios, which consider the global energy markets in 2050. In the foreword of its published report, Shell's Chief Executive, Jeroen van der Veer states:

> Never before has humanity faced such a challenging outlook for energy and the planet. This can be summed up in five words: 'more energy, less carbon dioxide'.

Shell has identified three key trends that are likely to significantly alter the energy landscape. It has termed these its 'three hard truths':

- There will be a surge in energy demand (global requirements are predicted to double by 2050) especially resulting from the growth in economic activity from both China and India.
- Traditional energy sources are struggling to keep up with demand.
- Current and future projected uses of energy will continue to raise carbon dioxide emissions and other greenhouse gases with adverse effects on the environment.

Given the above trends, which when compared can be seen to create obvious tensions, Shell has characterised the possible future energy landscape as 'TANIA' (there are no ideal answers).

From these trends, two scenarios have been developed, one entitled 'Scramble', the other, 'Blueprints'.

In the scenario of 'Scramble', Shell suggests that events will continue to outpace action. For the next decade, people from all walks of life will join the debate about energy and climate change, but for governments, security of energy supply and fears of losing economic ground will shape decision making and policy. The primary focus will be on meeting the needs of global demand and there will be little in the way of consideration of investing in more efficient means of providing energy until traditional sources become critically depleted. In a 'Scramble' future, focus on addressing greenhouse gas emissions will receive scant attention much before around 2020, by when an increasing frequency of climate shocks will force governments to belatedly respond to the needs of the natural environment. Even then, Shell believes that such responses will be localised, with both governments and firms taking individual action, with little framework for a co-ordinated, considered global response. Although by 2050 greenhouse gas emissions will have been reduced, it is argued that the efforts may be seen as too little too late.

In 'Blueprints', groups of seemingly disconnected people (e.g. politicians, environmentalists, venture capitalists, farmers and businesses) all begin to recognise the profitable potential of finding solutions to the challenges of economic development, energy security and environmental pollution at the same time. These seemingly disparate groups begin to collaborate together in localised and regionalised areas, motivated by recognising the need to take action before it's forced upon them by circumstance.

These actions receive public support, which then transfers into public pressure on governments for change. Buildings are made more energy efficient, and there are government efforts to reduce greenhouse gas emissions and improve air quality. Participating governments will use a range of individualised, local initiatives and policy investments, from tax breaks to subsidies, mandates, and investment and support for new 'cleaner' technologies. Whilst governments begin to take a holistic view of the challenges posed, multinational firms find international investment decisions and strategies difficult to implement given the patchwork of government initiatives. These firms begin to pressure local, national and international authorities to harmonise approaches towards energy consumption, supply and environmental management.

With harmonisation comes widespread adoption of good efficiency practices. Trading schemes for carbon dioxide emissions' rights begin to cover a critical mass of industry sectors in a critical mass of countries and transport becomes 'greener' through growth in vehicle engine hybrids and, later, full-electric vehicles.

Royal Dutch Shell does not indicate which of the two scenarios is most likely, but suggests that both are plausible. Shell is keen to indicate its preference for the 'Blueprints' scenario, which is a break from tradition, as the organisation has previously always presented a neutral view towards it scenarios.

 The Shell website (2008) can be found at: *www.shell.com*

Expert opinion: the Delphi method

To predict future developments or to build likely scenarios, some organisations turn to experts, an increasing number of whom work as consultants. These experts often operate as a group to produce an analysis which is presented to management in the form of a report or which emanates from a discursive technique known as **brainstorming**. Alternatively, the organisation may prefer to canvass the views of an anonymous panel of experts, using a technique known as the **Delphi method**, which was originally developed by the Rank Corporation in the United States to forecast likely military events.

In essence the Delphi approach involves eliciting opinions from a group of experts who operate individually, and anonymously, unaware of the other members of the group. Each expert is asked to respond to an initial set of questions and the answers are clarified and tabulated by a neutral investigator who uses them to generate a more refined set of questions that are then put to the experts. Following their replies, further revisions may occur and the respondents may be asked again to provide another set of predictions that take into account the information provided in the earlier replies. This process may continue for several rounds until a measure of convergence occurs between the views of the panel and a form of consensus is reached on likely future developments. As a technique the Delphi method tends to be expensive and time-consuming and there is no guarantee that a clear view will emerge. It can, however, be used to investigate any aspect of a firm's environment and to identify not only the effects of predicted changes, but also their causes, and this information may be incorporated into other forms of environmental analysis of both a qualitative and quantitative kind.

Cross-impact matrices

The **cross-impact matrix** provides a more complex means of assessing and forecasting environmental change than some of the other methods previously described. Under this approach, analysts identify a set of events that are forecast to occur within a given time period, and specify not only the expected timing of each event but also its probability of occurrence. Arranging these events in anticipated chronological order in rows and columns of a matrix (see Figure 18.4) permits attention to be focused on the interaction between the events and, in particular, on the extent to which one may influence the timing or likely occurrence of another.

As a means of predicting likely interactions between anticipated future developments, cross-impact analysis serves at least two significant purposes. First, it can be used to check the consistency of the various forecasts which go into it – such as the prediction of events and their relationships – given that inconsistencies will become apparent from an analysis of the results. Second, it provides a means of identifying events and trends that will have the greatest impact on subsequent developments, whether they be in individual segments of the environment or across a range of segments, as in the case of interactions between economic, technological, social and political factors.

SWOT or TOWS analysis

It is widely accepted that corporate performance is influenced by a combination of internal and external factors. These factors can be characterised as the organisation's internal 'strengths' and 'weaknesses' and its external 'opportunities' and 'threats'. Systematically analysing these factors as an aid to strategic decision making represents a form of situational analysis known commonly by the acronym **SWOT** (or **TOWS**).

Figure 18.4   A simple cross-impact matrix

Probability and timing	Event 1	Event 2	Event 3	Event 4	Event 5
Event 1 (probability/ timing)					
Event 2 (probability/ timing)					
Event 3 (probability/ timing)					
Event 4 (probability/ timing)					
Event 5 (probability/ timing)					

The starting-point for a SWOT analysis is usually a review of the organisation's internal strengths and weaknesses, which may be undertaken by management or by external consultants brought in to provide a more objective view. The identified factors which have been listed may then be given scores to indicate their importance, with the more significant issues receiving a larger score. This process is then repeated for the firm's external opportunities and threats in order to highlight those external factors which are likely to occur and which are expected to have an impact on the organisation's future position. The resultant SWOT grid can then be used to focus attention on the key environmental influences faced by the organisation and to consider how far current strategy is relevant to the changes taking place in the business environment.

It is worth pointing out that the analysis of opportunities and threats cannot be absolute, since what might at first appear to be an opportunity may not be so when viewed against the organisation's resources or its culture or the expectations of its stakeholders. Moreover, the true value of the SWOT approach lies not in the listing of influences but in their contribution to the formulation of appropriate organisation strategies. One means of focusing attention on the latter is to produce a SWOT (TOWS) matrix which matches the firm's opportunities and threats against its internal strengths and weaknesses (see Figure 18.5). The result is four sets of possible strategic alternatives – termed SO, ST, WO and WT strategies – which range from the positive exploitation of strengths in order to take advantage of opportunities to the essentially defensive strategy of minimising weaknesses and avoiding anticipated threats.

Figure 18.5   **A SWOT matrix**

INTERNAL ASPECTS / EXTERNAL ASPECTS	Strengths (S) List major organisational strengths (e.g. quality products)	Weaknesses (W) List major organisational weaknesses (e.g. poor distribution)
Opportunities (O) List major organisational opportunities (e.g. new markets)	**SO strategies**	**WO strategies**
Threats (T) List major organisational threats (e.g. competition)	**ST strategies**	**WT strategies**

Limitations to environmental analysis

The techniques described above represent some of the ways in which organisations can examine the changing business environment in an attempt to understand what changes are likely to occur, how these may affect the organisation and what responses would be appropriate in the circumstances. In short, the value of such analysis lies not only in the information provided but also in the process of gathering and evaluating it and in applying it to the task of strategic management.

Despite its potential value as a tool of decision-making, environmental analysis is not without its limitations and these need to be taken into account. For a start, analysing the business environment is not a precise science and does not eliminate uncertainty for an organisation, caused, for instance, by unanticipated events which do not follow the normal pattern. Nor should it be regarded by managers as a means of foretelling the future, allowing them to avoid their responsibilities as strategic planners and decision-makers by blaming problems on a deficiency in the application of a particular technique or on inaccuracies in the data provided.

Added to this, environmental analysis of itself is by no means a guarantee of organisational effectiveness, and can sometimes complicate the decision-making process by providing information which calls into question the intuitive feeling of experienced managers. The danger is that the analysis may become an end in itself and may obscure information and data coming from other sources, rather than being used in conjunction with them. Accordingly, its value in strategic thinking and strategic decision-making may not be exploited to its full potential and this may represent a lost opportunity to the organisation, as well as an inefficient and ineffective use of resources.

Sources of information

Researching the business environment can be a daunting task, given the extensive amount of information and statistical data available. To help in this direction the final section of this chapter outlines some of the key national and international information sources which are readily accessible to both students and businesses. While the list is by no means exhaustive, it gives a good indication of the wide range of assistance available to researchers and of the different formats in which information is published by government and non-government sources for different purposes. Much of this information is available in an electronic as well as a print format, with the latter a particularly good starting-point for students of business. The Internet is now an invaluable resource for business information.

Statistical sources

Statistical information is an important component of business research and students need to be aware of what is available, particularly as some data turn up in the most unexpected places. Three key guides in locating statistical information are:

1 *National Statistics – the official UK statistics site.* A portal to UK officially produced statistics. Some information is available on-line, at other times you will be referred to print publications, including the ones listed below (***www.statistics.gov.uk***).

2 *Sources of Unofficial UK Statistics.* Complied by David Mort, this book provides details of a large number of unofficial statistical publications from a wide variety of organisations (e.g. pressure groups, trade unions, professional associations).

3 *World Directory of Non-Official Statistical Sources.* Published by Euromonitor and a key guide to non-official sources in selected countries outside western Europe, the latter being covered by the *European Directory of Non-Official Statistical Sources.* The *Directory* concentrates particularly on sources dealing with consumer goods, consumer trends, key industries and national economic and business trends. It has a subject and a geographical index. Also available on the GMID web service.

Some of the main statistical sources are discussed below:

4 *Annual Abstract of Statistics.* Published by the ONS, this is an authoritative source of official statistics arranged under various headings, which include population, production, energy, transport, trade and public services. Figures usually cover a ten-year period and are presented in tabulated form. There is a detailed alphabetical index at the end. It is available to download at no charge from the National Statistics website (***www.statistics.gov.uk***).

5 *Consumer Europe.* Produced by Euromonitor and available on CD-ROM and via the Internet. This is a pan-European source of marketing statistics with the emphasis on consumer goods and consumer trends. The information examines the main product groups and includes predictions on future levels of consumption. It is split into two regions – 'Consumer Western Europe' and 'Consumer Eastern Europe'.

6 *Datastream.* A finance and economics on-line database, produced by Thomson Financial. Accounts for public companies around the world, as well as share prices and stock market indices are available. The economics databases cover a vast range of current and historical international economic series, including money supply, inflation and interest rates for 150 countries. Data are taken from many statistical sources, including OECD and the UK government, central banks and unofficial statistical sources.

7 *United Nations Economic Commission for Europe (UNECE).* Another source of European economic data can be found on the UNECE website (***www.unece.org/ stats/Welcome.html***). Data on national accounts, labour figures, gender and transport statistics can be accessed for individual countries and compared with other European, North American or central Asian countries.

8 *Economic & Labour Market Review.* Merging *Economic Trends and Labour Market Trends* in January 2007, this is a monthly publication by the ONS and a key guide to the current economic indicators (e.g. prices, unemployment, trade interest rates and exchange rates) and labour market data.

9 *Economist Intelligence Unit.* Reviewing the business environment for selected countries, the EIU produce Country Reports for around 195 countries. A more in-depth look is offered by their Country Forecasts, providing macroeconomic projections for the world's largest economies. The Country Data reports provide economic indicators, forecasts and statistics for 150 countries. Available in print or on-line.

10 *Employment in Europe*. Contains an excellent overview of employment issues in Europe. Published annually by the European Commission, with a different focus in each issue.

11 *Europa World Year Book*. A Routledge publication available in print and on-line. An annual book which has an A–Z listing of all countries, not just European countries as the title suggests.

12 *Europe in Figures: Eurostat Yearbook*. A comprehensive and useful introduction to statistical data on the European Union and its Member States. The yearbook is also a useful alternative if overwhelmed by the Eurostat website. Background data and over 500 statistical tables, graphs and maps are presented. Areas covered include the economy, education, the labour market, industry and services, international trade, transport and the environment. The yearbook is free to download from the Eurostat website (***http://epp.eurostat.ec.europa.eu***) where the most up-to-date statistical tables can also be found.

13 *European Economic Statistics*. A broad overview of the economic developments of European Union Member States. Key areas covered include government finances, balance of payments, foreign trade and the labour market. Commentary is also offered on topical issues arising from the data. It is available to download from the Eurostat website (***http://epp.eurostat.ec.europa.eu***).

14 *European Marketing Data and Statistics*. An annual publication by Euromonitor providing statistical information on the countries of western and eastern Europe. The data cover a wide range of market aspects – including demographic trends, economic indicators, trade, consumer expenditure, retailing – and often show trends over a 21-year period. The information is provided primarily in a spreadsheet format and there is an alphabetical index.

15 *Expenditure and Food Survey*. This annual ONS publication merges the Family Expenditure Survey and the National Food Survey and is available on the ONS website (***www.statistics.gov.uk***). The ONS has overall responsibility for the EFS but DEFRA sponsors the food data. The publication is a survey of spending and other aspects of finance and data on food consumption presented in detailed charts and tables. The EFS is primarily used to provide information for the Retail Prices Index.

16 *Financial Statistics*. A monthly publication by the ONS on a wide range of financial aspects including the accounts of the public and non-public sectors of the economy. Figures cover the latest month or quarter together with those of previous years.

17 *General Household Survey*. A continuous sample survey produced by the ONS, based on the financial year of the general population. The survey spans a wide range of household-related aspects – including housing, health, education and employment – and is widely used as a source of background information for central government decisions on resource allocation. Since 1994 it has been renamed 'Living in Britain: Results of the General Household Survey'. NB: There was a break in the years 1997/8 and 1999/2000.

18 *International Marketing Data and Statistics (IMDAS)*. An international compendium of statistical information on the Americas, Asia, Africa and Oceania published annually by Euromonitor. Information on demographics, economic trends, finance, trade, consumer expenditure and many other areas usually covers a 21-year trend period, and an alphabetical index is provided. Available on CD-ROM – 'World Marketing Data and Statistics'. See also ***www.euromonitor.com***.

19 *Marketing Pocket Book*. Published by NTC Publications. An essential source of statistics and information. Published annually. Sister publications include *European Marketing Pocket Book* and *Retail Pocket Book*.

20 *Monthly Digest of Statistics*. The key source of current information on national income, output and expenditure, population, employment, trade, prices and a range of other areas. Previous as well as current data are provided. Published by ONS and available on-line.

21 *Annual Survey of Hours and Earnings*. Replacing the *New Earnings Survey* in 2004 ASHE presents detailed data in tables on earnings and hours paid for employees within industries, occupations and regions. It is free to download from the ONS website (*www.statistics.gov.uk*).

22 *National Income and Expenditure*. Now known as the *United Kingdom National Accounts* (or 'Blue Book'). Published annually by ONS, it contains data on domestic and national output, income and expenditure, and includes a sector-by-sector analysis. Figures often cover ten years or more and an alphabetical index is provided. Available on CD-ROM and on-line.

23 *OECD Economic Outlook*. A periodic assessment of economic trends, policies and prospects in OECD and non-member countries. Published twice a year, the Outlook includes articles as well as figures, tables, charts and short-term projections, and looks at developments on a country-by-country basis. Available for subscribers on the Internet.

24 *OECD Economic Surveys*. An annual publication by the OECD providing individual country reports of the world's advanced industrial economies. Very useful. Available on CD-ROM.

25 *Regional Trends*. An annual ONS publication providing a wide range of information on social, demographic and economic aspects of the United Kingdom's standard planning regions, together with some data on the sub-regions and on the EU. The guide includes a subject index. Available on the Internet via *www.statistics.gov.uk*.

26 *Social Trends*. Another annual ONS publication, in this case looking at different aspects of British society, including population, education, environment, housing, leisure and transport. It provides a more detailed analysis of data produced for the *Annual Abstract of Statistics* and includes a large number of charts and diagrams. Information often spans a 15–20-year period and an alphabetical subject index is included. Available on the Internet via *www.statistics.gov.uk*.

27 *United Kingdom Balance of Payments*. Known as the 'Pink Book'. It is a comprehensive guide to the United Kingdom's external trade performance and contains a wide range of statistics covering a ten-year period. Available on the Internet (see *Social Trends*).

28 *United Nations Statistical Yearbook*. Written in both English and French, the *Yearbook* is a detailed international comparative analysis of UN member countries. Data cover a wide variety of topics, including international finance, transport and communications, population, trade and wages, and a World Statistical Summary is provided at the beginning.

29 *World Economic Outlook*. Usually published twice a year by the International Monetary Fund (IMF); the focus is on the analysis and projections of global economic developments in the short and medium terms. It also considers current world economic policy issues. It is available in print and also as a free download from the IMF website (*www.imf.org*) where other useful statistics can be found.

Other useful statistical sources

1 Most government departments publish statistics on their own websites. Of particular interest is:
   (a) *Department for Business, Enterprise and Regulatory Reform.* The successor to the Department of Trade and Industry has a useful statistics webpage (*http://stats.berr.gov.uk*) with a wide variety of information, including SME statistics, UK competitiveness indicators, construction and energy statistics and regional data, such as economic performance indicators.
   (b) *Bank of England.* For the very latest information on the UK interest rates and inflation the Bank of England website is invaluable (*www.bankofengland.co.uk*). Other financial data is also available as well as full text publications on surveys and working papers.

2 *Eurostat.* The Statistical Office of the European Communities (Eurostat) is responsible for producing data for the European Union. There are numerous links to information on areas including general and regional statistics, demography, economic development and trade statistics. All are available to view on the Eurostat website (*http://epp.eurostat.ec.europa.eu*).

3 *UK Data Archive.* The UK Data Archive (University of Essex) is a specialist national resource containing the largest collection of accessible computer-readable data in the social sciences and humanities in the UK. Users must register; minimal charges apply for data delivery. Most of the large survey data can be accessed on-line free by academic researchers via MIMAS (see *www.data-archive.ac.uk*).

4 *MIMAS.* Based at the University of Manchester, this is another data centre which provides on-line access to census information, international data and large-scale survey information (e.g. OECD, IMF).

5 *Sources of further information.* By selecting a gateway site, you will often find links to just the information you need much more quickly than by just using Google.
   (a) *Business information on the Internet.* A gateway maintained by Karen Blakeman, including links to websites covering most aspects of business (see *www.rba.co.uk/sources/index.htm*).
   (b) *Useful UK Statistics sites from the University of Glasgow Library.* Very thorough summary (see *www.lib.gla.ac.uk/depts/mops/stats/statistics_on_internet.shtml*).
   (c) *Subject guide to statistics at Warwick.* Although this listing also includes specialist databases (which may not be available without payment) it is a very clear and comprehensive list (see *www2.warwick.ac.uk/services/library/main/tealea/socsciall/lawofficialpublications/statistics/websites2/*).

Information sources

Information on the different aspects of the business environment can be found in a variety of sources, including books, newspapers and periodicals. These often provide a wealth of contemporary data and commentary which can be located relatively easily in most cases, using specialist databases designed to assist the researcher. While an increasing amount of information is available on the Internet, the fastest and most reliable way of finding what you want tends to be to use newspapers and magazines, which are often available electronically (and which are loved by librarians!). In the last few years more and more abstracting databases have moved over to the Web, and now also offer the full text of articles, thereby reducing the amount of time it takes to research a topic. ProQuest (see below) can be used to trace information, but there are other alternatives (e.g. LexisNexis). It is even possible to customise your business databases to cover the most popular titles in a particular library. But remember, the situation tends to change on a regular basis, so you need to keep up to date. Some key sources in this area are discussed below:

1 *RDS Business & Industry.* Covers worldwide trade and business news, sourcing their information from journals, national and international newspapers and industry newsletters. It is available as an on-line subscription database.
2 *Ebsco.* Ebsco have a range of business databases including the *Business Source* range that offer full text articles and abstracts in the areas of business, economics and management.
3 *Newspaper Index.* A very useful website (***www.newspaperindex.com***) giving on-line access to newspapers from around the world. The main international quality newspapers are available here, as well as the Sunday papers. Where an English translated website is available, this is indicated.
4 *Emerald.* An Internet version of all the journals published by MCB University Press; includes some keys titles like the *European Journal of Marketing*. Also includes abstracts from many other journals in the *Emerald* reviews section.
5 *FT Intelligence.* This on-line subscription database combines a ten-year rolling archive of the *Financial Times* and Europe Intelligence Wire (formally known as FT McCarthy). Especially good for European financial and economic news, it is a good starting point when researching current events.
6 *General BusinessFile ASAP.* On-line database used in business research, covering a wide range of academic and trade journals.
7 *IMID/MICWeb.* Based on the holdings of the Institute of Management's book and journal article databases which form part of the largest collection of resources on management in Europe, focusing on all aspects of management theory and practice. MICWeb is updated monthly, as is the IMID CD-ROM. Business students can join the Institute of Management and have access to the library services.
8 *ProQuest.* ProQuest have a series of databases useful for business students. Particularly noteworthy is ABI/Inform. Though not as large as some other business databases, ABI/Inform is noted for the quality of its abstracting and information retrieval.

Other useful sources

1 *Bank of England Quarterly Bulletin.* An assessment of economic developments in the United Kingdom and the rest of the world. It includes articles and speeches, together with general commentary on the economy, and is available from the Bank of England website.
2 *Bank Reviews.* Quarterly publications by some of the leading clearing banks and often available free on request. These include *Barclays Economic Review* and *Lloyds Economic Bulletin*.

3 *Business Studies Update*. A very helpful source of discussion on contemporary business issues. Publication of this resource has been transferred from Hidcote Press to the Business School at the University of Lincoln. Released annually, it is free to download from the University of Lincoln website (*www.lincoln.ac.uk/lbs/resources/update)*.

4 *CBI Industrial Trends Survey*. A quarterly guide to the state of UK manufacturing industry based on questionnaire responses by businesses. It provides a useful insight into business prospects and an indicator to future changes.

5 *Company Annual Reports*. Available on request from all public companies and some private ones. Many are available on-line through company websites or from the following sites:

   (a) *Annual Reports.com* offers free access to many popular American companies. Though you are unlikely to find some of the more obscure companies, this is still a useful resource (*www.annualreports.com*).

   (b) *CAROL* is an on-line service offering direct links to the financial pages of listed companies in Europe and the USA. This is a practical site for company balance sheets, profit and loss statements and financial highlights. Annual reports are also available to registered users (see *www.carol.co.uk*).

   (c) *Corporate information*. Gateway providing international coverage of company information including industry sector profiles, economic data and country and regional-specific searches (see *www.corporateinformation.com*).

   (d) *Financial Times Annual Reports Service* (*http://ftcom.ar.wilink.com/asp/ P002_search_ENG.asp*). The site is sponsored by the participating companies which can be searched for by either name or sector. The requested reports can be delivered either on-line or by mail (in some instances). There is also an alerting service to notify users when a specified report is issued.

   (e) *Wright research centre*. This site includes information on 18 000 companies in fifty countries. In many cases it includes ten years of financial data (see *www.wisi.com/ramainnew.htm*).

6 *Economics Update*. Another annual publication by Hidcote Press and designed to provide a review and discussion of contemporary issues relevant to students of economics and business.

7 *Ernst and Young's International Business Series*. Many are free to download from their website (*www.ey.com*). PriceWaterhouse Cooper produce a similar series also prefixed with the title 'Doing business in...' and are freely available from their website (*www.pwc.com*).

8 *European Business Review*. A pan-European journal published by MCB University Press. It includes articles, editorial comment, news reports and a discussion of recent publications. The journal also incorporates the *New European* which looks at the more cultural, political and environmental developments within Europe. Has CD-ROM and on-line facilities.

9 *European Journal of Marketing*. Another publication by MCB University Press, relevant particularly to students of international marketing. It includes abstracts in French, German and Spanish and offers an on-line service.

10 *Income Data Services*. A regular series of studies and reports on pay and other labour-market issues (e.g. teamworking, child care, redundancy), containing valuable up-to-date information and some statistical analysis. Available on the Internet via *www.incomesdata.co.uk*.

11 *Journal of Marketing*. A quarterly publication by the American Marketing Association and comprising articles together with recent book reviews in the field of marketing. Details of the journal and some sample articles can be found on the AMA website *www.marketingpower.com*.

12 *Kelly's Business Directory*. Marketed as a business-to-business supplier search engline, basic information is available free on their website (*www.kellysearch.co.uk*).

13 *Key British Enterprises*. A multi-volume compendium from Dun and Bradstreet giving details of Britain's top 50 000 companies. Companies are listed alphabetically and are also indexed by trade, product and geographical location. Available on the Internet via *www.dnb.co.uk*; also on CD-ROM.

14 *Kompass (United Kingdom)*. A multi-volume directory with details on companies including products and services, industrial trade names and employee numbers. The Kompass website (*www.kompass.com*) allows a product or company search in 66 countries worldwide; basic information is free.

15 *Management Decision*. Published ten times a year by MCB University Press. Looks at management strategy and issues. Available on CD-ROM and on-line.

16 *Marketing*. A weekly source of facts and articles on various aspects of marketing, presented in a journalistic style. Available on the Internet via *www.haymarket. com/marketing/marketing_magazine/default.aspx*.

17 *Marketing Intelligence*. Also known as *Mintel Marketing Intelligence* and an invaluable source of information and statistics on a wide range of products. Reports cover market factors, trends, market share, the supply structure and consumer characteristics, and frequently include forecasts of future prospects. Available on-line via *www.mintel.co.uk*.

18 *Retail Price Index – Headline Rate*. A site maintained by Devon County Council giving a table with the RPI (headline rate), month by month for the last 30 years. Available at *www.devon.gov.uk/economyrpi.htm*.

19 *The Economist*. A standard reference source, published weekly and examining economic and political events throughout the world. It is an invaluable publication for business students and regularly contains features on specific business-related topics. It has a useful update on basic economic indicators. Available on the Internet via *www.economist.co.uk* or *www.economist.com*.

20 *WARC Advertising and Marketing Knowledge*. The World Advertising Research Centre's Advertising and Marketing Knowledge database is a vast collection of case studies and articles from authoritative sources. It covers all areas of advertising, marketing and media activity. The database also contains demographic information on a wide range of countries. Available at *www.warc.com*.

21 *Who Owns Whom*. An annual publication which identifies parent companies and their subsidiaries. It is a very useful source of information for examining the pattern of corporate ownership in the United Kingdom. Companion volumes are also available covering other parts of the world.

A final comment

When researching a business topic you are particularly recommended to use library catalogue sites, especially the British Library catalogue (*www.bl.uk*) and COPAC (*http://copac.ac.uk*), which is the combined catalogue of major British academic libraries. WorldCat (*www.worldcat.org*) is an integration of over 10 000 library catalogues from across the world, so WorldCat could be useful when searching for more obscure international business information. You might also want to check references on Internet bookshops sites such as Blackwell's (*http://bookshop.blackwell.co. uk/jsp/welcome.jsp*) or *Amazon.co.uk*. For older material *Abe.co.uk* is useful as they specialise in older, out of print books.

Synopsis

As the chapter has demonstrated, there is a need for business organisations to monitor the environment in which they exist and operate and, where possible, to anticipate changes which are likely to affect the enterprise. Rather than being an optional extra, environmental analysis and scanning should be seen as an intrinsic part of strategic management and should ideally provide data and information that are used to guide the decision-making process. Many of these data and much of the information already exist in published form and/or can be easily gathered from both literary and electronic sources on a national and international basis. Analysing them is also possible, using a range of techniques which have been developed by businesses and academics over a considerable number of years.

Summary of key points

- A firm's business environment changes over time.

- Firms need to consider and anticipate potential changes in their general and operational environments in order to take advantage of opportunities and/or minimise possible threats.

- Environmental analysis should be seen as a key part of the strategic management process; ideally it should form part of the basis on which corporate decisions are taken.

- Such analysis can occur at both a societal level (e.g. through PESTLE analysis) and at a task level (e.g. through industry-based approaches) and can involve the use of a wide variety of established techniques.

- Key techniques include trend extrapolation, scenario writing, the Delphi approach, cross-impact matrices and SWOT analysis.

- In researching the business environment, students and practitioners can utilise a wide range of information sources, many of which are relatively inexpensive and readily accessible.

- Accessing this information has been made considerably easier with improvements in information technology, especially the Internet.

Co-opetition and the influence of the macroenvironment on industry analysis: the case of Sony Blu-ray

On 18 February 2008, Toshiba announced its withdrawal from the market of its HD-DVD range, leaving the path now clear for Sony and its Blu-ray DVDs to provide the sole standard for high definition or second generation DVDs.

The announcement brought to an end a near six-year format war between the rival giant organisations, which had resembled in many ways the format battle during the 1980s between Sony's Betamax and JVC's VHS.

At stake was a market that was worth nearly $25 billion a year.

Both Toshiba and Sony were intent on providing rival high definition DVDs to replace the existing DVD format which had first entered the market in late 1995. Back in 1993, Sony and Philips were developing a high density optical storage disk called the Multimedia Compact Disk (MMCD), whilst a consortium including Toshiba, JVC, Thomson, Pioneer, Mitsubishi, Matsushita, Hitachi, Pioneer and Time Warner was working on what it called the Super Density Disk (SDD). A format war was narrowly avoided after pressure from a number of computer manufacturers for the two camps to agree on a single standard. Ultimately, the SDD format won the day, and the DVD was subsequently introduced using much of the SDD technology.

The DVD proved hugely successful and sales of pre-recorded films now account for nearly 50 per cent of the total revenues of the Hollywood studios, although sales growth of DVDs has slowed dramatically as the product enters the maturity phase of its life cycle.

Sony first introduced its Blu-ray disk in 2002 at a trade show in Japan. The new Blu-ray disk had far more storage capacity than standard DVDs (25 or 50GB versus the 4.7GB of standard DVDs). This additional capacity would enable a Blu-ray DVD to contain not only far more material (for example, all three Lord of the Rings films and extras) on a single disk but also have far superior picture and sound quality. With the introduction of large flat screen LCD and plasma televisions, it was envisaged that DVDs with near cinematic audio and visual quality would be a natural complementor.

Meanwhile, Toshiba was developing its own HD-DVD format. Picture and sound quality would be virtually identical to the Blu-ray, but Toshiba was trusting that it would succeed over Sony as its production costs were significantly lower. The HD-DVD format built upon common production and manufacturing activities associated with the manufacture of standard DVDs.

Both disk formats were considered incompatible and both Sony and Toshiba realised that in order for either format to become the industry standard it would be necessary for both firms to enter into a series of collaborative arrangements with other organisations throughout the industry. The Hollywood studios and DVD player manufacturers would need to cooperate in order to compete.

In 2005, the Blu-ray Disk Association was formed; founding members included Sony, Pioneer Electronics, Sharp and Panasonic, along with Dell and Hewlett Packard, the two largest manufacturers of personal computers. Toshiba's rival HD-DVD format was supported by Sanyo, NEC and Microsoft. With both formats having dedicated DVD player manufacturers on board, focus then turned to two further critical industry sectors, the film studios and game consuls market.

In both areas, Sony had a distinct advantage. The Sony Corporation had owned the Columbia Tristar film studio since 1989, which was now the fourth largest Hollywood studio by box office revenue. Sony was also the market leader in sales of game consuls and was about to release the eagerly awaited PlayStation3 (PS3) in 2006. The PS3 would have an integrated Blu-ray DVD player.

The HD-DVD also had some significant supporters, most notably Bill Gates at Microsoft. In response to the challenge of the PlayStation3, Microsoft's Xbox360 would be compatible with the HD-DVD format, although 'gamers' would need to purchase a separate hard drive. The founder of Microsoft also had influence in Hollywood, as the co-owner of Dreamworks Animations, the sister company to Paramount Pictures.

By 2007, all but one of the major film studios had decided which DVD format they would support. Warner Bros, the largest studio, was the only one that was prepared to offer its films in both formats (see Table 18.2).

Table 18.2 The major film studios' choice of format

Studio	Market share by revenue	Format	
		HD-DVD	Blu-ray
Warner Bros/ New Line	19.7	✓	✓
Paramount	15.5	✓	
Disney/Buena Vista	14.0		✓
Sony/Columbia	12.9		✓
Universal	11.4	✓	
20th Century Fox	10.5		✓
Lionsgate	3.8		✓
MGM/UA	3.8		✓
Other	8.4		

Source: *The Economist*, 'Everything's gone Blu', 12 January 2008, p. 56.

With the battle for Hollywood's adoption of a favoured format for pre-recorded films finely balanced, the net result was confusion among the general public. Consumers had no idea which format would ultimately become the standard, and whilst the film studios would continue to sell new releases and their back catalogue in standard DVD, there seemed little logic in purchasing a dedicated high definition DVD player that would only be able to recognise one of the two new formats. Therefore, sales of both new format DVDs and DVD players remained negligible.

Sony's eventual victory was predominantly down to the success of its 2006 launched PS3. Globally, sales of PS3 since its introduction has risen to over 10.5 million and with the built-in Blu-ray player, the Blu-ray disk became the *de facto* standard. Toshiba's sales of HD-DVD players was languishing at nearer to 1 million, and the end was in sight when in late 2007 American retailers Wal-Mart and Best Buys, along with video rental firm Blockbuster, decided to cease orders of HD-DVDs due to low sales volumes. In January 2008, Warner Bros decided that it would also no longer have its films pre-recorded on the Toshiba format and would adopt exclusively the Blu-ray format. With minimal pre-recorded material now available on HD-DVD, and low purchase volumes of HD-DVD dedicated players, there was no alternative but for Toshiba to exit the market. The spoils of victory, however, cannot yet be savoured by Sony, for whilst the format war may be over, it now has to face a potentially far more significant threat as a result of technological change.

Technological developments in broadband speed and connectivity are now driving increasing demand for electronic distribution of content through downloading. Increasing bandwidth makes streaming and downloading of high definition video accessible to many. Whilst the Blu-ray DVD undoubtedly offers far enhanced viewing quality to standard DVDs, the drivers of customer demand now seem to be predicated upon convenience, speed and portability. MP3s, for example, are as popular, if not more so, than music CDs, despite the latter's superior audio quality. Meanwhile, media and IT firms, such as Apple and Netflix are making more and more video content available on-line with little or no compromise on quality.

How Sony, the Hollywood studios, Blu-ray player manufacturers and DVD retailers respond to the on-line challenge of digital distribution will ultimately determine if the DVD format war was a profitable strategy.

Case study questions

1 What in your view are the key environmental influences shaping corporate strategy in this industry?

2 What examples of co-opetition are evident in the case study?

Review and discussion questions

1 Discuss the costs and benefits to businesses of the introduction of a system for monitoring and analysing the changing external environment in which they operate.

2 To what extent do you agree with the proposition that only large firms should or can make use of the various techniques of environmental analysis?

3 Using a firm or organisation of your choice, attempt a 'SWOT' analysis. For example, can you apply such an analysis to the organisation in which you work or study?

4 Using the information sources discussed in the text, and any others with which you are familiar, provide a comparative analysis of consumer markets in at least eight leading European countries (including eastern Europe).

Assignments

1 You work for a medium-sized private company in the UK fashion industry (it can be on either the production or the retailing side). As a personal assistant to the managing director, your brief is to provide help and advice on various aspects of the firm's operations. You have recently become concerned about the lack of a system for monitoring changes in the business environment and have agreed to produce a report on the issue for the board of directors. In producing this report, you are required to identify both the costs and the benefits to the business of implementing a system of environmental scanning.

2 As a librarian in a college (or university) library, with responsibility for help and advice to students on business studies courses, you are frequently asked for guidance on how to access information and data on a particular company. Choosing any well-known company you wish, produce a diagrammatic representation (e.g. flow chart) of the steps you would advise students to undertake to get the information they require. At each step, indicate what type of information is available and how and from where it can be obtained.

Further reading

Brandenburger, A. and Nalebuff, B., 'The Right Game: Use Game Theory to Shape Strategy', *Harvard Business Review*, Jul–Aug, 1995, pp. 57–71.

Cook, M. and Farquharson, C., *Business Economics: Strategy and Applications*, Pitman, 1998.

Cooke, S. and Slack, N., *Making Management Decisions*, 2nd edition, Prentice Hall, 1991.

The Economist, 'There will be blood', 23 February 2008.

Edwards, C., 'RIP, HD-DVD', *Business Week*, 21 February 2008.

Fahey, L. and Narayanan, V. K., *Macroenvironmental Analysis for Strategic Management*, West Publishing, 1986.

Finlay, Paul. N., *Strategic Management: An Introduction to Business and Corporate Strategy*, Financial Times/Prentice Hall, 2000.

Grant, R. M., *Contemporary Strategy Analysis*, 6th edition, Blackwell Business, 2007.

Gupta, U. and Clarke, R., 'Theory and Applications of the Delphi Technique: A Bibliography (1975–1994)', *Technological Forecasting and Social Change*, Volume 53, 1996, pp. 185–211.

Jasmin, M. and Wolpin, S., 'Hollow victory for Blu-ray.' *Electronic Engineering Times*, 20 June 2008.

Johnson, G., Scholes, K. and Whittington, R., *Exploring Corporate Strategy*, 8th edition, Financial Times/Prentice Hall, 2008.

Proctor, T., 'Strategic marketing management for health management: cross impact matrix and TOWS', *Journal of Management in Medicine*, 14 (1), 2000, pp. 47–56.

Ringland, G., *Scenario Planning: Managing for the Future*, Wiley, 1998.

Rowe, G. and Wright, G., 'The Delphi Technique as a forecasting tool: issues and analysis', *International Journal of Forecasting*, Volume 15, 1999, pp. 353–375.

Snider, M., 'The DVD War', *Maclean's*, 10 January 2005.

Weihrich, H., 'Daimler-Benz's move towards the next century with the TOWS matrix', *European Business Review*, 93 (1), 1993, pp. 4–11.

Wheelen, T. L. and Hunger, J. D., *Strategic Management and Business Policy*, 11th edition, Pearson Education (US), 2008.

Worthington, I., Britton, C. and Rees, A., *Business Economics: Blending Theory and Practice*, 2nd edition, Financial Times/Prentice Hall, 2005, esp. Chapter 15.

web link

Web links and further questions are available on the website at:
www.pearsoned.co.uk/worthington

Chapter 4
The Demographic, Social and Cultural Context of Business

The demographic, social and cultural context of business

Ian Worthington

Organisations exist and function within society and consequently are subject to a variety of social influences. These influences, which include demography, social class and culture, can change over time and affect both the demand and supply side of the economy. Marketing organisations recognise and make use of these factors when segmenting markets for consumer goods and services.

Learning outcomes

Having read this chapter you should be able to:

● explain the notions of demography, social class, lifestyles, reference groups, culture and sub-culture

● identify key demographic and social trends that can affect organisations in the private, public and voluntary sectors

● provide examples of how demographic, social and cultural factors can influence both the demand and supply side of the economy

● outline the concept of market segmentation and demonstrate how marketing organisations can use demographic and socio-cultural variables to segment consumer markets

Key terms

ACORN
Ageing population
Birth rate
Cultural diversity
Culture
Death rate
Demographic time-bomb
Demography
Dependent population

Family life cycle
Geo-demographic
    segmentation
Lifestyles
Market segmentation
MOSAIC
Natural population change
Net migration
Primary reference group

Psychographic
    segmentation
Reference group
Secondary reference group
Social class
Social mobility
Sub-culture
VALS

Introduction

As previous chapters have demonstrated, human beings are a critical element of business activity both in their role as producers (e.g. workers, managers, entrepreneurs) and as consumers of outputs provided by the private, public and voluntary sectors. Put simply, business activity ultimately takes place because of and for people, a point well illustrated by the concept of the circular flow of income (CFI) (Chapter 5) and by the systems model introduced in Chapter 1. In order to more fully understand the environment in which business organisations exist and operate, it is important to consider how broader 'social' influences affect business organisations by examining how they can impact upon both the demand and supply side of the economy.

In this chapter we look at three such influences: demography, social aspects and the idea of culture and illustrate how these can affect both the amount and types of goods and services consumed within an economy and different aspects of the production process. In the next chapter, on the resource context, we examine people as a key factor of production and look at a number of areas associated with the concept of the workforce.

As the CFI model clearly shows, both the demand and supply side of the economy are interrelated (e.g. consider the notion of 'derived demand') and the same is often true for demographic, social and cultural influences. For example, in some countries, changing attitudes to female participation in the workforce (a socio-cultural factor) have helped to influence family sizes (a demographic factor) and this in turn has had implications for both the markets for goods and services and for human resources. To simplify the analysis, however, we have chosen to examine the different social influences and their impact on the economy separately but would encourage you to think of the various ways in which the different factors can be interconnected, both in themselves and with other macroenvironmental variables (e.g. the political environment).

The examples provided below are by no means exhaustive and you might like to think of others based on your own interest and/or experience (e.g. public administration students should consider the impact of a changing demographic and socio-cultural environment on the supply of and demand for public sector services such as education, pensions and healthcare). Moreover, the analysis can also be applied across different countries and cultures and ideally should seek to demonstrate the impact of socio-cultural and demographic change on business activity.

The demographic environment of business

Demography is the study of populations both in terms of their overall size and their structural characteristics. From a business point of view the key areas of interest include the age structure of a given population, its gender balance, its geographical distribution and the tendency for both the size and structure of the population to change over time. As noted above, demographic change can have important implications for both the demand and supply side of the economy and hence for organisations of all types.

The size of the population

A country's population normally increases over time and will vary according to such factors as changes in the birth and death rates and in the rate of net migration (see below). For example, the UK population in 1971 was just under 56 million, by 2008 this had risen to 60 million. Estimates suggest that by 2021 the UK will have a population of just under 64 million and that this could peak at almost 67 million by 2050 before it starts to fall back again (see below). In comparison, Russia's current population of around 145 million is projected to fall to about 100 million by 2050 as a result of a declining birth rate and a rising death rate in the wake of the country's economic collapse. If this occurs the world's biggest country will have fewer people than countries such as Uganda and Egypt. It is worth remembering, however, that future population changes are only projections and that these can vary considerably over time as new data become available. For example, in late 2007 the UK's Office for National Statistics provided three projections for the UK population by 2081: 63 million (lowest estimate); 108.7 million (highest estimate); 85 million (most likely estimate). These estimates show considerable variation and indicate how future population changes are relatively unpredictable, which can make forward planning difficult.

Table 6.1 indicates the wide variations that can occur in the size of national populations by examining a range of countries across the globe. Within the EU we can see that major member countries such as France, Germany, Italy and the UK all had populations over 50 million in 2008, while the majority of the new member states had populations below 10 million. These figures are dwarfed, however, by India and China, which had populations of around 1.1 billion and 1.3 billion respectively. Such differences in overall population size have important economic implications in areas such as potential market size, workforce availability, public expenditure, economic growth and international trade.

Table 6.1 Population size in selected countries, 2008

Country	Population (millions)
Germany	82.4
France	64.0
UK	60.9
Italy	58.1
Netherlands	16.6
Greece	10.7
Poland	38.5
Hungary	9.9
Slovakia	5.4
Malta	0.4
USA	303.8
India	1148.0
China	1330.0

Source: Various (including Eurostat).

The age and sex distribution of the population

In addition to examining the overall size of a country's population, demographers are also interested in its structural characteristics, including the balance between males and females and the numbers of people in different age categories. Table 6.2 provides illustrative data for the UK population by age and gender for selected age groups and intervals over the period 1971–2021. As can be seen from the figures in the right-hand column, women outnumber men in the UK population despite the fact that the annual number of male births slightly exceeds that of female births. Moreover, the data clearly point to an **ageing population**, with an increasing percentage of the population in the over 65 group and a decreasing percentage in the under 16 category. Projections suggest that by 2013 the number of over 65s in the UK population will exceed the number who are under 16, a trend which is sometimes described as the **demographic time-bomb** and which has important implications for both the private and public sectors, not least in terms of the overall demand for goods and services including 'public goods' such as education, healthcare, social services, state pensions and social security arrangements.

Table 6.2 Distribution of UK population by age and gender, 1971–2021, at selected intervals

	Under 16 (%)	35–44 (%)	55–64 (%)	Over 65 (%)	All ages (millions)
Males					
1971	27	12	11	10	27.2
2001	21	15	11	14	28.8
2021[1]	18	13	13	18	31.4
Females					
1971	24	11	12	16	28.8
2001	19	15	11	18	30.2
2021[1]	17	12	13	22	32.4

Note: [1] Projections.
Source: Adapted from *Social Trends* (2005).

It is worth noting that the UK's ageing population is a characteristic shared by many other countries, including those in the European Union. Data produced by Eurostat indicate similar trends in both the original EU-15 and in the new accession countries (Table 6.3). In comparison, both India and China have a much smaller percentage of the population in the over 65 category, the figures being 4.8 per cent and 7.4 per cent respectively for 2003.

Table 6.3 Percentage of EU populations aged 65 and over for selected EU countries, 1970–2006

Country	1970	1991	2003	2006
Germany	13	15	17	19
Belgium	13	15	17	17
Spain	9	14	17	17
Finland	9	13	15	16
Denmark	12	16	15	15
Estonia	12	12	16	17
Lithuania	10	11	15	15
Czech Republic	12	13	14	14
Slovakia	9	10	12	12
EU-27 average	12	14	16	17

Source: Adapted from Eurostat and ONS.

Other structural characteristics

Populations can also be examined in a number of other ways including their ethnicity and geographical distribution. For instance, in the 2001 population census in the UK, around 8 per cent of people surveyed described themselves as belonging to a minority ethnic group, with the largest grouping being Indian, accounting for almost 2 per cent of the total population and nearly 23 per cent of those in the ethnic minority category. The census data show that, in general, minority ethnic groups in the UK have a younger age structure than those in the 'White Group' and tend to be highly concentrated in large urban centres, particularly London. For the UK population as a whole, the majority of people live in England, with significant concentrations in regions such as the south-east, the Midlands, the north-west and the north-east, a fact which has important economic, political and social ramifications. Moreover, inter-regional movements of population, together with other factors such as international migration and differential birth and death rates, can result in significant local and regional variations in population over time with a knock-on effect for both the public and private sectors (for example, demand for housing and school places).

Population change

As the previous analysis indicates, populations can change in either size and/or structure, with important consequences for economic activity both within and between countries. The size and structure of a country's population depend on a number of variables, the most important of which are the birth rate, the death rate and the net migration rate.

The birth rate

Birth rates tend to be expressed as the number of live births per thousand of the population in a given year. In many countries this figure has been falling steadily over a long period of time for a number of reasons. These include:

- A trend towards smaller families as people become better off and health improves and death rates fall.
- The increased availability of contraception.
- The trend towards later marriages and later childbearing for social and/or economic reasons.
- Declining fertility rates.
- Changing attitudes towards women and work.

In some countries governments have offered financial and other incentives to married couples to try to reduce the birth rate (e.g. China) as a means of controlling population growth. In other countries incentives have been offered to try to reverse the actual or potential decline in the birth rate because of its economic consequences (e.g. France, Singapore). Declining birth rates are, of course, an important contributor to an ageing population; they can also have other consequences. For instance, a recent increase in the birth rate in the UK has led to a call by the Optimum Population Trust for British couples to restrict themselves to 2 children in order to reduce the impact of population growth on the natural environment.

The death rate

Like birth rates, **death rates** are usually measured per thousand of the population in a given year. For developed economies such as the UK this figure has tended to fall over time before reaching a plateau. Among the main contributors to this trend have been:

- Rising living standards, including better housing, sanitation and nutrition.
- Developments in medical technology and practice.
- Better education.
- Improved working conditions.

The difference between the birth rate and the death rate represents the **natural change** in the population (i.e. increase or decrease).

Net migration

Apart from the movement of population within a country (internal migration), people may move from one country to another for a variety of reasons. The balance between those leaving (emigrants) and those entering (immigrants) a country over a given period of time represents the rate of **net migration**. Along with changes in the birth and/or death rate, this can be a significant factor in population change and can have important consequences for the economy (e.g. the gain or loss of certain skills) and for the political system. In the UK, recent estimates (2007) suggest that around 70 per cent of the country's future population growth might come both directly and indirectly from migration, much of which is related to EU enlargement.

Influences on the rate of net migration include:

- Legal barriers (e.g. immigration laws).
- Economic migrancy.
- The numbers fleeing persecution.
- Government policy.
- Political developments.

Demographic change and business

Changes in the size and/or structure of a country's population can have important consequences for enterprises in the public, private and voluntary sectors both in the short and long term. Given increased globalisation and international trade, the impact of demographic change has an international as well as a national dimension for a growing number of trading organisations.

The following examples provide illustrations of how a changing demography can influence both the level and pattern of demand within an economy and in turn help to explain why changes can occur in a country's economic and industrial structure (see Chapter 12) and why some countries engage in international trade (see Chapter 16). Demographic change can also have important effects on the supply side of the economy.

You should try to think of other examples.

- As populations grow in size the demand for many types of goods and services also tends to grow (e.g. energy, consumer durables, food). A growing population also provides a larger workforce, other things being equal.
- An 'ageing population' increases the demand for a range of public, private and voluntary sector goods and services (e.g. healthcare, pensions, specialist holidays, sheltered housing). It also creates an increasingly **dependent population**.
- A declining birth rate influences the demand for education, children's products, childcare, certain TV programmes, comics, toys, etc. It can also reduce the numbers of young people available to enter the workforce to replace those who retire.
- Changes in the ethnic make-up of the population can affect the demand for particular food products, clothing and media services and can place increased demands on public authorities (e.g. documents printed in different languages). Some researchers also argue that a more diverse workforce can improve an organisation's performance.
- The regional redistribution of the population will affect the consumption of a range of goods and services including housing, education, healthcare, transport, energy and many day-to-day products. It can also affect prices (e.g. in the housing market) and the make-up of the local labour market.

On a more general level, it is also worth noting that demographic change can impact on a country's social as well as its economic structure and that this can result in increased (or reduced) demands on a range of organisations, particularly those in the public sector. For example, the growing imbalance being experienced in many countries between an increasing and dependent elderly population and a diminishing population of working age touches on many areas of public policy, from healthcare and social provision on the one hand to pensions and fiscal policy on the other. Governmental responses to the consequences of demographic change can have both direct and indirect consequences for a wide variety of organisations across the economy.

The social context

Since organisations exist and operate in society, they are subject to a variety of societal influences that operate at both a general and specific level. In this section we consider some of the key factors within an organisation's social environment, starting with the concept of social class. The notion that organisations also have responsibilities to society is examined in Chapter 9.

Social class

Throughout history, all societies have normally exhibited a certain degree of social and economic inequality that has given rise to the tendency to classify individuals into different social categories. For example, in India the 'caste system' has been an important source of social differentiation and one which has exerted a key influence over the life and opportunities available to members of the different castes. In other countries, including the United Kingdom, the categorisation of individuals has often been based around notions of **social class**, the idea of grouping people together who share a similar social status which is related to certain common features such as educational background, income and occupation. Whereas in some types of social system, movement between groups is either very difficult or impossible (e.g. the caste system), in others **social mobility** is frequently observed, with some individuals able to move relatively quickly between the different social strata (e.g. upper class, middle class, working class) as their personal circumstances change.

In practice, the process of allocating individuals to a particular class category has generally been based on socio-economic criteria such as income, wealth and occupational status. Advertisers and market researchers – including the Institute of Practitioners in Advertising – have tended to favour a scheme known as 'ABC1' (see Table 6.4) which uses an individual's occupation as a basis for allocation, the assumption being that a person's job is closely linked to key aspects of her/his attitudes and behaviour, including their choice of car, clothes, home furnishings, holidays, reading material and so on. There is even evidence to suggest that class might be influential in an individual's choice of retail outlets (e.g. different UK supermarket chains appear to attract customers from different socio-economic groups).[1]

Table 6.4 The ABC1 system of social grading

Social grading	Social status	Occupation
A	Upper middle class	Higher managerial, administrative and professional
B	Middle class	Intermediate managerial, administrative and professional
C1	Lower middle class	Supervisory or clerical, junior managerial, administrative and professional
C2	Skilled working class	Skilled manual workers
D	Working class	Semi and unskilled manual workers
E	Lowest subsistence level	State pensioners or widows, casual workers, lowest grade workers

Similar systems of classification have also been/are used for official purposes (e.g. the UK 10-year census of population). In the 1990s in the UK, government statistics used what was called the Registrar General's Social Scale – subsequently renamed 'Social Class based on Occupation' – to group the UK population into seven different categories according to their occupation (e.g. Group I was professional; Group II was managerial and technical; Group V was unskilled occupations). This system has now been replaced by NS-SEC (the National Statistics Socio-Economic Classifications) which again focuses on occupation as the key criterion for class allocation. NS-SEC is shown in Table 6.5. The figures in the right-hand column represent the socio-economic classification of the UK population of working age in the summer of 2003.[2]

Table 6.5 National Statistics Socio-Economic Classifications (NS-SEC)

Category	Occupation	Estimated % of working population in 2003
1	Higher managerial and professional occupations	10.8
1.1	Employers and managers in larger organisations (e.g. company directors, senior managers, senior civil servants, senior police and armed forces officers)	
1.2	Higher professionals such as doctors, lawyers, teachers, social workers, clergy	
2	Lower managerial/professional occupations including nurses, midwives, journalists, actors, musicians, prison officers, etc.	22.2
3	Intermediate occupations, for example clerks, secretaries, driving instructors	10.3
4	Small employers and own-account workers such as publicans, farmers, taxi drivers, window cleaners, painters and decorators	7.7
5	Lower supervisory, craft and related occupations including plumbers, printers, train drivers and butchers	9.4
6	Semi-routine occupations, for example shop assistants, hairdressers, bus drivers, cooks	13.3
7	Routine occupations such as labourers, couriers, waiters, refuse collectors	9.8
8	People who have never had paid work or are long-term unemployed	16.5

Source: Office of National Statistics.

While it would be unwise to assume that a factor such as a person's social class will invariably affect their choice of goods and services, empirical evidence reveals some interesting variations in the levels of expenditure on particular products among different groups in the UK population, a fact not lost on marketing organisations which often use socio-economic criteria as one way to segment a market (see below). According to data produced in the annual survey of Social Trends in the UK (see Table 6.6), total expenditure was highest among the managerial and professional group and was almost double that of people in the never worked/unemployed category. Within this overall pattern of expenditure some interesting data emerges, particularly with regards to priorities, as indicated by expenditure on different items by the different social groupings. For instance, expenditure on housing, fuel and power was highest among the never worked/long-term unemployed group while spending on health was highest among the managerial group. Note that some of the high levels of spending among the former group, in areas such as education and communication, are probably largely to do with the fact that this category also contains students.

Table 6.6 Household expenditure (£/week) by socio-economic classification of household, 2006

	Managerial and professional occupations	Intermediate occupations	Routine and manual occupations	Never worked and long-term unemployed[1]
Transport	100.81	70.18	52.49	41.76
Recreation and culture	82.65	67.35	54.46	31.95
Food and non-alcoholic drink	56.70	49.49	45.99	38.05
Housing, fuel and power	56.04	51.83	50.03	63.51
Restaurant and hotels	59.44	41.48	35.51	28.65
Clothing and footwear	35.25	25.45	22.44	25.98
Alcohol and tobacco	12.86	12.69	13.11	8.79
Communication	14.81	14.69	12.13	11.72
Education	15.84	5.24	2.58	15.85
Health	7.32	4.31	4.52	1.37
All household expenditure	676.37	513.81	418.01	323.11

Note: [1]This category includes students.
Source: Adapted from *Expenditure and Food Survey*, ONS.

Lifestyles

Another factor that can clearly affect people's attitudes and behaviour is the **lifestyle** that they choose to adopt. Lifestyles are basically concerned with the way in which people live and how they spend their money, decisions which are not necessarily always linked to their socio-economic position. Two individuals with the same occupation – and nominally in the same social class – may have entirely different lifestyles, a point well illustrated by examining two university lecturers. My own lifestyle is highly sophisticated, environmentally sensitive, artistic and cosmopolitan; that of a colleague – who happens to teach marketing – is narrow, parochial, philistine and consumption-driven. Then, what would one expect?!

Joking apart, lifestyle analysis provides another way of seeking to categorise and explain human behaviour, based on factors such as an individual's interests, activities and opinions as well as on their demographic characteristics. In essence, the proposition is that by examining distinctive patterns of consumer response, a marketing organisation can build up a clearer picture of an individual's habits, preferences and behaviour and by doing so can design more effective and appealing products, marketing programmes and/or communications that can be aimed at specific lifestyle groups.

While we should be cautious of over-generalising, the evidence suggests that in many countries the way in which people spend their time and money has changed considerably in recent decades as a result of changes in demography, working patterns, technology, income and a range of other factors. Once again we can illustrate this by looking at longitudinal data collected through the annual survey of social trends in the UK. These data show, for example, that:

● Cinema attendance in 2004 was the second highest figure in 30 years.
● In 2002/3 around 45 per cent of homes in the UK could access the Internet; this was four times the number in 1998/9. In 2007 84 per cent of households had Internet access with a broadband connection.

- UK residents took over 41 million holidays abroad in 2003, six times the number in 1971.
- Household spending on communications (including mobile phones) increased more than ninefold in real terms between 1971 and 2006.
- Between 1974 and 2005/6, household purchases of fruit in the UK increased by 77 per cent (measured in grams/person per week). Fruit juice purchases, for example, rose tenfold per week during this period.
- In 1993 80 per cent of men and 73 per cent of women held at least one plastic card (e.g. credit/debit/store card); by 2003 this had risen to 91 per cent and 90 per cent respectively.
- The number of licensed cars on Britain's roads more than doubled in the period 1971–2006.
- The number of households with regular use of two cars increased fourfold over the same period.
- In 1996/7 16 per cent of households had a mobile phone; by 2006 the figure was 80 per cent.
- About 60 per cent of homes had a CD player in 1996/7; by 2006 this had topped 80 per cent. During the same period sales of home computers grew from under 30 per cent to 67 per cent.
- Since 1974 UK consumers have halved their consumption of red meat and sales of butter, margarine and cooking fats have also fallen.
- During the period 1997–2003 the amount of household waste collected for recycling more than doubled while the amount of land dedicated to organic food production grew more than sevenfold. By 2006/7 recycling rates had reached 31 per cent.

If we take changing expenditure patterns in the UK as an indication of changes in lifestyles then there has been a discernible shift in emphasis from essential products such as food, housing, water and fuel to the less essential items such as communications, foreign travel, recreation and culture (see Table 6.7). For example, after allowing for inflation, UK household expenditure on food and drink rose by only 52 per cent between 1971 and 2006 whereas spending on communication rose by over nine times. Interestingly spending on alcohol and tobacco actually fell over the same period while spending on healthcare doubled, suggesting a shift in public concern towards a healthier lifestyle (see Mini case: Fit for purpose?).

Table 6.7 Volume of household expenditure on selected items, 1971–2006, expressed as index numbers (base year 1971)

Category of spending	1971	1991	2003	2006
Food and non-alcoholic drink	100	117	141	152
Alcohol and tobacco	100	92	91	89
Housing, water, fuel	100	138	156	160
Health	100	182	205	212
Communication	100	306	846	956
Recreation and leisure	100	283	610	783
Household expenditure abroad	100	298	712	763

Source: Adapted from ONS.

In light of the discussion on inflation in Chapter 5, it is worth noting that such changes in spending patterns over time are reflected in changes in the official 'basket of goods and services' used to calculate the Retail Prices Index in the UK. The 1980s saw CDs, CD players and condoms added to the basket, with computers, camcorders and mobile phone charges added in the next decade. By 2004/5 dishwater tablets had replaced dishwasher powder, wooden garden furniture sets had replaced plastic sets and leather sofas had replaced ordinary ones. More bizarrely, hamsters and popcorn bought in cinemas had been added to the index while baguettes, corned beef and writing paper were dropped (see e.g. the *Guardian*, 22 March 2005, p. 20). By 2007/8, the RPI contained fruit smoothies, USB sticks, peppers, muffins and small oranges and had discarded microwaves, TV repairs, washable carpets and 35 mm camera films. What does this tell us about the changing lifestyles and spending habits of UK citizens; are people in the UK getting healthier?

mini case   Fit for purpose?

One of the important social trends in recent years has been the move towards healthier lifestyles, a development which has been spurred on by concerns over the increased incidence of obesity, diabetes, heart disease and cancer – problems often associated with rising levels of affluence. Along with this trend have come numerous business opportunities including the growth in the number of fitness clubs, health farms and activity holidays and a general rise in the sale of products such as vitamin supplements, fruit juices, blood pressure monitors and books promoting healthier diets. Grocery retailers too have not been slow to exploit the new situation, offering a range of chilled, ready made 'healthier option' meals, often endorsed by a well-known personality (e.g. the UK grocery retailing chain Sainsbury's has used Jamie Oliver, the TV chef, to promote its products; Oliver has also been involved in a well-publicised campaign to improve the nutritional value of school meals in the UK).

As with any change of this kind there tend to be losers as well as winners. For example, according to research by Mintel, sales of the UK's favourite snack, the potato crisp, are in decline as consumers switch to products generally held to be healthier such as dried fruit, cereal bars and nuts. A particular concern for many consumers has been the high fat and high salt content of products such as crisps and this has driven some companies to produce low salt and/or low fat brands and to change the types of fat being used in the product in an effort to boost sales (e.g. the UK-based Walker's Snack Products has a variety cooked in olive oil). Interestingly enough, the apparent trend towards healthier eating in the UK stands in contrast to the experiences in some other European countries, particularly those bordering the Mediterranean (e.g. Italy, Greece, Spain and Portugal). Reports suggest that there has been something of a retreat from the 'Mediterranean diet' of fruit and vegetables and a move towards foods with high fat, sugar and salt content as a growing number of consumers in these countries are influenced by sedentary lifestyles, supermarket shopping and fast-food restaurants.

Many of the trends referred to above are, of course, mirrored in consumer aspirations and behaviour in other countries, particularly in respect of issues such as healthier lifestyles, increased foreign travel, greater access to communications technology and more environmentally friendly products (though not necessarily rodent purchases!). As the following examples illustrate, changes in consumer lifestyles can represent both an opportunity and a threat to trading organisations and can have important implications for businesses and countries alike.

- Coca-Cola has seen a decline in profits as consumers have switched to bottled water, fruit juice and other non-fizzy drinks as part of a healthier diet.
- GlaxoSmithkline has targeted the Italian market with its non-smoking products in the wake of the ban by the Italian government on smoking in public places.
- Beer consumption in Germany has dropped dramatically as young Germans reject a product that they evidently regard as 'uncool' and less healthy than some alternatives.
- Some French wine companies have introduced wine in cartons with a straw to attract the 'eat on the go' young consumer.
- Smoking restrictions in countries such as the UK, Germany, Italy and France have had an impact in various ways (e.g. increase in home drinking; rise in sales of patio heaters; reduced use of slot machines in public houses).
- Sales of Guinness to Africa (especially Nigeria) have grown substantially.
- China has overtaken the USA in sales of televisions and mobile phones and Chinese consumers are increasingly buying a wide range of western consumer goods from luxury confectionery and designer clothes to expensive cars and foreign beers).
- With a rapidly expanding economy and growing liberalisation in many areas of private life, the sex industry in China is booming (see e.g. the *Guardian*, 25 June 2005, p. 20). The country now provides 70 per cent of the world's sex toys and there is a growing (sic) domestic market.
- Sales of organic food are growing significantly across Europe and beyond. The global market for organic food in 2005 was worth about £15 billion, with Europe responsible for just under half.
- With the immense popularity of the iPod and iTunes (its online record store), Apple has become one of the world's fastest-growing brands.
- Other brands in the technology/lifestyle field that are increasing in value include BlackBerry, Google, Amazon, Yahoo and eBay.
- Social networking sites (e.g. Facebook; MySpace) have become very popular particularly in the UK where it is estimated that 25 per cent of adults use such sites around 23 times every month.

Other social influences

While it is important to consider the influence of broad social factors such as class and lifestyles, it is also worth remembering that consumers are individuals and that they are subject to influences that operate at a personal level. Such influences include the wide variety of individuals and groups with whom we come into contact during our lifetime and who may influence our attitudes, values, opinions and/or behaviour. Primary among these are our interactions within the family, with friends or work colleagues and through our involvement with sports and social clubs, religious organisations, trade unions and so on. Such groups are sometimes referred to as **reference groups**.

Groups that have a regular or direct (i.e. face-to-face) influence on us are known as **primary reference groups** while those whose influence tends to be more indirect and formal are known as **secondary reference groups**. The former, in particular, can be very influential in shaping our attitudes and behaviour including our decisions on consumption.

The importance of reference groups, especially family and friends, is recognised by both economists and marketers. Economists, for example, use the notion of 'households' (see Chapter 5) to indicate that the consumption of goods and services often takes place within a collective family framework, as in the case of groceries, holidays, vehicles and many other everyday products. Marketers use concepts such as the **family life cycle** to show changing patterns of consumption as the individual moves from being a child in a family to being a parent with different needs and responsibilities.

While it is difficult to be precise about when and how far an individual's demand is shaped by the family and other reference groups, it is not difficult to think of particular examples when this is likely to be the case. For many services such as builders, restaurants, hotels, hairdressers and car repairs, consumers often rely on the advice of a trusted friend or colleague and many firms can gain new business through such word-of-mouth recommendations. Equally, through membership and/or support of a particular group or club, individuals may be tempted to purchase particular goods and/or services (e.g. football kit, trainers, a CD, tickets), especially those with a desirable 'brand name' and endorsed by a well-known personality (e.g. sportsperson, musician, singer, film star). In such cases, the demand for the product is often less price sensitive (see Chapter 14) since it is a 'must have' product.

The cultural environment

Culture

The term **culture** generally refers to a complex set of values, norms, beliefs, attitudes, customs, systems and artefacts which are handed down from generation to generation through the process of socialisation and which influence how individuals see the world and how they behave in it. Defined in this way, culture can be seen to have at least three important features:

- it comprises both material (e.g. human artefacts such as buildings, literature, art, music) and abstract elements (e.g. rituals, symbols, values);
- it is socially learned and transmitted over time; and
- it influences human behaviour.

As a concept, 'culture' is often applied in a variety of circumstances at both the macro and micro level: terms such as 'western culture', 'Asian culture', 'European culture', 'New York City culture', 'youth culture', 'pop culture', 'entrepreneurial culture' and 'research culture' are just some of the examples of its usage in the modern world. What they have in common is that they imply certain shared aspects of human belief, understanding and behaviour that link individuals together into some form of definable group and/or range of activities.

In a business context, it can be easy to underestimate the degree to which a person's perceptions, attitudes and behaviour can be shaped by cultural influences, some of which may be relatively enduring (e.g. certain 'core' values and beliefs) while others may be more open to change (i.e. secondary beliefs and values). In the United States, for example, American citizens believe in the right of individuals to bear arms and this is enshrined in the US Constitution. The buying and selling of handguns and rifles is thus acceptable within American society, despite the fact that they are frequently used in violent crimes including robbery and murder. In other countries, trade in such weapons tends to be seen as highly questionable by most people and is usually heavily regulated by the government to certain types of weapons for use in acceptable pursuits such as hunting or rifle shooting. Cultural differences such as this can, of course, apply not only to the kinds of goods and services that are consumed (e.g. eating horsemeat in France is acceptable but not in the UK) but also to other aspects of both the production and consumption process and this can have important implications for an organisation's behaviour.

Examples include:

- Who decides what is bought, how it is bought or where it is bought (e.g. in some cultures women have predominantly been the purchasers of household products).
- What colours are acceptable (e.g. the colour associated with bereavement varies across cultures).
- How far harmonisation of products and marketing activities is feasible (e.g. the EUs perennial debates over what constitutes an acceptable definition of certain products such as sausages, Feta cheese, chocolate).
- What factors can enhance the prospect of a sale (e.g. bribes are acceptable in some cultures).
- How business is conducted (e.g. the length of negotiations, the meaning of a handshake).
- The method of communicating with the target audience (e.g. in the UK a single shared language allows organisations to use national media).
- How customer enquiries/complaints are dealt with (e.g. UK businesses using call centres in India often give their operators British names and train them to talk about everyday British preoccupations such as the weather and sport).

In effect, culture not only influences an individual's response to products and the nature of the buying and selling process, but it also exercises a significant influence on the structure of consumption within a given society. For companies which can gain acceptability on a global scale, despite cultural differences between countries, the potential benefits are huge (e.g. global brands such as Coca-Cola, McDonald's, Nike).

While the so-called 'Americanisation' of consumption is not to everyone's taste, other forms of cultural exportation are often more acceptable and can prove highly lucrative for the country concerned. In the UK, for example, overseas earnings from culture and arts-related tourism make a significant contribution to the country's 'invisible earnings' (see Chapter 16) and many other countries benefit in similar ways.

mini case   National cultures

Recognising and responding to cultural differences between countries can have an important impact on how successful organisations are in international trade. But is it possible to generalise about a country's culture?

One academic who has made a significant contribution in this area is Professor Geert Hofstede, who has developed a theory of culture which allows comparisons to be made between the main cultural characteristics in different countries. Hofstede's research is based on data collected from IBM employees across the world while he was working at the company as a psychologist. On the basis of his research Hofstede identified four cultural dimensions; later he added a fifth. These dimensions can be used to compare value systems at different levels, from the family through to the state.

The five cultural dimensions are as follows:

1 *Power distance* – this is concerned with the degree to which the members of a society accept an unequal or hierarchical power structure. In societies where the power distance is large there is a perception that inequality exists and subordinates tend to be more dependent on their superiors. This can result in an autocratic or paternalistic style of management or governance (e.g. in some African countries) which can evoke either positive or negative reactions. Where the power distance is small, individuals tend to see themselves more as equals and management/governance styles tend to be more consultative and less hierarchical (e.g. in northern European countries).

2 *Uncertainty avoidance* – this focuses on how members of society cope with uncertainty in their lives. Where levels of anxiety are generally high, this results in high uncertainty avoidance and people in these cultures are deemed to be more expressive and emotional (e.g. Latin American countries) than in low uncertainty avoidance countries (e.g. many Asian countries).

3 *Individualism* – refers to the extent to which individuals in society see themselves as independent and autonomous human beings or as part of a collectivity. High individualist countries tend to be countries such as the United States, the UK, Canada and Australia; low individualism is said to be prevalent in Asian and Latin American countries.

4 *Masculinity* – is concerned with how far a society is predisposed to aggressive and materialistic behaviour and is linked to gender role. Hofstede associates masculinity with toughness, assertiveness and materialism and with a predisposition to conflict and competition. Femininity, in contrast, is characterised as caring, sensitive and concerned with the quality of life; the result is a more accommodating style based on negotiation and compromise. Hofstede's analysis suggests the more masculine countries include Austria and Japan, while Scandinavian countries tend to be the most feminine.

5 *Long-term orientation* – relates to the degree to which a society embraces a long-term view and respect for tradition. In societies with a short-term orientation people tend to stress the 'here and now', typified by western countries. Eastern cultures, by comparison, are generally held to have a longer-term orientation that emphasises concern for the future and for tradition as well as the present.

One of the benefits of Hofstede's research is that it reminds us that cultural differences can and do occur between states and, as a result, there is no 'one-size-fits-all' style of management or governance that would be suitable across all countries. For companies which are multinational organisations, management styles and approaches in the country of origin may not necessarily be suitable in other parts of the organisation for cultural reasons. Vive la différence!

Sub-culture

A society is rarely, if ever, culturally homogeneous. Within every culture **sub-cultures** usually exist, comprising groups of individuals with shared value systems based on common experiences, origins and/or situations. These identifiable sub-groups may be distinguished by nationality, race, ethnicity, religion, age, class, geographical location or some other factor and their attitudes, behaviour, customs, language and artefacts often reflect sub-cultural differences. At times such differences can be relatively easily accommodated and ultimately may become institutionalised through the legal and/or political process (e.g. the Scottish and Welsh Assemblies – see Chapter 4). At other times sub-cultural differences can be the source of a considerable degree of conflict between various sub-groups, resulting in serious divisions within a society and even in war and genocide.

The UK provides a good example of the notion of **cultural diversity** and can be used to illustrate how this can influence the demand for goods and services. In addition to nationality groups such as the Irish, Scots and Welsh, the country has provided a home for successive generations of immigrants from around the globe and this has created a rich mix of ethnic and other sub-groups, often concentrated in particular parts of the country and having their own language, traditions and lifestyles. In Leicester, for example, where a significant proportion of the population is of Asian origin, there is a substantial Asian business community, part of which has developed to cater specifically for the local ethnic population (e.g. halal butchers, saree shops), as well as attracting custom from the wider community (e.g. Indian restaurants). Many Asian businesses in Leicester are small, family owned enterprises, employing members of the extended family in keeping with cultural traditions. Aspects such as the organisation and financing of the business, its network of relationships and the working conditions for staff are also frequently influenced by cultural values, traditions and norms, although changes in these areas are becoming more apparent, especially among second and third generation Asian-owned enterprises.

Application: market segmentation

Marketers have long recognised the importance of demographic, social and cultural factors in shaping people's demand for goods and services. This is exemplified by the concept of **market segmentation**.

In essence, market segmentation refers to the practice of dividing a market into distinct groups of buyers who share the same or similar attitudes and patterns of behaviour and who might require separate products or marketing to meet their particular needs. By segmenting a market into its broad component parts, businesses should be able to focus their marketing efforts more effectively and efficiently, for example by developing product offerings and marketing programmes which meet the requirements of the different market segments.

Markets can be segmented in a variety of ways and this tends to differ between consumer markets and those which involve business to business transactions. Table 6.8 below outlines some of the major variables used in segmenting consumer markets. As the table indicates, demographic, social and cultural factors provide a basis for identifying distinct market segments within the markets for consumer goods and services. In practice, of course, marketers may use either one (e.g. demography) or a combination (e.g. age, location and social class) of different variables to segment a market they are seeking to target.

Table 6.8 Methods of segmenting consumer markets

Type of segmentation	Key segmentation variables	Examples
Demographic	Age, gender, religion, ethnic group, family size, family life cycle stage	Children's products, ethnic foods, 18–30 holidays, retirement homes, cars
Socio-economic	Social class, income, occupation	Luxury products, convenience services, discount goods
Geographic	Country, region, urban/suburban/ rural, town/city, climate	Country clothing, air conditioning, regional specialities
Geo-demographic	House type and location	Conservatories, lawn mowers
Psychographic	Lifestyles, values, personality	Health/healthier products, cosmetics, cigarettes
Mediagraphic	Media habits (e.g. papers read)	Specialist magazines, eco-friendly holidays
Behavioural	Behavioural characteristics including time/occasion of purchase, loyalty, user status, benefits sought, attitude to product, etc.	Mother's day products, disposable cameras, toothpaste

A good example of combining the different variables is provided by the notion of **geo-demographic segmentation** which focuses on the relationship between an individual's geographical location and her/his demographic characteristics, given that close links frequently exist between a person's place and type of residence and factors such as income, family size and attitudes. One well-known scheme of this type is **ACORN** (A Classification Of Residential Neighbourhoods) which uses 40 variables from population census data to differentiate residential areas. Another is **MOSAIC**, developed by Experian, which draws on a variety of data sources (e.g. census data, financial data, property characteristics, demographic information) and uses a range of sophisticated analytical techniques to produce household profiles at full postcode level. Under the MOSAIC scheme, UK households are currently divided into 11 groups with names such as 'Symbols of Success', 'Suburban Comfort' and 'Grey Perspectives' and these are then further sub-divided into 61 types, again with interesting and evocative names including 'Golden Empty Nesters', 'Sprawling Subtopia' and 'Childfree Serenity'. For a fuller description of MOSAIC and Experian's other products (e.g. commercial MOSAIC) and methodology you should access the company's website at *http://www.experian.co.uk* and follow the links.

With regard to factors such as social class and lifestyles, these tend to be grouped under the notion of **psychographic segmentation**, an approach which has attracted considerable attention in recent years given the reciprocal link between lifestyles and consumption indicated above. Lifestyle segments can be developed either as 'off-the-shelf' products by marketing agencies/management consultancies or can be customised for/by individual companies, although the latter often tend to be both complex and expensive to design. One established and popular example of the former is **VALS** (Values And Lifestyles) developed by SRI International. Under this model, individuals are allocated to different categories on the basis of a combination of demographic and lifestyle factors such as age, education, income and levels of self-confidence and then these categories are grouped into a number of broader segments which reflect a category's predominant orientations. Thus, under VALS 2, the three broad groups identified were (1) people who were *principle-orientated* (i.e. guided by their views of how the world should be); (2) people who were *status-orientated* (i.e. guided by the opinions and actions of others); (3) people who were *action-orientated* (i.e. guided by the desire for social and physical activity, variety in life and risk taking). Again you can gain further information on this scheme by visiting the SRI website at ***www.sric_bi.com***.

Synopsis

All organisations are an integral part of the society in which they exist and carry out their activities and as a result they are affected by a range of influences emanating from the demographic, social and cultural environment. These influences can change over time and help to shape both the demand and supply side of business activity. Businesses and other organisations need to be aware of and respond to the process of societal change and to the opportunities and threats that such change can engender.

Summary of key points

- Organisations exist and operate within society and are subject to a variety of demographic and socio-cultural influences.

- Demography is concerned with population variables, including population size, structure and distribution.

- Changes in demography are primarily related to changes in birth and/or death and/or net migration rates.

- Demographic change can affect both the demand and supply side of the economy.

- The social context of business includes factors such as social class, lifestyles and reference group influences. The consumption of goods and services in an economy can be linked to such factors.

- The cultural environment of business comprises those institutions and other forces which help to shape society's basic attitudes, values, perceptions, preferences and behaviour.

- Societies usually also contain sub-cultures which can influence a person's beliefs, attitudes and actions.

- Like demography and social factors, cultural influences can change over time and can affect organisations. Businesses need to be sensitive to such change.

- The importance of demographic, social and cultural factors in business can be illustrated by the concept of market segmentation.

case study | The effects of an ageing population

There is no doubt that the world's population is ageing. In 2000 there were 69 million people in the world over the age of 80 years and this is the fastest growing segment of the population (see Table 6.9). By 2050 it is estimated that this figure will have risen to 379 million, which represents 4 per cent of the world's population. In 2000 many countries already had higher percentages of over 80s including Sweden (5.1 per cent), Norway and Britain (both 4 per cent). In Japan (the fastest ageing country in the 1990s) it is predicted that by 2015 over 25 per cent of the population will be over 65 years of age.

Table 6.9 shows that in all parts of the world the fastest growing segments are the older ones; for the more developed countries reductions in the size of the 0 to 59 age groups are predicted. The predictions are made on the assumption that present trends in life expectancy and fertility rates will continue.

Why is the world population ageing?

There are two main causes – increased life expectancy and lower fertility rates. Figure 6.1 shows the fertility rates and Figure 6.2 shows the life expectancy for the same groups of the world's population between 1950 and 2050.

Fertility rates have fallen dramatically in all parts of the world since 1950 and this trend is expected to continue into the future although some countries may buck the trend in certain years (e.g. fertility rates in the UK increased in the period 2001–7). Conversely life expectancy has risen in all parts of the world and is also expected to continue to do so. Putting these two trends together means that the average age of the world population is increasing. (The factors behind these changes have already been discussed in this chapter.) There are of course wide differences between countries but the general picture is one of convergence.

What are the implications of the ageing population for business?

Production

Demand patterns vary a great deal with age and if the grey population is increasing in size businesses will have to respond to the changing demands. If the American experience is repeated in the rest of the world the grey population will spend more on education and leisure services. Many retirees take the opportunity to return to education to pursue their interests.

Table 6.9 Projected growth rates between 2000 and 2050, percentages

	0–14	15–59	60+	80+
World	0.15	0.79	2.35	3.40
More developed countries	−0.34	−0.42	1.07	2.23
Less developed countries	0.21	1.01	2.87	4.22
Least developed countries	1.26	2.38	3.37	4.07

Sources: *World Population Prospects*, United Nations, 2000.

Table 6.10 gives an example of how the level of weekly expenditure on selected products can vary by age. It can be seen that the older age groups spent less on beer and cider, cigarettes and visiting the cinema or theatre but more on holidays in the UK and medical insurance than the younger age groups.

As businesses respond to these changes there will be a shift of resources towards the service sector and

this will bring about further change in industrial structure (see Chapter 12).

Marketing

Demographic change has long been recognised as an important part of the marketing environment and one that needs continual monitoring. This is especially the case in the USA where the trends now evident in

Figure 6.1   Projected fertility rates between 1950 and 2050

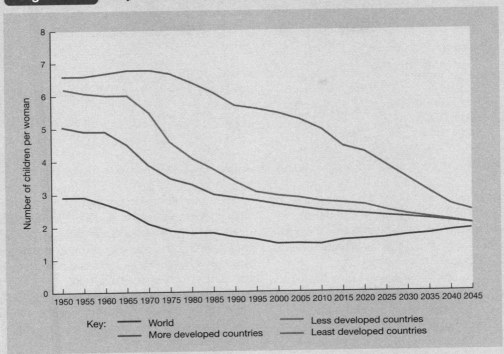

Source: United Nations, 2000.

Figure 6.2   Projected life expectancy between 1950 and 2050

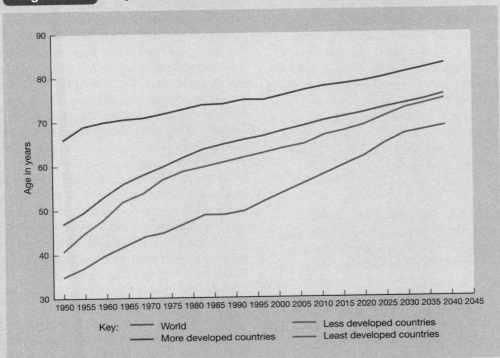

Source: United Nations, 2000.

Table 6.10 Expenditure on selected products by age of head of household, UK, 2002, £ per week

	Under 30	30 to 49	50 to 64	65+
Eating out at restaurant	9.30	11.60	11.50	11.40
Take away meals	4.90	4.80	2.90	2.20
Beer and cider	9.90	10.60	10.80	5.10
Cigarettes	5.60	6.80	6.10	4.80
Visit cinema/theatre	1.30	1.50	1.30	1.20
Holiday in the UK	1.50	2.30	2.70	5.80
Holiday abroad	5.50	12.50	14.50	11.20
Medical insurance	0.40	0.80	1.70	3.20

Source: Adapted from www.statistics.gov.uk/CC1/SearchRes.asp?tem=household+expenditure+age.

Europe started earlier and where the older population is large, affluent and with a great deal of market power. Older consumers have been dubbed 'woofs' by marketeers – well off older folk – and are accepted as an important part of the market.

Those currently in their 40s have been dubbed the 'third agers'. As they reach the 50–75 year age group they will have more free time, have better health, more money and higher expectations than their predecessors. The third agers in the USA have much higher demand than their predecessors for education and leisure services – they make heavy use of sports centres, cinemas and evening classes.

Demography is also important to marketers in the segmentation of markets and there are numerous examples of where age is the segregating factor. In recognition of the different needs and wants of the different age groups in the holiday market there is the 18–30 holiday company which caters for young people while Saga Holidays cater for the over 50s. Interestingly, given the comments already made, Saga Holidays is now offering the kind of holidays often associated with younger travellers – like elephant riding in Nepal for example.

HRM

A greying population has implications for HR strategies within organisations, especially in those industries which have traditionally employed young people. There will be fewer young people entering the labour market for two reasons: first there are fewer of them and second a higher percentage is now staying on at school. Other sources of labour will need to be found to meet the demand. At the same time people are continuing to retire early; in the USA only a half of men between the ages of 60 and 65 are still working

and in some European countries the percentage is much lower. Policies implemented in the 1980s and 1990s by organisations downsizing have created a 'retire early' culture among many, and some pension rules which penalise individuals who wish to work beyond retirement age have worked to exacerbate this. The combination of fewer younger people coming into the workforce and more people leaving early means that employers in many countries are facing a contracting market.

One possibility is the increased participation of older people in the labour force. This means that ageist HRM practices will have to change. Employers often view older workers as more expensive, less flexible and lacking in the required skills, but statistics show that the over-40s age group receives less training than other groups. Many studies in this area have shown that age makes no difference to the ability to acquire new skills with training. It is often the case that older workers are more reliable, are more experienced and have less absenteeism than younger workers. Many employers all around the world are recognising this and are implementing policies which positively encourage older workers.

The employment of older people will call for changes in recruitment practices. The retention of labour will become more important for organisations and therefore training and development will take on greater significance. Work will need to be made more attractive, with more part-time or temporary contracts. This might also overcome the cost implication of having older employees who are higher up incremental pay scales.

From 2006 age discrimination has been banned in the EU under an EU directive but market forces are already making some companies adopt a different approach to older workers.

Financial

There are financial implications of an ageing population. The Potential Support Ratio (PSR) shows the number of persons aged 15 to 64 years per one person of 65 years and over. It gives an indication of the dependency burden of an ageing population on the working population. This fell from 12:1 to 9:1 between 1950 and 2002 and is forecast to fall further to 4:1 by the year 2050 (see Table 6.11).

Again Table 6.11 shows a similar pattern all over the world – there will be an increasing financial burden on people of working age as a result of ageing populations. Within the overall figures there are marked differences. In Japan for instance, the ratio is forecast to fall from 4:1 in 2002 to 1:1 in 2050. In the USA, where immigration is generally higher (and therefore ageing is less pronounced), the ratio is forecast to fall from 5:1 to 3:1.

Table 6.11 Projected Potential Support Ratio, 2002 and 2050

	2002	2050
World	9:1	4:1
More developed countries	5:1	2:1
Less developed countries	12:1	5:1
Least developed countries	17:1	10:1

Source: United Nations, 2002.

This means that a higher proportion of the population will depend upon a smaller proportion of the population for support – in terms of resources for health care and the payment of pensions. Many countries are looking at their pension provisions to try to reduce the cost of dependency. In the UK for example there has been a shift in the burden of pension provision from the state to individuals and many companies have ended their 'final salary' pension schemes. Nevertheless, it is still estimated that to meet the demand for pensions of the ageing population by 2030 the UK needs a 5 per cent annual growth rate in GDP. This is much higher than growth rates have been. In the past in the UK, state pensions have been paid out of current taxation but this is likely to change so that state pensions will be funded from investments. Changes in the retirement age also help to reduce the cost of dependency.

In addition to the cost of pensions, an increase in the average age of a population has implications for health care and the cost of health care. Although this case study makes the point that the greying population is fitter and healthier than ever before, there are of course implications for the demand for health care. For example, the percentage of 65-year-olds in the UK with Altzheimer's disease is 5 per cent, and this rises to 20 per cent in the over-80s. Therefore there is a need for greater provision for health care, whether this is done by the state or by individuals.

As well as these major changes the ageing populations will mean changes in:

- popular culture, which for some time has been dominated by youth;
- crime rates – as most crime is carried out by younger people, crime rates should fall;
- family relationships – with falling birth rates and longer life expectancy the 'beanpole' family structure will become the norm.

It is clear from this discussion that the ageing population being experienced by much of the world has big implications for business in many diverse areas.

Case study questions

1 Think of some examples of goods and services for which demand will rise as a consequence of an ageing population. How should marketers address this new buyer segment?

2 What types of policy can organisations use to:
   (a) encourage the older worker to stay in employment for longer?
   (b) recruit older workers into the workplace?

Review and discussion questions

1 What is meant by an 'ageing' population? Examine some of the key ways in which an ageing population can affect the supply side of the economy.

2 In a country of your own choice, identify some of the major social trends over the last decade. How are these trends reflected in changing patterns of consumption?

3 What is meant by the term 'culture'? To what extent do you agree with the proposition that globalisation could destroy local cultural diversity?

4 Why do marketers segment markets? Give examples of particular markets where demographic segmentation might be appropriate.

Assignments

1 Assume you work in the HR department of a large retail organisation that is seeking to replace staff who are about to retire. Because of demographic and other trends you anticipate problems in recruiting school leavers in sufficient numbers. Produce a report outlining the problem to senior executives and suggest possible solutions. Provide justifications for your recommendations.

2 Choose three countries from different continents. Produce data to show the age distribution of the population in each of the countries in a given year. Account for any differences in the age profile of the three countries and suggest ways in which these differences might affect their respective economies in both the short and the long term.

Notes and references

1 See e.g. Worthington, I., Britton, C. and Rees, A., *Economics for Business: Blending Theory and Practice*, 2nd edition, Financial Times/Prentice Hall, 2005, pp. 86–9.

2 The figure for long-term unemployment includes students and others who are not officially in paid employment (e.g. housewives).

Further reading

Hofstede, G., *Culture's Consequences: Comparing Values, Behaviors, Institutions and Organizations Across Nations*, 2nd edition, Sage, 2003.

Hofstede, G., *Cultures and Organizations: Software of the Mind*, 2nd edition, McGraw-Hill, 2004.

Kotler, P., Wong, V., Saunders, J. and Armstrong, G., *Principles of Marketing*, 4th European edition, Financial Times/Prentice Hall, 2005, Chapter 10.

Masterson, R. and Pickton, D., *Marketing: An Introduction*, McGraw-Hill, 2004, Chapter 4.

Morrison, J., *The International Business Environment*, Palgrave, 2002, Chapters 5 and 6.

Office of National Statistics, *Social Trends 38*, Palgrave Macmillan, 2008. Available free online.

Worthington, I., 'The Social and Economic Context', in Rose, A. and Lawton, A., *Public Services Management*, Financial Times/Prentice Hall, 1999, pp. 26–43.

web
link

Web links and further questions are available on the website at:
www.pearsoned.co.uk/worthington

PART TWO
The Macroeconomic Environment

Chapter 5
The Macroeconomic Environment

The macroeconomic environment

Ian Worthington

Business organisations operate in an economic environment which shapes, and is shaped by, their activities. In market-based economies this environment comprises variables which are dynamic, interactive and mobile and which, in part, are affected by government in pursuit of its various roles in the economy. As a vital component in the macroeconomy, government exercises a significant degree of influence over the flow of income and hence over the level and pattern of output by the public and private sectors. Other key influences include a country's financial institutions and the international economic organisations and groupings to which it belongs or subscribes.

Learning outcomes

Having read this chapter you should be able to:

- compare alternative economic systems and their underlying principles and discuss the problems of transition from a centrally planned to a market-based economy
- illustrate flows of income, output and expenditure in a market economy and account for changes in the level and pattern of economic activity
- analyse the role of government in the macroeconomy, including government macroeconomic policies and the objectives on which they are based
- explain the role of financial institutions
- identify the key international economic institutions and organisations which influence the business environment in open, market economies

Key terms

Accelerator effect
Aggregate monetary demand
Balance of payments
Capital market
Capitalist economy
Central bank
Centrally planned economy
Circular flow of income model
Consumer Price Index (CPI)
Consumer sovereignty
Crowding out
Cyclical unemployment
Deindustrialisation
Direct controls
Direct taxation
Economic growth
Economic scarcity
Economics
Exchange rate
Factory gate prices
Financial intermediaries

Fiscal policy
Free-market economy
Full employment
G8 nations
Government spending
Gross domestic product
Headline inflation
Income flows
Indirect taxation
Inflation
Injections
Interest rates
Leakages
Macroeconomic analysis
Macroeconomic environment
Microeconomic analysis
Monetary aggregates
Monetary policies
Money market
Money stock
Multiplier effect

National Debt
Opportunity cost
Public sector net borrowing (PSNB)
Real cost
Real flows
Real interest rates
Real national income
Recession
Retail Price Index (RPI)
State bank
Stock exchange
Structural unemployment
Technological unemployment
Underlying rate of inflation
Wages/prices inflationary spiral
Withdrawals

Introduction

By 2008 many of the world's economies were facing substantial economic problems as a result of rising oil prices, increased food and energy costs and the aftermath of the 'credit crunch' in the United States. In countries across the globe the talk was predominantly of 'recession' and the impact on the consumer, businesses and the public finances of a downturn in economic activity. In an effort to boost the US economy, the Bush administration provided a $168bn (£86bn) economic stimulus package, using tax refunds for around 130 million US households, in an effort to boost consumer spending. The evidence suggests that the US government's fiscal response had some impact on consumer behaviour, with some retailers (e.g.Wal-Mart) reporting an increase in like-for-like sales in the period after households received their refund cheques. In other areas of the US economy, however, the picture was less rosy, with many businesses experiencing extremely tough trading conditions as consumers reduced their spending to cope with higher domestic bills for food, petrol and energy and the global crisis in financial markets continued to cause considerable uncertainty about future economic prospects.

What this simple example is designed to demonstrate is the intimate relationship between business activity and the wider economic context in which it takes place, and a glance at any quality newspaper will provide a range of similar illustrations of this interface between business and economics. What is important at this point is not to understand the complexities of global economic forces or their effect on businesses, but to appreciate in broad terms the importance of the **macroeconomic environment** for business organisations and, in particular, the degree of compatibility between the preoccupations of the entrepreneur and those of the economist. To the economist, for example, a recession is generally marked by falling demand, rising unemployment, a slowing down in economic growth and a fall in investment. To the firm, it usually implies a loss of orders, a likely reduction in the workforce, a decline in output (or a growth in stocks) and a general reluctance to invest in capital equipment and/or new projects.

Much of the detailed discussion of the economic aspects of business can be found in Parts Three and Four. In this chapter the focus is on the broader question of the economic structure and processes of a market-based economy and on the macroeconomic influences affecting and being affected by business activity in this type of economic system. As suggested in the previous chapter, an understanding of the overall economic context within which businesses operate and its core values and principles is central to any meaningful analysis of the business environment.

Three further points are worth highlighting at this juncture. First, business activity not only is shaped by the economic context in which it takes place, but helps to shape that context; consequently the success or otherwise of government economic policy depends to some degree on the reactions of both the firms and the markets (e.g. the stock market) which are affected by government decisions. Second, economic influences operate at a variety of spatial levels, as illustrated by the opening paragraph, and governments can find that circumstances largely or totally beyond their control can affect businesses either favourably or adversely. Third, the economic (and for that matter, political) influence of industry and commerce can be considerable and this ensures that business organisations – both individually and collectively – usually constitute one of the chief pressure groups in democratic states. This political and economic relationship between government and business is discussed more fully in Part 8.

Economic systems

The concept of economic scarcity

Like politics, the term **economic** tends to be used in a variety of ways and contexts to describe certain aspects of human behaviour, ranging from activities such as producing, distributing and consuming, to the idea of frugality in the use of a resource (e.g. being 'economical' with the truth). Modern definitions stress how such behaviour, and the institutions in which it takes place (e.g. households, firms, governments, banks), are concerned with the satisfaction of human needs and wants through the transformation of resources into goods and services which are consumed by society. These processes are said to take place under conditions of **economic scarcity**.

The economist's idea of 'scarcity' centres on the relationship between a society's needs and wants and the resources available to satisfy them. In essence, economists argue that whereas needs and wants tend to be unlimited, the resources which can be used to meet those needs and wants are finite and accordingly no society at any time has the capacity to provide for all its actual or potential requirements. The assumption here is that both individual and collective needs and wants consistently outstrip the means available to satisfy them, as exemplified, for instance, by the inability of governments to provide instant health care, the best roads, education, defence, railways, and so on, at a time and place and of a quality convenient to the user. This being the case, 'choices' have to be made by both individuals and society concerning priorities in the use of resources, and every choice inevitably involves a 'sacrifice' (i.e. forgoing an alternative). Economists describe this sacrifice as the **opportunity cost** or **real cost** of the decision that is taken (e.g. every pound spent on the health service is a pound not spent on some other public service) and it is one which is faced by individuals, organisations (including firms), governments and society alike.

From a societal point of view the existence of economic scarcity poses three serious problems concerning the use of resources:

1 What to use the available resources for? That is, what goods and services should be produced (or not produced) with the resources (sometimes described as the 'guns v. butter' argument)?
2 How best to use those resources? For example, in what combinations, using what techniques and what methods?
3 How best to distribute the goods and services produced with them? That is, who gets what, how much and on what basis?

In practice, of course, these problems tend to be solved in a variety of ways, including barter (voluntary, bilateral exchange), price signals and the market, queuing and rationing, government instruction and corruption (e.g. resources allocated in exchange for personal favours), and examples of each of these solutions can be found in most, if not all, societies, at all times. Normally, however, one or other main approach to resource allocation tends to predominate and this allows analytical distinctions to be made between different types of economic system. One important distinction is between those economies which are centrally planned and those which operate predominantly through market forces, with prices forming the integrating mechanism. Understanding this distinction is fundamental to an examination of the way in which business is conducted and represents the foundation on which much of the subsequent analysis is built.

The centrally planned economy

In this type of economic system – associated with the post-Second World War socialist economies of eastern Europe, China, Cuba and elsewhere – most of the key decisions on production are taken by a central planning authority, normally the state and its agencies. Under this arrangement, the state typically:

● owns and/or controls the main economic resources;
● establishes priorities in the use of those resources;
● sets output targets for businesses which are largely under state ownership and/or control;
● directs resources in an effort to achieve these predetermined targets; and
● seeks to co-ordinate production in such a way as to ensure consistency between output and input demands.

The fact that an economy is centrally planned does not necessarily imply that all economic decisions are taken at central level; in many cases decision making may be devolved to subordinate agencies, including local committees and enterprises. Ultimately, however, these agencies are responsible to the centre and it is the latter which retains overall control of the economy and directs the use of scarce productive resources.

The problem of co-ordinating inputs and output in a modern planned economy is, of course, a daunting task and one which invariably involves an array of state planners and a central plan or blueprint normally covering a number of years (e.g. a five-year plan). Under such a plan, the state planners would establish annual output targets for each sector of the economy and for each enterprise within the sector and would identify the inputs of materials, labour and capital needed to achieve the set targets and would allocate resources accordingly. Given that the outputs of some industries (e.g. agricultural machinery) are the inputs of others (e.g. collective farms), it is not difficult to see how the overall effectiveness of the plan would depend in part on a high degree of co-operation and co-ordination between sectors and enterprises, as well as on good judgement, good decisions and a considerable element of good luck. The available evidence from planned economies suggests that none of these can be taken for granted and each is often in short supply.

Even in the most centralised of economies, state planning does not normally extend to telling individuals what they must buy in shops or how to use their labour, although an element of state direction at times may exist (e.g. conscription of the armed forces). Instead, it tends to condition *what* is available for purchase and the *prices* at which exchange takes place, and both of these are essentially the outcome of political choices, rather than a reflection of consumer demands. All too often consumers tend to be faced by queues and 'black markets' for some consumer products and overproduction of others, as state enterprises strive to meet targets frequently unrelated to the needs and wants of consumers. By the same token, businesses which make losses do not have to close down, as the state would normally make additional funds available to cover any difference between sales revenue and costs. This being the case, the emphasis at firm level tends to be more on meeting targets than on achieving efficiency in the use of resources and hence a considerable degree of duplication and wastage tends to occur.

In such an environment, the traditional entrepreneurial skills of efficient resource management, price setting and risk taking have little, if any, scope for development and managers behave essentially as technicians and bureaucrats, administering decisions largely made elsewhere. Firms, in effect, are mainly servants of the state and their activities are conditioned by social and political considerations, rather than by the needs of the market – although some market activity normally occurs in planned economies (especially in agriculture and a number of private services). Accordingly, businesses and their employees are not fully sensitised to the needs of the consumer and as a result quality and choice (where it exists) may suffer, particularly where incentives to improved efficiency and performance are negligible. Equally, the system tends to encourage bribery and corruption and the development of a substantial black market, with differences in income, status and political influence being an important determinant of individual consumption and of living standards.

The free-market economy

The **free-market** (or **capitalist**) **economy** stands in direct contrast to the centrally planned system. Whereas in the latter the state controls most economic decisions, in the former the key economic agencies are private individuals (sometimes called 'households') and firms, and these interact in free markets, through a system of prices, to determine the allocation of resources.

The key features of this type of economic system are as follows:

● Resources are in private ownership and the individuals owning them are free to use them as they wish.
● Firms, also in private ownership, are equally able to make decisions on production, free from state interference.
● No blueprint (or master plan) exists to direct production and consumption.
● Decisions on resource allocation are the result of a decentralised system of markets and prices, in which the decisions of millions of consumers and hundreds of thousands of firms are automatically co-ordinated.
● The consumer is sovereign, i.e. dictates the pattern of supply and hence the pattern of resource allocation.

In short, the three problems of what to produce, how to produce and how to distribute are solved by market forces.

The diagram in Figure 5.1 illustrates the basic operation of a market economy. In essence, individuals are owners of resources (e.g. labour) and consumers of products; firms are users of resources and producers of products. What products are produced – and hence how resources are used – depends on consumers, who indicate their demands by purchasing (i.e. paying the price) or not purchasing, and this acts as a signal to producers to acquire the resources necessary (i.e. pay the price) to meet the

Figure 5.1 The market economy

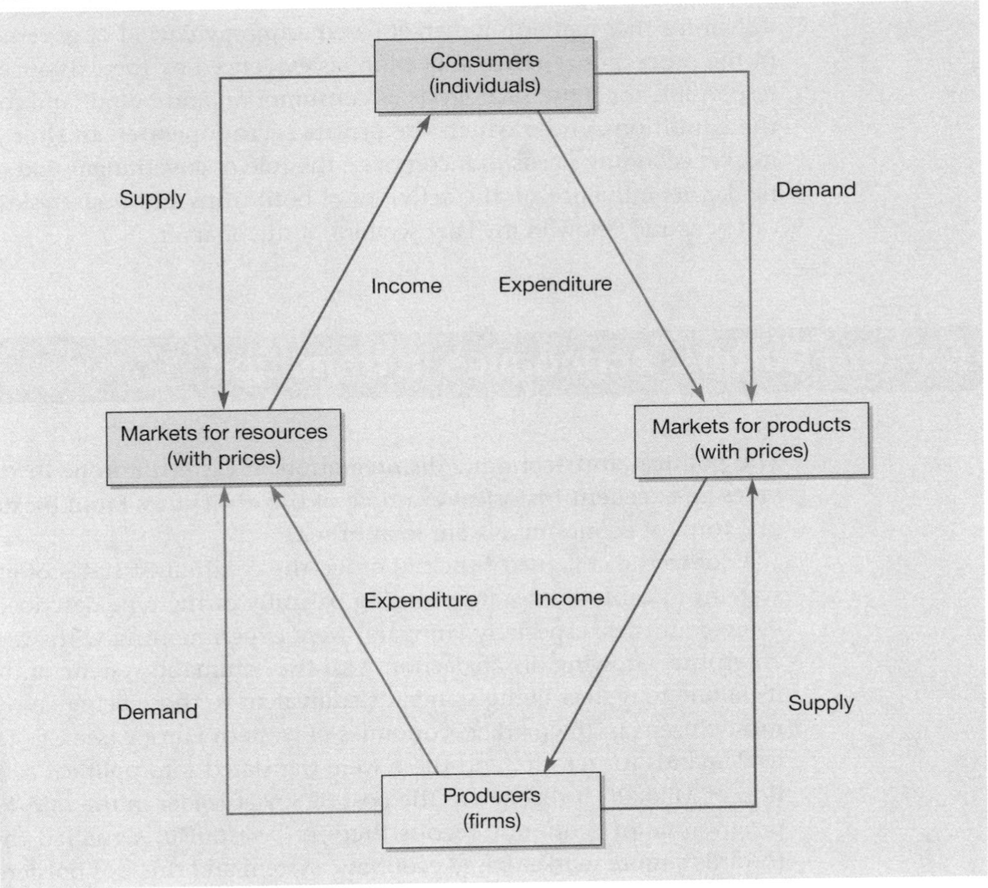

preferences of consumers. If consumer demands change, for whatever reason, this will cause an automatic reallocation of resources, as firms respond to the new market conditions. Equally, competition between producers seeking to gain or retain customers is said to guarantee that resources are used efficiently and to ensure that the most appropriate production methods (i.e. how to produce) are employed in the pursuit of profits.

The distribution of output is also determined by market forces, in this case operating in the markets for productive services. Individuals supplying a resource (e.g. labour) receive an income (i.e. a price) from the firms using that resource and this allows them to purchase goods and services in the markets for products, which in turn provides an income for firms that can be spent on the purchase of further resources (see below). Should the demand for a particular type of productive resource increase – say, as a result of an increase in the demand for the product produced by that resource – the price paid to the provider of the resource will tend to rise and hence, other things being equal, allow more output to be purchased. Concomitantly, it is also likely to result in a shift of resources from uses which are relatively less lucrative to those which are relatively more rewarding.

This matching of supply and demand through prices in markets is described in detail in Chapter 14 and the analysis can also be applied to the market for foreign currencies (see Chapter 16). In practice, of course, no economy operates entirely in the manner suggested above; firms after all are influenced by costs and supply decisions as well as by demand and generally seek to shape that demand, as well as simply responding to it. Nor for that matter is a market-based economy devoid of government involvement in the process of resource allocation, as evidenced by the existence of a public sector responsible for substantial levels of consumption and output and for helping to shape the conditions under which the private sector operates. In short, any study of the market economy needs to incorporate the role of government and to examine, in particular, its influence on the activities of both firms and households. Such an analysis can be found below in the later sections of this chapter.

Eastern Europe: economies in transition

The political and economic disintegration of eastern Europe in the late 1980s provides an excellent historical example of the difficulties faced by states moving from one form of economic system to another.

Prior to the collapse of the old order, the communist states of eastern Europe had systems of centralised state planning basically of the type described above, although some countries, especially Hungary, were experimenting with various forms of free enterprise. Growing dissatisfaction with the command system, and in particular with its failure to deliver living standards equivalent to those being enjoyed at the time by most citizens in the market economies of western Europe (see e.g. Table 5.1), gave rise to demands for reform, and these were translated into political action with the election of Mikhail Gorbachev to the post of Soviet leader in the mid-1980s. Gorbachev's programme of economic reconstruction (*perestroika*) signalled the start of a move towards a more market-based economic system and this was bolstered by his commitment to greater openness (*glasnost*) and democratic reform. By the late 1980s and early 1990s, the old Soviet empire had effectively ceased to exist and the newly independent states, almost without exception, had committed themselves to radical economic change of a kind unthinkable just a few years before.

Table 5.1 Comparative economic indicators, 1988

	Population (million)	GDP ($ billion)	GDP per capita ($)
East Germany	17	156	9360
Czechoslovakia	16	118	7600
Hungary	11	69	6500
Bulgaria	9	51	5630
Poland	37	207	5540
Romania	23	94	4120
European Union	325	4745	14609
West Germany	61	1202	19575

Source: *The Amex Bank Review*, November 1989.

For states anxious to move from an entrenched system of state planning to a market-based economic system, the obstacles can be formidable and can help to slow down the progress of economic (and political) reform. Among the problems faced by eastern European countries in the transitionary phase were:

- The need to create a legal and commercial framework to support the change to a market economy (e.g. company laws, laws on property rights, competition, external trade, the development of an appropriate accounting system).
- The need to establish different forms of free enterprise and to develop financial institutions capable of providing risk and venture capital, at commercial rates of return.
- The need to develop truly competitive markets, free from state control and protection.
- The need to liberalise labour markets and to develop entrepreneurial skills in a workforce traditionally demotivated by the old bureaucratic system.
- The need to allow prices to move to levels determined by market forces, rather than by political decision.
- The need to achieve macroeconomic stability as markets become more open both internally and externally.
- The need to reduce the burden of international debt.
- The need to attract substantial overseas investment to assist in the rebuilding of the collapsed old socialist economies.

Meeting these requirements was not made any easier by economic collapse and the perceived need on the part of some reformers to bring about rapid economic change whatever the consequences. In Russia, in particular, widespread bribery, corruption and criminal activity have helped to undermine an economy struggling with economic and political instability that appears endemic. The recent (2008) problems between Russia and Georgia have also had an effect, with foreign investors withdrawing billions of dollars of foreign investment from Russia because of the risks involved.

Evidence suggests that, given these and other requirements, the process of systemic change is destined to be long and painful for some countries and will be subject to political as well as economic developments, many of which are as yet unpredictable. Central to this process will be the attitude of western countries towards such issues as debt relief, financial assistance, investment and other forms of help, and perhaps understandably the approach thus far has been relatively cautious, particularly given the relative uncertainty that comes from dealing with countries historically perceived to be adversaries. For example, a contemporary analysis by the accountants Ernst & Young in 1992 suggested that the uncertainty was at its greatest in countries such as Russia, Ukraine and Albania and at its least in Hungary, the then Czechoslovakia and Poland, where reforms were often further down the road (see Table 5.2). Hungary's high notional score, for instance, was justified by its relative degree of political and economic stability and its favourable attitude to foreign investment, backed by a legal framework to encourage it. In contrast, in Albania – one of the most rigid of the old communist regimes – political and economic instability, limited business opportunities and a reluctance to change were seen as considerable obstacles to involvement on the part of western companies and governments.

Table 5.2 Eastern Europe: A comparative risk analysis

	Business opportunities	Political risk	Credit rating	Status of economy	Stability of local economy	Business infrastructure	Total
Hungary	2	1	2	3	2	2	12
Czechoslovakia	2	3	2	3	2	2	14
Poland	2	3	3	3	3	2	16
Baltic States	4	3	3	4	3	3	20
Bulgaria	4	3	4	4	3	3	21
Romania	4	4	4	4	4	3	23
Russia and Ukraine	1	4	5	5	4	4	23
Albania	5	4	4	5	5	4	27

Note: Countries are rated on a scale 1 to 5, where low scores are best and high scores worst.
Source: Adapted from the *Daily Telegraph*, 13 May 1992.

With regard to western corporate involvement, in practice this has taken a variety of forms including direct acquisition, joint ventures (which tend to carry tax advantages) and the development of local distribution networks, and much of it has been undertaken by multinational companies seeking to establish market share and to gain low-cost production sites. Coca-Cola, Pepsico, Levi Strauss, Philip Morris, BAT, Mars, Unilever, McDonald's, Procter & Gamble and General Electric have been just some of the organisations that have sought to take advantage of the growing demand for western consumer goods, and Hungary, Poland and the former Czechoslovakia have proved favourable locations for much of the investment. There is no doubt that the case for further investment has been significantly strengthened with the recent process of enlargement within the EU (see Chapter 16) that has involved a number of the old eastern European planned economies. By the same token, political instability in some parts of the old Soviet Empire (see above) acts as a disincentive for foreign investors who can find the risks beginning to outweigh the anticipated benefits.

Politico-economic synthesis

The economic problem of resource allocation, described above, clearly has a political dimension, given its focus on the ownership, control and use of wealth-producing assets within society. This allows links to be made between a country's chosen economic system and its political regime. A useful way of representing possible relationships is illustrated in Figure 5.2. As suggested in Chapter 4, political systems can be characterised as ranging from democratic to authoritarian, depending on the degree of public involvement in decision-making processes. Similarly, economic systems can be seen to range from free market to planned, according to the level of state intervention in the process of resource allocation. This two-dimensional model thus provides for four major combinations of politico-economic systems, ranging from democratic–free-market on the one hand (quadrant 1) to authoritarian–planned on the other (quadrant 3).

Figure 5.2   Politico-economic systems

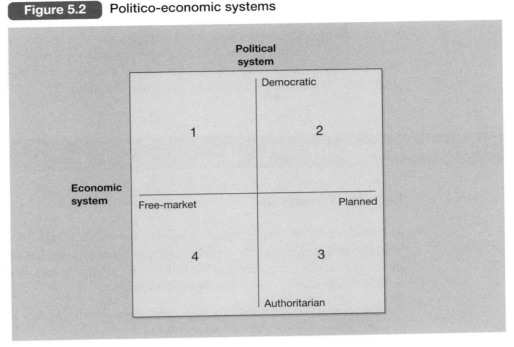

In applying this model to specific cases, it is clear that free-market approaches to resource allocation are predominantly associated with democratic states. Such a link is not surprising. Democracy, after all, includes the notion of individuals being able to express their preferences through the ballot box and having the opportunity to replace one government with another at periodic intervals. In free markets similar processes are at work, with individuals effectively 'voting' for goods and services through the price system and their expressed preferences being reflected in the pattern of resource allocation.

A link between authoritarian regimes and planned economic systems can equally be rationalised, in that government control over the political system is considerably facilitated if it also directs the economy through the ownership and/or control of the means of production, distribution and exchange. In effect, the relative absence of democratic mechanisms, such as free elections and choice between alternative forms of government, is echoed in the economic sphere by the inability of individuals to exercise any real influence over resource allocation. At the extreme, this could involve a government ban on any forms of free enterprise and total government control of the pattern of output and consumption in an economy which is devoid of effective consumer sovereignty.

In practice, of course, the picture is much more complicated than suggested by this simple dichotomy. Some authoritarian states, for instance, have predominantly capitalist economic systems (quadrant 4), while some democratic countries have a substantial degree of government intervention (i.e. moving them towards quadrant 2), either by choice or from necessity (e.g. wartime). Added to this, even in states where the political or economic system appears to be the same, considerable differences can occur at an operational and/or institutional level and this gives each country a degree of uniqueness not adequately portrayed by the model. That said, it is still the case that the basic congruity between democracy and free-market systems represents a powerful and pervasive influence in the business environment of the world's principal democratic states. The process of economic reform – as in eastern Europe – accordingly tends to be accompanied by corresponding pressures for political change and these are often resisted by regimes not prepared to give up their political and economic powers and their élite status.

The macroeconomy

Levels of analysis

As indicated above, economics is concerned with the study of how society deals with the problem of scarcity and the resultant problems of what to produce, how to produce and how to distribute. Within this broad framework the economist typically distinguishes between two types of analysis:

1 **Microeconomic analysis**, which is concerned with the study of economic decision taking by both individuals and firms.
2 **Macroeconomic analysis**, which is concerned with interactions in the economy as a whole (i.e. with economic aggregates).

The microeconomic approach is exemplified by the analysis of markets and prices undertaken in Chapter 14 which shows, for example, how individual consumers in the market for beer might be affected by a price change. This analysis could be extended to an investigation of how the total market might respond to a movement in the price, or how a firm's (or market's) decisions on supply are affected by changes in wage rates or production techniques or some other factor. Note that in these examples, the focus of attention is on decision-taking by individuals and firms in a single industry, while interactions between this industry and the rest of the economy are ignored: in short, this is what economists call a 'partial analysis'.

In reality, of course, all sectors of the economy are interrelated to some degree. A pay award, for example, in the beer industry (or in a single firm) may set a new pay norm that workers in other industries take up and these pay increases may subsequently influence employment, production and consumer demand in the economy as a whole, which could also have repercussions on the demand for beer. Sometimes such repercussions may be relatively minor and so effectively can be ignored. In such situations the basic microeconomic approach remains valid.

In contrast, macroeconomics recognises the interdependent nature of markets and studies the interaction in the economy as a whole, dealing with such questions as the overall level of employment, the rate of inflation, the percentage growth of output in the economy and many other economy-wide aggregates – exemplified, for instance, by the analysis of international trade in Chapter 16 and by the macroeconomic model discussed below. It should be pointed out, however, that while the distinction between the micro and macro approaches remains useful for analytical purposes, in many instances the two become intertwined. UK Chancellor Nigel Lawson's decision (in 1988) to cut the top rate of income tax from 60 per cent to 40 per cent was presented at the time as a means of boosting the economy by providing incentives for entrepreneurs – clearly a macroeconomic proposition. However, to investigate the validity of the Chancellor's view, it is necessary to lean heavily on microeconomic analysis to see how lower taxation might influence, say, an individual's preference for work over leisure. Given that macroeconomic phenomena are the result of aggregating the behaviour of individual firms and consumers, this is obviously a common situation and one which is useful to bear in mind in any study of either the firm or the economy as a whole.

The 'flows' of economic activity

Economic activity can be portrayed as a flow of economic resources into firms (i.e. productive organisations), which are used to produce output for consumption, and a corresponding flow of payments from firms to the providers of those resources, who use them primarily to purchase the goods and services produced. These flows of resources, production, income and expenditure accordingly represent the fundamental activities of an economy at work. Figure 5.3 illustrates the flow of resources and of goods and services in the economy – what economists describe as **real flows**.

In effect, firms use economic resources to produce goods and services, which are consumed by private individuals (private domestic consumption) or government (government consumption) or by overseas purchasers (foreign consumption) or by other firms (capital formation). This consumption gives rise to a flow of expenditures that represents an income for firms, which they use to purchase further resources in order to produce further output for consumption. This flow of income and expenditures is shown in Figure 5.4.

Figure 5.3   'Real flows' in the economy

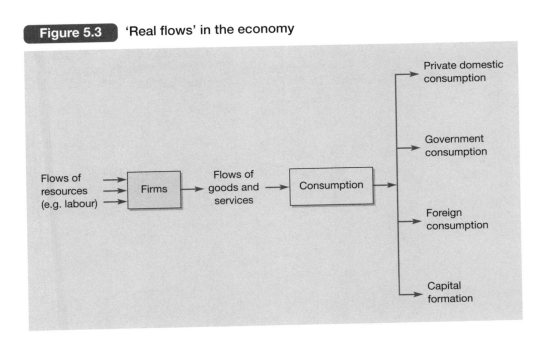

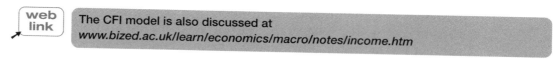

The CFI model is also discussed at
www.bized.ac.uk/learn/economics/macro/notes/income.htm

Figure 5.4   Income flows in the economy

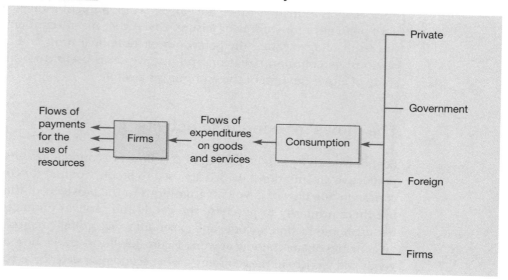

The interrelationship between **income flows** and real flows can be seen by combining the two diagrams into one, which for the sake of simplification assumes only two groups operate in the economy: firms as producers and users of resources, and private individuals as consumers and providers of those resources (see Figure 5.5). Real flows are shown by the arrows moving in an anti-clockwise direction, income flows by the arrows flowing in a clockwise direction.

Figure 5.5   A simplified model of real flows and income flows

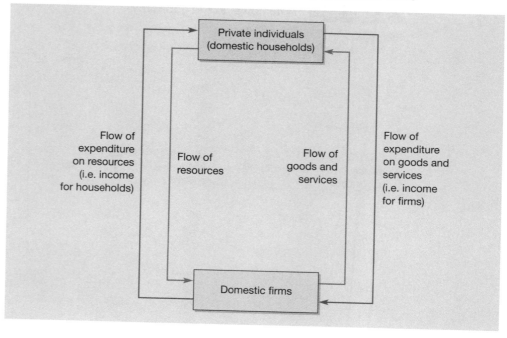

Despite a degree of over-simplification, the model of the economy illustrated in Figure 5.5 is a useful analytical tool which highlights some vitally important aspects of economic activity which are of direct relevance to the study of business. The model shows, for example, that:

1 Income flows around the economy, passing from households to firms and back to households and on to firms, and so on, and these income flows have corresponding real flows of resources, goods and services.
2 What constitutes an income to one group (e.g. firms) represents an expenditure to another (e.g. households), indicating that income generation in the economy is related to spending on consumption of goods and services and on resources (e.g. the use of labour).
3 The output of firms must be related to expenditure by households on goods and services, which in turn is related to the income the latter receive from supplying resources.
4 The use of resources (including the number of jobs created in the economy) must also be related to expenditure by households on consumption, given that resources are used to produce output for sale to households.
5 Levels of income, output, expenditure and employment in the economy are, in effect, interrelated.

From the point of view of firms, it is clear from the model that their fortunes are intimately connected with the spending decisions of households and any changes in the level of spending can have repercussions for business activity at the micro as well as the macro level. In the late 1980s, for instance, the British economy went into recession, largely as a result of a reduction in the level of consumption that was brought about by a combination of high interest rates, a growing burden of debt from previous bouts of consumer spending, and a decline in demand from some overseas markets also suffering from recession. While many businesses managed to survive the recession, either by drawing from their reserves or slimming down their operations, large numbers of firms went out of business, as orders fell and costs began to exceed revenue. As a result, output in the economy fell, unemployment grew, investment by firms declined, and house prices fell to a point where some houseowners owed more on their mortgage than the value of their property (known as 'negative equity'). The combined effect of these outcomes was to further depress demand, as individuals became either unwilling or unable to increase spending and as firms continued to shed labour and to hold back on investment. By late 1992, few real signs of growth in the economy could be detected, unemployment stood at almost 3 million, and business confidence remained persistently low.

The gradual recovery of the British economy from mid-1993 – brought about by a return in consumer confidence in the wake of a cut in interest rates – further emphasises the key link between consumption and entrepreneurial activity highlighted in the model. Equally, it shows, as did the discussion on the recession, that a variety of factors can affect spending (e.g. government policy on interest rates) and that spending by households is only one type of consumption in the real economy. In order to gain a clearer view of how the economy works and why changes occur over time, it is necessary to refine the basic model by incorporating a number of other key variables influencing economic activity. These variables – which include savings, investment spending, government spending, taxation and overseas trade – are discussed below.

Changes in economic activity

The level of spending by consumers on goods and services produced by indigenous firms is influenced by a variety of factors. For a start, most households pay tax on income earned, which has the effect of reducing the level of income available for consumption. Added to this, some consumers prefer to save (i.e. not spend) a proportion of their income or to spend it on imported products, both of which mean that the income of domestic firms is less than it would have been had the income been spent with them. Circumstances such as these represent what economists call a **leakage** (or **withdrawal**) from the **circular flow of income** and help to explain why the revenue of businesses can fluctuate over time (see Figure 5.6).

At the same time as such 'leakages' are occurring, additional forms of spending in the economy are helping to boost the potential income of domestic firms. Savings by some consumers are often borrowed by firms to spend on investment in capital equipment or plant or premises (known as investment spending) and this generates income for firms producing capital goods. Similarly, governments use taxation to spend on the provision of public goods and services (public or government expenditure) and overseas buyers purchase products produced by indigenous firms (export spending). Together, these additional forms of spending represent an **injection** of income into the circular flow (see Figure 5.7).

Figure 5.6 The circular flow of income with 'leakages'

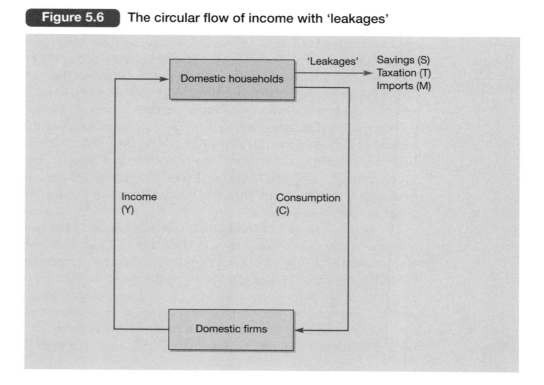

Figure 5.7 The circular flow of income with 'injections' added

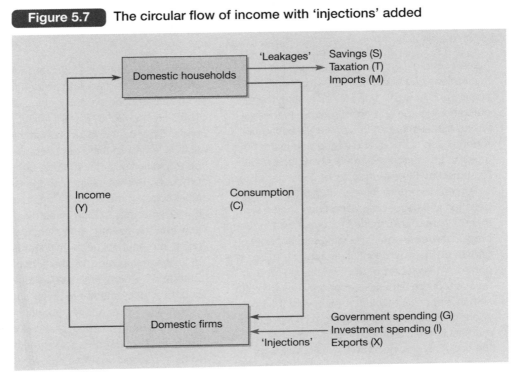

While the revised model of the economy illustrated in Figure 5.7 is still highly simplified (e.g. consumers also borrow savings to spend on consumption or imports; firms also save and buy imports; governments also invest in capital projects), it demonstrates quite clearly that fluctuations in the level of economic activity are the result of changes in a number of variables, many of which are outside the control of firms or governments. Some of these changes are autonomous (i.e. spontaneous), as in the case of an increased demand for imports, while others may be deliberate or overt, as when the government decides to increase its own spending or to reduce taxation in order to stimulate demand. Equally, from time to time an economy may be subject to 'external shocks', such as the onset of recession among its principal trading partners or a significant price rise in a key commodity (e.g. oil price rises in 2007/8), which can have an important effect on internal income flows. Taken together, these and other changes help to explain why demand for goods and services constantly fluctuates and why changes occur not only in an economy's capacity to produce output, but also in its structure and performance over time.

It is important to recognise that where changes in spending do occur, these invariably have consequences for the economy that go beyond the initial 'injection' or 'withdrawal' of income. For example, a decision by government to increase spending on infrastructure would benefit the firms involved in the various projects and some of the additional income they receive would undoubtedly be spent on hiring labour. The additional workers employed would have more income to spend on consumption and this would boost the income for firms producing consumer goods, which in turn may hire more staff, generating further consumption and so on. In short, the initial increase in spending by government will have additional effects on income and spending in the economy, as the extra spending circulates

mini case   A change in economic fortunes

Macroeconomic analysis helps to explain how fluctuations can occur in the level of economic activity and how this impacts on employment, outcome, income and consumption. In the real world, actual changes in a country's economic fortunes can occur over differing periods of time and can be triggered by a variety of factors, as illustrated by the experiences of Japan and Brazil.

After a decade or more of stagnation and deflation in its economy, Japan has shown signs in recent years of a sustained recovery with industrial production, consumer spending and economic growth positive, while inflation appears to be under control. At least part of the explanation for the recovery of the Japanese economy has been the shift in emphasis towards trading with the booming economies in Asia and away from its traditional markets in the US. According to Japanese officials, the economy has become far more stable as Japanese businesses have shifted their attention towards trade with countries such as China, where annual rates of economic growth are on average around 10 per cent.

Brazil, too, has shown that, over time, even apparently intractable economic difficulties can be overcome. In the late 1980s and early 1990s the country was plagued with an inflation problem, with average price rises reaching 490 per cent by 1993. By mid-2008, Brazil's inflation rate was under 5 per cent and its economy was booming, thanks largely to the global demand for commodities such as iron ore, biofuels and food products. Recent oil finds off the Brazilian coast have boosted the economy's future prospects considerably, as foreign investment continues to flow into the country. One measure of the country's rising international economic status was the award of 'investment grade' by the financial rating agency Standard & Poor which helped to push the country's stock market to an all-time high.

While global economic conditions (e.g. the global downturn in 2008) and unsolved economic problems (e.g. Japan's government debt) appear to be impacting upon the recovery process, what these two examples illustrate is that improvements in an economy's performance often take a considerable time. This fact is not always captured well in economists' models of how the macroeconomy operates.

from households to firms and back again. Economists refer to this as the **multiplier effect** to emphasise the reverberative consequences of any increase or decrease in spending by consumers, firms, governments or overseas buyers.

Multiple increases in income and consumption can also give rise to an '**accelerator effect**, which is the term used to describe a change in investment spending by firms as a result of a change in consumer spending. In the example above it is possible that the increase in consumption caused by the increase in government spending may persuade some firms to invest in more stock and capital equipment to meet increased consumer demands. Demand for capital goods will therefore rise, and this could cause further increases in the demand for industrial products (e.g. components, machinery) and also for consumer goods, as firms seek to increase their output to meet the changing market conditions. Should consumer spending fall, a reverse accelerator may occur and the same would apply to the multiplier as the reduction in consumption reverberates through the economy and causes further cuts in both consumption and investment. As Peter Donaldson has suggested, everything in the economy affects everything else; the economy is dynamic, interactive and mobile and is far more complex than implied by the model used in the analysis above.[1]

Government and the macroeconomy: objectives

Notwithstanding the complexities of the real economy, the link between business activity and spending is clear to see. This spending, as indicated above, comes from consumers, firms, governments and external sources and collectively can be said to represent total demand in the economy for goods and services. Economists frequently indicate this with the following notation:

Aggregate Monetary Demand = Consumer spending + Investment spending
+ Government spending + Export spending
– Import spending

or $$AMD = C + I + G + X - M$$

Within this equation, consumer spending (C) is regarded as by far the most important factor in determining the level of total demand.

While economists might disagree about what are the most significant influences on the component elements of AMD, it is widely accepted that governments have a crucial role to play in shaping demand, not only in their own sector but also on the market side of the economy. Government policies on spending and taxation, or on interest rates, clearly have both direct and indirect influences on the behaviour of individuals and firms, which can affect both the demand and supply side of the economy in a variety of ways. Underlying these policies are a number of key objectives which are pursued by government as a prerequisite to a healthy economy and which help to guide the choice of policy options. Understanding the broad choice of policies available to government, and the objectives associated with them, is of prime importance to students of the business environment.

Most governments appear to have a number of key economic objectives, the most important of which are normally the control of inflation, the pursuit of economic growth, a reduction in unemployment, the achievement of an acceptable balance of payments situation, controlling public (i.e. government) borrowing, and a relatively stable exchange rate.

Controlling inflation

Inflation is usually defined as an upward and persistent movement in the general level of prices over a given period of time; it can also be characterised as a fall in the value of money. For governments of all political complexions reducing such movements to a minimum is seen as a primary economic objective (e.g. the current UK government's target for 'underlying inflation' was 2.5 per cent. Under the new Consumer Prices Index the target is now 2 per cent).

Monitoring trends in periodic price movements tends to take a number of forms; in the UK these have included:

1 The use of a **Retail Price Index (RPI)**, which measures how an average family's spending on goods and services is affected by price changes. The RPI has traditionally been the measure used for **headline inflation** in the UK and includes mortgage interest payments.

2 An examination of the **underlying rate of inflation**, which excludes the effects of mortgage payments (known as RPIX in the UK).
3 Measuring **factory gate prices**, to indicate likely future changes in consumer prices.
4 Comparing domestic inflation rates with those of the United Kingdom's chief overseas competitors, as an indication of the international competitiveness of UK firms.

With regard to the latter, the UK now uses a new measure of inflation known as the **Consumer Prices Index (CPI)** to allow for a more direct comparison of the inflation rate in the UK with that of the rest of Europe. The CPI excludes a number of items that have historically been part of the RPIX, especially items relating to housing costs (e.g. mortgage interest payments and council tax).

In addition, changes in **monetary aggregates**, which measure the amount of money (and therefore potential spending power) in circulation in the economy, and movements of exchange rates (especially a depreciating currency – *see* Chapter 16) are also seen as a guide to possible future price increases, as their effects work through the economy.

Explanations as to why prices tend to rise over time vary considerably, but broadly speaking fall into two main categories. First, supply-siders tend to focus on rising production costs – particularly wages, energy and imported materials – as a major reason for inflation, with firms passing on increased costs to the consumer in the form of higher wholesale and/or retail prices. Second, demand-siders, in contrast, tend to emphasise the importance of excessive demand in the economy, brought about, for example, by tax cuts, cheaper borrowing or excessive government spending, which encourages firms to take advantage of the consumer's willingness to spend money by increasing their prices. Where indigenous firms are unable to satisfy all the additional demand, the tendency is for imports to increase. This may not only cause further price rises, particularly if imported goods are more expensive or if exchange rate movements become unfavourable, but also can herald a deteriorating balance of payments situation and difficult trading conditions for domestic businesses.

Government concern with inflation – which crosses both party and state boundaries – reflects the fact that rising price levels can have serious consequences for the economy in general and for businesses in particular, especially if a country's domestic inflation rates are significantly higher than those of its main competitors. In markets where price is an important determinant of demand, rising prices may result in some businesses losing sales, and this can affect turnover and may ultimately affect employment if firms reduce their labour force in order to reduce their costs. Added to this, the uncertainty caused by a difficult trading environment may make some businesses unwilling to invest in new plant and equipment, particularly if interest rates are high and if inflation looks unlikely to fall for some time. Such a response, while understandable, is unlikely to improve a firm's future competitiveness or its ability to exploit any possible increases in demand as market conditions change.

Rising prices may also affect businesses by encouraging employees to seek higher wages in order to maintain or increase their living standards. Where firms agree to such wage increases, the temptation, of course, is to pass this on to the consumer in the form of a price rise, especially if demand looks unlikely to be affected to any great extent. Should this process occur generally in the economy, the result may be a **wages/prices inflationary spiral**, in which wage increases push up prices which push up wage increases which further push up prices and so on. From an international competitive point of view, such an occurrence, if allowed to continue unchecked, could be disastrous for both firms and the economy. Thankfully, such an occurence tends to be relatively uncommon in most economies but, as the problems in Zimbabwe illustrate, hyperinflation can have disastrous consequences for a country's economy and its population (in mid-2008, for example, annual inflation in Zimbabwe was estimated at around 40 million per cent!).

Economic growth

Growth is an objective shared by governments and organisations alike. For governments, the aim is usually to achieve steady and sustained levels of non-inflationary growth, preferably led by exports (i.e. export-led growth). Such growth is normally indicated by annual increases in **real national income** or **gross domestic product** (where 'real' = allowing for inflation, and 'gross domestic product (GDP)' = the economy's annual output of goods and services measured in monetary terms).[2] To compensate for changes in the size of the population, growth rates tend to be expressed in terms of real national income per capita (i.e. real GDP divided by population).

Exactly what constitutes desirable levels of growth is difficult to say, except in very broad terms. If given a choice, governments would basically prefer:

- steady levels of real growth (e.g. 3–4 per cent p.a.), rather than annual increases in output which vary widely over the business cycle;
- growth rates higher than those of one's chief competitors; and
- growth based on investment in technology and on increased export sales, rather than on excessive government spending or current consumption.

It is worth remembering that, when measured on a monthly or quarterly basis, increases in output can occur at a declining rate and GDP growth can become negative. In the United Kingdom, for example, a **recession** is said to exist following two consecutive quarters of negative GDP.

From a business point of view, the fact that increases in output are related to increases in consumption suggests that economic growth is good for business prospects and hence for investment and employment, and by and large this is the case. The rising living standards normally associated with such growth may, however, encourage increased consumption of imported goods and services at the expense of indigenous producers, to a point where some domestic firms are forced out of business and the economy's manufacturing base becomes significantly reduced (often called **deindustrialisation**). Equally, if increased consumption is based largely on excessive state spending, the potential gains for businesses may be offset by the need to increase interest rates to fund that spending (where government borrowing is involved) and by the tendency of government demands for funding to **crowd out** the private sector's search for investment capital. In such cases, the short-term benefits from government-induced consumption may be more than offset by the medium- and long-term problems for the economy that are likely to arise.

Where growth prospects for the economy look good, business confidence tends to increase, and this is often reflected in increased levels of investment and stock holding and ultimately in levels of employment. In Britain, for example, the monthly and quarterly surveys by the Confederation of British Industry (CBI) provide a good indication of how output, investment and stock levels change at different points of the business cycle and these are generally seen as a good indication of future business trends, as interpreted by entrepreneurs. Other indicators – including the state of the housing market and construction generally – help to provide a guide to the current and future state of the economy, including its prospects for growth in the short and medium term.

The CBI's website address is *www.cbi.org.uk*

Reducing unemployment

In most democratic states the goal of **full employment** is no longer part of the political agenda; instead government pronouncements on employment tend to focus on job creation and maintenance and on developing the skills appropriate to future demands. The consensus seems to be that in technologically advanced market-based economies some unemployment is inevitable and that the basic aim should be to reduce unemployment to a level which is both politically and socially acceptable.

As with growth and inflation, unemployment levels tend to be measured at regular intervals (e.g. monthly, quarterly, annually) and the figures are often adjusted to take into account seasonal influences (e.g. school-leavers entering the job market). In addition, the statistics usually provide information on trends in long-term unemployment, areas of skill shortage and on international comparisons, as well as sectoral changes within the economy. All of these indicators provide clues to the current state of the economy and to the prospects for businesses in the coming months and years, but need to be used with care. Unemployment, for example, tends to continue rising for a time even when a recession is over; equally, it is not uncommon for government definitions of unemployment to change or for international unemployment data to be based on different criteria.

The broader social and economic consequences of high levels of unemployment are well documented: it is a waste of resources, it puts pressure on the public services and on the Exchequer (e.g. by reducing tax yields and increasing public expenditure on welfare provision), and it is frequently linked with growing social and health problems. Its implication for businesses, however, tends to be less clear-cut. On the one hand, a high level of unemployment implies a pool of labour available for firms seeking workers (though not necessarily with the right skills), generally at wage levels lower than when a shortage of labour occurs. On the other hand, it can also give rise to a fall in overall demand for goods and services which could exacerbate any existing deflationary forces in the economy, causing further unemployment and with it further reductions in demand. Where this occurs, economists tend to describe it as **cyclical unemployment** (i.e. caused by a general deficiency in demand) in order to differentiate it from unemployment caused by a deficiency in demand for the goods produced by a particular industry (**structural unemployment**) or by the introduction of new technology which replaces labour (**technological unemployment**).

A favourable balance of payments

A country's **balance of payments** is essentially the net balance of credits (earnings) and debits (payments) arising from its international trade over a given period of time (see Chapter 16). Where credits exceed debits a balance of payments surplus exists; the opposite is described as a deficit. Understandably governments tend to prefer either equilibrium in the balance of payments or surpluses, rather than deficits. However, it would be fair to say that for some governments facing persistent balance of payments deficits, a sustained reduction in the size of the deficit may be regarded as signifying a 'favourable' balance of payments situation.

Like other economic indicators, the balance of payments statistics come in a variety of forms and at different levels of disaggregation, allowing useful comparisons to be made not only on a country's comparative trading performance, but also on the international competitiveness of particular industries and commodity groups or on the development or decline of specific external markets. Particular emphasis tends to be given to the balance of payments on current account, which measures imports and exports of goods and services and is thus seen as an indicator of the competitiveness of an economy's firms and industries. Sustained current account surpluses tend to suggest favourable trading conditions, which can help to boost growth, increase employment and investment and create a general feeling of confidence amongst the business community. They may also give rise to surpluses which domestic firms can use to finance overseas lending and investment, thus helping to generate higher levels of corporate foreign earnings in future years.

While it does not follow that a sustained current account deficit is inevitably bad for the country concerned, it often implies structural problems in particular sectors of its economy or possibly an exchange rate which favours importers rather than exporters. Many observers believe, for instance, that the progressive decline of Britain's visible trading position after 1983 was an indication of the growing uncompetitiveness of its firms, particularly those producing finished manufactured goods for consumer markets at home and abroad. By the same token, Japan's current account trade surplus of around $120 billion in late 1995 was portrayed as a sign of the cut-throat competition of Japanese firms, particularly those involved in producing cars, electrical and electronic products, and photographic equipment.

Controlling public borrowing

Governments raise large amounts of revenue annually, mainly through taxation, and use this income to spend on a wide variety of public goods and services (see below). Where annual revenue exceeds government spending, a budget surplus occurs and the excess is often used to repay past debt (formerly known in the United Kingdom as the 'public sector debt repayment' or PSDR). The accumulated debt of past and present governments represents a country's **National Debt**. In the UK this stood at over £500 billion in 2007 which was approximately 38 per cent of GDP.

In practice, most governments often face annual budget deficits rather than budget surpluses and hence have a 'public sector borrowing requirement' or PSBR (now known in the UK as **public sector net borrowing** or **PSNB**). While such deficits are not inevitably a problem, in the same way that a small personal over-draft is not necessarily critical for an individual, large scale and persistent deficits are generally seen as a sign of an economy facing current and future difficulties which require urgent government action. The overriding concern over high levels of public borrowing tends to be focused on:

1 Its impact on interest rates, given that higher interest rates tend to be needed to attract funds from private sector uses to public sector uses.
2 The impact of high interest rates on consumption and investment and hence on the prospects of businesses.
3 The danger of the public sector 'crowding out' the private sector's search for funds for investment.
4 The opportunity cost of debt interest, especially in terms of other forms of public spending.
5 The general lack of confidence in the markets about the government's ability to control the economy and the likely effect this might have on inflation, growth and the balance of payments.
6 The need to meet the 'convergence criteria' laid down at Maastricht for entry to the single currency (e.g. central government debt no higher than 3 per cent of GDP).

The consensus seems to be that controlling public borrowing is best tackled by restraining the rate of growth of public spending rather than by increasing revenue through changes in taxation, since the latter could depress demand.

A stable exchange rate

A country's currency has two values: an internal value and an external value. Internally, its value is expressed in terms of the goods and services it can buy and hence it is affected by changes in domestic prices. Externally, its value is expressed as an **exchange rate** which governs how much of another country's currency it can purchase (e.g. £1 = $2 or £1 = €1.20). Since foreign trade normally involves an exchange of currencies, fluctuations in the external value of a currency will influence the price of imports and exports and hence can affect the trading prospects for business, as well as a country's balance of payments and its rate of inflation (see Chapter 16).

On the whole, governments and businesses involved in international trade tend to prefer exchange rates to remain relatively stable, because of the greater degree of certainty this brings to the trading environment; it also tends to make overseas investors more confident that their funds are likely to hold their value. To this extent, schemes which seek to fix exchange rates within predetermined levels (e.g. the ERM), or which encourage the use of a common currency (e.g. the euro), tend to have the support of the business community, which prefers predictability to uncertainty where trading conditions are concerned.

mini case   Digging in for the long term

For firms engaged in international trade, the strength of the currency (i.e. the exchange rate) is an important consideration (see e.g. Chapter 16). As the value of one currency changes against other currencies, this usually alters the price of imported/exported products and this can make them more/less attractive to potential customers. To mitigate the impact of exchange rate changes, some firms engage in a process known as hedging, which basically involves trying to reduce or eliminate exchange rate risks, for example by buying a proportion of a currency forward (i.e. before it is needed) at an agreed price. An alternative strategy is to consider producing the product in different locations (e.g. setting up manufacturing facilities in other countries) which can offset some of the impact of currency fluctuations, as well as providing other potential benefits to a business.

A good example of the latter approach is provided by JCB, the UK-owned private company famous for its yellow construction equipment (e.g. diggers). In the 1990s, the company's business was mainly based in the UK and parts of western Europe, but faced with a limited market and a strengthening pound which made exporting difficult, the firm decided to seek a global presence by investing in manufacturing abroad. Focusing first on the US, JCB built a plant in Georgia in the late 1990s to exploit the US market; this was followed by further plants in Sao Paulo in Brazil and new plants in India near Mumbai. It also acquired a German construction firm in 2005 and opened a further factory near Shanghai in 2006, thereby adding to its global reach.

In addition to the potential currency benefits of operating in different countries, JCB has also gained a number of other advantages, including establishing a global brand name, access to low-cost suppliers and to developing markets, and reducing freight costs and tariff barriers. Globalisation, in short, can offer businesses many 'opportunities', but we must not forget that it can also give rise to substantial 'threats' at the corporate level, not least the danger of low-cost competitors invading one's own markets.

Government and the macroeconomy: policies

Governments throughout Europe and beyond play various key roles in their respective economies. These include the following functions:

- consumer of resources (e.g. employer, landowner);
- supplier of resources (e.g. infrastructure, information);
- consumer of goods and services (e.g. government spending);
- supplier of goods and services (e.g. nationalised industries);
- regulator of business activity (e.g. employment laws, consumer laws);
- regulator of the economy (e.g. fiscal and monetary policies); and
- redistributor of income and wealth (e.g. taxation system).

The extent of these roles, and their impact on the economy in general and on business in particular, varies from country to country as well as over time.

Despite the economic significance of these roles, in most market-based economies democratically elected governments prefer levels and patterns of production and consumption to be determined largely by market forces, with a minimum of government interference. This approach is exemplified by the philosophical stance of the UK and

US governments in the 1980s, that became colloquially known as 'Thatcherism' (UK) and 'Reaganomics' (USA). At the same time, the recognition that market forces alone are unable to guarantee that an economy will automatically achieve the objectives established by governments has meant that state intervention – to curb inflation, encourage growth, reduce unemployment, correct a balance of payments or budgetary problem or restore currency stability – invariably occurs to some degree in all countries. In broad terms, this intervention usually takes three main forms, described as fiscal policy, monetary policy and direct controls. These policy instruments – or 'instrumental variables' – and their effects on the business community are discussed below.

Fiscal policy

As indicated above, each year governments raise and spend huge amounts of money. The UK government's estimates for 2008, for example, suggest that **government spending** will be about £618 billion and is to be allocated in the manner illustrated in Figure 5.8. This spending will be funded mainly from **taxation (direct and indirect)**, and national insurance contributions (see Figure 5.9). The PSNB is estimated at £43 billion.

Figure 5.8   The allocation of UK government spending, 2008 budget

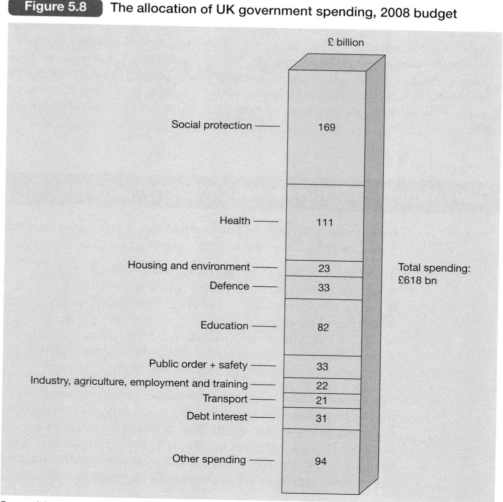

Source: Adapted from Budget Statement, 2008.

Figure 5.9 Sources of government revenue, 2008 budget

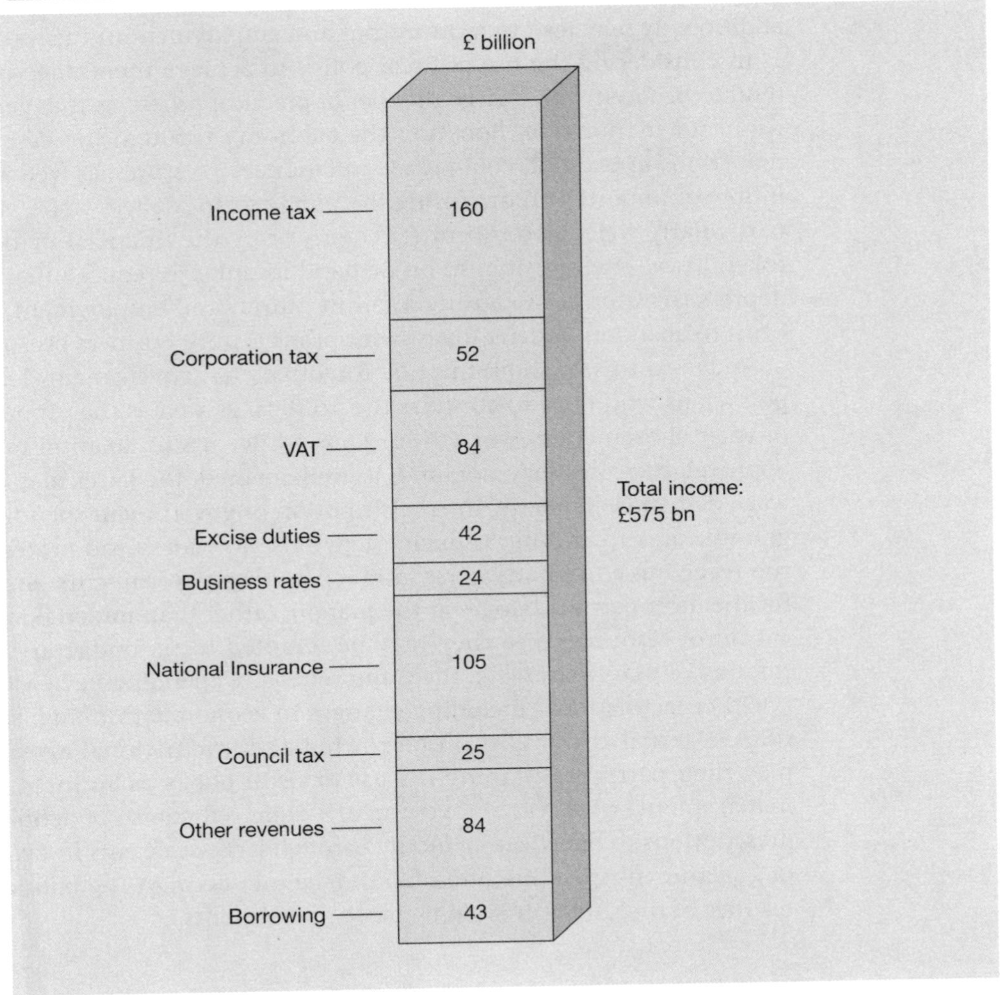

£ billion

Source	£ billion
Income tax	160
Corporation tax	52
VAT	84
Excise duties	42
Business rates	24
National Insurance	105
Council tax	25
Other revenues	84
Borrowing	43

Total income: £575 bn

Source: Adapted from Budget Statement, 2008.

Fiscal policy involves the use of changes in government spending and taxation to influence the level and composition of aggregate demand in the economy and, given the amounts involved, this clearly has important implications for business. Elementary circular flow analysis suggests, for instance, that reductions in taxation and/or increases in government spending will inject additional income into the economy and will, via the multiplier effect, increase the demand for goods and services, with favourable consequences for business. Reductions in government spending and/or increases in taxation will have the opposite effect, depressing business prospects and probably discouraging investment and causing a rise in unemployment.

Apart from their overall impact on aggregate demand, fiscal changes can be used to achieve specific objectives, some of which will be of direct or indirect benefit to the business community. Reductions in taxes on company profits and/or increases in tax allowances for investment in capital equipment can be used to encourage business to increase investment spending, hence boosting the income of firms producing industrial products and causing some additional spending on consumption.

Similarly, increased government spending targeted at firms involved in exporting, or at the creation of new business, will encourage increased business activity and additionally may lead to more output and employment in the economy.

In considering the use of fiscal policy to achieve their objectives, governments tend to be faced with a large number of practical problems that generally limit their room for manoeuvre. Boosting the economy through increases in spending or reductions in taxation could cause inflationary pressures, as well as encouraging an inflow of imports and increasing the public sector deficit, none of which would be particularly welcomed by entrepreneurs or by the financial markets. By the same token, fiscal attempts to restrain demand in order to reduce inflation will generally depress the economy, causing a fall in output and employment and encouraging firms to abandon or defer investment projects until business prospects improve.

Added to this, it should not be forgotten that government decision-makers are politicians who need to consider the political as well as the economic implications of their chosen courses of action. Thus while cuts in taxation may receive public approval, increases may not, and, if implemented, the latter may encourage higher wage demands. Similarly, the redistribution of government spending from one pro- gramme area to another is likely to give rise to widespread protests from those on the receiving end of any cuts; so much so that governments tend to be restricted for the most part to changes at the margin, rather than undertaking a radical reallo- cation of resources and they may be tempted to fix budgetary allocations for a number of years ahead (e.g. the Comprehensive Spending Review in the UK).

Other factors too – including changes in economic thinking, self-imposed fiscal rules, external constraints on borrowing and international agreements – can also play their part in restraining the use of fiscal policy as an instrument of demand management, whatever a government's preferred course of action may be. Simple prescriptions to boost the economy through large-scale cuts in taxation or increases in government spending often fail to take into account the political and economic realities of the situation faced by most governments.

Monetary policy

Monetary policy seeks to influence monetary variables such as the money supply or rates of interest in order to regulate the economy. While the supply of money and interest rates (i.e. the cost of borrowing) are interrelated, it is convenient to con- sider them separately.

As far as changes in **interest rates** are concerned, these clearly have implications for business activity, as circular flow analysis demonstrates. Lower interest rates not only encourage firms to invest as the cost of borrowing falls, but also encourage consumption as disposable incomes rise (predominantly through the mortgage effect) and as the cost of loans and overdrafts decreases. Such increased consump- tion tends to be an added spur to investment, particularly if inflation rates (and, therefore **'real' interest rates**) are low and this can help to boost the economy in the short term, as well as improving the supply side in the longer term.[3]

Raising interest rates tends to have the opposite effect – causing a fall in con- sumption as mortgages and other prices rise, and deferring investment because of the additional cost of borrowing and the decline in business confidence as consumer spending falls. If interest rates remain persistently high, the encouragement given to savers and the discouragement given to borrowers and spenders may help to generate a recession, characterised by falling output, income, spending and employment and by increasing business failure.

Changes in the **money stock** (especially credit) affect the capacity of individuals and firms to borrow and, therefore, to spend. Increases in money supply are generally related to increases in spending and this tends to be good for business prospects, particularly if interest rates are falling as the money supply rises. Restrictions on monetary growth normally work in the opposite direction, especially if such restrictions help to generate increases in interest rates which feed through to both consumption and investment, both of which will tend to decline.

As in the case of fiscal policy, government is usually able to manipulate monetary variables in a variety of ways, including taking action in the money markets to influence interest rates and controlling its own spending to influence monetary growth. Once again, however, circumstances tend to dictate how far and in what way government is free to operate. Attempting to boost the economy by allowing the money supply to grow substantially, for instance, threatens to cause inflationary pressures and to increase spending on imports, both of which run counter to government objectives and do little to assist domestic firms. Similarly, policies to boost consumption and investment through lower interest rates, while welcomed generally by industry, offer no guarantee that any additional spending will be on domestically produced goods and services, and also tend to make the financial markets nervous about government commitments to control inflation in the longer term (see below, 'The role of the central bank').

This nervousness among market dealers reflects the fact that in modern market economies a government's policies on interest rates and monetary growth cannot be taken in isolation from those of its major trading partners and this operates as an important constraint on government action. The fact is that a reduction in interest rates to boost output and growth in an economy also tends to be reflected in the exchange rate; this usually falls as foreign exchange dealers move funds into those currencies which yield a better return and which also appear a safer investment if the market believes a government is abandoning its counterinflationary policy. As the UK government found in the early 1990s, persistently high rates of interest in Germany severely restricted its room for manoeuvre on interest rates for fear of the consequences for sterling if relative interest rates got too far out of line.

Direct controls

Fiscal and monetary policies currently represent the chief policy instruments used in modern market economies and hence they have been discussed in some detail. Governments, however, also use a number of other weapons from time to time in their attempts to achieve their macroeconomic objectives. Such weapons, which are designed essentially to achieve a specific objective – such as limiting imports or controlling wage increases – tend to be known as **direct controls**. Examples of such policies include:

- *Incomes policies*, which seek to control inflationary pressures by influencing the rate at which wages and salaries rise.
- *Import controls*, which attempt to improve a country's balance of payments situation, by reducing either the supply of, or the demand for, imported goods and services (see Chapter 16).
- *Regional and urban policies*, which are aimed at alleviating urban and regional problems, particularly differences in income, output, employment, and local and regional decline (see Chapter 13).

A brief discussion of some of these policy instruments is found at various points in the text below. Students wishing to study these in more detail are recommended to consult the books referred to at the end of this chapter.

The role of financial institutions

Interactions in the macroeconomy between governments, businesses and consumers take place within an institutional environment that includes a large number of financial intermediaries. These range from banks and building societies to pension funds, insurance companies, investment trusts and issuing houses, all of which provide a number of services of both direct and indirect benefit to businesses. As part of the financial system within a market-based economy, these institutions fulfil a vital role in channelling funds from those able and willing to lend, to those individuals and organisations wishing to borrow in order to consume or invest. It is appropriate to consider briefly this role of financial intermediation and the supervision exercised over the financial system by the central bank, before concluding the chapter with a review of important international economic institutions.

Elements of the financial system

A financial system tends to have three main elements:

1 *Lenders and borrowers* – these may be individuals, organisations or governments.
2 *Financial institutions*, of various kinds, which act as intermediaries between lenders and borrowers and which manage their own asset portfolios in the interest of their shareholders and/or depositors.
3 *Financial markets*, in which lending and borrowing takes place through the transfer of money and/or other types of asset, including paper assets such as shares and stock.

Financial institutions, as indicated above, comprise a wide variety of organisations, many of which are public companies with shareholders. Markets include the markets for short-term funds of various types (usually termed **money markets**) and those for long-term finance for both the private and public sectors (usually called the **capital market**). **Stock exchanges** normally lie at the centre of the latter, and constitute an important market for existing securities issued by both companies and government.

The vital role played by **financial intermediaries** in the operation of the financial system is illustrated in Figure 5.10 and reflects the various benefits which derive from using an intermediary rather than lending direct to a borrower (e.g. creating a large pool of savings; spreading risk; transferring short-term lending into longer-term borrowing; providing various types of funds transfer services). Lenders on the whole prefer low risk, high returns, flexibility and liquidity, while borrowers prefer to minimise the cost of borrowing and to use the funds in a way that is best suited to their needs. Companies, for example, may borrow to finance stock or work-in-progress or to meet short-term debts and such borrowing may need to be as flexible as possible. Alternatively, they may wish to borrow in order to replace plant and equipment or to buy new premises – borrowing which needs to be over a much longer term and which hopefully will yield a rate of return which makes the use of the funds and the cost of borrowing worthwhile.

The process of channelling funds from lenders to borrowers often gives rise to paper claims, which are generated either by the financial intermediary issuing a claim to the lender (e.g. when a bank borrows by issuing a certificate of deposit) or by the borrower issuing a claim to the financial intermediary (e.g. when government sells stock to a financial institution). These paper claims represent a liability to the issuer and an asset to the holder and can be traded on a secondary market (i.e. a market for existing securities), according to the needs of the individual or organisation holding the paper claim. At any point, financial intermediaries tend to hold a wide range of such assets (claims on borrowers), which they buy or sell ('manage') in order to yield a profit and/or improve their liquidity position. Decisions of this kind, taken on a daily basis, invariably affect the position of investors (e.g. shareholders) and customers (e.g. depositors) and can, under certain circumstances, have serious consequences for the financial intermediary and its stakeholders (e.g. the bad debts faced by western banks in the late 1980s and early 1990s).

Figure 5.10   **The role of financial intermediaries**

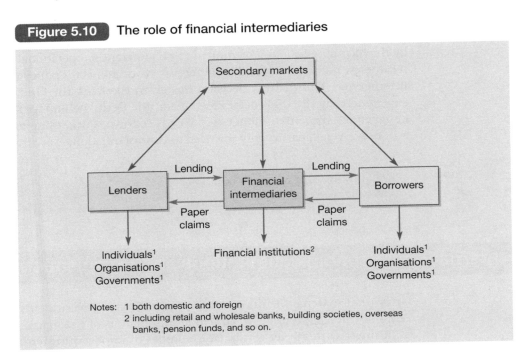

Notes: 1 both domestic and foreign
        2 including retail and wholesale banks, building societies, overseas banks, pension funds, and so on.

Given the element of risk, it is perhaps not surprising that some financial institutions tend to be conservative in their attitude towards lending on funds deposited with them, especially in view of their responsibilities to their various stakeholders. UK retail banks, for instance, have a long-standing preference for financing industry's working capital rather than investment spending, and hence the latter has tended to be financed largely by internally generated funds (e.g. retained profits) or by share issues. In comparison, banks in Germany, France, the United States and Japan tend to be more ready to meet industry's medium- and longer-term needs and are often directly involved in regular discussions with their clients concerning corporate strategy, in contrast to the arm's length approach favoured by many of their UK counterparts.[4]

The role of the central bank

A critical element in a country's financial system is its **central** or **state bank**; in the United Kingdom this is the Bank of England. Like most of its overseas counterparts, the Bank of England exercises overall supervision over the banking sector with the aim of maintaining a stable and efficient financial framework as part of its contribution to a healthy economy. Its activities have a significant influence in the financial markets (especially the foreign exchange market, the gilts market and the sterling money market). These activities include the following roles:

- banker to the government;
- banker to the clearing banks;
- manager of the country's foreign reserves;
- manager of the national debt;
- manager of the issue of notes and coins;
- supervisor of the monetary sector; and
- implementer of the government's monetary policy.

In the last case, the Bank's powers were significantly enhanced following the decision by the incoming Labour government (1997) to grant it 'operational independence' to set interest rates and to conduct other aspects of monetary policy free from Treasury interference. This historic decision has given the Bank the kind of independence experienced by the US Federal Reserve and the Deutsche Bundesbank and has been designed to ensure that monetary policy is conducted according to the needs of the economy overall, particularly the need to control inflation.

For further information on the Bank of England you should consult
www.bankofengland.co.uk

International economic institutions and organisations

Given that external factors constrain the ability of governments to regulate their economy, it is appropriate to conclude this analysis of the macroeconomic context of business with a brief review of a number of important international economic institutions and organisations which affect the trading environment. Foremost among these is the European Union, which is examined at length in Chapters 4 and 16. In the discussions below, attention is focused on the International Monetary Fund (IMF), the Organisation for Economic Co-operation and Development (OECD), the European Bank for Reconstruction and Development (EBRD), the World Trade Organisation (WTO) and the World Bank (IBRD).

The International Monetary Fund (IMF)

The IMF is an international organisation currently of 184 member countries. It came into being in 1946 following discussions at Bretton Woods in the USA which sought to agree a world financial order for the post-Second World War period that would avoid the problems associated with the worldwide depression in the inter-war years. In essence, the original role of the institution – which today incorporates most countries in the world – was to provide a pool of foreign currencies from its member states that would be used to smooth out trade imbalances between countries, thereby promoting a structured growth in world trade and encouraging exchange rate stability. In this way, the architects of the Fund believed that the danger of international protectionism would be reduced and that all countries would consequently benefit from the boost given to world trade and the greater stability of the international trading environment.

The IMF's website is *www.imf.org*

While this role as international 'lender of last resort' still exists, the IMF's focus in recent years has tended to switch towards international surveillance and to helping the developing economies with their mounting debt problems and assisting eastern Europe with reconstruction, following the break-up of the Soviet empire.[5] It has also been involved in the past in trying to restore international stability following the global economic turmoil in Asia and elsewhere and some countries would like it to adopt a more enhanced global surveillance role in the wake of the global credit crisis (2008). To some extent its position as an international decision-making body has been diminished by the tendency of the world's leading economic countries to deal with global economic problems outside the IMF's institutional framework. The United States, Japan, Germany, France, Italy, Canada, Britain and Russia now meet regularly as the **Group of Eight (G8)** leading industrial economies to discuss issues of mutual interest (e.g. the environment, eastern Europe). These world economic summits, as they are frequently called, have tended to supersede discussions in the IMF and as a result normally attract greater media attention.

The Organisation for Economic Co-operation and Development (OECD)

The OECD came into being in 1961, but its roots go back to 1948 when the Organisation for European Economic Co-operation (OEEC) was established to co-ordinate the distribution of Marshall Aid to the war-torn economies of western

Europe. Today it comprises 30 members, drawn from the rich industrial countries and including the G7 nations, Australia, New Zealand and most other European states. Collectively, these countries account for less than 20 per cent of the world's population, but produce around two-thirds of its output – hence the tendency of commentators to refer to the OECD as the 'rich man's club'. Currently talks are under way to expand the membership of the Organisation to include other countries such as Chile, Russia and Israel.

> **web link**
>
> You can access the OECD's website at *www.oecd.org*

In essence the OECD is the main forum in which the governments of the world's leading industrial economies meet to discuss economic matters, particularly questions concerned with promoting stable growth and freer trade and with supporting development in poorer non-member countries. Through its council and committees, and backed by an independent secretariat, the organisation is able to take decisions which set out an agreed view and/or course of action on important social and economic issues of common concern. While it does not have the authority to impose ideas, its influence lies in its capacity for intellectual persuasion, particularly its ability through discussion to promote convergent thinking on international economic problems. To assist in the task, the OECD provides a wide variety of economic data on member countries, using standardised measures for national accounting, unemployment and purchasing-power parities. It is for these data – and especially its economic forecasts and surveys – that the organisation is perhaps best known.

The European Bank for Reconstruction and Development (EBRD)

The aims of the EBRD, which was inaugurated in April 1991, are to facilitate the transformation of the states of central and eastern Europe and beyond from centrally planned to free-market economies and to promote political and economic democracy, respect for human rights and respect for the environment. It is particularly involved with the privatisation process, technical assistance, training and investment in upgrading of the infrastructure and in facilitating economic, legal and financial restructuring. It works in co-operation with its members, private companies and organisations such as the IMF, OECD, the World Bank and the United Nations.

> **web link**
>
> Information on the EBRD can be obtained at *www.ebrd.com*

The World Trade Organisation (WTO)

The World Trade Organisation, which came into being on 1 January 1995, superseded the General Agreement on Tariffs and Trade (the GATT), which dated back to 1947. Like the IMF and the International Bank for Reconstruction and

Development (see below), which were established at the same time, the GATT was part of an attempt to reconstruct the international politico-economic environment in the period after the end of the Second World War. Its replacement by the WTO can be said to mark an attempt to put the question of liberalising world trade higher up the international political agenda.

The WTO can be accessed at *www.wto.org*

With a membership of around 150 states (plus other observers), the WTO is a permanent international organisation charged with the task of liberalising world trade within an agreed legal and institutional framework. In addition it administers and implements a number of multilateral agreements in fields such as agriculture, textiles and services and is responsible for dealing with disputes arising from the Uruguay Round Final Act. It also provides a forum for the debate, negotiation and adjudication of trade problems and in the latter context is said to have a much stronger and quicker trade compliance and enforcement mechanism than existed under the GATT. See also Chapter 16.

The World Bank (IBRD)

Established in 1945, the World Bank (more formally known as the International Bank for Reconstruction and Development or IBRD) is a specialised agency of the United Nations, set up to encourage economic growth in developing countries through the provision of loans and technical assistance. The IBRD currently has over 180 members.

The IBRD can be accessed at *www.worldbank.org* and *http://web.worldbank.org*

The European Investment Bank (EIB)

The European Investment Bank was created in 1958 under the Treaty of Rome and is the financing institution of the European Union. Its main task is to contribute to the integration, balanced development and the economic and social cohesion of EU Member States. Using funds raised on the markets, it finances capital projects which support EU objectives within the European Union and elsewhere. Its interests include environmental schemes, projects relating to transport and energy and support for small and medium-sized enterprises.

For further information on the EIB see *www.eib.org*

Synopsis

Business and economics are inextricably linked. Economics is concerned with the problem of allocating scarce productive resources to alternative uses – a fundamental aspect of business activity. In market-based economies, this problem of resource allocation is largely solved through the operation of free markets, in which price is a vital ingredient. The existence of such markets tends to be associated primarily, though not exclusively, with democratic political regimes.

In all democratic states, government is a key component of the market economy and exercises considerable influence over the level and pattern of business activity – a point illustrated by the use of elementary circular flow analysis. A government's aims for the economy help to shape the policies it uses and these policies have both direct and indirect consequences for business organisations of all kinds.

In examining the economic context in which firms exist, due attention needs to be paid to the influence of a wide range of institutions and organisations, some of which operate at international level. Equally, as markets become more open and business becomes more global, the fortunes of firms in trading economies become increasingly connected and hence subject to fluctuations that go beyond the boundaries of any individual state.

Summary of key points

- Business activity exists in and is affected by the broader macroeconomic environment; it also helps to shape that environment.

- Economics is concerned with how societies allocate scarce economic resources to alternative uses and the 'real costs' of the choices that are made.

- Broadly speaking two main approaches to the problem of resource allocation exist: state planning and the market.

- Most economies in the world are market-based economies which operate through a price mechanism. Within such economies the state also plays a key role in some allocative decisions.

- In market economies economic activity essentially involves 'real flows' and corresponding flows of income and expenditure between producers and consumers.

- Combining these flows into a simple model of the macroeconomy illustrates that income basically flows round the economy in a circular motion.

- Levels of income in the economy are related to levels of output, expenditure and employment.

- Changes in the level of economic activity can be explained by examining changes in one or more of the key economic variables such as consumer spending, saving, government decisions on state spending/taxation and external trade.

- Within the macroeconomy, governments often play a key role in influencing both the levels and patterns of demand in pursuit of their macroeconomic objectives.

- Key government objectives usually include controlling inflation, promoting economic growth, reducing unemployment, and creating a stable macroeconomic environment.

- To pursue these objectives governments use a range of policies, most notably fiscal and monetary policies.

- Government policy decisions take place within a broader economic and financial framework which includes the influence of financial institutions and markets and the requirements which accrue from membership of different supranational and international organisations.

case study — Toyota UK

Toyota's origins can be traced back to the early twentieth century when the inventor of Japan's first automatic loom, Sakidu Toyoda, established a spinning and weaving company. By the 1930s, using funds from selling patent rights to a British machine maker, the company had begun to invest in automotive technology research and soon produced its first prototype passenger vehicle. In August 1937, Kiichiro Toyoda, the son of the original owner, established the Toyota Motor Company, beginning mass production at its Koromo plant in 1938, just before the outbreak of the Second World War.

Despite experiencing considerable difficulties in the post-war period, Toyota recommenced production and began to build up a sales network to market its vehicles. In 1950, the company was split into two parts – production and sales – with the Toyota Motor Company the manufacturing arm of the organisation. Using techniques which have subsequently been emulated by other large companies (e.g. total quality control, just-in-time), Toyota began to increase its output and sales and was beginning to make significant inroads into overseas markets by the mid-1960s. By 1982, when the sales and manufacturing arms of the organisation merged to form the Toyota Motor Corporation, export sales of vehicles had exceeded domestic registrations and Toyota had grown into a large multinational corporation with a range of interests in various parts of the world.

For much of the early post-war period, Toyota focused its attention on the American market and established sales facilities in California in 1957, to be followed by a design base in 1973 and a joint production venture with General Motors in 1984. Less than two years later, the Corporation established its first wholly owned production plant at Georgetown in Kentucky, from which the first of many US-built Toyotas emerged in 1988.

Toyota's development in post-war Europe proceeded along broadly similar lines, with the company establishing local sales and distribution networks, followed by design and production facilities. Initially, production took place under licence (e.g. in Portugal in 1968) or through joint ventures (e.g. with Volkswagen in 1989) and was restricted to commercial vehicles and fork-lift trucks. By the late 1980s, however, the company had signalled its intention of establishing a passenger vehicle manufacturing facility in Europe, as part of its programme of overseas market development. This plant was opened in mid-1992 at Burnaston near Derby and was followed by the opening of an engine plant at Deeside, North Wales, some months later.

Toyota's decision to establish production facilities in Europe is best understood against the political and economic realities of the period. Japan's post-war success in export markets had, by the 1980s, given rise to a huge Japanese balance of payments surplus that was bitterly resented by US and European governments and became the focus of attention in numerous meetings of the G7 countries. As part of this success, the Japanese car industry was under

▶

pressure from US and European car manufacturers and their governments to restrain exports, and this ultimately culminated in a system of agreed voluntary restraints (known as VERs) by Japanese car producers, for fear of more draconian measures. Since these restraints did not apply to vehicles produced by Japanese factories overseas ('transplants'), establishing a manufacturing presence outside Japan made sound commercial and political sense. This was particularly true in western Europe, where the EU's Common External Tariff made cars imported from Japan more expensive to consumers and hence relatively less competitive than locally produced vehicles.

The EU's decision to establish a 'single market' within the Union added a further impetus to the decision by Japanese car manufacturers (and others) to seek a European presence. The fact that the United Kingdom was a favoured location for Toyota – and for many other Japanese companies – is not difficult to explain. Apart from providing direct access to the largest single market for motor vehicles in the world, the United Kingdom had a substantial market in its own right and a developed vehicle manufacturing industry with a significant parts and component sector. Added to this, the favourable response given to direct foreign investment by United Kingdom national and local government – including the use of financial and other inducements – made the United Kingdom an attractive proposition and a location of minimal risk for investing multinational corporations.

As far as the choice of Burnaston was concerned, this seems to have been dictated by economic and commercial rather than political factors, although Derbyshire County Council actively lobbied the parent company and offered it a number of inducements to locate in the Midlands. Being centrally placed in Britain and close to the M1, Burnaston offered direct access to all parts of the country and a relatively quick route to the Continent, via the ports and the Channel Tunnel. It also boasted a highly skilled local workforce, a developed infrastructure and a large site with room for further expansion.

There is no doubt that the multi-million Toyota development in Derbyshire has had a considerable impact on the local economy. Apart from the jobs created in building and operating the car plant, further employment has been created directly among local component suppliers and indirectly amongst those involved in providing services and materials and from the extra spending resulting from the growth of jobs. The area has also benefited from the prestige of having attracted a famous company to invest and this has encouraged investment by some other overseas organisations. How far these gains will ultimately be at the expense of the other car-producing areas of Britain still remains to be seen, but economic analysis suggests they may prove significant, particularly as global forces are increasingly shaping the international car industry and making it a highly competitive environment in which to do business.

Case study questions

1 What do you think are the key factors which have made the UK an attractive location for direct foreign investment?

2 To what extent do you think the expansion of the European Union will affect future inward investment decisions?

web link Toyota UK's website is *www.toyotauk.com*

Review and discussion questions

1 To what extent do you agree with the proposition that the market economy is the 'best' form of economic system? Do you have any reservations?

2 Explain how interest rates could be used to boost the economy. Why, then, do governments frequently hesitate to take such steps?

3 Using circular flow analysis, suggest why a large programme of capital expenditure by government (e.g. on new motorways, roads, railways) will benefit businesses. How could such a programme be financed?

4 Which businesses are likely to benefit from a recovery in a country's housing market?

Assignments

1 Imagine you work in the economic development unit of a local authority. Produce a draft report outlining the benefits to the local economy of encouraging direct inward investment. Indicate any disadvantages.

2 You are a trainee journalist on a regional or national newspaper. As part of your first big assignment, you have been asked to provide information on the 'privatisation' of eastern European economies. Using journals and newspapers, provide a scrapbook of information indicating the different ways in which western companies have sought to exploit business opportunities in eastern Europe.

Notes and references

1 Donaldson, P. and Farquhar, J., *Understanding the British Economy*, Penguin, 1988, p. 84.

2 See also the concept of Gross Value Added (GVA) which is an important measure in the estimation of GDP. National Statistics Online has a good explanation of GVA.

3 Real interest rates allow for inflation.

4 See, for example, Neale, A. and Haslam, C., *Economics in a Business Context*, Chapman & Hall, 1991, p. 141.

5 The role of assisting reconstruction in eastern Europe is also undertaken by the European Bank for Reconstruction and Development (EBRD). See text below.

Further reading

Begg, D. and Ward, D., *Economics for Business*, 2nd revised edition, McGraw-Hill, 2006.

Donaldson, P. and Farquhar, J., *Understanding the British Economy*, Penguin, 1991.

Ferguson, K., Essential Economics: *A Guide for Business Students*, Palgrave, 2004.

Griffiths, A. and Wall, S. (eds), *Applied Economics*, 11th edition, Financial Times/Prentice Hall, 2007.

Griffiths, A. and Wall, S., *Economics for Business and Management*, 2nd revised edition, FT/Prentice Hall, 2008.

Macdonald, N. T., *Macroeconomics and Business: An Interactive Approach*, International Thomson Publishing, 1999.

Mulhearn, C., Vane, H.R. and Eden, J., *Economics for Business*, Palgrave, 2001.

Neale, A., Haslam, C. and Johal, S., *Economics in a Business Context*, Thomson Learning, 3rd edition, 2000.

Worthington, I., Britton, C. and Rees, A., *Economics for Business: Blending Theory and Practice*, 2nd edition, Financial Times/Prentice Hall, 2005.

web
link

Web links and further questions are available on the website at:

www.pearsoned.co.uk/worthington

Chapter 6
The National Economy

The national economy

We turn now to *macroeconomics*. This will be the subject for this second part of the book. As we have already seen, microeconomics focuses on *individual* markets. In macroeconomics we take a much loftier view. We examine the economy as a whole. We still examine demand and supply, but now it is the *total* level of spending in the economy and the total level of production. In other words, we examine *aggregate demand* and *aggregate supply*.

In particular, we will be examining three key issues. The first is national output. What determines the size of national output? What causes it to grow? Why do growth rates fluctuate? Why do economies sometimes surge ahead and at other times languish in recession?

The second issue is employment and unemployment. What causes unemployment? If people who are unemployed want jobs, and if consumers want more goods and services, then why does our economy fail to provide a job for everyone who wants one?

Then there is the issue of inflation. Why is it that the general level of prices always seems to rise, and only rarely fall? Why is inflation a problem, and would it be a good thing or a bad thing if prices *did* fall? Why do countries' central banks, such as the Bank of England, set targets for the rate of inflation?

In this chapter, after a preliminary look at the range of macroeconomic issues, we then focus on national output. We will see how national output tends to grow over time, but nevertheless fluctuates from year to year. Then, in Sections 7.4 to 7.6, we develop two simple models to explain how national output in any one year is determined.

After studying this chapter, you should be able to answer the following questions:

- What are the key macroeconomic issues faced by all countries?
- What are the various flows of incomes around the economy? What causes these flows to expand or contract?
- What is meant by 'the business cycle' and how does the actual output produced in the economy relate to what could potentially be produced?
- What determines the rate of economic growth over the long term?
- What determines the level of national output at any one time?
- How do we measure national output?
- What is the effect on the economy of an increase in spending? Will output increase; will prices increase; or will there be some combination of the two?

7.1 MACROECONOMIC ISSUES

What are the major economic problems that economies as a whole suffer from?

Economic growth

Definition

Rate of economic growth
The percentage increase in output over a 12-month period.

Governments try to achieve high **rates of economic growth** over the long term: in other words, growth that is sustained over the years and is not just a temporary phenomenon. Table 7.1 shows the average annual growth in output between 1960 and 2006 for selected economies. As you can see, the differences between countries are quite substantial.

Governments also try to achieve *stable* growth, avoiding both recessions and excessive short-term growth that cannot be sustained. In practice, however, this can often prove difficult to achieve.

> ***Economies suffer from inherent instability.*** As a result, economic growth and other macroeconomic indicators tend to fluctuate. This is **Threshold Concept 12**. It is a threshold concept because it is vital to recognise the fundamental instability in market economies. Analysing the ups and downs of the 'business cycle' occupies many macroeconomists.
>
> **Key Idea 28**
>
> **TC 12**

Figure 7.1 shows how growth rates have fluctuated over the years for four economies. Note that 'EU15' stands for the 15 countries that were members of the EU prior to the accession of 10 new members in 2004. As you can see, in all four cases there has been considerable volatility in their economies.

| **Table 7.1** | Economic growth, unemployment and inflation in selected economies |

	France	Germany	Italy	Japan	UK	USA	EU(15)	OECD[1]	Brazil	Malaysia	Singapore
Growth (average % per year)											
1960–9	7.5	4.4	5.3	10.9	2.9	4.3	3.5	4.6	5.4	6.5	8.8
1970–9	3.2	2.6	3.8	4.3	2.0	2.8	3.2	3.6	8.1	7.9	8.3
1980–9	2.2	1.8	2.4	4.0	2.4	2.5	2.2	2.6	3.0	5.8	6.1
1990–9	1.7	2.2	1.5	1.7	2.1	3.0	2.1	2.6	1.8	6.9	7.7
2000–6	2.0	1.1	1.2	1.6	2.5	2.8	1.9	2.5	2.7	5.2	4.5
Unemployment (average %)											
1960–9	1.5	0.9	5.1	1.3	2.2	4.1	2.5	2.5	n/a	n/a	n/a
1970–9	3.7	2.3	6.4	1.7	4.5	6.1	4.0	4.3	n/a	n/a	n/a
1980–9	9.0	5.9	9.5	2.5	10.0	7.2	9.3	7.3	n/a	6.2	3.6
1990–9	10.6	7.7	10.4	3.7	8.1	5.8	9.2	6.9	9.3	3.4	2.8
2000–6	9.2	8.6	8.5	4.4	4.9	5.2	7.7	6.5	12.2	3.5	3.9
Inflation (average % per year)											
1960–9	4.2	3.2	4.4	4.9	4.1	2.8	3.7	3.1	46.1	−0.3	1.1
1970–9	9.4	5.0	13.9	9.0	13.0	6.8	10.3	9.2	30.6	7.3	5.9
1980–9	7.3	2.9	11.2	2.5	7.4	5.5	7.4	8.9	332.2	2.2	2.5
1990–9	2.0	2.2	4.7	0.8	3.9	2.4	3.3	4.4	847.0	3.6	1.9
2000–6	1.6	1.4	2.5	−0.7	1.9	2.3	2.1	2.4	8.4	1.5	0.7

[1] The Organisation for Economic Co-operation and Development: the 30 major industrial countries (excluding Russia, but including Turkey and Mexico)

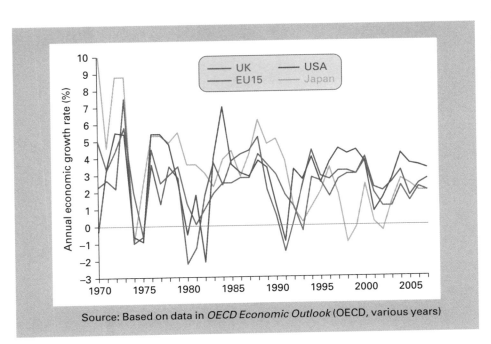

Figure 7.1
Growth rates in selected industrial economies

Unemployment

Reducing unemployment is another major macroeconomic aim of governments, not only for the sake of the unemployed themselves, but also because it represents a waste of human resources and because unemployment benefits are a drain on government revenues.

Unemployment in the 1980s and early 1990s was significantly higher than in the 1950s, 1960s and 1970s. Then, in the late 1990s and early 2000s, it fell in some countries, such as the UK and USA. In others, such as Germany and France, it remained stubbornly high. This is illustrated in Figure 7.2, which shows unemployment rates (as a percentage of the labour force) for the same four economies.

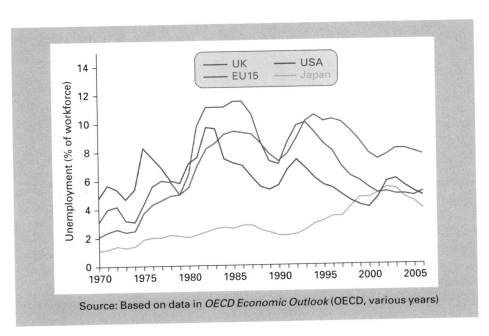

Figure 7.2
Unemployment rates in selected industrial economies

Figure 7.3
Inflation rates in
selected industrial
economies

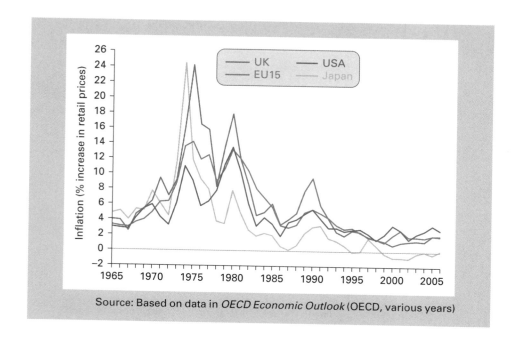

Source: Based on data in *OECD Economic Outlook* (OECD, various years)

You can also see that unemployment has fluctuated over the years with the ups and downs of the respective economies. For example, UK unemployment rose in the recessions of the early 1980s and early 1990s and fell in the boom of the late 1980s and mid-to-late 1990s.

Inflation

By inflation we mean a general rise in prices throughout the economy. Government policy here is to keep inflation both low and stable. One of the most important reasons for this is that it will aid the process of economic decision making. For example, businesses will be able to set prices and wage rates, and make investment decisions with far more confidence.

Today we are used to **inflation rates** of around 2 or 3 per cent per year, but it was not long ago that inflation in most developed countries was in double figures. In 1975, UK inflation reached 24 per cent. Figure 7.3 illustrates inflation rates in the same four economies.

In most developed countries, governments have a particular target for the rate of inflation. In the UK the target is 2 per cent. The Bank of England then adjusts interest rates to try to keep inflation on target (we see how this works in Chapter 10).

The balance of payments

A country's **balance of payments account** records all transactions between the residents of that country and the rest of the world. These transactions enter as either debit items or credit items. The debit items include all payments *to* other countries: these include the country's purchases of imports, the spending on investment it makes abroad, and the interest and dividends paid to people abroad who have invested in the country. The credit items include all receipts *from* other countries: from the sales of exports, from inward investment expenditure, and from interest and dividends earned from abroad.

The sale of exports and any other receipts earn foreign currency. The purchase of imports or any other payments abroad use up foreign currency. If we start to spend more foreign currency than we earn, one of two things must happen. Both are likely to be a problem.

The balance of payments will go into deficit.   In other words, there will be a shortfall of foreign currencies. The government will therefore have to borrow money from abroad, or draw on its foreign currency reserves to make up the shortfall. This is a problem because, if it goes on too long, overseas debts will mount, along with the interest that must be paid; and/or reserves will begin to run low.

The exchange rate will fall.   The exchange rate is the rate at which one currency exchanges for another. For example, the exchange rate of the pound into the dollar might be £1 = \$1.60.

  If the government does nothing to correct the balance of payments deficit, then the exchange rate must fall: for example, to \$1.55 or \$1.50, or lower. (We will show just why this is so in Chapter 12.) A falling exchange rate is a problem because it pushes up the price of imports and may fuel inflation. Also, if the exchange rate fluctuates, this can cause great uncertainty for traders and can damage international trade and economic growth.

In order to achieve the goals of high and sustainable economic growth, low unemployment, low inflation, a satisfactory balance of payments and stable exchange rates, the government (or central bank[1]) may seek to control several 'intermediate' variables. These include taxes, government expenditure, interest rates and the supply of money. We will be looking at the relationship between all these in the coming chapters.

> ### Definition
>
> **Exchange rate**
> The rate at which one national currency exchanges for another. The rate is expressed as the amount of one currency that is necessary to purchase *one unit* of another currency (e.g. €1.55 = £1).

Recap

1. Macroeconomics, like microeconomics, looks at issues such as output, employment and prices; but it looks at them in the context of the whole economy.

2. The four main macroeconomic goals that are generally of most concern to governments are economic growth, reducing unemployment, keeping inflation low and stable, and avoiding balance of payments and exchange rate problems.

THE CIRCULAR FLOW OF INCOME   7.2

Why does money go round and round from firms to consumers and back again?

KI 27
p201

Unfortunately, the pursuit of any one of the four objectives that we have identified may make at least one of the others worse. For example, attempts to increase the rate of economic growth by giving tax cuts so as to boost consumer spending, and thereby encourage investment, may lead to higher inflation. It is thus important to understand the relationship between the four objectives.

---

[1] The central bank is banker to the government and the banks as a whole (see Section 8.2). In most countries the central bank operates monetary policy by setting interest rates and influencing the supply of money. The central bank in the UK is the Bank of England; in the eurozone it is the European Central Bank (ECB) and in the USA it is the Federal Reserve Bank (the 'Fed').

Figure 7.4
The circular flow of income

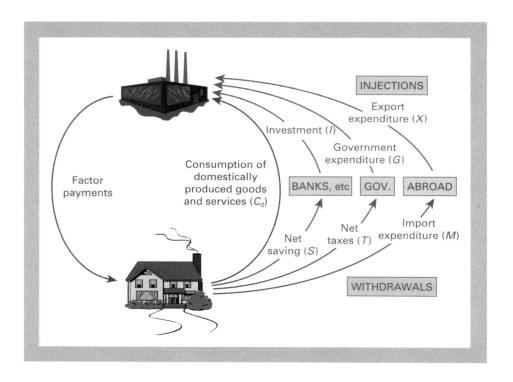

One way in which the objectives are linked is through their relationship with **aggregate demand (*AD*)**. This is the total spending on goods and services made within the country ('domestically produced goods and services') over a given period of time (normally a year). This spending consists of four elements: consumer spending on domestically produced goods and services (C_d), investment expenditure within the country by firms (I), government spending on goods and services (such as health, education and transport) (G), and the expenditure by residents abroad on this country's exports (X). Thus:[2]

$$AD = C_d + I + G + X$$

To show how the four objectives are related to aggregate demand, we can use a simple model of the economy. This is the *circular flow of income*, and is shown in Figure 7.4. It is an extension of the model we looked at back in the Introduction (see Figure I.5 on page 14).

In the diagram, the economy is divided into two major groups: *firms* and *households*. Each group has two roles. Firms are producers of goods and services; they are also the employers of labour and other factors of production. Households (which include all individuals) are the consumers of goods and services; they are also the suppliers of labour and various other factors of production. In the diagram there is an inner flow and various outer flows of incomes between these two groups.

---

[2] Investment, government expenditure and export expenditure are also only on domestically produced goods and services (and thus strictly speaking should also be written with a subscript 'd'). If, alternatively, we were also to include in C, I, G and X any component of expenditure going on imports, we would then have to subtract imports (M) again to get back to aggregate demand. Thus another way of writing aggregate demand is $AD = C + I + G + X - M$ (where each of C, I, G and X includes expenditure on both domestic *and* imported goods and services).

Before we look at the various parts of the diagram, a word of warning. Do not confuse *money* and *income*. Money is a stock concept. At any given time, there is a certain quantity of money in the economy (e.g. £1 billion). But that does not tell us the level of national *income*. Income is a flow concept (as is expenditure). It is measured as so much *per period of time*.

> **Stocks and flows.** A stock is a quantity of something at a given point in time. A flow is an increase or decrease in something over a specified period of time. This is an important distinction and a common cause of confusion. **Key Idea 29**

The relationship between money and income depends on how rapidly the money circulates: its 'velocity of circulation'. (We will examine this concept in detail later on.) If there is £1 billion of money in the economy and each £1 on average is paid out as income five times per year, then annual national income will be £5 billion.

The inner flow, withdrawals and injections

The inner flow

Firms pay money to households in the form of wages and salaries, dividends on shares, interest and rent. These payments are in return for the services of the factors of production – labour, capital and land – that are supplied by households. Thus, on the left-hand side of Figure 7.4, money flows directly from firms to households as 'factor payments'.

Households, in turn, pay money to domestic firms when they **consume domestically produced goods and services** (C_d). This is shown on the right-hand side of the inner flow. There is thus a circular flow of payments from firms to households to firms and so on.

If households spend *all* their incomes on buying domestic goods and services, and if firms pay out *all* this income they receive from consumers as factor payments to domestic households, and if the velocity at which money circulates does not change, the flow will continue at the same level indefinitely. The money just goes round and round at the same speed and incomes remain unchanged.

In the real world, of course, it is not as simple as this. Not all income gets passed on round the inner flow; some is *withdrawn*. At the same time, incomes are injected into the flow from outside. Let us examine these withdrawals and injections.

> **Pause for thought**
>
> *Would this argument still hold if prices rose?*

Withdrawals (W)

There are three forms of **withdrawals** (or 'leakages' as they are sometimes called).

Net saving (S). Saving is income that households choose not to spend but to put aside for the future. Savings are normally deposited in financial institutions such as banks and building societies. This is shown in Figure 7.4. Money flows from households to 'banks, etc'. What we are seeking to measure here, however, is the net flow from households to the banking sector. We therefore have to subtract from saving any borrowing or drawing on past savings by households to arrive at the net saving flow. Of course, if household borrowing exceeded saving, the net flow would be in the other direction: it would be negative.

Definitions

The consumption of domestically produced goods and services (C_d) The direct flow of money payments from households to firms.

Withdrawals (W) (or leakages) Incomes of households or firms that are not passed on round the inner flow. Withdrawals equal net saving (S) plus net taxes (T) plus import expenditure (M): $W = S + T + M$

Net taxes (T). When people pay taxes (to either central or local government), this represents a withdrawal of money from the inner flow in much the same way as saving: only in this case people have no choice. Some taxes, such as income tax and employees' national insurance contributions, are paid out of household incomes. Others, such as VAT and excise duties, are paid out of consumer expenditure. Others, such as corporation tax, are paid out of firms' incomes before being received by households as dividends on shares. (For simplicity, however, we show taxes being withdrawn at just one point. It does not affect the argument.)

When, however, people receive *benefits* from the government, such as working tax credit, child benefit and pensions, the money flows the other way. Benefits are thus equivalent to a 'negative tax'. These benefits are known as transfer payments. They transfer money from one group of people (taxpayers) to others (the recipients).

In the model, 'net taxes' (*T*) represents the *net* flow to the government from households and firms. It consists of total taxes minus benefits.

Import expenditure (M). Not all consumption is of totally home-produced goods. Households spend some of their incomes on imported goods and services, or on goods and services using imported components. Although the money that consumers spend on such goods initially flows to domestic retailers, it will eventually find its way abroad, either when the retailers or wholesalers themselves import the goods, or when domestic manufacturers purchase imported inputs to make their products. This expenditure on imports constitutes the third withdrawal from the inner flow. This money flows abroad.

Total withdrawals are simply the sum of net saving, net taxes and the expenditure on imports:

$$W = S + T + M$$

Injections (J)

Only part of the demand for firms' output (i.e. aggregate demand) arises from consumers' expenditure. The remainder comes from other sources outside the inner flow. These additional components of aggregate demand are known as injections (*J*). There are three types of injection.

Investment (I). This is the flow of money that firms spend which they obtain from various financial institutions – either past savings or loans, or through a new issue of shares. They may invest in plant and equipment or may simply spend the money on building up stocks of inputs, semi-finished or finished goods.

Government expenditure (G). When the government spends money on goods and services produced by firms, this counts as an injection. Examples of such government expenditure include spending on roads, hospitals and schools. (Note that government expenditure in this model does not include state benefits. These transfer payments, as we saw above, are the equivalent of negative taxes and have the effect of reducing the *T* component of withdrawals.)

Export expenditure (X). Money flows into the circular flow from abroad when residents abroad buy our exports of goods and services.

Total injections are thus the sum of investment, government expenditure and exports:

$$J = I + G + X$$

Aggregate demand, which is the total spending on output, is thus $C_d + J$.

Definitions

Transfer payments
Moneys transferred from one person or group to another (e.g. from the government to individuals) without production taking place.

Injections (J)
Expenditure on the production of domestic firms coming from outside the inner flow of the circular flow of income. Injections equal investment (*I*) plus government expenditure (*G*) plus expenditure on exports (*X*).

The relationship between withdrawals and injections

There are indirect links between saving and investment via financial institutions, between taxation and government expenditure via the government (central and local), and between imports and exports via foreign countries. These links, however, do not guarantee that $S = I$ or $G = T$ or $M = X$.

Take investment and saving. The point here is that the decisions to save and invest are made by different people, and thus they plan to save and invest different amounts. Likewise the demand for imports may not equal the demand for exports. As far as the government is concerned, it may choose not to make $T = G$. It may choose not to spend all its tax revenues: to run a 'budget surplus' ($T > G$); or it may choose to spend more than it receives in taxes: to run a 'budget deficit' ($G > T$) – by borrowing to make up the difference.

Thus planned injections (J) may not equal planned withdrawals (W).

The circular flow of income and the four macroeconomic objectives

If planned injections are not equal to planned withdrawals, what will be the consequences? If injections exceed withdrawals, the level of expenditure will rise: there will be a rise in aggregate demand. This extra spending will increase firms' sales and thus encourage them to produce more. Total output in the economy will rise. Thus firms will pay out more in wages, salaries, profits, rent and interest. In other words, national income will rise.

The rise in aggregate demand will have the following effects upon the four macroeconomic objectives:

- There will be economic growth. The greater the initial excess of injections over withdrawals, the bigger will be the rise in national income.
- Unemployment will fall as firms take on more workers to meet the extra demand for output.
- Inflation will tend to rise. The greater the rise in aggregate demand relative to the capacity of firms to produce, the more will firms find it difficult to meet the extra demand, and the more likely they will be to raise prices.
- The exports and imports part of the balance of payments will tend to deteriorate. The higher demand sucks more imports into the country, and higher domestic inflation makes exports less competitive and imports relatively cheaper compared with home-produced goods. Thus imports will tend to rise and exports will tend to fall.

> **Pause for thought**
>
> What will be the effect on each of the four objectives if planned injections are less than planned withdrawals?

Equilibrium in the circular flow

When injections do not equal withdrawals, a state of disequilibrium will exist. This will set in train a process to bring the economy back to a state of equilibrium where injections are equal to withdrawals.

To illustrate this, let us consider the situation again where injections exceed withdrawals. Perhaps there has been a rise in business confidence so that investment has risen. Or perhaps there has been a tax cut so that withdrawals have fallen. As we have seen, the excess of injections over withdrawals will lead to a rise in national income. But as national income rises, so households will not only spend more on domestic goods (C_d), but also save more (S), pay more taxes (T) and buy more imports (M). In other words, withdrawals will rise. This will continue until they have risen to equal injections. At that point, national income will stop rising, and so will withdrawals. Equilibrium has been reached.

For the rest of this chapter, we focus largely on what determines the level of national output and its rate of growth over time. In other words, we focus mainly on the first of the above four issues. In doing so, we will touch on the other three, but we will save a detailed analysis of them until later. We look at unemployment and inflation in Chapter 9 and at the balance of payments and exchange rates in Chapter 12.

Recap

1. The circular flow of income model depicts the flows of money round the economy. The inner flow shows the direct flows between firms and households. Money flows from firms to households in the form of factor payments, and back again as consumer expenditure on domestically produced goods and services.
2. Not all incomes get passed on directly round the inner flow. Some is withdrawn in the form of saving, some is paid in taxes, and some goes abroad as expenditure on imports.
3. Likewise not all expenditure on domestic firms is by domestic consumers. Some is injected from outside the inner flow in the form of investment expenditure, government expenditure and expenditure on the country's exports.
4. Planned injections and withdrawals are unlikely to be the same.
5. If injections exceed withdrawals, national income will rise. As a result, unemployment will tend to fall, inflation will tend to rise, imports will tend to rise and exports fall. The reverse will happen if withdrawals exceed injections.
6. If injections exceed withdrawals, the rise in national income will lead to a rise in withdrawals. This will continue until $W = J$. At this point the circular flow will be in equilibrium.

7.3 ECONOMIC GROWTH AND THE BUSINESS CYCLE

Is a country's economic growth likely to be constant over time?

The distinction between actual and potential growth

Before examining the causes of economic growth, it is essential to distinguish between *actual* and *potential* economic growth.

Actual growth is the percentage annual increase in national output or '*gross domestic product*' (GDP) as it is called. When statistics on GDP growth rates are published, it is actual growth they are referring to. (We examine the measurement of GDP in the appendix to this chapter.)

When there is inflation, we have to be careful in assessing how much national output is increasing. GDP in year 2 may be higher in money terms (i.e. at current prices) than in year 1, but this may be partly, or even wholly, the result of higher prices. Thus GDP in money terms may have risen by 5 per cent, but if inflation is 3 per cent, *real* growth in GDP will be only 2 per cent. In other words, the volume of output will be only 2 per cent higher.

The distinction between nominal and real figures. Nominal figures are those using current prices, interest rates, etc. Real figures are figures corrected for inflation. This distinction is so important in assessing economic data that it is another of our **Threshold Concepts** (no. 13).

Key Idea 30

TC 13

Potential growth is the speed at which the economy *could* grow. It is the percentage annual increase in the economy's *capacity* to produce: the rate of growth in potential output.

Potential output (i.e. potential GDP) is the level of output when the economy is operating at 'normal capacity utilisation'. This allows for firms having a planned degree of spare capacity to meet unexpected demand or for hold-ups in supply. It also allows for some unemployment as people move from job to job. Potential output is thus somewhat below full-capacity output, which is the absolute maximum that could be produced with firms working flat out.

The difference between actual and potential output is known as the **output gap**. Thus if actual output exceeds potential output, the output gap is positive: the economy is operating above normal capacity utilisation. If actual output is below potential output, the output gap is negative: the economy is operating below normal capacity utilisation. Box 7.1 looks at the output gap since 1980 for four major industrial economies.

> *Long-term growth in a country's output depends on a growth in the quantity and/or productivity of its resources.* Potential economic growth depends on the country's resources, technology and productivity. This is crucial to understanding what underlies the wealth of nations and why some countries have faster growth rates that others. It forms the 14th of our **Threshold Concepts.**
>
> **Key Idea 31**
> **TC 14**

If the potential growth rate exceeds the actual growth rate, there will be an increase in spare capacity and an increase in unemployment: there will be a growing gap between potential and actual output. To close this gap, the actual growth rate would temporarily have to exceed the potential growth rate. In the long run, however, the actual growth rate will be limited to the potential growth rate.

There are thus two major issues concerned with economic growth: the short-run issue of ensuring that actual growth is such as to keep actual output as close as possible to potential output; and the long-run issue of what determines the rate of potential economic growth.

Growth and the production possibility curve

The distinction between actual and potential growth in output can be illustrated on a production possibility diagram. If you remember, a production possibility curve shows all the possible combinations of two goods that can be produced at any one time (see pages 11–14). For purposes of illustration, we could lump all goods and services together into two categories: for example, agricultural goods (good X) and manufactured goods and services (good Y).

The production possibility curve itself shows full-capacity output. Potential *growth*, then, is illustrated by a shift outwards of the curve (e.g. curve I to curve II in Figure 7.5). Actual growth is represented by a movement outwards of the production point (e.g. from point *a* to point *b*).

In the short run, actual growth can arise from a fuller use of resources (e.g. a movement from point *a* to point *b*). This would involve taking up slack in the economy: using machinery more fully and reducing unemployment. For actual growth to be sustained over a number of years, however, there would also have to be an increase in potential output. In other words, to get beyond point *b* in Figure 7.5, the production possibility curve itself would have to shift outwards beyond curve I.

Figure 7.5
Growth and
the production
possibility curve

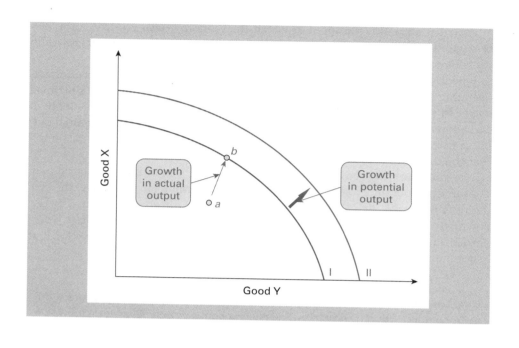

Actual economic growth and the business cycle

Although growth in potential output varies to some extent over the years – depending on the rate of advance of technology, the level of investment and the discovery of new raw materials – it nevertheless tends to be much more steady than the growth in actual output.

Actual growth tends to fluctuate. In some years there is a high rate of economic growth: the country experiences a boom. In other years, economic growth is low or even negative: the country experiences a recession.[3] This cycle of booms and recessions is known as the **business cycle or trade cycle**.

There are four 'phases' of the business cycle. They are illustrated in Figure 7.6.

1. *The upturn.* In this phase, a contracting or stagnant economy begins to recover, and growth in actual output resumes.
2. *The rapid expansion.* During this phase there is rapid economic growth: the economy is booming. A fuller use is made of resources, and the gap between actual and full-capacity output narrows.
3. *The peaking out.* During this phase, growth slows down or even ceases.
4. *The slowdown, recession or slump.* During this phase there is little or no growth or even a decline in output. Increasing slack develops in the economy.

A word of caution: do not confuse a high *level* of output with a high *rate of growth* in output. The level of output is highest in phase 3. The rate of growth in output is highest in phase 2 (i.e. where the curve is steepest).

Long-term output trend. A line can be drawn showing the trend of national output over time (i.e. ignoring the cyclical fluctuations around the trend). This is shown as the dashed line in Figure 7.6. If, over time, firms on average operate with a 'normal' degree of capacity utilisation, the trend output line will be the same as the potential

Definition

Business cycle or trade cycle
The periodic fluctuations of national output round its long-term trend.

---

[3] In official statistics, a recession is defined as when an economy experiences falling national output (negative growth) for two or more quarters.

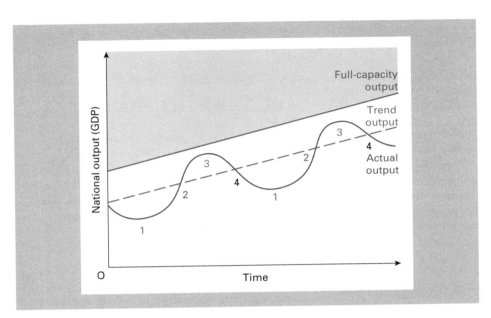

Figure 7.6
The business cycle

output line. If the average level of capacity that is unutilised stays constant from one cycle to another, the trend line will have the same slope as the full-capacity output line. In other words, the trend (or potential) rate of growth will be the same as the rate of growth of capacity.

If, however, the level of unutilised capacity changes from one cycle to another, then the trend line will have a different slope from the full-capacity output line. For example, if unemployment and unused industrial capacity *rise* from one peak to another, or from one trough to another, the trend line will move further away from the full-capacity output line (i.e. it will be less steep).

> **Pause for thought**
>
> *If the average percentage (as opposed to the average level) of capacity that was unutilised remained constant, would the trend line have the same slope as the potential output line?*

The business cycle in practice

The business cycle illustrated in Figure 7.6 is a 'stylised' cycle. It is nice and smooth and regular. Drawing it this way allows us to make a clear distinction between each of the four phases. In practice, however, business cycles are highly irregular. They are irregular in two ways.

The length of the phases.   Some booms are short lived, lasting only a few months or so. Others are much longer, lasting perhaps three or four years. Likewise some recessions are short while others are long.

The magnitude of the phases.   Sometimes in phase 2 there is a very high rate of economic growth, perhaps 4 per cent per annum or more. On other occasions in phase 2 growth is much gentler. Sometimes in phase 4 there is a recession, with an actual decline in output (e.g. in the early 1980s and early 1990s). On other occasions, phase 4 is merely a 'pause', with growth simply being low.

Nevertheless, despite the irregularity of the fluctuations, cycles are still clearly discernible, especially if we plot *growth* on the vertical axis rather than the *level* of output. This is done in Figure 7.7 (which is the same as Figure 7.1). It shows the business cycles in selected industrial economies from 1970 to 2007.

Box 7.1

Output gaps

An alternative measure of excess or deficient demand

If the economy grows, how fast and for how long can it grow before it runs into inflationary problems? On the other hand, what minimum rate must be achieved to avoid rising unemployment?

To answer these questions, economists have developed the concept of 'output gaps'.[1] As we have seen, the output gap is the difference between actual output and potential output. If actual output is below potential output (the gap is negative), there will be a higher than normal level of unemployment as firms are operating below their normal level of capacity utilisation. There will, however, be a downward pressure on inflation, resulting from a lower than normal level of demand for labour and other resources. If actual output is above potential output (the gap is positive), there will be excess demand and a rise in inflation. Generally, the gap will be negative in a recession and positive in a boom. In other words, output gaps follow the course of the business cycle.

The diagram shows output gaps for four countries from 1980 to 2007. As you can see, there was a large positive output gap in the UK in the late 1980s. This corresponded to a rapid rise in output and inflation and a fall in unemployment. You will also see that there was a large negative output gap in Japan in the early 2000s. This corresponded to a

[1] See Giorno et al., 'Potential output, output gaps and structural budget balances', *OECD Economic Studies*, no. 24, 1995: 1

deep recession, high unemployment and inflation just below zero (i.e. a slight decline in prices).

Over the long term, the rate of economic growth will be approximately the same as the rate of growth in potential output. In other words, over the years, the average output gap will tend towards zero.

But how do we measure the output gap? There are two possible methods.

Measuring trend growth. The simplest way of calculating the output gap is by measuring the trend growth rate of the economy (i.e. the average growth rate over the course of the business cycle: see Figure 7.6 on page 245) and then seeing how much actual output differs from trend output. The assumption here is that the potential level of output grows steadily. This is, in fact, a major weakness of this method. Technological innovations tend to come in waves, generating surges in an economy's sustainable output. Rates of innovation, in turn, depend upon how flexible the economy is in adapting to such new technologies and how much investment takes place in equipment using this technology and in training labour in the necessary skills.

Business surveys. An alternative way to measure the output gap is to ask businesses directly. However, survey-based evidence can provide only a broad guide to rates of capacity utilisation and whether there is deficient or excess demand. Survey evidence tends to focus on specific sectors, which might, or might not, be indicative of the capacity position of the economy as a whole.

Causes of fluctuations in actual growth

The major determinants of variations in the rate of actual growth in the *short run* are variations in the growth of aggregate demand.

A rapid rise in aggregate demand will create shortages. This will tend to stimulate firms to increase output, thereby reducing slack in the economy. Likewise, a reduction in aggregate demand will leave firms with increased stocks of unsold goods. They will therefore tend to reduce output.

Aggregate demand and actual output, therefore, fluctuate together in the short run. A boom is associated with a rapid rise in aggregate demand: the faster the rise

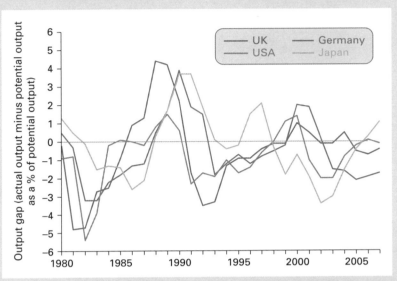

Source: Based on data in *Economic Outlook* (OECD, various years)

Output gaps in selected countries: 1980–2007

Evidence for the UK. The trend growth rate in the UK was about 2.7 per cent per year over the full economic cycle to 2005 (i.e. from 1991: the equivalent point in the previous cycle). But whereas the economy in 1991/2 was suffering quite a severe recession, with negative growth for six of the eight quarters from 1990 quarter 3, in 2005 the economy was experiencing a relatively mild slowdown (economic growth was 1.7 per cent). This reflects the fact that cyclical fluctuations in the UK have become less severe in recent years.

The question is whether the greater stability in the UK economy is encouraging a climate that will lead to a long-term increase in investment and hence a long-term increase in potential growth.

? *Under what circumstances would potential output (i.e. a zero output gap) move further away from the full-capacity output ceiling shown in Figure 7.6?*

in aggregate demand, the higher the short-run growth rate. A recession, by contrast, is associated with a reduction in aggregate demand.

A rapid rise in aggregate demand, however, is not enough to ensure a continuing high level of growth over a *number* of years. Without an expansion of potential output too, rises in actual output must eventually come to an end as spare capacity is used up.

In the long run, therefore, there are two determinants of actual growth:

- The growth in aggregate demand. This determines whether potential output will be realised.
- The growth in potential output.

Figure 7.7
Growth rates in selected industrial economies: 1970–2007

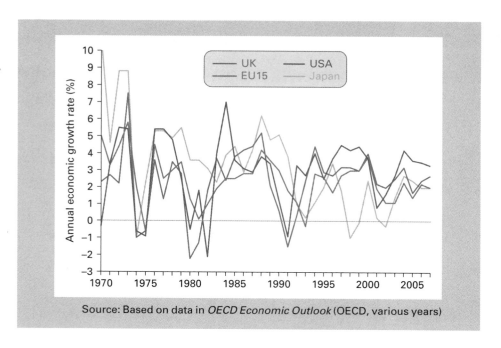

Source: Based on data in *OECD Economic Outlook* (OECD, various years)

Potential economic growth

We now turn to the *supply* question. Here we are concerned with the capacity of the economy to produce. There are two main determinants of potential output: (a) the amount of resources available and (b) their productivity.

Increases in the quantity of resources

Capital.   The nation's output depends on its stock of capital. An increase in this stock (through investment) will increase output. Generally, the higher the rate of investment, the faster will the stock of capital increase. The rise in output that results will depend on the productivity of capital: how much extra capital you need to produce extra output.

Over the long term, if investment is to increase, then saving must increase in order to finance that investment. Put another way, people must be prepared to forgo a certain amount of consumption in order to allow resources to be diverted into producing more capital goods: factories, machines, etc.

Labour.   If there is an increase in the working population, there will be an increase in potential output. This increase in working population may result from a larger 'participation rate': a larger proportion of the total population in work or seeking work. For example, if a greater proportion of women with children decide to join the labour market, the working population will rise.

Alternatively, a rise in the working population may be the result of an increase in total population. There is a problem here. If a rise in total population does not result in a greater *proportion* of the population working, output *per head of the population* may not rise at all. In practice, many developed countries are faced with a growing proportion of their population above retirement age, and thus a potential *fall* in output per head of the population.

Land and raw materials.   The scope for generating growth here is usually very limited. Land is virtually fixed in quantity. Land reclamation schemes and the opening up of marginal land can add only tiny amounts to GDP. Even if new raw materials are discovered (e.g. oil), this will result only in *short-term growth*: i.e. while the rate of extraction is building up. Once the rate of extraction is at a maximum, economic growth will cease. Output will simply remain at the new higher level, until eventually the raw materials begin to run out. Output will then fall back again.

The problem of diminishing returns. If a single factor of production increases in supply while others remain fixed, diminishing returns will set in (see pages 83–5). For example, if the quantity of capital increases with no increase in other factors of production, then diminishing returns to capital will set in. The rate of return on capital will fall. Unless *all* factors of production increase, therefore, the rate of growth is likely to slow down.

Then there is the problem of the environment. If a rise in labour and capital leads to a more *intensive* use of land and natural resources, the resulting growth in output may be environmentally unsustainable.

The solution to the problem of diminishing returns is for there to be an increase in the *productivity* of resources.

Increases in the productivity of resources

Technological improvements can increase the productivity of capital. Much of the investment in new machines is not just in extra machines, but in superior machines producing a higher rate of return. Consider the microchip revolution of recent years. Modern computers can do the work of many people and have replaced many machines that were cumbersome and expensive to build. Improved communications (such as e-mail and the Internet) have reduced the costs of transmitting information. The high-tech world of today would seem a wonderland to a person of 100 years ago.

As a result of technical progress, the productivity of capital has tended to increase over time. Similarly, as a result of new skills, improved education and training, and better health, the productivity of labour has also tended to increase over time.

But technical progress on its own is not enough. There must also be the institutions and attitudes that encourage *innovation*. In other words, the inventions must be exploited.

> **Pause for thought**
>
> *Will the rate of actual growth have any effect on the rate of potential growth?*

Policies to achieve growth

How can governments increase a country's growth rate? Policies differ in two ways.

First, they may focus on the demand side or the supply side of the economy. In other words, they may attempt to create sufficient *aggregate demand* to ensure that firms wish to invest and that potential output is realised. Alternatively, they may seek to increase *aggregate supply* by concentrating on measures to increase potential output: measures to encourage research and development, innovation and training.

Second, they may be market-orientated or interventionist policies. Many economists and politicians, especially those on the political right, believe that the best environment for encouraging economic growth is one where private enterprise is allowed to flourish: where entrepreneurs are able to reap substantial rewards from investment in new techniques and new products. Such economists therefore advocate policies designed to free up the market. Others, however, argue that a free market will be subject to considerable cyclical fluctuations. The resulting uncertainty will discourage investment. Such economists, therefore, tend to advocate active intervention by the government to reduce these fluctuations.

Box 7.2

The costs of economic growth

Is more necessarily better?

For many developing countries economic growth is a necessity if they are to remove mass poverty. When the majority of their population is underfed, poorly housed, with inadequate health care and little access to education, few would quarrel with the need for an increase in productive potential. The main query is whether the benefits of economic growth will flow to the mass of the population, or whether they will be confined to the few who are already relatively well-off.

For developed countries the case for economic growth is less clear-cut. Economic growth is usually measured in terms of the growth in national output valued in prices as given by the market. The problem is that there are many 'goods' and 'bads' that are not included when measuring national output. Economic growth, therefore, is not the same as growth in a nation's *welfare*. True, there can be major advantages of economic growth, and certainly, other things being equal, the majority of the population wants higher levels of production and consumption. But it is important to recognise the costs of economic growth. Indeed, some people regard these costs as so serious that they advocate a policy of *zero economic growth*.

So, what are the benefits and costs of economic growth?

The benefits of growth

Increased levels of consumption. Provided economic growth outstrips population growth, it will lead to higher real income per head. This can lead to higher levels of consumption of goods and services. If human welfare is related to the level of consumption, then growth provides an obvious gain to society.

It can help avoid other macroeconomic problems. People have aspirations to rising living standards. Without a growth in productive potential, people's demands for rising incomes are likely to lead to higher inflation, balance of payments crises (as more imports are purchased), industrial disputes, etc. Growth in productive potential helps to meet these aspirations and avoid macroeconomic crises.

It can make it easier to redistribute incomes to the poor. If incomes rise, the government can redistribute incomes from the rich to the poor *without the rich losing*. For example, as people's incomes rise, they automatically pay more taxes. These extra revenues for the government can be spent on programmes to alleviate poverty.

Without a continuing rise in national income the scope for helping the poor is much more limited.

Society may feel that it can afford to care more for the environment. As people grow richer, they may become less preoccupied with their own private consumption and more concerned to live in a clean environment. The regulation of pollution tends to be tougher in developed countries than in the developing world.

KI 19
p177

The costs of growth

In practice, more consumption may not make people happier; economies may be no less crisis-riven; income may not be redistributed more equally; the environment may not be better protected. More than this, some people argue that growth may worsen these problems and create additional problems besides.

The current opportunity cost of growth. To achieve faster growth, firms will probably need to invest

TC 1
p7

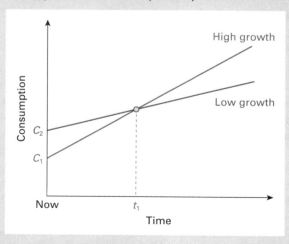

High- and low-growth paths

more. This will require financing. The finance can come from a higher saving rate or higher taxes. Either way, there must be a cut in consumption. In the short run, therefore, higher growth leads to *less* consumption, not more.

In the diagram, assume that consumption is currently at a level of C_1. Its growth over time is shown by the line out from C_1. Now assume that the government pursues a policy of higher growth. Consumption has to *fall* to finance the extra investment. Consumption falls to, say, C_2. The growth in consumption is now shown by the line out from C_2. Not until time t_1 is reached (which may be several years into the future) does consumption overtake the levels it would have reached with the previous lower growth rate.

Growth may simply generate extra demands. 'The more people have, the more they want.' If this is so, more consumption may not increase people's happiness at all. It is often observed that rich people tend to be miserable!

Social effects. Many people claim that an excessive pursuit of material growth by a country can lead to a more greedy, more selfish and less caring society. As society becomes more industrialised, violence, crime, loneliness, stress-related diseases, suicides, divorce and other social problems are likely to rise.

Environmental costs. A richer society may be more concerned for the environment, but it is also likely to do more damage to it. The higher the level of consumption, the higher is likely to be the level of pollution and waste. What is more, many of the environmental costs are likely to be underestimated due to a lack of scientific knowledge. Acid rain and the depletion of the ozone layer have been two examples.

Non-renewable resources. If growth involves using a greater amount of resources, rather than using the same amount of resources more efficiently, certain non-renewable resources will run out more rapidly. Unless viable alternatives can be found for various minerals and fossil fuels, present growth may lead to shortages for future generations.

Effects on the distribution of income. While some people may gain from a higher standard of living, others are likely to lose. If the means to higher growth are greater incentives (such as cuts in higher rates of income tax), then the rich might get richer, with little or no benefits 'trickling down' to the poor.

Growth involves changes in production: both in terms of the goods produced and in terms of the techniques used and the skills required. The more rapid the rate of growth, the more rapid the rate of change. People may find that their skills are no longer relevant. Their jobs may be replaced by machines. People may thus find themselves unemployed, or forced to take low-paid, unskilled work.

Conclusion

So should countries pursue growth? The answer depends on (a) just what costs and benefits are involved, (b) what weighting people attach to them, and (c) how opposing views are to be reconciled. A problem is that the answer involves a judgement about what a 'desirable' society should look like, and that depends on your point of view. Generally, however, the electorate seems to want economic growth. As long as that is so, governments will tend to pursue policies to achieve growth. That is why we need to study the causes of growth and the policies that governments can pursue.

One thing the government can do is to view the problem as one of *constrained optimisation*. It sets constraints: levels of environmental protection, minimum wages, maximum rates of depletion of non-renewable resources, etc. It then seeks policies that will maximise growth, while keeping within these constraints.

1. *Is a constrained optimisation approach a practical solution to the possible costs of economic growth?*
2. *Are worries about the consequences of economic growth a 'luxury' that only rich countries can afford?*

Chapter 10 looks at various macroeconomic policies: both demand-side and supply-side.

For the remainder of this chapter, we focus on the determination of actual output and why it fluctuates. Later, in Section 9.7, we look more closely at the long-term position and ask what determines long-term growth rates: in other words, what determines the growth in potential output.

Recap

1. Actual growth must be distinguished from potential growth. The actual growth rate is the percentage annual increase in the output that is actually produced, whereas potential growth is the percentage annual increase in the capacity of the economy to produce (whether or not it is actually produced).

2. Actual growth will fluctuate with the course of the business cycle. The cycle can be broken down into four phases: the upturn, the expansion, the peaking out, and the slowdown or recession. In practice, the length and magnitude of these phases vary: the cycle is thus irregular.

3. Actual growth is determined by potential growth and by the level of aggregate demand. If actual output is below potential output, actual growth can temporarily exceed potential growth, if aggregate demand is rising sufficiently. In the long term, however, actual output can grow only as fast as potential output will permit.

4. Potential growth is determined by the rate of increase in the *quantity* of resources: capital, labour, land and raw materials; and by the *productivity* of resources. The productivity of capital can be increased by technological improvements and the more efficient use of the capital stock; the productivity of labour can be increased by better education, training, motivation and organisation.

5. Whether governments can best achieve rapid growth through market-orientated or interventionist policies is highly controversial.

7.4 THE EQUILIBRIUM LEVEL OF NATIONAL INCOME

What determines the level of a country's output in the short run?

The analysis of this and the next section is based on the theory developed by John Maynard Keynes in the 1930s (see Box 7.3), a theory that has had a profound influence on economics. Keynes argued that, without government intervention to steer the economy, countries could lurch from unsustainable growth to deep and prolonged recessions. Keynesian analysis of output and employment can be explained most simply in terms of the circular flow of income diagram. Figure 7.8 shows a simplified version of the circular flow that we looked at in Section 7.2.

If injections (J) do not equal withdrawals (W), a state of disequilibrium exists. What will bring them back into equilibrium is a change in national income and employment.

Start with a state of equilibrium, where injections equal withdrawals. If there is now a rise in injections – say, firms decide to invest more – aggregate demand ($C_d + J$) will be higher. Firms will respond to this increased demand by using more labour and other resources, and thus paying out more incomes (Y) to households. Household consumption will rise and so firms will sell more.

Firms will respond by producing more, and thus using more labour and other resources. Household incomes will rise again. Consumption and hence production

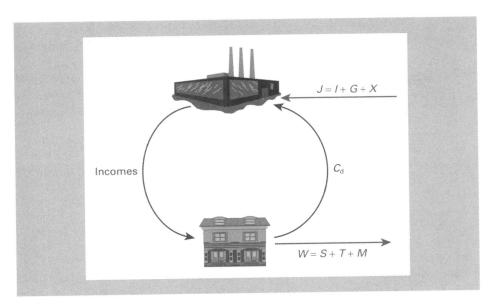

Figure 7.8
The circular flow of income

will rise again, and so on. There will thus be a multiplied rise in incomes and employment. This is known as the multiplier effect and is an example of the 'principle of cumulative causation'.

> ***The principle of cumulative causation.*** An initial event can cause an ultimate effect that is much larger. This phenomenon of things building on themselves occurs throughout market economies. It is a fundamental principle in economics and is the 15th and final **Threshold Concept**
>
> Key Idea 32
> TC 15

The process, however, does not go on for ever. Each time household incomes rise, households save more, pay more taxes and buy more imports. In other words, withdrawals rise. When withdrawals have risen to match the increase in injections, equilibrium will be restored and national income and employment will stop rising. The process can be summarised as follows:

$$J > W \rightarrow Y\uparrow \rightarrow W\uparrow \text{ until } J = W$$

Similarly, an initial fall in injections (or rise in withdrawals) will lead to a multiplied fall in national income and employment:

$$J < W \rightarrow Y\downarrow \rightarrow W\downarrow \text{ until } J = W$$

Thus equilibrium in the circular flow of income can be at *any* level of output and employment.

Showing equilibrium with a Keynesian diagram

Equilibrium can be shown on a 'Keynesian' diagram. This plots various elements of the circular flow of income (such as consumption, withdrawals, injections and aggregate demand) against national income (i.e. GDP). There are two approaches to finding equilibrium: the withdrawals and injections approach and the income and expenditure approach. Let us examine each in turn.

Box 7.3   **Exploring Economics**

The Keynesian revolution

'In the long run we're all dead'

Up until the early 1920s, economists generally believed that there could be no such thing as mass unemployment. The reasoning of these 'classical' economists was simple: if there was unemployment in any given labour market, then all that was necessary was for a fall in real wage rates and firms, as a result, could afford to take on more workers. The unemployment would be largely eliminated.

But in the early 1920s, the UK plunged into a deep recession that persisted until the outbreak of the Second World War in 1939. The UK was followed in 1929 by many other countries after the crash on the US stock exchange (the 'Wall Street crash'). The world experienced 'the Great Depression'.

How did the classical economists explain what had seemed impossible? They argued that, as a result of growing unionisation, wage rates were not sufficiently flexible downwards. What was needed was a willingness on the part of workers to accept wage cuts, so as to 'price themselves into employment'. What would also help would be an increase in saving, so as to provide a greater fund of money for businesses to borrow for investment: investment that would get the economy growing again.

What was *not* needed, they argued, was an increase in government spending (a problem, given the growing expenditure on unemployment benefits as the number of unemployed rose). Increased government expenditure would mean more government borrowing (if higher taxes were to be avoided), and this would divert funds away from the private sector. Private investment would be 'crowded out' by increased government spending.

Keynes's response

This analysis was criticised by John Maynard Keynes. In 1936 his *General Theory of Employment, Interest and Money* was published. Probably no other economist and no other book has ever had such a profound influence on the subject of economics and on the policies pursued by governments. Indeed, throughout the 1950s and 1960s, governments in the UK and the USA, and many other countries too, considered themselves to be 'Keynesian'.

Full employment, maintained Keynes, was not a natural state of affairs. The economy could slide into a depression, and stay there. To achieve full employment, the government would have to intervene actively in the economy to ensure a sufficient level of aggregate demand. With government intervention, however, a depression would become merely a *short-term* problem – a problem that the intervention could cure.

The classical economists seemed more concerned with the *long* term: with issues of efficiency, productivity and *potential* output. Keynes was not particularly interested in the long-run future of the world. 'Take care of the short run and the long run will look after itself' might have been Keynes's maxim. Keynes himself put it more succinctly: 'In the long run we are all dead'.

Keynes's solution to mass unemployment

Keynes argued that the solution to mass unemployment was for the government to spend *more*, not less. Rather than raising taxes, or increasing borrowing from the general public, it could pay for the extra spending by expanding the money supply. Extra spending would stimulate firms to produce more and to take on more workers.

As more people were employed, so they would spend more. This would encourage firms to produce even more, and to take on even more workers. There would be a 'multiplied' rise in income and employment.

After the Second World War, 'Keynesianism' became the new orthodoxy and remained so for more than 20 years. Governments of both parties accepted responsibility for ensuring that aggregate demand was kept at a sufficiently high level to maintain full, or near full, employment.

? *If the economy were at the peak of the boom (phase 3 in Figure 7.6 on page 245), what would be the likely results of an increase in government expenditure with no corresponding increase in taxes?*

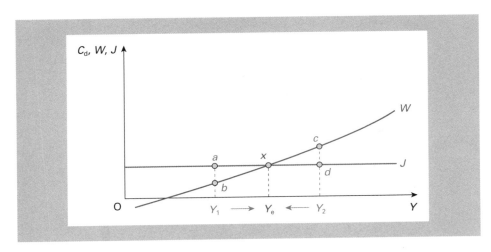

Figure 7.9
Deriving equilibrium
national income:
withdrawals and
injections approach

The withdrawals and injections approach

In Figure 7.9, national income (Y) is plotted on the horizontal axis. Withdrawals (W) and injections (J) are plotted on the vertical axis.

As national income rises, so withdrawals (saving, taxes and imports) will rise. Thus the withdrawals curve slopes upwards. But the amounts that businesses plan to invest, that the government plans to spend and that overseas residents plan to import from the UK (i.e. UK exports) are all only slightly affected by the current level of UK national income. Thus injections, for simplicity, are assumed to be independent of national income. The injections line, therefore, is drawn as a horizontal straight line. (This does not mean that injections are constant over time: merely that they are constant with respect to national income. If injections rise, the whole line will shift upwards.)

Withdrawals equal injections at point X in the diagram. Equilibrium national income is thus Y_e. If national income were below this level, say at Y_1, injections would exceed withdrawals (by an amount $a - b$). This additional net expenditure injected into the economy would encourage firms to produce more. This in turn would cause national income to rise. But as people's incomes rose, so they would save more, pay more taxes and buy more imports. In other words, withdrawals would rise. There would be a movement up along the W curve. This process would continue until $W = J$ at point x.

If, on the other hand, national income were initially at Y_2, withdrawals would exceed injections (by an amount $c - d$). This deficiency of demand would cause production and hence national income to fall. As it did so, there would be a movement down along the W curve until again point x was reached.

The income and expenditure approach

In Figure 7.10 two continuous lines are shown. The 45° line out from the origin plots $C_d + W$ against Y. It is a 45° line because, by definition, $Y = C_d + W$. To understand this, consider what can happen to national income: either it must be spent on domestically produced goods (C_d) or it must be withdrawn from the circular flow – there is nothing else that can happen to it. Thus if Y were £100 billion, then $C_d + W$ must also be £100 billion. If you draw a line such that whatever value is plotted on the horizontal axis (Y) is also plotted on the vertical axis ($C_d + W$), the line will be at 45° (assuming that the axes are drawn to the same scale).

Figure 7.10
Deriving equilibrium
national income:
national income and
aggregate expenditure
approach

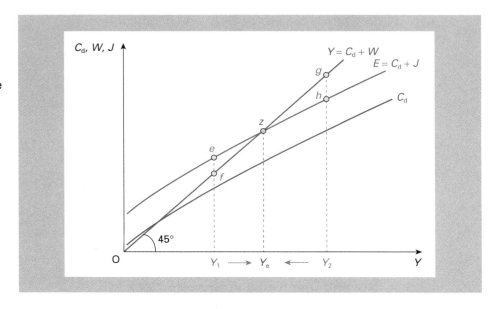

The other continuous line plots aggregate demand. In this diagram it is known as the *aggregate expenditure line* (*E*). It consists of $C_d + J$: in other words, the total spending on the product of domestic firms (see Figure 7.8).

To show how this line is constructed, consider the brown line. This shows C_d. It is flatter than the 45° line. The reason is that for any given rise in national income, only *part* will be spent on domestic product, while the remainder will be withdrawn: i.e. C_d rises less quickly than Y. The *E* line consists of $C_d + J$. But we have assumed that J is constant with respect to changes in Y. Thus the *E* line is simply the C_d line shifted upwards by the amount of J.

If aggregate expenditure exceeded national income, at say Y_1, there would be excess demand in the economy (of $e - f$). In other words, people would be buying more than was currently being produced. Firms would thus find their stocks dwindling and would therefore increase their level of production. In doing so, they would employ more factors of production. National income would thus rise. As it did so, C_d and hence E would rise. There would be a movement up along the *E* line. But because not all the extra income would be consumed (i.e. some would be withdrawn), expenditure would rise less quickly than income: the *E* line is flatter than the *Y* line. As income rises towards Y_e, the gap between Y and E gets smaller. Once point z is reached, $Y = E$. There is then no further tendency for income to rise.

If national income exceeded aggregate expenditure, at say Y_2, there would be insufficient demand for the goods and services currently being produced ($g - h$). Firms would find their stocks of unsold goods building up. They would thus respond by producing less and employing fewer factors of production. National income would thus fall and go on falling until Y_e was reached.

Note that if Y and E, and W and J were plotted on the same diagram, point z (in Figure 7.10) would be vertically above point x (in Figure 7.9).

Pause for thought

(a) Why does $a - b$ in Figure 7.9 equal $e - f$ in Figure 7.10?

(b) Why does $c - d$ in Figure 7.9 equal $g - h$ in Figure 7.10?

Recap

1. In the simple Keynesian model, equilibrium national income is where withdrawals equal injections, and where national income equals the total expenditure on domestic products: where $W = J$ and where $Y = E$.

2. The relationships between national income and the various components of the circular flow of income can be shown on a diagram, where national income is plotted on the horizontal axis and the various components of the circular flow are plotted on the vertical axis.

3. Equilibrium national income can be shown on this diagram either at the point where the W and J lines cross, or where the E line crosses the 45° line (Y).

THE MULTIPLIER

7.5

What will be the effect on output of a rise in spending?

When injections rise (or withdrawals fall), this will cause national income to rise. But by how much? The answer is that there will be a *multiplied* rise in income: i.e. national income will rise by more than the rise in injections (or fall in withdrawals). The size of the multiplier is given by the letter k, where:

$$k = \Delta Y / \Delta J$$

Thus if injections rose by £10 million (ΔJ) and as a result national income rose by £30 million (ΔY), the multiplier would be 3.

But what determines the size of the rise in income (ΔY)? In other words, what determines the size of the multiplier? This can be shown graphically using either the withdrawals and injections approach or the income and expenditure approach. (You may omit one, if you choose.)

The withdrawals and injections approach

Assume that injections rise from J_1 to J_2 in Figure 7.11. Equilibrium will move from point a to point b. Income will thus rise from Y_{e_1} to Y_{e_2}. But this rise in income (ΔY) is bigger than the rise in injections (ΔJ) that caused it. This is the multiplier effect. It is given by $(c - a)/(b - c)$ (i.e. $\Delta Y/\Delta J$).

It can be seen that the size of the multiplier depends on the *slope of the W curve*. The flatter the curve, the bigger will be the multiplier: i.e. the bigger will be the rise in national income from any given rise in injections. The slope of the W curve is given by $\Delta W/\Delta Y$. This is the proportion of a rise in national income that is withdrawn, and is known as the marginal propensity to withdraw (mpw).

The point here is that the less is withdrawn each time money circulates, the more will be re-circulated and hence the bigger will be the rise in national income. The size of the multiplier thus varies inversely with the size of the mpw. The bigger the mpw, the smaller the multiplier; the smaller the mpw, the bigger the multiplier. In fact the multiplier formula is simply the inverse of the mpw:

$$k = 1/mpw$$

Thus if the mpw were ¼, the multiplier would be 4. So if J increased by £10 million, Y would increase by £40 million. To understand why, consider what must

TC 15
p253

Definitions

Multiplier
The number of times by which a rise in national income (ΔY) exceeds the rise in injections (ΔJ) that caused it: $k = \Delta Y/\Delta J$

Marginal propensity to withdraw
The proportion of an increase in national income that is withdrawn from the circular flow of income: $mpw = \Delta W/\Delta Y$

Multiplier formula
The formula for the multiplier is: $k = 1/mpw$ or $1/(1 - mpc_d)$

Figure 7.11
The multiplier: a shift in injections

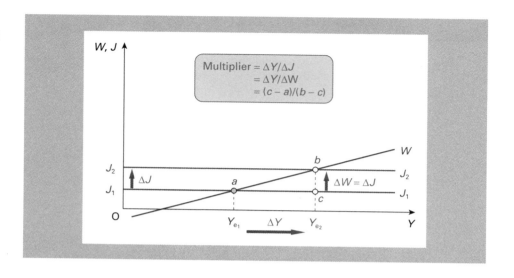

happen to withdrawals. Injections have risen by £10 million, thus withdrawals must rise by £10 million to restore equilibrium ($J = W$). But with an *mpw* of ¹/₄, this £10 million rise in withdrawals must be one-quarter of the rise in national income that has resulted from the extra injections. Thus Y must rise by £40 million.

An alternative formula uses the concept of the marginal propensity to consume domestically produced goods (*mpc*$_d$). This is the proportion of a rise in national income that is spent on domestically produced goods, and thus is not withdrawn. Thus if a quarter of a rise in national income is withdrawn, the remaining three-quarters will re-circulate as C_d. Thus:

$$mpw + mpc_d = 1$$

and

$$mpw = 1 - mpc_d$$

Thus the alternative formula for the multiplier is:

$$k = 1/(1 - mpc_d)$$

But why is the multiplier given by the formula 1/*mpw*? This can be illustrated by referring to Figure 7.11. The *mpw* is the slope of the W line. In the diagram this is given by the amount $(b - c)/(c - a)$. The multiplier is defined as $\Delta Y/\Delta J$. In the diagram this is the amount $(c - a)/(b - c)$. But this is merely the inverse of the *mpw*. Thus the multiplier equals 1/*mpw*.[4]

The income and expenditure approach

Pause for thought

Think of two reasons why a country might have a steep E line, and hence a high value for the multiplier.

Assume in Figure 7.12 that injections rise by £20 billion. The expenditure line thus shifts upward by £20 billion to E_2. The same effect would be achieved by withdrawals falling by £20 billion, and hence consumption of domestically produced goods rising by

---

[4] In some elementary textbooks, the formula for the multiplier is given as 1/*mps* (where *mps* is the marginal propensity to save: the proportion of a rise in income saved). The reason for this is that it is assumed (for simplicity) that there is only one withdrawal, namely saving, and only one injection, namely investment. As soon as this assumption is dropped, 1/*mps* becomes the wrong formula.

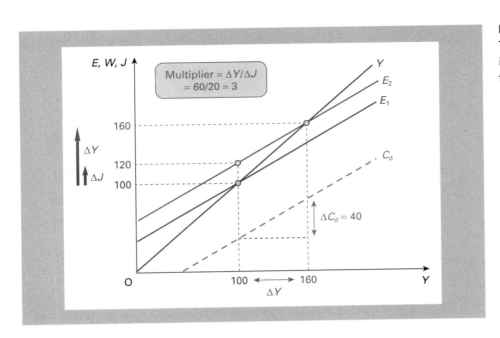

Figure 7.12
The multiplier: a shift
in the expenditure
function

£20 billion. Equilibrium national income rises by £60 billion, from £100 billion to £160 billion (where the E_2 line crosses the Y line).

What is the size of the multiplier? It is $\Delta Y/\Delta J$: in other words, £60bn/£20bn = 3. This can be derived from the multiplier formula:

$$k = \frac{1}{1 - mpc_d}$$

The mpc_d is given by $\Delta C_d/\Delta Y = $ £40bn/£60bn $ = {}^2/_3$ (i.e. the slope of the C_d line). Thus:

$$k = \frac{1}{1 - {}^2/_3} = \frac{1}{{}^1/_3} = 3$$

The multiplier: a numerical illustration

The multiplier effect does not work instantaneously. When there is an increase in injections, whether investment, government expenditure or exports, it takes time before this brings about the full multiplied rise in national income.

Consider the following example. Let us assume for simplicity that the mpw is $^1/_2$. This will give an mpc_d of $^1/_2$ also. Let us also assume that investment (an injection) rises by £160 million and stays at the new higher level. Table 7.2 shows what will happen.

As firms purchase more machines and construct more factories, the incomes of those who produce machines and those who work in the construction industry will increase by £160 million. When this extra income is received by households, whether as wages or profits, half will be withdrawn ($mpw = {}^1/_2$) and half will be spent on the goods and services of domestic firms. This increase in consumption thus generates additional incomes for firms of £80 million over and above the initial £160 million (which is still being generated in each time period). When this additional £80 million of incomes is received by households (round 2), again half will be withdrawn and half will go on consumption of domestic product. This increases national income by a further £40 million (round 3). And so each time we go around the circular flow of income, national income increases, but by only half as much as the previous time ($mpc_d = {}^1/_2$).

Round	ΔJ (£m)	ΔY (£m)	ΔCd (£m)	ΔW (£m)
Table 7.2	The multiplier 'round'			
1	160	160	80	80
2	–	80	40	40
3	–	40	20	20
4	–	20	10	10
5	–	10	5	5
6	–	5	.	.
.	.	.	.	.
$1 \to \infty$		320	160	160

If we add up the additional income generated in each round (assuming the process goes on indefinitely), the total will be £320 million: twice the rise in injections. The multiplier is 2.

The bigger the mpc_d (and hence the smaller the mpw), the more will expenditure rise each time national income rises, and hence the bigger will be the multiplier.

Recap

1. If injections rise (or withdrawals fall), there will be a multiplied rise in national income. The multiplier is defined as $\Delta Y/\Delta J$. Thus if a £10 million rise in injections led to a £50 million rise in national income, the multiplier would be 5.

2. The size of the multiplier depends on the marginal propensity to withdraw (mpw). The smaller the mpw, the less will be withdrawn each time incomes are generated round the circular flow, and thus the more will go round again as *additional* demand for domestic product. The multiplier formula is $1/mpw$ or $1/(1 - mpc_d)$.

7.6   AGGREGATE DEMAND AND SUPPLY

What determines the level of output and the level of prices in an economy?

In the previous two sections, we have assumed that a rise in aggregate demand will be reflected purely in terms of an increase in national output (GDP). We have assumed that prices will not change. In practice, a rise in aggregate demand is likely to lead to a rise not only in GDP, but also in prices throughout the economy. To demonstrate this we use an aggregate demand and supply diagram. This is shown in Figure 7.13.

As with demand and supply curves for individual goods, we plot price on the vertical axis, except that now it is the *general* price level; and we plot quantity on the horizontal axis, except that now it is the *total quantity of national output* (GDP). Let us examine each curve in turn.

The aggregate demand curve

Remember what we said about aggregate demand in the previous section. It is the total level of spending on the country's products, and consists of four elements:

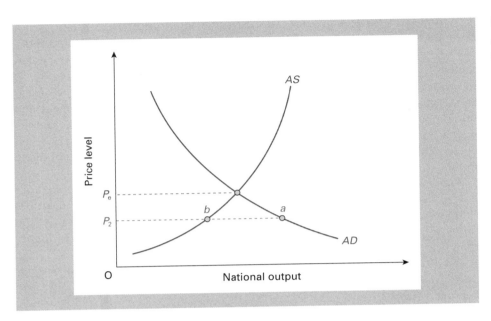

Figure 7.13
Aggregate demand
and aggregate supply

consumer spending on domestic products (C_d), private investment within the country (I), government expenditure on domestic goods and services (G), and expenditure on the country's exports (X). Thus:

$$AD = C_d + I + G + X$$

The aggregate demand curve shows how much national output (GDP) will be demanded at each level of prices. The level of prices in the economy is shown by a price index (see Web Appendix A).

But why will the *AD* curve slope downwards: why will people demand fewer products as prices rise? There are three main reasons:

- If prices rise, people will be encouraged to buy fewer of the country's products and more imports instead (which are now relatively cheaper); the country will also sell fewer exports (which are now less competitive). Thus imports (a withdrawal) will rise and exports (an injection) will fall. Aggregate demand, therefore, will be lower.

- As prices rise, people will need more money to pay for their purchases. With a given supply of money in the economy, this will have the effect of driving up interest rates (we will explore this in Chapter 8). The effect of higher interest rates will be to discourage borrowing and encourage saving. Both will have the effect of reducing spending and hence reducing aggregate demand.

- If prices rise, the value of people's savings will be eroded. They may thus save more (and spend less) to compensate. This is known as the **real balance effect**.

The aggregate supply curve

The aggregate supply curve shows the amount of goods and services that firms are willing to supply at any level of prices, other things remaining the same. The main variables that we hold constant when drawing the aggregate supply curve are wage rates, the prices of other inputs, technology, the labour force and the capital stock. Because these things obviously do change over time, by holding them constant we are analysing the *short-run* aggregate supply curve.

Definition

Real balance effect
As the price level rises, the value of people's money assets falls. They therefore spend less in their attempt to protect the real value of their savings.

Why do we assume that wage rates and other input prices are constant? Wage rates are frequently determined by a process of collective bargaining and, once agreed, will typically be set for a whole year, if not two. Even if they are not determined by collective bargaining, wage rates often change relatively infrequently. So too with the price of other inputs: except in perfect, or near-perfect, markets (such as the market for various raw materials), firms supplying capital equipment and other inputs tend to change their prices relatively infrequently. They do not immediately raise them when there is an increase in demand or lower them when demand falls. Thus there is a 'stickiness' in both wage rates and the price of many inputs.

The short-run aggregate supply curve slopes upwards (as in Figure 7.13). In other words, the higher the level of prices, the more will be produced. The reason is simple: because we are holding wages and other input prices constant, as the prices of firms' products rise their profitability at each level of output will be higher than before. This will encourage them to produce more.

But what *limits* the increase in aggregate supply in response to an increase in prices? In other words, why is the aggregate supply curve not horizontal? There are two main reasons:

■ Diminishing returns. With some factors of production fixed in supply, notably capital equipment, firms experience diminishing returns from their other factors, and hence have an upward-sloping marginal cost curve. In microeconomic analysis the upward-sloping cost curves of firms explain why the supply curves of individual goods and services slope upwards. Here in macroeconomics we are adding the supply curves of all goods and services and thus the aggregate supply curve also slopes upwards.
■ Growing shortages of certain variable factors. As firms collectively produce more, even inputs that can be varied may increasingly become in short supply. Skilled labour may be harder to find, for example.

Thus rising costs explain the upward-sloping aggregate supply curve. The more steeply costs rise as production increases, the less elastic will the aggregate supply curve be. It is likely that, as the level of GDP increases, and as full capacity is approached, so marginal costs will rise faster. The aggregate supply curve will thus tend to get steeper (as shown in Figure 7.13).

Equilibrium

The equilibrium price level will be where aggregate demand equals aggregate supply. To demonstrate this, consider what would happen if aggregate demand exceeded aggregate supply: for example, at P_2 in Figure 7.13. The resulting shortages throughout the economy would drive up prices. This would cause a movement up *along* both the *AD* and *AS* curves until *AD* = *AS*, at a price level of P_e.

Shifts in the AD or AS curves

If there is a change in the price level there will be a movement *along* the *AD* and *AS* curves. If any other determinant of *AD* or *AS* changes, the respective curve will shift. The analysis here is very similar to shifts and movements along demand and supply curves in individual markets (see pages 32 and 37).

The aggregate demand curve will shift if there is a change in any of its components – C_d, *I*, *G* or *X*. Thus if the government decides to spend more, or if customers spend more as a result of lower taxes, or if business confidence increases so that firms decide to invest more, the *AD* curve will shift to the right. A fall in any of these will cause the *AD* curve to shift to the left.

Similarly, the aggregate supply curve will shift if there is a change in any of the variables that are held constant when we plot the curve. Several of these variables, notably technology, the labour force and the stock of capital, change only slowly in the short run – normally shifting the curve gradually to the right. The wage rate (and other input prices) can change significantly in the short run, however, and are thus the major causes of shifts in the short-run supply curve.

What effect will an increase in the average wage rate have on the aggregate supply curve? Wages account for around 70% of firms' costs. If, therefore, wages increase, costs increase and profitability falls, and this reduces the amount that firms wish to produce at any level of prices. Thus the aggregate supply curve shifts to the left. A similar effect will occur if other input prices increase. A dramatic example of such a shift took place in 2002–5 when the price of oil tripled (see Box 4.3).

> **Pause for thought**
>
> *Give some examples of events that could shift (a) the AD curve to the left; (b) the AS curve to the right.*

Effect of a shift in the aggregate demand curve

 If there is an increase in aggregate demand, the *AD* curve will shift to the right. This will lead to a combination of higher prices and higher output, depending on the elasticity of the *AS* curve. The more elastic the *AS* curve, the more will output rise relative to prices. We will consider the shape of the *AS* curve in more detail in Chapter 9.

What we shall see is that the aggregate supply curve in the long run is generally much less elastic than the short-run curve and may well be vertical.

The relationship between the *AD/AS* and Keynesian diagrams

Now that we have introduced the argument that a rise in aggregate demand can lead to a rise not only in national output (GDP) but also in the price level, how does this affect the relationship between our two models: the *AD/AS* model and the Keynesian model? This is examined in Figure 7.14. Initial equilibrium is at Y_1 in both parts of the diagram, where $AD_1 = AS$ and where E_1 crosses the 45° line.

Now let us assume that there is a rise in aggregate demand. The *E* line shifts initially to E_2 in diagram (b). If this rise in demand were to lead to a full multiplied rise in real income, equilibrium income would rise to Y_2. But we are now assuming that only part of the rise in aggregate demand results in higher output, with the remainder resulting in higher prices. In other words, we are assuming that the *AS* curve is upward sloping.

In diagram (a), the rise in aggregate demand has shifted the *AD* curve from AD_1 to AD_2. Part of this increase in demand is reflected in higher prices – the price level rises to P_2 – and only *part* is reflected in higher output. Equilibrium real income therefore rises only to Y_3 and not Y_2. In other words, it does not rise by the full extent of the multiplier.

 In diagram (b), the effect of the higher prices is to reduce the real value of expenditure (*E*). In other words, a given amount of money buys fewer goods. If there is no compensating increase in money supply (which would shift the *AD* curve further to the right in diagram (a)), the *E* line must fall to the point where it intersects the 45° line at a real income of Y_3: the *E* line must fall to E_3.

Clearly, what happens to the money supply has an important influence on national output and the price level. The next chapter explores the role of money in the economy.

> **Pause for thought**
>
> *If money supply did increase sufficiently for the E line to remain at E_2, what would be the position of the new AD curve?*

Figure 7.14
Allowing for higher prices in the Keynesian and *AD/AS* diagrams

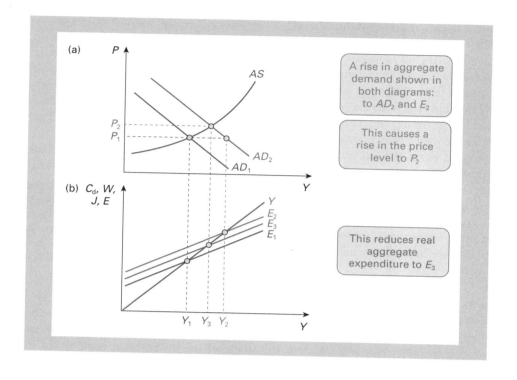

(a) A rise in aggregate demand shown in both diagrams: to AD_2 and E_2

This causes a rise in the price level to P_2

This reduces real aggregate expenditure to E_3

Recap

1. Equilibrium in the economy occurs where aggregate demand equals aggregate supply.

2. A diagram can be constructed to show aggregate demand and aggregate supply, with the price level on the vertical axis and national output (GDP) on the horizontal axis.

3. The *AD* curve is downward sloping, meaning that aggregate demand will be lower at a higher price level. The reason is that at higher prices: (a) there will be more imports and fewer exports; (b) interest rates will tend to be higher, resulting in reduced borrowing and increased saving; (c) people will be encouraged to save more to maintain the value of their savings.

4. The *AS* curve is upward sloping because the higher prices resulting from higher demand will encourage firms to produce more (assuming that factor prices and technology are fixed).

5. A change in the price level will cause a movement along the *AD* and *AS* curves. A change in any other determinant of either *AD* or *AS* will cause a shift in the respective curve.

6. The amount that prices and output rise as a result of an increase in aggregate demand will depend on the shape of the *AS* curve.

7. A rise in aggregate demand, to the extent that it results in higher prices, will not have a full multiplier effect on real national income. This can be shown by combining the Keynesian and *AD/AS* diagrams.

APPENDIX: MEASURING NATIONAL INCOME AND OUTPUT

Three routes: one destination

To assess how fast the economy has grown we must have a means of *measuring* the value of the nation's output. The measure we use is *gross domestic product* (GDP).

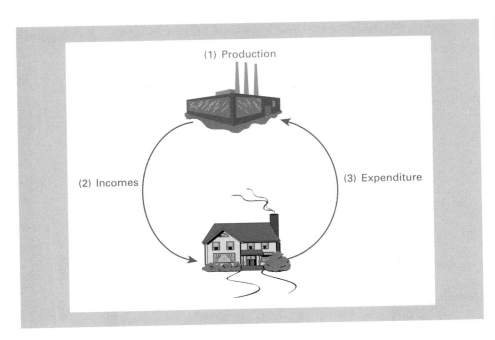

Figure 7.A1
The circular flow
of national income
and expenditure

GDP can be calculated in three different ways, which should all result in the same figure. These three methods are illustrated in the simplified circular flow of income shown in Figure 7.A1.

The product method

The first method of measuring GDP is to add up the value of all the goods and services produced in the country, industry by industry. In other words, we focus on firms and add up all their production. This method is known as the *product method*.

In the national accounts these figures are grouped together into broad categories such as manufacturing, construction and distribution. The figures for the UK economy for 2005 are shown in Figure 7.A2(a).

When we add up the output of various firms we must be careful to avoid *double counting*. For example, if a manufacturer sells a television to a retailer for £200 and the retailer sells it to the consumer for £300, how much has this television contributed to GDP? The answer is *not* £500. We do not add the £200 received by the manufacturer to the £300 received by the retailer: that would be double counting. Instead we either just count the final value (£300) or the value added at each stage (£200 by the manufacturer + £100 by the retailer).

The sum of all the values added by all the various industries in the economy is known as **gross value added (GVA) at basic prices**.

How do we get from GVA to GDP? The answer has to do with taxes and subsidies on products. Taxes paid on goods and services (such as VAT and duties on petrol and alcohol) and any subsidies on products are *excluded* from gross value added (GVA), since they are not part of the value added in production. Nevertheless the way GDP is measured throughout the EU is at *market prices*: i.e. at the prices actually paid at each stage of production. Thus **GDP at market prices** (sometimes referred to simply as GDP) is GVA *plus* taxes on products *minus* subsidies on products.

Definitions

Gross value added (GVA) at basic prices
The sum of all the values added by all industries in the economy over a year. The figures exclude taxes on products (such as VAT) and include subsidies on products.

Gross domestic product (GDP) (at market prices)
The value of output produced within a country over a 12-month period in terms of the prices actually paid. GDP = GVA + taxes on products − subsidies on products.

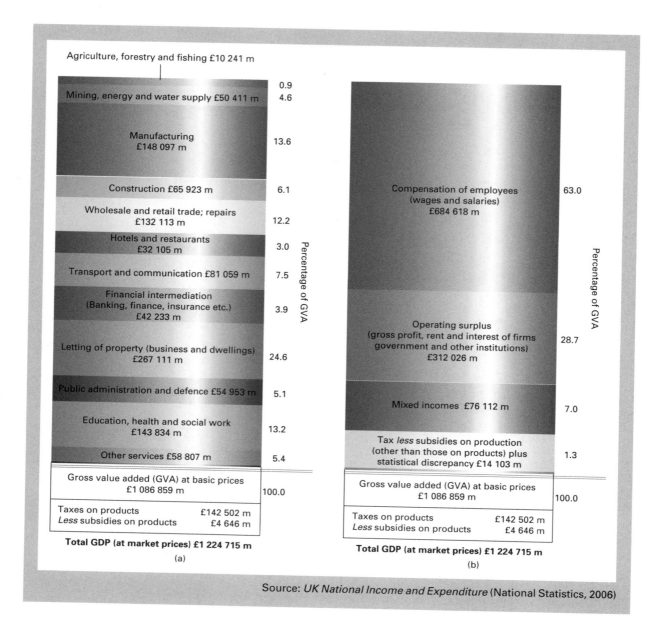

Agriculture, forestry and fishing £10 241 m — 0.9

Mining, energy and water supply £50 411 m — 4.6

Manufacturing £148 097 m — 13.6

Construction £65 923 m — 6.1

Wholesale and retail trade; repairs £132 113 m — 12.2

Hotels and restaurants £32 105 m — 3.0

Transport and communication £81 059 m — 7.5

Financial intermediation (Banking, finance, insurance etc.) £42 233 m — 3.9

Letting of property (business and dwellings) £267 111 m — 24.6

Public administration and defence £54 953 m — 5.1

Education, health and social work £143 834 m — 13.2

Other services £58 807 m — 5.4

Percentage of GVA

Gross value added (GVA) at basic prices £1 086 859 m — 100.0

Taxes on products £142 502 m
Less subsidies on products £4 646 m

Total GDP (at market prices) £1 224 715 m
(a)

Compensation of employees (wages and salaries) £684 618 m — 63.0

Operating surplus (gross profit, rent and interest of firms government and other institutions) £312 026 m — 28.7

Mixed incomes £76 112 m — 7.0

Tax *less* subsidies on production (other than those on products) plus statistical discrepancy £14 103 m — 1.3

Percentage of GVA

Gross value added (GVA) at basic prices £1 086 859 m — 100.0

Taxes on products £142 502 m
Less subsidies on products £4 646 m

Total GDP (at market prices) £1 224 715 m
(b)

Source: *UK National Income and Expenditure* (National Statistics, 2006)

Figure 7.A2
UK GDP: 2005

The income method

The second approach is to focus on the incomes generated from the production of goods and services. A moment's reflection will show that this must be the same as the sum of all values added at each stage of production. Value added is simply the difference between a firm's revenue from sales and the costs of its purchases from other firms. This difference is made up of wages and salaries, rent, interest and profit. In other words, it consists of the incomes earned by those involved in the production process.

Since GVA is the sum of all values added, it must also be the sum of all incomes generated: the sum of all wages and salaries, rent, interest and profit.

Figure 7.A2(b) shows how these incomes are grouped together in the official statistics. As you can see, the total is the same as that in Figure 7.A2(a), even though the components are quite different.

Note that we do not include *transfer payments* such as social security benefit and pensions. Since these are not payments for the production of goods and services, they are excluded from GVA. Conversely, part of people's gross income is paid in income taxes. Since it is this *gross* (pre-tax) income that arises from the production of goods and services, we count wages, profits, interest and rent *before* the deduction of income taxes.

As with the product approach, if we are working out GVA, we measure incomes before the payment of taxes on products or the receipt of subsidies on products, since it is these pre-tax-and-subsidy incomes that arise from the value added by production. When working out GDP, however, we add in these taxes and subtract these subsidies to arrive at a *market price* valuation.

The expenditure method

The final approach to calculating GDP is to add up all expenditure on final output (which will be at market prices). This will include the following:

■ Consumer expenditure (C). This includes all expenditure on goods and services by households and by non-profit institutions serving households (NPISH) (e.g. clubs and societies).
■ Government expenditure (G). This includes central and local government expenditure on final goods and services. Note that it includes non-marketed services (such as health and education), but excludes transfer payments, such as pensions and social security payments.
■ Investment expenditure (I). This includes investment in capital, such as buildings and machinery. It also includes the value of any increase (+) or decrease (–) in inventories, whether of raw materials, semi-finished goods or finished goods.
■ Exports of goods and services (X).
■ Imports of goods and services (M). These have to be *subtracted* from the total in order to leave just the expenditure on *domestic* product. In other words, we subtract the part of consumer expenditure, government expenditure and investment that goes on imports. We also subtract the imported component (e.g. raw materials) from exports.

$$GDP \text{ (at market prices)} = C + G + I + X - M$$

Table 7.A1 shows the calculation of UK GDP by the expenditure approach.

Table 7.A1 UK GDP at market prices by category of expenditure: 2005	£ million	% of GDP
Consumption expenditure of households and NPISH (C)	791 302	64.6
Government final consumption (G)	267 530	21.8
Gross capital formation (I)	209 187	17.1
Exports of goods and services (X)	322 298	26.3
Imports of goods and services (M)	–366 540	–29.9
Statistical discrepancy	938	0.1
GDP at market prices	**1 224 715**	**100.0**

Source: *UK National Income and Expenditure* (National Statistics, 2006)

Box 7.4

The Human Development Index (HDI)

A measure of human welfare?

GDP is not a complete measure of a country's economic welfare – nor is it meant to be. So is there any alternative that takes other factors into account and gives a more complete picture of human wellbeing?

Since 1990, the United Nations Development Program (UNDP) has published an annual Human Development Index (HDI). This is an attempt to provide a more broadly based measure of development than GDP. HDI is a score from 0 to 1 and is based on three sets of variables: (1) life expectancy at birth; (2) education (a weighted average of adult literacy (two-thirds) and average years of schooling (one-third)); and (3) real GDP per head.

The GDP element is measured in US dollars and is adjusted to take into account inflation and the purchasing power of each country's currency. In other words, a 'purchasing-power parity exchange rate' is used. This is the rate of exchange into the US dollar that would allow a given amount of the domestic currency to buy the same amount of goods in the USA as at home. The GDP figures are also adjusted to take into account the fact that the human value of an extra dollar is less to rich countries than to poor countries.

Countries are then placed in one of three groups according to their HDI: high human development (0.8 to 1.0), medium human development (0.5 to 0.799) and low human development (below 0.5).

The table opposite, based on the 2005 *Human Development Report*, gives the HDIs for selected countries and their rankings. It also gives rankings

for GDP per capita. The final column shows the divergence between the two rankings. A positive number shows that a country has a higher ranking for HDI than GDP per capita. As can be seen, the rankings differ substantially in some cases between the two measures. For some countries, such as Australia, Sweden, Ecuador, China and Madagascar, GDP understates their relative level of human development, whereas for others, such as the United Arab Emirates, Saudi Arabia, South Africa and Angola, GDP per capita overstates their relative level of human development. Thus Angola's GDP per capita is nearly three times that of Madagascar and yet its HDI is lower.

The point is that countries with similar levels of national income may use that income quite differently.

Recently, work has been done to adjust HDI figures for various other factors, such as overall income distribution, gender inequalities and inequalities by region or ethnic group. Thus the overall HDI can be adjusted downwards to reflect greater degrees of inequality. Alternatively separate HDIs can be produced for separate regions, ethnic groups or women and men within a country.

1. For what reasons are HDI and per-capita GDP rankings likely to diverge?
2. Why do the United Arab Emirates, Saudi Arabia and South Africa have such a large negative figure in the final column of the table?

From GDP to national income

Gross national income

Some of the incomes earned in the country will go abroad. These include wages, interest, profit and rent earned in this country by foreign residents and remitted abroad, and taxes on production paid to foreign governments and institutions (e.g. the EU). On the other hand, some of the incomes earned by domestic residents will come from abroad. Again, these can be in the form of wages, interest, profit or rent, or in the form of subsidies received from governments or institutions abroad. Gross *domestic* product, however, is concerned with those incomes generated *within* the country, irrespective of ownership. If, then, we are to take 'net income from abroad'

Country	HDI ranking	HDI	GDP per head (PPP$)	GDP (PPP$) ranking	GDP (PPP$) rank minus HDI rank
High human development					
Norway	1	0.963	37 670	3	2
Australia	3	0.955	29 632	10	7
Canada	5	0.949	30 677	5	2
Sweden	6	0.949	26 750	20	14
Ireland	8	0.946	37 738	2	−6
USA	10	0.944	37 562	4	−6
UK	15	0.939	27 147	18	3
Singapore	25	0.907	24 481	21	−4
United Arab Emirates	41	0.849	22 420	23	−18
Medium human development					
Russia	62	0.795	9 230	59	−3
Brazil	63	0.792	7 790	64	1
Saudi Arabia	77	0.772	13 226	44	−33
Ecuador	82	0.759	3 641	112	30
China	85	0.755	5 003	96	11
South Africa	120	0.658	10 346	52	−68
India	127	0.602	2 892	118	−9
Pakistan	135	0.527	2 097	130	−5
Low human development					
Madagascar	146	0.499	809	170	24
Angola	160	0.445	2 344	126	−34
Malawi	165	0.404	605	176	11
Sierra Leone	176	0.298	548	177	1
Niger	177	0.281	835	165	−8

Source: *Human Development Indicators*, Table 1 (*Human Development Report 2005*) (http://hdr.undp.org/reports/global/2005/)

into account (i.e. these inflows minus outflows), we need a new measure. This is gross national income (GNY).[5] It is defined as follows:

GNY at market prices = GDP at market prices + Net income from abroad

Thus GDP focuses on the value of domestic production, whereas GNY focuses on the value of incomes earned by domestic residents.

Definition

Gross national income (GNY)
GDP plus net income from abroad.

---

[5] In the official statistics, this is referred to as *GNI*. We use *Y* to stand for income, however, to avoid confusion with investment.

Table 7.A2 UK GDP, GNY and NNY at market prices: 2005	
	£ million
Gross domestic product (GDP)	**1 224 715**
Plus net income from abroad	28 846
Gross national income (GNY)	**1 253 561**
Less capital consumption (depreciation)	−131 093
Net national income (NNY)	**1 112 468**

Source: *UK National Income and Expenditure* (National Statistics, 2006)

Definitions

Depreciation
The decline in value of capital equipment due to age or wear and tear.

Net national income (NNY)
GNY minus depreciation.

Households' disposable income
The income available for households to spend: i.e. personal incomes after deducting taxes on incomes and adding benefits.

Net national income

The measures we have used so far ignore the fact that each year some of the country's capital equipment will wear out or become obsolete: in other words, they ignore capital **depreciation**. If we subtract an allowance for depreciation (or 'capital consumption') we get **net national income** (NNY).

NNY at market prices = GNY at market prices − Depreciation

Table 7.A2 shows GDP, GNY and NNY figures for the UK.

Households' disposable income

Finally, we come to a term called **households' disposable income**. It measures the income people have available for spending (or saving): i.e. after any deductions for income tax, national insurance, etc. have been made. It is the best measure to use if we want to see how changes in household income affect consumption.

Pause for thought

1. *Should we include the sale of used items in the GDP statistics? For example, if you sell your car to a garage for £2000 and it then sells it to someone else for £2500, has this added £2500 to GDP, or nothing at all, or merely the value that the garage adds to the car: i.e. £500?*
2. *What items are excluded from national income statistics which would be important to take account of if we were to get a true indication of a country's standard of living?*

How do we get from GNY at market prices to households' disposable income? We start with the incomes that firms receive[6] from production (plus income from abroad) and then deduct that part of their income that is *not* distributed to households. This means that we must deduct taxes that firms pay – taxes on goods and services (such as VAT), taxes on profits (such as corporation tax) and any other taxes – and add in any subsidies they receive. We must then subtract allowances for depreciation and any undistributed profits. This gives us the gross income that households receive from firms in the form of wages, salaries, rent, interest and distributed profits.

To get from this what is available for households to spend, we must subtract the money that households pay in income taxes and national insurance contributions, but add all benefits to households such as pensions and child benefit.

Households' disposable income = GNY at market prices − Taxes paid by firms
+ Subsidies received by firms − Depreciation
− Undistributed profits − Personal taxes
+ Benefits

---

[6] We also include income from any public-sector production of goods or services (e.g. health and education) and production by non-profit institutions serving households.

Questions

1. The table shows index numbers for real GDP (national output) for various countries (200 = 100).
   Using the formula $G = (Y_t - Y_{t-1})/Y_{t-1} \times 100$ (where G is the rate of growth, Y is the index number of output, t is any given year and $t-1$ is the previous year):

   (a) Work out the growth rate for each country for each year from 2001 to 2005.
   (b) Plot the figures on a graph. Describe the pattern that emerges.

	2000	2001	2002	2003	2004	2005
USA	100.0	100.8	102.7	105.8	110.5	114.1
Japan	100.0	100.4	100.1	102.6	106.7	108.9
Germany	100.0	101.0	101.1	101.0	102.2	103.6
France	100.0	102.1	103.2	103.7	105.9	108.0
UK	100.0	102.3	104.1	106.4	109.8	112.7

Sources: Various

2. For simplicity, taxes are shown as being withdrawn from the inner flow of the circular flow of income (see Figure 7.4 on page 238) at just one point. In practice, different taxes are withdrawn at different points. At what point of the flow would the following be paid: (a) income taxes people pay on the dividends they receive on shares; (b) VAT; (c) business rates; (d) employees' national insurance contributions?

3. In terms of the UK circular flow of income, do the following represent changes in (i) net injections, (ii) net withdrawals or (iii) neither? If there is uncertainty, explain your assumptions.

   (a) Firms are forced to take a cut in profits in order to give a pay rise.
   (b) Firms spend more money on research.
   (c) The government increases personal tax allowances.
   (d) The general public invests more money in building societies.
   (e) UK investors earn higher dividends on overseas investments.
   (f) The government purchases US military aircraft.
   (g) People save less in order to finance increased spending on holidays abroad.
   (h) People save less in order to finance increased spending on UK holidays.
   (i) The government increases its expenditure and finances it by borrowing from the general public.
   (j) The government increases its expenditure and finances it by printing more money.

4. Will the rate of actual growth have any effect on the rate of potential growth?

5. Figure 7.6 on page 245 shows a decline in actual output in recessions. Redraw the diagram, only this time show a mere slowing-down of growth in phase 4.

6. Why do cyclical swings seem much greater when we plot growth, rather than the level of output, on the vertical axis?

7. At what point of the business cycle is the country now? What do you predict will happen to growth over the next two years? On what basis do you make your prediction?

8. For what possible reasons may one country experience a persistently faster rate of economic growth than another?

9. An economy is currently in equilibrium. The following figures refer to elements in its national income accounts.

	£bn
Consumption (total)	60
Investment	5
Government expenditure	8
Imports	10
Exports	7

   (a) What is the current equilibrium level of national income?
   (b) What is the level of injections?
   (c) What is the level of withdrawals?
   (d) Assuming that tax revenues are £7 billion, how much is the level of saving?
   (e) If national income now rises to £80 billion and, as a result, the consumption of domestically produced goods rises to £58 billion, what is the mpc_d?
   (f) What is the value of the multiplier?
   (g) Given an initial level of national income of £80 billion, now assume that spending on exports rises by £4 billion, spending on investment rises by £1 billion and government expenditure falls by £2 billion. By how much will national income change?

10. What is the relationship between the mpc_d and the mpw?

11. Assume that the multiplier has a value of 3. Now assume that the government decides to increase

aggregate demand in an attempt to reduce unemployment. It raises government expenditure by £100 million with no increase in taxes. Firms, anticipating a rise in their sales, increase investment by £200 million, of which £50 million consists of purchases of foreign machinery. How much will national income rise? (Assume no other changes in injections.)

12. On a Keynesian diagram, draw three W lines of different slopes, all crossing the J line at the same point. Now draw a second J line above the first. Mark the original equilibrium and all the new ones corresponding to each of the W lines. Using this diagram, show how the size of the multiplier varies with the *mpw*.

13. Why does the slope of the E line in a Keynesian diagram equal the mpc_d? (Clue: draw an mpc_d line.)

14. On a Keynesian diagram, draw two E lines of different slopes, both crossing the Y line at the same

point. Now draw another two E lines, parallel with the first two and crossing each other vertically above the point where the first two crossed. Using this diagram, show how the size of the multiplier varies with the mpc_d.

15. What factors could explain why some countries have a higher multiplier than others?

16. In what way will the nature of aggregate supply influence the effect of a change in aggregate demand on prices and real national income?

17. What shape do you think the aggregate supply curve would be at the current output if the economy were in a deep recession?

18. Referring to Figure 7.13 on page 261, assume that the price level is currently above the equilibrium. Explain how the price level would return to its equilibrium level.

Additional case studies on the *Essentials of Economics* MyEconLab (www.pearsoned.co.uk/sloman)

7.1 Introducing theories of economic growth. An overview of classical and more modern theories of growth (a more detailed account of economic growth is given in Section 9.7).

7.2 Classical 'remedies' for unemployment. How the policies advocated by the classical economists to cure unemployment would, according to Keynes, make the problem worse.

7.3 The paradox of thrift. How saving more can make the country worse off.

7.4 John Maynard Keynes (1883–1946). Profile of the great economist.

7.5 Keynes's views on the consumption function. An analysis of how the assumptions made by Keynes affect the shape of the consumption function.

7.6 Deriving the multiplier formula. Using simple algebra to show how the multiplier formula is derived.

7.7 The GDP deflator. An examination of how GDP figures are corrected to take inflation into account.

7.8 Simon Kuznets and the system of national income accounting. This looks at the work of Simon Kuznets, who devised the system of national income accounting that is used around the world. It describes some of the patterns of economic growth that he identified.

7.9 Comparing national income statistics. The importance of taking the purchasing power of local currencies into account.

7.10 Taking into account the redistributive effects of growth. This case shows how figures for economic growth can be adjusted to allow for the fact that poor people's income growth would otherwise count for far less than rich people's.

7.11 The use of ISEW. An alternative measure to GDP for estimating economic welfare.

Sections of chapter covered in *WinEcon* – Sloman, *Essentials of Economics*

Essentials of Economics section	*WinEcon* section
7.1	7.1
7.2	7.2
7.3	7.3
7.4	7.5
7.5	7.6
7.6	7.6
Appendix	7.4

Websites relevant to this chapter

Numbers and sections refer to websites listed in the Web Appendix and hotlinked from MyEconLab. Visit:

www.pearsoned.co.uk/sloman

- For news articles relevant to this chapter, see the *Economics News Articles* link from MyEconLab.
- For general news on macroeconomic issues, both national and international, see websites in section A, and particularly A1–5. See also links to newspapers worldwide in A38, 43 and 44, and the news search feature in Google at A41. See also A42 for links to economics news video and audio worldwide.
- For macroeconomic data, including data on economic growth and the business cycle, see links in B1 or 2; also see B4 and 12. For UK data, see B3 and 34. For EU data, see G1 > *The Statistical Annex*. For US data, see *Current economic indicators* in B5 and the *Data* section of B17. For international data, see B15, 21, 24, 31, 33 and 40. For links to data sets, see B28; I14.
- For information on the development of ideas, see C12, 18; see also links under *Methodology and History of Economic Thought* in C14; and links to economists in I4 and 17. See also sites I7 and 11 > *Economic Systems and Theories* > *History of Economic Thought*.
- For a model of the economy (based on the Treasury model), see *The Virtual Economy* (site D1). In addition to the model, where you can devise your own Budget, there are worksheets and outlines of theories and the work of famous economists.
- For national income statistics for the UK (Appendix), see B1, *1. National Statistics* > the fourth link > *Economy* > *United Kingdom Economic Accounts* and *United Kingdom National Accounts – The Blue Book*.
- For the Human Development Index (Box 7.4) see site H17.
- For student resources relevant to this chapter, see sites C1–7, 9, 10, 19.

Web Appendix

7.1   Using GDP statistics. How well do GDP statistics measure a country's standard of living?

Chapter 7
Macroeconomic Policy

Macroeconomic policy

In this chapter we look at various types of policy the government or central bank can use to tackle the macroeconomic problems of low and fluctuating economic growth, unemployment and inflation.

In the first three sections we focus on the control of aggregate demand, and start in Section 10.1 by looking at fiscal policy. This involves altering taxes and/or government spending. Cutting taxes or increasing government expenditure will increase aggregate demand, while increasing taxes or cutting government expenditure will reduce aggregate demand.

We then turn to monetary policy. In the past this involved attempts to manage aggregate demand through control of the money supply. Today, monetary policy generally involves the control of interest rates. We see how the central bank achieves this and the problems in attempting to control aggregate demand in this way.

Then in Section 10.3 we put fiscal and monetary policy together and ask whether governments should even attempt to manage aggregate demand on a regular basis with the aim of ironing out the ups and downs of the business cycle. Or should the government adopt targets for the public finances (in the case of fiscal policy) and inflation (in the case of monetary policy) and then just stick to them?

The chapter finishes by turning to the supply side. It looks at various policies that aim to increase *potential* output, and hence shift the aggregate supply curve to the right, and to reduce equilibrium unemployment. As we shall see, some of these policies involve 'freeing-up' the market; such policies, not surprisingly, are advocated by the political right. Other supply-side policies involve government investment in training and infrastructure and tend to be more favoured by the political centre and left.

After studying this chapter, you should be able to answer the following questions:

■ What are the different types of macroeconomic policy that governments or central banks can use to control the economy?

■ How can fiscal policy be used to alter the level of aggregate demand? What are the strengths and drawbacks of using fiscal policy to (a) stabilise the economy; (b) cure fundamental disequilibria?

■ How is monetary policy operated by the central bank? How does it alter the money supply? How does it control interest rates?

■ How successful is monetary policy likely to be in controlling (a) aggregate demand and (b) inflation?

■ Should fiscal and monetary policy be frequently adjusted in an attempt to stabilise the economy? Or should fiscal and monetary rules be set by the government and then rigidly followed?

■ What types of supply-side policy are available to governments? What are their strengths and weaknesses?

10.1   FISCAL POLICY

How can government expenditure and taxation be used to affect the level of economic activity?

Fiscal policy involves the government manipulating the level of government expenditure and/or rates of tax so as to affect the level of aggregate demand. An *expansionary* fiscal policy will involve raising government expenditure (an injection into the circular flow of income) or reducing taxes (a withdrawal from the circular flow). This will increase aggregate demand and lead to a *multiplied* rise in national income. A *contractionary* fiscal policy will involve cutting government expenditure and/or raising taxes.

During the 1950s and 1960s, when fiscal policy was seen by both governments and economists as the major way of controlling the economy, it was used to perform two main functions.

■ To prevent the occurrence of *fundamental* disequilibria in the economy. In other words, expansionary fiscal policy could be used to prevent mass unemployment, such as that experienced in the Great Depression of the 1930s or in east and south-east Asia, Russia and Brazil in the late 1990s. Likewise contractionary fiscal policy could be used to prevent excessive inflation, such as that experienced in many countries in the early 1970s.

■ To smooth out the fluctuations in the economy associated with the business cycle. This would involve reducing government expenditure or raising taxes during the boom phase of the cycle. This would dampen down the expansion and prevent 'overheating' of the economy with its attendant rising inflation and deteriorating balance of trade. Conversely, during the recessionary phase, as unemployment grew and output declined, the government should cut taxes or raise government expenditure in order to boost the economy. If these stabilisation policies were successful, they would amount merely to fine tuning. Problems of excess or deficient demand would never be allowed to get severe. Any movement of aggregate demand away from a steady growth path would be immediately 'nipped in the bud'.

Deficits and surpluses

Central government deficits and surpluses

Since an expansionary fiscal policy involves raising government expenditure and/or lowering taxes, this has the effect of either increasing the budget deficit or reducing the budget surplus. A budget deficit in any one year is where central government's expenditure exceeds its revenue from taxation. A budget surplus is where tax revenues exceed central government expenditure. With the exception of short periods (1969–70, 1987–90 and 1998–2001), governments in the UK, like most governments around the world, have run budget deficits.

Public-sector deficits and surpluses

To get a better view of the overall stance of fiscal policy – just how expansionary or contractionary it is – we would need to look at the deficit or surplus of the entire public sector: namely, central government, local government and public corporations.

If the public sector spends more than it earns (through central and local taxes and the revenues of public corporations, etc.) the amount of this deficit is known

Table 10.1 UK public-sector deficits (+) / surpluses (−): selected years 1982–2005

	1982	1984	1986	1988	1990	1992	1994	1996	1998	2000	2002	2004	2005
PSNCR (£bn)	5.3	10.3	2.6	−11.5	−1.3	28.6	39.4	24.8	−6.4	−37.5	18.3	41.4	41.4
% of GDP	1.9	3.2	0.7	−2.4	−0.2	4.7	5.8	3.3	−0.7	−3.9	1.7	3.6	3.4

Source: www.statistics.gov.uk (National Statistics): Series RURQ and YBHA.

Table 10.2 General government deficits/surpluses and debt as a percentage of GDP

Country	General government deficits (−) or surpluses (+)			General government debt		
	Average 1991–5	Average 1996–2000	Average 2001–5	Average 1991–5	Average 1996–2000	Average 2001–5
Belgium	−6.5	−1.3	+0.1	139.2	125.2	105.9
France	−4.7	−2.6	−3.2	51.2	68.3	71.0
Germany	−2.9	−1.7	−3.6	46.6	61.6	64.8
Greece	−11.2	−4.0	−4.2	99.3	108.9	112.1
Ireland	−2.5	+2.1	+0.2	90.8	55.8	31.4
Italy	−9.9	−3.1	−2.7	127.6	131.0	120.8
Japan	−1.6	−5.8	−6.9	75.0	113.2	156.5
Netherlands	−3.5	−0.2	−2.2	91.6	79.6	64.3
Sweden	−7.4	+1.1	+0.8	74.9	76.9	61.7
UK	−6.0	−0.3	−2.2	44.7	50.9	42.6
USA	−4.5	0.0	−3.5	73.8	66.9	61.8
Euro area	−5.2	−2.1	−2.5	70.9	80.8	77.4

Source: Various

as the **public-sector net cash requirement (PSNCR)** (previously known as the public-sector borrowing requirement (PSBR)). The reason for the name 'public-sector net cash requirement' is simple. If the public sector runs a deficit in the current year of, say, £1 billion, then it will have to borrow £1 billion this year (require 'cash') in order to finance it (see Chapter 8 for methods of government borrowing). Table 10.1 shows UK PSNCR from 1982 to 2005.

If the public sector runs a surplus (a negative PSNCR), then this will be used to reduce the accumulated debts from the past. The accumulated debts of central and local government are known as the **general government debt**. Table 10.2 shows general government deficits and debt for various countries.

The use of fiscal policy

Automatic fiscal stabilisers

To some extent, government expenditure and taxation will have the effect of *automatically* stabilising the economy. For example, as national income rises, the amount of tax people pay automatically rises. This rise in withdrawals from the circular flow of income helps to dampen down the rise in national income. This effect will be bigger if taxes are progressive (i.e. rise by a bigger percentage than national income). Some government expenditure will have a similar effect. For example, total government expenditure on unemployment benefits will fall if rises in national income cause a fall in unemployment. This again will have the effect of dampening the rise in national income.

Discretionary fiscal policy

Automatic stabilisers cannot *prevent* fluctuations; they merely reduce their magnitude. If there is a *fundamental* disequilibrium in the economy or substantial fluctuations in national income, these automatic stabilisers will not be enough. The government may thus choose to *alter* the level of government expenditure or the rates of taxation. This is known as discretionary fiscal policy. Box 10.1 looks at an example of discretionary fiscal policy in the USA. Web Case 10.6 examines the use of discretionary fiscal policy in Japan from 1991 to the present day.

If government expenditure on goods and services (roads, health care, education, etc.) is raised, this will create a full multiplied rise in national income. The reason is that all the money gets spent and thus all of it goes to boosting aggregate demand.

Cutting taxes (or increasing benefits), however, will have a smaller effect on national income than raising government expenditure on goods and services by the same amount. The reason is that cutting taxes increases people's *disposable* incomes, of which only *part* will be spent. Part will be withdrawn into extra saving, imports and other taxes. In other words, not all the tax cuts will be passed on round the circular flow of income as extra expenditure. Thus if one-fifth of a cut in taxes is withdrawn and only four-fifths is spent, the tax multiplier will only be four-fifths as big as the government expenditure multiplier.

> **Pause for thought**
>
> *Why will the multiplier effect of government transfer payments, such as child benefit, pensions and social security benefits, be less than the full multiplier effect from government expenditure on goods and services?*

> **Definitions**
>
> **Discretionary fiscal policy**
> Deliberate changes in tax rates or the level of government expenditure in order to influence the level of aggregate demand.
>
> **Crowding out**
> Where increased public expenditure diverts money or resources away from the private sector.

The effectiveness of fiscal policy

There are two main problem areas with discretionary fiscal policy. The first concerns the *magnitude* of the effects of policy measures. If G or T is changed, how much will *total* injections and withdrawals change? What will be the size of the resulting multiplier effect? How much will the change in aggregate demand affect output and employment, and how much will it affect prices?

The second concerns the *timing* of the effects. How quickly can policy be changed and how quickly will the changes affect the economy?

Problems of magnitude

Before changing government expenditure or taxation, the government will need to calculate the effect of any such change on national income, employment and inflation. Predicting these effects, however, is often very unreliable for a number of reasons.

Predicting the effect of changes in government expenditure

A rise in government expenditure of £x may lead to a rise in total injections (relative to withdrawals) that is smaller than £x. This will occur if the rise in government expenditure *replaces* a certain amount of private expenditure. For example, a rise in expenditure on state education may dissuade some parents from sending their children to private schools. Similarly, an improvement in the National Health Service may lead to fewer people paying for private treatment.

Crowding out.   Another reason for the total rise in injections being smaller than the rise in government expenditure is a phenomenon known as crowding out. If the

Box 10.1

Managing the US economy

Attempts in the early 2000s to get the economy expanding again

Since the start of 2001, the US Federal Reserve, led by Alan Greenspan, had been fighting a sharp slow-down in the US economy. Interest rates had been cut seven times from their level of 6½ per cent at the beginning of the year to 3½ per cent in August. By September 2001, the economy seemed to be starting to recover.

The attacks on 11 September brought this modest recovery to an abrupt halt. At this point, many analysts were suggesting that it might be necessary to lower rates close to zero in order to kick-start the economy. Even then the success of such a strategy was not guaranteed.

At this point, it was decided that a measure of discretionary fiscal policy was required in order to help reduce pressure on the Federal Reserve and its use of interest rates to pump-prime the economy.

Following a meeting at the end of September 2001, Alan Greenspan advised Congress that a fiscal stimulus of $100 billion, or 1 per cent of US GDP, was advisable. The Stimulus Bill proposed cutting personal taxation from 27 to 25 per cent, and offering tax exemption to business on moneys used for new investment. The Democrats were opposed to the personal tax cuts, which would go largely to the rich. A compromise was reached in March 2002

when a stimulus package of $51 billion passed into law, consisting mainly of tax incentives to business.

Such was the delay in passing the Stimulus Bill that recovery began to occur without it. With continued reductions in interest rates, which by December 2001 had been cut 11 times and, at 1¾ per cent, were at the lowest level since the presidency of John F. Kennedy in the 1960s, the economy seemed to be bouncing back. Economic growth was 1.9 per cent in 2002, 3.0 per cent in 2003 and 4.4 per cent in 2004.

But it was not just the Stimulus Bill and the interest rate cuts that were boosting the economy. Fiscal policy generally was becoming more and more expansionary as the size of the budget deficit increased. Tax cuts totalling over $650 billion were given between 2001 and 2004 (71.7 per cent of which went to the richest 20 per cent, 26.4 per cent to the richest 1 per cent and just 0.2 per cent to the poorest 20 per cent). In 2004, the total tax cuts during this period had the effect of increasing the budget deficit from 1.6 to 3.5 per cent of GDP.

? *Which is likely to give a bigger boost to aggregate demand: tax cuts of a given amount targeted to (a) the rich, or (b) the poor?*

government relies on **pure fiscal policy** – that is, if it does not finance an increase in the budget deficit by increasing the money supply – it will have to borrow the money from the non-bank private sector. It will thus be competing with the private sector for finance and will have to offer higher interest rates. This will force the private sector too to offer higher interest rates, which may discourage firms from investing and individuals from buying on credit. Thus government borrowing crowds out private borrowing. In the extreme case, the fall in consumption and investment may completely offset the rise in government expenditure, with the result that aggregate demand does not rise at all.

Predicting the effect of changes in taxes

A cut in taxes, by increasing people's real disposable income, increases not only the amount they spend but also the amount they save. The problem is that it is not easy to predict the relative size of these two increases. In part it will depend on whether people feel that the cut in tax is only temporary, in which case they may simply

TC9
p68

save the extra disposable income, or permanent, in which case they may adjust their consumption upwards.

Predicting the resulting multiplied effect on national income

Even if the government *could* predict the net *initial* effect on injections and withdrawals, the ultimate effect on national income will still be hard to predict for the following reasons:

- The size of the *multiplier* may be difficult to predict, since it is difficult to predict how much of any rise in income will be withdrawn. In other words, it is difficult to predict the size of the *mpw*. For example, the amount of a rise in income that households save or consume will depend on their expectations about future price and income changes.

- Induced investment through the *accelerator* (see page 336) is also extremely difficult to predict. It may be that a relatively small fiscal stimulus will be all that is necessary to restore business confidence, and that induced investment will rise substantially. In such a case, fiscal policy can be seen as a 'pump primer'. It is used to *start* the process of recovery, and then the *continuation* of the recovery is left to the market. But for pump priming to work, businesspeople must *believe* that it will work. Business confidence can change very rapidly and in ways that could not have been foreseen a few months earlier.

Random shocks

Forecasts cannot take into account the unpredictable, such as the attack on the World Trade Center in New York in September 2001. Unfortunately, unpredictable events do occur and may seriously undermine the government's fiscal policy.

Pause for thought

Give some other examples of 'random shocks' that could undermine the government's fiscal policy.

The problem of timing

Fiscal policy can involve considerable time lags. It may take time to recognise the nature of the problem before the government is willing to take action; tax or government expenditure changes take time to plan and implement – changes will have to wait until the next Budget to be announced and may come into effect some time later; the effects of such changes take time to work their way through the economy via the multiplier and accelerator.

If time lags are long enough, fiscal policy could even be *de*stabilising. Expansionary policies taken to cure a recession may not come into effect until the economy has *already* recovered and is experiencing a boom. Under these circumstances, expansionary policies are quite inappropriate: they simply worsen the problems of overheating. Similarly, contractionary policies taken to prevent excessive expansion may not take effect until the economy has already peaked and is plunging into recession. The contractionary policies only deepen the recession.

This problem is illustrated in Figure 10.1. Path (a) shows the course of the business cycle without government intervention. Ideally, with no time lags, the economy should be dampened in stage 2 and stimulated in stage 4. This would make the resulting course of the business cycle more like path (b), or even, if the policy were perfectly stabilising, a straight line. With time lags, however, contractionary policies taken in stage 2 may not come into effect until stage 4, and expansionary policies taken in stage 4 may not come into effect until stage 2. In this case the resulting course of the business cycle will be more like path (c). Quite obviously,

Figure 10.1
Fiscal policy:
stabilising or
destabilising?

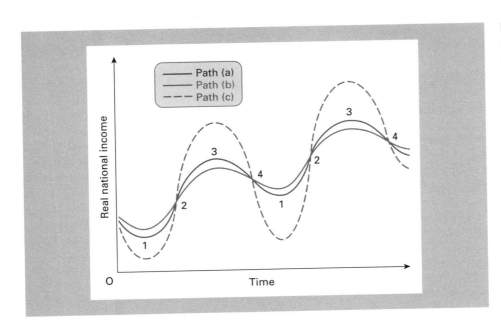

in these circumstances 'stabilising' fiscal policy actually makes the economy *less* stable.

If the fluctuations in aggregate demand can be forecast, and if the lengths of the time lags are known, then all is not lost. At least the fiscal measures can be taken early and their delayed effects can be taken into account.

Fiscal rules

Given the problems of pursuing active fiscal policy, many governments today take a much more passive approach. Instead of changing the policy as the economy changes, a rule is set for the level of public finances. This rule is then applied year after year, with taxes and government expenditure being planned to meet that rule. For example, a target could be set for the PSNCR, with government expenditure and taxes being adjusted to keep the PSNCR at or within its target level. Fiscal (and monetary) rules are examined in more detail in Section 10.3.

The approach to fiscal policy in the UK

Since 1998, the UK government has set targets for government expenditure, not for just one year, but for a three-year period. Does this mean, therefore, that fiscal policy as a means of adjusting aggregate demand had been abandoned? In one sense, this is the case. The government is now committed to following its 'golden rule', whereby public-sector receipts should cover all current spending, averaged over the course of the business cycle (see Box 10.2).

But despite this apparent rejection of short-term discretionary fiscal adjustments, there is still a role for automatic fiscal stabilisers: with deficits rising in a recession and falling in a boom. There is also still the possibility, within the golden rule, of financing additional investment by borrowing, thereby providing a stimulus to a sluggish economy.

The golden rule also permits increased government expenditure (or tax cuts) if there is a budget surplus. Thus in the 2001 Budget the Chancellor announced spending increases of 3.7 per cent per year for three years. The effect was to provide

Box 10.2

Following the golden rule

Fiscal policy in a straitjacket?

If the government persistently runs a budget deficit, the national debt will rise. If it rises faster than GDP, it will account for a growing proportion of GDP. There is then likely to be an increasing problem of 'servicing' this debt: i.e. paying the interest on it. The government could find itself having to borrow more and more to meet the interest payments, and so the national debt could rise faster still. As the government borrows more and more, so it has to pay higher interest rates to attract finances. If it is successful in this, borrowing and hence investment by the private sector could be crowded out (see page 358–9).

Recognising these problems, many governments in recent years have attempted to reduce their debts.

Preparing for EMU

In signing the Maastricht Treaty in 1992, the EU countries agreed that to be eligible to join the single currency (i.e. the euro), they should have sustainable deficits and debts. This was interpreted as follows: the general government deficit should be

no more than 3 per cent of GDP and general government debt should be no more than 60 per cent of GDP, or should at least be falling towards that level at a satisfactory pace.

But in the mid-1990s, several of the countries that were subsequently to join the euro had deficits and debts substantially above these levels (see the figure). Getting them down proved a painful business. Government expenditure had to be cut and taxes increased. Fiscal policy, unfortunately, proved to be powerful! Unemployment rose and growth remained low.

The EU Stability and Growth Pact

In June 1997, at the European Council in Amsterdam, the EU countries agreed that governments adopting the euro should seek to balance their budgets (or even aim for a surplus) averaged over the course of the business cycle, and that deficits should not exceed 3 per cent of GDP in any one year. A country's deficit is permitted to exceed 3 per cent only if its GDP has declined by at least 2 per

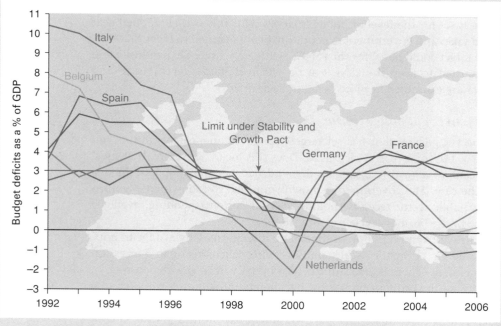

Source: based on data in *European Economy Statistical Annex* (European Commission)

(a) Getting budget deficits down

cent (or 0.75 per cent with special permission from the Council of Ministers). Otherwise, countries with deficits exceeding 3 per cent are required to make deposits of money with the European Central Bank. These then become fines if the excessive budget deficit is not eliminated within two years.

There are two main aims of targeting a zero budget deficit over the business cycle. The first is to allow automatic stabilisers to work without 'bumping into' the 3 per cent deficit ceiling in years when economies are slowing. The second is to allow a reduction in government debts as a proportion of GDP (assuming that GDP grows on average at around 2–3 per cent per year).

The main criticism of aiming for a zero deficit over the cycle has been that this would mean a further reduction in deficits, which by the start of the euro in 1999 were typically only just meeting the 3 per cent ceiling. In other words, meeting the zero deficit target would mean further deflationary fiscal policies: something that most political leaders in Europe felt to be inappropriate at a time when there were fears of a world recession.

Later the criticisms turned on whether the Pact was flexible enough. From 2002, both Germany and

France breached the 3 per cent ceiling (see diagram (a)). This was partly the result of slow growth and rising unemployment, and hence falling tax revenue and rising benefit payments. Not surprisingly, both countries were reluctant to cut government expenditure to bring the deficit in line for fear of dampening an already sluggish economy. Despite various promises by the two countries to rein in expenditure, they continued to have deficits in excess of 3 per cent.

Eventually, in March 2005 a deal was reached between European finance ministers. This allowed Germany to exclude reunification costs and France to exclude military and aid costs from the calculation of government expenditure. This compromise brought the deficits of the two countries below the 3 per cent ceiling and allowed them to escape having to adopt tighter fiscal policy.

Labour's golden rule

The Labour government in the UK has adopted a similar approach to that of the Stability and Growth Pact. Under its 'golden rule', the government pledges that over the economic cycle, it will borrow only to invest (e.g. in roads, hospitals and schools)

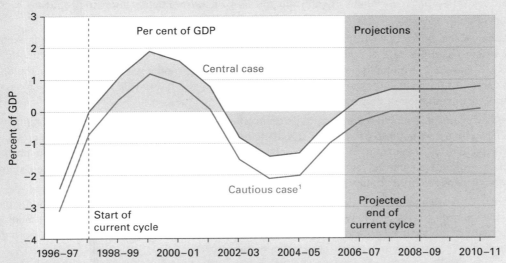

[1] *Cautious case assumes trend output 1 percentage point lower in relation to actual output than the central case.*

Source: *Financial Statement and Budget Report* (HM Treasury 2006)

(b) Cyclically adjusted surplus on UK current budget

and not to fund current spending (e.g. on wages, administration and benefits). Investment is exempted from the zero borrowing rule because it contributes towards the growth of GDP. Indeed, in its 1998 'Comprehensive Spending Review', the government announced that government investment expenditure would double as a percentage of GDP. The government has also set itself the target of maintaining a stable public-sector debt/GDP ratio below 40 per cent.

To allow the golden rule to operate, government departments are set three-year spending limits and each has separate current and capital (investment) budgets.

As with the Stability and Growth Pact, the argument is that by using an averaging rule over the cycle, automatic stabilisers will be allowed to work. Deficits of receipts over current spending can occur when the economy is in recession or when growth is sluggish (as in 2001–3), helping to stimulate the economy. Surpluses can occur in boom periods (as in 1998–2000), helping to dampen the economy (see diagram (b)).

As with the Stability and Growth Pact, however, a major concern is whether the policy provides too much of a straitjacket. Does it prevent the government using substantial discretionary boosts to the economy at times of serious economic slowdown?

? *What effects will government investment expenditure have on public-sector debt (a) in the short run; (b) in the long run?*

a stimulus to the economy just at a time when the world economy was slowing down. This helped to make the slowdown in UK economic growth in the period 2001–3 much less severe than in many other countries.

Recap

1. An expansionary fiscal policy involves raising government expenditure and/or reducing taxes. A contractionary fiscal policy involves the reverse.

2. The government's fiscal policy determines the size of the budget deficit or surplus and the size of the public-sector deficit (PSNCR) or surplus.

3. Automatic fiscal stabilisers are tax revenues that rise and government expenditures that fall as national income rises. They have the effect of reducing the size of the multiplier and thus reducing cyclical upswings and downswings.

4. Discretionary fiscal policy is where the government deliberately changes taxes or government expenditure in order to alter the level of aggregate demand. Changes in government expenditure on goods and services will have a full multiplier effect. Changes in taxes and benefits will have a smaller multiplier effect as some of the tax/benefit changes will merely affect other withdrawals and thus have a smaller net effect on consumption of domestic product.

5. There are problems in predicting the magnitude of the effects of discretionary fiscal policy. Expansionary fiscal policy can act as a pump primer and stimulate increased private expenditure, or it can crowd out private expenditure. The extent to which it acts as a pump primer depends crucially on business confidence – something that is very difficult to predict beyond a few weeks or months. The extent of crowding out depends on monetary conditions and the government's monetary policy.

6. There are five possible time lags involved with fiscal policy: the time lag before the problem is diagnosed, the lag between diagnosis and new measures being announced, the lag between announcement and implementation, the lag while the multiplier and accelerator work themselves out, and the lag before consumption responds fully to new economic circumstances.

7. Today many governments prefer a more passive approach towards fiscal policy. Targets are set for one or more measures of the public-sector finances, and then taxes and government expenditure are adjusted so as to keep to the target.

MONETARY POLICY   10.2

How can the supply of money and interest rates be controlled?

Each month the Bank of England's Monetary Policy Committee meets to set interest rates. The event gets considerable media coverage. Pundits, for two or three days before the meeting, try to predict what the MPC will do and economists give their 'considered' opinions about what the MPC *ought* to do.

The fact is that changes in interest rates have gained a central significance in macroeconomic policy. And it is not just in the UK. Whether it is the European Central Bank setting interest rates for the eurozone countries, or the Federal Reserve Bank setting US interest rates, or any other central bank around the world choosing what the level of interest rates should be, monetary policy is seen as having a major influence on a whole range of macroeconomic indicators.

But is monetary policy simply the setting of interest rates? In reality, it involves the central bank intervening in the money market to ensure that the interest rate that has been announced is also the *equilibrium* interest rate.

The policy setting

In framing its monetary policy, the government must decide on what the goals of the policy are. Is the aim simply to control inflation, or does the government wish also to affect output and employment, or does it want to control the exchange rate?

The government must also decide where monetary policy fits into the total package of macroeconomic policies. Is it seen as the major or even sole macroeconomic policy instrument, or is it merely one of several?

A decision also has to be made about who is to carry out the policy. There are three possible approaches here.

In the first, the government both sets the policy and decides the measures necessary to achieve it. Here the government would set the interest rate, with the central bank simply influencing money markets to achieve this rate. This first approach was used in the UK before 1997.

The second approach is for the government to set the policy *targets*, but for the central bank to be given independence in deciding interest rates. This is the approach adopted in the UK today. The government has set a target rate of inflation of 2 per cent, but then the MPC is free to choose the rate of interest.

The third approach is for the central bank to be given independence not only in carrying out policy, but in setting the policy targets themselves. The ECB, within the statutory objective of maintaining price stability over the medium term, decides on (a) the target rate of inflation – currently that inflation for the eurozone should be kept close to 2 per cent, and (b) the target rate of growth in money supply. It then sets interest rates to meet these targets.

Finally, there is the question of whether the government or central bank should take a long-term or short-term perspective. Should it adopt a target for inflation or money supply growth and stick to it come what may? Or should it adjust its policy as circumstances change and attempt to 'fine-tune' the economy?

We will be looking primarily at *short-term* monetary policy: that is, policy used to keep to a set target for inflation or money supply growth, or policy used to smooth out fluctuations in the business cycle. It is important first, however, to take a longer-term perspective. Governments will generally want to prevent an excessive growth in the money supply over the longer term. If money supply does grow rapidly, then inflation is likely to be high.

Control of the money supply over the medium and long term

One of the major sources of monetary growth is government borrowing. If the government wishes to prevent excessive growth in the money supply over the longer term, therefore, it will have to be careful not to have an excessively high PSNCR (see page 357).

The precise effect of government borrowing on the money supply will depend on how the PSNCR is financed. If it is financed by borrowing from the Bank of England or by the sale of Treasury bills to the banking sector, the money supply will increase. If, however, it is financed by selling bills or gilts outside the banking sector or by selling gilts to the banks, the money supply will not increase (see pages 290–1).

If there is no increase in money supply, however, the increased demand for loans by the government will 'crowd out' lending to the private sector. To attract money the government will have to offer higher interest rates on gilts. This will force up private-sector interest rates and reduce private-sector borrowing and investment. This is known as financial crowding out.

If governments wish to reduce monetary growth and yet avoid financial crowding out, they must therefore reduce the level of the PSNCR.

Issues with medium- and long-term monetary control

Once inflation is at or near its target level, longer-term control of the monetary base is largely a matter of ensuring that government borrowing is kept in check. Keeping bank lending under control is achieved by *short-term* measures to keep inflation at its target rate (see below).

In the early years, however, when a government is embarking on a policy of bringing inflation down there can be serious problems. When the Thatcher government in 1980 adopted a policy of medium-term monetary control, inflation was 18 per cent.

The higher the initial rate of inflation, and the more rapidly the government wishes to reduce it, the bigger the problems can be. The government must cut the PSNCR, but this will be a contractionary *fiscal* policy. This could lead to a recession, given that inflation may be slow to fall.

The less successful a government is in controlling the public-sector deficit, the more it will have to borrow through bond issue, to prevent money supply growing too fast. This will mean high interest rates and the problem of crowding out, and a growing burden of public-sector debt with interest on it that has to be paid from taxation, from further cuts in government expenditure, or from further borrowing.

It is for reasons such as these that in 1998 the UK Chancellor adopted his 'golden rule' of fiscal policy. Similarly, under the EU Stability and Growth Pact (see Box 10.2) eurozone countries are required to aim for a zero government deficit over the business cycle, so that in times of economic slowdown the deficit will not exceed 3 per cent – the limit set for deficits under the Pact. A problem with this rule is that if a recession or slowdown persists, the deficit is likely to breach the 3 per cent limit (as happened in France, Germany and some other EU countries in 2003). There then may have to be deflationary cuts in expenditure or rises in taxation, just at a time when a boost to aggregate demand is called for.

Short-term monetary measures

Inflation may be off target. Alternatively, the government (or central bank) may wish to alter its monetary policy. What can it do? Various techniques could be used.

Definition

Financial crowding out
Where an increase in government borrowing diverts money away from the private sector.

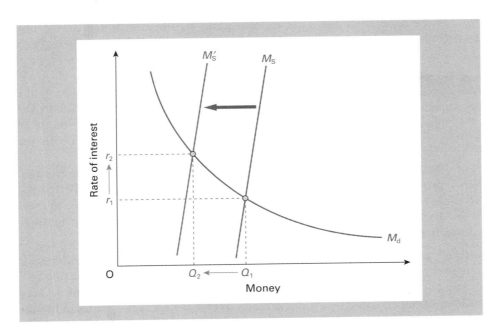

Figure 10.2
The demand for and supply of money

These can be grouped into three categories: (a) altering the money supply; (b) altering interest rates; (c) rationing credit. These are illustrated in Figure 10.2, which shows the demand for and supply of money. The equilibrium quantity of money is initially Q_1 and the equilibrium interest rate is r_1.

Assume that the central bank wants to tighten monetary policy in order to reduce inflation. It could (a) seek to shift the supply of money curve to the left, e.g. from M_S to M_S' (resulting in the equilibrium rate of interest rising from r_1 to r_2), (b) raise the interest rate directly from r_1 to r_2, and then manipulate the money supply to reduce it to Q_2, or (c) keep interest rates at r_1, but reduce money supply to Q_2 by rationing the amount of credit granted by banks and other institutions.

Credit rationing was widely used in the past, especially during the 1960s. The aim was to keep interest rates low, so as not to discourage investment, but to limit the amount of credit granted to more risky business customers and/or to consumers. In the UK, the Bank of England could order banks to abide by such a policy, although in practice it always relied on persuasion. The government also, from time to time, imposed restrictions on hire purchase credit, by specifying minimum deposits or maximum repayment periods.

Such policies are not used today. They stifle competition and prevent efficient banks from expanding. Hire-purchase controls may badly hit certain industries (e.g. cars and other consumer durables), whose products are bought largely on hire-purchase credit. What is more, with the deregulation and globalisation of financial markets, it would be virtually impossible to ration credit. If one financial institution was controlled, borrowers could simply go elsewhere.

We thus focus on controlling the money supply and controlling interest rates.

Techniques to control the money supply

There are four possible techniques that a central bank could use to control money supply. They have one major feature in common: they involve manipulating the liquid assets of the banking system. The aim is to influence the total money supply by affecting the amount of credit that banks can create.

Open-market operations. **Open-market operations** are the most widely used of the four techniques around the world. They alter the monetary base. This then affects the amount of credit banks can create and hence the level of broad money (M4 in the UK).

`KI 6` `p27`

Open-market operations involve the sale or purchase by the central bank of government securities (bonds or bills) in the open market. These sales or purchases are *not* in response to changes in the PSNCR, and are thus best understood in the context of an unchanged PSNCR.

If the central bank wishes to *reduce* the money supply, it will sell more securities. When people buy these securities, they pay for them with cheques drawn on banks. Thus banks' balances with the central bank are reduced. If this brings bank reserves below their prudent ratio, banks will reduce advances. There will be a multiple contraction of credit and hence of (broad) money supply.

`TC 15` `p253`

Definitions

Open-market operations
The sale (or purchase) by the authorities of government securities in the open market in order to reduce (or increase) money supply.

Funding
Where the authorities alter the balance of bills and bonds for any given level of government borrowing.

Minimum reserve ratio
A minimum ratio of specified liquid assets to deposits (either total or selected) that the central bank requires banks to hold.

Reduced central-bank lending to the banks. The central bank in most countries is prepared to provide extra money to banks (through gilt repos, rediscounting bills or straight loans). In some countries, it is the policy of the central bank to keep its interest rate to banks below market rates, thereby encouraging banks to borrow (or sell back securities) whenever such facilities are available. By cutting back the amount it is willing to provide, the central bank can reduce banks' liquid assets and hence the amount of credit they can create.

In other countries, such as the UK and the eurozone countries, it is not so much the amount of money made available that is controlled, but rather the rate of interest (or discount). The higher this rate is relative to other market rates, the less will banks be willing to borrow, and the lower, therefore, will be the monetary base. Raising this rate, therefore, has the effect of reducing the money supply.

Funding. Rather than focusing on controlling the monetary base (as in the case of the above two techniques), an alternative is for the central bank to alter the overall liquidity position of the banks. An example of this approach is a change, by the central bank, in the balance of **funding** government debt. To reduce money supply the central bank issues more bonds and fewer bills. Banks' balances with the central bank will be little affected, but to the extent that banks hold fewer bills, there will be a reduction in their liquidity and hence a reduction in the amount of credit created. Funding is thus the conversion of one type of government debt (liquid) into another (illiquid).

Variable minimum reserve ratios. In some countries (such as the USA), banks are required to hold a certain proportion of their assets in liquid form. The assets that count as liquid are known as 'reserve assets'. These include assets such as balances in the central bank, bills of exchange, certificates of deposit and money market loans. The ratio of such assets to total liabilities is known as the **minimum reserve ratio**. If the central bank raises this ratio (in other words, requires the banks to hold a higher proportion of liquid assets), then banks will have to reduce the amount of credit. The money supply will fall.

Difficulties in controlling money supply

Targets for the growth in broad money were an important part of UK monetary policy from 1976 to 1985. Money targets were then abandoned and have not been used since. The European Central Bank targets the growth of M3 (see Box 10.4), but this is a subsidiary policy to that of setting interest rates in order to keep inflation under control. If, however, a central bank did choose to target money supply as its main monetary policy, how would the policy work?

Assume that money supply is above target and that the central bank wishes to reduce it. It would probably use open-market operations: i.e. it would sell more bonds or bills. The purchasers of the bonds or bills would draw liquidity from the banks. Banks would then supposedly be forced to cut down on the credit they create. But is it as simple as this?

The problem is that banks will normally be unwilling to cut down on loans if people want to borrow – after all, borrowing by customers earns profits for the banks. Banks can always 'top up' their liquidity by borrowing from the central bank and then carry on lending. True, they will have to pay the interest rate charged by the central bank, but they can pass on any rise in the rate to their customers.

The point is that as long as people *want* to borrow, banks and other financial institutions will normally try to find ways of meeting the demand. In other words, in the short run at least, the supply of money is to a large extent demand-determined. It is for this reason that central banks prefer to control the *demand* for money by controlling interest rates.

Techniques to control interest rates

The approach to monetary control today in most countries is to focus directly on interest rates. Normally an interest rate change will be announced, and then open-market operations will be conducted by the central bank to ensure that the money supply is adjusted so as to make the announced interest rate the *equilibrium* one. Thus, in Figure 10.2 (on page 367), the central bank might announce a rise in interest rates from r_1 to r_2 and then conduct open-market operations to ensure that the money supply is reduced from Q_1 to Q_2.

Let us assume that the central bank decides to raise interest rates. What does it do? In general, it will seek to keep banks short of liquidity. This will happen automatically on any day when tax payments by banks' customers exceed the money they receive from government expenditure. This excess is effectively withdrawn from banks and ends up in the government's account at the central bank. Even when this does not occur, sales of bills by the central bank will effectively keep the banking system short of liquidity.

This 'shortage' can then be used as a way of forcing through interest rate changes. Banks will obtain the necessary liquidity from the central bank through repos or by selling it back bills. The central bank can *choose the rate of interest to charge* (i.e. the repo rate or the bill rediscount rate). This will then have a knock-on effect on other interest rates throughout the banking system. (See Box 10.3 for more details on just how the Bank of England manipulates interest rates on a day-to-day basis.)

The effectiveness of changes in interest rates

Even though central bank adjustment of the repo rate is the current preferred method of monetary control in most countries, it is not without its difficulties. The problems centre on the nature of the demand for loans. If this demand is (a) unresponsive to interest rate changes or (b) unstable because it is significantly affected by other determinants (such as anticipated income or foreign interest rates), then it will be very difficult to control by controlling the rate of interest.

 Problem of an inelastic demand for loans. If the demand for loans is inelastic, as in Figure 10.3, any attempt to reduce demand (e.g. from Q_1 to Q_2) will involve large rises in interest rates (r_1 to r_2). The problem will be compounded if the demand shifts to the right, due, say, to a consumer-spending boom. High interest rates lead to the following problems:

What goes on at Threadneedle Street?

The Bank of England does not attempt to control money supply directly. Instead it seeks to control short-term interest rates by conducting open-market operations in the gilt repo and discount markets. These operations, as we shall see, determine short-term interest rates, which will then have a knock-on effect on longer-term rates, as returns on different forms of assets must remain competitive with each other.

Let us assume that the Monetary Policy Committee of the Bank of England is worried that inflation is set to rise, perhaps because there is excessive growth in the money supply. It thus decides to raise interest rates. What does the Bank of England do?

The first thing is that it will *announce* a rise in interest rates. But it must do more than this. It must back up the announcement by using open-market operations to ensure that its announced interest rate is the *equilibrium rate*. In fact, it has to conduct open-market operations every day to keep interest rates at the level it chooses.

How do these open-market operations work? In general, the Bank of England seeks to keep banks short of liquidity. It achieves this through its weekly sales of Treasury bills to the banks and other financial institutions (collectively known as the Bank's 'counterparties').

The counterparties thus have to borrow from the Bank of England. They do this by entering into sale and repurchase agreements (repos). This entails them selling gilts to the Bank, with an agreement that they will repurchase them from the Bank at a fixed date in the future (typically two weeks). The difference between the sale and repurchase prices will be set by the Bank of England to reflect its chosen rate of interest. By the Bank determining the repo rate in this way, there will then be a knock-on effect on other interest rates throughout the banking system.

Each morning at 9.45 the Bank of England forecasts that day's liquidity shortage. Unless the shortage is too small to necessitate action, it then provides liquidity through open-market operations: i.e. through repos or the repurchasing of bills. The rate charged is that set by the MPC. At 2.30, the Bank revises its forecasts of the market's liquidity shortage, and if necessary undertakes a further round of open-market operations.

Then, at 3.30, it publishes a final update for the day's liquidity shortage, and if necessary makes a further repo facility available, normally on an overnight basis and normally at 1 per cent above the rate set by the MPC. The rate is higher because the Bank expects its counterparties to obtain liquidity at the 9.45 and 2.30 rounds. The 3.30 round is designed to cater for any unforeseen late shortage.

Finally, at 4.20, after the market has closed, banks may apply for additional overnight liquidity through repos to allow the process of clearing to be completed. The Bank will charge them anything from the MPC's agreed repo rate to $1\frac{1}{2}$ per cent above that rate.

Although there is usually a shortage of liquidity in the banking system, on some days there may be a *surplus*. To prevent this driving market interest rates down, the Bank will invite its counterparties to bid for outright purchase of short-dated Treasury bills (i.e. ones part-way through their life) at prices set by the Bank to reflect its current (above-equilibrium) interest rate: i.e. at prices lower than the market would otherwise set. At such prices, the Bank has no difficulty in selling them and hence in 'mopping up' the surplus liquidity.

? *Assume that the Bank of England wants to reduce interest rates. Trace through the process during the day by which it achieves this.*

- They may discourage investment and hence long-term growth.
- They add to the costs of production, to the costs of house purchase and generally to the cost of living. They are thus cost-inflationary.
- They are politically unpopular, since the general public do not like paying higher interest rates on overdrafts, credit cards and mortgages.

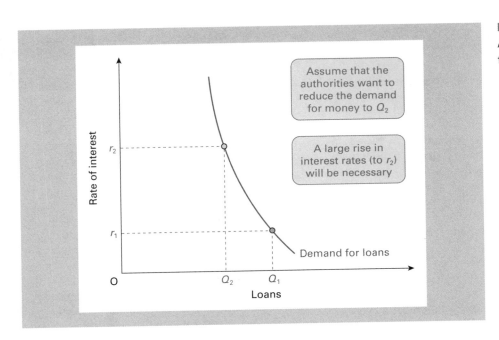

Figure 10.3
An inelastic demand for loans

- The necessary bond issue to restrain liquidity will commit the government to paying high rates on these bonds for the next 20 years or so.
- High interest rates encourage inflows of money from abroad. This drives up the exchange rate. (We examine this in Section 12.2.) A higher exchange rate makes domestic goods expensive relative to goods made abroad. This can be very damaging for export industries and industries competing with imports. Many firms in the UK have suffered badly in recent years from a high exchange rate, caused partly by higher interest rates in the UK than in the eurozone and the USA.

Evidence suggests that the demand for loans may indeed be quite inelastic, especially in the short term. Although investment *plans* may be curtailed by high interest rates, *current* borrowing by many firms cannot easily be curtailed. Similarly, while high interest rates may discourage householders from taking on *new* mortgages, existing mortgages are unlikely to be reduced. What is more, although high interest rates may discourage many firms from taking out long-term fixed-interest loans, some firms may merely switch to shorter-term variable-interest loans.

 Problem of an unstable demand.   Accurate monetary control requires the authorities to be able to predict the demand curve for money (in Figure 10.2). Only then can they set the appropriate level of interest rates. Unfortunately, the demand curve may shift unpredictably, making control very difficult. The major reason is *speculation*:

- If people think interest rates will rise and bond prices fall, in the meantime they will demand to hold their assets in liquid form. The demand for money will rise.
- If people think exchange rates will rise, they will hold the domestic currency while it is still relatively cheap. The demand for money will rise.
- If people think inflation will rise, the transactions demand for money may rise. People plan to spend more while prices are still relatively low.
- If people think the economy is going to grow faster, the demand for loans will increase as firms seek to increase their investment.

It is very difficult for the central bank to predict what people's expectations will be. Speculation depends considerably on world political events, rumour and 'random shocks'.

Box 10.4

Monetary policy in the eurozone

The role of the ECB

The European Central Bank (ECB) is based in Frankfurt and is charged with operating the monetary policy of those EU countries that have adopted the euro. Although it has the overall responsibility for the eurozone's monetary policy, the central banks of the individual countries, such as the Bank of France and Germany's Bundesbank, have not been abolished. They are responsible for distributing euros and for carrying out the ECB's policy with respect to institutions in their own countries. The whole system of the ECB and the national central banks is known as the European System of Central Banks (ESCB).

In operating the monetary policy of a 'euro economy' roughly the size of the USA, and in being independent from national governments, the ECB's power is enormous. So what is the structure of this giant on the European stage, and how does it operate?

The structure of the ECB

The ECB has two major decision-making bodies: the Governing Council and the Executive Board.

■ The Governing Council consists of the members of the Executive Board and the governors of the central banks of each of the eurozone countries. The Council's role is to set the main targets of monetary policy and to oversee the success (or otherwise) of that policy.

■ The Executive Board consists of a president, a vice-president and four other members. Each serves for an eight-year, non-renewable term. The Executive Board is responsible for implementing the decisions of the Governing Council and for preparing policies for the Council's consideration. Each member of the Executive Board has a responsibility for some particular aspect of monetary policy.

The ECB is one of the most independent central banks in the world. It has very little formal accountability to elected politicians. Although its president can be called before the European Parliament, the Parliament has virtually no powers to influence the ECB's actions. Also its deliberations are secret. Unlike meetings of the Bank of England's Monetary Policy Committee, the minutes of the Council meetings are not published.

The targets of monetary policy

The overall responsibility of the ECB is to achieve price stability in the eurozone. The target is a rate of inflation below, but close to, 2 per cent over the medium term. It is a weighted *average* rate for all 12 members, not a rate that has to be met by each member individually.

The ECB also sets a reference value for the annual growth of M3, the broad measure of the money

Pause for thought

Assume that the central bank announces a rise in interest rates and backs this up with open-market operations. What determines the size of the resulting fall in aggregate demand?

If the demand curve shifts very much, and if it is inelastic, then monetary control will be very difficult. Furthermore, the central bank will have to make frequent and sizeable adjustments to interest rates. These fluctuations can be very damaging to business confidence and may discourage long-term investment.

The net result of an inelastic and unstable demand for money is that substantial interest rate changes may be necessary to bring about the required change in aggregate demand. An example occurred in 2001 when the US Federal Reserve, seeing the economy moving rapidly into recession, had to cut interest rates several times. At the beginning of 2001, the US 'federal funds rate' was 6 per cent. By the end of the year it had been reduced to a mere 1.75 per cent.

supply (see Box 8.3 on page 288). This was set at $4\frac{1}{2}$ per cent at the launch of the euro in 1999 and was still the same value in 2006. The reference value is not a rigid target, but is used as a guide to whether monetary policy is consistent with long-run price stability. In setting the reference value, three things are taken into account: the target for inflation, assumptions about the rate of growth of GDP (assumed to have a trend growth rate of 2 to $2\frac{1}{2}$ per cent per year) and the velocity of circulation of M3 (see page 288) (assumed to be declining at a rate of between $\frac{1}{2}$ and 1 per cent per year).

On the basis of its inflation target and M3 reference value, the ECB then sets the rates of interest. It sets three rates: a rate for 'refinancing operations' of the ESCB (i.e. the rate of interest charged by the ESCB for liquidity on offer to banks, largely through repos); a (higher) 'last-resort rate'; and a (lower) 'deposit rate' (the rate paid to banks for depositing surplus liquidity with the ESCB). In January 2006, these rates were 2.25, 3.25 and 1.25 per cent respectively.

Interest rates are set by the Governing Council by simple majority. In the event of a tie, the president has the casting vote.

The operation of monetary policy

The ECB sets a minimum reserve ratio. It argues that this gives greater stability to the system and reduces the need for day-to-day intervention by the ECB. The ECB argues that if there were no minimum reserves, with banks free to use as much of their reserves with the ESCB as they choose, then they would do so if there was an upsurge in demand from customers. After all, the banks know that they can always *borrow* from the ESCB to meet any liquidity requirements. In such a situation, the ECB would be forced to rely much more on open-market operations to prevent excessive lending by banks to their customers, and hence excessive borrowing from the ESCB, and this would mean much greater fluctuations in interest rates.

The minimum reserve ratio is not designed to be used to make *changes* in monetary policy. In other words, it is not used as a *variable* minimum reserves ratio, and for this reason is set at a low level of 2 per cent.

The main instrument for keeping the ECB's desired interest rate as the equilibrium rate is open-market operations in government bonds and other recognised assets, mainly in the form of repos. These repo operations are conducted by the national central banks, which must ensure that the repo rate does not rise above the last-resort rate or below the deposit rate.

What are the arguments for and against publishing the minutes of the meetings of the ECB's Governing Council and Executive Board?

Using monetary policy

It is impossible to use monetary policy as a precise means of controlling aggregate demand. It is especially weak when it is pulling against the expectations of firms and consumers, and when it is implemented too late. However, if the authorities operate a tight monetary policy firmly enough and long enough, they should eventually be able to reduce lending and hence aggregate demand, and with it, inflation. But there will inevitably be time lags and imprecision in the process.

An expansionary monetary policy is even less reliable. If the economy is in recession, no matter how low interest rates are driven, people cannot be forced to borrow if they do not wish to. Firms will not borrow to invest if they predict a continuing recession.

A particular difficulty in using interest rate reductions to expand the economy arises if the repo rate is nearly zero but this is still not enough to stimulate the economy. The problem is that (nominal) interest rates cannot be negative, for clearly nobody would be willing to lend in these circumstances. Japan was in such a situation in the early 2000s. It was caught in what is known as the liquidity trap.

Despite these problems, changing interest rates can be quite effective. After all, they can be changed very rapidly. There are not the time lags of implementation that there are with fiscal policy. Indeed, since the early 1990s, most governments or central banks in OECD countries have used interest rate changes as the major means of keeping aggregate demand and inflation under control.

In the UK, the eurozone and many other countries, a target is set for the rate of inflation. As we have seen, in the UK and the eurozone the target is 2 per cent. If forecasts suggest that inflation is going to be above the target rate, the government or central bank raises interest rates. The advantage of this is that it sends a very clear message to people that inflation *will* be kept under control. People will therefore be more likely to adjust their expectations accordingly and keep their borrowing in check.

Recap

1. Controlling the growth in the money supply over the longer term will normally involve governments attempting to restrict the size of the budget deficit. This will be difficult to do, however, in a period of recession.

2. In the short term, the government or central bank can use monetary policy to restrict the growth in aggregate demand in one of three ways: (a) reducing money supply directly; (b) reducing the demand for money by raising interest rates; (c) rationing credit. Credit rationing has not been used in recent years.

3. The money supply can be reduced directly by using open-market operations. This involves the central bank selling more government securities and thereby reducing banks' reserves when their customers pay for the securities from their bank accounts. Alternatively, the central bank could reduce the amount it is prepared to lend to banks (other than as a last-resort measure). Or it could use funding, by increasing the sale of bonds relative to bills, thereby reducing banks' liquid assets. Finally it could operate a system of variable minimum reserve ratios. Increasing these would force banks to cut back on the amount of credit they create.

4. The money supply is difficult to control precisely, however, and even if the government is successful in controlling the money supply, there then arises the problem of severe fluctuations in interest rates if the demand for money fluctuates and is relatively inelastic.

5. The current method of control in the UK and many other countries involves the central bank influencing interest rates by its operations in the repo and discount markets. The central bank keeps banks short of liquidity, and then supplies them with liquidity, largely through repos, at its chosen interest rate (repo rate). This then has a knock-on effect on interest rates throughout the economy.

6. There are problems with this approach too. With an inelastic demand for loans, there may have to be substantial changes in interest rates in order to bring the required change in aggregate demand. What is more, controlling aggregate demand through controlling interest rates is made even more difficult as a result of *fluctuations* in the demand for money. These fluctuations are made more severe by speculation against changes in interest rates, exchange rates, the rate of inflation, etc.

7. Nevertheless, controlling interest rates is a way of responding rapidly to changing forecasts, and it can be an important signal to markets that inflation will be kept under control – especially when, as in the UK and the eurozone, there is a firm target for the rate of inflation.

DEMAND-SIDE POLICY   10.3

What will be the effect of attempts by the government to control the level of spending in the economy?

Attitudes towards demand management

The debate over the management of demand has shifted ground somewhat in recent years. There is less debate today over the relative merits of fiscal and monetary policy. There is general agreement now that a *combination* of fiscal and monetary policies will have a more powerful effect on demand than just relying on one of the two policies. For example, a policy of cutting the size of the public-sector deficit by reducing government expenditure and/or increasing taxes (fiscal policy) will enable the central bank much more easily to restrain the growth of the money supply (monetary policy), which in turn will help to reinforce the fiscal policy.

The debate today is much more concerned with whether the government ought to pursue an active ('discretionary') demand management policy at all, or whether it ought merely to adhere to a set of policy rules.

The case for rules

The case against discretionary policy centres on the problem of time lags. Both fiscal and monetary policies can involve long and variable time lags, which can make the policy at best ineffective and at worst destabilising. Taking the measures *before* the problem arises, and thus lessening the problem of lags, is no answer since forecasting tends to be unreliable.

By setting and sticking to rules, however, and then not interfering further, the government can provide a sound monetary framework in which firms are not cushioned from market forces, and are therefore encouraged to be efficient. By the government or central bank setting a clear target either for the growth of money supply, or for the rate of inflation, and then resolutely sticking to it, people's expectations of inflation will be reduced, thereby making the target easier to achieve.

This sound and stable monetary environment, with no likelihood of sudden expansionary or contractionary policy, will encourage firms to take a longer-term perspective, and plan ahead. This could then lead to increased capital investment and long-term growth.

The optimum situation is for all the major countries to adhere to mutually consistent rules, so that their economies do not get out of line. This will create more stable exchange rates and provide the climate for world growth.

Advocates of this point of view in the 1970s and 1980s were monetarists, but in recent years support for the setting of targets has become widespread. As we have seen, in both the UK and the eurozone countries, targets are set for both inflation and public-sector deficits.

The case for discretion

Keynesians reject the argument that rules provide the environment for high and stable growth. Demand, argue Keynesians, is subject to many and sometimes violent shocks: e.g. changes in expectations, domestic political events (such as an impending election), world economic factors (such as the world economic slowdown of 2001–3) or world political events (such as a war). The resulting shifts in injections or withdrawals cause the economy to deviate from a stable full-employment growth path.

Any change in injections or withdrawals will lead to a cumulative effect on national income via the multiplier and accelerator and via changing expectations. These effects take time and interact with each other, and so a process of expansion or contraction can last many months before a turning point is eventually reached.

TC 15
p253

Since shocks to demand occur at irregular intervals and are of different magnitudes, the economy is likely to experience cycles of irregular duration and of varying intensity.

Given that the economy is inherently unstable and is buffeted around by various shocks, Keynesians argue that the government needs actively to intervene to stabilise the economy. Otherwise, the uncertainty caused by unpredictable fluctuations will be very damaging to investment and hence to long-term economic growth (quite apart from the short-term effects of recessions on output and employment).

TC 12
p234

Difficulties with choice of target

Assume that the government or central bank sets an inflation target. Should it then stick to that rate, come what may? Might not an extended period of relatively low inflation warrant a lower inflation target? The government must at least have the discretion to *change* the rules, even if only occasionally.

Then there is the question of whether success in achieving the target will bring success in achieving other macroeconomic objectives, such as low unemployment and stable economic growth. The problem is that something called Goodhart's law is likely to apply. The law, named after Charles Goodhart, formerly of the Bank of England, states that attempts to control an *indicator* of a problem may, as a result, make it cease to be a good indicator of the problem.

Targeting inflation may make it become a poor indicator of the state of the economy. If people believe that the central bank will be successful in achieving its inflation target, then those expectations will feed into their inflationary expectations, and not surprisingly the target will be met. But that target rate of inflation may now be consistent with both a buoyant and a depressed economy. In other words, the Phillips curve may become *horizontal*. An example occurred in 2001/2 when the UK economy slowed down considerably and yet there was virtually no change in the rate of inflation. Thus achieving the inflation target may not tackle the much more serious problem of creating stable economic growth and an environment that will therefore encourage long-term investment.

> **Goodhart's law.** Controlling a symptom (i.e. an indicator) of a problem will not cure the problem. Instead, the indicator will merely cease to be a good indicator of the problem.

Key Idea 33

Use of a Taylor rule. For this reason, many economists have advocated the use of a Taylor rule,[1] rather than a simple inflation target. A Taylor rule takes two objectives into account – (1) inflation and (2) either real national income or unemployment – and seeks to get the optimum degree of stability of the two. The degree of

---

[1] Named after John Taylor, from Stanford University, who proposed that for every 1 per cent that GDP rises above sustainable GDP, real interest rates should be raised by 0.5 percentage point and for every 1 per cent that inflation rises above its target level, real interest rates should be raised by 0.5 percentage point (i.e. nominal rates should be raised by 1.5 percentage points).

Definitions

Goodhart's law
Controlling a symptom of a problem, or only part of the problem, will not cure the problem: it will simply mean that the part that is being controlled now becomes a poor indicator of the problem.

Taylor rule
A rule adopted by a central bank for setting the rate of interest. It will raise the interest rate if (a) inflation is above target or (b) real national income is above the sustainable level (or unemployment is below the equilibrium rate). The rule states how much interest rates will be changed in each case.

importance attached to each of the two objectives can be decided by the government or central bank. The central bank adjusts interest rates when either the rate of inflation diverges from its target or the level of real national income (or unemployment) diverges from its sustainable (or equilibrium) level.

Take the case where inflation is above its target level. The central bank following a Taylor rule will raise the rate of interest. It knows, however, that this will reduce real national income. This, therefore, limits the amount that the central bank is prepared to raise the rate of interest. The more weight it attaches to stabilising inflation, the more it will raise the rate of interest. The more weight it attaches to stabilising real national income, the less it will raise the rate of interest.

Thus the central bank has to trade off inflation stability against real income stability.

Current demand-side policy in the UK

Fiscal policy

Since 1998, the government has set targets for government expenditure, not for just one year, but for a three-year period. Does this mean, therefore, that fiscal policy as a means of adjusting aggregate demand has been abandoned? In one sense, this is the case. The government is now committed to following its 'golden rule', whereby public-sector receipts should cover all current spending, averaged over the course of the business cycle (see Box 10.2). In fact, in supporting sticking to the golden rule, the Chancellor explicitly rejected Keynesian fine-tuning:

> In today's deregulated, liberalised financial markets, the Keynesian fine tuning of the past, which worked in relatively sheltered, closed national economies and which tried to exploit a supposed long-term trade-off between inflation and unemployment, will simply not work.[2]

But despite this apparent rejection of short-term discretionary fiscal adjustments, there is still a role for *automatic* fiscal stabilisers: with deficits rising in a recession and falling in a boom. There is also still the possibility, within the golden rule, of financing additional *investment* by borrowing, thereby providing a stimulus to a sluggish economy.

The golden rule also permits increased government expenditure (or tax cuts) if there is a budget surplus. Thus in the 2001 Budget the Chancellor announced spending increases of 3.7 per cent per year for three years. The effect was to provide a stimulus to the economy just at a time when the world economy was slowing down. This helped to make the slowdown in economic growth in the period 2001–3 much less severe in the UK than in many other countries.

Monetary policy

Since 1992, both Conservative and Labour governments have used monetary policy to achieve a target rate of inflation. The Conservative government chose both the target (to be within a range of 1 to 4 per cent) and also the rate of interest felt necessary to achieve that target. The interest rate, however, was chosen in consultation with the Governor of the Bank of England and was based on forecasts of the rate of inflation. The Chancellor met monthly with the Governor to discuss interest rates, and the minutes of the meetings were published six weeks later, in order to give transparency to the process.

---

[2] Extract from the Chancellor's Mansion House speech, 11 June 1998.

Box 10.5

Inflation targeting

The fashion of the age

More and more countries are turning to inflation targeting as their main macroeconomic policy. The table gives the targets for a selection of countries (as of 2006).

Part of the reason is the apparent failure of discretionary macroeconomic policies. Discretionary fiscal and monetary policies suffer from time lags, from being used for short-term political purposes and from failing to straighten out the business cycle. But if discretionary policies have seemed not to work, why choose an inflation target rather than a target for the money supply or the exchange rate?

Inflation targets

Country	Inflation target (%)	Details
Australia	2–3	Average over the business cycle
Brazil	4.5	Tolerance band of ±2 percentage points
Canada	1–3	6–8-quarter horizon
Chile	2–4	Over 12 to 24 months
Czech Republic	3	Tolerance band of ±1 percentage point
Eurozone	<2 but close to it	Average for eurozone as a whole; over medium term
Hungary	3.5	Tolerance band of ±1 percentage point
Iceland	2.5	Tolerance band of ±1.5 percentage points
Israel	1–3	
Mexico	3	Tolerance band of ±1 percentage point
New Zealand	1–3	On average over the medium term
Norway	2.5	Over 1–3 years
Peru	2.5	Tolerance band of ±1 percentage point
Poland	2.5	Tolerance band of ±1 percentage point
South Africa	3–6	
South Korea	2.5–3.5	
Sweden	2	1–2-year horizon; tolerance band of ±1 percentage point
Switzerland	<2 but close to it	
Thailand	0–3.5	
UK	2	2-year horizon; tolerance band of ±1 percentage point

Source: Adapted from Reserve Bank of Australia (http://www.rba.gov.au/Education/monetary_policy.html)
Figures are current to mid-2005 and readers should refer to The Reserve Bank of Australia website for any updates.

In 1997, the incoming Labour government set the target at $2^1/_2$ per cent for RPIX inflation. (This was changed to 2 per cent for CPI inflation in December 2003.) Unlike its predecessor, however, the government decided to make the Bank of England independent. Indeed, this was the first action taken by the Chancellor when the government came to power.

But why did the government give up its right to set interest rates? First, there is the political advantage of taking 'blame' away from the government if interest rates need to be raised in order to prevent inflation rising above its target. Second, an independent central bank, free to set interest rates in order to achieve a clear target, is more likely to be consistent in pursuit of this objective than a government concerned about its popularity. Then there is the question of transparency in decision making.

If inflation is more than 1 percentage point higher or lower than the target, an open letter will be sent by the Governor to the Chancellor so that the public is fully informed as to why the divergence has occurred; the policy action being

Money supply targets were adopted by many countries in the 1980s, including the UK, and this policy too was largely a failure. Money supply targets proved very difficult to achieve. As we have seen, money supply depends on the amount of credit banks create, and this is not easy for the authorities to control. Then, even if money supply is controlled, this does not necessarily mean that aggregate demand will be controlled: the velocity of circulation may change. Nevertheless, many countries do still target the money supply, although in most cases it is not the main target. In a study of 91 countries by the Bank of England in 1999, of the 55 that targeted inflation, 31 also targeted the money supply (see Web Case 10.12).

Exchange-rate targets, as we shall see in Chapter 12, may have serious disadvantages if the equilibrium exchange rate is not the one that is being targeted. The main instrument for keeping the exchange rate on target is the rate of interest. For example, if the exchange rate target were £1 = $1.50, and the exchange rate were currently £1 = $1.40, then interest rates would be raised. This would cause an inflow of money into the economy and hence push up the exchange rate. But if the rate of interest is being used to achieve an exchange rate target, it cannot be used for other purposes, such as controlling aggregate demand or inflation. Raising interest rates to achieve an exchange rate target may lead to a recession.

Inflation targets have proved relatively easy to achieve. There may be problems at first, if the actual rate of inflation is way above the target level. The high rates of interest necessary to bring inflation down may cause a recession. But once inflation has been brought down and the objective is then simply to maintain it at the target level, most countries have been relatively successful. And the more successful they are, the more people will expect this success to be maintained, which in turn will help to ensure this success.

So, are there any problems with inflation targeting? Ironically, one of the main problems lies in its success. With worldwide inflation having fallen, and with global trade and competition helping to keep prices down, there is now less of a link between inflation and the business cycle. Booms no longer seem to generate the inflation they once did. Gearing interest-rate policy to maintaining low inflation could still see economies experiencing unsustainable booms, followed by recessions. Inflation may be controlled, but the business cycle may not be.

KI 33
p376

? *Why may there be problems in targeting (a) both inflation and money supply; (b) both inflation and the exchange rate?*

taken to deal with it; the period within which inflation is expected to return to the target; and how this approach meets the government's monetary policy objectives. Monetary policy decision-making is now among the most transparent and accountable in the world.[3]

Transparency is enhanced by the publication of the minutes of the monthly meetings of the Bank of England's Monetary Policy Committee at which interest rates are set. One of the main purposes of transparency is to convince people of the seriousness with which the Bank will adhere to its targets. This, it is hoped, will keep people's *expectations* of inflation low: the lower expected inflation is, the lower will be the actual rate of inflation.

TC 9
p68

---

[3] *The Government's Overall Economic Strategy* (http://www.hm-treasury.gov.uk/pub/html/ e_info/ overview/1_goes.html).

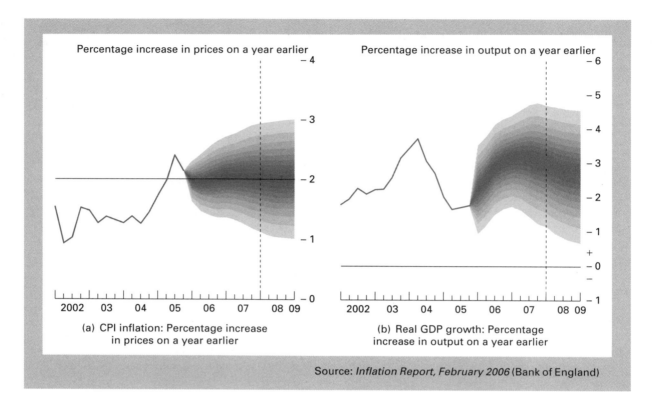

Percentage increase in prices on a year earlier

(a) CPI inflation: Percentage increase in prices on a year earlier

Percentage increase in output on a year earlier

(b) Real GDP growth: Percentage increase in output on a year earlier

Source: *Inflation Report, February 2006* (Bank of England)

Figure 10.4
Fan chart of CPI inflation and GDP growth projections (made in Q1 2006) based on market interest rate expectations

The operation of the inflation target rule. The Bank of England uses a rule that is apparently simpler than the Taylor rule, but in reality is more sophisticated. The Bank of England targets inflation alone; in this sense the rule is simpler. But the inflation figure on which it bases its interest rate decisions is the forecast rate of inflation, not the current rate; in this sense it is more sophisticated.

The Bank of England publishes a quarterly *Inflation Report*, which contains projections for inflation for the next three years. These projections assume that interest rates follow market expectations. They form the basis for the Monetary Policy Committee's monthly deliberations. If the projected inflation in 24 months' time is off-target, the MPC will change interest rates accordingly.

Two key projections of the MPC are shown in the Bank of England's *Inflation Report*, which is published each quarter. These are shown in Figure 10.4. They are known as 'fan charts'. The first plots the forecast range of inflation. The second plots the forecast range of real GDP growth. In each case, the darkest central band represents a 10 per cent likelihood, as does each of the eight subsequent pairs of lighter areas out from the central band. Thus inflation and GDP growth are considered to have a 90 per cent probability of being within the fan. The bands get wider as the time horizon is extended, indicating increasing uncertainty about the outcome. Also, the less reliable are considered to be the forecasts by the MPC, the wider will be the fan. The dashed line indicates the two-year target point. Thus in quarter 1 of 2006, the 2 per cent inflation target was for quarter 1 of 2008.

Although projections are made for GDP growth, these are to help inform the forecast for inflation. GDP growth is not itself an explicit target.

As it has turned out, inflation targeting has been successful in its prime purpose: keeping inflation at or near its target. For the

Pause for thought

If people believe that the central bank will be successful in keeping inflation on target, does it matter whether a simple inflation rule or a Taylor rule is used? Explain.

whole period from 1997 to 2006, the chosen measure of inflation never diverged by more than 1 percentage point from the target. In the light of the history of macro-economic management over the past 60 years, this would seem remarkable.

A rules-based approach to demand-side policy?

With monetary policy geared to an inflation target and fiscal policy geared to following the golden rule, there seems to be virtually no scope for discretionary demand-management policy. Rules appear to have replaced discretion.

When there are ever more rapid financial flows across the world that are unpredictable and uncertain, the answer is to ensure stability through establishing the right long-term policy objectives and to build credibility in the policy through well-understood procedural rules that are followed for fiscal and monetary policy.[4]

> **Pause for thought**
>
> Do you agree that 'ever more rapid financial flows across the world that are unpredictable and uncertain' make Keynesian discretionary fiscal (and monetary) policy less suitable? Explain.

There is, however, a new form of fine-tuning: the frequent adjustment of interest rates – not to smooth out the business cycle, but to make sure that the inflation rule is adhered to. Nevertheless, with automatic fiscal stabilisers still operating and with interest rate changes to stabilise inflation also having the effect of stabilising aggregate demand, the degree of cyclical fluctuations has been less in recent years. In the 10 years to 2005, annual economic growth has not fallen below 1.8 per cent or risen above 3.9 per cent.

Recap

1. The case against discretionary policy is that it involves unpredictable time lags, which can make the policy destabilising. The government may as a result overcorrect. Also the government may ignore the long-run adverse consequences of policies designed for short-run political gain.
2. The case in favour of rules is that they help to reduce inflationary expectations and thus create a stable environment for investment and growth.
3. The case against sticking merely to inflation rules is that they may not allow adjustment to an economic slowdown. Keynesians thus argue that the government must have the discretion to change its policy as circumstances demand.
4. Since 1992, both Conservative and Labour governments in the UK have pursued a largely rules-based demand-side policy.
5. Fiscal policy is geared to achieving a balanced budget over the course of the business cycle. The only exception to this is borrowing for public *investment*. Monetary policy is geared to achieving a target rate of inflation of 2 per cent. The Bank of England adjusts interest rates in order to keep to this target.

SUPPLY-SIDE POLICY 10.4

How might the government attempt to control the level of output and employment directly?

Supply-side policies, as the name suggests, focus on aggregate supply. If successful, they will shift the aggregate supply curve to the right, thus increasing output for

[4] Extract from the Chancellor's Mansion House speech, 11 June 1998.

any given level of prices (or reducing the price level for any given level of output). They may also shift the Phillips curve to the left, reducing the rate of unemployment for any given rate of inflation.

Unemployment and supply-side policies

Equilibrium unemployment – frictional, structural, etc. – is caused by various rigidities or imperfections in the market. There is a mismatching of aggregate supply and demand, and vacancies are not filled despite the existence of unemployment. Perhaps workers have the wrong qualifications, or are poorly motivated, or are living a long way away from the job, or are simply unaware of the jobs that are vacant. Generally, the problem is that labour is not sufficiently mobile, either occupationally or geographically, to respond to changes in the job market. Labour supply for particular jobs is too inelastic.

Supply-side policies aim to influence labour supply. They aim to make workers more responsive to changes in job opportunities. Alternatively, they may aim to make employers more adaptable and willing to operate within existing labour constraints.

Inflation and supply-side policies

If inflation is caused by cost-push pressures, supply-side policy can help to reduce these cost pressures in two ways:

- By reducing the power of unions and/or firms (e.g. by anti-monopoly legislation) and thereby encouraging more competition in the supply of labour and/or goods.
- By encouraging increases in productivity through the retraining of labour, or by investment grants to firms, or by tax incentives, etc.

Growth and supply-side policies

Supply-side economics focuses on *potential* output. Supply-side policies aim to increase the total quantity of factors of production (e.g. policies designed to encourage the building of new factories), or they can be used to encourage greater productivity of factors of production (e.g. policies to encourage the training of labour, or incentives for people to work harder). Box 9.5 examined the link between productivity and economic growth.

Supply-side policies can take various forms. They can be *market orientated* and focus on ways of 'freeing up' the market, such as encouraging private enterprise, risk taking and competition: policies that provide incentives and reward initiative, hard work and productivity. Alternatively, they can be *interventionist* in nature and focus on means of counteracting the deficiencies of the free market. Thus supply-side policies are advocated across the political and economic spectrum.

First we will examine market-orientated policies. Then we will turn to interventionist policies.

Market-orientated supply-side policies

Radical market-orientated supply-side policies were first adopted in the early 1980s by the Thatcher government in the UK and the Reagan administration in the USA, but were subsequently copied by other right and centre-right governments around the world. The essence of these policies is to encourage and reward individual enterprise and initiative, and to reduce the role of government; to put more reliance on market forces and competition, and less on government intervention and regulation.

Table 10.3	Total general government expenditure as a percentage of GDP						
	1961–70	1971–80	1981–85	1986–90	1991–95	1996–2000	2001–05
Belgium	33.7	49.6	61.7	55.7	54.7	51.4	50.6
Germany	37.0	46.0	47.7	45.0	48.6	48.5	48.2
France	38.3	42.4	51.6	51.3	54.0	53.8	53.5
Japan	–	26.8	34.2	32.7	34.5	38.9	39.0
Netherlands	39.9	48.6	57.3	54.8	52.9	46.2	47.3
Sweden	–	52.8	65.0	58.5	65.6	61.3	57.5
UK	36.5	46.0	49.0	42.0	45.0	40.2	43.0
USA	29.1	32.6	35.6	35.8	36.2	33.4	34.3

Source: Adapted from *European Economy Statistical Annex* (Commission of the European Union)

Note that total expenditure in this table includes transfer payments as well as expenditure on final goods and services

Reducing government expenditure

The desire by many governments to cut government expenditure is not just to reduce the PSNCR and hence reduce the growth of money supply; it is also an essential ingredient of their supply-side strategy.

In most countries the size of the public sector, relative to national income, grew substantially up until the mid-1980s (see Table 10.3). A major aim of Conservative governments throughout the world has been to reverse this trend. The public sector is portrayed as more bureaucratic and less efficient than the private sector. What is more, it is claimed that a growing proportion of public money has been spent on administration and other 'non-productive' activities, rather than on the direct provision of goods and services.

Two things are needed, it is argued: (a) a more efficient use of resources within the public sector and (b) a reduction in the size of the public sector. This would allow private investment to increase with no overall rise in aggregate demand. Thus the supply-side benefits of higher investment could be achieved without the demand-side costs of higher inflation.

In practice, governments have found it very difficult to cut their expenditure without cutting services and the provision of infrastructure.

Tax cuts: the effects on labour supply and employment

Cutting the marginal rate of income tax was a major objective of the Thatcher and Major governments (1979–97). In 1979, the standard rate of income tax in the UK was 33 per cent and the top rate was 83 per cent. By 1997 the standard rate was only 23 per cent (with a starting rate of just 20 per cent), and the top rate was only 40 per cent. The Blair government continued with this policy. In 2006 the standard rate was 22 per cent and the starting rate was only 10 per cent. Cuts in the marginal rate of income tax are claimed to have many beneficial effects: for example, people work longer hours; more people wish to work; people work more enthusiastically; unemployment falls; employment rises. The evidence regarding the truth of these claims, however, is less than certain.

For example, do more people wish to work? This applies largely to second income-earners in a family, mainly women. A rise in after-tax wages may encourage more women to look for jobs. It may now be worth the cost in terms of transport, child minders, family disruption, etc. However, the effect of a 1 or 2 per cent cut in income tax rates is likely to be negligible. A more significant effect may be achieved by raising tax allowances: the amount of income that can be earned before taxes are paid. Part-time workers, especially, could end up paying no taxes.

Whether people will be prepared to work longer hours is also questionable. On the one hand, each hour worked will be more valuable in terms of take-home pay, and thus people may be encouraged to work more and have less leisure time. This is a substitution effect (see page 179): people substitute work for leisure. On the other hand, a cut in income tax will make people better off, and therefore they may feel less need to do overtime than before. This is an income effect (see page 179): they can afford to work less. The evidence on these two effects suggests that they just about cancel each other out. Anyway, for many people there is no such choice in the short run. There is no chance of doing overtime or working a shorter week. In the long run, there may be some flexibility in that people can change jobs.

One of the main arguments is that tax cuts, especially at the lower end (by having a low starting rate of tax, or high personal allowances), will help to reduce unemployment. If income taxes are cut (especially if unemployment benefits are also cut), there will be a bigger difference between after-tax wage rates and unemployment benefit. More people will be motivated to take jobs rather than remain unemployed.

> **Pause for thought**
>
> *If taxes as a proportion of national income have risen since 1979, does this mean that there can have been no positive incentive effects of the various tax measures taken by first the Conservative and then the Labour governments?*

Tax cuts for business and other investment incentives

A number of financial incentives can be given to encourage investment. Market-orientated policies seek to reduce the general level of taxation on profits, or to give greater tax relief to investment.

A cut in corporation tax (the tax on business profits) will increase after-tax profits. This will leave more funds for ploughing back into investment. Also the higher after-tax return on investment will encourage more investment to take place. In 1983 the main rate of corporation tax in the UK stood at 52 per cent. A series of reductions have taken place since then, and by 2006 the rate was 30 per cent for large companies and 19 per cent for small ones, with a 0 per cent starting rate.

Reducing the power of labour

The argument here is that, if labour costs to employers are reduced, their profits will probably rise. This could encourage and enable more investment and hence economic growth. If the monopoly power of labour is reduced, then cost-push inflation will also be reduced.

The Thatcher government took a number of measures to curtail the power of unions. These included the right of employees not to join unions, preventing workers taking action other than against their direct employers and enforced secret ballots on strike proposals. It set a lead in resisting strikes in the public sector.

As labour markets have become more flexible, with increased part-time working and short-term contracts, and as the process of globalisation has exposed more companies to international competition, so this has further eroded the power of labour in many sectors of the economy (see Box 5.2 on page 168).

Reducing welfare

New classical economists claim that a major cause of unemployment is the small difference between the welfare benefits of the unemployed and the take-home pay of the employed. This causes voluntary unemployment (i.e. frictional unemployment). People are caught in a 'poverty trap': if they take a job, they lose their benefits (see page 181).

A dramatic solution to this problem would be to cut unemployment benefits. A major problem with this approach, however, is that with changing requirements for labour skills, many of the redundant workers from the older industries are simply not qualified for new jobs that are created. What is more, the longer people are unemployed, the more demoralised they become. Employers would probably be prepared to pay only very low wages to such workers. To persuade these unemployed people to take low-paid jobs, the welfare benefits would have to be slashed. A 'market' solution to the problem, therefore, may be a very cruel solution. A fairer solution would be an interventionist policy: a policy of retraining labour.

Another alternative is to make the payment of unemployment benefits conditional on the recipient making a concerted effort to find a job. In the Jobseeker's Allowance introduced in 1996, claimants must be available for and actively seeking work, and must complete a jobseeker's agreement, which sets out the types of work the person is willing to do, and the plan to find work. Payment can be refused if the claimant refuses to accept the offer of a job. Similarly, under the employment and support allowance, which replaced incapacity benefit in 2006, those assessed as 'capable of work with help' are assisted in finding work by employment advisers. Anyone refusing such help has their benefits reduced.

Policies to encourage competition

If the government can encourage more competition, this should have the effect of increasing national output and reducing inflation. Five major types of policy have been pursued under this heading.

Privatisation. If privatisation simply involves the transfer of a natural monopoly to private hands (e.g. the water companies), the scope for increased competition is limited. However, where there is genuine scope for increased competition (e.g. in the supply of gas and electricity), privatisation can lead to increased efficiency, more consumer choice and lower prices (see Box 6.2 on pages 208–9).

Alternatively, privatisation can involve the introduction of private services into the public sector (e.g. private contractors providing cleaning services in hospitals, or refuse collection for local authorities). Private contractors may compete against each other for the franchise. This may well lower the cost of provision of these services, but the quality of provision may also suffer unless closely monitored. The effects on unemployment are uncertain. Private contractors may offer lower wages and thus may use more labour. But if they are trying to supply the service at minimum cost, they may employ less labour.

Deregulation. This involves the removal of monopoly rights: again, largely in the public sector. The deregulation of the bus industry, opening it up to private operators, is a good example of this initiative. An example in the private sector was the so-called Big Bang on the Stock Exchange in 1986. Under this, the monopoly power of 'jobbers' to deal in stocks and shares on the Stock Exchange was abolished. In addition, stockbrokers now compete with each other in the commission rates they charge, and on-line share dealing has become commonplace.

Introducing market relationships into the public sector. This is where the government tries to get different departments or elements within a particular part of the public sector to 'trade' with each other, so as to encourage competition and efficiency. The best-known examples are within health and education.

The process often involves 'devolved budgeting'. For example, in the UK, under the locally managed schools scheme (LMS), schools have become self-financing. Rather than the local authority meeting the bill for teachers' salaries, the schools have to manage their own budgets. The objective is to encourage them to cut costs, thereby reducing the burden on council tax payers. However, one result is that schools have tended to appoint inexperienced (and hence cheaper) teachers rather than those who can bring the benefits of their years of teaching.

Another example is in the National Health Service. In 2003, the government introduced a system of 'foundation trusts'. Hospitals can apply for foundation trust status. If successful, they are given much greater financial autonomy in terms of purchasing, employment and investment decisions. Applications are judged by Monitor, the independent health regulator. By 2006, there were 33 foundation trusts. Critics argue that funds have been diverted to foundation hospitals away from the less well-performing hospitals where greater funding could help that performance.

The Private Finance Initiative (PFI). This is where a private company, after a competitive tender, is contracted by a government department or local authority to finance and build a project, such as a new road or a prison. The government then pays the company to maintain and/or run it, or simply rents the assets from the company. The public sector thus becomes a purchaser of services rather than a direct provider itself.

The aim of these 'public–private partnerships' (PPPs) is to introduce competition (through the tendering process) and private-sector expertise into the provision of public services (see Web Case 10.17). It is hoped that the extra burden to the taxpayer of the private-sector profits will be more than offset by gains in efficiency. Critics, however, claim that PPPs have resulted in poorer quality of provision and that cost control has often been poor too, resulting in a higher burden for the taxpayer in the long term.

Free trade and capital movements. The opening-up of international trade and investment is central to a market-orientated supply-side policy. One of the first measures of the Thatcher government (in October 1979) was to remove all controls on the purchase and sale of foreign currencies, thereby permitting the free inflow and outflow of capital, both long-term and short-term. Most other industrialised countries also removed or relaxed exchange controls during the 1980s and early 1990s.

The Single European Act of 1987, which came into force in 1993, was another example of international liberalisation. As we shall see in Section 11.5, it created a 'single market' in the EU: a market without barriers to the movement of goods, services, capital and labour.

Interventionist supply-side policies

The basis of the case for government intervention is that the free market is likely to provide too little research and development, training and investment.

There are potentially large external benefits from research and development (see page 193). Firms investing in developing and improving products, and especially firms engaged in more general scientific research, may produce results that provide benefits to many other firms. Thus the *social* rate of return on investment may be much higher than the private rate of return. Investment that is privately unprofitable for a firm may therefore still be economically desirable for the nation.

Similarly, investment in training may continue yielding benefits to society that are lost to the firms providing the training when the workers leave.

Investment often involves risks. Firms may be unwilling to take those risks, since the costs of possible failure may be too high. When looked at nationally, however, the benefits of investment might well have substantially outweighed the costs, and thus it would have been socially desirable for firms to have taken the risk. Successes would have outweighed failures.

Box 10.6 **Case Studies and Applications**

Unemployment and supply-side policies

Two successful approaches

Although some countries, such as Germany and France have found that unemployment has remained stubbornly high at around 10 per cent, others have had much more success in reducing unemployment through appropriate supply-side policies.

In 2006, the *OECD* put countries into four groups according to their policies towards labour markets. The first two groups have been successful in cutting unemployment. The other two have not.

The first group, labelled "mainly English-speaking" by the OECD (Japan, South Korea and Switzerland are honorary Anglophones), tends to have weaker job protection, less generous unemployment benefits and thinner tax wedges than the average. Its employment rate is comfortably higher than the OECD average; its jobless rate [5.3 per cent] is comfortably lower [than the OECD average of 7.5 per cent]. In the second, "northern European" group (Scandinavia, the Netherlands, Austria and Ireland), taxes and unemployment benefits are high and workers hard to fire. Yet the average employment rate is a little higher than the first group's and the unemployment rate a little lower [4.8 per cent].

There are two reasons why the second group can match the first. Their product markets are, like those of the first group, fairly loosely regulated, making the whole economy more dynamic. And they spend much more on schemes intended to ensure that the unemployed try hard to find work: in return for high benefits, they must accept

that their search for a job will be closely watched and that some work-seeking programmes may be compulsory. That high unemployment benefits are a disincentive to seek work is not in doubt; but it seems that a sufficiently diligent and well-funded employment service can offset their effects. . . .

Countries in the third group—mainly southern European ones, plus France and Germany—tend to pay high benefits too. But they have not offset these with labour-market programmes on the scale of the second group, and their product markets are more protected. [Unemployment in this group averages 9.0 per cent.]

In the last group, which includes the Czech Republic, Poland and Slovakia, benefits are low. But workers are not especially easy to fire; little is spent on pushing the jobless into work; and product markets are more regulated than in any other group. [Unemployment in this group averages 15.1 per cent.][1]

1. How would you classify the approaches of the first two groups in terms of 'market-orientated' or 'interventionist'?
2. Is there an even more effective approach to reducing unemployment that uses elements of each?

[1] 'Intricate workings', *The Economist* (17/6/06)

Even when firms do wish to make such investments, they may find difficulties in raising finance. Banks may be unwilling to lend. Alternatively, if firms rely on raising finance by the issue of new shares, this makes them very dependent on the stock market performance of their shares. This depends largely on current profitability and expected profitability in the near future, not on *long-term* profitability.

Types of interventionist supply-side policy

Nationalisation. This is the most extreme form of intervention, and one that most countries have now rejected, given the world-wide trend of privatisation. Nevertheless, many countries have stopped short of privatising certain key transport and power industries, such as the railways and electricity generation. Having these industries under public ownership may result in higher investment than if they were under private ownership. Thus French governments have invested heavily in the state-owned railway system. This has resulted in fast, efficient rail services, with obvious benefits to rail users and the economy generally.

Box 10.7

A New Approach to Industrial Policy

Encouraging competitiveness

As with many other areas of economic policy, industrial policy throughout most of the world has undergone a radical reorientation in recent years. The government's role has shifted from one of direct intervention in the form of subsidies and protecting industry from competition, to one of focusing upon the external business environment and the conditions that influence its competitiveness.

The reasons for such a change are both philosophical and structural:

■ The rise of the political right in the 1980s led to a shift away from interventionist and towards market-based supply-side policy.

■ Growing government debt and a desire to curb public expenditure acted as a key incentive to reduce the state's role in industrial affairs. This is argued to have been one of the driving forces behind the European privatisation process since the 1980s.

■ Industry, during the 1980s, became progressively more global in its outlook. As such, its investment decisions were increasingly being determined by external environmental factors, especially the technology, productivity and labour costs of its international competitors.

The new approach to industrial policy, being widely adopted by many advanced countries, is to focus on improving those factors that shape a nation's competitiveness. This involves shifting away from particular sectors to targeting what are referred to as 'framework conditions for industry'. Policies include the following:

■ The promotion of investment in physical and human capital. Human capital in particular, and

the existence of a sound skills base, are seen as crucial for attracting global business and ensuring long-run economic growth.

■ A reduction in non-wage employment costs, such as employers' social security and pension contributions. Many governments see these costs as too high and as a severe limitation on competitiveness and employment creation.

■ The promotion of innovation and the encouragement of greater levels of R&D.

■ Support for small and medium-sized enterprises (SMEs). SMEs have received particular attention due to their crucial role in enhancing innovation, creating employment and contributing to skills development, especially in high-tech areas.

■ The improvement of infrastructure. This includes both physical transport, such as roads and railways, as well as information highways.

■ The protection of intellectual property by more effective use of patents and copyright. By reinforcing the law in these areas it is hoped to encourage firms to develop new products and commit themselves to research.

These policies, if they are to be truly effective, are likely to require co-ordination and integration, since they represent a radical departure from traditional industrial policy.

? 1. In what senses could these new policies be described as (a) non-interventionist; (b) interventionist?

2. Does globalisation, and in particular the global perspective of multinational corporations, make industrial policy in the form of selective subsidies and tax relief more or less likely?

Direct provision. Improvements in infrastructure, such as a better motorway system, can be of direct benefit to industry. Alternatively, the government could provide factories or equipment to specific firms.

Funding research and development. Some 31 per cent of UK R&D is financed by the government, but around half of this has been concentrated in the fields of defence, aerospace and the nuclear power industry. As a result, there has been little government sponsorship of research in the majority of industry. Since the mid-1970s, however, there have been a number of government initiatives in the field of information technology. Even so, the amount of government support in this field has been very small compared with in Japan, France and the USA. What is more, the amount of support declined between the mid-1980s and the late 1990s.

In 1999, however, the Labour government introduced a system of tax credits for small firms that invest in research and development. Then, in 2002, tax relief of 20 per cent of R&D expenditures by large firms was introduced.

Private-sector R&D is generally lower in the UK than in other major industrialised countries. Of the companies in the top 700 R&D spenders in the world in 2004, US companies' R&D as a percentage of sales was 4.9 per cent. For German companies the figure was 4.3 per cent, for Japanese companies it was 4.2 per cent, for French companies it was 3.1 per cent, while for UK companies it was only 2.3 per cent (see Web Case 9.19).

Training and education.   The government may set up training schemes, or encourage educational institutions to make their courses more vocationally relevant, or introduce new vocational qualifications (such as the GNVQs, NVQs and foundation degrees in the UK). Alternatively, the government can provide grants or tax relief to firms which themselves provide training schemes. The UK invests little in training programmes compared with most of its industrial competitors. Alternative approaches to training in the UK, Germany, France and the USA are examined in Web Case 10.18).

Assistance to small firms.   UK governments in recent years have recognised the importance of small firms to the economy and have introduced various forms of advisory services, grants and tax concessions. For example, small firms pay a 19 per cent rate of corporation tax compared with 30 per cent for larger companies. In addition, small firms are subject to fewer planning and other bureaucratic controls than large companies. Support to small firms in the UK is examined in Web Case 10.19.

Advice and persuasion.   The government may engage in discussions with private firms in order to find ways to improve efficiency and innovation. It may bring firms together to exchange information, so as to co-ordinate their decisions and create a climate of greater certainty. It may bring firms and unions together to try to create greater industrial harmony.

Information.   The government may provide various information services to firms: technical assistance, the results of public research, information on markets, etc.

> **Pause for thought**
>
> *How might a new classical economist criticise these various forms of interventionist supply-side policy?*

Recap

1. Market-orientated supply-side policies aim to increase the rate of growth of aggregate supply and reduce the rate of unemployment by encouraging private enterprise and the freer play of market forces.

2. Reducing government expenditure as a proportion of GDP is a major element of such policies.

3. Tax cuts can be used to encourage more people to take up jobs, to work longer hours and to work more enthusiastically. The effects of tax cuts will depend on how people respond to incentives.

4. Reducing the power of trade unions and a reduction in welfare benefits, especially those related to unemployment, may force workers to accept jobs at lower wage rates, thereby decreasing equilibrium unemployment.

5. Other examples of market-orientated supply-side policy include privatisation, competitive tendering for public-sector contracts, deregulation, the Private Finance Initiative and free trade and capital movements.

6. Interventionist supply-side policy can take the form of grants for investment and research and development, advice and persuasion, the direct provision of infrastructure and the provision, funding or encouragement of various training schemes.

Questions

1. How does the size of (a) the budget deficit and (b) the general government debt vary with the course of the business cycle?

2. How would the withdrawals curve shift in each of the following cases? (a) A reduction in the basic rate of tax. (b) An increase in personal allowances.

3. Under what circumstances is a rise in taxes likely to have a disincentive effect?

4. What factors determine the effectiveness of discretionary fiscal policy?

5. Give some examples of changes in one injection or withdrawal that can affect others.

6. Why is it difficult to use fiscal policy to 'fine-tune' the economy?

7. If the government buys back £1 million of maturing bonds from the general public and then, keeping the total amount of its borrowing the same, raises £1 million by selling bills to banks, what will happen to the money supply?

8. Assume that a bank has the simplified balance sheet shown in the table, and is operating at its desired liquidity ratio. Now assume that the central bank repurchases £5 million of government bonds on the open market. Assume that the people who sell the bonds all have their accounts with this bank.

Liabilities	£m	Assets	£m
Deposits	100	Balances with central bank	10
		Advances	90
	100		100

(a) Draw up the new balance sheet directly after the purchase of the bonds.
(b) Now draw up the eventual balance sheet after all credit creation has taken place.

(c) Would there be a similar effect if the central bank rediscounted £5 billion of bills?
(d) How would such open-market operations affect the rate of interest?

9. What effect would a substantial increase in the sale of government bonds and bills have on interest rates?

10. Why would it be difficult for a central bank to predict the precise effect on money supply of open-market operations?

11. Imagine you were called in by the government to advise on whether it should adopt a policy of targeting the money supply. What advice would you give and how would you justify the advice?

12. Imagine you were called in by the government to advise on whether it should attempt to prevent cyclical fluctuations by the use of fiscal policy. What advice would you give and how would you justify the advice?

13. Is there a compromise between purely discretionary policy and adhering to strict targets?

14. Under what circumstances would adherence to inflation targets lead to (a) more stable interest rates, (b) less stable interest rates than pursuing discretionary demand management policy?

15. Why might market-orientated supply-side policies have undesirable side-effects on aggregate demand?

16. If supply-side measures led to a 'shake-out' of labour and a resulting reduction in overstaffing, but also a resulting rightward shift in the Phillips curve, would you judge the policy a success?

17. What types of tax cut are likely to create the greatest (a) incentives, (b) disincentives to effort?

18. In what ways can interventionist supply-side policy work *with* the market, rather than against it? What are the arguments for and against such a policy?

Additional case studies on the *Essentials of Economics* MyEconLab (www.pearsoned.co.uk/sloman)

10.1 **The national debt.** This explores the question of whether it matters if a country has a high national debt.

10.2 **Fine-tuning in 1959 and 1960.** This looks at two Budgets in the era of Keynesian 'fine-tuning'.

10.3 **Trends in public expenditure.** This case examines attempts to control public expenditure in the UK and relates them to the crowding-out debate.

10.4 **The crowding-out effect.** The circumstances in which an increase in public expenditure can replace private expenditure.

10.5 **Injections against the contagion.** The use of discretionary fiscal policy in the late 1990s.

10.6 **Discretionary fiscal policy in Japan.** How the Japanese government used fiscal policy on various occasions throughout the 1990s and early 2000s in an attempt to bring the economy out of recession.

10.7 **Central banking and monetary policy in the USA.** This case examines how the Fed conducts monetary policy.

10.8 **Monetary policy in the eurozone.** This is a more detailed examination of the role of monetary policy and the ECB than that contained in Box 10.4.

10.9 **Effective monetary policy versus banking efficiency and stability.** This case examines potential conflicts between banking stability, efficiency and the effective operation of monetary policy.

10.10 **Should central banks be independent of government?** An examination of the arguments for and against independent central banks.

10.11 **Goodhart's law.** An examination of the difficulty of controlling aggregate demand by setting targets for the money supply.

10.12 **Monetary targeting: its use around the world.** An expanded version of Box 10.5.

10.13 **Managing the macroeconomy.** This considers whether there have been conflicts of objectives in recent UK macroeconomic policy.

10.14 **Controlling inflation in the past.** This case study looks at the history of prices and incomes policies in the UK.

10.15 **UK industrial performance.** This examines why the UK has had a poorer investment record than many other industrial countries and why it has suffered a process of 'deindustrialisation'.

10.16 **The supply-side revolution in the USA.** 'Reaganomics' and the birth of radical-right supply-side policy in the USA.

10.17 **Assessing PFI.** Has this been the perfect solution to funding investment for the public sector without raising taxes?

10.18 **Alternative approaches to training and education.** This compares the approaches to training and education – a crucial element in supply-side policy – in the UK, France, Germany and the USA.

10.19 **Assistance to small firms in the UK.** An examination of current government measures to assist small firms.

10.20 **Small-firm policy in the EU.** This looks at the range of support available to small and medium-sized firms in the EU.

10.21 **Welfare to work.** An examination of the policy of the UK Labour government whereby welfare payments are designed to encourage people into employment.

Sections of chapter covered in *WinEcon* – Sloman, *Essentials of Economics*

Essentials of Economics section	*WinEcon* section
10.1	10.1
10.2	10.2
10.3	–
10.4	–

Websites relevant to this chapter

Numbers and sections refer to websites listed in the Web Appendix and hotlinked from MyEconLab. Visit:

www.pearsoned.co.uk/sloman

- For news articles relevant to this chapter, see the *Economics News Articles* link from MyEconLab.
- For general news on national economies, the international economy and fiscal policy, see websites in section A, and particularly A1–5. See also links to newspapers worldwide in A38, 43 and 44, and the news search feature in Google at A41. See also links to economics news video and audio in A42.
- For data on economic growth, employment and the business cycle, see links in B1 or 2; also see B4 and 12. For UK data, see B3 and 34. For EU data, see G1 > *The Statistical Annex*. For US data, see *Current economic indicators* in B5 and the *Data* section of B17. For international data, see B15, 21, 24, 31, 33. For links to data sets, see B28; I14.
- For information on the development of ideas, see C12, 18; see also links under *Methodology and History of Economic Thought* in C14; and links to economists in I4 and 17. See also sites I7 and 11 > *Economic Systems and Theories* > *History of Economic Thought*.
- For a model of the economy (based on the Treasury model), see *The Virtual Economy* (site D1). In addition to the model, where you can devise your own Budget, there are worksheets and outlines of theories and the work of famous economists.
- For information on UK fiscal policy and government borrowing, see sites E30, 36, F2. See also sites A1–8 at Budget time. For fiscal policy in the eurozone, see *Public Finances in EMU* in H1.
- Sites I7 and 11 contain links to fiscal policy: go to *Macroeconomics* > *Macroeconomic Policy* > *Taxes and Taxation*.
- For monetary policy in the UK, see F1 and E30. For monetary policy in the eurozone, see F6 and 5. For monetary policy in the USA, see F8. For monetary policy in other countries, see the respective central bank site in section F.
- For links to sites on money and monetary policy, see the *Financial Economics* sections in I4, 7, 11, 17.
- For demand-side policy in the UK, see the latest Budget Report (e.g. section on maintaining macro-economic stability) at site E30.
- For inflation targeting in the UK and eurozone see sites F1 and 6.
- For the current approach to UK supply-side policy, see the latest Budget Report (e.g. sections on productivity and training) at site E30. See also sites E5 and 9.
- For support for a market-orientated approach to supply-side policy see C17.
- For information on training in the UK and Europe, see sites D7, E5, G5, 14; and E34.
- For information on the support for small business in the UK see site E38.
- For student resources relevant to this chapter, see sites C1–7, 9, 10, 19. See also '2nd floor – economic policy' in site D1. Also see sites D10 (*The Virtual Chancellor*) and D11 (*The Virtual Bank of Biz/ed*). See also the *Labour market reforms* simulation in D3.

Web Appendix

10.1 *ISLM analysis of fiscal and monetary policy.* This appendix uses the *ISLM* model to show the effects of fiscal and monetary policy on national income according to various assumptions about the *IS* and *LM* curves. (For an explanation of *ISLM* analysis, see Web Appendix 8.2

PART THREE

The Microeconomic Environment

Chapter 8
The Market System

The market system

Chris Britton

As part of their normal production activity, businesses are involved in buying (inputs – like labour and raw materials) and selling (outputs – the finished product). Buying and selling take place in markets and although there are many different types of market the basic analysis remains the same.

Learning outcomes

Having read this chapter you should be able to:

- explain the working of the market system
- apply the theory to the real world
- demonstrate the importance of key concepts like elasticity to business
- discuss the wider economic effects of changes in market forces

Key terms

Buyers' market	Equilibrium quantity	Market system
Complements	Excess demand	Normal goods
Cross-price elasticity	Excess supply	Price ceiling
Demand	Factor market	Price controls
Demand curve	Free market	Price elasticity
Effective demand	Income elasticity	Price floor
Effective supply	Inelasticity	Product market
Elasticity	Inferior goods	Sellers' market
Elasticity of demand	'Law of demand'	Substitutes
Elasticity of supply	'Law of supply'	Supply
Equilibrium price	Market	Supply curve

Introduction

As indicated in Chapter 5, the market system is an economy in which all of the basic economic choices are made through the market. The **market** is a place where buyers and sellers of a product are brought together. The nature and location of the market depends on the product. For example, within your local town there is likely to be a vegetable market where you would go to buy vegetables. Here, buyers and sellers meet face to face in the same location, but this is not always the case. The market for used cars might be the local newspaper classified section; the sale of stocks and shares passes through a broker so that the buyer never meets the seller. There are many different types of market, involving different buyers and sellers. Firms sell the goods and services they produce to households on the **product markets**, while in the **factor markets** firms are buying resources such as labour and raw materials. The discussion in this chapter will concentrate on the product markets but much of the analysis could also be applied to the factor markets.

A **free market** system is one in which the basic economic choices are made through the market, without any intervention by the government. In reality, markets are not completely free; governments intervene in markets for many reasons and in many different ways (see Chapter 17), but in this chapter such intervention will be ignored.

The market mechanism

In every market there will be a buyer and a seller, and somehow they have to be brought together so that a sale can take place. The market mechanism is the way in which this takes place in a market economy. In the product market, the buyer is the household and the seller is the firm. In economic language the household **demands** the good or service and the firm **supplies** the good or service. Each of these will be considered separately first and then brought together.

Demand

The quantity demanded refers to the quantity of a good or service that households are willing and able to purchase at a particular price. This definition shows that it is **effective demand** that is important; although many people would like to own a Rolls-Royce they could not afford it and so their demand is not effective on the market. The demand for a good or service depends on a number of factors, the most important of which are:

- the price of the good;
- the prices of other goods;
- disposable income; and
- tastes.

Table 14.1 The demand for 'Real Brew' draught beer

Price (£ per pint)	Quantity demanded (000s of pints/week)
0.90	83
1.00	70
1.10	58
1.20	48
1.30	40
1.40	35
1.50	32

To begin with, the relationship between quantity demanded and price will be looked at, assuming that the other factors above remain the same. This assumption will be relaxed in the subsequent analysis.

Table 14.1 shows what happens to the quantity demanded of beer as the price per pint goes up. Note that demand is measured over some period of time. The information is then presented in a graphical form in Figure 14.1; the line joining the various combinations of price and quantity demanded is called a **demand curve**. The demand curve shows that if all of the other factors which influence demand are constant then as price goes up, quantity demanded goes down. This is commonly referred to as **the law of demand**. What happens when price rises is that some individuals will cut down their consumption of beer and others may switch to other types of beer. There are some goods where this relationship might not hold:[1] for example, in the stock market where a rise in share prices might lead to the expectation of further price rises and therefore an increase in demand on the part of those wishing to make a capital gain. However, these exceptions are rare and it is therefore safe to assume that the law of demand holds.

If the price of beer changes, there is a movement along the demand curve. For example, if the price of beer goes up from 90p a pint to £1.00 a pint, the quantity demanded goes down from 83 000 pints per week to 70 000 pints per week. In drawing the demand curve the assumption was made that other factors affecting demand are constant. If this assumption is relaxed, what happens to the demand curve?

Figure 14.1 A demand curve for 'Real Brew' draught beer

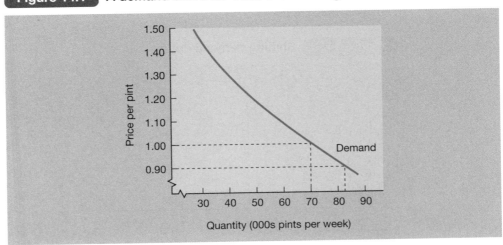

Price of other goods

The quantity of beer consumed will be affected by the prices of other goods. These other goods are likely to be **substitutes** or **complements**. A substitute for beer may be lager, and if the price of lager goes down, some individuals may switch from beer to lager; thus the demand for beer goes down. What happens to the demand curve is that at all price levels, the demand for beer is now lower. Thus the demand curve shifts to the left, indicating that at £1.00 per pint only 60 000 pints of beer are demanded per week. If the price of a substitute goes up, there will be an increase in the demand for beer. The demand curve moves to the right. These movements are shown in Figure 14.2. The closer the goods are as substitutes and the greater the change in the price of the substitute, the greater will be the shift in the demand curve.

A complementary good is one which tends to be consumed with another good. For beer, it is possible that individuals eat crisps or smoke cigarettes at the same time as drinking beer. The relationship is the opposite of that for substitutes. If the price of a complement goes up, individuals might be less likely to drink beer, and demand will fall. The demand curve moves to the left. If the price of a complement goes down, the demand for beer will rise. Again the closer the goods are as complements, and the greater the price change of that complement, the greater will be the shift in the demand curve.

Disposable income

Changes in disposable income will clearly affect demand. If the economy moves into recession, then retail sales and the housing market might suffer. As incomes increase once the economy recovers, then such sectors will pick up again. Higher incomes will lead to increased consumption of most goods. If your income is boosted, how will this affect your consumption? You might buy more textbooks, and probably spend more money on leisure activities and clothes. Most students might also drink an extra pint of beer per week. Thus an increase in disposable income will lead to an increase in demand for these goods, indicated by a rightward shift in the demand curve. As incomes fall the demand for these goods will fall, indicated by a leftward shift in the demand curve. These types of goods are called **normal goods**.

Figure 14.2 Shifting demand curves

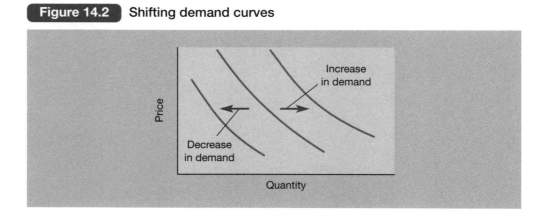

There are goods, however, that experience a fall in demand as a result of income increases. These goods are called **inferior goods**. A good example is hard toilet paper; as individuals become richer, they are likely to substitute more expensive soft toilet paper, and thus the demand for hard toilet paper will fall.

Tastes

Taste includes attitudes and preferences of consumers, and will be affected by such things as fashion, and advertising campaigns by producers or by governments. For example, a successful advertising campaign by the government pointing out the effects of smoking would cause tastes to change and demand for cigarettes to fall.

The demand curve, then, is downward sloping, indicating that as the price of the good rises the quantity demanded by households falls, shown by a *movement along the demand curve*. Changes in the other determining factors lead to *movements of the demand curve*.

Supply

The other side of the market is the supply side. In the market for goods and services it is the firm that is the supplier. The quantity supplied of a good is defined as the quantity that firms are willing and able to supply to the market at a particular price. Again notice the wording of the definition is such that it only includes **effective supply** and, as with demand, it is measured over a specific time period.

The quantity supplied to the market depends on a number of factors, the most important of which are:

● the price of the good;
● the prices of other goods;
● the prices of the resources used to produce the good;
● technology;
● expectations; and
● number of suppliers.

In the same way as for demand, all factors other than price will be assumed to be constant and the relationship between quantity supplied and price will be considered first.

Table 14.2 provides some information on price and quantity supplied of beer. The same information is represented graphically in Figure 14.3; the line joining the points together is called the **supply curve**. The upwards-sloping curve illustrates **the law of supply**. This states that, as the price of a good rises, the quantity that firms are willing to supply also rises. This is because if costs are constant as we have assumed, then higher prices must mean higher profits to the firm.

Note that there is no supply at a price below 90p per pint; this is the minimum price required by the producer to produce the beer. If the price per pint changes there is a movement along the supply curve in the same way as for demand. If any of the other factors listed above change there will be a movement of the supply curve.

Table 14.2 The supply of 'Real Brew' draught beer

Price (£ per pint)	Quantity supplied (000s of units/week)
0.90	0
1.00	35
1.10	43
1.20	48
1.30	55
1.40	60
1.50	68

Other prices

The supply of one good can be influenced by the price of another. For example, if the brewery in which Real Brew beer is brewed is also producing lager, then an increase in the price of lager (with the price of beer remaining the same) will encourage the firm to produce less beer and more lager, as lager is now more profitable to produce. The supply curve for beer would shift to the left, indicating that at every possible price, less is now supplied than before. If the price of lager fell, the supply of beer would increase. This is shown by a rightward shift of the supply curve. The size of the shift would depend upon the degree to which the goods could be substituted for each other in production, and the size of the price change. These shifts are illustrated in Figure 14.4.

Goods can also be complements in their production process; for example, beef and leather hides. An increase in the price of beef would increase not only the supply of beef but also the supply of hides. There would be a corresponding shift in the supply curve for hides.

Figure 14.3 The supply of 'Real Brew' draught beer

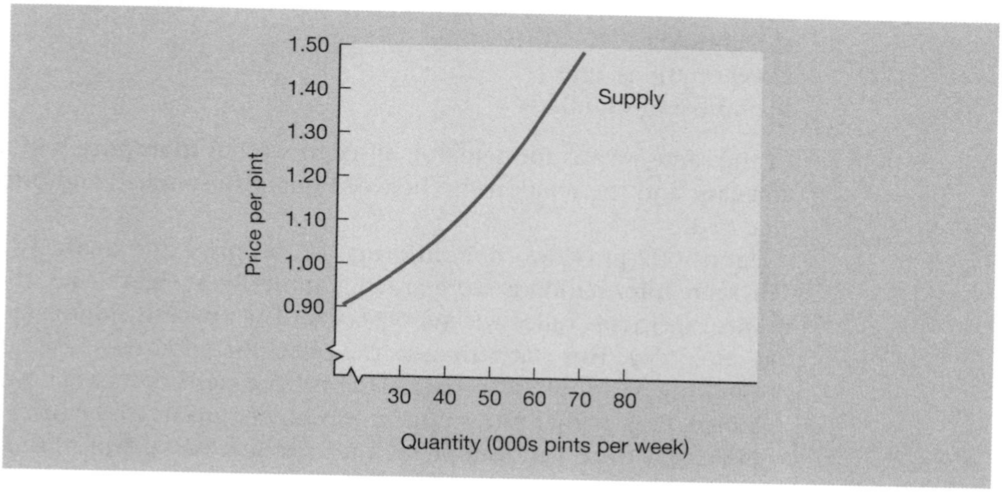

Figure 14.4   Shifting supply curves

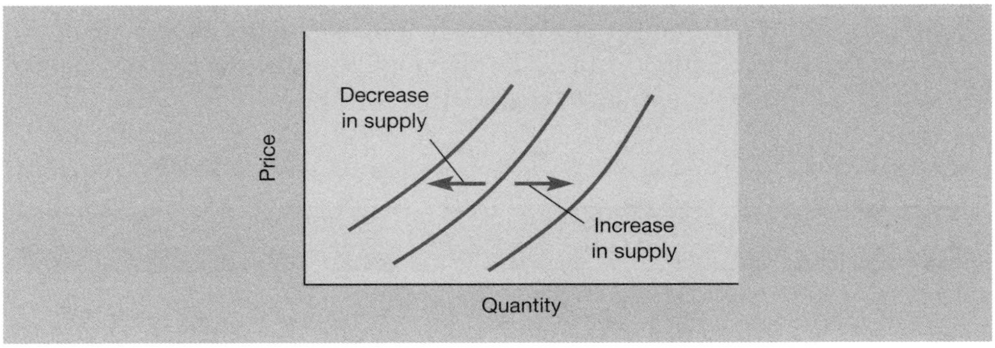

The prices of the resources used in the production of the good

If any of the costs of production (wages, rent, rate of interest, and so on) increased, then the profitability of that good at each price would fall and there would be a tendency for supply to be reduced. The supply curve would move to the left. If costs of production fell there would be an increase in supply and a rightward movement of the supply curve. The extent of the shift depends upon the size of the price change, the significance of that factor in production, and the degree to which the factor could be substituted for another factor.

Technology

As illustrated in Chapter 7, technical development in all aspects of production has led to great improvements in output per worker. Such improvements generally result in either more being produced with the same resources, or the same being produced with fewer. In most cases it would also lead to a substitution of one factor of production for another. For example, car production becomes less labour intensive as robotic techniques take over. Even such a product as traditional British beer has benefited from significant technical improvements in production. The effect of such advances would result in increased supply at each price level and hence a movement of the supply curve to the right.

Business expectations

Expectations play a crucial role in the decision making of firms. Good expectations of the future would encourage firms to invest in new plant and machinery, which would increase their productive potential. Chancellors of the Exchequer are occasionally accused of trying to 'talk the economy up': that is, they may paint a rosy picture of the current and future state of the economy in the hope that this will enhance business expectations, and help pull the economy out of recession. If business does become increasingly confident, or perhaps more inclined to take risks, then this would shift the supply curve to the right. The reverse would shift it to the left.

The number of suppliers

As the number of suppliers in a market increases the supply will rise; the supply curve shifts to the right. If suppliers leave the market, supply will fall and the supply curve moves to the left.

Price determination

The market is the place where buyers and sellers meet and where demand and supply are brought together. The information on demand and supply is combined in Table 14.3 and presented graphically in Figure 14.5.

Table 14.3 The supply and demand for 'Real Brew' draught beer

Price (£ per pint)	Quantity demanded (000s/wk)	Quantity supplied (000s/wk)
0.90	83	0
1.00	70	35
1.10	58	43
1.20	48	48
1.30	40	55
1.40	35	60
1.50	32	68

The equilibrium price

At a price of £1.20, the quantity demanded is the same as the quantity supplied at 48 000 pints per week. At this price the amount that consumers wish to buy is the

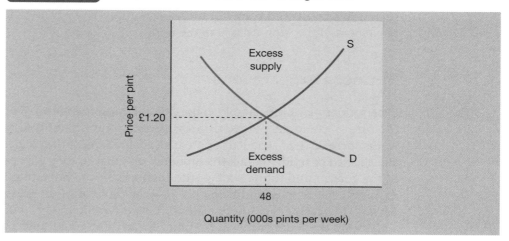

Figure 14.5   The market for 'Real Brew' draught beer

same as the amount that producers wish to sell. This price is called the **equilibrium price** and the quantity being bought and sold is called the **equilibrium quantity**. The point of equilibrium can be seen on the diagram at the point where the demand and supply curves cross.

At price levels above £1.20 the quantity that producers wish to supply is greater than the quantity consumers wish to buy. There is **excess supply** and the market is a 'buyers' market'. At prices less than £1.20 consumers wish to buy more than producers wish to supply. There is **excess demand** and the market is a **sellers' market**.

In competitive markets, situations of excess demand or supply should not exist for long as forces are put into motion to move the market towards equilibrium. For example, if the price level is £1.30 per pint, there is excess supply and producers will be forced to reduce the price in order to sell their beer. Consumers may be aware that they are in a **buyers' market** and offer lower prices, which firms might accept. For one or both of these reasons, there will be a tendency for prices to be pushed back towards the equilibrium price. The opposite occurs at prices below equilibrium and price is pushed upwards towards equilibrium.

Shifts in demand and supply

So long as the demand and supply curves in any market remain stationary, the equilibrium price should be maintained. However, there are numerous factors that could shift either or both of these curves. If this were to happen, then the old equilibrium would be destroyed and the market should work to a new equilibrium. How does this happen?

In Figure 14.6 the original equilibrium price for Real Brew draught beer is P_1. Assume that the demand curve moves from D_1 to D_2. This increase in demand could be due to a variety of factors already mentioned. For example, the price of a rival drink may have increased; disposable income could have risen; or sales may have benefited from a successful advertising campaign. In any event, at the old equilibrium price there now exists an excess of demand over supply of Q_1Q_3. It is likely that price will be bid upwards in order to ration the shortage in supply. As

Figure 14.6   A shift in the demand curve

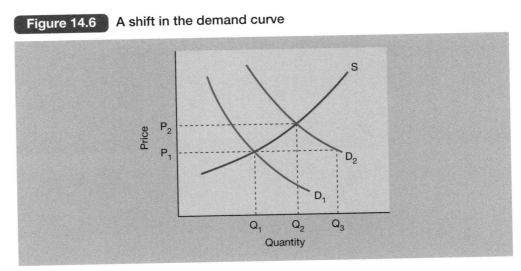

price rises, demand is choked off and supply exhausted. Eventually, there is a movement to a new equilibrium of P_2. At this new price both supply and demand at Q_2 are higher than they were at the previous equilibrium. If, alternatively, the demand curve had shifted to the left, then the process would have been reversed and the new equilibrium would have been at a level of demand and supply less than Q_1, with a price below P_1. Illustrate this process diagrammatically for yourself.

In Figure 14.7 there is a shift in the supply curve from S_1 to S_2. Refer back in this chapter to envisage specific reasons for such a shift. At the original equilibrium price of P_1 there would now be an excess supply over demand of Q_1Q_3. Price would therefore fall in a free market. As it does, demand will be encouraged and supply diminished. Eventually there will be a new equilibrium at P_2 with a higher quantity demanded and supplied than at the previous equilibrium. If the supply curve had instead shifted to the left, then market forces would have resulted in a lower quantity supplied and demanded than before. Once again, illustrate this diagrammatically for yourself.

The analysis so far has been relatively straightforward; it has been assumed that either the demand or the supply curve moves alone. However, it is likely that in any given time period both curves could move in any direction and perhaps even more than once.

Given the many factors that may shift both the demand and the supply curves, it is easy to imagine that markets can be in a constant state of flux. Just as the market is moving towards a new equilibrium, some other factor may change, necessitating an adjustment in an opposite direction. Given that such adjustment is not immediate, and that market conditions are constantly changing, it may be the case that equilibrium is never actually attained. It is even possible that the very process of market adjustment can be destabilising.[2] The constant movement of price implied by the analysis may also be detrimental to business. The firm might prefer to keep price constant in the face of minor changes in demand and supply.

Figure 14.7 A shift in the supply curve

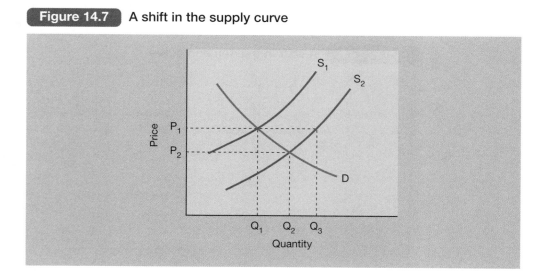

mini case   The price of gold

Gold as a commodity has always had a particular historical economic importance and its price is very volatile. Over 84 per cent of the gold mined each year goes into the production of jewellery, but it is the role of gold as a store of wealth that gives it such volatility. Until the 1970s the US, the UK and many other countries pegged their currencies to the value of gold – 'the gold standard'. As a result, central banks kept stocks of gold, as well as other currencies, which gives gold increased importance as a commodity.

The price of gold has been increasing since 2001 to hit $1000 per ounce in March 2008. By June the price had fallen to $880 per ounce. Explanations for these movements in gold prices can be found in the theory of demand and supply.

Supply factors

First, as a natural resource, the supply of gold is inelastic; it is mined in over 60 countries but the amount mined is small and getting smaller each year. This means that the supply curve will be inelastic (see below) – SS in Figure 14.8. Any changes in demand will have a bigger impact upon price than if the supply curve was elastic. Draw a more elastic supply curve in Figure 14.8 and see what impact that has on price.

Once the gold standard had been rejected by countries, their central banks started to sell off some of their stocks of gold; this led to increases in market supply and therefore falls in the price of gold. You should be able to draw this on a demand and supply diagram.

Demand factors

The increase in the price of gold that took place between 2001 and 2008 has mainly been down to demand factors:
- there has been higher demand for gold from oil-producing countries such as Russia and Qatar, which do not wish to hold the surpluses they have accumulated in dollars (from exporting oil), which by 2008 was a weakened currency;

- an increasingly wealthy Chinese population has been buying gold as a store of wealth;
- western pension funds have also been very active in the closed exchanges where they can buy 'shares' in gold bars.

The effect of increasing demand is shown in Figure 14.8. Increases in demand from D_1 to D_2 to D_3 cause price to increase fairly sharply.

Figure 14.8   The market for gold

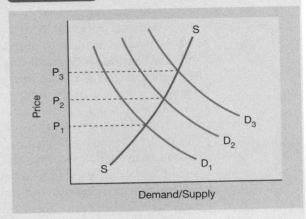

At the time of writing, the price of gold had already fallen from its peak of $1000 per ounce and the main reason for this was the stabilising of the US$. It is clear that the forces of demand and supply are very evident in the market for gold and the supply characteristics make its price more susceptible to changes in demand. This may change in the future as deep-sea mining equipment should go into action in 2010, and if gold is found in significant quantities, the supply of gold will become more elastic. Shocks to the global financial system (e.g. the global financial crisis in 2007/8) also affect the price of gold as investors look for 'safe havens' for their money. Historically, gold has been seen as one such safe haven.

Price controls

Governments occasionally take the view that a particular equilibrium price is politically, socially or economically unacceptable. In such circumstances, one course of action is the imposition of **price controls**. This involves the institutional setting of prices at either above or below the true market equilibrium. For example, if it was felt that the equilibrium price of a good was too high, then the government might try to impose a lower price on the market. This would now be the maximum acceptable price or **price ceiling**. Price may not rise above this ceiling. Alternatively, the equilibrium price could be seen as too low. In this case, a higher price, or **price floor** is imposed, below which price should not fall.

Figure 14.9 illustrates the market for a basic foodstuff. Imagine that it is wartime and the disruption has shifted the supply curve to the left. This could be largely due to a movement of resources away from the production of this good and towards munitions. The free market price at P_1 is seen to be unacceptably high relative to the pre-war price, and the decision is made to impose a price ceiling of P_2. It is hoped that such a ceiling will alleviate the problems of consumers who could not afford the free market price. The problem now is that at the price ceiling only Q_3 units will be supplied, whereas demand is for Q_2. The volume of output Q_3Q_2 therefore represents an excess of demand over supply. Many customers are frustrated in their desire to purchase that good. To help bring order to the situation, a system of rationing might be introduced. This could allocate the limited output between the many customers in a more orderly fashion than 'first come, first served'. For example, one unit could be allocated per person and priority could be given to the old and the sick. This does not solve the problem of excess demand. It is commonly found in such situations that illegal trading starts to emerge at a price above the ceiling. To obtain the good many would be willing to pay a higher price. This is commonly referred to as black market trading.

Figure 14.10 illustrates the market for a specific type of labour. The downward-sloping demand curve indicates that, at lower wages, employers will wish to take on additional workers. The supply curve shows how more people will offer themselves for work as wage rates increase. At the intersection of the curves, the market

Figure 14.9   Imposition of a price ceiling

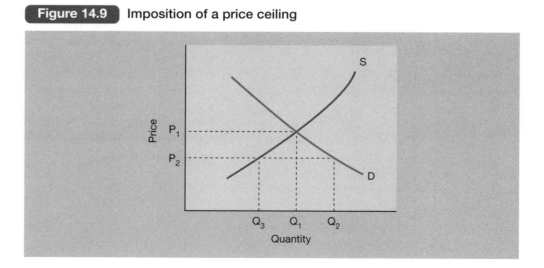

Figure 14.10 Imposition of a price floor

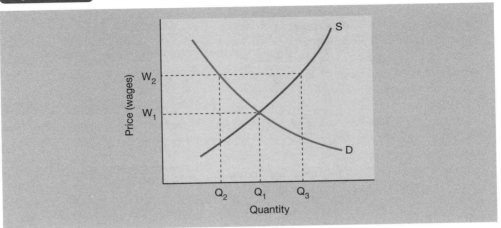

is in equilibrium. Imagine that this equilibrium wage is seen to be too low, and the authorities seek to impose a minimum wage of W_2. Employers are not permitted to pay any less than this amount. It is hoped that the policy will improve the welfare of workers by raising their living standards to some acceptable level.

At this minimum wage, employment becomes more attractive, and Q_3 persons seek employment. On the other hand, employers only wish to take on Q_2 workers. There is now a situation of excess supply. Only Q_2 find work, the remainder Q_2Q_3 are unsuccessful. The policy has actually reduced the level of employment from Q_1 to Q_2. In such a situation, there will be a temptation to flout the legislation. For example, unscrupulous employers observing the ranks of unemployed would realise that many would willingly work at less than the minimum wage.

The above examples illustrate the problems that arise once price is imposed away from its equilibrium. Further examples of such price controls would include the guaranteed minimum prices to farmers within the Common Agricultural Policy (CAP) of the European Union (see case study at the end of Chapter 12 of the previous edition of this book), and various post-war attempts to control the cost of rented accommodation at a price affordable to the low paid. The former has been associated with overproduction and the need to control the mountains of excess supply, while the latter tended to result in landlords taking their properties off the rental market in order to seek more profitable returns. The success of such policies requires careful control and monitoring. In many circumstances, it might be better to consider alternative ways of achieving the policy goals.

mini case   What can be done about rising food prices?

Rising world food prices (see case study at the end of the chapter) have implications for the whole world, but especially for poorer countries where incomes are low and the demand for food is high; 2008 has seen food riots in countries from Mexico to Pakistan to Burkina Faso. Even consumers in the USA have seen the rationing of rice in supermarkets. What can governments do? Demand and supply diagrams can be used to analyse some of the possibilities.

1 Price controls

One possibility is the introduction of a maximum price ceiling below the equilibrium price – at P in Figure 14.11.This has been done in India for a number of years on a range of goods and several Far Eastern countries on petrol. In 2008 the Chinese government has frozen the price of certain essential goods. There are two main problems with the use of price ceilings. First, as described in the text, there is now excess demand at the enforced price level and no incentive for more to be produced so this may lead to greater food shortages.

Figure 14.11 Price ceiling

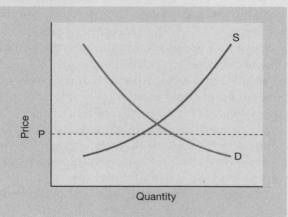

Second, this type of price control is expensive and cannot be maintained in the long run. For example, it is estimated that the cost of the price ceiling on petrol in Malaysia is 10 per cent of government spending.

2 Rationing

In the face of food shortages, one possibility is that rationing will take place so that individuals will only be allowed a certain quantity of the product in question. This would be more equitable than a first-come, first-served basis for distribution or black market trading where the rich have more market power than the poor. The problem with food markets is that they are not free markets; there are trading blocs and trading rules which prevent an equitable distribution of food worldwide.

3 Subsidies

Farmers could be paid subsidies to increase their production of foodstuffs. These are shown in Figure 14.12.

Figure 14.12 Payment of subsidies

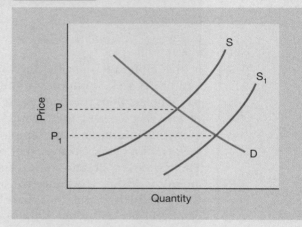

The payment of a subsidy to a producer is like the opposite of a tax – it means that the costs of production are lower so that supply can be increased. The supply curve moves from S to S_1 and price falls. This overcomes the first problem with price controls – the lack of incentive to increase production. The use of demand and supply diagrams show how problems with the market mechanism can be addressed in theory. The problem is that we live in the real world and the solutions to the food crisis are more likely to be political rather than economic. For example, will the west turn away from the use of biofuels? Will trade policies be changed so that the worldwide distribution of food can be more equitable?

Elasticity of demand

It has been shown that as long as other factors affecting demand remain constant, a decrease in price would be expected to increase the quantity demanded by consumers. This knowledge is obviously of importance to business, in that it implies that sales will expand as the good becomes more price competitive. It does not, however, say anything about the degree to which sales might increase. As prices change, will demand change by a large or a small amount? At the end of the day, will the extra sales bring in more or less total revenue? In short, a measure is needed of the responsiveness of demand to price changes. In the same way the responsiveness of quantity demanded to other factors like income or other prices can also be measured. It is also important to be aware of the responsiveness of supply to changes in prices. All of these are measured by the concept of **elasticity**.

Price elasticity of demand

Figure 14.13 illustrates two different-shaped demand curves and shows the effect of a price increase from 40p to 60p in each case. On the left-hand diagram, the increase in price causes demand to fall from 25 to 20 units. Total revenue received by the producer (i.e. price multiplied by the number of units sold) changes from £10.00 (40p × 25 units) to £12.00 (60p × 20 units). As illustrated, the area A represents the gain in revenue as a result of the price change, while B shows the loss of revenue. In this case there is a clear net gain. The reason for this is that the significance of the price rise is greater than the fall in demand. Compare this with the right-hand diagram. The same price rise now causes total revenue to fall from £20.00 (40p × 50 units) to £6.00 (60p × 10 units). The loss of revenue, area B^1, is clearly greater than the gain in revenue, area A^1. There is a net loss of revenue. This is a situation where the decrease in demand is of greater significance than the increase in price.

The traditional way of measuring the responsiveness of demand to a change in price is via the concept of **price elasticity**, the formula being:

$$\text{Price elasticity of demand (Ep)} = \frac{\text{Percentage change in quantity demanded}}{\text{Percentage change in price}}$$

$$Ep = \frac{\% \text{ change QD}}{\% \text{ change P}}$$

The significance of this formula lies in whether the value of price elasticity is greater or less than 1. If it is greater, then the percentage change in quantity demanded is greater than the percentage change in price. Demand is referred to as being relatively **elastic**, or responsive to price changes. If, on the other hand, the percentage change in quantity demanded is less than the percentage change in price, then price elasticity will be less than 1. Demand is now referred to as being relatively **inelastic**, and demand is not very responsive to price changes.

The higher or lower the value of price elasticity, the greater or lesser the responsiveness of demand to the price change. Table 14.4 demonstrates the connection between price elasticity and total revenue. It will be observed that if price elasticity is greater than 1, then there is a negative relationship between price changes and total revenue. For example, an increase in price results in a decrease in total revenue. Whereas, if elasticity is less than 1, then there is a positive relationship.

Table 14.4 Elasticity and total revenue

Elasticity	Price change	Change in total revenue
Elastic	Upward	Downward
	Downward	Upward
Inelastic	Upward	Upward
	Downward	Downward

Calculating elasticity

From the information portrayed in Figure 14.13, in the left-hand diagram price rose from 40p to 60p and demand fell from 25 to 20 units; thus:

$$Ep = \frac{\% \text{ change QD}}{\% \text{ change P}} = \frac{5/25 \times 100}{20/40 \times 100} = \frac{20\%}{50\%} = 0.4$$

This shows that demand is inelastic. One problem with this measurement is that if you measured elasticity when price fell from 60p to 40p the answer would be different:

$$Ep = \frac{\% \text{ change in QD}}{\% \text{ change in P}} = \frac{5/20 \times 100}{20/60 \times 100} = \frac{25\%}{33.3\%} = 0.75$$

The reason for this variation is that the percentage change in each case is being measured from a different base. When price rises from 20p to 40p, this is a 50 per cent rise. Yet when it falls from 60p to 40p this is only a 33.3 per cent fall. The value of elasticity therefore varies. To avoid this ambiguity, elasticity is measured as the percentage change from the average value of price and quantity before and after the change, that is:

$$\% \text{ change} = \frac{\text{Change in value} \times 100}{\text{Average value}}$$

Figure 14.13   Responsiveness of demand to a price change

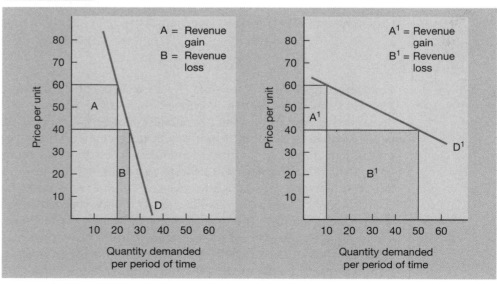

Quantity demanded per period of time

The value of elasticity for the price increase and decrease must now be identical:

$$Ep = \frac{\% \text{ change QD}}{\% \text{ change P}} = \frac{5/22.5 \times 100}{20/50 \times 100} = \frac{22.2\%}{40\%} = 0.55$$

The determinants of elasticity

There are a number of factors which determine how responsive quantity demanded is to price changes. First, the nature of the good and how it is viewed by consumers. A good which is a necessity will have a low value of elasticity, as an increase in price will not have a very big impact on the quantity consumed. Goods like cigarettes will have inelastic demand because they are habit forming. The tastes of consumers will be important: whether they view a television, for example, as a necessity or a luxury will determine the value of elasticity. Another factor is whether substitutes are available for the good or not. If there is no substitute for a particular good and the household wishes to continue to consume it, an increase in price will have little effect on the level of demand. Other factors include the importance of the good in the household's total expenditure. The smaller the proportion of the household's budget which is spent on a particular good, the smaller will be the effect on demand of any change in price.

Income elasticity of demand

Income elasticity of demand is a measure of the responsiveness of quantity demanded to changes in income. It can be negative in the case of inferior goods, where an increase in income leads to a fall in the demand for a good, or positive in the case of a normal good, where an increase in income leads to an increase in demand. There is also a difference between luxuries and necessities. Luxuries will have positive income elasticities with values over 1. This means that an increase in income will cause an increase in demand for that good and that a 1 per cent increase in income will cause a more than 1 per cent increase in demand. A necessity on the other hand will also have a positive income elasticity but its value will lie somewhere between 0 and 1, showing that an increase in income of 1 per cent causes an increase in demand by less than 1 per cent.

Income elasticity is calculated in a similar way to price elasticity except that it is income which is changing rather than the price of the good:

$$\text{Income elasticity} = \frac{\% \text{ change in quantity demanded}}{\% \text{ change in income}}$$

The effect of changes in income on the overall level of expenditure depends upon the type of the good being considered, as Table 14.5 shows.

Table 14.5 Income elasticity and total expenditure

Type of good	Income elasticity	Change in total expenditure brought about by an increase in income of 1%
Inferior	Negative	Downward
Normal	Positive	Upward
Luxury	Positive and above 1	Upward by more than 1%
Necessity	Positive between 0 and 1	Upward by less than 1%

Cross-price elasticity of demand

Cross-price elasticity of demand is a measure of how the demand for one good is affected by changes in the prices of other goods. It is calculated with the formula:

$$\frac{\text{Cross-price}}{\text{elasticity}} = \frac{\text{\% change in quantity demanded of good X}}{\text{\% change in the price of good Y}}$$

Like income elasticity it can be positive or negative depending this time upon the nature of the relationship between the goods. If the goods are substitutes for one another, as the price of Y goes up, the quantity demanded of X will also rise, as consumers substitute the relatively cheaper good (e.g. margarine for butter). Therefore cross-price elasticity will be positive. If the goods are complements, as the price of Y rises the demand for X will fall and cross-price elasticity will be a negative value. The size will depend upon how closely the goods are related, either as substitutes or complements.

Elasticity of supply

The concept of elasticity can be applied to supply as well as demand, and is a measurement of how responsive quantity supplied is to changes in the price of a good. Figure 14.14 illustrates two differently shaped supply curves and the effect of the same price change in each case.

Elasticity of supply is measured with the following formula:

$$\text{Elasticity of supply} = \frac{\text{\% change in quantity supplied}}{\text{\% change in price}}$$

The higher the numerical value, the more responsive is supply to changes in price.

The main determinants of the elasticity of supply for a good are the nature of the production process and the time-scale in question. It may well be easier to increase the supply of manufactured goods than agricultural goods, given the nature of the production processes involved. Even agricultural goods can be increased in supply, given time to replant stock, so supply is more responsive to price changes in the longer time period.

Figure 14.14   Responsiveness of supply to a price change

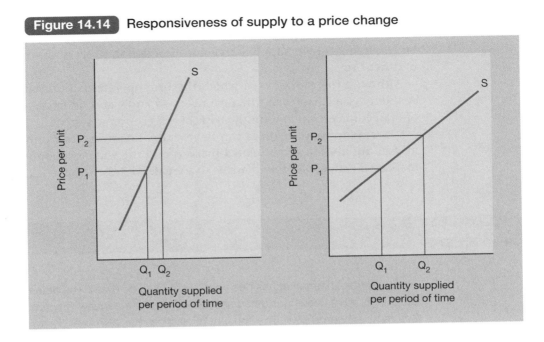

The importance of the market to business

All firms operate in markets, whether they are localised, national or international. Although firms might be able to influence the market conditions that face them, they need a knowledge of their own markets and how markets fit together in the market economy. Firms often have a range of products and they need to be aware of the differing conditions in each of their markets. They need a knowledge of the shape and position of the demand curve they face, including knowledge of the following aspects:

● The nature of the good they produce.
● The way in which it is viewed by consumers.
● The factors which affect the demand for their good.
● Any changes likely in the future which will affect the market.
● Any likely government intervention in the market.

Only through this information can the firm hope to retain markets, expand existing markets and move into new ones.

An understanding is also needed of the concept of elasticity of demand. Knowing how the demand for its product responds to changes in its price will help the firm in its pricing policy. Measures of income elasticity help the firm in forecasting the effects of changes in income on the demand for its products. Economic growth will affect markets with high income elasticities much more than markets with low income elasticities. This knowledge will also help the firm in developing its marketing strategy. For example, goods with low income elasticities could be marketed as 'economical', thus hopefully increasing the market share.

If the firm wishes to be successful in existing markets and to expand into new markets, as well as detailed knowledge of demand conditions, it also needs to know about its own supply curve and production process and the supply curves of other firms.

Although the economy in which the firm operates is not a totally free market economy (see Chapter 5), the firm needs to know and understand the importance of market forces which form the basis of our economic system.

Changes in market forces can have dramatic effects, not only on the affected market but also on other related markets and the wider economy. Changes in one market will affect all other markets to a greater or lesser degree.

Synopsis

In this chapter, the market has been examined in some detail. The determinants of demand and supply have been considered and the effects on the market of changes in any of these factors have been shown. The concept of elasticity has also been examined and calculated and the importance of all these issues to business has been demonstrated.

Summary of key points

- In a free market both the quantity being traded and the price of a product are determined by the forces of demand and supply.

- The demand for a good or service depends upon a number of factors, including price, the price of other goods, the income of consumers, tastes and so on.

- The supply of a good or service also depends upon a range of influences, including price, the costs of production, technology and the number of suppliers.

- Changes in demand and supply cause changes in the price of the product and the quantity being traded.

- Where demand and supply are equal, the market is said to be in equilibrium.

- Where this occurs, equilibrium price and quantity result.

- Intervention in the market mechanism can take the form of minimum or maximum prices, taxation or subsidy.

- Elasticity is a measure of the responsiveness of demand or supply to various factors, including price, income and the price of other goods.

- It is important for businesses to be aware of the demand and supply characteristics of the good or service they are producing.

case study   The international food crisis

2008 saw rapidly increasing food prices worldwide. The price of wheat rose 130 per cent in the year up to March 2008 and has risen threefold since 2000. The price of wheat jumped by 25 per cent in one day in February 2008. The cost of 1 tonne of Thai rice rose by 30 per cent in April 2008. The price rises are not confined to cereals; dairy and meat prices are also rising as feed costs of cattle rise. These price rises have important implications for many people – especially the poor, who are being priced out of the market. Demand and supply diagrams can be used to analyse the reasons for the price rises. They can also be used to consider the remedies. Reasons put forward are as follows.

1 Growing demand for food

It is estimated that the world's richest 20 per cent consumes 16 times more food than the world's poorest 20 per cent. The growing affluence of countries like India and China has led to a massive increase in the demand for foodstuffs. Added to this is the growth in the world population, estimated to rise from 6.6 billion in 2008 to 9.2 billion in 2050. These factors push the demand for food upwards.

The supply of foodstuffs is fairly inelastic (as it takes time to increase supply) so the supply curve in Figure 14.15 is shown as very steep (S). Increases in demand (D_1, D_2, D_3 etc.) push price upwards, the inelastic nature of supply makes this happen quicker.

2 Global warming

Many countries are experiencing adverse weather conditions which have contributed to a fall in the supply of many agricultural products. In Canada (the second largest wheat exporter in the world) drought is expected to reduce the harvest by a quarter in 2008. Australia (third largest producer) has been experiencing a drought for the last 5 years which has led to a fall in annual production of 25 million tonnes of grain in 2000 to 9.8 million in 2006.

Figure 14.16 demonstrates this effect. With demand constant, the falls in supply lead to increases in price. Of course, given the above discussion, demand is not constant and so the effects are intensified.

3 Palm oil and biofuel

The demand for palm oil is rising for two main reasons: because consumers are demanding more non-hydrogenated oil in foodstuffs; and, second, because palm oil can be used in biofuel and the demand for that is increasing. It is impossible for farmers to increase the production of palm oil as drought and flooding in the countries that produce palm oil have reduced the crop and it takes eight years for a palm oil tree to mature before supply can be increased. Whether supply should be increased at all is in dispute as the use of land for the production of palm oil reduces the amount of food that can be

Figure 14.15   Increased demand for food

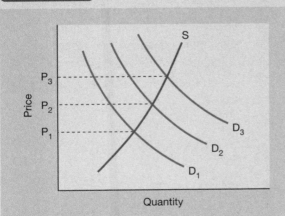

Figure 14.16   The effect of global warming

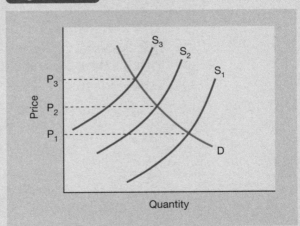

grown and Greenpeace argue that the carbon dioxide released by the deforestation that has taken place to plant palm oil trees is more than the savings in CO_2 from the use of biofuels. Land used for biofuel production is not being used for food production. It is estimated that the USA now devotes a third of its output of maize to car fuel. Figure 14.16 shows the impact of this on food prices.

All of these factors and more are impacting on the price of food at the same time, so the combined effect is even bigger and, at the time of writing, there is no indication of these problems abating. In the normal operation of the market mechanism, increasing prices indicate to the producers that resources should be switched to produce more in order to meet the excess demand. Given the factors

mentioned above, this is not likely to happen. This means that action needs to be taken by governments or supra-national organisations. Possible remedies can also be analysed using demand and supply diagrams, and this has been done in the second mini case study in this chapter.

Case study questions

1 What has happened in the market for food since the writing of this case study? Use demand and supply diagrams to analyse this.

2 A solution used by some grain exporters has been to restrict the export of grain in order to feed their own populations. How could you show this using a demand and supply diagram?

 web link   Information is available from *www.wfp.org* and *www.fao.org*

Review and discussion questions

1 Show the effects on the market for houses of the following:
   (a) a fall in income levels;
   (b) a rise in the rate of interest;
   (c) the lack of a 'feel good factor' in the economy.

2 Considering the market for CDs, show the effects of the following changes using demand and supply diagrams:
   (a) an increase in the number of people owning CD players;
   (b) a fall in the cost of producing CDs; and
   (c) a movement away from releasing music on LP and towards releasing music on CD.

3 Have the changes you predicted in your answers to questions 1 and 2 actually happened in the real world? If not, why not?

Assignments

1   You are a journalist on a local newspaper and have been asked to write an article on the current state of the housing market in your locality. You should identify factors which influence house prices in general and more specifically in your region. The following information from the Nationwide house price index may help (*www.nationwide.co.uk/hpi*).

Region	Average house prices, quarter 1, 2008	% change since quarter 4, 2007
East Anglia	£179 868	−2
East Midlands	£153 066	−1.3
London	£296 772	−2.3
North	£132 439	−0.6
North West	£154 124	−3.1
South East	£211 119	−1.6
South West	£196 711	−3.1
Scotland	£149 834	−0.9
Wales	£151 499	−2.2
West Midlands	£160 715	−2.5
Yorkshire and Humberside	£151 764	−1.9
UK	£179 363	−2.5

2   You work in the marketing department of a company that produces light bulbs. The company is considering increasing the price of its light bulbs by 20 per cent. At present a 100 watt light bulb costs 80p. The only information that is available is a study carried out in the previous year on the sensitivity of sales to price, the results of which are shown opposite:

Price	Sales (million)
80p	5800
100p	4000

Write a report for your manager on the likely effects of the proposed price increase, explaining the concept of elasticity of demand and the factors which are likely to affect it for this product.

Notes and references

1   In such cases the demand curve would be upward sloping, indicating that as price rises demand rises. Other examples include 'snob goods', which are consumed because of their price.

2   In the markets described in this chapter there is an automatic tendency for the market to move back towards equilibrium once it is disturbed. However, it is possible for the demand and supply curves to be so shaped that once the market is disturbed it tends to move away from equilibrium rather than towards it. This is called the cobweb model. The interested reader should look at R. Lipsey, *An Introduction to Positive Economics*, Weidenfeld & Nicolson, 1989.

Further reading

Begg, D., Fischer, S. and Dornbusch, R., *Economics*, 7th edition, McGraw-Hill, 2003.

Griffiths, A. and Wall, S., *Applied Economics: An Introductory Course*, 10th edition, Financial Times Prentice Hall, 2004.

Lipsey, R. and Chrystal, A., *Economics*, 10th edition, Oxford University Press, 2004.

Worthington, I., Britton, C., and Rees, A., *Economics for Business: Blending Theory and Practice*, 2nd edition, Financial Times/Prentice Hall, 2005.

Web links and further questions are available on the website at:
www.pearsoned.co.uk/worthington

Chapter 9
Markets, Demand and Supply

Markets, demand and supply

In this first half of the book we focus on microeconomics. Despite being 'small economics' – in other words, the economics of the individual parts of the economy, rather than the economy as a whole – it is still concerned with many of the big issues of today.

We will study why the pattern of production and consumption changes over time; why some people are rich and others poor; why our lives seem to be dominated by market forces beyond our control. We will look at the world of big business at one extreme and highly competitive markets at the other. We will look at many of the seemingly intractable problems we face: from the growing problem of pollution, to our limited power as consumers, to the widening inequality of incomes in society.

In this chapter, we examine how different economies of the world answer the key microeconomic questions of 'what to produce', 'how to produce' and 'for whom to produce'.

We start by looking at how economies would work if they were run totally by the government and did not rely on markets at all. We then look at the other extreme and consider economies that rely totally on the market. We will look at how markets work. We will examine what determines how much of any product gets produced and sold, and why some goods rise in price, whereas others fall. In the process we will be looking at one of the most important theories in the whole of economics: the theory of supply and demand.

After studying this chapter, you should be able to answer the following questions:

- How do different economic systems tackle the problem of scarcity?
- How do markets operate?
- What determines the amount that consumers buy of a product?
- What determines how much producers supply of a product?
- How are market prices determined and when are they likely to rise or fall?
- How do markets respond to changes in demand or supply?
- What are the major strengths and weaknesses of a free-market economy?

1.1 ECONOMIC SYSTEMS

How do countries differ in the way their economies are organised?

All societies are faced with the problem of scarcity. They differ considerably, however, in the way they tackle the problem. One important difference between societies is in the degree of government control of the economy.

At the one extreme lies the completely planned or command economy, where all the economic decisions are taken by the government.

At the other extreme lies the completely free-market economy. In this type of economy there is no government intervention at all. All decisions are taken by individuals and firms. Households decide how much labour and other factors to supply, and what goods to consume. Firms decide what goods to produce and what factors to employ. The pattern of production and consumption that results depends on the interactions of all these individual demand and supply decisions.

In practice, all economies are a mixture of the two. It is therefore the *degree* of government intervention that distinguishes different economic systems. Thus in the former communist countries of eastern Europe the government played a large role, whereas in the United States the government plays a much smaller role.

It is nevertheless useful to analyse the extremes in order to put the different mixed economies of the real world into perspective.

We start by having a brief look at the command economy. Then for the rest of this chapter we will see how a free-market economy operates. In subsequent chapters we will examine the various ways in which governments intervene in market economies: i.e. we will look at the various forms of mixed market economy.

The command economy

The command economy is usually associated with a socialist or communist economic system, where land and capital are collectively owned. The state plans the allocation of resources at three important levels:

- It plans the allocation of resources between current consumption and investment for the future. By sacrificing some present consumption and diverting resources into investment, it could increase the economy's growth rate. The amount of resources it chooses to devote to investment will depend on its broad macroeconomic strategy: the importance it attaches to growth as opposed to current consumption.

- At a microeconomic level it plans the output of each industry and firm, the techniques that will be used and the labour and other resources required by each industry and firm.

   In order to ensure that the required inputs are available, the state would probably conduct some form of input–output analysis. All industries are seen as users of *inputs* from other industries and as producers of *output* for consumers or other industries. For example, the steel industry uses inputs from the coal and iron-ore industries and produces output for the vehicle and construction industries. Input–output analysis shows, for each industry, the sources of all its inputs and the destination of all its output. By its use the state attempts to match up the inputs and outputs of each industry so that the planned demand for each industry's product is equal to its planned supply.

- It plans the distribution of output between consumers. This will depend on the government's aims. It may distribute goods according to its judgement of people's *needs*; or it may give more to those who produce more, thereby providing an *incentive* for people to work harder.

It may distribute goods and services directly (for example, by a system of rationing); or it may decide the distribution of money incomes and allow individuals to decide how to spend them. If it does the latter, it may still seek to influence the pattern of expenditure by setting appropriate prices: low prices to encourage consumption, and high prices to discourage consumption.

Assessment of the command economy

With central planning, the government could take an overall view of the economy. It could direct the nation's resources in accordance with specific national goals.

High growth rates could be achieved if the government directed large amounts of resources into investment. Unemployment could be largely avoided if the government carefully planned the allocation of labour in accordance with production requirements and labour skills. National income could be distributed more equally or in accordance with needs. The social repercussions of production and consumption (e.g. the effects on the environment) could be taken into account, provided the government was able to predict these effects and chose to take them into account.

In practice, a command economy could achieve these goals only at considerable social and economic cost. The reasons are as follows:

- The larger and more complex the economy, the greater the task of collecting and analysing the information essential to planning, and the more complex the plan. Complicated plans are likely to be costly to administer and involve cumbersome bureaucracy.
- If there is no system of prices, or if prices are set arbitrarily by the state, planning is likely to involve the inefficient use of resources. It is difficult to assess the relative efficiency of two alternative techniques that use different inputs, if there is no way in which the value of those inputs can be ascertained. For example, how can a rational decision be made between an oil-fired and a coal-fired furnace if the prices of oil and coal do not reflect their relative scarcity?
- It is difficult to devise appropriate incentives to encourage workers and managers to be more productive without a reduction in quality. For example, if bonuses are given according to the quantity of output produced, a factory might produce shoddy goods, since it can probably produce a larger quantity of goods by cutting quality. To avoid this problem, a large number of officials may have to be employed to check quality.
- Complete state control over resource allocation would involve a considerable loss of individual liberty. Workers would have no choice where to work; consumers would have no choice what to buy.
- The government might enforce its plans even if they were unpopular.
- If production is planned, but consumers are free to spend money incomes as they wish, then there will be a problem if the consumer wishes change. Shortages will occur if consumers decide to buy more, and surpluses will occur if they decide to buy less.

Most of these problems were experienced in the former USSR and the other Eastern bloc countries, and were part of the reason for the overthrow of their communist regimes (see Box 1.1).

> **Pause for thought**
>
> *Queues were a common feature of the former Soviet Union. Why do you think they were so commonplace? Is a system of queuing a fair way of allocating scarce goods and resources?*

Box 1.1

The rise and fall of planning in the former Soviet Union

When everything didn't go according to plan

Early years

The Bolsheviks under the leadership of Lenin came to power in Russia with the October revolution of 1917. The Bolsheviks, however, were opposed by the White Russians and civil war ensued.

During this period of *War Communism*, the market economy was abolished. Industry and shops were nationalised; workers were told what jobs to do; there were forced requisitions of food from peasants to feed the towns; the money economy collapsed as rampant inflation made money worthless; workers were allocated goods from distribution depots.

With the ending of the civil war in 1921, the economy was in bad shape. Lenin embarked on a *New Economic Policy*. This involved a return to the use of markets. Smaller businesses were returned to private hands, and peasants were able to sell their food rather than having it requisitioned. The economy began to recover.

Lenin died in 1924 and Stalin came to power.

The Stalinist system

The Soviet economy underwent a radical transformation from 1928 onwards. The key features of the Stalinist approach were collectivisation, industrialisation and central planning.

Collectivisation of agriculture

Peasant farms were abolished and replaced by large-scale collective farms where land was collectively owned and worked. Collectivisation initially caused massive disruption and famine, with peasants slaughtering their animals rather than giving them up to the collective. People died in their thousands. Despite an initial fall in output, more food

was provided for the towns, and many workers left the land to work in the new industries.

In addition to the collective farms, state farms were established. These were owned by the state and were run by managers appointed by the state. Workers were paid a wage rather than having a share in farm income.

Both collective and state farms were given quotas of output that they were supposed to deliver for which the state would pay a fixed price.

Industry and central planning

A massive drive to industrialisation took place. To achieve this a vast planning apparatus was developed. At the top was *Gosplan*, the central planning agency. This prepared five-year plans and annual plans.

The five-year plans specified the general direction in which the economy was to move. The annual plans gave the details of just what was to be produced and with what resources for some 200 or so key products. Other products were planned at a lower level – by various industrial ministries or regional authorities.

The effect was that all factories were given targets that had to be achieved. It was the task of the planning authorities to ensure that the targets were realistic: that there were sufficient resources to meet the targets. The system operated without the aid of the price mechanism and the profit motive. The main incentive was the bonus: bonuses were paid to managers and workers if targets were achieved.

In the early years, very high growth rates were achieved; but this was at a cost of low efficiency. The poor flow of information from firms to the planners led to many inconsistencies in the plans. The targets were often totally unrealistic, and as a result there

The free-market economy

Free decision making by individuals

The free-market economy is usually associated with a pure capitalist system, where land and capital are privately owned. All economic decisions are made by households and firms, which are assumed to act in their own self-interest. The following assumptions are usually made:

were frequent shortages and sometimes surpluses. With incentives purely geared to meeting targets, there was little product innovation and goods were frequently of poor quality and finish.

The limits of planning

Although most resources were allocated through planning, there were nevertheless some goods that were sold in markets. Any surpluses above their quota that were produced by collective farms could be sold in collective farm markets (street markets) in the towns. In addition, the workers on collective farms were allowed to own their own small private plots of land, and they too could sell their produce in the collective farm markets.

A large 'underground economy' flourished in which goods were sold on the black market and in which people did second 'unofficial' jobs (e.g. as plumbers, electricians or garment makers).

Gorbachev's reforms

Stalin died in 1953. The planning system, however, remained largely unchanged until the late 1980s.

During the 1970s growth had slowed down and by the time Mikhail Gorbachev came to power in 1985 many people were pressing for fundamental economic reforms. Gorbachev responded with his policy of *perestroika* (economic reconstruction), which among other things included the following:

- Making managers more involved in preparing their own plans rather than merely being given instructions.
- Insisting that firms cover their costs of production. If they could not, the state might refuse to bale them out and they could be declared bankrupt. The aim of this was to encourage firms to be more efficient.
- Improving the incentive system by making bonuses more related to genuine productivity. Workers had come to expect bonuses no matter how much or how little was produced.
- Organising workers into small teams or 'brigades' (typically of around 10–15 workers). Bonuses were then awarded to the whole brigade according to its productivity. The idea was to encourage people to work more effectively together.
- Stringent checks on quality by state officials and the rejection of substandard goods.
- Allowing one-person businesses and co-operatives (owned by the workers) to be set up.
- A greater willingness by the state to raise prices if there were substantial shortages.

These reforms, however, did not halt the economic decline. What is more, there was now an unhappy mix of planning and the market, with people unclear as to what to expect from the state. Many managers resented the extra responsibilities they were now expected to shoulder and many officials saw their jobs threatened. Queues lengthened in the shops and people became increasingly disillusioned with *perestroika*.

Following a failed coup in 1991, in which hard-line communists had attempted to reimpose greater state control, and with the consequent strengthening of the position of Boris Yeltsin, the Russian president and the main advocate of more radical reforms, both the Soviet Union and the system of central planning came to an end.

Russia embarked upon a radical programme of market reforms in which competition and enterprise were intended to replace state central planning (see Web Case 1.5).

- Firms seek to maximise profits.
- Consumers seek to get the best value for money from their purchases.
- Workers seek to maximise their wages relative to the human cost of working in a particular job.

It is also assumed that individuals are free to make their own economic choices; consumers are free to decide what to buy with their incomes; workers are free to choose where and how much to work; firms are free to choose what to sell and what production methods to use.

The resulting supply and demand decisions of firms and households are transmitted to each other through their effect on *prices*.

The price mechanism

The **price mechanism** works as follows. Prices respond to *shortages* and *surpluses*. Shortages cause prices to rise. Surpluses cause prices to fall.

If consumers decide they want more of a good (or if producers decide to cut back supply), demand will exceed supply. The resulting *shortage* will encourage sellers to *raise* the price of the good. This will act as an incentive for producers to supply more, since production will now be more profitable. At the same time, it will discourage consumers from buying so much. *The price will continue rising until the shortage has thereby been eliminated.*

If, on the other hand, consumers decide they want less of a good (or if producers decide to produce more), supply will exceed demand. The resulting *surplus* will encourage sellers to *reduce* the price of the good. This will act as a disincentive for producers, who will supply less, since production will now be less profitable. It will encourage consumers to buy more. *The price will continue falling until the surplus has thereby been eliminated.*

This price, where demand equals supply, is called the **equilibrium price**. By **equilibrium** we mean a point of balance or a point of rest: in other words, a point towards which there is a tendency to move.

The same analysis can be applied to factor markets. If the demand for a particular type of labour exceeds its supply, the resulting shortage will drive up the wage rate (i.e. the price of labour) as employers compete with each other for labour. The rise in the wage rate will have the effect of curbing firms' demand for that type of labour and encouraging more workers to take up that type of job. Wages will continue rising until demand equals supply: until the shortage is eliminated. Likewise if there is a surplus of a particular type of labour, the wage will fall until demand equals supply.

As with price, the wage rate where the demand for labour equals the supply is known as the *equilibrium* wage rate.

The response of demand and supply to changes in price illustrates a very important feature of how economies work:

> **People respond to incentives.** It is important, therefore, that incentives are appropriate and have the desired effect. This is another of our **Threshold Concepts**. For details, visit MyEconLab.

The effect of changes in demand and supply

How will the price mechanism respond to changes in consumer demand or producer supply? After all, the pattern of consumer demand changes. For example, people may decide they want more mountain bikes and fewer racers. Likewise the pattern of supply also changes. For example, changes in technology may allow the mass production of microchips at lower cost, while the production of hand-built furniture becomes relatively expensive.

In all cases of changes in demand and supply, the resulting changes in *price* act as both *signals* and *incentives*.

Definitions

The price mechanism
The system in a market economy whereby price changes that occur in response to changes in demand and supply have the effect of making demand equal to supply.

Equilibrium price
The price where the quantity demanded equals the quantity supplied: the price where there is no shortage or surplus.

Equilibrium
A position of balance. A position from which there is no inherent tendency to move away.

A change in demand. A rise in demand is signalled by a rise in price. This then acts as an incentive for firms to produce more of the good: the quantity supplied rises. Firms divert resources from goods with lower prices relative to costs (and hence lower profits) to those goods that are more profitable.

A fall in demand is signalled by a fall in price. This then acts as an incentive for firms to produce less: such goods are now less profitable to produce. Thus the quantity supplied falls.

A change in supply. A rise in supply is signalled by a fall in price. This then acts as an incentive for consumers to buy more: the quantity demanded rises. A fall in supply is signalled by a rise in price. This then acts as an incentive for consumers to buy less: the quantity demanded falls.

> ***Changes in demand or supply cause markets to adjust.*** Whenever such changes occur, the resulting 'disequilibrium' will bring an automatic change in prices, thereby restoring equilibrium (i.e. a balance of demand and supply).

The interdependence of markets

The interdependence of goods and factor markets. A rise in demand for a good will raise its price and profitability. Firms will respond by supplying more. But to do this they will need more inputs. Thus the demand for the inputs will rise, which in turn will raise the price of the inputs. The suppliers of inputs will respond to this incentive by supplying more. This can be summarised as follows:

1. Goods market
   - Demand for the good rises.
   - This creates a shortage.
   - This causes the price of the good to rise.
   - This eliminates the shortage by choking off some of the demand and encouraging firms to produce more.
2. Factor market
   - The increased supply of the good causes an increase in the demand for factors of production (i.e. inputs) used in making it.
   - This causes a shortage of those inputs.
   - This causes their prices to rise.
   - This eliminates their shortage by choking off some of the demand and encouraging the suppliers of inputs to supply more.

Goods markets thus affect factor markets.

It is common in economics to summarise an argument like this by using symbols. It is a form of shorthand. Figure 1.1 summarises this particular sequence of events.

Interdependence exists in the other direction too: factor markets affect goods markets. For example, the discovery of raw materials will lower their price. This will lower the production costs of firms using these raw materials and increase the supply of the finished goods. The resulting surplus will lower the price of the good, which will encourage consumers to buy more.

The interdependence of different goods markets. A rise in the price of one good will encourage consumers to buy alternatives. This will drive up the price of alternatives. This in turn will encourage producers to supply more of the alternatives.

> **Pause for thought**
> *Summarise this last paragraph using symbols like those in Figure 1.1.*

Figure 1.1
The price mechanism:
the effect of a rise in
demand

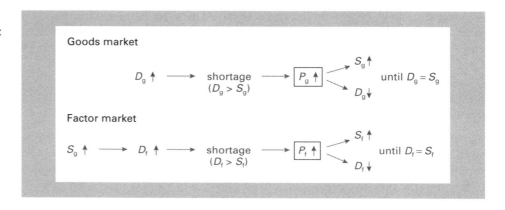

Interdependence and the public interest. Even though all individuals are merely looking to their own self-interest in the free-market economy, they are in fact being
encouraged to respond to the wishes of others through the incentive of the price
mechanism. For example, if consumers want more of a product, firms will supply
more – not out of the goodness of their hearts, but because it is profitable to do so.
It is often claimed that this is a major advantage of a free-market economy. We will
be examining this claim in subsequent chapters.

Competitive markets

For the rest of this chapter we will examine the working of the price mechanism in
more detail. We will look first at demand, then at supply, and then we will put the
two together to look at the determination of price.

The markets we will be examining are highly competitive markets, with many
firms competing against each other. In economics we call this **perfect competition**.
This is where consumers and producers are too numerous to have any control over
prices: they are **price takers**.

In the case of consumers, this means that they have to accept the prices as given
for the things that they buy. On most occasions this is true. For example, when
you get to the supermarket checkout you cannot start haggling with the checkout
operator over the price of a can of beans or a tub of margarine.

In the case of firms, perfect competition means that producers are too small and
face too much competition from other firms to be able to raise prices. Take the case
of farmers selling wheat. They have to sell it at the current market price. If individually they try to sell at a higher price, no one will buy, since purchasers of
wheat (e.g. flour millers) can get all the wheat they want at the market price.

Of course, many firms *do* have the power to choose their prices. This does not
mean that they can simply charge whatever they like. They will still have to take
account of overall consumer demand and their competitors' prices. Ford, when
setting the price of its Focus cars, will have to ensure that they remain competitive
with Astras, Golfs, 307s, etc. Nevertheless, most firms have some flexibility in
setting their prices: they have a degree of 'market power'.

If this is the case, then why do we study *perfect* markets, where firms are price
takers? One reason is that they provide a useful approximation to the real world
and give us many insights into how a market economy works. Many markets do
function very similarly to the markets we shall be describing.

Another is that perfect markets provide an ideal against which to compare the
real world. It is often argued that perfect markets benefit the consumer, whereas
markets dominated by big business may operate against the consumer's interests.
For example, the consumer may end up paying higher prices in a market dominated by just a few firms than in one operating under perfect competition.

Definitions

**Perfect competition
(preliminary definition)**
A situation where the
consumers and
producers of a product
are price takers. (There
are other features of a
perfectly competitive
market; these are
examined in Chapter 4.)

Price taker
A person or firm with
no power to be able to
influence the market
price.

Recap

1. The economic systems of different countries vary according to the extent to which they rely on the market or the government to allocate resources.

2. At the one extreme, in a command economy, the state makes all the economic decisions. It plans how many resources to allocate for present consumption and how many for investment for future output. It plans the output of each industry, the methods of production it will use and the amount of resources it will be allocated. It plans the distribution of output between consumers.

3. A command economy has the advantage of being able to address directly various national economic goals, such as rapid growth and the avoidance of unemployment and inequality. A command economy, however, is likely to be inefficient: a large bureaucracy will be needed to collect and process information; prices and the choice of production methods are likely to be arbitrary; incentives may be inappropriate; shortages and surpluses may result.

4. At the other extreme is the free-market economy. In this economy, decisions are made by the interaction of demand and supply. Price changes act as the mechanism whereby demand and supply are balanced. If there is a shortage of a product, its price will rise until the shortage is eliminated. If there is a surplus, its price will fall until that is eliminated.

5. For the rest of this chapter we will be studying perfect markets. These are markets where both producers and consumers are price takers.

DEMAND 1.2

How much will people buy of any item?

The relationship between demand and price

The headlines announce, 'Major crop failures in Brazil and East Africa: coffee prices soar.' Shortly afterwards you find that coffee prices have doubled in the shops. What do you do? Presumably you will cut back on the amount of coffee you drink. Perhaps you will reduce it from, say, six cups per day to two. Perhaps you will give up drinking coffee altogether.

This is simply an illustration of the general relationship between price and consumption: *when the price of a good rises, the quantity demanded will fall.* This relationship is known as the **law of demand**. There are two reasons for this law:

- People will feel poorer. They will not be able to afford to buy so much of the good with their money. The purchasing power of their income (their *real income*)[1] has fallen. This is called the **income effect** of a price rise.
- The good will now be dearer relative to other goods. People will thus switch to alternative or 'substitute' goods. This is called the **substitution effect** of a price rise.

Similarly, when the price of a good falls, the quantity demanded will rise. People can afford to buy more (the income effect), and they will switch away from consuming alternative goods (the substitution effect).

Therefore, returning to our example of the increase in the price of coffee, we will not be able to afford to buy as much as before, and we will probably drink more tea, cocoa, fruit juices or even water instead.

> ### Definitions
>
> **The law of demand**
> The quantity of a good demanded per period of time will fall as price rises and will rise as price falls, other things being equal.
>
> **Income effect**
> The effect of a change in price on quantity demanded arising from the consumer becoming better or worse off as a result of the price change.
>
> **Substitution effect**
> The effect of a change in price on quantity demanded arising from the consumer switching to or from alternative (substitute) products.

---

[1] 'Real income' is income measured in terms of its purchasing power: i.e. after taking price changes into account. Thus if prices doubled and your money income stayed the same, your real income would have halved. In other words, you would only be able to buy half as much as before with your income.

Table 1.1	The demand for potatoes (monthly)			
	Price (pence per kg) (1)	Tracey's demand (kg) (2)	Darren's demand (kg) (3)	Total market demand (tonnes: 000s) (4)
A	20	28	16	700
B	40	15	11	500
C	60	5	9	350
D	80	1	7	200
E	100	0	6	100

A word of warning: be careful about the meaning of the words **quantity demanded**. They refer to the amount consumers are willing and able to purchase at a given price over a given period (e.g. a week, or a month, or a year). They do *not* refer to what people would simply *like* to consume. You might like to own a luxury yacht, but your demand for luxury yachts will almost certainly be zero at the current price.

The demand curve

Consider the hypothetical data in Table 1.1. The table shows how many kilos of potatoes per month would be purchased at various prices.

Columns (2) and (3) show the **demand schedules** for two individuals, Tracey and Darren. Column (4), by contrast, shows the total **market demand schedule**. This is the total demand by all consumers. To obtain the market demand schedule for potatoes, we simply add up the quantities demanded at each price by *all* consumers: i.e. Tracey, Darren and everyone else who demands potatoes. Notice that we are talking about demand *over a period of time* (not at a *point* in time). Thus we would talk about daily demand, or weekly demand, or annual demand or whatever.

The demand schedule can be represented graphically as a **demand curve**. Figure 1.2 shows the market demand curve for potatoes corresponding to the schedule in Table 1.1. The price of potatoes is plotted on the vertical axis. The quantity demanded is plotted on the horizontal axis.

Point *E* shows that at a price of 100p per kilo, 100 000 tonnes of potatoes are demanded each month. When the price falls to 80p we move down the curve to point *D*. This shows that the quantity demanded has now risen to 200 000 tonnes per month. Similarly, if the price falls to 60p we move down the curve again to point *C*: 350 000 tonnes are now demanded. The five points on the graph (*A–E*) correspond to the figures in columns (1) and (4) of Table 1.1. The graph also enables us to read off the likely quantities demanded at prices other than those in the table.

A demand curve could also be drawn for an individual consumer. Like market demand curves, individuals' demand curves generally slope downwards from left to right: the lower the price of a product, the more is a person likely to buy.

Two points should be noted at this stage:

- In textbooks, demand curves (and other curves too) are only occasionally used to plot specific data. More frequently they are used to illustrate general theoretical arguments. In such cases, the axes will simply be price and quantity, with the units unspecified.
- The term demand 'curve' is used even when the graph is a straight line! In fact, when using demand curves to illustrate arguments we frequently draw them as straight lines – it's easier.

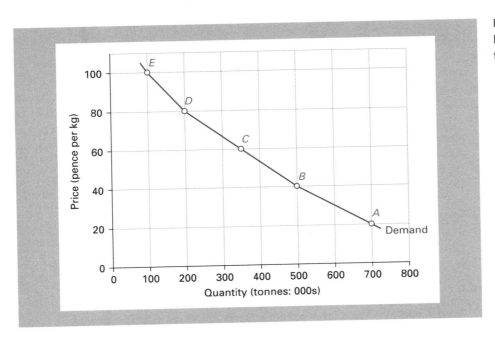

Figure 1.2
Market demand curve for potatoes (monthly)

Other determinants of demand

Price is not the only factor that determines how much of a good people will buy. Demand is also affected by the following:

Tastes. The more desirable people find the good, the more they will demand. Tastes are affected by advertising, by fashion, by observing other consumers, by considerations of health and by the experiences from consuming the good on previous occasions.

The number and price of substitute goods (i.e. competitive goods). The higher the price of substitute goods, the higher will be the demand for this good as people switch from the substitutes. For example, the demand for coffee will depend on the price of tea. If tea goes up in price, the demand for coffee will rise.

The number and price of complementary goods. **Complementary goods** are those that are consumed together: cars and petrol, shoes and polish, fish and chips. The higher the price of complementary goods, the fewer of them will be bought and hence the less will be the demand for this good. For example, the demand for electricity will depend on the price of electrical goods. If the price of electrical goods goes up, so that fewer are bought, the demand for electricity will fall.

Income. As people's incomes rise, their demand for most goods will rise. Such goods are called **normal goods**. There are exceptions to this general rule, however. As people get richer, they spend less on **inferior goods** such as cheap margarine, and switch to better-quality goods.

Distribution of income. If national income were redistributed from the poor to the rich, the demand for *luxury* goods would rise. At the same time, as the poor got poorer they might have to turn to buying inferior goods, whose demand would thus rise too.

Expectations of future price changes. If people think that prices are going to rise in the future, they are likely to buy more now before the price does go up.

To illustrate these six determinants, let us look at the demand for butter:

Definitions

Substitute goods
A pair of goods which are considered by consumers to be alternatives to each other. As the price of one goes up, the demand for the other rises.

Complementary goods
A pair of goods consumed together. As the price of one goes up, the demand for both goods will fall.

Normal good
A good whose demand rises as people's incomes rise.

Inferior good
A good whose demand falls as people's incomes rise.

- Tastes: if it is heavily advertised, demand is likely to rise. If, on the other hand, there is a cholesterol scare, people may demand less for health reasons.
- Substitutes: if the price of margarine goes up, the demand for butter is likely to rise as people switch from one to the other.
- Complements: if the price of bread goes up, people will buy less bread and hence less butter to spread it on.
- Income: if people's incomes rise, they may well turn to consuming butter rather than margarine, or feel that they can afford to spread butter more thickly on their bread.
- Income distribution: if income is redistributed away from the poor, they may have to give up consuming butter and buy cheaper margarine instead, or simply buy less butter and use it more sparingly.
- Expectations: if it is announced in the news that butter prices are expected to rise in the near future, people are likely to buy more now and stock up their freezers while current prices last.

Movements along and shifts in the demand curve

A demand curve is constructed on the assumption that 'other things remain equal' (sometimes known by the Latin term *ceteris paribus*). In other words, it is assumed that none of the determinants of demand, other than price, changes.[2] The effect of a change in price is then simply illustrated by a movement along the demand curve: for example, from point *B* to point *D* in Figure 1.2 when the price of potatoes rises from 40p to 80p per kilo.

What happens, then, when one of these other determinants does change? The answer is that we have to construct a whole new demand curve: the curve shifts. If a change in one of the other determinants causes demand to rise – say, income rises – the whole curve will shift to the right. This shows that at each price, more will be demanded than before. Thus in Figure 1.3 at a price of *P*, a quantity of Q_0 was

Figure 1.3
An increase in demand

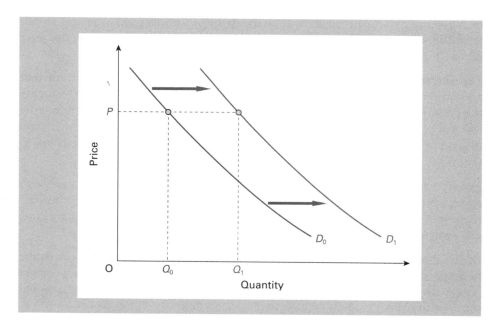

2 We make this assumption to keep the analysis simple at the outset. We can then drop the assumption by changing things one at a time and seeing what happens.

| Box 1.2 | Exploring Economics |

Getting satisfaction

The relationship between marginal utility and the demand curve

When you buy something, it's normally because you want it. You want it because you expect to get pleasure, satisfaction or some other sort of benefit from it. This applies to everything from chocolate bars, to bus journeys, to CDs, to jeans, to insurance. Economists use the term 'utility' to refer to the benefit we get from consumption.

Clearly, the nature and amount of utility that people get vary from one product to another, and from one person to another. But there is a simple rule that applies to virtually all people and all products. *As you consume more of a product, and thus become more satisfied, so your desire for additional units of it will decline.*

Economists call this rule the principle of diminishing marginal utility.

> **The principle of diminishing marginal utility.** The more of a product a person consumes over a given period of time, the less will be the additional utility gained from one more unit. **Key Idea 7**

For example, the second cup of tea in the morning gives you less additional satisfaction than the first cup. The third cup gives less still. We call the additional utility you get from consuming an extra unit of a product the marginal utility (*MU*). So the rule says that the marginal utility will fall as we consume more of a product over a given period of time.

There is a problem, however, with the concept of marginal utility. How can it be measured? After all, we cannot get inside each other's heads to find out just how much pleasure we are getting from consuming a product! One way round the problem is to measure marginal utility in money terms: in other words, the amount that a person would be prepared to pay for one more unit of a product. Thus if you were prepared to pay 30p for an extra packet of crisps per week, then we would say that your marginal utility from consuming it is 30p. As long as you are prepared to pay more or the same as the actual price, you will buy an extra packet. If you are not prepared to pay that price, you will not.

We can now see how this relates to a downward-sloping demand curve. As the price of a good falls, it will be worth buying extra units. You will buy more because the price will now be below the amount you are prepared to pay: i.e. price is less than your marginal utility. But as you buy more, your marginal utility from consuming each extra unit will get less and less. How many extra units do you buy? You will stop when the marginal utility has fallen to the new lower price of the good: when *MU = P*.

Marginal utility analysis is explored further in Web Appendix 1.1. An alternative approach to analysing demand, known as 'indifference analysis', is explored in Web Appendix 1.2.

> **?**
> 1. How will your marginal utility from the consumption of electricity be affected by the number of electrical appliances you own?
> 2. How will your marginal utility from the consumption of butter depend on the amount of margarine you consume?
> 3. If a good were free, what would your marginal utility be from consuming it?

TC2 p10

Definitions

Principle of diminishing marginal utility
As more units of a good are consumed, additional units will provide less additional satisfaction than previous units.

Marginal utility (*MU*)
The extra satisfaction gained from consuming one extra unit of a good within a given time period.

originally demanded. But now, after the increase in demand, Q_1 is demanded. (Note that D_1 is not necessarily parallel to D_0.)

If a change in a determinant other than price causes demand to fall, the whole curve will shift to the left.

To distinguish between shifts in and movements along demand curves, it is usual to distinguish between a change in *demand* and a change in the *quantity demanded*. A shift in demand is referred to as a **change in demand**, whereas a movement along the demand curve as a result of a change in price is referred to as a **change in the quantity demanded**.

Definitions

Change in demand
The term used for a shift in the demand curve. It occurs when a determinant of demand *other* than price changes.

Change in the quantity demanded
The term used for a movement along the demand curve to a new point. It occurs when there is a change in price.

Recap

1. When the price of a good rises, the quantity demanded per period of time will fall. This is known as the 'law of demand'. It applies both to individuals' demand and to the whole market demand.

2. The law of demand is explained by the income and substitution effects of a price change.

3. The relationship between price and quantity demanded per period of time can be shown in a table (or 'schedule') or as a graph. On the graph, price is plotted on the vertical axis and quantity demanded per period of time on the horizontal axis. The resulting demand curve is downward sloping (negatively sloped).

4. Other determinants of demand include tastes, the number and price of substitute goods, the number and price of complementary goods, income, the distribution of income and expectations of future price changes.

5. If price changes, the effect is shown by a movement along the demand curve. We call this effect 'a change in the quantity demanded'.

6. If any other determinant of demand changes, the whole curve will shift. We call this effect 'a change in demand'. A rightward shift represents an increase in demand; a leftward shift represents a decrease in demand.

1.3 SUPPLY

How much of any item will firms want to produce?

Supply and price

Imagine you are a farmer deciding what to do with your land. Part of your land is in a fertile valley. Part is on a hillside where the soil is poor. Perhaps, then, you will consider growing vegetables in the valley and keeping sheep on the hillside.

Your decision will largely depend on the price that various vegetables will fetch in the market and likewise the price you can expect to get from sheep and wool. As far as the valley is concerned, you will plant the vegetables that give the best return. If, for example, the price of potatoes is high, you will probably use a lot of the valley for growing potatoes. If the price gets higher, you may well use the whole of the valley, perhaps being prepared to run the risk of potato disease. If the price is very high indeed, you may even consider growing potatoes on the hillside, even though the yield per hectare is much lower there.

In other words, the higher the price of a particular crop, the more you are likely to grow in preference to other crops. This illustrates the general relationship between supply and price: *when the price of a good rises, the quantity supplied will also rise*. There are three reasons for this:

■ As firms supply more, they are likely to find that beyond a certain level of output costs rise more and more rapidly. Only if the price rises will it be worth producing more and incurring these higher costs.

In the case of the farm we have just considered, once potatoes have to be grown on the hillside, the costs of producing them will increase. Also, if the land has to be used more intensively, say by the use of more and more fertilisers, again the costs of producing extra potatoes are likely to rise quite rapidly. It is the same for manufacturers. Beyond a certain level of output, costs are likely to rise rapidly as workers have to be paid overtime and as machines approach capacity working. If higher output involves higher costs of production, producers will need to get a higher price if they are to be persuaded to produce extra output.

■ The higher the price of the good, the more profitable it becomes to produce. Firms will thus be encouraged to produce more of it by switching from the production of less profitable goods.

■ Given time, if the price of a good remains high, new producers will be encouraged to set up in production. Total market supply thus rises.

The first two determinants affect supply in the short run. The third affects supply in the long run. We distinguish between short-run and long-run supply in Chapter 2 (page 64).

The supply curve

The amount that producers would like to supply at various prices can be shown in a **supply schedule**. Table 1.2 shows a monthly supply schedule for potatoes, both for an individual farmer (farmer X) and for all farmers together (the whole market).

The supply schedule can be represented graphically as a **supply curve**. A supply curve may be an individual firm's supply curve or a market curve (i.e. that of the whole industry).

Figure 1.4 shows the *market* supply curve of potatoes. As with demand curves, price is plotted on the vertical axis and quantity on the horizontal axis. Each of the points *a–e* corresponds to a figure in Table 1.2. For example, a price rise from 60p per kilo to 80p per kilo will cause a movement along the supply curve from point *c* to point *d*: total market supply will rise from 350 000 tonnes per month to 530 000 tonnes per month.

Definitions
Supply schedule A table showing the different quantities of a good that producers are willing and able to supply at various prices over a given time period. A supply schedule can be for an individual producer or group of producers, or for all producers (the market supply schedule).
Supply curve A graph showing the relationship between the price of a good and the quantity of the good supplied over a specified period of time.

Table 1.2	The supply of potatoes (monthly)		
	Price of potatoes (pence per kg)	Farmer X's supply (tonnes)	Total market supply (tonnes: 000s)
a	20	50	100
b	40	70	200
c	60	100	350
d	80	120	530
e	100	130	700

Figure 1.4
Market supply curve of
potatoes (monthly)

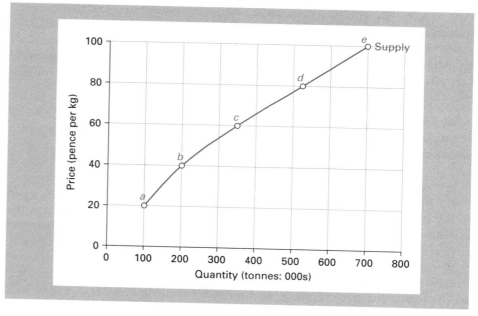

Not all supply curves will be upward sloping (positively sloped). Sometimes they will be vertical, or horizontal, or even downward sloping. This will depend largely on the time period over which firms' response to price changes is considered. This question is examined in Chapter 2 in the section on the elasticity of supply (Section 2.3) and in more detail in Chapters 3 and 4.

Other determinants of supply

Like demand, supply is not simply determined by price. The other determinants of supply are as follows:

The costs of production. The higher the costs of production, the less profit will be made at any price. As costs rise, firms will cut back on production, probably switching to alternative products whose costs have not risen so much.
    The main reasons for a change in costs are:

- Change in input prices: costs of production will rise if wages, raw material prices, rents, interest rates or any other input prices rise.
- Change in technology: technological advances can fundamentally alter the costs of production. Consider, for example, how the microchip revolution has changed production methods and information handling in virtually every industry in the world.
- Organisational changes: various cost savings can be made in many firms by re-organising production.
- Government policy: costs will be lowered by government subsidies and raised by various taxes.

Definition

Substitutes in supply
These are two goods where an increased production of one means diverting resources away from producing the other.

The profitability of alternative products (substitutes in supply). If some alternative product (a **substitute in supply**) becomes more profitable to supply than before, producers are likely to switch from the first good to this alternative. Supply of the first good falls. Other goods are likely to become more profitable if their prices rise or their costs of production fall. For example, if the price of carrots goes up, or the cost of producing carrots comes down, farmers may decide to produce more carrots. The supply of potatoes is therefore likely to fall.

The profitability of goods in joint supply. Sometimes when one good is produced, another good is also produced at the same time. These are said to be **goods in joint supply**. An example is the refining of crude oil to produce petrol. Other grade fuels will be produced as well, such as diesel and paraffin. If more petrol is produced, due to a rise in demand, then the supply of these other fuels will rise too.

> **Definition**
>
> **Goods in joint supply**
> These are two goods where the production of more of one leads to the production of more of the other.

Nature, 'random shocks' and other unpredictable events. In this category we would include the weather and diseases affecting farm output, wars affecting the supply of imported raw materials, the breakdown of machinery, industrial disputes, earthquakes, floods and fire, and so on.

The aims of producers. A profit-maximising firm will supply a different quantity from a firm that has a different aim, such as maximising sales. For most of the time we shall assume that firms are profit maximisers.

Expectations of future price changes. If price is expected to rise, producers may temporarily reduce the amount they sell. Instead they are likely to build up their stocks and release them on to the market only when the price does rise. At the same time they may plan to produce more, by installing new machines, or taking on more labour, so that they can be ready to supply more when the price has risen.

> **Pause for thought**
>
> *By reference to each of the above determinants of supply, identify what would cause (a) the supply of potatoes to fall and (b) the supply of leather to rise.*

The number of suppliers. If new firms enter the market, supply is likely to rise.

Movements along and shifts in the supply curve

The principle here is the same as with demand curves. The effect of a change in price is illustrated by a movement along the supply curve: for example, from point *d* to point *e* in Figure 1.4 when price rises from 80p to 100p. Quantity supplied rises from 530 000 to 700 000 tonnes per month.

If any other determinant of supply changes, the whole supply curve will shift. A rightward shift illustrates an increase in supply. A leftward shift illustrates a decrease in supply. Thus in Figure 1.5, if the original curve is S_0, the curve S_1 represents an

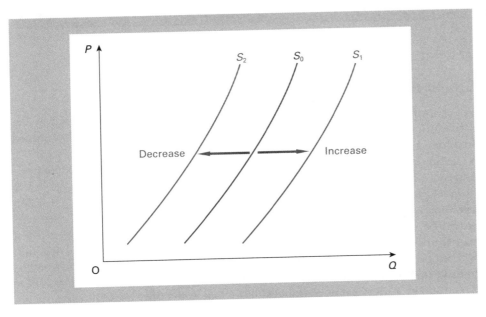

Figure 1.5
Shifts in the supply curve

increase in supply (more is supplied at each price), whereas the curve S_2 represents a decrease in supply (less is supplied at each price).

A movement along a supply curve is often referred to as a **change in the quantity supplied**, whereas a shift in the supply curve is simply referred to as a **change in supply**.

Definitions

Change in the quantity supplied
The term used for a movement along the supply curve to a new point. It occurs when there is a change in price.

Change in supply
The term used for a shift in the supply curve. It occurs when a determinant *other* than price changes.

Recap

1. When the price of a good rises, the quantity supplied per period of time will usually also rise. This applies both to individual producers' supply and to the whole market supply.

2. There are two reasons in the short run why a higher price encourages producers to supply more: (a) they are now willing to incur higher costs per unit associated with producing more; (b) they will switch to producing this product instead of now less profitable ones. In the long run there is a third reason: new producers will be attracted into the market.

3. The relationship between price and quantity supplied per period of time can be shown in a table (or schedule) or as a graph. As with a demand curve, price is plotted on the vertical axis and quantity per period of time on the horizontal axis. The resulting supply curve is upward sloping (positively sloped).

4. Other determinants of supply include the costs of production, the profitability of alternative products, the profitability of goods in joint supply, random shocks and expectations of future price changes.

5. If price changes, the effect is shown by a movement along the supply curve. We call this effect 'a change in the quantity supplied'.

6. If any determinant *other* than price changes, the effect is shown by a shift in the whole supply curve. We call this effect 'a change in supply'. A rightward shift represents an increase in supply; a leftward shift represents a decrease in supply.

1.4   THE DETERMINATION OF PRICE

How much of any item will actually be bought and sold and at what price?

Equilibrium price and output

We can now combine our analysis of demand and supply. This will show how the actual price of a product and the actual quantity bought and sold are determined in a free and competitive market.

Let us return to the example of the market demand and market supply of potatoes, and use the data from Tables 1.1 and 1.2. These figures are given again in Table 1.3.

What will be the price and output that actually prevail? If the price started at 20p per kilogram, demand would exceed supply by 600 000 tonnes (*A* – *a*). Consumers would be unable to obtain all they wanted and would thus be willing to pay a higher price. Producers, unable or unwilling to supply enough to meet the demand, will be only too happy to accept a higher price. The effect of the shortage, then, will be to drive up the price. The same would happen at a price of 40p per kilogram. There would still be a shortage; price would still rise. But as the price rises, the quantity demanded falls and the quantity supplied rises. The shortage is progressively eliminated.

Table 1.3	The market demand and supply of potatoes (monthly)	
Price of potatoes (pence per kg)	**Total market demand (tonnes: 000s)**	**Total market supply (tonnes: 000s)**
20	700 (A)	100 (a)
40	500 (B)	200 (b)
60	350 (C)	350 (c)
80	200 (D)	530 (d)
100	100 (E)	700 (e)

What would happen if the price started at a much higher level: say at 100p per kilogram? In this case supply would exceed demand by 600 000 tonnes (*e* – *E*). The effect of this surplus would be to drive the price down as farmers competed against each other to sell their excess supplies. The same would happen at a price of 80p per kilogram. There would still be a surplus; price would still fall.

In fact, only one price is sustainable. This is the price where demand equals supply: namely 60p per kilogram, where both demand and supply are 350 000 tonnes. When supply matches demand the market is said to **clear**. There is no shortage and no surplus.

As we saw on page 26, the price where demand equals supply is called the equilibrium price. Remember that by equilibrium we mean a point of balance or a point of rest: in other words, a point towards which there is a tendency to move. In Table 1.3, if the price starts at other than 60p per kilogram, there will be a tendency for it to move towards 60p. The equilibrium price is the only price at which producers' and consumers' wishes are mutually reconciled: where the producers' plans to supply exactly match the consumers' plans to buy.

> **Definition**
>
> **Market clearing**
> A market clears when supply matches demand, leaving no shortage or surplus.

> *Equilibrium is the point where conflicting interests are balanced.* Only at this point is the amount that demanders are willing to purchase the same as the amount that suppliers are willing to supply. It is a point which will be automatically reached in a free market through the operation of the price mechanism. This is another of our **Threshold Concepts**. For details, visit MyEconLab.
>
> **Key Idea 8**
> **TC 5**

Demand and supply curves

The determination of equilibrium price and output can be shown using demand and supply curves. Equilibrium is where the two curves intersect.

Figure 1.6 shows the demand and supply curves of potatoes corresponding to the data in Table 1.3. Equilibrium price is P_e (60p) and equilibrium quantity is Q_e (350 000 tonnes).

At any price above 60p, there would be a surplus. Thus at 80p there is a surplus of 330 000 tonnes (*d* – *D*). More is supplied than consumers are willing and able to purchase at that price. Thus a price of 80p fails to clear the market. Price will fall to the equilibrium price of 60p. As it does so, there will be a movement along the demand curve from point *D* to point *C*, and a movement along the supply curve from point *d* to point *c*.

At any price below 60p, there would be a shortage. Thus at 40p there is a shortage of 300 000 tonnes (*B* – *b*). Price will rise to 60p. This will cause a movement along the supply curve from point *b* to point *c* and along the demand curve from point *B* to point *C*.

Point *Cc* is the equilibrium: where demand equals supply.

KI 6
p27

Figure 1.6
The determination of
market equilibrium
(potatoes: monthly)

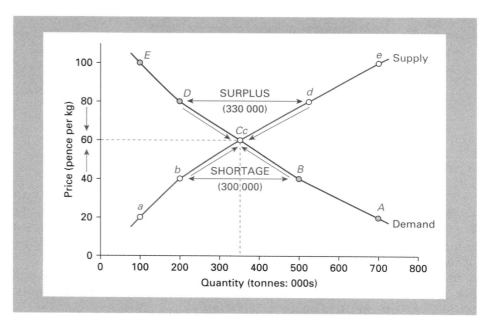

Movement to a new equilibrium

The equilibrium price will remain unchanged only so long as the demand and
supply curves remain unchanged. If either of the curves shifts, a new equilibrium
will be formed.

A change in demand

If one of the determinants of demand changes (other than price), the whole
demand curve will shift. This will lead to a movement along the supply curve to the
new intersection point.

For example, in Figure 1.7, if a rise in consumer incomes led to the demand curve
shifting to D_2, there would be a shortage of $h - g$ at the original price P_{e_1}. This would
cause price to rise to the new equilibrium P_{e_2}. As it did so, there would be a movement

Figure 1.7
Effect of a shift in the
demand curve

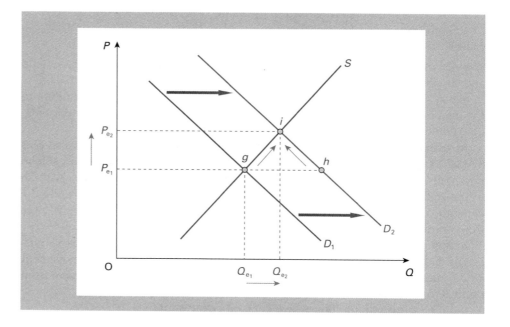

Figure 1.8
Effect of a shift in
the supply curve

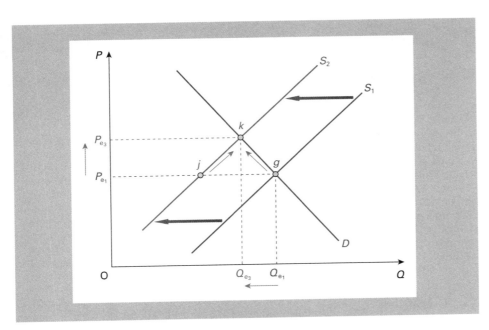

along the supply curve from point *g* to point *i*, and along the new demand curve
(D_2) from point *h* to point *i*. Equilibrium quantity would rise from Q_{e_1} to Q_{e_2}.

The effect of the shift in demand, therefore, has been a movement along the
supply curve from the old equilibrium to the new: from point *g* to point *i*.

A change in supply

Likewise, if one of the determinants of supply changes (other than price), the whole
supply curve will shift. This will lead to a movement *along* the *demand* curve to the
new intersection point.

For example, in Figure 1.8, if costs of production rose, the supply curve would
shift to the left: to S_2. There would be a shortage of *g* – *j* at the old price of P_{e_1}. Price
would rise from P_{e_1} to P_{e_3}. Quantity would fall from Q_{e_1} to Q_{e_3}. In
other words, there would be a movement along the demand
curve from point *g* to point *k*, and along the new supply
curve (S_2) from point *j* to point *k*.

To summarise: a shift in one curve leads to a movement along
the other curve to the new intersection point.

Sometimes a number of determinants might change. This
may lead to a shift in *both* curves. When this happens, equilibrium simply moves from the point where the old curves inter-
sected to the point where the new ones intersect.

> **Pause for thought**
>
> *Is the following statement true?*
> 'An increase in demand will cause an
> increase in price. This increase in price
> will cause a reduction in demand, until
> demand is reduced back to its original
> level.' Explain your answer and try
> using a demand and supply diagram
> to illustrate what is going on.

Recap

1. If the demand for a good exceeds the supply, there will be a shortage. This will lead to a rise in the price
   of the good.
2. If the supply of a good exceeds the demand, there will be a surplus. This will lead to a fall in the price.
3. Price will settle at the equilibrium. The equilibrium price is the one that clears the market: the price where
   demand equals supply.
4. If the demand or supply curve shifts, this will lead either to a shortage or to a surplus. Price will therefore
   either rise or fall until a new equilibrium is reached at the position where the supply and demand curves
   now intersect

Box 1.3

The UK housing market

The home-buyer's big dipper

If you are thinking of buying a house sometime in the future, then you may well follow the fortunes of the housing market with some trepidation. In the late 1980s there was a housing price explosion in the UK: in fact, between 1984 and 1989 house prices *doubled*. After several years of falling or gently rising house prices in the early and mid-1990s, there was another boom from 1996 to 2003, with house prices rising by 26 per cent per year at the peak (in the 12 months to January 2003). For many, owning a home of their own was becoming a mere dream.

House prices since the early 1980s

The diagram shows what happened to house prices in the period 1983 to 2003. The height of each bar measures the percentage by which average house prices rose in that particular year. You can see that house price inflation was very high in the late 1980s, reaching a peak of 23.3 per cent in 1988.

In their rush to buy a house before prices rose any further, many people in this period borrowed as much as they were able. Building societies and banks at that time had plenty of money to lend and were only too willing to do so. Many people, therefore, took out very large mortgages. In 1983 the average new mortgage was 2.08 times average annual earnings. By 1989 this figure had risen to 3.44.

After 1989 there followed a period of *falling* prices. From 1990 to 1995, house prices fell by 12.2 per cent. Many people now found themselves in a position of *negative equity*. This is the situation where the size of mortgage is greater than the value of the house. In other words, if they sold their house, they would end up still owing money! For this reason many people found that they could not move house.

Then in 1996, house prices began to recover and for the next three years rose moderately – by around 5 per cent per annum. But then they started rising rapidly again, and by 2002, house price inflation had returned to rates similar to those in the 1980s. Was this good news or bad news? For those who had been trapped in negative equity, it was good news. It was also good news for old people who wished to move into a retirement home and who had a house to sell. It was bad news for the first-time buyer, however! As we shall see in many parts of this book, what is good news for one person is often bad news for another.

The determinants of house prices

House prices are determined by demand and supply. If demand rises (i.e. shifts to the right) or if supply falls (i.e. shifts to the left), the equilibrium price of houses will rise. Similarly, if demand falls or supply rises, the equilibrium price will fall.

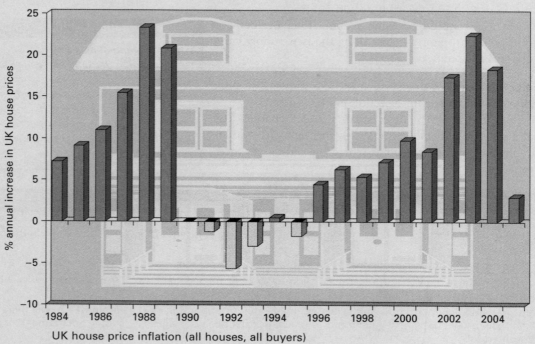

UK house price inflation (all houses, all buyers)

KI 6
p27

So why did house prices rise so rapidly in the 1980s, only to fall in the early 1990s and then rise rapidly again in the late 1990s and early 2000s? The answer lies primarily in changes in the *demand* for housing. Let us examine the various factors that affected the demand for houses.

Incomes (actual and anticipated). The second half of the 1980s was a period of rapidly rising incomes. The economy was experiencing an economic 'boom'. Many people wanted to spend their extra incomes on housing: either buying a house for the first time, or moving to a better one. What is more, many people thought that their incomes would continue to grow, and were thus prepared to stretch themselves financially in the short term by buying an expensive house, confident that their mortgage payments would become more and more affordable over time.

The early 1990s, by contrast, was a period of recession, with rising unemployment and much more slowly growing incomes. People had much less confidence about their ability to afford large mortgages. The mid-1990s onwards saw incomes rising again.

The desire for home ownership. Mrs Thatcher (Prime Minister from 1979 to 1991) put great emphasis on the virtues of home ownership: a home-owning democracy. Certainly, the mood of the age was that it was very desirable to own your own home. This fuelled the growth in demand in the 1980s.

The cost of mortgages. During the second half of the 1980s, mortgage interest rates were generally falling. This meant that people could afford larger mortgages, and thus afford to buy more expensive houses. In 1989, however, this trend was reversed. Mortgage interest rates were now rising. Many people found it difficult to maintain existing payments, let alone take on a larger mortgage. From 1996 to 2003 mortgage rates were generally reduced again, once more fuelling the demand for houses.

The availability of mortgages. In the late 1980s, mortgages were readily available. Banks and building societies were prepared to accept smaller deposits on houses, and to grant mortgages of $3\frac{1}{2}$ times a person's annual income, compared with $2\frac{1}{2}$ times in the early 1980s. In the early 1990s, however, banks and building societies were more cautious about granting mortgages. They were aware that, with falling house prices, rising unemployment and the growing problem of negative equity, there was an increased danger that borrowers would default on payments. With the recovery of the economy in the mid-1990s, however, and with a growing number of mortgage lenders, mortgages became more readily available and for greater amounts relative to people's income.

Speculation. In the 1980s, people generally believed that house prices would continue rising. This encouraged people to buy as soon as possible, and to take out the biggest mortgage possible, before prices went up any further. There was also an effect on supply. Those with houses to sell held back until the last possible moment in the hope of getting a higher price. The net effect was for a rightward shift in the demand curve for houses and a leftward shift in the supply curve. The effect of this speculation, therefore, was to help bring about the very effect that people were predicting (see Section 2.5).

In the early 1990s, the opposite occurred. People thinking of buying houses held back, hoping to buy at a lower price. People with houses to sell tried to sell as quickly as possible before prices fell any further. Again the effect of this speculation was to aggravate the change in prices – this time a fall in prices.

Then, in the late 1990s and early 2000s, the return of rapidly rising house prices encouraged people to buy more rapidly again, once more adding fuel to house price inflation. From 2001 to 2003 the speculation was compounded by worries about falling stock market prices (see Box 1.4). Many investors turned to buying property instead of shares.

What of the future?

By mid 2004, the boom in house prices seemed to be coming to an end. People were becoming increasingly worried about taking on large mortgage debt. And with house price inflation slowing down, speculation could go into reverse. It seemed unlikely that there would be a house price crash, however, with interest rates edging lower. Indeed, annual house price inflation bottomed out at just under 3 per cent in mid-2005 and by mid-2006 had risen to 5 per cent.

?

1. Draw supply and demand diagrams to illustrate what was happening to house prices (a) in the second half of the 1980s and the late 1990s and early 2000s; (b) in the early 1990s.
2. Are there any factors on the supply side that influence house prices?
3. Find out what has happened to house prices over the past two years. Attempt an explanation of what has happened.

Box 1.4

Stock market prices

Demand and supply in action

Firms that are quoted on the stock market (see Web Case 3.1) can raise money by issuing shares. These are sold on the 'primary stock market'. People who own the shares receive a 'dividend' on them, normally paid six-monthly. This varies with the profitability of the company.

People or institutions that buy these shares, however, may not wish to hold on to them for ever. This is where the 'secondary stock market' comes in. It is where existing shares are bought and sold. There are stock markets, primary and secondary, in all the major countries of the world.

There are more than 2700 companies whose shares are listed on the London Stock Exchange, and shares are traded each Monday to Friday (excluding Bank Holidays). The prices of shares depend on demand and supply. For example, if the demand for Tesco shares at any one time exceeds the supply on

offer, the price will rise until demand and supply are equal. Share prices fluctuate throughout the trading day and sometimes price changes can be substantial.

To give an overall impression of share price movements, stock exchanges publish share price indices. The best-known one in the UK is the FTSE 100, which stands for the 'Financial Times Stock Exchange' index of the 100 largest companies' shares. The index represents an average price of these 100 shares. The chart shows movements in the FTSE 100 from 1995 to 2006. The index was first calculated on 3 January 1984 with a base level of 1000 points. It reached a peak of 6930 points on 30 December 1999 and fell to 3287 on 12 March 2003.

But what causes share prices to change? Why were they so high in 1999, but under half that value just three years later? The answer lies in the determinants of the demand and supply of shares.

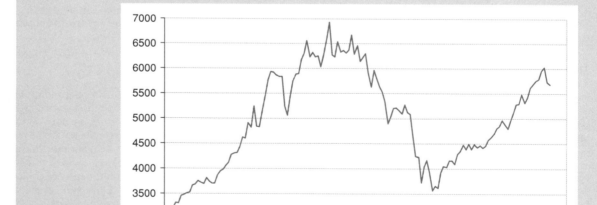

Financial Times Stock Exchange Index (FTSE) (3/1/1984 = 1000)

Demand

There are four main factors that affect the demand for shares.

The price of and/or return on substitutes. The main substitutes for shares in specific companies are other shares. Thus if, in comparison with other shares, Tesco shares are expected to pay high dividends relative to the share price, people will buy Tesco shares. As far as shares in general are concerned, the main substitutes are other forms of saving. Thus if the interest rate on savings accounts in banks and building societies fell, people with such accounts would be tempted to take their money out and buy shares instead.

Incomes. If the economy is growing rapidly and people's incomes are thus rising rapidly, they are likely to buy more shares. Thus in the mid-to-late 1990s, when UK incomes were rising at an average annual rate of over 3 per cent, share prices rose rapidly (see chart). As growth rates fell in the early 2000s, so share prices fell.

Wealth. 'Wealth' is people's accumulated savings and property. Wealth rose in the 1990s and many people used their increased wealth to buy shares.

Expectations. In the mid-to-late 1990s, people expected share prices to go on rising. They were optimistic about continued growth in the economy and that certain sectors, such as leisure and hightech industries, would grow particularly strongly. But as people bought shares, this pushed their prices up even more, thereby fuelling further speculation that they would go on rising and encouraging further share buying. In the early 2000s, by contrast, confidence was shaken. Most countries experienced a slowing down in economic growth, or even a recession (a fall in national output). This combined with other negative factors, such as the 11 September 2001 attack on the World Trade Center and various corporate scandals, such as the accounting fraud concerning the giant US company Enron, caused share prices to plummet. As people anticipated

further price falls, so they held back from buying, thereby pushing prices even lower.

Supply

The factors affecting supply are largely the same as those affecting demand, but in the opposite direction.

If the return on alternative forms of saving falls, people with shares are likely to hold on to them, as they represent a better form of saving. The supply of shares to the market will fall. If incomes or wealth rise, people again are likely to want to hold on to their shares. As far as expectations are concerned, if people believe that share prices will rise, they will hold on to the shares they have. Supply to the market will fall, thereby pushing up prices. If, however, they believe that prices will fall, they will sell their shares now before prices do fall. Supply will increase, driving down the price.

Share prices and business

Companies are crucially affected by their share price. If a company's share price falls, this is taken as a sign that 'the market' is losing confidence in the company. This will make it more difficult to raise finance, not only by issuing additional shares in the primary market, but also from banks. It will also make the company more vulnerable to a takeover bid. This is where one company seeks to buy out another by offering to buy all its shares. A takeover will succeed if the owners of more than half of the company's shares vote to accept the offered price. Shareholders are more likely to agree to the takeover if the company's shares have not being doing very well recently.

If the rate of economic growth in the economy is 3 per cent in a particular year, why are share prices likely to rise by more than 3 per cent that year?

1.5 THE FREE-MARKET ECONOMY

How well does it serve us?

Advantages of a free-market economy

The fact that a free-market economy functions automatically is one of its major advantages. There is no need for costly and complex bureaucracies to co-ordinate economic decisions. The economy can respond quickly to changing demand and supply conditions.

When markets are highly competitive, no one has great power. Competition between firms keeps prices down and acts as an incentive to firms to become more efficient. The more firms there are competing, the more responsive they will be to consumer wishes.

The more efficiently firms can combine their factors of production, the more profit they will make. The more efficiently workers work, the more secure will be their jobs and the higher their wages. The more carefully consumers decide what to buy, the greater the value for money they will receive.

Thus people pursuing their own self-interest through buying and selling in competitive markets helps to minimise the central economic problem of scarcity, by encouraging the efficient use of the nation's resources in line with consumer wishes. From this type of argument, the following conclusion is often drawn by defenders of the free market:

'The pursuit of private gain results in the social good.' This is obviously a highly significant claim and has profound moral implications (see Threshold Concepts 5 and 6).

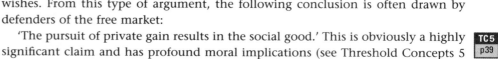

People gain from voluntary interaction. When people buy from or sell to other people, or when they are employed by or employ other people, both parties will gain from the interaction. This is the sixth of our **Threshold Concepts.**

Key Idea 9

TC 6

Problems with a free-market economy

In practice, however, markets do not achieve maximum efficiency in the allocation of scarce resources, and governments feel it necessary to intervene to rectify this and other problems of the free market. The problems of a free market are as follows:

■ Competition between firms is often limited. A few giant firms may dominate an industry. In these cases they may charge high prices and make large profits. Rather than merely responding to consumer wishes, they may attempt to persuade consumers by advertising. Consumers are particularly susceptible to advertisements for products that are unfamiliar to them.

■ Lack of competition and high profits may remove the incentive for firms to be efficient.

■ Power and property may be unequally distributed. Those who have power and/or property (e.g. big business, unions, landlords) will gain at the expense of those without power and property.

■ The practices of some firms may be socially undesirable or have adverse environmental consequences. For example, a chemical works may pollute the environment.

- Some socially desirable goods would simply not be produced by private enterprise. What firm would build and operate a lighthouse, unless it were paid for by the government?
- A free-market economy may lead to macroeconomic instability. There may be periods of recession with high unemployment and falling output, and other periods of rising prices.
- Finally, there is the ethical objection that a free-market economy, by rewarding self-interested behaviour, may encourage selfishness, greed, materialism and the acquisition or pursuit of power.

We shall be examining these various problems in more detail in later chapters.

The mixed economy

Because of the problems of both free-market and command economies, all real-world economies are a mixture of the two systems. The economies of the former communist bloc all used the market mechanism to some extent. All market economies involve some degree of government intervention.

> ***Government intervention may be able to rectify various failings of the market.*** Government intervention in the market can be used to achieve various economic objectives that may not be best achieved by the market. Governments are not perfect, however, and their actions may bring adverse as well as beneficial consequences.
>
> **Key Idea 10**
>
> **TC 7**

The fact that government intervention can, at least in principle, correct market failures is the seventh of our fifteen Threshold Concepts.

In mixed market economies, the government may control the following:

- **Relative prices** of goods and inputs, by taxing or subsidising them or by direct price controls.
- Relative incomes, by the use of income taxes, welfare payments or direct controls over wages, profits, rents, etc.
- The pattern of production and consumption, by the use of legislation (e.g. making it illegal to produce unsafe goods), by direct provision of goods and services (e.g. education and defence), by taxes and subsidies or by nationalisation.
- The macroeconomic problems of unemployment, inflation, lack of growth, balance of trade deficits and exchange rate fluctuations, by the use of taxes and government expenditure, the control of bank lending and interest rates, the direct control of prices, and the control of the foreign exchange rate.

> **Definition**
>
> **Relative price**
> The price of one good compared with another (e.g. good X is twice the price of good Y).

Just how the government intervenes, and what the effects of the various forms of intervention are, will be examined in detail in later chapters.

The relative merits of alternative mixtures of government and the market depend on the weight attached to various political and economic goals: goals such as liberty, equality, efficiency in production, the fulfilling of consumer wishes, economic growth and full employment. No one type of mixed market economy is likely to be superior in all respects.

> **Pause for thought**
>
> *Why do governments on the political right tend to intervene less in markets than governments on the political left? Does this mean that whether something is an economic 'problem' depends on your perspective?*

Box 1.5

The coffee crisis

An unfair bean count?

The cultivating, processing and retailing of coffee is a big industry. In the late 1990s and early 2000s the world supply of coffee rose relative to demand, causing a slump in the price. The graph below shows the trend in the average price of coffee (there are many varieties and prices) between 1996 and 2006. The price rose from $1.00 per lb in January 1996 to $1.80 per lb in July 1997. Subsequently it fell more or less continuously reaching around $44 in 2002.

In this period the supply of coffee increased by around 3.6 per cent a year, outstripping the 1.5 per cent annual increase in demand. The growth in supply was largely caused by new plantings in Vietnam and Brazil. In 2002 world demand was estimated to be around 106 million bags. Current supply was 113 million bags but world stocks of coffee stood at 40 million bags.

So in five years the price of coffee fell by some 75 per cent. Then why, you might ask, hasn't the

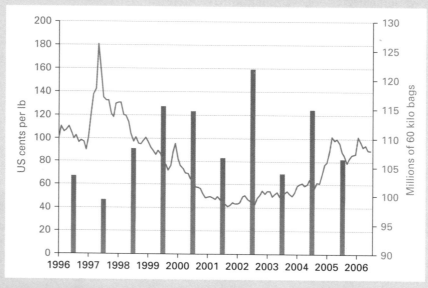

Coffee prices (average of all coffees) and output

Recap

1. A free-market economy functions automatically, and if there is plenty of competition between producers, this can help to protect consumers' interests.

2. In practice, however, competition may be limited; there may be great inequality; there may be adverse social and environmental consequences; there may be macroeconomic instability.

3. All real-world economies are some mixture of the market and government intervention. Governments intervene in market economies in various ways in order to correct the failings of the free market. The degree and form of government intervention depend on the aims of governments and the nature of the problems they are attempting to tackle.

price of a latte or an espresso in your local Dome Café or Starbucks also fallen? Because of the £1.50 or £2.00 you pay for a cup of coffee only a very small part – maybe 10p – is accounted for by the coffee beans. The rest pays for the wages of staff, overheads, advertising and profits.

Fine, but why didn't the price of instant coffee in supermarkets fall noticeably? The answer here lies in the actions of coffee roasters. About a half of the world production of coffee is bought by just four huge companies – Kraft, Nestlé, Procter & Gamble, and Sara Lee. These companies did not, in general, pass on the reduction in the price of coffee to producers but substantially increased their profits. (We will be looking at the behaviour of large firms in Chapter 4, in the section on oligopoly.)

The effect on many coffee growers, who are mainly to be found in some of the world's poorest countries, was catastrophic. Many farmers were driven into debt; others left the land and migrated to cities, worsening the often appalling conditions there. Some farmers switched to growing illegal substances – coca in Vietnam, for example.

The International Coffee Organization (ICO) has developed some strategies to help growers out of the crisis. These include stimulating demand in new markets such as China and Russia and encouraging farmers to diversify into other crops. The growth in supply has slowed down in any case (see chart). Although efficient growers using up-to-date tech-

nology were still able to make a living out of coffee, many small growers could not cover their costs and stopped cultivating coffee.

The decline in supply, combined with a growth in demand, has led to a gradual rise in prices again (see chart). However, they still remain below the levels of the 1980s and 1990s. As the ICO's submission to the UN General Assembly in September 2005 stated:

In many countries reductions in the cash income of farmers means less money for basics such as medicine and education. In the latter area girls are particularly at risk of being kept from school. In El Salvador the World Food Programme has had to distribute emergency rations to 10 000 coffee-growing families. There have been widespread increases in unemployment. Moreover the crisis has led in many areas to abandonment of farms, population movement to urban areas and illegal migration. Problems of low prices have also increased incentives to plant narcotic drugs.

1. *What do you think caused the large increase in the price of coffee in 1997?*
2. *Use supply and demand diagrams to explain (a) the fall in coffee prices from 1997 to 2002; (b) the likely effect on coffee prices of the factors referred to in the final paragraph.*

The material in this box has largely been drawn from the ICO website, (www.ico.org/index.htm).

Questions

1. Using a chart similar to that in Figure 1.1 (on page 28), trace through the following effects: (a) a fall in demand for a good; (b) an increased supply of a factor of production. (In the case of (b) you will need to consider the factor market first, and then the goods market.)

2. Why do the prices of fresh vegetables fall when they are in season? Could an individual farmer prevent the price falling?

3. If you were the owner of a clothes shop, how would you set about deciding what prices to charge for each garment at the end-of-season sale?

4. The number of owners of mobile phones has grown rapidly and hence the demand for mobile phones has also grown rapidly. Yet the prices of mobile phones have fallen. Why?

5. Assume that oil begins to run out and that extraction becomes more expensive. Trace through

the effects of this on the market for oil and the market for other fuels.

6. This question is concerned with the supply of oil for central heating. In each case consider whether there is a movement along the supply curve (and in which direction) or a shift in it (and whether left or right).

   (a) New oil fields start up in production.
   (b) The demand for central heating rises.
   (c) The price of gas falls.
   (d) Oil companies anticipate an upsurge in demand for central heating oil.
   (e) The demand for petrol rises.
   (f) New technology decreases the costs of oil refining.
   (g) All oil products become more expensive.

7. The weekly demand and supply schedules for t-shirts (in millions) in a free market are as follows:

Price (£)	8	7	6	5	4	3	2	1
Quantity demanded	6	8	10	12	14	16	18	20
Quantity supplied	18	16	14	12	10	8	6	4

   (a) What is the equilibrium price and quantity?
   (b) Assume that changes in fashion cause the demand for t-shirts to rise by 4 million at each price. What will be the new equilibrium price and quantity? Has equilibrium quantity risen as much as the rise in demand? Explain why or why not.
   (c) Now plot the data in the table on a graph and mark the equilibrium. Also plot the new data corresponding to (b) and mark the new equilibrium.

8. On separate demand and supply diagrams for bread, sketch the effects of the following: (a) a rise in the price of wheat; (b) a rise in the price of butter and margarine; (c) a rise in the price of rice, pasta and potatoes. In each case, state your assumptions.

9. For what reasons might the price of foreign holidays rise? In each case identify whether these are reasons affecting demand or supply (or both).

10. If both demand and supply change, and if we know in which direction they have shifted but not how much, why is it that we will be able to predict the direction in which *either* price *or* quantity will change, but not both? (Clue: consider the four possible combinations and sketch them if necessary: (a) *D* left, *S* left; (b) *D* right, *S* right; (c) *D* left, *S* right; (d) *D* right, *S* left.)

11. What will happen to the equilibrium price and quantity of butter in each of the following cases? You should state whether demand or supply (or both) have shifted and in which direction. (In each case assume *ceteris paribus*.)

    (a) A rise in the price of margarine.
    (b) A rise in the demand for yoghurt.
    (c) A rise in the price of bread.
    (d) A rise in the demand for bread.
    (e) An expected rise in the price of butter in the near future.
    (f) A tax on butter production.
    (g) The invention of a new, but expensive, process for removing all cholesterol from butter, plus the passing of a law which states that all butter producers must use this process.

Additional case studies on the *Essentials of Economics* MyEconLab (www.pearsoned.co.uk/sloman)

1.1 **The interdependence of markets.** A case study in the operation of markets, examining the effects on a local economy of the discovery of a large coal deposit.
1.2 **Adam Smith (1723–90).** Smith, the founder of modern economics, argued that markets act like an invisible hand guiding production and consumption.
1.3 **Bentham and the philosophy of utilitarianism.** This looks at the historical and philosophical underpinning of the ideas of utility maximisation.
1.4 **Stocks and flows.** This examines one of the most important distinctions in economics and one that we shall come across on several occasions.
1.5 **Free-market medicine in Russia.** This examines the operation of the fledgling market economy in Russia and the successes and difficulties in moving from a planned to a market economy.

Sections of chapter covered in *WinEcon* – Sloman, *Essentials of Economics*

Essentials of Economics section	*WinEcon* section
1.1	1.1
1.2	1.2
1.3	1.3
1.4	1.4
1.5	–

Websites relevant to this chapter

Numbers and sections refer to websites listed in the Web Appendix and hotlinked from MyEconLab. Visit:

www.pearsoned.co.uk/sloman

- For news articles relevant to this chapter, see the *Economics News Articles* link from MyEconLab.
- For general news on markets, see websites in section A, and particularly A2, 3, 4, 5, 8, 9, 18, 24, 25, 26, 36. See also site A44 for links to economics news articles from newspapers worldwide.
- For links to sites on markets, see the relevant sections of I4, 7, 11, 17.
- For news on the Russian economy (Box 1.1), see sites A14, 15. See also the *Economic Systems and Theories > Transition Economies* section of sites I7 and 11.
- For data on the housing market (Box 1.3), see sites B7, 8, 11.
- For student resources relevant to this chapter, see sites C1–7, 9, 10, 19; D3.
- For sites favouring the free market, see C17 and E34.

Web Appendices

1.1 **Marginal utility theory.** This develops the analysis of Box 1.2 and shows how the marginal utility the consumer receives from a product affects demand.

1.2 **Indifference analysis.** This examines the choices consumers make between products and shows how these choices are affected by the prices of the products.

PART FOUR

Market Structures and Analysis of the Business Environment

Chapter 10

Market Structure

Market structure

Chris Britton

All businesses operate in a market which will be peculiar to that industry. Each market will have its own particular characteristics which depend upon many factors, and although it is not possible to have a model which describes every market, there are some economic models which provide some guidance to the kind of characteristics and behaviour that will be found in individual markets.

Learning outcomes

Having read this chapter you should be able to:

- explain the market structures of perfect competition, monopoly, oligopoly and monopolistic competition and indicate their implications for the behaviour of firms
- demonstrate the applicability of these predictions to the real world
- apply Porter's five-forces model to an analysis of the structure of industries
- understand the measurement of competition by concentration ratios
- survey differences in industrial concentration between industries, countries and over time
- indicate what determines market structure and what determines the behaviour of firms

Key terms

Abnormal profits	Market structure	Price competition
Average costs of production	Minimum efficient scale of production (MES)	Price discrimination
Barriers to entry		Price leadership
Barriers to exit	Monopolistic competition	Price maker
Cartel	Monopoly	Price taker
Collusion	Monopsony	Price war
Concentration ratio	Natural monopoly	Sticky prices
Contestable market	Non-price competition	Structure–conduct– performance model (S–C–P)
Differentiation	Normal profits	
Economies of scale	Oligopoly	
Five-forces model	Perfect competition	Transaction cost economics
Homogeneous products	Perfect knowledge	
Interdependence	Perfect mobility	

Introduction

In economics the behaviour and the performance of firms in an industry are thought to depend upon some basic structural characteristics. This view is exemplified by the **structure–conduct–performance model**, where structure determines conduct, which in turn determines performance. The basic elements included under these headings are given in Table 15.1.

The structure–conduct–performance model provides a good framework for classifying and analysing an industry. A simple example of the process can be seen in the soap powder industry. Here the market is dominated by two large producers, Unilever and Procter & Gamble. This apparent lack of competition gives rise to certain behavioural characteristics like the massive amount of advertising, the existence of many brand names and fairly uniform prices. This process will be considered in more detail later in the chapter, but the example serves to indicate the relationship between the structure of the market and the behaviour and ultimately the performance of firms in an industry.

For more information on these companies see *www.unilever.com* and *www.procterandgamble.com*

'**Market structure**' refers to the amount of competition that exists in a market between producers. The degree of competition can be thought of as lying along a continuum with very competitive markets at one end and markets in which no competition exists at all at the other end. This chapter looks at the two extremes (perfect competition and monopoly), and the market structures which exist between. The theory predicts the effects of market structure on behaviour and performance in those markets. However, as with the working of the market mechanism, the real world is often different from the theory and therefore this chapter will look at real markets and the relevance of the theory to the real world. The structure–conduct–performance model is open to criticism[1] since it says little about what determines structure in the first place. It also tends to view the firm as passive in the face of market structure, accepting the implications for conduct and performance, rather than actively trying to change and mould market structure. Michael Porter's 'five-forces model'[2] will be used to broaden out the analysis.

Table 15.1 Structure–conduct–performance model

Structural factors
- Amount of actual competition: (a) seller concentration; and (b) buyer concentration.
- Existence of potential competition.
- Cost conditions.
- Demand conditions.
- Existence of barriers to entry.

Conduct factors
- Pricing policy.
- Amount of advertising.
- Merger behaviour.
- Product differentiation.

Performance factors
- Profitability.
- Technological innovation.

Market structure is important not only because of the implications it has for conduct and performance but also because it has an impact upon the strategic possibilities which face the organisation, its ability to act strategically and the likely effects of such strategic behaviour (*see* Chapter 3).

In addition, this chapter will examine how the level of competition is measured in a market, how the level of competition varies between industries and countries, and how and why this has changed over time.

Market structures – in theory and practice

As mentioned above, market structures can be thought of as lying along a continuum with perfect competition at one end and monopoly at the other (*see* Figure 15.1). Both of these market structures are unrealistic representations of the real world, but are useful as benchmarks in assessing the degree of competition in a market. Between these two extremes lie other market structures, which are more realistic. Two will be described, oligopoly and monopolistic competition.

Perfect competition

This is the most competitive market structure. A number of conditions need to be fulfilled before **perfect competition** is said to exist. These conditions are as follows:

1. There are so many buyers and sellers in the market that no *one* of them can influence price through its activities.
2. The good being sold in the market is **homogeneous** (i.e. all units of the good are identical).
3. **Perfect knowledge** exists in the market. This means that producers have perfect knowledge of prices and costs of other producers and that consumers know the prices charged by all firms.
4. There exists **perfect mobility** of both the factors of production and consumers. This means that people, machines and land can be used for any purpose, and that consumers are free to purchase the good from any of the producers.
5. There are no **barriers to entry or exit** in the industry. There is nothing to prevent a new firm setting up production in the industry.

Figure 15.1   Market structures

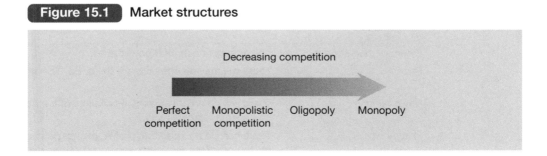

Naturally, this is a highly theoretical model and these conditions are unlikely to be all met in reality, but if they did, and the theory is followed through, the conclusion is that there will only be one price in the market for the good being sold. For example, if one firm is charging a higher price for the good than other firms, everyone in the market will know (because of perfect knowledge), and because the good is homogeneous and because of perfect mobility on the part of consumers, consumers will simply purchase the good from another firm. The firm that was charging a higher price will be forced to reduce the price of the good in order to sell it, or face mounting stocks of the good. There is therefore only one price for the good and this will be determined by *market* demand and supply – that is, total demand and total supply, no one consumer or producer having enough market power to influence the price. Accordingly, the firm is said to be a **price taker**.

Price determination in perfect competition

Firms need to cover costs of production and to earn a certain level of profits in order to stay in business. This minimum level of profits is called **normal profit**, and profits over and above this level are called **abnormal profits**. If the firm is trying to maximise its profits it will decide what level of output to produce by setting the cost of producing the last unit of the good equal to the revenue gained from selling the last unit: in economic terminology, where marginal cost equals marginal revenue. Included in cost would be elements of wages, rent, rates, interest, raw materials *and* normal profits. If these costs are not being covered the firm will be making a loss.

As there is only one price in perfect competition, the revenue derived from selling the last unit must be equal to its price. Therefore, the price of the good depends on the level of marginal cost.

In the short run, individual firms can earn abnormal profits, but these are not sustainable in the longer term. If one firm is earning abnormal profits, given the assumption of perfect knowledge, everyone will know and, since freedom of entry exists, other firms will enter the market in order to earn abnormal profits. This means that there is an increase in market supply and price will fall back to a level where abnormal profits have been competed away. Similarly when losses are being made, freedom of exit means that supply will be reduced and price will rise again until normal profits have been regained.

The implications of perfect competition for market behaviour and performance are summarised in Table 15.2. Perfect competition involves very restrictive assumptions,

Table 15.2 Implications of perfect competition for conduct and performance of firms in an industry

Extent of market power	The firm has no market power at all.
Price	There will only be one price for the good. The firm will be a 'price taker'.
Advertising	There will be no advertising, as all units of the good are the same and everyone knows this.
Profitability	There can be no abnormal profits, except possibly in the very short run if a producer reduces price and captures a larger share of the market.

which will rarely be fulfilled in the real world. The usefulness of the model lies in its role as an *ideal market* in which competition is at a maximum, rather than in its applicability to the real world.

An example of perfect competition?

The nearest example to perfect competition is probably the fruit and vegetable market in the centre of a large town. The goods will be fairly homogeneous, with perhaps slight variation in the quality. Knowledge will be almost perfect with respect to prices charged, as consumers could quickly walk around the market and ascertain the price of tomatoes, for example. Mobility of consumers is also high because the sellers are located in the same place. Thus the conditions for perfect competition nearly hold. The prediction is that there will be only one price for a particular good. Again this prediction is nearly fulfilled; the price of tomatoes tends to be rather similar across such a market, and when one trader reduces the price towards the end of the day, others tend to follow suit. Another market which is said to be close to perfect competition is the stock exchange, although with the increasing use of computers this is less likely to be true in the future.

Monopoly

Monopoly lies at the opposite end of the spectrum to competition. In its purest form a monopolistic market is one in which there is no competition at all; there is a single producer supplying the whole market. The monopolist has considerable market power and can determine price or quantity sold, but not both because he or she cannot control demand. The power of the monopolist depends on the availability of substitutes, and on the existence and height of barriers to entry. If there are no close substitutes for the good being produced, or if there are high barriers to entry, the power of the monopolist will be high and abnormal profits can be earned in the long run.

A monopolist could also be a group of producers acting together to control supply to the market: for example, a **cartel** such as OPEC (Organisation of Petroleum Exporting Countries).

 For information on OPEC see *www.opec.org*

In monopolistic markets the producer might be able to charge different prices for the same good: for example, on an aeroplane it is quite likely that there will be passengers sitting in the same class of seat having paid very different prices, depending upon where and when the tickets were bought. Essentially they are paying different prices for the same service, and the producer is said to be exercising **price discrimination**. Why is this possible? There are certain conditions that must hold for this type of price discrimination to occur. First, the market must be monopolistic and the producer must be able to control supply. Second, there must be groups of consumers with different demand conditions. For example, the demand for train travel by the commuter who works in London will be more inelastic than the demand of a student going to London for the day, who could use alternative forms of transport or even not go. This means that the willingness to pay among consumers will vary. The final condition necessary is that it must be possible to separate these groups in some way. For example, telephone companies are able to separate markets by time so that it is cheaper to phone after a certain time; British Rail used to separate groups by age for certain of its railcards.

The monopolist will maximise its profits by charging different prices in different markets. Price discrimination is often thought of as a bad thing as the monopolist is exploiting the consumer by charging different prices for the same good. But there are some advantages, in that it makes for better use of resources if cheap airline tickets are offered to fill an aeroplane which would otherwise have flown half-full. It can also lead to a more equitable solution in that higher-income users pay a higher price than lower-income users. The main problems with the notion of price discrimination is not that it is always a bad thing, but that it is the monopolist who has the power to decide who is charged what price.

Again the effects of monopoly on the behaviour and performance of the firm can be predicted (*see* Table 15.3). Like perfect competition, this is a highly theoretical model and is mainly used as a comparison with perfect competition to show the effects of the lack of competition.

Table 15.3 Implications of monopoly for conduct and performance of firms in an industry

Extent of market power	The firm has absolute market power.
Price	There will only be one price for the good, except in the case of price discrimination. The firm is a '**price maker**'.
Advertising	There will be no need for advertising, as there is only one firm producing the good.
Profitability	Abnormal profits can exist in the long run as there is no competition which might erode them away.

A comparison of perfect competition and monopoly

● It would be expected that price would be higher under monopoly than under perfect competition because of the absence of competition in the monopolistic market. It is argued, for example, that the large telephone companies (including BT) are overcharging the consumer. The benefits of the considerable technological advances that have been made in this area have not been passed on fully to the consumer. This can only be sustained by virtue of the monopolistic power of the companies. *But*, to counter this it could be argued that a monopolist is in a better position to reap the benefits of economies of scale, therefore it is possible that price might be lower.

● There might be less choice under monopoly since firms do not have to continually update their products in order to stay in business. *But*, it is also possible to think of examples where monopolies provide greater choice (e.g. in the case of radio stations), where under perfect competition all radio stations would cater for the biggest market, which would be for pop music. A monopolist, however, would be able to cover all tastes with a variety of stations.

● There is less incentive to innovate under monopoly, since the monopolist is subject to less competition. *But*, equally, a monopolist might have more incentive to innovate as it can reap the benefits in terms of higher profits. It may also have more resources to devote to innovation.

As can be seen there is not a clear set of arguments that imply that perfect competition is better than monopoly, and, as will be seen in Chapter 17, this is taken into account in UK competition policy.

An example of monopoly?

Although it is easy to think of examples of industries where the dominant firm has a great deal of monopoly power, there is no such thing as a pure monopoly, as substitutes exist for most goods. For example, British Rail used to have monopoly power in the market for rail travel, but there are many alternative forms of travel. This point highlights the difficulties of defining markets and industries discussed in Chapter 10. The nearest examples of monopolies are the old public utilities, like gas, electricity, water and so on, many of which have been privatised.

The government, in determining whether monopoly power exists in a market, has a working definition of what constitutes a monopoly. It is when 25 per cent of the market is accounted for by one firm or firms acting together. This would form grounds for investigation by the Competition Commission. The process of UK competition policy is discussed in Chapter 17 in more detail. The sources of monopoly power are the existence of barriers to entry and exit and the availability of substitutes (these will be discussed later in this chapter).

For information on the the operation of the Competition Commission see *www.competition-commission.org.uk*

Oligopoly

In both perfect competition and monopoly firms make independent decisions. In the case of monopoly there are no other firms in the industry to consider; in the case of perfect competition the firm has no power to affect the market at all. So for different reasons they act as though they have no rivals. This is not true in the case of oligopoly. **Oligopoly** is where a small number of producers supply a market in which the product is differentiated in some way. The characteristics of oligopoly are:

- A great deal of **interdependence** between the firms; each firm has to consider the likely actions of other firms when making its decisions.
- A lack of **price competition** in the market; firms are reluctant to increase their prices in case their competitors do not and they might lose market share. Firms are also reluctant to reduce their prices, in case other firms do the same and a price war results which reduces prices but leaves market share unchanged and so everyone is left worse off.[3]
- The lack of price competition means that different forms of **non-price competition** take place, such as branding or advertising. Oligopolists will sell their products not by reducing the price but through heavy advertising, brand names or special offers. The Premier points scheme was a good example of such non-price competition. The purchase of petrol from certain outlets gave the customer

points which were accumulated on their Premier points card and then redeemed for money-off vouchers to be spent at Argos. Table 15.4 shows the implications of oligopoly for conduct and performance of firms in an industry.

The way in which price is determined in an oligopolistic market is through either **price leadership** or some sort of **collusion**. Price leadership is where one firm takes the lead in setting prices and the others follow suit. The price leader is not necessarily the firm with the lowest cost, as it depends upon the power of the firm. So price could be set at a higher level than in a competitive market. Collusion is an explicit or implicit agreement between firms on price, which serves to reduce the amount of competition between firms. Collusion is illegal in most countries as it is seen as a form of restrictive practice, but this does not mean that collusion does not take place. A cartel is a form of collusion where firms come together to exercise joint market power. Cartels are now illegal in most countries, but the most famous of all is OPEC which has had a dramatic effect on the oil industry over the last 30 years. Collusive agreements, as well as possibly being harmful to the consumer, tend to be unstable as there is great temptation on the part of individual firms/countries to cheat. What is clear in the case of oligopoly is that once price is set there is a reluctance to change it. Therefore price competition is replaced by non-price competition of the sort mentioned above.

Table 15.4 Implications of oligopoly for conduct and performance of firms in an industry

Extent of market power	A great deal of market power.
Price	A stable price level. Prices set by price leadership or collusion.
Advertising	Much advertising and branding. Non-price competition is common.
Profitability	Abnormal profits can exist, their extent depends on the strength of competitors.

The most often quoted examples of oligopoly are the market for tobacco and the market for soap powder. Both of these markets are dominated by a very small number of producers and both exhibit the predicted characteristics. There is little price competition and price is fairly uniform in both markets. There is a high degree of non-price competition in both markets – high advertising, strong brand names and images, and the use of special offers or gifts at times in order to sell the goods.

Compared with monopoly and perfect competition, oligopoly is a much more realistic market structure, with many markets exhibiting the characteristics stated above. Table 15.5 gives a few examples.

Table 15.5 The top firms' share of the market in the UK (percentages)

Industry	Percentages
Cigarettes[a]	91*
Brewing[b]	89**
Sugar and artificial sweeteners[c]	79*
Ice cream[c]	68*
Jeans[c]	13*

Note: * Top three firms in the industry; ** Top five firms.
Source: [a] Keynote Report; 2007; [b] Keynote Report, 2008; [c] Mintel Report, 2008.

It is interesting to note that the market shares of the top firms in all of these industries have decreased since the publication of the last edition of this text. For three of these products, this has mainly been down to an increase in the market's share of own-brand products. For sugar there has been an increase of 20 per cent in the market's share of own brands between 2002 and 2006 and the corresponding figures are 22 per cent for jeans and 3 per cent for ice creams. More will be said about this later in the chapter.

For information and reports on specific industries see *www.mintel.co.uk* and *www.keynote.co.uk*

Monopolistic competition

A market structure of monopolistic competition exists when all of the conditions for perfect competition are met except for the existence of a homogeneous good, so that each firm has a monopoly over its own good but there is a great deal of competition in the market from other suppliers producing very similar products. In **monopolistic competition** the good is slightly **differentiated** in some way, either by advertising and branding or by local production. There does not have to be a technical difference between the two goods, which could be identical in composition, but there must be an 'economic difference' – that is, a difference in the way the goods are perceived by consumers. There is also some degree of consumer loyalty, so that if one firm reduces price, consumers might not necessarily move to that firm if they believe that the difference between the brands justifies the higher price. Abnormal profits can exist in the short run but cannot persist since new firms are free to enter the industry and compete away abnormal profit (*see* Table 15.6).

Table 15.6 Implications of monopolistic competition for conduct and performance of firms in an industry

Extent of market power	The firm has little market power.
Price	There will be small differences in price.
Advertising	There will be heavy advertising and branding.
Profitability	Small abnormal profits can exist in the short run but will be competed away in the longer run.

An example of monopolistic competition?

There are many examples of this type of industry: for example, the paint industry where ICI is the only producer of Dulux but there are many other types of paint on the market.

How accurate is the theory?

The implications of the theory of market structures for the behaviour and performance of firms are summarised in Table 15.7.

Table 15.7 Implications of theory for behaviour of firms

	Market power	Price	Advertising	Profitability
Perfect competition	None	One price	None	Only normal profits
Monopoly	Absolute	Price discrimination possible	None	Abnormal profits
Oligopoly	High	One price	High	Abnormal profits
Monopolistic competition	Little	Small differences in price	High	Only normal profits in long run

As argued above, both perfect competition and pure monopoly tend to be based on assumptions that are somewhat unrealistic and should be regarded as 'ideal types' of market structure, in the sense that they establish the boundaries within which true markets exist and operate, and against which they can be analysed. In contrast, oligopoly and monopolistic competition are much nearer to the types of market structure which can be found in the real world, and economic theory does appear to explain and predict behaviour in these markets to a certain extent. In oligopolistic markets, for example, price tends to be **sticky** and much of the competition between firms occurs in non-price ways, particularly branding, advertising and sales promotion (*see* Table 15.8). Occasionally, however, **price wars** do occur – as in the petrol market in the 1980s and more recently between the four biggest supermarkets.

Table 15.8 shows the top advertisers in the United Kingdom ranked for 2006; their ranks in 1994 are also given. The names in the list are familiar and largely expected from the predictions: for example, Procter & Gamble is one of the two companies which together with Unilever account for around 90 per cent of the market for washing powder. A less familiar name is Reckitt Benckiser which subsequently acquired Boots in 2007.

Table 15.8 Top advertisers in the UK, 2006

Rank 2006	Rank 1994	Advertiser	Total adspend (£000)
1	1	Procter & Gamble	181 023
2	3	Unilever	177 167
3	–	Central Office of Information Communication	140 758
4	36	L'Oréal Golden	120 121
5	48	British Sky Broadcasting	118 306
6	–	DFS Furniture	107 286
7	2	British Telecom	92 241
8	–	Orange	88 982
9	32	Reckitt Benckiser	83 790
10	19	Tesco	76 101

Source: Adapted from *Advertising Statistics Yearbook*, 1995 and 2007, Advertising Association, WARC.

For information on advertising see *www.adassoc.org.uk*

It is much more difficult to judge how accurate the behavioural implications are. Lack of data is one problem, as is the fact that only one structural characteristic has been considered here – the level of competition between producers. The other structural factors listed in Table 15.1 will also have an effect, like the level of demand, the degree of competition between the buyers and the degree of potential competition. Profitability, price and advertising, for instance, will be affected by the level of demand in the market.

Porter's five-forces model

Porter's model[4] says that the structure of an industry and the ability of firms in that industry to act strategically depend upon the relative strengths of five forces: current competition, potential competition, the threat of substitute products, the power of buyers and the power of suppliers. Each of these five forces will be examined in turn. The case study at the end of this chapter uses this model to analyse the airline industry.

Current competition

Current competition has already been considered under the heading of market structure but the important point to remember is that by acting strategically firms can change the structure of the industry. Firms in a highly competitive market might be unhappy with the lack of power they have over various factors like pricing and may through their strategic actions try to change the situation. If they are successful there will be a change in the level of current competition and therefore in market structure.

Potential competition (or threat of new entry)

It has been shown that market structure or current competition affects the behaviour of firms in an industry. However, looking at the number of firms in an industry does not provide the whole picture. It is possible that firms in an oligopolistic market might act in a way consistent with perfect competition because of the threat of potential competition. This threat can affect the behaviour of firms even if it does not happen. The degree of potential competition depends upon the existence and height of barriers to entry and exit.

Barriers to entry

Barriers to entry are any barriers which prevent or inhibit the entry of firms into the industry. There are several sources of barriers to entry.

Some industries are what are called **natural monopolies** in that the production process is such that competition would be wasteful. The old public utilities are good examples of these, as it would be very wasteful for there to be two national grid systems in the electricity industry.

Some production processes are subject to **economies of scale**. As firms grow in size, or as the scale of production increases, certain economies occur which serve to reduce the **average cost of production**. The scale of production can be increased in many ways, for example by increasing the capacity of the existing plant, by increasing the number of plants or by increasing the product range. Figure 15.2 shows how the average *cost* of production changes as the *scale* of production changes.

The downward-sloping part of the curve shows falling average cost or economies of scale. The upward-sloping part shows rising average cost or diseconomies of scale. Economies of scale reduce average cost and therefore benefit the producer and also the consumer if they are passed on in lower prices.

The sources of economies of scale are usually classified under three headings: technical; marketing; and financial.

Technical economies come from increased specialisation and indivisibilities. The larger the scale of production the more the production process can be broken down into its component parts and the greater the gain from specialisation. There are certain indivisibilities involved in production, which only large firms can benefit from. For example, a small firm cannot have half a production line as that is meaningless, but might not be big enough to use a whole production line. Another type of indivisibility is involved in the notion of fixed costs. Fixed costs like the cost of rates or the fees of an accountant, for example, remain the same irrespective of the level of production. Therefore the greater the level of production, the lower will be the average cost of items as it is being spread over a larger output.

Marketing economies come from spreading marketing costs over a larger output, so that average costs will be lower. The company can also take advantage of bulk buying, and will probably have a specialised department devoted to marketing.

Financial economies come from the fact that larger companies find it easier and often cheaper to borrow capital.

Added to these is *risk diversification* which is possible with larger companies as they may well have interests in other industries. All of these economies of scale give rise to falling average cost and therefore explain the downward-sloping part of the cost curve in Figure 15.2. Economies of scale are a very effective barrier to entry. If the incumbent firm in an industry has lower average cost as a result of economies of scale, it will be hard for a newcomer to compete effectively at a smaller scale of production. Gas, electricity and water are examples of this. The production processes of these goods are subject to economies of scale and it is therefore

Figure 15.2   A firm's average cost curve

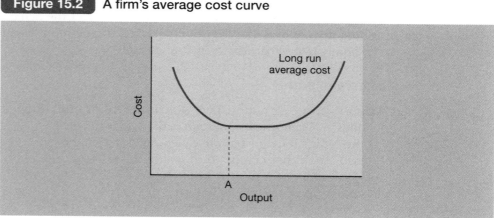

difficult for others to come into the market in competition with established firms. This is why such industries are called 'natural monopolies'.

Barriers to entry can be legal ones, as in the case of patents and franchises which serve to restrict competition and prevent new firms from entering an industry. Advertising and branding can also be barriers, in that industries where brand names are well established are difficult to enter without massive expenditure on advertising. Some industries require a high initial capital investment to enter, for example, dry cleaning, where the machinery is very expensive. Switching costs can also be regarded as a barrier to entry. If the consumer has to bear a cost in switching from one good to another that might be enough to deter the consumer from doing so and therefore serve as a barrier to entry. The recent practice of the building societies and banks of offering low fixed-rate mortgages with penalties for early withdrawal can be seen as an example of the introduction of switching costs into the market.

A **contestable market**[5] is one in which there are no barriers to entry or exit. This means that all firms (even potential entrants) have access to the same technology and there are therefore no cost barriers to entry. It also means that there are no sunk or unrecoverable costs which would prevent a firm leaving the industry. It follows that it is possible to ensure that firms behave in a competitive way, even if the market structure they operate in is imperfectly competitive, by ensuring that the market is contestable. What is regulating market behaviour then is not *actual* competition but *potential* competition.

mini case — Open Skies and Contestability

The 'Open Skies' agreement between the USA and the EU signed in 2007 and introduced in 2008 is a policy designed to make markets more contestable. It eases restrictions on air travel between the US and the EU so that any airline can fly to US destinations and not necessarily from its home nation, as was previously the case. British Airways can now fly from Paris to New York, whereas it could only fly from London Heathrow to New York. Similarly any US airline can do the same for European destinations.

This policy is not designed to break up existing companies or to introduce more competition into the market directly. It makes the market more contestable – it opens the market up for the possibility of competition. The agreement has led to structural changes in the market (see the case study at the end of this chapter for more details of the air industry). For example, as a direct result of this deal:

- British Airways has launched a new airline called OpenSkies which flies between Paris and New York.

- Virgin Atlantic has increased the number of flights from London to New York.
- Continental and Delta have started flying from London Heathrow to New York.

Theory predicts that more competition will lead to lower prices. Unfortunately this agreement has come into force at a time of rapidly rising oil prices so this is unlikely to happen – Virgin Atlantic has said that prices cannot be any lower. It is also argued by EU airlines that the agreement is unbalanced. US airlines can fly between EU destinations (from Paris to London for example) but EU airlines cannot do the same within the USA. In addition to this, US carriers are allowed to buy up their EU rivals but foreign ownership of US airlines is not allowed. The agreement is being introduced in stages and US markets should be completely open to competition by 2010; whether this happens or not will have to be seen.

Barriers to exit

Exit barriers are those which prevent or deter exit from an industry; they are mainly related to the cost of leaving the industry. The cost of exit depends upon how industry-specific the assets of the firm are. If we take physical assets as an example, a printing press is highly specific to the printing industry and could not be used for anything other than printing. There will be a second-hand market for printing presses but it would probably have to be sold at a loss, therefore incurring a high cost. A van, however, would be different, as it is still a physical asset but one that would not be specific to a particular industry, therefore the loss involved in selling would be less. Generally speaking, the more industry-specific an asset is the lower will be the second-hand value and the higher the cost of exit. An intangible asset like knowledge of the market or expenditure on research and development cannot be resold and must be left in the market, and therefore is a sunk cost – a non-recoverable cost.

Barriers to entry and exit can be 'innocent' or can be deliberately erected. Economies of scale can be regarded as innocent barriers to entry since they are inherent in the production process. Advertising and branding can be thought of as deliberately erected barriers to entry since they increase the expense of any firm entering the market. Similarly, the introduction of penalty clauses on mortgages is a deliberately erected barrier since it incurs switching costs for the consumer.

Where innocent barriers to entry or exit are low, potential competition will be high and firms within such a market are faced with the choice of accepting the situation or deliberately erecting some barriers. This is an example of strategic behaviour on the part of firms; whether it is attempted or not depends on the likelihood of success and the relative costs and benefits. It is another area where game theory is used to formulate strategic possibilities.[6]

The threat of substitute products

The threat from substitute products largely depends upon the nature of the good being traded in the market and the extent of product differentiation. It has a clear impact upon market structure, because if there are no substitutes for a good the producer of that good will face little competition and have a great deal of market power. However, as was seen earlier, even industries which appear to be pure monopolies like the former British Rail face competition from substitutes since there are other ways to travel. Much of the expenditure by firms to differentiate their products is designed to reduce the threat from substitute products.

The power of buyers

So far this chapter has concentrated on the competition between producers in a market, but the amount of competition between buyers will also have an impact on an industry. Markets will range from those where there are many buyers, as in the case of retailing, through markets where there are a small number of buyers, as in the case of car and parts manufacturers, to markets where there is only one buyer.

This latter type of market is called a **monopsony**, and it is the buyer who has a great deal of market power rather than the seller. An example of this is the coal industry, where the majority of output goes to the electricity producers. Increasingly in retailing the giant retailers are exerting a great deal of power over the manufacturers. TOYS 'R' US, the world's largest toy retailer, is involved very early on by manufacturers in the design process for new toys and as a result gets many exclusives that are not available in other toy shops.

The level of buyer power could be measured in the same way as seller power (*see* later in this chapter), but no data are collected centrally on the level of buyer concentration. It is clear, however, that there are many markets in which powerful buyers can and do exert a great deal of control over suppliers, and this power is an important source of marketing economies of scale. It is possible to put together the level of competition between producers and consumers in order to predict behaviour. For example, a market which consists of a single buyer and a single seller will have quite different characteristics from a market which has many buyers and sellers. The existence of strong buyers might have beneficial effects on the market as they could offset the power of strong producers or it could lead to higher seller concentration as sellers come together to counteract the power of the buyer.

In markets where there are strong sellers and weak buyers the producers' power can be offset by, for example, consumer advice centres or watch-dog bodies, as in the case of the former public utilities.

A distinction can be made between existing and potential customers. Existing customers are particularly significant to firms in industries where repeat orders are important or where goods are supplied on a regular basis, as in grocery retailing. It is no surprise that the large grocery retailers are using loyalty cards to increase the loyalty of existing customers. The power of existing customers is much lower where the firm supplies goods on a one-off basis, although the firm cannot disregard existing customers as this will affect its reputation and the ability to attract potential customers. Potential customers might be new to the market or can be buying from an existing competitor at present.

Power of suppliers

The power of suppliers over the firm is likely to be extremely important in certain markets, depending upon the nature of the product being supplied. For example: Is the product highly specialised? Is the same or similar product available from elsewhere? How important is the product in the production process? The importance of good and reliable supplies has assumed greater significance since firms have started to adopt just-in-time production methods. Reducing stock levels to reduce costs can only be effective if firms can depend upon their suppliers; hence there has been the development of partnership sourcing as firms develop long-term relationships with their suppliers.

Another important factor here is whether or not the firm itself can produce the components it needs in the production process. If it can the power of suppliers is greatly reduced. The decision as to whether to produce or to buy from a supplier is the subject of a relatively new area of economics called **transaction cost economics**.[7]

Measuring the degree of actual competition in the market

In industrial economics the level of competition in a market is measured by concentration ratios. These measure the percentage of value added, total output or employment that is produced by a stated number of the largest firms in the industry. The common numbers are three or five. The five-firm concentration ratio measures the percentage of employment or output accounted for by the five largest firms in the industry.

Table 15.9 shows the five-firm concentration ratios for a selection of industries in 2004 as measured by output.

Table 15.9 Five-firm concentration ratios for selected industries in the UK, 2004

Industry	Output (%)
Sugar and sugar by-products	99
Tobacco	99
Iron and steel	61
Pharmaceutical products	57
Rubber products	45
Leather goods	30
Footwear	25
Legal service	9
Other business services	5

Source: Adapted from Appendix 1, 'Concentration ratios for businesses by industry in 2004', Sanjiv Mahajan, *Economic Trends*, ONS, October 2006.

Although Table 15.9 shows only a small selection of industries, it does show that there is a wide variation in the degree of concentration across industries. Only two services industries are listed because there is a general lack of data on the service sector. Generally services are less concentrated than manufacturing industries because of the nature of the production process and the fact there is less scope for economies of scale. The differences between the market shares of sugar and tobacco in Tables 15.5 and 15.9 are due to the fact that the large producers also produce the own-brand labels.

While it is relatively easy to compare the level of concentration in particular industries over time it is more difficult to make any conclusion about the 'average' level of concentration (*see* Mini case: Concentration in this chapter). Table 15.10 gives an illustration of the percentage share of total employment and sales of the largest 100 private firms in the United Kingdom between 1979 and 1992. Although these are not concentration ratios as such, the data do provide an indication of how concentration has changed over time in aggregate. The change in the Standard Industrial Classification during this period has only a small impact on the figures. Note how the level of 'average' concentration decreased slightly during the first part of the period, reversing the trend of the first half of this century where industrial concentration increased. The reason for the decrease is largely the process of privatisation and the growth in the small-firm sector during the 1970s and 1980s.

Table 15.10 100 largest private enterprise groups

Year	Percentage share of total Employment	Sales
SIC(68)		
1979	12	18
SIC(80)		
1980	13	15
1981	13	16
1982	12	15
1983	12	16
1984	15	19
1985	9.5	14
1986	9.7	15.4
1987	10.8	17.1
1988	9.4	17.6
1989	12.1	21.6
1990	14.6	23.6
1991	14.9	21.2
1992	16.9	24.9

Source: *Census of Production*, various. Crown copyright. Reproduced by permission of the Controller of HMSO and of the Office for National Statistics, UK.

In the later part of the period concentration started to rise again, mainly due to the industrial restructuring taking place and the increased level of merger activity identified in Chapter 11. As the UK government ceased publication of these figures in 1992 it is difficult to assess what has happened to concentration more recently.

Making comparisons between different countries tends to be difficult because of this problem of 'averaging' concentration and because of national differences in the way in which data are collected and reported. Moreover official EU publications on industry have changed the way in which they report data, so comparisons over time are problematical. Available evidence suggests, however, that in the 1960s concentration increased in Europe and stabilised by the 1970s before declining in the last quarter of the twentieth century, as in the United Kingdom.

One of the main arguments for the creation and expansion of the Single European Market was that the bigger market would allow greater economies of scale through the growth in the size of firms. Chapter 11 has already identified an increase in merger activity in the EU in the late 1980s in the run-up to 1992 and Table 15.11 shows the change in the five-firm concentration ratios according to value added in selected sectors in the EU between 1986 and 1991.

Most sectors experienced an increase in concentration levels, although there are differences between the sectors. Aerospace is one sector where concentration increased by 20 per cent, mainly due to the growth of British Aerospace and Rolls-Royce. The level of concentration in the EU has risen as a result of increased merger activity and a competition policy which is torn between promoting competition by preventing market domination and the need to establish European competitiveness by encouraging it.

Despite the difficulties in comparing concentration ratios, the general view of industrial economists is that concentration is greater in the United Kingdom than in other member states.

Table 15.11 Five-firm concentration ratios on a value-added basis (%) for selected sectors in the EU

Sector	1986	1991	% change
Tobacco	58.39	59.16	0.76
Chemicals	42.25	41.48	−0.77
Rubber and plastic products	14.78	21.71	6.93
Iron and steel	47.21	82.31	35.10
Aerospace	51.24	71.97	20.72
Computers	34.08	33.17	−0.91
Drink	39.73	43.24	3.50
Food	16.92	20.37	3.45
Printing and publishing	19.20	19.34	0.14

Source: Commission of the European Communities, *European Economy*, no. 57, 1994. Reproduced by permission of the Office for Official Publications of the European Communities.

mini case   Concentration

Although it is difficult to talk about the 'average' level of concentration in a country, the government in the UK produced data on the percentage share of the largest 100 enterprises in employment and output up to 1992 (*see* Table 15.10). These data show that concentration increased in the first half of this century but has stabilised and even fallen at times. A report in 2002[8] found that the concentration of industry in the EU had reduced both geographically and industrially in the last quarter of the twentieth century. Between 1970 and 2000 there was less geographical concentration of industry in France, Germany and the UK (63 per cent in 1970 and 58 per cent in 2000). Using the Gini coefficient to measure concentration[9] there had been a small fall in concentration in manufacturing as a whole and also in the majority of industries. The most concentrated industries were motor vehicles, motorcycles, aircraft, electrical apparatus, chemicals, petroleum and coal products. It is also true that the relative importance of the small firm to both output and employment has increased over recent years at the expense of larger organisations. What are the reasons for these changes?

The main benefits to result from increased size and concentration are the economies of scale discussed in the text. The techniques of mass production which produced standardised goods at low cost rely upon the economies of specialisation and division of labour. Although there are many industries which are still dominated by very large organisations, the recent trends in firm size and concentration indicate that smaller firms are increasingly able to compete with large firms. In unsegmented markets where the product is standardised the techniques of mass production are still appropriate, but increasingly there is a movement to a more flexible approach to manufacturing. This has been called the 'Japanisation' of industry.

● Changes in consumer demand have led to a demand for a bigger range of products so that markets are increasingly segmented and there is greater product differentiation. Under such conditions the benefits of economies of large-scale production have little significance, and large-scale organisations are less responsive to changes in demand than small firms. The use of 'flexible manufacturing systems' gives much greater flexibility in production and enables firms to produce a wider range of products at lower cost than traditional methods of production.

● Developments in information technology like Computer Aided Design (CAD) and Computer Aided Manufacturing (CAM) have exacerbated this trend since they serve to reduce the minimum efficient scale of production and make economies of scale possible at lower levels of output. Thus small firms can benefit from economies of scale in the same way as large firms. CAD and CAM make possible the manufacture of different products so that the product mix can be altered quickly.

- Economies of scope exist where a firm can produce two or more products at a lower per unit cost than if it produced each product separately. They result where related activities use similar labour and equipment and where producing related goods is a way of using up excess capacity. The economies

stem from the spreading of fixed costs over larger output. Since economies of scope are not due to increased scale of production they can be realised by large and small firms alike. One small firm industry which has benefited from economies of scope is executive recruitment consultancy, where firms increasingly offer a range of related services like training audits and succession planning.

- Techniques like just-in-time production are more accessible to small firms since they eradicate the need for keeping large inventories and the associated costs of storage.

Reasons for high concentration

Many industries in the United Kingdom are highly concentrated and it is believed that the United Kingdom has higher concentration ratios than other large industrial countries. Why are there different market structures between industries?

Referring back to Figure 15.2, the point at which the curve becomes horizontal (A in diagram) is called the **minimum efficient scale of production** or **MES**. It is the point at which all economies of scale have been reaped by the firm, and the point at which firms that wish to maximise their efficiency must operate.

The higher the MES relative to the total output of the industry, the fewer will be the number of firms operating in an industry and therefore the higher will be the level of concentration. For example, if the MES in an industry is half of the industry output, the industry could only support two firms, as smaller firms could not achieve low enough costs to compete with the large firms.

As the scale of production continues to increase, average costs eventually start to rise. This is due to diseconomies of scale, which are mostly attributed to managerial inefficiencies. These are the difficulties faced by management in controlling, co-ordinating and communicating in a large organisation.

Firms in every industry will face differing average cost curves and therefore market structures will be different. In services, for example, because of the nature of the product, the scope for economies of scale is small and, accordingly, the MES is small relative to the size of the total market and the industries tend to be unconcentrated. The level of concentration in manufacturing tends to be much higher because of the nature of the production process and the scope for economies of scale.

The size of the MES is not the only explanation of why there are different market structures. If it was, one might expect that the same industry would have similar levels of concentration in different countries, but this is not the case, as indicated above. The strength of the five forces will differ greatly between industries and will therefore give many different structures. Obviously government policy can influence the type of market structure, and this will differ between countries. It is also true that the significance of barriers to entry varies between countries. Empirical results from West Germany and the United Kingdom show that in both countries barriers to entry are high, but that in the United Kingdom advertising is the most important barrier, while in West Germany it is economies of scale.

Synopsis

In this chapter, four different market structures were considered that embraced the whole spectrum of competition: perfect competition; monopoly; oligopoly; and monopolistic competition. Each of these market structures gives predictions about the behaviour of firms in those markets. Generally the more realistic of these market structures predict well what happens in the real world. This analysis was then incorporated into Porter's five-forces model which includes further factors largely ignored by traditional economic theory. Nevertheless, these factors are particularly important in certain industries, like the power of the giant retailers as buyers and the importance of potential customers to industries where the level of repeat business is high.

The amount of competition in a market is measured using concentration ratios and evidence on concentration was examined both within the United Kingdom and between countries as far as that was possible.

Summary of key points

- There are four different market structures identified by business economists. These are (arranged with most competitive first): perfect competition, monopolistic competition, oligopoly and monopoly.

- Perfect competition is a market structure which is very competitive and where the producers are 'price takers'.

- Pure monopoly is a market structure with a single producer that is a 'price maker'.

- Monopolistic competition is a market structure where there is a great deal of competition but where the product is slightly differentiated, so producers have a little market power.

- Oligopoly is a market structure where there is a small number of large producers, interdependent in their decision making. This is a common market structure.

- The determinants of market structure include the existence and height of barriers to entry and exit and the existence of economies of scale.

- Knowledge of market structure gives some indication of likely behaviour of firms with respect to factors like pricing and advertising.

case study A Porter's five-force analysis of the airline industry

Like many other industries in 2008, the airline industry is under threat from a variety of sources. Increasing oil prices, the credit crunch and environmental concerns are just three of the issues which are having a dramatic effect on the industry. How will these affect the industry? This case study uses Porter's five-forces model to analyse this.

Current competition

There are hundreds of airlines in the world. Some are very big like British Airways and American Airways and some are smaller like the low-cost airlines Ryanair and easyJet. The rising price of oil is having a dramatic effect on market structure. In the year up to September 2008, 26 airlines had gone out of business. Rising fuel prices impact more on the smaller airlines as they typically operate older aircraft which are less fuel efficient. More casualties are expected by the end of 2008, especially among the 70 smaller airlines operating in Europe.

The credit crunch is also having an effect: IATA estimates that in 2008 global passenger capacity grew faster than the demand for seats. Even national flag carriers are having problems; at the time of writing it is not clear whether the attempts to save Alitalia will be successful. Problems faced by holiday companies also impact on the airline industry. The collapse of XL Leisure Group in 2008 left 85 000 holidaymakers stranded and a further 200 000 without a holiday. One way in which airlines try to protect themselves and provide 'seamless travel' to their customers is through the formation of strategic alliances. There are three main alliances.

The Open Skies agreement has opened the door to possible strategic alliances between airlines and one was under consideration at the end of 2008 – between American Airlines, British Airways and Iberia. This has been heralded as the advent of the global mega-alliance.

Power of buyers

There are two main reasons for air travel – leisure and business. It is estimated that business travel accounts for around 15 per cent of air travel and leisure 85 per cent. Over the last 50 years the demand for air travel has increased greatly. Demographic factors, including

Table 15.12 Major airline alliances, 2008

Oneworld Alliance	Aer Lingus, American Airlines, British Airways, Cathay Pacific, Finnair, Iberia, Japan Airlines, LAN, Malév, Royal Jordanian, Qantas
Star Alliance	Air Canada, Air China, Air New Zealand, ANA, Asian Airlines, Austrian Airlines, BMI, LOT Polish Airlines, Lufthansa, Scandinavian Airlines, Shanghai Airlines, Singapore Airlines, South African Airlines, Spanair, TAP Portugal, Thai Airways International, United Airlines, US Airways
Sky Team	Aeroflot, Aeromexico, Air France, Alitalia, China Southern, Continental Airlines, CSA Czech Airlines, Delta Airlines, KLM, Korean Air, Northwest Airlines

increased life expectancy and better health, have meant that all ages travel more than before. The average growth rate in air travel over the last 20 years is around 5 per cent per annum.[10] Both travel for leisure and travel for business are cyclical and will depend upon economic growth and this demand is highly susceptible to external forces. There was a sharp drop in air travel after 11 September 2001, for example (see Chapter 1), and the effects of the credit crunch will be felt on the volume of air travel. It is generally believed that the demand for leisure travel is price elastic: as prices go down travel increases sharply (and vice versa). It is also generally believed that business travel is price inelastic, that business travellers are less concerned about what they pay as someone else picks up the bill (this is questionable given the extent to which the low-cost, no-frills airlines have expanded in the business market).

The annual growth rate in the numbers of passengers carried has fallen from 12 per cent in 2004 to 5 per cent in 2007. Table 15.13 shows the breakdown of air travel by area and predicted growth rates up to 2011, and it can be seen that these are variable. There has been faster growth in the developing countries, especially China.

▶

Table 15.13 Air traffic by area

Area	Percentage of global air traffic in 2007	Growth rate forecast 2007–2011
Europe	40	+5.0
Asia/Pacific	28	+5.9
North America	17	+4.2
Middle East	7	+6.8
Latin America	4	+4.4
Africa	3	+5.6

Source: Adapted from IATA, 2008.

Another issue which might impact on the level of demand for air travel is the environmental impact of flying. The International Civil Aviation Organisation has a carbon emission calculator on its website. The UK government has announced that it will introduce a new tax which will replace the current air-passenger duty in 2009. The new tax will be much higher than the current tax and it is argued that it represents a more realistic assessment of the environmental costs of air travel.

Power of suppliers

There are two main organisations which dominate the supply of aircraft to airlines – Boeing Company (US based) and Airbus SAS (European based). Both companies have full order books but are experiencing delays in production. Airbus has delayed deliveries of its A380 because of wiring problems and Boeing is experiencing ongoing industrial action by employees. Another supplier of importance is the oil industry – oil represents a third of the operating costs of the airlines. Because of rises in the oil price, the price of jet fuel rose by 80 per cent between 2007 and 2008.

Threat of new entry

The threat of new entry is low because the airline business carries very high fixed costs – there are the costs of purchasing and maintaining the aeroplanes and the cost of landing at airports. All of these are fixed costs which do not change if an aircraft is half-empty. Airspace was deregulated in the 1970s in the USA and in the 1990s in Europe, such that any qualified airline can fly anywhere in the EU without government agreement.

This increased the level of competition and allowed the smaller low-cost airlines to establish themselves. The Open Skies agreement has also reduced barriers to entry for competition by existing airlines if not by new companies. In order to fly, airlines have to pay airport charges and these are very high especially in the bigger airports (this is why the low-cost airlines often operate to and from smaller, less well known airports) and this may be prohibitive. The problems with Terminal 5 at Heathrow in 2008 led to delays in the transfer of BA flights to the new terminal and a backlog of airlines waiting to take up BA's empty slots.

Threat of substitutes

For international travel there is really no substantial competition to air travel; sea travel accounted for only 10 per cent of international trips in 2007. Domestically, the airlines are in competition with all other sorts of travel and there is evidence from the UK that between 2003 and 2007, the fastest growing mode of transport for domestic destinations was railways (up from 6.2 per cent to 7.1 per cent). This growth took place at the expense of road travel rather than air travel, which remained static. Europe has been opened up as a destination for railway travel with the opening of the Channel Tunnel.

The low-cost airlines are cheaper than other methods of travel and of course much faster. The fact that in Europe countries are joined and the rail network is more developed may in part explain why the low-cost airlines do not yet have much of the market (5 per cent) compared with the UK (20 per cent) and the USA (22 per cent).

The Future

The airline industry is experiencing a period of rapid structural change for a number of reasons, which have been considered above. It is argued by many commentators that this restructuring is necessary and that the industry that emerges will be much stronger.

Case study questions

1 Why is there unlikely to be a price war between the low-cost providers in the airline industry?

2 What might be the effect on the industry of the proposed strategic alliance between British Airways, American Airlines and Iberia mentioned in the text?

web link

For further details see e.g. *www.iata.org*; *www.icao.org*; *www.oneworld.com*; *www.staralliance.com*; *www.skyteam.com*

Review and discussion questions

1 Use Porter's five-forces model to analyse two industries of your choice. Try to choose industries which have contrasting market structures.

2 What economies of scale are likely to exist in retailing?

3 Think of examples of a market which is very competitive and a market which is not very competitive. Does the behaviour of the firms in these markets comply with the predictions in Table 15.7?

4 Why are goods like washing powders and coffee advertised more heavily than goods like matches or bread?

Assignments

1 You are working in the strategic planning department of a large recorded music producer and have been asked to write a briefing document for a board meeting on the structure of the industry. Use either the S–C–P model or Porter's five-forces model as a framework for this briefing. (Sources of information: Competition Commission reports, the previous editions of this book, media and local libraries, Mintel and Keynote.)

2 You are working in the local consumer advice centre which each week produces an information sheet giving the prices of a typical 'basket of goods' in local shops. Choose ten branded items (like Nescafé, for example) to constitute your basket of goods and survey three types of retail outlet: a small corner shop, a mini-market on a local main road and a large supermarket. Design an information sheet and present the information you have gathered in the form of a table. Include a list of bullet points which might explain any differences in price.

Notes and references

1 See Hay, D. A. and Morris, D. J., *Industrial Economics: Theory and Evidence*, Oxford University Press 1979, for a summary of the criticisms which are beyond the scope of this book.

2 Porter, M., *Competitive Strategy: Techniques for Analyzing Industries and Competitors*, The Free Press, New York, 1980.

3 For a full discussion of this, see Begg, D., Fischer, S. and Dornbusch, R., *Economics*, 7th edition, McGraw-Hill, 2003.

4 Porter, M., *Competitive Strategy: Techniques for Analyzing Industries and Competitors*, The Free Press, New York, 1980.

5 Baumol, W. J., Panzar, J. C. and Willig, R. D., *Contestable Markets and the Theory of Industry Structure*, Harcourt Brace Jovanovich, 1988.

6 In this context students should note the use of game theory to model and predict the behaviour of firms in oligopolistic markets. For a simple introduction to this area, see Griffiths, A. and Wall, S., *Applied Economics: An Introductory Course*, 9th edition, Financial Times/Prentice Hall, 2001.

7 Williamson, O. E., 'The Economics of Organisation: The Transaction Cost Approach', *American Journal of Sociology*, 87 (3), 1981, pp. 548–77.

8 'Location and Concentration of Industries' *European Economy Special Report* no. 2, 2002.

9 Worthington, I., Britton, C. and Rees, A., *Economics for Business; Blending Theory and Practice*, 2nd edition, Financial Times/Prentice Hall, 2005.

10 Keynote Report on Airlines, 2008.

Further reading

Begg, D., Fischer, S. and Dornbusch, R., *Economics*, 8th edition, McGraw-Hill, 2005.

Griffiths, A. and Wall, S., *Applied Economics: An Introductory Course*, 10th edition, Financial Times/Prentice Hall, 2004.

Jones, T. T. and Cockerill, T. A. J., *Structure and Performance of Industries*, Philip Allan, 1984.

Worthington, I., Britton, C. and Rees, A., *Economics for Business: Blending Theory and Practice*, 2nd edition, Financial Times/Prentice Hall, 2005.

web link

Web links and further questions are available on the website at:
www.pearsoned.co.uk/worthington

Chapter 11

Market Structures

Market structures

As we saw in Section 3.4, a firm's profits are maximised where its marginal cost equals its marginal revenue: $MC = MR$. But we will want to know more than this.

What determines the *amount* of profit that a firm will make? Will its profits be large, or just enough for it to survive, or so low that it will be forced out of business? Will the price charged to the consumer be high or low? And, more generally, will the consumer benefit from the decisions a firm makes?

The answers to these questions depend on the amount of competition that a firm faces. A firm in a highly competitive environment will behave quite differently from a firm facing little or no competition. In particular, a firm facing competition from many other firms will be forced to keep its prices down and be as efficient as possible, simply to survive.

Even if a firm faces only one or two rivals, competition might be quite intense. Firms might put a lot of effort into producing more efficiently or into developing new or better products in order to gain a larger share of the market. They may, however, collude with each other to keep prices up.

When firms face little or no competition (like the local water company or a major pharmaceutical company), they may have considerable power over prices and we may end up paying a lot more.

In this chapter we look at different types of market and how well they serve the consumer.

After studying this chapter, you should be able to answer the following questions:

- What determines the degree of market power of a firm?
- Why does operating under conditions of perfect competition make being in business a constant battle for survival?
- How do firms get to become monopolies and remain so?
- At what price and output will a monopolist maximise profits and how much profit will it make?
- How well or badly do monopolies serve the consumer compared with competitive firms?
- How are firms likely to behave when there are just a few of them competing ('oligopolies')? Will they engage in all-out competition or will they collude with each other?
- What strategic games are oligopolists likely to play in their attempt to out do their rivals?
- Explain why firms may charge different consumers different prices for an identical product.

4.1 THE DEGREE OF COMPETITION

How much competition does a firm face?

It is traditional to divide industries into categories according to the degree of competition that exists between the firms within the industry. There are four such categories.

At one extreme is **perfect competition** where there are very many firms competing. Each firm is so small relative to the whole industry that it has no power to influence price. It is a price taker. At the other extreme is **monopoly**, where there is just one firm in the industry, and hence no competition from *within* the industry. In the middle come **monopolistic competition**, which involves quite a lot of firms competing and where there is freedom for new firms to enter the industry, and **oligopoly**, where there are only a few firms and where entry of new firms is restricted.

To distinguish more precisely between these four categories, the following must be considered:

■ How freely can firms enter the industry: is entry free or restricted? If it is restricted, just how great are the barriers to the entry of new firms?
■ The nature of the product. Do all firms produce an identical product, or do firms produce their own particular brand or model or variety?
■ The degree of control the firm has over price. Is the firm a price taker or can it choose its price, and if so, how will changing its price affect its profits? What we are talking about here is the nature of the demand curve it faces. How elastic is it? If the firm puts up its price, will it lose (a) all its sales (a horizontal demand curve), or (b) a large proportion of its sales (a relatively elastic demand curve), or (c) just a small proportion of its sales (a relatively inelastic demand curve)?

TC8
p64

> **Market power benefits the powerful at the expense of others.** When firms have market power over prices, they can use this to raise prices and profits above the perfectly competitive level. Other things being equal, the firm will gain at the expense of the consumer. Similarly, if consumers or workers have market power they can use this to their own benefit.   Key Idea 16

Table 4.1 shows the differences between the four categories.

The market structure under which a firm operates will determine its behaviour. Firms under perfect competition behave quite differently from firms that are monopolists, which behave differently again from firms under oligopoly or monopolistic competition.

This behaviour (or 'conduct') in turn affects the firm's performance: its prices, profits, efficiency, etc. In many cases it also affects other firms' performance: *their* prices, profits, efficiency, etc. The collective conduct of all the firms in the industry affects the whole industry's performance.

Economists thus see a causal chain running from market structure to the performance of that industry.

Structure → Conduct → Performance

First we look at the two extreme market structures: perfect competition and monopoly (Sections 4.2 and 4.3). Then we turn to look at the two intermediate cases of monopolistic competition and oligopoly (Sections 4.4 and 4.5).

Table 4.1	Features of the four market structures				
Type of market	Number of firms	Freedom of entry	Nature of product	Examples	Implication for demand curve for firm
Perfect competition	Very many	Unrestricted	Homogeneous (undifferentiated)	Cabbages, carrots (these approximate to perfect competition)	Horizontal. The firm is a price taker
Monopolistic competition	Many/several	Unrestricted	Differentiated	Builders, restaurants	Downward sloping, but relatively elastic. The firm has some control over price
Oligopoly	Few	Restricted	1. Undifferentiated or 2. Differentiated	1. Cement 2. Cars, electrical appliances	Downward sloping, relatively inelastic but depends on reactions of rivals to a price change
Monopoly	One	Restricted or completely blocked	Unique	Many prescription drugs, local water company	Downward sloping, more inelastic than oligopoly. The firm has considerable control over price

These two intermediate cases are sometimes referred to collectively as **imperfect competition**. The vast majority of firms in the real world operate under imperfect competition. It is still worth studying the two extreme cases, however, because they provide a framework within which to understand the real world. Some industries tend more to the competitive extreme, and thus their performance corresponds to some extent to perfect competition. Other industries tend more to the other extreme: for example, when there is one dominant firm and a few much smaller firms. In such cases their performance corresponds more to monopoly.

Definition

Imperfect competition The collective name for monopolistic competition and oligopoly.

Recap

1. There are four alternative market structures under which firms operate. In ascending order of firms' market power, they are: perfect competition, monopolistic competition, oligopoly and monopoly.

2. The market structure under which a firm operates affects its conduct, which in turn affects its performance.

PERFECT COMPETITION

4.2

What happens when there are very many firms all competing against each other? Is this good for us as consumers?

The theory of perfect competition illustrates an extreme form of capitalism. In it, firms are entirely subject to market forces. They have no power whatsoever to affect the price of the product. The price they face is determined by the interaction of demand and supply in the whole *market*.

Assumptions

The model of perfect competition is built on four assumptions:

TC 3
p11

- Firms are *price takers*. There are so many firms in the industry that each one produces an insignificantly small proportion of total industry supply, and therefore has *no power whatsoever* to affect the price of the product. It faces a horizontal demand 'curve' at the market price: the price determined by the interaction of demand and supply in the whole market.
- There is complete *freedom of entry* into the industry for new firms. Existing firms are unable to stop new firms setting up in business. Setting up a business takes time, however. Freedom of entry, therefore, applies in the long run.
- All firms produce an *identical product*. (The product is 'homogeneous'.) There is therefore no branding or advertising.
- Producers and consumers have *perfect knowledge* of the market. That is, producers are fully aware of prices, costs and market opportunities. Consumers are fully aware of price, quality and availability of the product.

> **Pause for thought**
>
> *It is sometimes claimed that the market for various stocks and shares is perfectly competitive, or nearly so. Take the case of the market for shares in a large company, such as BP. Go through each of the four assumptions above and see if they apply in this case. (Don't be misled by the first assumption. The 'firm' in this case is not BP itself, but rather the owners of the shares.)*

These assumptions are very strict. Few, if any, industries in the real world meet these conditions. Certain agricultural markets are perhaps closest to perfect competition. The market for certain fresh vegetables, such as potatoes, is an example. A potato grower is likely to face competition from so many others that he or she cannot affect the market price of any given variety of potatoes; there is freedom for farmers to set up in business growing potatoes; for any variety and grade of potatoes, each farmer produces a virtually identical product (potatoes are not branded by grower); knowledge of the market by both producers and consumers is very good.

The short-run equilibrium of the firm

TC5
p39

Definition

The short run under perfect competition
The period during which there is too little time for new firms to enter the industry.

In the short run, we assume that the number of firms in the industry cannot be increased; there is simply not time for new firms to enter the market.

Figure 4.1 shows a short-run equilibrium for both industry and a firm under perfect competition. Both parts of the diagram have the same scale for the vertical axis. The horizontal axes have totally different scales, however. For example, if the horizontal axis for the firm were measured in, say, thousands of units, the

Figure 4.1
Short-run equilibrium of industry and firm under perfect competition

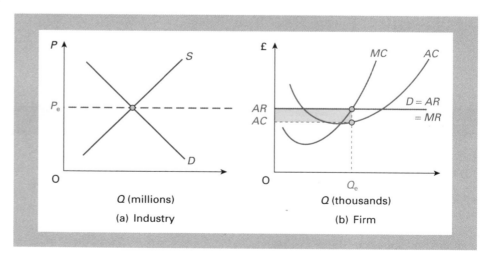

(a) Industry

(b) Firm

horizontal axis for the whole industry might be measured in millions or tens of millions of units, depending on the number of firms in the industry.

Let us examine the determination of price, output and profit in turn.

Price

The price is determined in the industry by the intersection of demand and supply. Being a price taker, the firm faces a horizontal demand (or average revenue) 'curve' at this price. It can sell all it can produce at the market price (P_e), but nothing at a price above P_e.

Output

The firm will maximise profit where marginal cost equals marginal revenue ($MR = MC$), at an output of Q_e. Note that, since the price is not affected by the firm's output, marginal revenue will equal price (see page 100 and Figure 3.4). Thus the firm's MR 'curve' and AR 'curve' (= demand 'curve') are the same horizontal straight line.

Profit

If the average cost (AC) curve (which includes normal profit) dips below the average revenue (AR) 'curve', the firm will earn supernormal profit. Supernormal profit per unit at Q_e is the vertical difference between AR and AC at Q_e. Total supernormal profit is the shaded rectangle in Figure 4.1 (i.e. profit per unit times quantity sold).

The short-run supply curve

The *firm's* short-run supply curve will be its (short-run) marginal cost curve. But why? A supply curve shows how much will be supplied at each price: it relates quantity to price. The marginal cost curve relates quantity to marginal cost. But, under perfect competition, given that $P = MR$, and $MR = MC$, P must equal MC. Thus the supply curve and the MC curve will follow the same line.

For example, in Figure 4.2(b), if price were P_1, profits would be maximised at Q_1 where $P_1 = MC$. Thus point a is one point on the supply curve. At a price of P_2, Q_2 would be produced. Thus point b is another point on the supply curve, and so on.

So, under perfect competition, the firm's supply curve depends entirely on production costs. This demonstrates why the firm's supply curve is upward sloping.

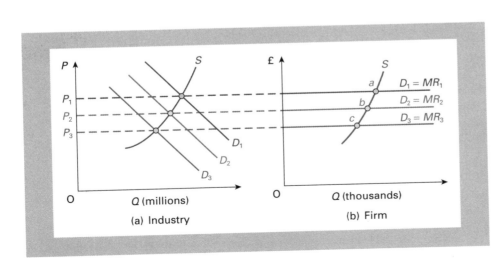

Figure 4.2
Deriving the short-run supply curve

Since marginal costs rise as output rises (due to diminishing marginal returns), a higher price will be necessary to induce the firm to increase its output.

Note that the firm will not produce at a price below AVC (see page 106 above). Thus the supply curve is only that portion of the MC curve above point e.

What will be the short-run supply curve of the whole *industry*? This is simply the sum of the short-run supply curves (and hence MC curves) of all the firms in the industry. Graphically this will be a *horizontal* sum, since it is *quantities* that are being added.

KI 19 p83

The long-run equilibrium of the firm

In the long run, if typical firms are making supernormal profits, new firms will be attracted into the industry. Likewise, if existing firms can make supernormal profits by increasing the scale of their operations, they will do so, since all factors of production are variable in the long run.

TC5 p39

The effect of the entry of new firms and/or the expansion of existing firms is to increase industry supply. This is illustrated in Figure 4.3. At a price of P_1 supernormal profits are earned. The industry supply curve will thus shift to the right as new firms enter. This in turn leads to a fall in price. Supply will go on increasing, and price falling, until firms are making only normal profits. This will be when price has fallen to the point where the demand 'curve' for the firm just touches the bottom of its long-run average cost curve. Q_L is thus the long-run equilibrium output of the firm, with P_L the long-run equilibrium price.

KI 6 p27

Since the $LRAC$ curve is tangential to (i.e. just touching) all possible short-run AC curves (see Section 3.2), the full long-run equilibrium will be as shown in Figure 4.4 where:

$$LRAC = AC = MC = MR = AR$$

The incompatibility of perfect competition and substantial economies of scale

Why is perfect competition so rare in the real world – if it even exists at all? One important reason for this has to do with economies of scale.

In many industries, firms may have to be quite large if they are to experience the full potential economies of scale. But perfect competition requires there to be *many* firms. Firms must therefore be small under perfect competition: too small in most cases for economies of scale.

Figure 4.3
Long-run equilibrium under perfect competition

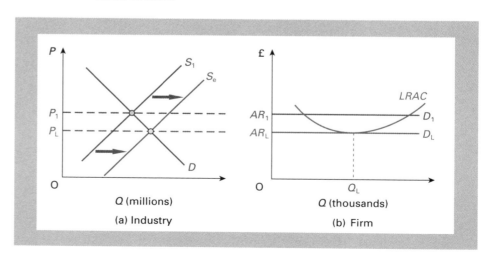

(a) Industry

(b) Firm

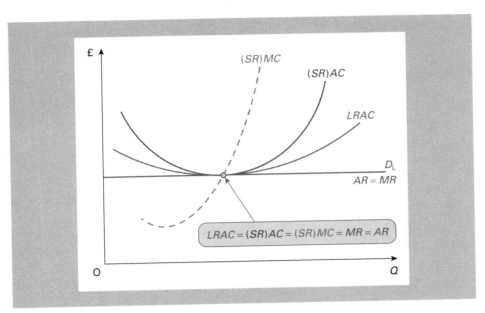

Figure 4.4
Long-run equilibrium
of the firm under
perfect competition

 Once a firm expands sufficiently to achieve economies of scale, it will usually gain market power. It will be able to undercut the prices of smaller firms, which will thus be driven out of business. Perfect competition is destroyed.

Perfect competition could exist in any industry, therefore, only if there were no (or virtually no) economies of scale.

Is perfect competition good for consumers?

Generally it is argued that perfect competition is a 'good thing', and that the more perfect an industry becomes the better. We explore the arguments in Section 4.3 (page 122) after we have looked at monopoly, but at this stage the main points in favour of perfect competition can be identified.

- Price equals marginal cost. Why is this desirable? To answer this, consider what would happen if they were not equal. If price were greater than marginal cost, this would mean that consumers were putting a higher value (P) on the production of extra units than they cost to produce (MC). Therefore more ought to be produced. If price were less than marginal cost, consumers would be putting a lower value on extra units than they cost to produce. Therefore less ought to be produced. When they are equal, therefore, production levels are just right. But, as we shall see later, it is only under perfect competition that $MC = P$.
- The combination of (long-run) production being at minimum average cost and the firm making only normal profit keeps prices at a minimum.
 - Perfect competition is a case of 'survival of the fittest'. Inefficient firms will be driven out of business, since they will not be able to make even normal profits. This encourages firms to be as efficient as possible and, where possible, to invest in new improved technology.

In general, it can be argued that perfectly competitive markets result in economic efficiency.

Economic efficiency is achieved when each good is produced at the minimum cost and where consumers get maximum benefit from their income.

Key
Idea
17

Box 4.1

E-commerce

A modern form of perfect competition?

The relentless drive towards big business in recent decades has seen many markets become more concentrated and increasingly dominated by large producers. And yet forces are at work that are undermining this dominance and bringing more competition to markets. One of these forces is *e-commerce*.

In this case study, we will consider just how far e-commerce is returning 'power to the people'.

Moving markets back towards perfect competition?

To see the extent to which e-commerce is making markets more competitive, let's look at the assumptions of perfect competition.

Large number of firms.   The growth of e-commerce has led to many new firms starting up in business. It's not just large firms like Amazon that are providing increased competition for established firms, but the thousands of small on-line companies that are being established every day. Many of these firms are selling directly to us as consumers. This is known as 'B2C' e-commerce (business-to-consumers). But many more are selling to other firms ('B2B'). More and more companies, from the biggest to the smallest, are transferring their purchasing to the Web and are keen to get value for money.

The reach of the Web is global. This means that firms, whether conventional or Web-based, are having to keep an eye on the prices and products of competitors in the rest of the world, not just in the local neighbourhood. Firms' demand curves are thus becoming very price-elastic. This is especially so for goods that are cheap to transport, or for services such as insurance and banking.

Perfect knowledge.   There are various ways in which e-commerce is adding to the consumer's knowledge. There is greater price transparency, with consumers able to compare prices on-line. On-line shopping agents such as Kelkoo, DealTime and Froogle can quickly locate a list of alternative suppliers. There is greater information on product availability and quality. Virtual shopping malls, full of e-retailers, place the high-street retailer under intense competitive pressure.

The pressure is even greater in the market for intermediate products. Many firms are constantly searching for cheaper sources of supply, and the Internet provides a cheap and easy means of conducting such searches.

Freedom of entry.   Internet companies often have lower start-up costs than their conventional rivals. Their premises are generally much smaller, with no 'shop-front' costs and lower levels of stock holding. Marketing costs can also be relatively low, especially given the ease with which companies can be located with search engines. Internet companies are often smaller and more specialist, relying on Internet 'outsourcing' (buying parts, equipment and other supplies through the Internet), rather than making everything themselves. They are also more likely to use delivery firms rather than having their own transport fleet. All

Recap

1. The assumptions of perfect competition are: a very large number of firms, complete freedom of entry, a homogeneous product and perfect knowledge of the good and its market by both producers and consumers.

2. In the short run, there is not time for new firms to enter the market, and thus supernormal profits can persist. In the long run, however, any supernormal profits will be competed away by the entry of new firms.

3. The short-run equilibrium for the firm will be where the price, as determined by demand and supply in the market, is equal to marginal cost. At this output the firm will be maximising profit.

4. The long-run equilibrium will be where the market price is just equal to firms' long-run average cost.

5. There can be no substantial economies of scale to be gained in a perfectly competitive industry. If there were, the industry would cease to be perfectly competitive as the large, low-cost firms drove the small, high-cost ones out of business.

this makes it relatively cheap for new firms to set up and begin trading over the Internet.

In fact, the distinction between firms and consumers is becoming increasingly blurred. With the rise of eBay, more and more people are finding going into business incredibly easy. Suddenly people are finding a market for all the junk they've collected over the years! As the eBay TV advertisement says, 'someone wants everything'. There are some 200 million registered eBay users worldwide, and hundreds of thousands of people make a full-time living from buying and selling on eBay. In 2006, there were nearly 400 000 stores hosted on eBay. Annual sales on eBay are worth over £25 billion.

Not only do these factors make markets more price-competitive, they also bring other benefits. Costs are driven down, as firms economise on stock holding, rely more on outsourcing and develop more efficient relationships with suppliers. 'Procurement hubs', on-line exchanges and trading communities are now well established in many industries. The competition also encourages innovation, which improves quality and the range of products.

Is there a limit to e-commerce?

In 20 years, will we be doing all our shopping on the Internet? Will the only shopping malls be virtual ones? Although e-commerce is revolutionising some markets, it is unlikely that things will go anything like that far.

The benefits of 'shop shopping' are that you get to see the good, touch it and use it. You can buy the good there and then, and take instant possession of it: you don't have to wait. Shopping is also an enjoyable experience. Many people like wandering round the shops, meeting friends, seeing what takes their fancy, trying on clothes, browsing through CDs and so on. 'Retail therapy' for many is an important means of 'de-stressing'.

On-line shopping is limited by the screen; Internet access may be slow and frustrating; 'surfing' may instead become 'wading'; you have to wait for goods to be delivered; and what if deliveries are late or fail completely?

Also costs might not be as low as expected. How efficient is it to have many small deliveries of goods? How significant are the lost cost savings from economies of scale that larger producers or retailers are likely to generate?

Nevertheless, e-commerce has made many markets, both retail and B2B, more competitive. This is especially so for services and for goods whose quality is easy to identify on-line. Many firms are being forced to face up to having their prices determined by the market.

1. *Why may the Internet work better for replacement buys than for new purchases?*
2. *Give three examples of products that are particularly suitable for selling over the Internet and three that are not. Explain your answer.*

MONOPOLY   4.3

What happens when there is only one firm in the market? Do we as consumers suffer?

What is a monopoly?

This may seem a strange question because the answer appears obvious. A monopoly exists when there is only one firm in the industry.

But whether an industry can be classed as a monopoly is not always clear. It depends how narrowly the industry is defined. For example, a textile company may have a monopoly on certain types of fabric, but it does not have a monopoly on fabrics in general. The consumer can buy fabrics other than those supplied by the company. A rail company may have a monopoly over rail services between two cities, but it does not have a monopoly over public transport between these two cities. People can travel by coach or air. They could also use private transport.

To some extent, the boundaries of an industry are arbitrary. What is more important for a firm is the amount of monopoly *power* it has, and that depends on the closeness of substitutes produced by rival industries. The Post Office before 2006 had a monopoly over the delivery of letters, but it faced competition in communications from telephone, faxes and e-mail.

Barriers to entry

For a firm to maintain its monopoly position, there must be barriers to the entry of new firms. As we shall see, barriers also exist under oligopoly, but in the case of monopoly they must be high enough to block the entry of new firms. Barriers can take various forms.

Economies of scale. If the monopolist's costs go on falling significantly up to the output that satisfies the whole market, the industry may not be able to support more than one producer. This case is known as natural monopoly. It is particularly likely if the market is small. For example, two bus companies might find it unprofitable to serve the same routes, each running with perhaps only half-full buses, whereas one company with a monopoly of the routes could make a profit. Electricity transmission via a national grid is another example of a natural monopoly.

Even if a market could support more than one firm, a new entrant is unlikely to be able to start up on a very large scale. Thus the monopolist that is already experiencing economies of scale can charge a price below the cost of the new entrant and drive it out of business. If, however, the new entrant is a firm already established in another industry, it may be able to survive this competition.

Economies of scope. A firm that produces a range of products is also likely to experience a lower average cost of production. For example, a large pharmaceutical company producing a range of drugs and toiletries can use shared research, marketing, storage and transport facilities across its range of products. These lower costs make it difficult for a new single-product entrant to the market, since the large firm will be able to undercut its price and drive it out of the market.

Product differentiation and brand loyalty. If a firm produces a clearly differentiated product, where the consumer associates the product with the brand, it will be very difficult for a new firm to break into that market. Rank Xerox invented, and patented, the plain paper photocopier. After this legal monopoly (see below) ran out, people still associated photocopiers with Rank Xerox. It is still not unusual to hear someone say that they are going to 'Xerox the article' or, for that matter, 'Hoover their carpet'. Other examples of strong brand image include Guinness, Kellogg's Cornflakes, Coca-Cola, Nescafé and Sellotape.

Lower costs for an established firm. An established monopoly is likely to have developed specialised production and marketing skills. It is more likely to be aware of the most efficient techniques and the most reliable and/or cheapest suppliers. It is likely to have access to cheaper finance. It is thus operating on a lower cost curve. New firms would therefore find it hard to compete and would be likely to lose any price war.

Definition

Natural monopoly
A situation where long-run average costs would be lower if an industry were under monopoly than if it were shared between two or more competitors.

Ownership of, or control over, key inputs or outlets.   If a firm governs the supply of vital inputs (say, by owning the sole supplier of some component part), it can deny access to these inputs to potential rivals. On a world scale, the de Beers company has a monopoly in fine diamonds because all diamond producers market their diamonds through de Beers.

Similarly, if a firm controls the outlets through which the product must be sold, it can prevent potential rivals from gaining access to consumers. For example, Birds Eye Wall's used to supply freezers free to shops on the condition that they stocked only Wall's ice-cream in them.

Legal protection.   The firm's monopoly position may be protected by patents on essential processes, by copyright, by various forms of licensing (allowing, say, only one firm to operate in a particular area) or by tariffs (i.e. customs duties) and other trade restrictions to keep out foreign competitors. Examples of monopolies protected by patents include most new medicines developed by pharmaceutical companies (e.g. anti-AIDS drugs), Microsoft's Windows operating systems, and agro-chemical companies, such as Monsanto, with various genetically modified plant varieties and pesticides.

Mergers and takeovers.   The monopolist can put in a takeover bid for any new entrant. The sheer threat of takeovers may discourage new entrants.

Aggressive tactics.   An established monopolist can probably sustain losses for longer than a new entrant. Thus it could start a price war, mount massive advertising campaigns, offer attractive after-sales service, introduce new brands to compete with new entrants, and so on.

Equilibrium price and output

Since there is, by definition, only one firm in the industry, the firm's demand curve is also the industry demand curve.

Compared with other market structures, demand under monopoly tends to be less elastic at each price. The monopolist can raise its price and consumers have no alternative firm to turn to within the industry. They either pay the higher price, or go without the good altogether.

Unlike the firm under perfect competition, the monopoly firm is thus a 'price maker'. It can choose what price to charge. Nevertheless, it is still constrained by its demand curve. A rise in price will reduce the quantity demanded.

As with firms in other market structures, a monopolist will maximise profit where $MR = MC$. In Figure 4.5 profit is maximised at Q_m. The supernormal profit obtained is shown by the shaded area.

These profits will tend to be larger the less elastic is the demand curve (and hence the steeper is the MR curve), and thus the bigger is the gap between MR and price (AR). The actual elasticity will depend on whether reasonably close substitutes are available in *other* industries. The demand for a rail service will be much less elastic (and the potential for profit greater) if there is no bus service to the same destination.

Since there are barriers to the entry of new firms, a monopolist's supernormal profits will not be competed away in the long run. The only difference, therefore, between short-run and long-run equilibrium is that in the long run the firm will produce where $MR = long-run MC$.

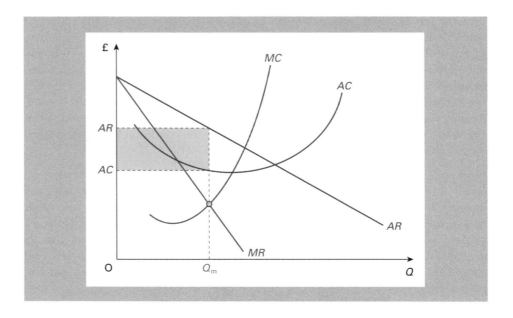

Monopoly versus perfect competition: which best serves the public interest?

Because it faces a different type of market environment, the monopolist will produce a quite different output and at a quite different price from a perfectly competitive industry.

Let us compare the two.

Short-run price and output. Figure 4.6 compares the profit-maximising position for an industry under monopoly with that under perfect competition. Note that we are comparing the monopoly with the whole *industry* under perfect competition. That way we can assume, for sake of comparison, that they both face the same

TC3
p11

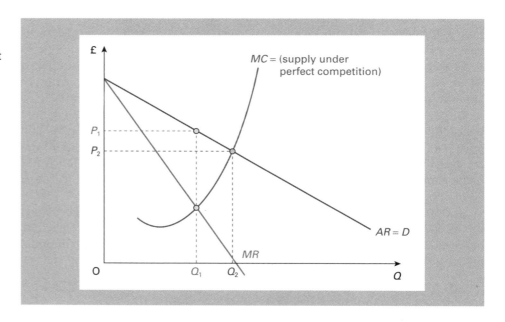

demand curve. We also assume for the moment that they both face the same cost curves.

The monopolist will produce Q_1 at a price of P_1. This is where $MC = MR$. If the same industry were under perfect competition, however, it would produce at Q_2 and P_2 – a higher output and a lower price. But why? The reason is that for each of the firms in the industry – and it is at this level that the decisions are made – marginal revenue is the same as price. Remember that the *firm* under perfect competition faces a perfectly elastic demand (*AR*) curve, which also equals *MR* (see Figure 4.1). Thus producing where $MC = MR$ also means producing where $MC = P$. When *all* firms under perfect competition do this, price and quantity in the *industry* will be given by P_2 and Q_2 in Figure 4.6.

In the short run, therefore, it would seem (other things being equal) that perfect competition better serves the consumer's interest than does monopoly.

Long-run price and output.   Under perfect competition, freedom of entry eliminates supernormal profit and forces firms to produce at the bottom of their *LRAC* curve. The effect, therefore, is to keep long-run prices down. Under monopoly, however, barriers to entry allow profits to remain supernormal in the long run. The monopolist is not forced to operate at the bottom of the *AC* curve. Thus, other things being equal, long-run prices will tend to be higher, and hence output lower, under monopoly.

Thus, again, it would *seem* that perfect competition better serves the consumer's interests. But this assumes that the cost curves are the *same* under both perfect competition and monopoly. Let us, therefore, turn to costs.

> ### Pause for thought
>
> If the shares in a monopoly (such as a water company) were very widely distributed among the population, would the shareholders necessarily want the firm to use its monopoly power to make larger profits?

Costs under monopoly.   The sheer survival of a firm in the long run under perfect competition requires that it uses the most efficient known technique, and develops new techniques wherever possible. The monopolist, however, sheltered by barriers to entry, can still make large profits even if it is not using the most efficient technique. It has less incentive, therefore, to be efficient. For this reason, costs may be *higher* under monopoly (another criticism of monopoly).

On the other hand, the monopoly may be able to achieve substantial economies of scale due to larger plant, centralised administration and the avoidance of unnecessary duplication (e.g. a monopoly water company would eliminate the need for several sets of rival water mains under each street). If this results in an *MC* curve substantially below that of the same industry under perfect competition, the monopoly may even produce a *higher* output at a *lower* price.

Another reason why a monopolist may operate with lower costs is that it can use part of its supernormal profits for research and development and investment. It may not have the same *incentive* to become efficient as the perfectly competitive firm which is fighting for survival, but it may have a much greater *ability* to become efficient than has the small firm with limited funds.

Although a monopoly faces no competition in the goods market, it may face an alternative form of competition in financial markets. A monopoly, with potentially low costs, which is currently run inefficiently, is likely to be subject to a takeover bid from another company. This **competition for corporate control**, as it is called, may thus force the monopoly to be efficient in order to prevent being taken over.

Innovation and new products.   The promise of supernormal profits, protected perhaps by patents, may encourage the development of new (monopoly) industries producing new products. It is this chance of making monopoly profits that encourages many people to take the risks of going into business.

> ### Definition
>
> **Competition for corporate control**
> The competition for the control of companies through takeovers.

Potential competition or potential monopoly? The theory of contestable markets

Potential competition

In recent years, economists have developed the theory of contestable markets. This theory argues that what is crucial in determining price and output is not whether an industry is *actually* a monopoly or competitive, but whether there is the real *threat* of competition.

If a monopoly is protected by high barriers to entry – say, it owns all the raw materials – then it will be able to make supernormal profits with no fear of competition.

If, however, another firm *could* take over from it with little difficulty, it will behave much more like a competitive firm. The threat of competition has a similar effect to actual competition.

As an example, consider a catering company that is given permission by a factory to run its canteen. The catering company has a monopoly over the supply of food to the workers in that factory. If, however, it starts charging high prices or providing a poor service, the factory could offer the running of the canteen to an alternative catering company. This threat may force the original catering company to charge 'reasonable' prices and offer a good service.

Perfectly contestable markets

> **Definition**
>
> **Perfectly contestable market**
> A market where there is free and costless entry and exit.

A market is **perfectly contestable** when the costs of entry and exit by potential rivals are zero, and when such entry can be made very rapidly. In such cases, the moment the possibility of earning supernormal profits occurs, new firms will enter, thus driving profits down to a normal level. The sheer threat of this happening, so the theory goes, will ensure that the firm already in the market will (a) keep its prices down, so that it just makes normal profits, and (b) produce as efficiently as possible, taking advantage of any economies of scale and any new technology. If the existing firm did not do this, entry would take place, and potential competition would become actual competition.

Contestable markets and natural monopolies

So why in such cases are the markets not *actually* perfectly competitive? Why do they remain monopolies?

The most likely reason has to do with economies of scale and the size of the market. To operate on a minimum efficient scale, the firm may have to be so large relative to the market that there is only room for one such firm in the industry. If a new firm does come into the market, then one or other of the two firms will not survive the competition. The market is simply not big enough for both of them.

If, however, there are no entry or exit costs, new firms will be perfectly willing to enter even though there is only room for one firm, provided they believe that they are more efficient than the existing firm. The existing firm, knowing this, will be forced to produce as efficiently as possible and with only normal profit.

The importance of costless exit

Setting up in a new business usually involves large expenditures on plant and machinery. Once this money has been committed, it becomes fixed costs. If these fixed costs are no higher than those of the existing firm, then the new firm could win the battle. But, of course, there is always the risk that it might lose.

But does losing the battle really matter? Can the firm not simply move to another market?

It does matter if there are substantial costs of exit. This will be the case if the capital equipment cannot be transferred to other uses – for example, a new blast furnace constructed by a new rival steel company. In this case, these fixed costs are known as **sunk costs**. The losing firm is left with capital equipment it cannot use. The firm may therefore be put off entering in the first place. The market is not perfectly contestable, and the established firm can make supernormal profit.

If, however, the capital equipment can be transferred, the exit costs will be zero (or at least very low), and new firms will be more willing to take the risks of entry. For example, a rival coach company may open up a service on a route previously operated by only one company, and where there is still only room for one operator. If the new firm loses the resulting battle, it can still use the coaches it has purchased. It simply uses them for a different route. The cost of the coaches is not a sunk cost.

Costless exit, therefore, encourages firms to enter an industry, knowing that, if unsuccessful, they can always transfer their capital elsewhere.

The lower the exit costs, the more contestable the market. This implies that firms already established in other similar markets may provide more effective competition against monopolists, since they can simply transfer capital from one market to another. For example, studies of airlines in the USA show that entry to a particular route may be much easier for an established airline, which can simply transfer planes from one route to another.

Contestability and the consumer's interests

The more contestable the market, the more will a monopoly be forced to act like a firm under perfect competition. If, therefore, a monopoly operates in a perfectly contestable market, it might bring the 'best of both worlds' for the consumer. Not only will it be able to achieve low costs through economies of scale, but also the potential competition will keep profits and hence prices down.

Recap

1. A monopoly is where there is only one firm in an industry. In practice it is difficult to determine where a monopoly exists because it depends on how narrowly an industry is defined.

2. Barriers to the entry of new firms will normally be necessary to protect a monopoly from competition. Such barriers include economies of scale (making the firm a natural monopoly or at least giving it a cost advantage over new (small) competitors), control over supplies of inputs or over outlets, patents or copyright, and tactics to eliminate competition (such as takeovers or aggressive advertising).

3. Profits for the monopolist will be maximised (as for other firms) where $MC = MR$.

4. If demand and cost curves are the same in a monopoly and a perfectly competitive industry, the monopoly will produce a lower output and at a higher price than the perfectly competitive industry.

5. On the other hand, any economies of scale will, in part, be passed on to consumers in lower prices, and the monopolist's high profits may be used for research and development and investment, which in turn may lead to better products at possibly lower prices.

6. Potential competition may be as important as actual competition in determining a firm's price and output strategy.

7. The threat of this competition is greater the lower are the entry and exit costs to and from the industry. If the entry and exit costs are zero, the market is said to be perfectly contestable. Under such circumstances an existing monopolist will be forced to keep its profits down to the normal level if it is to resist entry of new firms. Exit costs will be lower, the lower are the sunk costs of the firm.

Box 4.2

Microsoft, the Internet and the US Justice Department

Windows cleaning

On 18 May 1998, the US government initiated its biggest competition case for 20 years: it sued Microsoft, the world's largest software company. It accused Microsoft of abusing its market power and seeking to crush its rivals. By controlling the *Windows* operating software, Microsoft could force its own Internet browser, *Internet Explorer*, on to consumers and computer manufacturers.

The case against Microsoft had been building for many years, but it was with the release of *Windows 98* that the US government decided to act. The US Justice Department alleged that Microsoft had committed the following anti-competitive actions:

■ Back in May 1995, Microsoft attempted to collude with Netscape Communications to divide the Internet browser market. Netscape Communications refused.

■ Microsoft had forced personal computer manufacturers to install *Internet Explorer* in order to obtain a *Windows 95* operating licence.

■ Microsoft insisted that PC manufacturers conformed to a Microsoft front screen for Windows. This included specified icons, one of which was Microsoft's *Internet Explorer*.

■ It had set up reciprocal advertising arrangements with America's largest Internet service providers, such as America Online. Here Microsoft would promote America Online via Windows. In return, America Online would not promote Netscape's browsers.

Microsoft, in its defence, argued that the integration of its own browser into the Windows system was a natural part of the process of product innovation and development. Microsoft officials claimed that accusations of unfair trading practices were not founded: it was simply attempting to improve the quality of its product. If Microsoft was to do nothing with its Windows product, it would, over time, lose its dominant market position, and be replaced by a more innovative and superior product manufactured by a rival software producer.

In this respect, Microsoft could be seen to be operating in the consumer's interest. The argument is that, in an environment where technology is changing rapidly, Microsoft's control over standards gives the user a measure of stability, knowing that any new products and applications will be compatible with existing ones. In other words, new software can be incorporated into existing systems.

Network effects

The key issue in respect of Microsoft, then, was not so much the browser war, but far more fundamentally to do with the operating system, and how Microsoft used its ownership of this system to extend its leverage into other related high-technology markets.

An operating system attracts software developed around that operating system, thereby discouraging new competition since any alternative faces not only the challenge of creating a better operating system but competing against a whole array of already existing software applications. Businesses train employees in one technology and are reluctant to abandon that investment in training, while the existence of a pool of people trained in that technology encourages other businesses to adopt that technology. . . . These so-called 'network effects' give an incredible anti-competitive edge to companies like Microsoft that control so many different parts of the network.[1]

Network effects arise when consumers of a product benefit from it being used by *other* consumers. The more people who use it, the greater the benefit to each individual user. The problem for the con-

[1] N. Newman, *From Microsoft Word to Microsoft World: How Microsoft is building a global monopoly* (1997) www.netaction.org/msoft/world

sumer in such a scenario is that these network effects can lead to the establishment of a monopoly producer and hence to higher prices. There is also the problem of whether the best product is being produced by the monopolist. In such an instance, the consumer may be 'locked in' to using an inferior product or technology with limited opportunity (if any) to change.

Microsoft had been able to use consumer lock-in to drive competitors from the market. Where choice did exist, for example in Internet browsers, Microsoft was using its operating system dominance to promote its own product.

Court findings

A verdict was reached on 7 June 2000, when Federal Judge Thomas Penfield Jackson ruled that Microsoft be split in two to prevent it operating as a monopoly. One company would produce and market the Windows operating system; the other would produce and market the applications software, such as *Microsoft Office* and the Web browser, *Internet Explorer*.

Microsoft appealed against the judgment to the US Federal Appeals Court, which in June 2001 overturned the ruling and referred the case to a different judge for reconsideration. Judge Colleen Kollar-Kotelly urged both sides (Microsoft and the US Justice Department) to try to reach a settlement, and in November 2001 they did just that. They agreed that Microsoft would provide technical information about Windows to other companies to enable them to write software that would compete with Microsoft's own software. Also Microsoft would not be allowed to retaliate against computer manufacturers that installed rival products or removed icons for Microsoft applications.

Nine states, however, refused to sign up to the agreement and a further year went past before Judge Kollar-Kotelly gave her final ruling. Whilst she agreed with many of Judge Jackson's original findings, she did not require that Microsoft be split into two companies. Instead, she upheld the November 2001 agreement.

Legal action against Microsoft was not confined to the USA. In March 2004, the European Commission fined Microsoft a record €497 million for abusing its monopoly position. In addition Microsoft was ordered to issue a version of *Windows XP* without *Windows Media Player* (*WMP*). The argument was similar to the earlier ones used in the USA over browsers. This time it was claimed that by bundling *WMP* with *XP*, Microsoft was gaining an unfair advantage over competitor media players, such as *RealPlayer* and Apple's *QuickTime*.

In April 2006, Microsoft launched an appeal against the judgment, claiming that the EU's ruling violated international law by forcing the company to share information with rivals.

Meanwhile, other countries' competition authorities were acting against Microsoft. In 2006, the Korean Fair Trade Commission imposed a fine of 32.5 billion Korean won (£18.5 million) on the company and required it to provide two separate versions of Windows: one without Windows Media Player and Windows Messenger; the other with the two software products but carrying links to Web pages that allow consumers to download competing versions. Microsoft also appealed against this ruling.

You might want to follow subsequent events as the news unfolds (see section A of the Hotlinks section in MyEconLab).

?
1. *In what respects might Microsoft's behaviour be deemed to have been: (a) against the public interest; (b) in the public interest?*
2. *Being locked into a product or technology is only a problem if such a product can be clearly shown to be inferior to an alternative. What difficulties might there be in establishing such a case?*

4.4 MONOPOLISTIC COMPETITION

What happens if there are quite a lot of firms competing, but each firm tries to attract us to its particular product or service?

Very few markets in practice can be classified as perfectly competitive or as a pure monopoly. The vast majority of firms do compete with other firms, often quite aggressively, and yet they are not price takers: they do have some degree of market power. Most markets, therefore, lie between the two extremes of monopoly and perfect competition, in the realm of 'imperfect competition'. As we saw in Section 4.1, there are two types of imperfect competition: namely, monopolistic competition and oligopoly.

Monopolistic competition is nearer to the competitive end of the spectrum. It can best be understood as a situation where there are a lot of firms competing but where each firm does nevertheless have some degree of market power (hence the term 'monopolistic' competition): each firm has some discretion as to what price to charge for its products.

Assumptions

TC 3
p11

- There is *quite a large number of firms*. As a result each firm has only a small share of the market, and therefore its actions are unlikely to affect its rivals to any great extent. What this means is that each firm in making its decisions does not have to worry how its rivals will react. It assumes that what its rivals choose to do will *not* be influenced by what it does.

    This is known as the assumption of **independence**. (As we shall see later, this is not the case under oligopoly. There we assume that firms believe that their decisions *do* affect their rivals, and that their rivals' decisions will affect them. Under oligopoly we assume that firms are *inter*dependent.)
- There is *freedom of entry* of new firms into the industry. If any firm wants to set up in business in this market, it is free to do so.

In these two respects, therefore, monopolistic competition is like perfect competition.

TC 8
p64

- Unlike perfect competition, however, each firm produces a product or provides a service in some way different from its rivals. As a result it can raise its price without losing all its customers. Thus its demand curve is downward sloping, albeit relatively elastic given the large number of competitors to which customers can turn. This is known as the assumption of **product differentiation**.

Petrol stations, restaurants, hairdressers and builders are all examples of monopolistic competition.

A typical feature of monopolistic competition is that, although there are many firms in the industry, there is only one firm in a particular location. This applies particularly in retailing. There may be several newsagents in a town, but only one in a particular street. In a sense, therefore, it has a local monopoly. People may be prepared to pay higher prices there to avoid having to go elsewhere.

Definitions

Independence (of firms in a market)
Where the decisions of one firm in a market will not have any significant effect on the demand curves of its rivals.

Product differentiation
Where one firm's product is sufficiently different from its rivals' to allow it to raise the price of the product without customers all switching to the rivals' products. A situation where a firm faces a downward-sloping demand curve.

Pause for thought

An example of monopolistic competition is that of fast-food restaurants. What other businesses are in competition with fast-food restaurants and what determines the closeness of this competition?

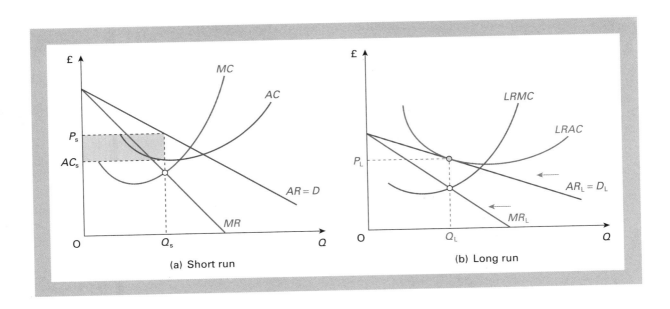

(a) Short run   (b) Long run

Figure 4.7
Equilibrium of the firm
under monopolistic
competition

Equilibrium of the firm

Short run

As with other market structures, profits are maximised at the output where $MC = MR$. The diagram is the same as for the monopolist, except that the AR and MR curves are more elastic. This is illustrated in Figure 4.7(a). As with perfect competition, it is possible for the monopolistically competitive firm to make supernormal profit in the short run. This is shown as the shaded area.

Just how much profit the firm will make in the short run depends on the strength of demand: the position and elasticity of the demand curve. The further to the right the demand curve is relative to the average cost curve, and the less elastic the demand curve is, the greater will be the firm's short-run profit. Thus a firm whose product is considerably differentiated from its rivals may be able to earn considerable short-run profits.

> **Pause for thought**
>
> *Which of these two items is a petrol station more likely to sell at a discount: (a) oil; (b) sweets? Why?*

Long run

If typical firms are earning supernormal profit, new firms will enter the industry in the long run. As new firms enter, they will take some of the customers away from the established firms. The demand for the established firms' product will therefore fall. Their demand (AR) curve will shift to the left, and will continue doing so as long as supernormal profits remain and thus new firms continue entering.

Long-run equilibrium will be reached when only normal profits remain: when there is no further incentive for new firms to enter. This is illustrated in Figure 4.7(b). The firm's demand curve settles at D_L, where it just touches the firm's $LRAC$ curve. Output will be Q_L: where $AR_L = LRAC$. (At any other output, $LRAC$ is greater than AR and thus less than normal profit would be made.)

Non-price competition

One of the biggest problems with the simple model in Figure 4.7 is that it concentrates on price and output decisions. In practice, the profit-maximising firm under monopolistic competition will also need to decide the exact variety of product to produce and how much to spend on advertising it. This will lead the firm to take part in non-price competition.

Non-price competition involves two major elements: product development and advertising.

The major aims of *product development* are to produce a product that will sell well (i.e. one in high or potentially high demand) and one that is different from rivals' products (i.e. has an inelastic demand due to lack of close substitutes). For shops or other firms providing a service, 'product development' takes the form of attempting to provide a service which is better than, or at least different from, that of rivals: personal service, late opening, certain lines stocked, and so on.

The major aim of *advertising* is to sell the product. This can be achieved not only by informing people of the product's existence and availability, but also by trying to persuade them to purchase it. Like product development, successful advertising will both increase demand and also make the firm's demand curve less elastic, since it stresses the specific qualities of this firm's product over its rivals' (see Box 2.3).

Product development and advertising not only increase a firm's demand and hence revenue, they also involve increased costs. So how much should a firm advertise, say to maximise profits?

For any given price and product, the optimal amount of advertising is where the revenue from *additional* advertising (MR_A) is equal to its cost (MC_A). As long as $MR_A > MC_A$, additional advertising will add to profit. But extra amounts spent on advertising are likely to lead to smaller and smaller increases in sales. Thus MR_A falls, until $MR_A = MC_A$. At that point no further profit can be made. It is at a maximum.

Pause for thought

*Why will additional advertising lead to
smaller and smaller increases in sales?*

Two problems arise with this analysis:

- The effect of product development and advertising on demand will be difficult for a firm to forecast.
- Product development and advertising are likely to have different effects at different prices. Profit maximisation, therefore, will involve the more complex choice of the optimum combination of price, type of product, and level and variety of advertising.

Monopolistic competition and the public interest

Comparison with perfect competition

It is often argued that monopolistic competition leads to a less efficient allocation of resources than perfect competition.

Figure 4.8 compares the long-run equilibrium positions for two firms. One firm is under perfect competition and thus faces a horizontal demand curve. It will produce an output of Q_1 at a price of P_1. The other is under monopolistic competition and thus faces a downward-sloping demand curve. It will produce the lower output of Q_2 at the higher price of P_2. A crucial assumption here is that a firm would have the *same* long-run average cost (*LRAC*) curve in both cases. Given this assumption, monopolistic competition has the following disadvantages:

- Less will be sold and at a higher price.
- Firms will not be producing at the least-cost point.

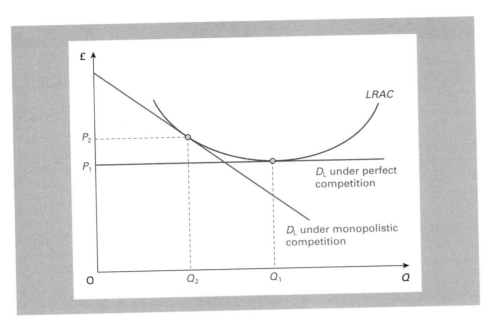

Figure 4.8
Long-run equilibrium
of the firm under
perfect and
monopolistic
competition

By producing more, firms would move to a lower point on their *LRAC* curve. Thus firms under monopolistic competition are said to have **excess capacity**. In Figure 4.8 this excess capacity is shown as $Q_1 - Q_2$. In other words, monopolistic competition is typified by quite a large number of firms (e.g. petrol stations), all operating at less than optimum output, and thus being forced to charge a price above that which they could charge if they had a bigger turnover. How often have you been to a petrol station and had to queue for the pumps?

So how does this affect the consumer? Although the firm under monopolistic competition may charge a higher price than under perfect competition, the difference may be very small. Although the firm's demand curve is downward sloping, it is still likely to be highly elastic due to the large number of substitutes. Furthermore, the consumer may benefit from monopolistic competition by having a greater variety of products to choose from. Each firm may satisfy some particular requirement of particular consumers.

Comparison with monopoly

The arguments are very similar here to those when comparing perfect competition and monopoly.

On the one hand, freedom of entry for new firms and hence the lack of long-run supernormal profits under monopolistic competition are likely to help keep prices down for the consumer and encourage cost saving. On the other hand, monopolies are likely to achieve greater economies of scale and have more funds for investment and research and development.

Definitions

Excess capacity (under monopolistic competition)
In the long run firms under monopolistic competition will produce at an output below their minimum-cost point.

1. Monopolistic competition occurs where there is free entry to the industry and quite a large number of firms operating independently of each other, but where each firm has some market power as a result of producing differentiated products or services.

2. In the short run, firms can make supernormal profits. In the long run, however, freedom of entry will drive profits down to the normal level. The long-run equilibrium of the firm is where the (downward-sloping) demand curve just touches the long-run average cost curve.

3. The long-run equilibrium is one of excess capacity. Given that the demand curve is downward sloping, the point where it just touches the *LRAC* curve will not be at the bottom of the *LRAC* curve. Increased production would thus be possible at *lower* average cost.

4. Firms under monopolistic competition may engage in non-price competition, in the forms of product development and advertising, in order to maintain an advantage over their rivals.

5. Monopolistically competitive firms, because of excess capacity, may have higher costs, and thus higher prices, than perfectly competitive firms, but consumers may gain from a greater diversity of products.

6. Monopolistically competitive firms may have fewer economies of scale than monopolies and conduct less research and development, but the competition may keep prices lower than under monopoly. Whether there will be more or less choice for the consumer is debatable.

4.5 OLIGOPOLY

What happens if there are just a few firms that dominate the market? Will they compete or get together?

Oligopoly occurs when just a few firms between them share a large proportion of the industry.

There are, however, significant differences in the structure of industries under oligopoly and similarly significant differences in the behaviour of firms. The firms may produce a virtually identical product (e.g. metals, chemicals, sugar, petrol). Most oligopolists, however, produce differentiated products (e.g. cars, soap powder, soft drinks, electrical appliances). Much of the competition between such oligopolists is in terms of the marketing of their particular brand.

The two key features of oligopoly

Despite the differences between oligopolies, there are two crucial features that distinguish oligopoly from other market structures.

Barriers to entry

Unlike firms under monopolistic competition, there are various barriers to the entry of new firms. These are similar to those under monopoly (see pages 120–1). The size of the barriers, however, will vary from industry to industry. In some cases entry is relatively easy, whereas in others it is virtually impossible.

Interdependence of the firms

Because there are only a few firms under oligopoly, each firm has to take account of the others. This means that they are mutually dependent: they are interdependent. Each firm is affected by its rivals' actions. If a firm changes the price or specification of its product, for example, or the amount of its advertising, the sales of its rivals

Definition

Interdependence (under oligopoly)
One of the two key features of oligopoly. Each firm will be affected by its rivals' decisions. Likewise its decisions will affect its rivals. Firms recognise this interdependence. This recognition will affect their decisions.

will be affected. The rivals may then respond by changing their price, specification or advertising. No firm can therefore afford to ignore the actions and reactions of other firms in the industry.

People often think and behave strategically. How you think others will respond to your actions is likely to influence your own behaviour. Firms, for example, when considering a price or product change will often take into account the likely reactions of their rivals.

Key Idea 18

It is impossible, therefore, to predict the effect on a firm's sales of, say, a change in the price of its product without first making some assumption about the reactions of other firms. Different assumptions will yield different predictions. For this reason there is no single generally accepted theory of oligopoly. Firms may react differently and unpredictably.

Competition and collusion

Oligopolists are pulled in two different directions:

■ The interdependence of firms may make them wish to *collude* with each other. If they can club together and act as if they were a monopoly, they could jointly maximise industry profits.

■ On the other hand, they will be tempted to *compete* with their rivals to gain a bigger share of industry profits for themselves.

These two policies are incompatible. The more fiercely firms compete to gain a bigger share of industry profits, the smaller these industry profits will become! For example, price competition drives down the average industry price, while competition through advertising raises industry costs. Either way, industry profits fall.

Sometimes firms will collude. Sometimes they will not. The following sections examine first **collusive oligopoly** (both open and tacit), and then **non-collusive oligopoly**.

Collusive oligopoly

KI 16
p112

When firms under oligopoly engage in collusion, they may agree on prices, market share, advertising expenditure, etc. Such collusion reduces the uncertainty they face. It reduces the fear of engaging in competitive price cutting or retaliatory advertising, both of which could reduce total industry profits.

A cartel

A formal collusive agreement is called a **cartel**. The cartel will maximise profits if it acts like a monopoly: if the members behave as if they were a single firm. This is illustrated in Figure 4.9.

The total market demand curve is shown with the corresponding market *MR* curve. The cartel's *MC* curve is the *horizontal* sum of the *MC* curves of its members (since we are adding the *output* of each of the cartel members at each level of marginal cost). Profits are maximised at Q_1 where $MC = MR$. The cartel must therefore set a price of P_1 (at which Q_1 will be demanded).

TC2
p10

Having agreed on the cartel price, the members may then compete against each other using *non-price competition*, to gain as big a share of resulting sales (Q_1) as they can.

Box 4.3

OPEC – the rise and fall and rise again of a cartel

The history of the world's most famous cartel

OPEC is probably the best known of all cartels. It was set up in 1960 by the five major oil-exporting countries: Saudi Arabia, Iran, Iraq, Kuwait and Venezuela. Its stated objectives were as follows:

- The co-ordination and unification of the petroleum policies of member countries.
- The organisation of means to ensure the stabilisation of prices, eliminating harmful and unnecessary fluctuations.

The years leading up to 1960 had seen the oil-producing countries increasingly in conflict with the international oil companies, which extracted oil under 'concessionary agreement'. Under this scheme, oil companies were given the right to extract oil in return for royalties. This meant that the oil-producing countries had little say over output and price levels.

Despite the formation of OPEC in 1960, it was not until 1973 that control of oil production was effectively transferred from the oil companies to the oil countries, with OPEC making the decisions on how much oil to produce and thereby determining its oil revenue. By this time OPEC consisted of 13 members.

OPEC's pricing policy over the 1970s consisted of setting a market price for Saudi Arabian crude (the market leader), and leaving other OPEC members to set their prices in line with this: a form of 'dominant firm' price leadership.

As long as demand remained buoyant, and was price inelastic, this policy allowed large price increases with consequent large revenue increases. In 1973/4, after the Arab–Israeli war, OPEC raised the price of oil from around $3 per barrel to over $12. The price was kept at roughly this level until 1979. And yet the sales of oil did not fall significantly.

After 1979, however, following a further increase in the price of oil from around $15 to $40 per barrel, demand did fall. This was largely due to the recession of the early 1980s (although this recession was in turn largely caused by governments' responses to the oil price increases).

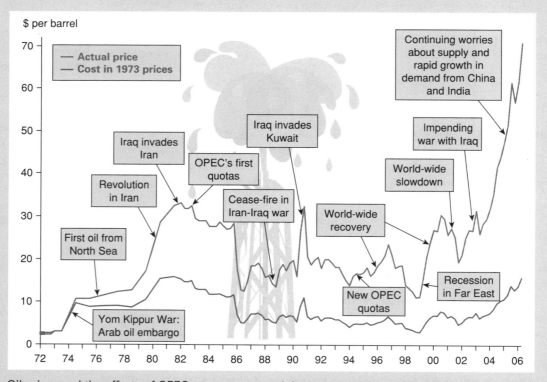

Oil prices and the effects of OPEC quotas, wars and the ups and downs of the world economy
Source: *OPEC Annual Statistical Bulletin 2006.*

Faced by declining demand, OPEC after 1982 agreed to limit output and allocate production quotas in an attempt to keep the price up. A production ceiling of 16 million barrels per day was agreed in 1984.

The cartel was beginning to break down, however, due to the following:

- The world recession and the resulting fall in the demand for oil.
- Growing output from non-OPEC members.
- 'Cheating' by some OPEC members which exceeded their quota limits.

With a glut of oil, OPEC could no longer maintain the price. The 'spot' price of oil (the day-to-day price at which oil trades on the open market) fell dramatically in 1986, as the graph shows.

The trend of lower oil prices was reversed in the late 1980s. With the world economy booming, the demand for oil rose and along with it the price. Then in 1990 Iraq invaded Kuwait and the Gulf War ensued. With the cutting off of supplies from Kuwait and Iraq, the supply of oil fell and there was a sharp rise in its price.

But with the ending of the war and the recession of the early 1990s, the price rapidly fell again and only slowly recovered as the world economy started expanding once more. On the demand side, the development of energy-saving technology plus increases in fuel taxes led to a relatively slow growth in consumption. On the supply side, the growing proportion of output supplied by non-OPEC members, plus the adoption in 1994 of a relatively high OPEC production ceiling of $24\frac{1}{2}$ million barrels per day, meant that supply kept pace with demand.

The situation for OPEC deteriorated further in the late 1990s, following a recession in the Far East. Oil demand fell by some 2 million barrels per day. By early 1999, the price had fallen to around $10 per barrel – a mere $2.70 in 1973 prices! In response, OPEC members agreed to cut production by 4.3 million barrels per day. The objective was to push the price back up to around $18–$20 per barrel. But, with the Asian economy recovering and the world generally experiencing more rapid economic growth, the price rose rapidly and soon overshot the $20 mark. By early 2000 it had reached $30: a tripling in price in just 12 months. With the world economy then slowing down, however, the price rapidly fell back, reaching $18 in November 2001.

In late 2001 the relationship between OPEC and non-OPEC oil producers changed. The ten members of the OPEC cartel decided to cut production by 1.5 million barrels a day. This followed an agreement with five of the major oil producers *outside* the cartel to reduce their output too, the aim being to push oil prices upwards and then stabilise them at around $25. The alliance between OPEC and non-OPEC oil producers was the first such instance of its kind in the oil industry. As a result, it seemed that OPEC might now once again be able to control the market for oil.

But how successfully could this arrangement cope with crisis? With worries over an impending war with Iraq and a strike in Venezuela, the price rose again in late 2002, passing the $30 mark in early 2003. OPEC claimed that it could maintain supply and prevent prices from surging even with an Iraq war, but with prices rising rapidly above $30, many doubted that it could.

From 2004 the situation worsened. There were supply concerns related to the situation in Iraq, Saudi Arabia, Russia and Nigeria. At the same time there was a rapid growth in demand from countries such as China and India. OPEC tried to relax the quotas, but found it difficult to adjust supply sufficiently quickly to make any real difference to the price. By 2006, the price had passed the $70 mark. Many analysts were predicting a price of over $100 per barrel within a year or two.

The history of OPEC illustrates the difficulty of using supply quotas to achieve a particular price. With demand being price inelastic but income elastic (responsive to changes in world income), and with considerable speculative movements in demand, the equilibrium price for a given supply quota can fluctuate wildly.

1. What conditions facilitate the formation of a cartel? Which of these conditions were to be found in the oil market in (a) the early 1970s; (b) the mid-1980s; (c) the early 2000s?
2. Could OPEC have done anything to prevent the long-term decline in real oil prices since 1981?
3. Many oil analysts are predicting a rapid decline in world oil output in 10 to 20 years as world reserves are depleted. What effect is this likely to have on OPEC's behaviour?

Figure 4.9
Profit-maximising
cartel

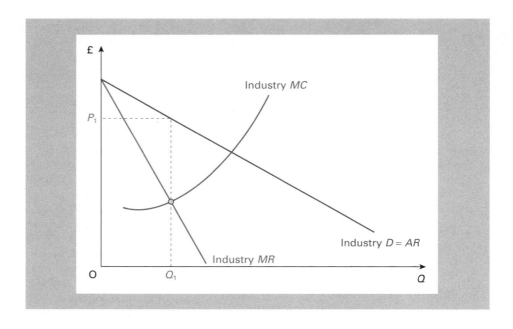

TC9
p68

Pause for thought

If this 'fair' solution were adopted, what effect would it have on the industry MC curve in Figure 4.9?

Definitions

Quota (set by a cartel)
The output that a given member of a cartel is allowed to produce (production quota) or sell (sales quota).

Tacit collusion
Where oligopolists take care not to engage in price cutting, excessive advertising or other forms of competition. There may be unwritten 'rules' of collusive behaviour, such as price leadership.

Dominant firm price leadership
Where firms (the followers) choose the same price as that set by a dominant firm in the industry (the leader).

Alternatively, the cartel members may somehow agree to divide the market between them. Each member would be given a **quota**. The sum of all the quotas must add up to Q_1. If the quotas exceeded Q_1, either there would be output unsold if price remained fixed at P_1, or the price would fall.

But if quotas are to be set by the cartel, how will it decide the level of each individual member's quota? The most likely method is for the cartel to divide the market between the members according to their current market share. That is the solution most likely to be accepted as 'fair'.

In many countries, including the UK, cartels are illegal. They are seen by the government as a means of driving up prices and profits, and thereby as being against the public interest. Where open collusion is illegal, firms may simply break the law, or get round it. For example, in November 2001, the EU imposed record fines totalling €855.2 million on eight pharmaceutical companies for meeting secretly to fix the prices of vitamins (see Web Case 4.12). Alternatively, firms may stay within the law, but still *tacitly* collude by watching each other's prices and keeping theirs similar. Firms may tacitly 'agree' to avoid price wars or aggressive advertising campaigns.

Tacit collusion

One form of **tacit collusion** is where firms keep to the price that is set by an established leader. The leader may be the largest firm: the firm that dominates the industry. This is known as **dominant firm price leadership**. Alternatively, the price leader may simply be the one that has proved to be the most reliable to follow: the one that is the best barometer of market conditions. This is known as **barometric firm price leadership**.

Dominant firm price leadership. How does the leader set the price? This depends on the assumptions it makes about its rivals' reactions to its price changes. If it assumes that rivals will simply follow it by making exactly the same percentage price changes up or down, then a simple model can be constructed. This is illustrated in

Figure 4.10
A price leader aiming
to maximise profits for
a given market share

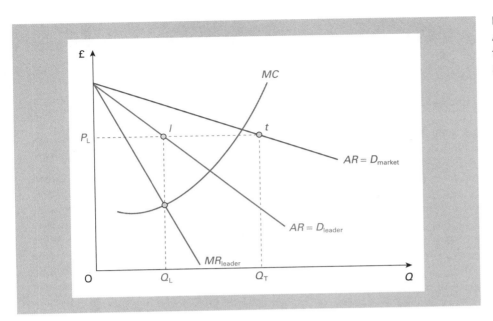

Figure 4.10. The leader assumes that it will maintain a constant market share (say, 50 per cent).

The leader will maximise profits where its marginal revenue is equal to its marginal cost. It knows its current position on its demand curve (say, point *a*). It then estimates how responsive its demand will be to industry-wide price changes and thus constructs its demand and *MR* curves on that basis. It then chooses to produce Q_L at a price of P_L: at point *l* on its demand curve (where $MC = MR$). Other firms then follow that price. Total market demand will be Q_T, with followers supplying that portion of the market not supplied by the leader: namely, $Q_T - Q_L$.

There is one problem with this model. That is the assumption that the followers will want to maintain a constant market share. It is possible that if the leader raises its price, the followers may want to supply more at this new price. On the other hand, the followers may decide merely to maintain their market share for fear of invoking retaliation from the leader, in the form of price cuts or an aggressive advertising campaign.

Barometric firm price leadership. A similar exercise can be conducted by a barometric firm. Although the firm is not dominating the industry, its price will be followed by the others. It merely tries to estimate its demand and *MR* curves – assuming, again, a constant market share – and then produces where $MR = MC$ and sets price accordingly.

In practice, which firm is taken as the barometer may frequently change. Whether we are talking about oil companies, car producers or banks, any firm may take the initiative in raising prices. If the other firms are merely waiting for someone to take the lead – say, because costs have risen – they will all quickly follow suit. For example, if one of the bigger building societies or banks raises its mortgage rates by 1 per cent, this is likely to stimulate the others to follow suit.

Other forms of tacit collusion An alternative to having an established leader is for there to be an established set of simple 'rules of thumb' that everyone follows. One such example is **average cost pricing**. Here producers, instead of equating *MC* and *MR*, simply add a certain percentage for profit on top of average costs. Thus, if average costs rise by 10 per cent, prices will automatically be raised by 10 per cent. This

Box 4.4   Case Studies and Applications

Supermarket wars

Genuine competition or tacit collusion?

Food retailing in the UK is a good example of oligopoly. As the chart shows, the largest four supermarket chains have a combined market share of more than 75 per cent. What is more, for many consumers there are only one or two supermarkets within their area.

In 1999, the government's Office of Fair Trading (OFT) (see page 207) identified three major areas where the supermarkets gain from the use (or abuse) of market power: (i) barriers to entry to new competitors, (ii) the relationship between the large supermarket chains and their suppliers, and (iii) the lack of effective price competition.

Barriers to entry. The most important barrier to entry is the difficulty in getting planning permission to open a new supermarket. Also, the large economies of scale and the huge buying power of the established supermarkets would make it virtually impossible for a new player to match their low costs.

Relationships between supermarkets and their suppliers. One of the most contentious issues concerns the major supermarket chains' huge buying and selling power. They have been able to drive costs down by forcing suppliers to offer discounts. Many suppliers, such as growers, have found their profit margins cut to the bone. However, these cost savings have not been passed on from supplier to shopper.

Lack of effective price competition. The supermarket chains have adopted a system of 'shadow pricing', a form of tacit collusion whereby they all observe each other's prices and ensure that they remain at similar levels – often similarly high levels rather than similarly low levels! This has limited the extent of true price competition, and the resulting high prices have seen profits grow as costs have been driven ever downwards.

Supermarkets *do* compete on price, and since the £6.4 billion takeover in 1999 of Asda by Wal-Mart, the world's largest retailer, price wars in the supermarket sector have become more cut-throat. Asda has slashed prices on hundreds of products. Tesco in response, striving to maintain its position as the UK's number one supermarket retailer, launched its own price-cutting campaign. It was determined not to get left behind in the price war.

But intense price competition tends to be only over basic items, such as the own-brand 'value' products. To get to the basic items, you normally have to pass the more luxurious ones, which are much more highly priced! Supermarkets rely on shoppers making impulse buys of the more expensive lines: lines that have much higher profit margins.

In May 2006, the OFT decided to refer the big four supermarkets to the Competition Commission for investigation. In particular the OFT was worried about their increased power: they had significant land holdings, which could block competition; some aspects of their pricing behaviour (such as below-cost selling on certain lines) could distort competition; the opening of convenience stores, such as Tesco Metro, Tesco Express and Sainsbury's Local, was driving independent retailers from the market – between 2000 and 2004, 7337 independent retailers went out of business.

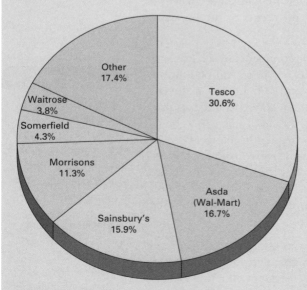

UK supermarket food market share (2006)

?
1. *In what forms of tacit collusion are supermarket chains likely to engage?*
2. *In what ways can convenience stores compete with supermarkets?*

is a particularly useful rule of thumb in times of inflation, when all firms will be experiencing similar cost increases.

Another rule of thumb is to have certain **price benchmarks**. Thus clothes may sell for £9.95, £14.95, £19.95, etc. (but not £12.31, £16.42 or £20.04). If costs rise, then firms simply raise their price to the next benchmark, knowing that other firms will do the same.

Rules of thumb can also be applied to advertising (e.g. you do not criticise other firms' products, only praise your own); or to the design of the product (e.g. lighting manufacturers tacitly agreeing not to bring out an everlasting light bulb).

Factors favouring collusion

Collusion between firms, whether formal or tacit, is more likely when firms can clearly identify with each other or some leader and when they trust each other not to break agreements. It is easier for firms to collude if the following conditions apply:

- There are only very few firms, all well known to each other.
- They are open with each other about costs and production methods.
- They have similar production methods and average costs, and are thus likely to want to change prices at the same time and by the same percentage.
- They produce similar products and can thus more easily reach agreements on price.
- There is a dominant firm.
- There are significant barriers to entry and thus there is little fear of disruption by new firms.
- The market is stable. If industry demand or production costs fluctuate wildly, it will be difficult to make agreements, partly due to difficulties in predicting and partly because agreements may frequently have to be amended. There is a particular problem in a declining market where firms may be tempted to undercut each other's price in order to maintain their sales.
- There are no government measures to curb collusion.

Non-collusive oligopoly: the breakdown of collusion

In some oligopolies, there may be only a few (if any) factors favouring collusion. In such cases, the likelihood of price competition is greater.

Even if there is collusion, there will always be the temptation for individual oligopolists to 'cheat', by cutting prices or by selling more than their allotted quota. The danger, of course, is that this would invite retaliation from the other members of the cartel, with a resulting price war. Price would then fall and the cartel could well break up in disarray.

When considering whether to break a collusive agreement, even if only a tacit one, a firm will ask: (1) 'How much can we get away with without inviting retaliation?' and (2) 'If a price war does result, will we be the winners? Will we succeed in driving some or all of our rivals out of business and yet survive ourselves, and thereby gain greater market power?'

 The position of rival firms, therefore, is rather like that of generals of opposing armies or the players in a game. It is a question of choosing the appropriate *strategy*: the strategy that will best succeed in outwitting your opponents. The strategy a firm adopts will, of course, be concerned not just with price but also with advertising and product development.

Pause for thought

If a firm has a typically shaped average cost curve and sets prices 10 per cent above average cost, what will its supply curve look like?

Definition

Price benchmark
A price that is typically used. Firms, when raising a price, will usually raise it from one benchmark to another.

Figure 4.11
The Cournot model of
duopoly: Firm A's
profit-maximising
position

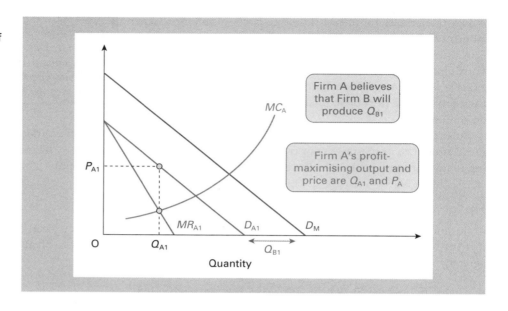

Non-collusive oligopoly: assumptions about rivals' behaviour

Even though oligopolists might not collude, they will still need to take account of rivals' likely behaviour when deciding their own strategy. In doing so they will probably look at rivals' past behaviour and make assumptions based on it. There are three well-known models, each based on a different set of assumptions.

Assumption that rivals produce a given quantity: the Cournot model

One assumption is that rivals will produce a particular quantity. This is most likely when the market is stable and the rivals have been producing a relatively constant quantity for some time. The task, then, for the individual oligopolist is to decide its own price and quantity, given the presumed output of its competitors.

The earliest model based on this assumption was developed by the French economist Augustin Cournot[1] in 1838. The Cournot model (which is developed in Web Appendix 4.2) takes the simple case of just two firms (a duopoly) producing an identical product: for example, two electricity-generating companies supplying the whole country.

This is illustrated in Figure 4.11, which shows the profit-maximising price and output for Firm A. The total market demand curve is shown as D_M. Assume that Firm A believes that its rival, Firm B, will produce Q_{B1} units. Thus Firm A perceives its own demand curve (D_{A1}) to be Q_{B1} units less than total market demand. In other words, the horizontal gap between D_M and D_{A1} is Q_{B1} units. Given its perceived demand curve of D_{A1}, its marginal revenue curve will be MR_{A1} and the profit-maximising output will be Q_{A1}, where $MR_{A1} = MC_A$. The profit-maximising price will be P_{A1}.

If Firm A believed that Firm B would produce *more* than Q_{B1}, its perceived demand and *MR* curves would be further to the left and the profit-maximising quantity and price would both be lower.

Profits in the Cournot model.   Industry profits will be *less* than under a monopoly or a cartel. The reason is that price will be lower than the monopoly price. This can be

TC3
p11

TC9
p68

Definitions

Cournot model
A model of duopoly where each firm makes its price and output decisions on the assumption that its rival will produce a particular quantity.

Duopoly
An oligopoly where there are just two firms in the market.

---

[1] See http://cepa.newschool.edu/het/profiles/cournot.htm for a profile of Cournot and his work.

seen from Figure 4.11. If this were a monopoly, then to find the profit-maximising output, we would need to construct an *MR* curve corresponding to the market demand curve (D_M). This would intersect with the *MC* curve at a higher output than Q_{A1} and a *higher* price (given by D_M).

Nevertheless, profits in the Cournot model will be higher than under perfect competition, since price is still above marginal cost.

Assumption that rivals set a particular price: the Bertrand model

An alternative assumption is that rival firms set a particular price and stick to it. This scenario is more realistic when firms do not want to upset customers by frequent price changes or want to produce catalogues which specify prices. The task, then, for a given oligopolist is to choose its own price and quantity in the light of the prices set by rivals.

The most famous model based on this assumption was developed by another French economist, Joseph Bertrand, in 1883. Bertrand again took the simple case of a duopoly, but his conclusions apply equally to oligopolies with three or more firms.

The outcome is one of price cutting until all supernormal profits are competed away. The reason is simple. If Firm A assumes that its rival, Firm B, will hold price constant, then Firm A should undercut this price by a small amount and as a result gain a large share of the market. At this point, Firm B will be forced to respond by cutting its price. What we end up with is a price war until price is forced down to the level of average cost, with only normal profits remaining.

Nash equilibrium. The equilibrium outcome in either the Cournot or Bertrand models is not in the *joint* interests of the firms. In each case, total profits are less than under a monopoly or cartel. But, in the absence of collusion, the outcome is the result of each firm doing the best it can, given its assumptions about what its rivals are doing. The resulting equilibrium is known as a Nash equilibrium, after John Nash, a US mathematician (and subject of the film *A Beautiful Mind*) who introduced the concept in 1951.

In practice, when competition is intense, as in the Bertrand model, the firms may seek to collude long before profits have been reduced to a normal level. Alternatively firms may put in a takeover bid for their rival(s).

The kinked demand-curve assumption

In 1939 a theory of non-collusive oligopoly was developed simultaneously on both sides of the Atlantic: in the USA by Paul Sweezy and in Britain by R. L. Hall and C. J. Hitch. This kinked demand theory has since become perhaps the most famous of all theories of oligopoly. The model seeks to explain how it is that, even when there is no collusion at all between oligopolists, prices can nevertheless remain stable.

The theory is based on two asymmetrical assumptions:

- If an oligopolist cuts its price, its rivals will feel forced to follow suit and cut theirs, to prevent losing customers to the first firm.
- If an oligopolist raises its price, however, its rivals will *not* follow suit since, by keeping their prices the same, they will thereby gain customers from the first firm.

On these assumptions, each oligopolist will face a demand curve that is *kinked* at the current price and output (see Figure 4.12). A rise in price will lead to a large fall in sales as customers switch to the now relatively lower-priced rivals. The firm will thus be reluctant to raise its price. Demand is relatively elastic above the kink. On the other hand, a fall in price will bring only a modest increase in sales, since rivals

Definitions

Nash equilibrium
The position resulting from everyone making their optimal decision based on their assumptions about their rivals' decisions. Without collusion, there is no incentive for any firm to move from this position.

Takeover bid
Where one firm attempts to purchase another by offering to buy the shares of that company from its shareholders.

Kinked demand theory
The theory that oligopolists face a demand curve that is kinked at the current price: demand being significantly more elastic above the current price than below. The effect of this is to create a situation of price stability.

Figure 4.12
Kinked demand for a
firm under oligopoly

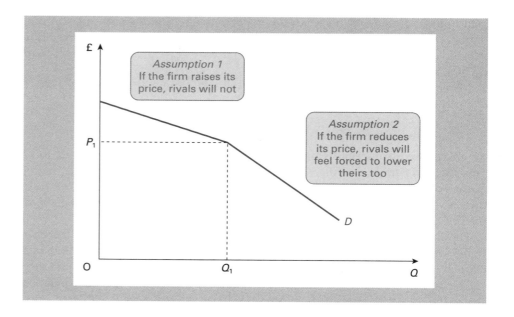

Figure 4.13
Stable price under
conditions of a kinked
demand curve

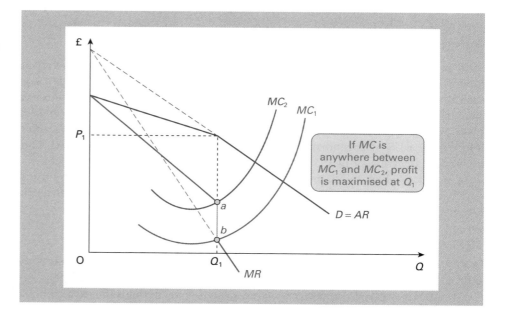

lower their prices too and therefore customers do not switch. The firm will thus also be reluctant to lower its price. Demand is relatively inelastic below the kink. Thus oligopolists will be reluctant to change prices at all.

This price stability can be shown formally by drawing in the firm's marginal revenue curve, as in Figure 4.13.

To see how this is done, imagine dividing the diagram into two parts either side of Q_1. At quantities less than Q_1 (the left-hand part of the diagram), the *MR* curve will correspond to the shallow part of the *AR* curve. At quantities greater than Q_1 (the right-hand part), the *MR* curve will correspond to the steep part of the *AR* curve. To see how this part of the *MR* curve is constructed, imagine extending the steep part of the *AR* curve back to the vertical axis. This and the corresponding *MR* curve are shown by the dotted lines in Figure 4.13.

		X's price	
		£2.00	£1.80
Y's price	£2.00	**A** £10m each	**B** £5m for Y £12m for X
	£1.80	**C** £12m for Y £5m for X	**D** £8m each

Table 4.2 Profits for firms X and Y at different prices

As you can see, there will be a gap between points *a* and *b*. In other words, there is a vertical section of the *MR* curve between these two points. Profits are maximised where *MC* = *MR*. Thus, if the *MC* curve lies anywhere between MC_1 and MC_2 (i.e. between points *a* and *b*), the profit-maximising price and output will be P_1 and Q_1. Thus prices will remain stable *even with a considerable change in costs*.

Non-collusive oligopoly: game theory

As we have seen, the behaviour of a firm under non-collusive oligopoly depends on how it thinks its rivals will react to its decisions. Economists use **game theory** to examine the best strategy a firm can adopt for each assumption about its rivals' behaviour.

Simple dominant strategy games

The simplest case is where there are just two firms with identical costs, products and demand. They are both considering which of two alternative prices to charge. Table 4.2 shows typical profits they could each make.

Let us assume that at present both firms (X and Y) are charging a price of £2 and that they are each making a profit of £10 million, giving a total industry profit of £20 million. This is shown in the top left-hand cell (A).

Now assume they are both (independently) considering reducing their price to £1.80. In making this decision they will need to take into account what their rival might do, and how this will affect them. Let us consider X's position. In our simple example there are just two things that its rival, firm Y, might do. Either Y could cut its price to £1.80, or it could leave its price at £2. What should X do?

One alternative is to go for the *cautious* approach and think of the worst thing that its rival could do. If X kept its price at £2, the worst thing for X would be if its rival Y cut its price. This is shown by cell C: X's profit falls to £5 million. If, however, X cut its price to £1.80, the worst outcome would again be for Y to cut its price, but this time X's profit only falls to £8 million. In this case, then, if X is cautious, it will *cut its price to £1.80*. Note that Y will argue along similar lines, and if it is cautious, it too will cut its price to £1.80. This policy of adopting the safer strategy is known as **maximin**. Following a maximin strategy, the firm will opt for the alternative that will maximise its minimum possible profit.

An alternative strategy is to go for the *optimistic* approach and assume that your rivals react in the way most favourable to you. Here the firm goes for the strategy

TC 9
p68

Definitions

Maximax
The strategy of choosing the policy that has the best possible outcome.

Dominant strategy game
Where the *same* policy is suggested by different strategies.

Prisoners' dilemma
Where two or more firms (or people), by attempting independently to choose the best strategy for whatever the other(s) are likely to do, end up in a worse position than if they had co-operated in the first place.

Credible threat (or promise)
One that is believable to rivals because it is in the threatener's interests to carry it out.

that yields the highest possible profit. In X's case this again means cutting price, only this time on the optimistic assumption that firm Y will leave its price unchanged. If firm X is correct in its assumption, it will move to cell B and achieve the maximum possible profit of £12 million. This strategy of going for the maximum possible profit is known as **maximax**. Note that again the same argument applies to Y. Its maximax strategy will be to cut price and hopefully end up in cell C.

Given that in this 'game' *both* approaches, maximin and maximax, lead to the *same* strategy (namely, cutting price), this is known as a **dominant strategy game**. The result is that the firms will end up in cell D, earning a lower profit (£8 million each) than if they had charged the higher price (£10 million each in cell A).

As we saw, the equilibrium outcome of a game where there is no collusion between the players (cell D in this game) is known as a Nash equilivrium. The Nash equilibrium in this game is cell D.

In our example, collusion rather than a price war would have benefited both firms. Yet, even if they did collude, both would be tempted to cheat and cut prices. This is known as the **prisoners' dilemma**. An example is given in Box 4.5.

More complex games with no dominant strategy

More complex 'games' can be devised with more than two firms, many alternative prices, differentiated products and various forms of non-price competition (e.g. advertising). In such cases, the cautious (maximin) strategy may suggest a different policy (e.g. do nothing) from the high-risk (maximax) strategy (e.g. cut prices substantially).

In complex and changing situations, firms may alter their tactics in the light of new circumstances. Thus in some cases firms may compete hard for a time (in price or non-price terms) and then realise that maybe no one is winning. Firms may then jointly raise prices and reduce advertising. Later, after a period of tacit collusion, competition may break out again. This may be sparked off by the entry of a new firm, by the development of a new product design, by a change in market demand, or simply by one or more firms no longer being able to resist the temptation to 'cheat'. In short, the behaviour of particular oligopolists may change quite radically over time.

The importance of threats and promises

In many situations, an oligopolist will make a threat or promise that it will act in a certain way. As long as the threat or promise is **credible** (i.e. its competitors believe it), the firm can gain and it will influence its rivals' behaviour.

Take the simple situation where a large oil company, such as Esso, states that it will match the price charged by any competitor within a given radius. Assume that competitors believe this 'price promise' but also that Esso will not try to *undercut* their price. In the simple situation where there is only one other filling station in the area, what price should it charge? Clearly it should charge the price that would maximise its profits, assuming that Esso will charge the *same* price. In the absence of other filling stations in the area, this is likely to be a relatively high price.

Now assume that there are several filling stations in the area. What should the company do now? Its best bet is probably to charge the same price as Esso and hope that no other company charges a lower price and forces Esso to cut its price. Assuming that Esso's threat is credible, other companies are likely to reason in a similar way.

Pause for thought

Assume that there are two major oil companies operating filling stations in an area. The first promises to match the other's prices. The other promises to sell at 1p per litre cheaper than the first. Describe the likely sequence of events in this 'game' and the likely eventual outcome. Could the promise of the second company be seen as credible?

Box 4.5   **Case Studies and Applications**

The prisoners' dilemma

Game theory is relevant not just to economics. A famous non-economic example is the prisoners' dilemma.

Nigel and Amanda have been arrested for a joint crime of serious fraud. Each is interviewed separately and given the following alternatives:

- First, if they say nothing, the court has enough evidence to sentence both to a year's imprisonment.
- Second, if either Nigel or Amanda *alone* confesses, he or she is likely to get only a three-month sentence but the partner could get up to ten years.
- Third, if both confess, they are likely to get three years each.

What should Nigel and Amanda do?

Let us consider Nigel's dilemma. Should he confess in order to get the short sentence (the maximax strategy)? This is better than the year he would get for not confessing. There is, however, an even better reason for confessing. Suppose Nigel doesn't confess but, unknown to him, Amanda does confess. Then Nigel ends up with the long sentence. Better than this is to confess and to get no more than three years: this is the safest (maximin) strategy.

Amanda is in the same dilemma. The result is simple. When both prisoners act selfishly by confessing, they both end up in position D with relatively long prison terms. Only when they collude will they end up in position A with relatively short prison terms, the best combined solution.

Of course the police know this and will do their best to prevent any collusion. They will keep Nigel and Amanda in separate cells and try to persuade each of them that the other is bound to confess.

Thus the choice of strategy depends on:

- Nigel's and Amanda's risk attitudes: i.e. are they 'risk lovers' or 'risk averse'?
- Nigel's and Amanda's estimates of how likely the other is to own up.

> 1. *Why is this a dominant strategy 'game'?*
> 2. *How would Nigel's choice of strategy be affected if he had instead been involved in a joint crime with Jeremy, Pauline, Diana and Dave, and they had all been caught?*

Let us now look at two real-world examples of the prisoners' dilemma.

Standing at concerts

When people go to some public event, such as a concert or a match, they often stand in order to get a better view. But once people start standing, everyone is likely to do so: after all, if they stayed sitting, they would not see at all. In this Nash equilibrium, most people are worse off, since, except for tall people, their view is likely to be worse and they lose the comfort of sitting down.

Too much advertising

Why do firms spend so much on advertising? If they are aggressive, they do so to get ahead of their rivals (the maximax approach). If they are cautious, they do so in case their rivals increase their advertising (the maximin approach). Although in both cases it may be in the individual firm's best interests to increase advertising, the resulting Nash equilibrium is likely to be one of excessive advertising: the total spent on advertising (by all firms) is not recouped in additional sales.

> Give one or two other examples (economic or non-economic) of the prisoners' dilemma.

	Amanda's alternatives	
	Not confess	Confess
Nigel's alternatives Not confess	A Each gets 1 year	C Nigel gets 10 years / Amanda gets 3 months
Confess	B Nigel gets 3 months / Amanda gets 10 years	D Each gets 3 years

Alternatives for Nigel and Amanda

Figure 4.14
A decision tree

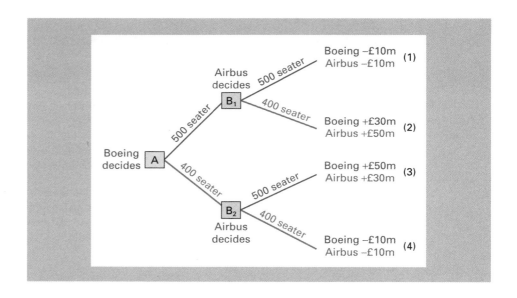

The importance of timing

Most decisions by oligopolists are made by one firm at a time rather than simultaneously by all firms. Sometimes a firm will take the initiative. At other times it will respond to decisions taken by other firms.

Take the case of a new generation of large passenger aircraft that can fly further without refuelling. Assume that there is a market for a 500-seater version of this type of aircraft and a 400-seater version, but that the market for each size of aircraft is not big enough for the two manufacturers, Boeing and Airbus, to share it profitably. Let us also assume that the 400-seater market would give an annual profit of £50 million to a single manufacturer and that the 500-seater would give an annual profit of £30 million, but that if both manufacturers produced the same version, they would each make an annual loss of £10 million.

Assume that Boeing announces that it is building the 400-seater plane. What should Airbus do? The choice is illustrated in Figure 4.14. This diagram is called a **decision tree** and shows the sequence of events. The small square at the left of the diagram is Boeing's decision point (point A). If it had decided to build the 500-seater plane, we would move up the top branch. Airbus would now have to make a decision (point B_1). If it too built the 500-seater plane, we would move to outcome 1: a loss of £10m for both manufacturers. Clearly, with Boeing building a 500-seater plane, Airbus would choose the 400-seater plane: we would move to outcome 2, with Boeing making a profit of £30m and Airbus a profit £50m. Airbus would be very pleased!

Boeing's best strategy at point A, however, would be to build the 400-seater plane. We would then move to Airbus's decision point B_2. In this case, it is in Airbus's interests to build the 500-seater plane. Its profit would be only £30m (outcome 3), but this is better than the £10m loss if it too built the 400-seater plane (outcome 4). With Boeing deciding first, the Nash equilibrium will thus be outcome 3.

There is clearly a **first-mover advantage** here. Once Boeing has decided to build the more profitable version of the plane, Airbus is forced to build the less profitable one. Naturally, Airbus would like to build the more profitable one and be the first mover. Which company succeeds in going first depends on how advanced they are in their research and development and in their production capacity.

KI 18
p133

More complex decision trees. The aircraft example is the simplest version of a decision tree, with just two companies and each one making only one key decision. In many business situations, much more complex trees could be constructed. The 'game' would be more like chess, with many moves and several options on each move. If there were more than two companies, the decision tree would be more complex still.

Oligopoly and the consumer

If oligopolists act collusively and jointly maximise industry profits, they will in effect be acting together as a monopoly. In such cases, prices may be very high. This is clearly not in the best interests of consumers.

Furthermore, in two respects, oligopoly may be more disadvantageous than monopoly:

- Depending on the size of the individual oligopolists, there may be less scope for economies of scale to mitigate the effects of market power.
- Oligopolists are likely to engage in much more extensive advertising than a monopolist.

These problems will be less severe, however, if oligopolists do not collude, if there is some degree of price competition, and if barriers to entry are weak.

Also, the power of oligopolists in certain markets may to some extent be offset if they sell their product to other powerful firms. Thus oligopolistic producers of baked beans or soap powder sell a large proportion of their output to giant supermarket chains, which can use their market power to keep down the price at which they purchase these products. This phenomenon is known as **countervailing power**.

In some respects, oligopoly has *advantages* to society over other market structures:

- Oligopolists, like monopolists, can use part of their supernormal profit for research and development. Unlike monopolists, however, oligopolists will have a considerable *incentive* to do so. If the product design is improved, this may allow the firm to capture a larger share of the market, and it may be some time before rivals can respond with a similarly improved product. If, in addition, costs are reduced by technological improvement, the resulting higher profits will improve the firm's capacity to withstand a price war.
- Non-price competition through product differentiation may result in greater choice for the consumer. Take the case of stereo equipment. Non-price competition has led to a huge range of different products of many different specifications, each meeting the specific requirements of different consumers.

It is difficult to draw any general conclusions, since oligopolies differ so much in their performance.

3. They are more likely to collude if there are few of them; if they are open with each other; if they have similar products and cost structures; if there is a dominant firm; if there are significant entry barriers; if the market is stable; and if there is no government legislation to prevent collusion.

4. Collusion can be open or tacit.

5. A formal collusive agreement is called a 'cartel'. A cartel aims to act as a monopoly. It can set price and leave the members to compete for market share, or it can assign quotas. There is always a temptation for cartel members to 'cheat' by undercutting the cartel price if they think they can get away with it and not trigger a price war.

6. Tacit collusion can take the form of price leadership. This is where firms follow the price set by either a dominant firm in the industry or one seen as a reliable 'barometer' of market conditions. Alternatively, tacit collusion can simply involve following various rules of thumb such as average cost pricing and benchmark pricing.

7. Even when firms do not collude they will still have to take into account their rivals' behaviour. In the Cournot model firms assume that their rivals' output is given and then choose the profit-maximising price and output in the light of this assumption. The resulting price and profit are lower than under monopoly, but still higher than under perfect competition. In the Bertrand model firms assume that their rivals' price is given. This will result in prices being competed down until only normal profits remain.

8. In the kinked-demand curve model, firms are likely to keep their prices stable unless there is a large shift in costs or demand.

9. Non-collusive oligopolists will have to work out a price strategy. Game theory examines various strategies that firms can adopt when the outcome of each is not certain. They can adopt a low-risk 'maximin' strategy of choosing the policy that has the least-bad worst outcome, or a high-risk 'maximax' strategy of choosing the policy with the best possible outcome, or some compromise. Either way, a 'Nash' equilibrium is likely to be reached which is not in the best interests of the firms collectively. It will entail a lower level of profit than if they had colluded.

10. An oligopolist is likely to be more profitable if its rivals take its threats seriously. It is important here that its threats are credible.

11. Timing can be vitally important for the success of an oligopolist. There is often a 'first-mover advantage' for the company that beats its rivals to the market with a new product.

12. Whether consumers benefit from oligopoly depends on the particular oligopoly and how competitive it is; whether there is any countervailing power; whether the firms engage in extensive advertising and of what type; whether product differentiation results in a wide range of choice for the consumer; and how much of the profits are ploughed back into research and development. Since these conditions vary substantially from oligopoly to oligopoly, it is impossible to state just how well or how badly oligopoly in general serves the consumer's interest.

4.6   PRICE DISCRIMINATION

In what situations will firms be able to charge different prices to different consumers? How will we as consumers benefit or lose from the process?

Definition

Price discrimination
Where a firm sells the same product at different prices.

Up to now we have assumed that a firm will sell its output at a single price. Sometimes, however, firms may practise **price discrimination**. This is where consumers are grouped into two or more independent markets and a separate price is charged in each market, even though there is no difference in costs of production or supply. Examples include different-priced seats on buses for adults and children, different prices for the same seats on aircraft (depending on when they are booked), and different prices charged for the same product in different countries or different parts of the same country. (There are other forms of price discrimination, but this – known as 'third-degree price discrimination' – is the most common.)

Conditions necessary for price discrimination to operate

As we shall see, a firm will be able to increase its profits if it can engage in price discrimination. But under what circumstances will it be able to charge discriminatory prices? There are three conditions that must be met:

- The firm must be able to set its price. Thus price discrimination will be impossible under perfect competition, where firms are price takers.
- The markets must be separate. Consumers in the low-priced market must not be able to resell the product in the high-priced market. For example, children must not be able to resell a half-priced child's cinema ticket for use by an adult.

- Demand elasticity must differ in each market. The firm will charge the higher price in the market where demand is less elastic, and thus less sensitive to a price rise.

Advantages to the firm

Price discrimination allows the firm to earn a higher revenue from any given level of sales. Figure 4.15 represents a firm's demand curve. If it is to sell 200 units without price discrimination, it must charge a price of P_1. The total revenue it earns is shown by the blue area. If, however, it can practise price discrimination by selling 150 of those 200 units at the higher price of P_2, it will gain the pink area in addition to the blue area.

Another advantage the firm gains by price discrimination is that it may be able to use it to drive competitors out of business. If a firm has a monopoly in one market (e.g. the home market), it may be able to charge a high price due to its relatively inelastic demand, and thus make high profits. If it is under oligopoly in another market (e.g. the export market), it may use the high profits in the first market to

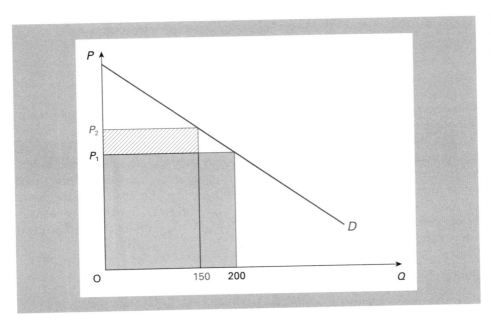

Figure 4.15
Third-degree price discrimination

Box 4.6 **Exploring Economics**

Profit-maximising prices and output for a price-discriminating firm

Identifying different prices in different markets

Assuming that a firm wishes to maximise profits, what discriminatory prices should it charge and how much should it produce?

Assume that the firm sells an identical product in two separate markets X and Y with demand and MR curves as shown in the diagrams.

Diagram (c) shows the MC and MR curves for the firm as a whole. This MR curve is found by adding the amounts sold in the two markets at each level of MR (in other words, the horizontal addition of the two MR curves). Thus, for example, with output of 1000 units in market X and 2000 in market Y, making 3000 in total, revenue would increase by £5 if one extra unit were sold, whether in market X or Y.

Total profit is maximised where $MC = MR$: i.e. at an output of 3000 units in total. This output must then be divided between the two markets so that MC is equal to MR in each market: i.e. $MC = MR = £5$ in each market. MR must be the same in both markets, otherwise revenue could be increased by switching output to the market with the higher MR.

The profit-maximising price in each market will be given by the relevant demand curve. Thus, in market X, 1000 units will be sold at £9 each, and in market Y, 2000 units will be sold at £7 each.

? *Why is the higher price charged in the market with the less elastic demand curve?*

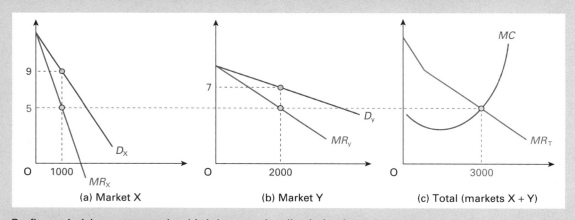

(a) Market X   (b) Market Y   (c) Total (markets X + Y)

Profit-maximising output under third-degree price discrimination

---

subsidise a very low price in the oligopolistic market, thus forcing its competitors out of business.

Large bus companies in the UK have been accused of doing this. They use the profits made from the high fares on routes where they face no competition to subsidise fares on routes where they do face competition, often from a small rival attempting to break into the market. The aim is to drive the small company out of business. Sometimes on these routes, the large company charges fares that are below cost (thereby making a temporary loss on these routes). This practice is known as **predatory pricing**.

Price discrimination and the consumer

No clear-cut decision can be made over the desirability of price discrimination from the point of view of the consumer. Some people will benefit from it; others will lose. Those paying the higher price will probably feel that price discrimination is unfair to them. On the other hand, those charged the lower price may thereby be able to obtain a good or service they could otherwise not afford: e.g. concessionary bus fares for senior citizens.

Competition. As explained above, a firm may use price discrimination to drive competitors out of business. On the other hand, it might use its profits from its high-priced market to break into another market and withstand a possible price war. Competition is thereby increased.

Profits. Price discrimination raises a firm's profits. This could be seen to be against the interests of the consumer, especially if the average price of the product is raised. On the other hand, the higher profits may be reinvested and lead to lower costs in the future.

Recap

1. Price discrimination is where a firm sells the same product at different prices in different markets.

2. Price discrimination allows the firm to earn a higher revenue from a given level of sales.

3. Some people will gain from price discrimination; others will lose. It is likely to be particularly harmful when it is used as a means of driving competitors from the market (predatory pricing).

Questions

1. A perfectly competitive firm faces a price of £14 per unit. It has the short-run cost schedule shown at the bottom of this page.

   (a) Copy the table and put in additional rows for average cost and marginal cost at each level of output. (Enter the figures for marginal cost in the space between each column.)
   (b) Plot *AC*, *MC* and *MR* on a diagram.
   (c) Mark the profit-maximising output.
   (d) How much (supernormal) profit is made at this output?
   (e) What would happen to the price in the long run if this firm were typical of others in the industry? Why would we need to know information about long-run average cost in order to give a precise answer to this question?

2. If the industry under perfect competition faces a downward-sloping demand curve, why does an individual firm face a horizontal demand curve?

3. On a diagram similar to Figure 4.3, show the long-run equilibrium for both firm and industry under perfect competition. Now assume that the demand for the product falls. Show the short-run and long-run effects.

Output	0	1	2	3	4	5	6	7	8
TC (£)	10	18	24	30	38	50	66	91	120

4. If supernormal profits are competed away under perfect competition, why will firms have an incentive to become more efficient?

5. Is it a valid criticism of perfect competition to argue that it is incompatible with economies of scale?

6. As an illustration of the difficulty in identifying monopolies, try and decide which of the following are monopolies: British Telecom; your local evening newspaper; a water company; the village post office; the Royal Mail; Interflora; the London Underground; ice-creams in the cinema; Guinness; food sold in a train buffet car; Tipp-Ex; the board game 'Monopoly'.

7. Try this brain teaser. A monopoly would be expected to face an inelastic demand. After all, there are no direct substitutes. And yet, if it produces where $MR = MC$, MR must be positive, and demand must therefore be elastic. Therefore the monopolist must face an elastic demand! Can you solve this conundrum?

8. For what reasons would you expect a monopoly to charge (a) a higher price, and (b) a lower price than if the industry were operating under perfect competition?

9. In which of the following industries are exit costs likely to be low: (a) steel production; (b) market

gardening; (c) nuclear power generation; (d) specialist financial advisory services; (e) production of fashion dolls; (f) production of a new drug; (g) contract catering; (h) mobile discos; (i) car ferry operators? Are these exit costs dependent on how narrowly the industry is defined?

10. Think of three examples of monopolies (local or national) and consider how contestable their markets are.

11. Think of ten different products or services and estimate roughly how many firms there are in the market. You will need to decide whether 'the market' is a local one, a national one or an international one. In what ways do the firms compete in each of the cases you have identified?

12. Assume that a monopolistically competitive industry is in long-run equilibrium. On a diagram like Figure 4.7, show the effect of a fall in demand on a firm's price and profit in (a) the short run and (b) the long run.

13. Imagine there are two types of potential customer for jam sold by a small food shop. The one is the person who has just run out and wants some now. The other is the person who looks in the cupboard, sees that the pot of jam is less than half full and thinks, 'I will soon need some more.' How will the price elasticity of demand differ between these two customers?

14. Why may a food shop charge higher prices than supermarkets for 'essential items' and yet very similar prices for delicatessen items?

15. Firms under monopolistic competition generally have spare capacity. Does this imply that if, say, half of the petrol stations were closed down, the consumer would benefit? Explain.

16. Will competition between oligopolists always reduce total industry profits?

17. In which of the following industries is collusion likely to occur: bricks, beer, margarine, cement, crisps, washing powder, blank audio or video cassettes, carpets?

18. Devise a box diagram like that in Table 4.2 (on page 143), only this time assume that there are three firms each considering the two strategies of keeping price the same or reducing it by a set amount. Is the game still a 'dominant strategy game'?

19. Which of the following are examples of effective countervailing power?

    (a) Power stations buying coal from a large mining company.
    (b) A large office hiring a photocopier from Rank Xerox.
    (c) Marks and Spencer buying clothes from a garment manufacturer.
    (d) A small village store (but the only one for miles around) buying food from a wholesaler.

    Is it the size of the purchasing firm that is important in determining its power to keep down the prices charged by its suppliers?

20. If a cinema could sell all its seats to adults in the evenings at the end of the week, but only a few on Mondays and Tuesdays, what price discrimination policy would you recommend to the cinema in order for it to maximise its weekly revenue?

21. Think of two examples of price discrimination. In what ways do the consumers gain or lose? What information would you need to be certain in your answer?

Additional case studies on the *Essentials of Economics* MyEconLab (www.pearsoned.co.uk/sloman)

4.1   **Is perfect best?** An examination of the meaning of the word 'perfect' in perfect competition.
4.2   **B2B electronic marketplaces.** This case study examines the growth of firms trading with each other over the Internet (business to business or 'B2B') and considers the effects on competition.
4.3   **Concentration ratios.** One way of measuring the degree of market power in an industry.
4.4   **Competition in the pipeline.** Monopoly in the supply of gas in the UK.
4.5   **X-inefficiency.** A type of inefficiency suffered by many large firms, resulting in a wasteful use of resources.
4.6   **Airline deregulation in the USA and Europe.** Whether the deregulation of various routes has led to more competition and lower prices.

4.7 Edward Chamberlin (1899–1967). The birth of the monopolistic competition model.

4.8 The motor vehicle repair and servicing industry. A case study of monopolistic competition.

4.9 Curry wars. Monopolistic competition in the take-away food market.

4.10 Bakeries: oligopoly or monopolistic competition? A case study on the bread industry, showing that small-scale local bakeries can exist alongside giant national bakeries.

4.11 Oligopoly in the brewing industry. A case study showing how the UK brewing industry is becoming more concentrated.

4.12 The global vitamin cartel. A case study showing oligopolistic collusion in the production and sale of vitamins.

4.13 Cartels set in concrete, steel and cardboard. This examines some of the best-known Europe-wide cartels of recent years.

4.14 Merger activity. This examines mergers in Europe: their causes and consequences.

4.15 A product's life cycle. How market conditions vary at different stages in a product's life.

4.16 Peak load pricing. An example of price discrimination.

4.17 How do UK companies set prices? A summary of the findings of a Bank of England survey on how firms set prices in practice.

Sections of chapter covered in *WinEcon* – Sloman, *Essentials of Economics*

Essentials of Economics section	*WinEcon* section
4.1	4.1
4.2	4.2
4.3	4.3
4.4	4.4
4.5	4.5
4.6	4.6

Websites relevant to this chapter

Numbers and sections refer to websites listed in the Web Appendix and hotlinked from MyEconLab. Visit:

www.pearsoned.co.uk/sloman

- For news articles relevant to this chapter, see the *Economics News Articles* link from MyEconLab.
- For general news on companies and markets, see websites in section A, and particularly A2, 3, 4, 5, 8, 9, 18, 24, 25, 26, 36. See also A38, 43 and 44 for links to newspapers worldwide; and A42 for links to economics news video and audio.
- For sites that looks at competition and market power, see B2 (third link); E4, 10, 18; G7, 8. See also links in I7, 11, 14 and 17.
- For regulation of the gas industry, see E16.
- For a site on game theory, see A40 including its home page. See also D4; C20; I17 and 4 (in the EconDirectory section).

Web Appendices

4.1 Measuring monopoly power. An examination of how the degree of monopoly power possessed by a firm can be measured.

4.2 The Cournot model. An extension of the analysis given in the text.

Chapter 12

Size Structure of Firms

Size structure of firms

Chris Britton

Businesses range in size from the single proprietor at one extreme to the large multinational at the other which employs thousands of people over several countries. The structure of these businesses will be very different and the problems they face will vary as a result of the differences in size. The size structure of business will depend on many factors which range from choice (the sole proprietor may choose to remain small) to external factors which are beyond the control of the firm.

Learning outcomes

Having read this chapter you should be able to:

● outline the size structure of UK industry

● provide reasons for why organisations grow in size

● demonstrate the way in which organisations grow and the methods of finance

● explain the limitations to growth

● survey the level of merger activity in the United Kingdom and the European Union

● demonstrate the role and importance of the small-firm sector

● discuss the idea of networking between firms

Key terms

Capital market	External growth	Networking
Concentration	Flexible firm	Profit
Conglomerate merger	Gearing	Small firm
Debentures	Horizontal merger	Stock Exchange
Diseconomies of scale	Industrial concentration	Subcontracting
Diversification	Internal growth	Takeover
Dividends	Joint venture	Vertical integration
Enterprise	Merger	Virtual organisation
Equity	Money market	
Establishment	Multinational corporation	

Introduction

There has been an increase in the level of industrial concentration in the United Kingdom over the last one hundred years. In 1909 the largest hundred companies produced 16 per cent of manufacturing output; by 1990 this had risen to around 30 per cent. Such an increase in the size of business organisations gives rise to worries about the concentration of power in the hands of a few producers and abuses of this power. If the companies are multinationals, they may be beyond the control even of national governments. More recently the trend towards greater concentration has been reversed, and there seems to be a movement towards employment in smaller units. This chapter will look at the size structure of British industry and the reasons for such a structure, with some international comparisons. It will consider the role of small and large firms in the economy. It will also examine the reasons for growth, the ways in which organisations grow, the financing of growth and the limits to growth. It will also consider the relatively more recent trend towards co-operation in production, rather than competition, through activities like joint ventures and networking.

The size structure of UK industry

When looking at the size of firms it is important to define the terms used in official data. The firm, or 'enterprise', is the organisation as a whole, and it might be comprised of several units or 'establishments'. Small firms like the corner shop will mostly be enterprises with only one establishment. Large firms like Sainsbury's will have many establishments as they have branches in most towns.

There are many different ways to measure the size of firms. Common measures used are turnover, the value of output, the capital employed or the level of employment. Such measurement is beset by problems, not least the difficulty of defining the small firm, as will be seen later in this chapter. The three measures mentioned above might give conflicting pictures, as an industry which is becoming increasingly mechanised will probably have rising levels of average capital employed and output but falling average levels of employment. Table 11.1 shows the 'top ten' companies in the United Kingdom using two of these measures and it illustrates the point that different measures of the size of a firm will give different rankings.

Some of these names will be familiar to the reader while others are less so. Compass Group plc, for example, is a food service organisation which provides catering and support services to its clients.

The most common measure of size used is the level of employment. Table 11.2 shows the size structure of units in all industries by the number of employees in the United Kingdom in 2006. The table shows that smaller firms predominate in terms of numbers, with 98.4 per cent of firms employing fewer than 100 employees. In terms of employment, however, these firms account for only 34.0 per cent of the total level of employment in manufacturing. At the other end of the scale establishments with over 500 employees account for only 0.3 per cent of the total number but 54.6 per cent of total employment. The pattern of size structure varies across industries and over time. In the last 20 to 30 years there seems to have been an increase in the importance of small firms and a decline in the importance of large firms in their contribution to employment. In 1980 establishments with fewer than 200 employees accounted for 31.9 per cent of total employment and establishments with more than 500 employees accounted for 49.8 per cent. The comparable figures from Table 11.2 are 38.7 per cent and 54.6 per cent. Even the short period of time from 1991 to 2000 saw a shift in the importance of small firms. There was an increase of 188 968 in the number of units employing fewer than 20 people, while there was a decrease of 13 332 in the number of units employing more than 20 employees. A similar pattern emerges with employment, with an increase in employment of 313 800 in the smaller units and a decrease in employment of 882 800 in the larger units.

Many of the large companies listed in Table 11.1 operate in more than one country and are therefore multinationals. **Multinational corporations** strictly defined are enterprises operating in a number of countries and having production or service facilities outside the country of their origin.[1] Multinationals pose particular problems for governments and economies because of their size. They are considered later in this chapter.

Table 11.1 The ten largest companies in the UK, 2007

Ranking by turnover	Ranking by employment
1 Tesco plc	1 Compass Group plc
2 Vodafone Group plc	2 Group 4 Securicor plc
3 BP International plc	3 Tesco plc
4 Tesco Stores plc	4 HSBC Holdings plc
5 Aviva plc	5 Unilever plc
6 Unilever plc	6 Royal Mail Holdings plc
7 WPP 2005 Ltd	7 Royal Mail Group plc
8 BT Group plc	8 Sainsbury's Supermarkets Ltd
9 British Telecommunications plc	9 Tesco Stores Ltd
10 J. Sainsbury plc	10 The Royal Bank of Scotland Group plc

Source: *Key British Enterprises*, 2007.

Table 11.2 Size structure of UK industry by employment, 2006

Employment size group	Number of units	% of total	Employment (000s)	% of total
1–9	1 064 170	83.0	3 906	15.2
10–19	118 120	9.2	1 638	6.4
20–49	60 575	4.7	1 874	7.3
50–99	18 925	1.5	1 316	5.1
100–199	9 120	0.7	1 217	4.7
200–499	5 510	0.4	1 691	6.6
500 and over	4 415	0.3	14 065	54.6

Source: Adapted from Table 1, *http://stats.berr.gov.uk/ed/sme/smestats2006.xls* 'UK whole economy'! A1

Organisational growth

The reasons for organisational growth

Firms grow in size for many reasons; growth could be an explicit objective of management or could be necessary for the successful operation of the firm:

- Growth could be a managerial objective if it brings benefits to management such as greater security and higher remuneration.
- It could be that the market in which the business operates is expanding and growth is necessary to maintain market share. This is especially the case as markets become more international.
- Growth enables the organisation to reap the benefits of economies of scale (see Chapter 15).
- Growth enables firms to diversify into other markets, which means that risk can be spread further.
- Industries which are capital intensive will of necessity be comprised of large firms.
- In the area of product development it is possible that the necessary research and development could only be carried out by large companies.
- Growth could be pursued as a defensive strategy, as a reaction to the activities of competitors.

Table 11.3 provides an illustration of how the stated objectives of EU firms for engaging in merger activity can change over time and gives some indication of the reasons for growth. Much of this shift can be explained by changing market conditions which resulted from the creation of the Single European Market in 1992. The relaxation of trade restrictions in the run-up to 1992 encouraged much greater competition, and hence expansion and strengthening of market position have assumed much greater importance since 1985, together accounting for nearly 75 per cent of mergers. It was expected that the increased competition would force companies to concentrate more upon their core activities and as a result diversification as a motive for merger fell from 17.6 per cent in 1985 to 2.1 per cent of cases in 1992.

Table 11.3 Main motives for mergers in Europe, 1985–1992

Motive	% of times mentioned			
	1985–86	*1989–90*	*1990–91*	*1991–92*
Expansion	17.1	26.9	27.7	32.4
Diversification	17.6	3.0	2.8	2.1
Strengthening market position	10.6	45.3	48.2	44.4
Rationalisation and synergies	46.5	17.7	13.3	16.2
Research and development	2.4	0.6	0	0
Other	5.9	6.4	8.0	5.0

Source: *European Economy*, no. 57, 1994. Reproduced by permission of the Office for Official Publications of the European Communities.

The OECD[2] recognises that there are efficiencies involved in growth and it classifies these into 'static' and 'dynamic' efficiencies. Static efficiencies are one-off improvements such as economies of scale in production. Dynamic efficiences are those that enable improvements in cost, quality, service or new product development on an ongoing basis. In considering the benefits of a takeover or merger, for example, it may be that the dynamic efficiences will eventually overtake the initially bigger static efficiences. Examples of dynamic efficiences include:

● Economies of scale and scope in R&D.
● Better risk-spreading especially for R&D.
● Increased financial resources for R&D.
● Better intellectual property rights protection.

In industrial economics firm size is seen as a function of growth. It is suggested that although there is no limit on the size of a firm there are limits on the rate of expansion. Growth rates are seen to depend on different things by different theorists, including the availability of finance, the level of consumer demand and the limitations of management. These theories, however, are primarily concerned with large firms and their development. Small firms are seen as potentially large firms that failed to grow for some reason or other. One interesting theory of growth is the stages model, where the firm is seen as passing through various stages in its development from small sole proprietor/partnership through the decision to expand into a large organisation. This again is a 'grow or fail' theory which does not apply well to industries which are dominated by successful small firms, as will be seen later in the chapter.

mini case   Mars and Wrigley

In May 2008 Mars surprised the market by taking over Wrigley in a $23 billion deal. The takeover was a friendly one and was negotiated in less than three weeks. Unusually, both companies are private family-owned businesses which possibly meant that there were compatibilities which made the takeover more feasible and meant that the decision-making timescale could be short. What will the takeover mean for both companies?

For Mars, it enables diversification into a new market – chewing gum has a much healthier image than other confectionary and the dental benefits of chewing gum are well documented. The gum market has a higher growth rate than other forms of confectionary – 20 per cent in 2007. Wrigley has a big presence in Asia and China in particular, where growth in the confectionary market is particularly high, and Mars will be able to tap into these distribution networks. The new company will take the market leader's position away from Cadbury's Trident brand with 14 per cent of the world market against 10 per cent (Cadbury).

For Wrigley, the premium offered over its share price was generous (28 per cent) and the takeover will bring access to more extensive distribution networks. Wrigley will be a standalone subsidiary which means that managers at Wrigley are allowed to keep their jobs and to remain in the location of their HQ. Bill Wrigley, the company's executive chairman, said that 'this combined entity will have the resources and critical mass to explore new geographies and categories that might have been beyond our reach in the past'.

The takeover will have implications for other companies in the market – Cadbury for example. Commentators cannot agree whether the Mars–Wrigley takeover has made Cadbury a more likely takeover target or predator, as it will retain the number 1 position outside the USA. Nestlé and Kraft have been identified as possible companies for either possibility. There is also speculation of an alliance with Hershey's, which holds 43 per cent of the US chocolate markets, a company that Cadbury has held talks with in the past.

Methods of growth

Firms grow in size internally as part of normal business operation or externally through takeover and merger.

Internal growth

Growth is a natural process for many firms that start small, capture a segment of the market and then continue to expand either by producing more of the same goods or by extending their product lines. The advantage of **internal growth** over external growth is that the company grows within the existing structure of management; there are none of the problems of bringing together two different management systems. There might also be economies of scale from building a bigger plant that might not be available when companies merge and plant size does not change. Set against these, internal growth has certain disadvantages and this is why most of the growth in the size of organisations has occurred through external growth.

External growth

Growth by acquisition is called **external growth** and occurs through **takeover** or **merger**. A merger is the voluntary coming together of two companies with the agreement of the management of both companies, the result of which is the creation of a new legal identity. A takeover is where one company makes an offer to the shareholders of another. If the management of the threatened company resist it is called a hostile takeover, but if the price offered to shareholders is high enough they will accept. Takeover bids can be and have been successfully fought off by the management of the second firm. A holding company is a new company that is formed to acquire assets in other companies. The acquired companies retain their independent identities but are directed by the holding company.

   External growth can be seen to have a number of advantages:

1 It is fast, so that productive capacity can be increased very quickly.
2 The acquiring firm has access to an established management team and system.
3 If the shares of the acquiring company have sufficiently high values relative to the acquired firm, there might be no need for additional cash to be raised.
4 The purchase of existing assets could be cheaper than building new productive capacity.

But set against these is the fact that the process might not be an easy one; it is a difficult job to merge two companies smoothly and successfully and there are likely to be many teething problems. Research by Coopers & Lybrand (now PriceWaterhouse Coopers) found that top executives regarded half of the takeovers in which they had been involved as failures. The main reasons for failure were lack of planning and managerial problems.

Although the definitions of merger and takeover are clear enough, it is often difficult to tell them apart in practice and they are usually put together in official publications under the heading of acquisitions. In order to understand fully the motivation for mergers and takeovers it is important to recognise that there are different types of mergers.

Horizontal mergers

A **horizontal merger** is where a combination between firms at the same stage in a production process takes place; for example, between two car manufacturers or between two brewers. The vast majority of mergers that take place are of this type and many of our largest companies have been formed through horizontal merger. Examples include mergers between banks and building societies. The motives for this type of merger are:

- *To benefit from economies of scale.* Horizontal mergers allow the merged firms a greater level of specialisation and the benefits of other economies of scale (see Chapter 15).
- *Greater market share.* When firms come together there will be a reduction in competition in the market and the resulting firm will have a much larger share of the market.
- *Rationalisation of output.* If the level of demand for a good is shrinking, merger between the producers could be necessary in order to rationalise output.
- *Reaction to competitors.* In markets where mergers are taking place, companies may feel that they have to do the same in order to maintain their market position.

The takeover of the American company Anheuser–Busch (which makes Budweiser) by Belgian company InBev (which makes Stella Artois) in 2008 is an example of a horizontal takeover (see International business in action: 'A lot of bottle').

Vertical mergers

A vertical merger involves firms at different stages of the same production process. It is vertical since it runs along the production process from extraction of raw materials to distribution. An example would be a merger between a car manufacturer and a metal-pressing company. **Vertical integration** can take place 'backwards' towards the beginning of the production process or 'forwards' towards the end of it and it can occur for several reasons:

1 In the case of backwards integration, to control the supplies of raw materials with respect to their quantity and quality. This brings greater security to the acquiring firm.
2 To restrict supplies of the raw materials to competitors.
3 In the case of forwards integration, to control the quality of the outlets for the finished product. Manufacturers finance the majority of advertising and they might well feel that a forwards merger would enable them to ensure that the good was being sold in the most appropriate setting.
4 In both cases, economies of scale are possible if different parts of the production process are brought together.
5 Again, vertical mergers can be carried out as a reaction to the activities of competitors.

An example of a vertical takeover is the proposed aquisition of Continental (a German tyre producer) by Ashaeffler (a maker of car parts, especially ball bearings) in 2008.

Conglomerate mergers

These mergers are neither vertical nor horizontal but involve a merger between firms involved in producing different goods. The bid made during 2008 by advertising giant WPP for the market research group TNS would be an example of a conglomerate merger, although the markets are highly complementary. The main motivation for this type of merger is diversification. It reduces the risk involved in producing for only one market and allows the firm to spread risk further. It can also provide the firm with another option if the original market declines in size.

As far as the economy is concerned, the main gains of mergers are in increased efficiency resulting from economies of scale and also the increased scope for research and development. A common view is that merger and takeover activity serves the purpose of rationalising business. The weak businesses go and the strong survive. Even when a takeover is carried out for the purpose of asset stripping this will be the case.

Growth by merger and takeover

Growth through merger and takeover first appeared in the USA over a hundred years ago and merger activity tends to come in waves (see the discussion later in this chapter). Five periods of heightened merger activity have been identified in the USA:

- The period 1880 to 1905 – this coincided with the proliferation of the joint stock company and the international establishment of stock exchanges. This period was characterised by mergers of a horizontal nature.
- The 1920s – at this time the mergers were largely vertical in nature, as manufacturers took control of both suppliers and distributors.
- The 1960s – mergers in this period were mainly about diversification and the establishment of conglomerates.
- The post-1980 period – this wave of activity took place in a period of recession and was largely about cost-cutting and rationalisation.
- The late 1990s – as companies in mature industries attempted to become global operators. The pace of this surge of activity slowed for a period after September 11th 2001, but by 2004 the boom in activity had restarted.
- Early 2000s – from 2004 to 2007 the boom continued until the credit crunch in the USA caused a sharp fall in merger activity, including a 36 per cent decline in the first half of 2008.

The first two periods of heightened merger activity in the USA had little effect in Europe; however, there were waves of activity in Europe which coincided with the last two. The first wave of merger activity in Europe came in the 1960s after obstacles to trade were removed by the establishment of the EEC in 1957. The second wave of mergers came in the 1980s in the run-up to the establishment of the Single European Market in 1992. As yet there is little evidence of an increase in merger activity as a result of EMU in Europe.

The most recent surge of activity in the USA did not reach the EU until 2005 – the value of mergers and acquisitions in Europe in the first quarter of 2005 was three times higher than the same period in 2004 and there are several pending large deals. The motivation for this activity seems to be the synergies achieved through mergers with similar companies – it seems that national companies are trying to become European companies.

The recent fall in merger activity seen in the USA has been echoed in Europe (e.g. 35.4 per cent decline in activity in the first half of 2008) which is suffering from the same economic malaise. The only part of the world not affected as yet is Asia where the value of deals rise by 27.4 per cent in the same time period.

Finance for growth

Internal sources

As part of its operation the firm will generate income in the form of **profit**. Part of this profit will be distributed in the form of **dividends** to shareholders, the rest can be used for reinvestment and to finance growth. Although this is seen as a relatively easy and cheap source of finance, it does carry an opportunity cost and therefore should be judged on its rate of return like any other source of finance. Table 11.4 shows that internal funds were the largest single source of finance for industry during the 1990s. It also shows that the totals available and the pattern of sources vary a great deal from year to year. (This data is no longer compiled by the Office for National Statistics.)

Table 11.4 Sources of funds for industry, 1990, 1994 and 1997 (£ million)

Source	1990	1994	1997
Internal funds	33 838	61 406	56 363
Banks and other short-term borrowing	19 911	−4 841	6 630
Loans and mortgages	9 120	4 557	4 384
Ordinary shares	1 880	8 495	19 616
Debentures and preference shares	6 367	1 008	10 640
Other capital issues	7 485	5 067	10 526
Other overseas investment	11 233	−1 400	25 938
Other	1 444	3 766	953
Total	91 278	78 056	135 050

Source: *Financial Statistics*, January 1993, 1996 and 1999. Crown copyright 1999. Reproduced by permission of the Controller of HMSO and of the Office for National Statistics, UK.

External sources

As the size and availability of retained earnings will be limited, most firms will also have to seek other sources of finance for expansion. There are many external sources of finance and a typical firm's capital structure will comprise a combination of these. The sources are as follows.

Banks

Banks provide short- and medium-term finance to companies in the form of loans or overdrafts. The relative cost of these depends upon how the firm wishes to use the funds. Loans carry a lower rate of interest but the interest is paid on the whole amount, while the interest on overdrafts is only paid on the amount drawn. British banks have been criticised by many for failing to provide longer-term finance for business, as banks do in other countries.

Capital market

The **capital market** is the place where stocks and shares are traded and is therefore a key provider of long-term finance to firms. The main institution in the capital market is the **Stock Exchange**. The capital market is made up of two parts: the primary part which involves the buying and selling of new stocks and shares; and the secondary part which involves the buying and selling of existing stocks and shares. It is therefore the primary part of the market that is the source of finance for firms. The secondary part of the market is, however, also important in this process as individuals and organisations are more likely to buy stocks and shares with the knowledge that there is a ready market on which they can be traded at a later date.

The main institutions that buy stocks and shares are the insurance companies, pension funds, investment trusts, unit trusts and other large financial institutions such as building societies.

A new issue of shares takes place when an existing company needs extra finance or when a company becomes a public limited company.

Types of stocks and shares

1 *Preference shares.* These are shares in a company which carry a fixed dividend. Holders have preference over other shareholders in the payment of dividends and on the liquidation of the firm. Preference shares usually carry no voting rights, and so holders have little influence over how the company is run.
2 *Ordinary shares.* Ordinary shares are called the '**equity**' of the company. They do not usually carry a fixed dividend; the company declares a dividend, depending upon its performance in that year. This means that in good years ordinary shareholders could receive high dividends, while in bad years possibly none at all. Ordinary shares are therefore more risky than preference shares, and in recognition of this they usually carry voting rights, so that holders can exercise some influence over how the company is run.
3 *Debentures.* **Debentures** or loan stock are bonds which are given in exchange for a loan to the company. The company agrees to repay the borrowed amount at some date in the future and to make annual payments of interest in the meantime. Interest on debentures is paid before payment of any dividends and the interest is allowable against tax. A debenture holder is a creditor of the company, a shareholder is an owner of the company.

New issue of shares

A company will go to an issuing house or merchant bank which will advise it on the type and number of shares to issue, the price at which they should be offered and other matters. They will often carry out the issue of shares on behalf of the firm. A new issue of shares is not a big source of finance for growth as it is fairly expensive; retained earnings are more convenient and cheaper. Also the amount of information that is required from companies which issue shares to the general public can act as a disincentive.

It is worth noting that in the UK the Stock Market has two main equity markets: the main market and the Alternative Investment Market (AIM). The main market deals in the shares of the large and well-established companies. The Alternative Investment Market provides an opportunity for growing smaller companies to raise capital and have their shares traded in a market without the considerable expense of a full market listing.

Money market

The **money markets** provide short-term finance for companies, often for as brief a period as overnight.

Government and other institutions

The government is a source of finance for firms. Through its regional policy it gives tax allowances, loans, grants and training allowances to firms in certain parts of the country (see Chapter 13). It has many schemes for helping business, particularly small businesses. This will be covered more fully later in this chapter.

Other sources

Other sources include trade credit and hire purchase (i.e. receiving assets now and paying later). This is only a small source of finance for companies. As Table 11.4 shows, industry draws a fairly high proportion of its funding from overseas. This includes finance from many different sources, including individuals, governments, financial institutions overseas and companies.

Firms will typically go for a mixture of different types of finance. The exact combination will depend upon many factors, including their relative costs, their availability and the desired capital structure of the firm. A firm's desired capital structure will largely depend upon the type of market in which it operates. The different types of finance are classified under the two headings of debt and equity. Debt refers to all types of capital on which payments have to be made each year regardless of how the firm has performed; this would include loans and preference shares. Equity refers to ordinary shares where the payment of a dividend depends upon the performance of the firm. As a source of finance, debt is generally cheaper but it is also more risky since in bad years the firm will have to meet the interest payments. The ratio of debt to equity is called the **gearing** of the company. Debt is not well suited to firms in industries where profits fluctuate and such firms will have lower gearing than those in more stable markets.

Limits to growth

Several factors tend to act as a limit to organisational growth:

- To finance growth, excessive borrowing might have taken place and the firm may have trouble meeting debt repayments; therefore there is increased risk of bankruptcy.
- A serious constraint to growth might be the abilities of management. As organisations grow in size they may experience **diseconomies of scale**, which are mainly to do with managerial problems, like communication and control.
- If the size of the market for the product is stagnant or declining it may be both unnecessary and impossible for the firm to grow.
- Government policies, too, can have an important impact on growth. Every government has policies on competition which seek to limit anti-competitive practices and which normally regulate merger activity (see Chapter 17).

Merger activity in the United Kingdom

There are two common ways of measuring the level of merger activity – by the number of transactions or by the total value of the transactions. Figure 11.1 shows the level of merger activity in the UK according to the number of companies acquired in the UK by UK companies. It can be seen that there was a sharp rise in

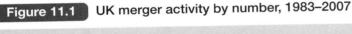

Figure 11.1   UK merger activity by number, 1983–2007

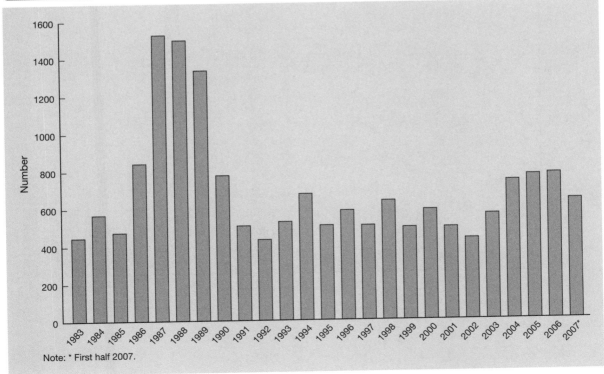

Note: * First half 2007.

Source: *www.statistics.gov.uk.*

merger activity in the mid-1980s and a downturn in 1989. The cyclical pattern continues into the 1990s but the amplitude is reduced. This cyclical pattern is repeated in other countries and in the EU as a whole and it implies that the level of mergers is in some way related to the state of the economy. The rise in the mid-1980s was due partly to an improvement in the state of the economy and partly to the liberalisation of the financial markets, which made finance for takeover bids more freely available. The fall in 1989 was due partly to the recession and partly to the problems that some companies subsequently experienced by overstretching themselves in the mid-1980s. The subsequent rise in the level of merger activity was due to the restructuring which took place in many diverse industries in the 1990s like the financial services sector and the public utilities.[3]

Figure 11.2 shows the level of merger activity in the UK according to the value of the transactions, and the same cyclical path can be discerned although the peaks and troughs do not exactly coincide with the number of transactions. The use of the value of the transactions as a measure of merger activity is problematic in that it will be distorted by any very high-value deals that take place, as in 1995–7 and 2000 when the number of transactions fell but their value rose. The first half of 2007 showed record activity but by the end of the year markets had slowed because of the impact of the global financial crisis (see International business in action: 'The global financial crisis').

Figure 11.2 UK merger activity by value, 1983–2007

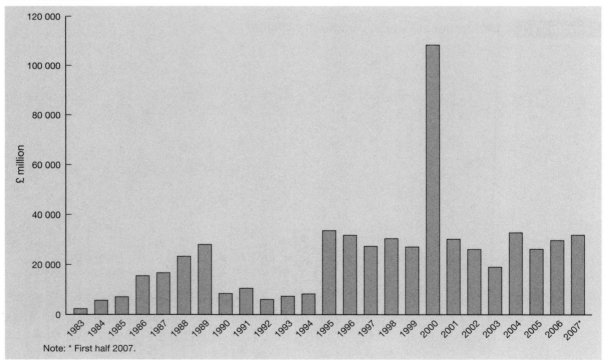

Note: * First half 2007.

Source: *www.statistics.gov.uk.*

Global merger activity

The same pattern seen in the UK data is also evident in the EU and the world as a whole (see Table 11.5). There was a decline in merger and acquisitions in the early 2000s followed by a surge in activity in 2004. During the 1990s the boom in merger activity was dominated by the telecommunications sector, while in the 2004/5 recovery the activity was taking place mainly in the financial services sector.

Table 11.5 Cross-border mergers and acquisitions to and from OECD countries, 1999–2007 ($ billion)

Year	Outwards	Inwards
1999	801	775
2000	1166	1136
2001	606	585
2002	376	410
2003	321	338
2004	422	444
2005	673	635
2006	847	818
2007	1028	1033

Source: Adapted from Table 2.3, *International Investment Perspectives*, OECD, 2007.

The high volume of merger and acquisition activity in the first half of 2007 meant that it was a record year even though the pace slowed in the second half of the year as the credit crunch took hold – worldwide mergers and acquisitions totalled $4.5 trillion, a 24 per cent increase over 2006. The global financial crisis has had an impact on the level of merger and acquisition activity – the value of global mergers and acquisitions was $729.9 billion in the first quarter of 2008 (down by 24.2 per cent on the previous year) and the lowest level since the third quarter of 2006. In quarter 2 the level of activity was down by 36 per cent.[4] It is difficult to predict what will happen in the second half of 2008, but the consensus among commentators is that the level of activity will be 25 per cent lower than in 2007.

Small firms

There are serious problems in the analysis of the small-firm sector, including the lack of data over a long period of time and the problem of defining exactly what is a **small firm**. The Bolton Report,[5] published in 1971, was the report of a committee set up to look into the role of small firms in the UK economy. It used various definitions for statistical purposes, depending upon the industry being considered, on the grounds that what is small in one industry might be large in another. Table 11.6 shows the size distribution of firms based on their turnover for a selection of industries for 2007.

Table 11.6 Size of companies by turnover across different industries, 2007 (%)

Industry	Turnover size ('000)		
	up to £250	£250–£500	over £500
Agriculture, forestry and fishing	86	9	5
Mining and quarrying and public utilities	40	10	50
Manufacturing	53	14	33
Construction	70	13	17
Wholesaling	48	14	38
Retailing	63	19	18
Financial services	49	11	40
Business services	76	10	15

Source: Adapted from Table B2.2, *UK Business Activity by Size and Location*, National Statistics, 2007.

It is clear from Table 11.6 that the definition of 'big' will vary with the industry. In the Bolton Report the definition used for small firms in manufacturing was 'less than 200 employees', while in construction it was 'less than 25 employees'. In some industries turnover limits were chosen while in others a mixture of employment and turnover was used. Although this is confusing and makes comparison between industries and countries difficult, it was accepted that there could not be a single definition which would apply to all sectors. The EU in 1994 recommended to its members that they use 'less than 250 employees' as the definition of a small to medium-sized enterprise (SME), in order to facilitate the easy comparison of data across member states. A further refinement of the definition used by Eurostat based on numbers employed is shown in Table 11.7.

Table 11.7 Classification of firms by employment size

Number of employees	Type of firm
0–9	micro businesses
10–99	small enterprises
100–499	medium-sized enterprises
500+	large enterprises

Applying this definition to Table 11.2, it can be seen that 83 per cent of manufacturing firms in the UK are micro businesses, 15.4 per cent are small, 1.1 per cent are medium sized and 0.3 per cent are large. Although there are some national differences (the southern-most countries have relatively more micro businesses than the northern countries) the pattern of size structure is similar in the EU as a whole – 92 per cent of all enterprises are micro businesses, 7.4 per cent are small, 0.5 per cent are medium sized and 0.1 per cent are large.[6]

It is important to note that the definition of SME used within the EU changed in 2005. For grant-aid purposes an SME must have no more than 25 per cent of its capital owned by a larger enterprise and must meet specific criteria with regard to numbers of employees, turnover or balance sheet totals. A 'micro firm' is one with 0–9 employees, a maximum annual turnover of 2 million euros or a maximum balance sheet total also of 2 million euros. The equivalent figures for a 'small firm' are

10–49 employees, 10 million euros turnover or 10 million euros balance sheet total; for a 'medium-sized firm' 50–249 employees, 50 million euros turnover or 43 million euros balance sheet total. Using these definitions it is estimated that 99 per cent of all enterprises in the EU (prior to enlargement) were SMEs and that they provided around 65 million jobs.

No matter how small firms are defined, they will suffer from similar problems, which are very different from those faced by larger companies.

Trends in the small-firm sector

The percentage share of small establishments in total manufacturing employment in the UK was in decline for the 1930s up to the early 1970s, when its importance increased dramatically.[7] In recent years the percentage has stayed around 40 per cent. Table 11.2 showed that for UK industry small firms are very important in terms of the number of businesses, accounting for 99 per cent of total firms. Even though they were less important in terms of employment, they still accounted for 39 per cent of total employment. Figure 11.3 shows the share of employment of small firms by sector; as can be seen, there is a great deal of variation between sectors.

Reasons for the growth in the small-firm sector

There has clearly been a resurgence in the importance of the small-firm sector which appears to have been more pronounced in the United Kingdom than in other countries. Why? Some causal factors are as follows:

Figure 11.3   Share of small firms in employment by sector, 2007

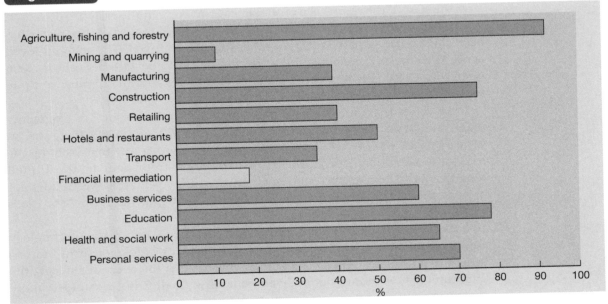

Source: Adapted from Figure 3, UKN 08/92, BERR, 2008.

1 *The changing pattern of industry.* In Chapter 12 it is shown that there has been a change in the industrial structure of the United Kingdom away from manufacturing and towards services. Since many services are dominated by small firms, there will be a corresponding change in average firm size. However, this does not provide the full explanation as there has been a growth in the share of small firms even in the manufacturing sector. And it does not explain the international differences since there have been similar changes in industrial structure in other countries too.

2 *Changes in consumer spending habits.* A move from mass-produced goods to more specialised products puts small firms at an advantage as they can react more quickly to changes in demand and shorter product life cycles.

3 *Flexible specialisation and the growth of subcontracting.* A debate which started in the late 1980s centres round the idea of the **flexible firm**.[8] As a result of the recession of the early 1980s there was a drive by firms to reduce their costs in order to remain competitive. One way of reducing overhead costs was to move to a flexible firm structure whereby the firm's activities are divided into core and peripheral activities. The core activities, which are central to the activities of the firm, would be kept 'in-house' and carried out by full-time permanent workers. The peripheral activities would be carried out by temporary workers or would be subcontracted. The firm has then reduced its overheads and can react to peaks in demand by increasing the amount of temporary labour it uses or increasing the amount of **subcontracting**. This might also have had the effect of increasing the relative importance of the small-firm sector.

4 *Reorganisation and job reduction.* There has been an increase in the phenomenon of downsizing by organisations in an attempt to reduce costs. Ninety per cent of large companies have reorganised and cut jobs since 1985.

5 *Government policy.* After the Bolton Report there was a much greater interest in the role of the small firm in the regeneration of the economy and in the provision of jobs. But most of the initiatives designed to help the small firm came after the start of the resurgence of the small-firm sector in the early 1970s.

6 *The growth in self-employment.* A part of the growth in the small-firm sector has been due to the growth in the number of self-employed. The self-employed accounted for 9.8 per cent of the workforce in 1984 and 11.8 per cent in 2006 (see Table 11.8). This represents a 20 per cent increase in the number of those self-employed over this period.

   The level of self-employment is likely to be related to the level of unemployment, so that as unemployment rose during the 1970s and 1980s there was an increase in the level of self-employment. This goes a long way to explaining the international differences as the growth in self-employment in the United Kingdom has far outstripped that in other countries. Again, however, it does not provide the full explanation as business births were growing in the late 1960s when unemployment was falling.

7 *Technological change.* Changes in technology, particularly information technology and the miniaturisation of components, has made it possible for small firms to benefit to a similar extent to large firms. This has had the effect of reducing the importance of economies of scale and enabling small firms to compete more effectively with large ones.

Table 11.8 Percentage of workforce self-employed, 1984–2006 (UK)

Year	% self-employed
1984	9.8
1985	10.0
1986	10.0
1987	10.9
1988	11.3
1989	12.1
1990	12.3
1991	11.9
1992	11.3
1993	11.2
1994	11.7
1995	11.6
1996	11.6
1997	11.5
1998	10.9
1999	10.8
2000	10.6
2001	11.3
2002	11.2
2003	11.6
2004	11.7
2005	11.6
2006	11.8

Source: Adapted from *Annual Abstract of Statistics* (various), ONS, UK.

8 *Competitive forces.* As far as the international differences are concerned, the Bolton Report found that industry in the United Kingdom was biased towards large size in comparison with other countries. So what may have happened as a result of competitive forces is that the balance of industry in the United Kingdom has moved towards the norm of other countries.

The role of the small-firm sector

The growing importance of the small-firm sector implies that small firms do have a valuable role in the economy apart from being a mere provider of employment. The areas in which the small firm has advantages over large firms are those where there are:

1 *Clearly defined small markets.* It is not worthwhile for large firms to enter such markets since there are no economies of scale and no scope for mass production.
2 *Specialist, quality, non-standardised products.* Again it would not be worth a large firm entering such a market as the benefits of large-scale production cannot be reaped.
3 *Geographically localised markets.* For example, the small corner shop.
4 *Development of new ideas.* It is often argued that the small firm is the 'seedbed' of ideas and that, because of greater motivation and commitment on the part of the owner of the small firm, it is very conducive to invention and innovation.

Aid to the small-firm sector

The thinking on small firms has changed over time. Initially they were viewed favourably, but after the Second World War the dominant thinking was that large-scale production could take advantage of large economies of scale and that costs would be lower and production more efficient. It was not until more recently that the interest in the small-firm sector has increased again. The main reasons for the renewed interest are seen in the results of empirical studies which have shown that the role of the small firm is greater than previously thought in areas such as innovation, the balance of payments and employment.

The main argument for giving support to the small-firm sector is that it has a valuable role to play in the economy. In the 1980s and 1990s, for example, small firms were seen as a mechanism for reducing the very high levels of unemployment. Between 1983 and 1993 the small-firm sector created 2.5 million jobs. The basic premise for support is that small firms are at a disadvantage with respect to large businesses in areas such as raising capital, research and development and risk bearing. The 2007 EU Observatory Survey of SMEs in Europe found that there were three main problems facing small firms:

- The burden of regulation – reported as acting as a constraint by 36 per cent of SMEs within Europe. It is estimated that large firms spend €1 per employee on regulatory compliance compared to €10 for SMEs. All EU governments had introduced measures to reduce this burden and the Commission has a commitment to reduce the administrative demands on small businesses by 25 per cent.
- Access to finance – including cash flow problems resulting from late or non-payment of bills. In the UK all public limited companies are required by law to state in their annual reports the average length of time it takes to pay their bills. The Federation of Small Business in the UK publishes a 'name and shame' list of slow payers.
- Access to new markets – between 1996 and 2004 it has been estimated that 60 per cent of the UK's productivity growth came from exporting firms. Only 8 per cent of European SMEs report turnover from exports.

Government policy

Within the UK national policy for small firms has increasingly become a vital component of governmental attempts to create a competitive economy capable of achieving sustainable economic growth. To this end policy initiatives in recent years have become more focused and have tended to adopt a multi-agency approach, aimed at improving the environment in which small businesses emerge and grow, and at fostering enterprise and innovation. Key developments over the last decade or so have included:

- *Business Link* – a national network of 'one-stop shops' to provide information and support to small firms.
- *Direct Access Government* – a 'one-stop shop' on the Internet that provides businesses with access to regulatory guidance and forms.
- *The Enterprise Zone* – another Internet-based initiative to help firms with finding

information on issues such as finance, exporting, technology, innovation and management.

- *The Teaching Company Scheme (TCS)* – the government's premier technology transfer mechanisms for linking UK higher education establishments and businesses.
- *The SMART Awards* – designed to promote technological development and innovation.

There have also been a number of legislative and fiscal changes aimed at reducing the burdens on small businesses (e.g. levels of corporation tax). Some of the more recent developments have included the launch of the University for Industry (UfI), the Enterprise Fund, the University Challenge Fund, the Small Business Service (SBS) and the EU SME Initiative. The latter – introduced in December 1997 – was designed to assist SMEs in rural areas or areas of industrial decline to become more competitive in overseas markets. There have also been attempts to reduce the flow and improve the quality of regulation affecting smaller businesses and an action plan to make the UK the number one location for starting and growing a business.

As the mini case 'the small-firm sector' illustrates, the UK government's 2008 Enterprise Strategy provides a framework of five key 'enablers' aimed at developing an enhanced enterprise culture in the UK. Among the measures proposed under the strategy are a net reduction in the regulatory burden on small firms (of 25 per cent by 2010); changes to the insolvency rules; cross-border mentoring and work placements in SMEs; a women's enterprise campaign; a global entrepreneurship week; a National Enterprise Academy; improvements in the Business Link and business support services; changes to the Small Firms Loans Guarantee Scheme; expansion of the Enterprise Capital Fund; a refocused Small Business Research Initiative; changes to public procurement processes to help SMEs gain access to public contracts. Further information on government small-firm policy is available via the Department of Business Entreprise and Regulatory Reform website (*www.berr.gov.uk*).

mini case   The small-firm sector

Over the years the UK government, like most others, has introduced policies designed to aid the small-firm sector. The latest initiative launched in March 2008 is the Enterprise Strategy, designed to make the UK the most enterprising economy in the world and the best place to start and grow a business. The Strategy aims to boost enterprise skills and to increase knowledge, to help both new and existing business to grow and to ease the burden of regulations, especially on small firms. Five key enablers are identified:

- building an enterprise culture – to provide everyone with the understanding of enterprise so that ideas can be turned into wealth;
- knowledge and skills – encouraging enterprise throughout education, starting in primary schools and continuing through universities to become embedded in the workplace;
- access to finance – to ensure that entrepreneurs and small businesses have both the knowledge and the opportunity to access finance to advance their enterprise;
- regulatory framework – legislation will be kept to a minimum and regulatory burdens reduced;
- business innovation – ensuring that UK business can capitalise on global trends through help in developing innovative products and processes.

Although not specifically aimed at the SME sector, policies proposed under each of the five enablers should have a positive effect on small businesses as two of the five enablers are identified as particular problems for small firms – access to finance and the burden of regulation.

Networking between firms

A more recent trend in industry which is well documented is towards co-operation rather than competition.[9] This co-operation can take many forms: for example, subcontracting, networking (both formal and informal) and joint ventures. Such co-operation can be (and is) used by large as well as small and medium-sized enterprises. For large companies it is a way to grow and diversify without risk. For smaller firms it allows them to stay small but at the same time to benefit from some of the advantages of large-scale production like specialisation.

Subcontracting

There has been an increase in the amount of subcontracting, where firms do not carry out the whole of the production process themselves but subcontract some of their activities to other firms. This represents a rejection of vertical integration and it is related to the notion of the flexible firm mentioned earlier. Subcontracting goes some way to explaining the phenomenal growth rate in 'business services' that occurred in the 1980s. It is increasingly common for businesses to subcontract specialist work in areas such as human resource management to outside consultancies. 'Partnering' between companies and consultancies is becoming more common where the consultancy is retained on a semi-permanent basis to give advice on a whole range of human resource matters from recruitment to planning for succession. This will obviously boost the small-firm sector. There has also been an increase in 'partnership sourcing' as large firms are developing long-term relationships between themselves and their suppliers. This phenomenon brings benefits to the large firms in the form of reducing stock levels and associated costs and facilitating just-in-time production methods. It also brings benefits to small firms, many of which are the suppliers, in the form of greater security.

Networking

Networking refers to the relationships that exist between organisations and the people within those organisations. These relationships can be of different types, both formal and informal, and there is increasing recognition of the importance of these relationships, especially to small firms (e.g. they may be based on the exchange of goods and services, like the relationship between a firm and its supplier or client). Subcontracting is an example of this kind of network but there are other links not based on exchange, like the relationship between a firm and the bank manager or other advisers. There are also informal links between the entrepreneur and family and friends, and between entrepreneurs in different organisations. There might also be co-operative links between firms. This can be seen in the market for executive recruitment where there has been a growth in the links between consultancies, particularly for international work. The creation of the Single European Market and the increased internationalisation of business left the smaller consultancies in a weak position relative to the large international recruitment firms like Korn Ferry International, which have branches in most European countries. The smaller consultancies have reacted by forming networks. There are basically two types of network:

1 Where firms are members of a network but where the network has a different name from the individual firms and the firms operate under their own name (i.e. the network has an identity of its own). The members are independent firms that co-operate in carrying out their business. There are 16 such groups in Europe including EMA Partners International and AMROP Heuer Group.
2 Where firms are part of a network of independent firms but where the network does not have a separate identity and the firms operate under their own names. There are ten such groups in Europe.

For information on companies mentioned see *www.kornferry.com*, *www.ema-partners.com* and *www.amrop.com*

The firm is seen as existing within a spider's web of relationships, as Figure 11.4 shows. It is possible for two firms to be linked in a variety of ways; in one market they may be competitors, in the next co-operators, customers in another and suppliers in another.

Networking has taken on greater significance because of changes that are taking place in the economy, which include the reversal of the trend towards higher industrial concentration, the adoption of Japanese methods of production, the decline of 'mass markets' and technological change that requires greater specialisation than previously. All of these changes favour the formation of networks.

The role of strategic alliances between firms has been recognised, especially in the small-firm sector where expansion through other means is often impossible and in the process of internationalisation.[10]

Figure 11.4 A typical network

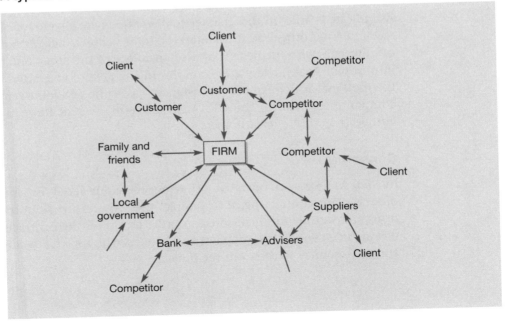

The virtual organisation

The **virtual organisation** is a network-based structure built on partnerships where a small core operating company outsources most of its processes. It is a network of small companies which specialise in various aspects of production. The organisation can be very big in trading terms but very small in the numbers of permanent staff. The process is typically mediated by information technology.

The main benefit of the virtual structure is that it helps organisations to deal with uncertainty. When virtual organisations are managed properly they can simultaneously increase efficiency, flexibility and responsiveness to changes in market conditions. The organisation is reaping the benefits of specialisation without having to develop those specialisms itself. Therefore overhead costs are minimised, as too are training costs and support costs. Information technology assumes many of the co-ordinating and managing roles that managers and committees carry out in large organisations. Information technology enables communication and the sharing of information across geographical boundaries. It is often the case, however, that the creation of a virtual organisation is driven solely by cost considerations rather than strategic considerations, in which case the benefits might not be realised. There will be a loss of control over outsourced activities and it may actually cost more to manage such activities. The organisation can become locked into contracts and specific relationships so that flexibility is reduced. There may be a lack of commitment of key resources (i.e. contractors) to the company and the loss of a contractor will be very serious.

There is some evidence that the incidence of virtual organisations is on the increase, facilitated by developments in information technology. It is a matter of 'wait and see' if this will become the dominant organisational structure in the future.

Joint ventures

As indicated earlier in this chapter, **joint ventures** are a good way for firms to diversify and enter other countries' markets. Joint ventures benefit both parties as each can diversify with the benefit of the experience of the other, and the level of risk is minimised. Again, there are examples in the area of executive recruitment. The International Search Group, for instance, was set up as a joint venture between five companies in France, the UK, Austria, Germany and Italy in order to offer a European service to its customers.

Consortia

In some industries co-operative behaviour has come about for particular reasons. In process plant contracting, for example, the projects are often too large for single firms and so they form consortia in order to bid for the contract. The consortium will include contractors, suppliers and bankers who together will have the expertise and the resources to carry out the project.

Multinationals

At the opposite end of the scale from the very small business are companies which have the capability to produce goods or services in more than one country but where control usually resides in a central location. **Multinationals** are often well-known household names, as the examples below illustrate:

- UK multinationals – BP, Glaxosmithkline.
- European multinationals – Nestlé, Volkswagen.
- USA multinationals – General Motors, IBM.

These multinationals are huge organisations and their market values often exceed the GNP of many of the countries in which they operate. They are estimated to account for a quarter of the world's output.

The growth in the multinationals is due to relaxation of exchange controls making it easier to move money between countries, and the improvements in communication which make it possible to run a worldwide business from one country. See Chapter 3 for a full discussion of the operation of multinational enterprises.

 web link

For information on the companies mentioned on this page see: *www.bp.com, www.gsk.com, www.nestle.com, www.vw.com, www.gm.com* and *www.ibm.com*

Synopsis

This chapter has looked at the size structure of industry in the United Kingdom and Europe as a whole. It examined the motives for and the methods of growth, as well as the sources of finance for such growth. The role of the small firm was considered, as too was the role of the multinational. Although many industries are dominated by huge companies, the trend seems to be moving away from growth towards a process of disintegration for a variety of reasons. As a result of this trend there has been an upsurge in the small-firm sector, and an increase in the level of co-operative behaviour between firms.

Summary of key points

- The size structure of firms varies greatly within industries, within a country and between countries.
- Firms can grow internally through organic growth or externally through merger and takeover.
- There are many motivations for growth, including increased market share, the reaping of economies of scale, the diversification of risk.

- Growth can be financed internally through reinvested profits or externally through banks, the capital market and the money market.

- There are limits to organisational growth, such as diseconomies of scale.

- The level of merger activity in the UK and in Europe follows a cyclical pattern and is related to economic conditions.

- The small-firm sector is an important source of output and employment, and this importance has increased over time.

- Many factors have influenced the growth of the small-firm sector, including the changing pattern of industries, changes in demand, technological change, the trend towards increased subcontracting and government policy.

- At the other end of the size spectrum, multinational corporations have a massive impact on world output and employment through their activities.

case study

Grocery retailing in the UK

The grocery retailing market in the UK is dominated by four major players. Table 11.9 shows the market shares of the major firms in 2007. As the table illustrates, out of the four, Tesco is the clear market leader.

Table 11.9 Market share for grocery retailing in the UK, 2007

Retailer	Market share %
Tesco	27
Asda	14.5
Sainsbury	14
Morrisons	10
Somerfield	4
Co-op Group	4
M & S	4
Waitrose	3.5
Iceland	2
Lidl	2
Aldi	1.8
Netto	1
Others	12.2

The grocery retailing market is one dominated by large firms; the market is an oligopoly (see Chapter 15) as four major players account for over 65 per cent of the market and their behaviour exhibits some of the characteristics of an oligopoly, as will be seen later on in this case study. Another group of retailers of interest in Table 11.9 comprises Iceland, Lidl, Aldi and Netto – these are the discounters. They offer a much reduced range of products (around 2000 instead of the 30,000 offered by the big supermarkets) at a discounted price. In the UK they hold a small part of the market but in other European countries they play a much more important role – in Germany, for example, the discounters account for 40 per cent of the market. The 'Others' category in Table 11.9 includes all the small local and corner shop grocery retailers.

Tesco has diversified into many different areas including electricals, clothing, finance, insurance and telecommunications. It has 2000 stores and is still growing at a high rate. It is estimated that in 2008, Tesco accounts for £1 in every £7 spent by the British public. Tesco is also the third biggest employer in the UK and has recently become the biggest non-food retailer in the UK. It is the fourth biggest retailer in the world behind Wal-Mart (which owns Asda), Carrefour and Home Depot. It has diversified internationally and now has more floor space outside the UK than in the UK. It has a presence in local markets through its Tesco Expresses and the One Stops.

Has Tesco become too big?

By 2008 the British public's love affair with Tesco appeared to be reaching an end, with claims from many different quarters that Tesco had become too big. The criticisms have become increasingly loud and vociferous:

- For many years, Tesco has been accused of predatory behaviour with respect to planning rules and regulations. It has been very active in lobbying local councillors and politicians and has been accused of forcing the small corner shops out of business.
- In the USA Barak Obama has criticised Tesco for its relationship with trade unions.
- In the UK Tesco has come under fire for not meeting RSPCA standards of care for the chickens sold in its stores.
- It has been accused of importing food from Zimbabwe and exploiting workers in India.

There is even an organisation of pressure groups with an interest in the activities of Tesco called the Tescopoly Alliance which serves as a rallying point for anti-Tesco feeling.

In addition to this negative publicity, the three Fs (rising food prices, rising fuel prices and the world financial crisis) has led to changes in consumer behaviour as households try to cut back on their spending. There is evidence that consumers are moving away from the big four supermarkets towards the discount stores like Aldi, Iceland and Lidl. The market share of Aldi rose to 2.9 per cent in 2008. The discounters work by offering only around 2000 products at much lower prices than the big four supermarkets. Tesco has responded by dramatically cutting the prices of 3000 basic foodstuffs. As the market is an oligopoly, economic theory suggests that the other large players will do the same and there is evidence that this is happening as both Sainsbury and Asda have reduced the price of basic food items. Commentators are predicting that this is the start of a full-scale price war – only time will tell.

Although its sheer size provides Tesco some immunity from these factors, the general view of Tesco is of a giant that does not listen to either its critics or its customers. All of this is not good news for Tesco. The situation is reminiscent of the early 1990s in the UK, when the then market leader – Sainsbury – appeared to become arrogant and not interested in listening to its customers. Its near demise left the market clear for Tesco to expand.

Case study questions

1 Why do small corner supermarkets manage to survive in the grocery retail market?

2 Has there been a price war between the big four supermarkets in the UK?

Review and discussion questions

1 What impact is the global financial crisis ('credit crunch') likely to have on merger and acquisition behaviour?

2 Can you see any dangers in the creation of super utilities (large, diversified organisations which supply a range of utilities – gas, electricity and water)?

3 What advantages does networking bring to small firms and the economy as a whole?

4 How has the balance between large and small firms in manufacturing changed in the last ten years? Do you expect these trends to continue?

Assignments

1 You are an information officer at your local business advice centre and you have been given the job of designing and writing a leaflet aimed at the proprietors of small firms, outlining the government aid that is available to small businesses. Your brief is to keep the leaflet short and readable but with maximum information. (Information on government aid will be available at your local library or business advice centre.)

2 As part of 'Business Week' you have been asked to give a short talk to local sixth-formers doing Business Studies A-level on the size structure of UK industry. Prepare your talk by choosing two industries, describing and giving reasons for the typical size structure of the firms in those industries.

Notes and references

1 *Penguin Dictionary of Economics.*

2 See OECD, *Dynamic Efficiencies in Merger Analysis*, May 2008.

3 *See* case study in Chapter 8 of the 2nd edition of this book.

4 Thomson merger news available at www.thomsonmergernews.com

5 *The Bolton Committee Report*, HMSO, 1971.

6 *Panorama of EU Industry*, 1994, European Commission.

7 See Figures 9.4 in the 5th edition of this book.

8 Atkinson, J., 'Flexibility, uncertainty and manpower management', Report no. 89, Institute of Manpower Studies, 1984.

9 Pyke, F., 'Co-operative practices among small and medium-sized establishments', *Work, Employment and Society*, 2 (3), September 1988.

10 See case study at the end of Chapter 13 of the 2nd edition of this book.

Further reading

Griffiths, A. and Wall, S., *Applied Economics*, 11th edition, Financial Times/Prentice Hall, 2005.

Stanworth, J. and Gray, C., *Bolton 20 Years On: The Small Firm in the 1990s*, Chapman, 1991.

web link

Web links and further questions are available on the website at:
www.pearsoned.co.uk/worthington

PART FIVE

Demand, Elasticity and Revenue

Chapter 13

Markets in Action

Markets in action

In this chapter we explore the working of markets in more detail. We start by examining one of the most important concepts in the whole of economics – that of elasticity (Sections 2.1–2.4).

A bumper harvest may seem like good news for farmers: after all, they will be able to sell more. But is it good news? Although they will sell more, the effect of the increased supply will be to drive down the price – and that's bad news for farmers! So will the increased sales (the good news) be enough to compensate for the reduction in price (the bad news)? Will farmers end up earning more or less from their bumper harvest? It all depends on just how much the price falls, and this depends on the *price elasticity of demand* for their produce. This is a measure of how *responsive* demand is to a change in price.

It is not just the responsiveness of *demand* that is important in determining the functioning of markets. It is also the responsiveness of *supply*. Why, do you think, do some firms respond to a rise in price by producing a lot more, whereas others only produce a little more? Is it simply because of different technologies? We will discover just what influences the price elasticity of supply in Section 2.3.

The chapter closes by looking at what happens if governments set about *controlling* prices. Why will shortages occur if the government sets the price too low, or surpluses if it sets it too high? When might governments feel that it is a good idea to fix prices?

After studying this chapter, you should be able to answer the following questions:

- How responsive is consumer demand to changes in prices and changes in incomes?
- How responsive is firms' output to a change in price?
- How does this responsiveness (or 'elasticity') of demand and supply affect the working of markets?
- Why are markets likely to be more responsive in the long run than in the short run to changes in demand or supply?
- How will people respond if they anticipate a change in price?
- What will happen if the government sets a price either above or below the market equilibrium?

2.1   PRICE ELASTICITY OF DEMAND

How responsive is demand to a change in price?

When the price of a good rises, the quantity demanded will fall. That much is fairly obvious. But in most cases we will want to know more than this. We will want to know just *how much* the quantity demanded will fall. In other words, we will want to know how *responsive* demand is to a rise in price.

Take the case of two products: oil and cauliflowers. In the case of oil, a rise in price is likely to result in only a slight fall in the quantity demanded. If people want to continue driving, they have to pay the higher prices for fuel. A few may turn to riding bicycles, and some people may try to make fewer journeys, but for most people, a rise in the price of petrol and diesel will make little difference to how much they use their cars.

In the case of cauliflowers, however, a rise in price may lead to a substantial fall in the quantity demanded. The reason is that there are alternative vegetables that people can buy. Many people, when buying vegetables, are very conscious of their prices and will buy whatever is reasonably priced.

We call the responsiveness of demand to a change in price the **price elasticity of demand**. If we know the price elasticity of demand for a product, we can predict the effect on price and quantity of a shift in the *supply* curve for that product. For example, we can predict the effect of the bumper harvest that we considered at the beginning of the chapter.

Figure 2.1 shows the effect of a shift in supply with two quite different demand curves (*D* and *D'*). Curve *D'* is more elastic than curve *D* over any given price range. In other words, for any given change in price, there will be a larger change in quantity demanded along curve *D'* than along curve *D*.

Assume that initially the supply curve is S_1, and that it intersects with both demand curves at point *a*, at a price of P_1 and a quantity of Q_1. Now supply shifts to S_2. What will happen to price and quantity? In the case of the less elastic demand curve *D*, there is a relatively large rise in price (to P_2) and a relatively small fall in quantity (to Q_2): equilibrium is at point *b*. In the case of the more elastic demand

Definition

Price elasticity of demand
The responsiveness of quantity demanded to a change in price.

KI 6
p27

TC 3
p11

Figure 2.1
Market supply and demand

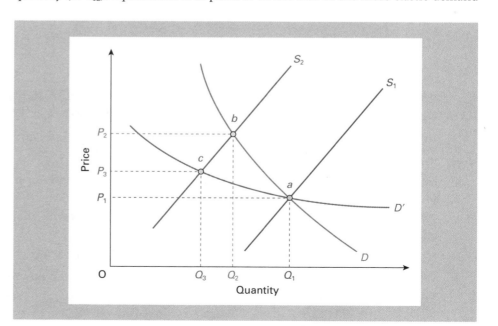

curve D', however, there is only a relatively small rise in price (to P_3) but a relatively large fall in quantity (to Q_3): equilibrium is at point c.

Measuring the price elasticity of demand

What we want to compare is the size of the change in quantity demanded with the size of the change in price. But since price and quantity are measured in different units, the only sensible way we can do this is to use percentage or proportionate changes. This gives us the following **formula for the price elasticity of demand** ($P\varepsilon_D$) for a product: percentage (or proportionate) change in quantity demanded divided by the percentage (or proportionate) change in price. Putting this in symbols gives:

$$P\varepsilon_D = \frac{\%\Delta Q_D}{\%\Delta P}$$

where ε (the Greek epsilon) is the symbol we use for elasticity, and Δ (the capital Greek delta) is the symbol we use for 'a change in'.

Thus if a 40 per cent rise in the price of oil caused the quantity demanded to fall by a mere 10 per cent, the price elasticity of oil over this range would be:

$$-10\%/40\% = -0.25$$

On the other hand, if a 5 per cent fall in the price of cauliflowers caused a 15 per cent rise in the quantity demanded, the price elasticity of demand for cauliflowers over this range would be:

$$15\%/-5\% = -3$$

Cauliflowers have a more elastic demand than oil, and this is shown by the figures. But just what do these two figures show? What is the significance of minus 0.25 and minus 3?

Interpreting the figure for elasticity

The use of proportionate or percentage measures

Elasticity is measured in proportionate or percentage terms for the following reasons:

- It allows comparison of changes in two qualitatively different things, and thus which are measured in two different types of unit: i.e. it allows comparison of *quantity* changes with *monetary* changes.
- It is the only sensible way of deciding *how big* a change in price or quantity is. Take a simple example. An item goes up in price by £1. Is this a big increase or a small increase? We can answer this only if we know what the original price was. If a can of beans goes up in price by £1, that is a huge price increase. If, however, the price of a house goes up by £1, that is a tiny price increase. In other words, it is the percentage or proportionate increase in price that we look at in deciding how big a price rise it is.

The sign (positive or negative)

Demand curves are generally downward sloping. This means that price and quantity change in opposite directions. A *rise* in price (a positive figure) will cause a *fall* in the quantity demanded (a negative figure). Similarly a *fall* in price will cause a *rise* in the quantity demanded. Thus when working out price elasticity of demand

Pause for thought

Why will the price elasticity of demand for a particular brand of a product (e.g. Texaco) be greater than that for the product in general (e.g. petrol)? Is this difference the result of a difference in the size of the income effect or the substitution effect?

we either divide a negative figure by a positive figure, or a positive figure by a negative. Either way, we end up with a negative figure.

The value (greater or less than 1)

If we now ignore the negative sign and just concentrate on the value of the figure, this tells us whether demand is elastic or inelastic.

- Elastic demand ($\varepsilon > 1$). This is where a change in price causes a proportionately larger change in the quantity demanded. In this case the value of elasticity will be greater than 1, since we are dividing a larger figure by a smaller figure.
- Inelastic demand ($\varepsilon < 1$). This is where a change in price causes a proportionately smaller change in the quantity demanded. In this case elasticity will be less than 1, since we are dividing a smaller figure by a larger figure.
- Unit elastic demand ($\varepsilon = 1$). This is where price and quantity demanded change by the same proportion. This will give an elasticity equal to 1, since we are dividing a figure by itself.

Determinants of price elasticity of demand

The price elasticity of demand varies enormously from one product to another. Table 2.1 gives some examples. But why do some products have a highly elastic demand, whereas others have a highly *in*elastic demand? What determines price elasticity of demand?

The number and closeness of substitute goods. This is the most important determinant. The more substitutes there are for a good, and the closer they are, the more will people switch to these alternatives when the price of the good rises: the greater, therefore, will be the price elasticity of demand.

Returning to our examples of oil and cauliflowers, there is no close substitute for oil and thus demand is relatively inelastic. There are plenty of alternatives to cauliflowers, however, and thus demand is relatively elastic.

The proportion of income spent on the good. The higher the proportion of our income we spend on a good, the more we will be forced to cut consumption when its price rises: the bigger will be the income effect and the more elastic will be the demand.

Thus salt has a very low price elasticity of demand. We spend such a tiny fraction of our income on salt, that we would find little difficulty in paying a relatively large percentage increase in its price: the income effect of a price rise would be very small. By contrast, there will be a much bigger income effect when a major item of expenditure rises in price. For example, if mortgage interest rates rise (the 'price' of loans for house purchase), people may have to cut down substantially on their demand for housing, being forced to buy somewhere smaller and cheaper, or to live in rented accommodation.

The time period. When price rises, people may take time to adjust their consumption patterns and find alternatives. The longer the time period after a price change, then the more elastic is the demand likely to be.

To illustrate this, let us return to our example of oil. Between December 1973 and June 1974 the price of crude oil quadrupled, which led to similar increases in the prices of petrol and other oil products (such as central heating oil). Over the next few months, there was only a very small fall in the consumption of oil

Table 2.1	Estimates of price elasticity of demand for the USA
Product	**Price elasticity of demand**
Food	−0.21
Medical services	−0.22
Housing	
Rental	−0.18
Owner occupied	−1.20
Electricity	−1.14
Cars	−1.20
Beer	−0.26
Wine	−0.88
Cigarettes	−0.35
Transatlantic air travel	−1.30
Imports	−0.58

Source: W. Nicholson, *Intermediate Microeconomics*, 9th edition (South-Western, 2004)

products. Demand was highly inelastic. The reason was that people still wanted to drive their cars and heat their houses.

Over time, however, as the higher oil prices persisted, new fuel-efficient cars were developed and many people switched to smaller cars or moved closer to their work. Similarly, people switched to gas or solid fuel central heating, and spent more money insulating their houses to save on fuel bills. Demand was thus much more elastic in the long run.

Recap

1. Price elasticity of demand is a measure of the responsiveness of demand to a change in price.
2. It is defined as the proportionate (or percentage) change in quantity demanded divided by the proportionate (or percentage) change in price. Given that demand curves are downward sloping, price elasticity of demand will have a negative value.
3. If quantity changes proportionately more than price, the figure for elasticity will be greater than 1 (ignoring the sign): demand is elastic. If the quantity changes proportionately less than price, the figure for elasticity will be less than 1 (again, ignoring the sign): demand is inelastic. If quantity and price change by the same proportion, the elasticity has a value of (minus) 1: demand is unit elastic.
4. Demand will be more elastic the greater the number and closeness of substitute goods, the higher the proportion of income spent on the good, and the longer the time period that elapses after the change in price.

PRICE ELASTICITY OF DEMAND AND CONSUMER EXPENDITURE   2.2

How much do we spend on a good at a given price?

One of the most important applications of price elasticity of demand concerns its relationship with the total amount of money that consumers spend on a product. **Total consumer expenditure (TE)** is simply price times quantity purchased.

$$TE = P \times Q$$

For example, if consumers buy 3 million units (Q) at a price of £2 per unit (P), they will spend a total of £6 million (TE). Note that total consumer expenditure will be the same as the **total revenue** (TR) received by firms from the sale of the product (before any taxes or other deductions).

What will happen to consumer expenditure (and hence firms' revenue) if there is a change in price? The answer depends on the price elasticity of demand.

Elastic demand

As price rises so quantity demanded falls, and vice versa. When demand is elastic, quantity demanded changes proportionately more than price. Thus the change in quantity has a bigger effect on total consumer expenditure than does the change in price. For example, when the price rises, there will be such a large fall in consumer demand that less will be spent than before. This can be summarised as follows:

- P rises; Q falls proportionately more; therefore TE falls.
- P falls; Q rises proportionately more; therefore TE rises.

In other words, total expenditure changes in the same direction as *quantity*.

This is illustrated in Figure 2.2(a). The areas of the rectangles in the diagram represent total expenditure. But why? The area of a rectangle is its height multiplied by its length. In this case, this is price multiplied by quantity purchased, which, as we have seen, gives total expenditure.

Demand is elastic between points *a* and *b*. A rise in price from £4 to £5 causes a proportionately larger fall in quantity demanded: from 20 million to 10 million. Total expenditure *falls* from £80 million (the blue area) to £50 million (the striped area).

When demand is elastic, then a rise in price will cause a fall in total consumer expenditure and thus a fall in the total revenue that firms selling the product receive. A reduction in price, however, will result in consumers spending more, and hence firms earning more.

Inelastic demand

When demand is inelastic, it is the other way around. Price changes proportionately more than quantity. Thus the change in price has a bigger effect on total consumer expenditure than does the change in quantity. To summarise the effects:

Definitions

Total consumer expenditure on a product (*TE*) (per period of time)
The price of the product multiplied by the quantity purchased:
$TE = P \times Q$

Total revenue (*TR*) (per period)
The total amount received by firms from the sale of a product, before the deduction of taxes or any other costs. The price multiplied by the quantity sold.
$TR = P \times Q$.

Pause for thought

If a firm faces an elastic demand curve, why will it not necessarily be in the firm's interests to produce more? (Clue: you will need to distinguish between revenue and profit. We will explore this relationship in the next chapter.)

Figure 2.2
Price elasticity of demand and total expenditure

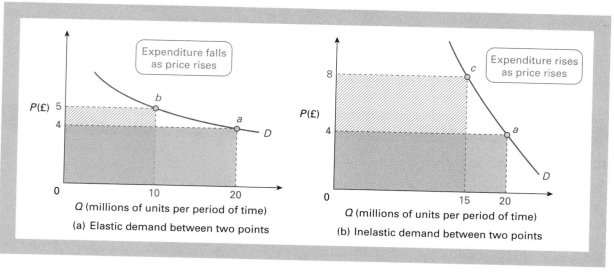

(a) Elastic demand between two points

(b) Inelastic demand between two points

■ *P* rises; *Q* falls proportionately less; therefore *TE* rises.
■ *P* falls; *Q* rises proportionately less; therefore *TE* falls.

In other words, total consumer expenditure changes in the same direction as *price*.

This is illustrated in Figure 2.2(b). Demand is inelastic between points *a* and *c*. A rise in price from £4 to £8 causes a proportionately smaller fall in quantity demanded: from 20 million to 15 million. Total expenditure *rises* from £80 million (the blue shaded area) to £120 million (the striped area).

In this case, firms' revenue will increase if there is a rise in price, and fall if there is a fall in price.

Box 2.1   **Exploring Economics**

Competition, price and revenue

Shall we put up our price?

When you buy a can of drink on a train, or an ice-cream in the cinema, or a bottle of wine in a restaurant, you may well be horrified by its price. How can they get away with it?

The answer is that these firms are *not* price takers. They can choose what price to charge. We will be examining the behaviour of such firms in Chapter 4, but here it is useful to see how price elasticity of demand can help to explain their behaviour.

Take the case of the can of drink on the train. If you are thirsty, and if you haven't brought a drink with you, then you will have to get one from the train's bar, or go without. There is no substitute. What we are saying here is that the demand for drink on the train is inelastic at the normal shop price. This means that the train operator can put up the price of its drinks, and food too, and earn *more* revenue.

Generally, the less the competition a firm faces, the lower will be the elasticity of demand for its products, since there will be fewer substitutes (competitors) to which consumers can turn. The lower the price elasticity of demand, the higher is likely to be the price that the firm charges.

When there is plenty of competition, it is quite a different story. Petrol stations in the same area may compete fiercely in terms of price. One station may hope that by reducing its price by 1p, or even 0.1p, per litre below that of its competitors, it can attract customers away from them. With a highly elastic demand, a small reduction in price may lead to a substantial increase in their revenue. The problem is, of course, that when they *all* reduce prices, no firm wins. No one attracts customers away from the others! In this case it is the customer who wins.

?
1. *Why may a restaurant charge very high prices for wine and bottled water and yet quite reasonable prices for food?*
2. *Why are clothes with designer labels so much more expensive than 'own brand' clothes from a chain store, even though they may cost a similar amount to produce?*

Special cases

Figure 2.3 shows three special cases: (a) a totally inelastic demand ($P\varepsilon_D = 0$); (b) an infinitely elastic demand ($P\varepsilon_D = -\infty$); and (c) a unit elastic demand ($P\varepsilon_D = -1$).

Totally inelastic demand. This is shown by a vertical straight line. No matter what happens to price, quantity demanded remains the same. It is obvious that the more the price rises, the bigger will be the level of consumer expenditure. Thus in Figure 2.3(a) consumer expenditure will be higher at P_2 than at P_1.

Infinitely elastic demand. This is shown by a horizontal straight line. At any price above P_1 in Figure 2.3(b) demand is zero. But at P_1 (or any price below) demand is 'infinitely' large.

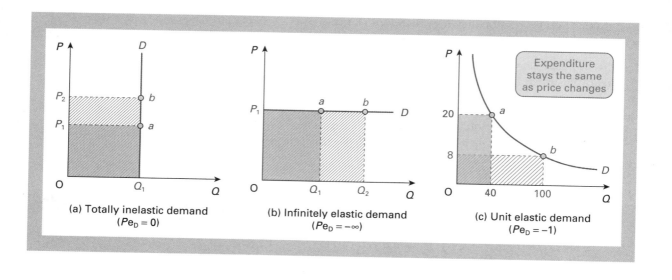

Figure 2.3
Price elasticity of demand: special cases

(a) Totally inelastic demand ($Pe_D = 0$)

(b) Infinitely elastic demand ($Pe_D = -\infty$)

(c) Unit elastic demand ($Pe_D = -1$)

This seemingly unlikely demand curve is in fact relatively common for an *individual producer*. In a perfect market, as we have seen, firms are small relative to the whole market (like the small-scale grain farmer). They have to accept the price as given by supply and demand in the *whole market*, but at that price they can sell as much as they produce. (Demand is not *literally* infinite, but as far as the firm is concerned it is.) In this case, the more the individual farmer produces, the more revenue will be earned. In Figure 2.3(b), more revenue is earned at Q_2 than at Q_1.

Unit elastic demand. This is where price and quantity change in exactly the same proportion. Any rise in price will be exactly offset by a fall in quantity, leaving total revenue unchanged. In Figure 2.3(c) the striped area is exactly equal to the blue shaded area: in both cases total expenditure is £800.

You might have thought that a demand curve with unit elasticity would be a straight line at 45° to the axes. Instead it is a curve. The reason for its particular shape is that the proportionate *rise* in quantity must equal the proportionate *fall* in price (and vice versa). As we move down the demand curve, in order for the *proportionate* change in both price and quantity to remain constant there must be a bigger and bigger *absolute* rise in quantity and a smaller and smaller absolute fall in price. For example, a rise in quantity from 200 to 400 is the same proportionate change as a rise from 100 to 200, but its absolute size is double. A fall in price from £5 to £2.50 is the same percentage as a fall from £10 to £5, but its absolute size is only half.

> **Pause for thought**
>
> Two customers go to the fish counter at a supermarket to buy some cod. Neither looks at the price. Customer A orders 1 kilo of cod. Customer B orders £3 worth of cod. What is the price elasticity of demand of each of the two customers?

Recap

1. The total expenditure on a product is found by multiplying the quantity sold by the price of the product.

2. When demand is price elastic, a rise in price will lead to a reduction in total expenditure on the good and hence a reduction in the total revenue of producers.

3. When demand is price inelastic, a rise in price will lead to an increase in total expenditure on the good and hence an increase in the total revenue of producers.

Box 2.2   **Exploring Economics**

The measurement of elasticity

We have defined price elasticity as the percentage or proportionate change in quantity demanded divided by the percentage or proportionate change in price. But how, in practice, do we measure these changes for a specific demand curve?

A common mistake that students make is to think that you can talk about the elasticity of a whole *curve*. The mistake here is that in most cases the elasticity will vary along the length of the curve.

Take the case of the demand curve illustrated in Figure (a). Between points *a* and *b*, total expenditure rises ($P_2Q_2 > P_1Q_1$): demand is thus elastic between these two points. Between points *b* and *c*, however, total expenditure falls ($P_3Q_3 < P_2Q_2$). Demand here is inelastic.

Normally, then, we can refer to the elasticity only of a *portion* of the demand curve, not of the *whole* curve.

There is, however, an exception to this rule. This is when the elasticity just so happens to be the same all the way along a curve, as in the three special cases illustrated in Figure 2.3.

Although we cannot normally talk about the elasticity of a whole curve, we can nevertheless talk about the elasticity between any two points on it. Remember the formula we used was:

$$\frac{\text{\% or proportionate } \Delta Q}{\text{\% or proportionate } \Delta P} \quad \text{(where } \Delta \text{ means 'change in')}$$

The way we measure a *proportionate* change in quantity is to divide that change by the level of Q: i.e. $\Delta Q/Q$. Similarly, we measure a proportionate change in price by dividing that change by the level of P: i.e. $\Delta P/Q$. Price elasticity of demand can thus now be rewritten as:

$$\frac{\Delta Q}{Q} \div \frac{\Delta P}{P}$$

But just what value do we give to P and Q? Consider the demand curve in figure (b). What is the elasticity of demand between points *m* and *n*? Price has fallen by £2 (from £8 to £6), but what is the proportionate change? Is it –2/8 or –2/6? The convention is to express the change as a proportion of the average of the two prices, £8 and £6: in other words to take the mid-point price, £7. Thus the proportionate change is –2/7.

Similarly the proportionate change in quantity between points *m* and *n* is 10/15, since 15 is mid-way between 10 and 20.

Thus using the **average (or 'mid-point') formula**, elasticity between *m* and *n* is given by:

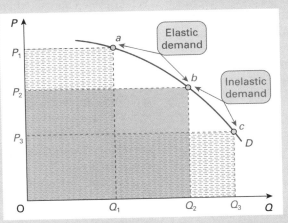

(a) Different elasticities along different portions of a demand curve

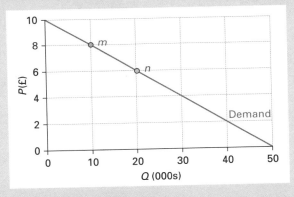

(b) Measuring elasticity

$$\frac{\Delta Q}{\text{average } Q} \div \frac{\Delta P}{\text{average } P} = \frac{10}{15} \div \frac{-2}{7} = -2.33$$

Since 2.33 is greater than 1, demand is elastic between *m* and *n*.

? *Referring again to Figure (b), what is the price elasticity of demand between a price of (a) £6 and £4; (b) £4 and £2? What do you conclude about the elasticity of a straight-line demand curve as you move down it?*

In this box we have looked at the measurement of elasticity over a segment of the demand curve. This gives what is known as 'arc elasticity'. An alternative is to measure elasticity at a single point on the demand curve. This gives, not surprisingly, what is known as 'point elasticity'. This method is examined in Web Appendix 2.1.

2.3 PRICE ELASTICITY OF SUPPLY

How responsive is supply to a change in price?

When price changes, there will be not only a change in the quantity demanded, but also a change in the quantity *supplied*. Frequently we will want to know just how responsive quantity supplied is to a change in price. The measure we use is the **price elasticity of supply**.

Figure 2.4 shows two supply curves. Curve S_2 is more elastic between any two prices than curve S_1. Thus, when price rises from P_1 to P_2 there is a larger increase in quantity supplied with S_2 (namely, Q_1 to Q_3) than there is with S_1 (namely, Q_1 to Q_2). For any shift in the demand curve there will be a larger change in quantity supplied and a smaller change in price with curve S_2 than with curve S_1. Thus the effect on price and quantity of a shift in the demand curve will depend on the price elasticity of supply.

The formula for the price elasticity of supply ($P\varepsilon_S$) is: the percentage (or proportionate) change in quantity supplied divided by the percentage (or proportionate) change in price. Putting this in symbols gives:

$$P\varepsilon_S = \frac{\%\Delta Q_S}{\%\Delta P}$$

In other words, the formula is identical to that for the price elasticity of demand, except that quantity in this case is quantity *supplied*. Thus if a 10 per cent rise in price caused a 25 per cent rise in the quantity supplied, the price elasticity of supply would be:

$$25\%/10\% = 2.5$$

and if a 10 per cent rise in price caused only a 5 per cent rise in the quantity, the price elasticity of supply would be:

Figure 2.4
Supply curves with different price elasticity of supply

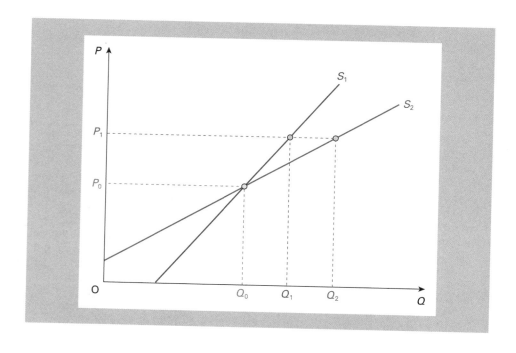

$$5\%/10\% = 0.5$$

In the first case, supply is elastic ($P\varepsilon_s > 1$); in the second it is inelastic ($P\varepsilon_s < 1$). Notice that, unlike the price elasticity of demand, the figure is positive (assuming that the supply curve is upward sloping). This is because price and quantity supplied change in the *same* direction.

Box 2.3   **Case Studies and Applications**

Advertising and its effect on the demand curve

How to increase sales and price

When we are told that brand X will make us more beautiful, enrich our lives, wash our clothes whiter, give us get-up-and-go, give us a new taste sensation or make us the envy of our friends, just what are the advertisers up to? 'Trying to sell the product', you may reply. In fact there is a bit more to it than this. Advertisers are trying to do two things:

- Shift the product's demand curve to the right.
- Make it less price elastic.

This is illustrated in the diagram.

D_1 shows the original demand curve with price at P_1 and sales at Q_1. D_2 shows the curve after an advertising campaign. The rightward shift allows an increased quantity (Q_2) to be sold at the original price. If the demand is also made highly inelastic, the firm can also raise its price and still have a substantial increase in sales. Thus in the diagram, price can be raised to P_2 and sales will be Q_3 – still substantially above Q_1. The total gain in revenue is shown by the shaded area.

How can advertising bring about this new demand curve?

Shifting the demand curve to the right

This will occur if the advertising brings the product to more people's attention and if it increases people's desire for the product.

Making the demand curve less elastic

This will occur if the advertising creates greater brand loyalty. People must be led to believe (rightly or wrongly) that competitors' brands are inferior. This will allow the firm to raise its price above that of its rivals with no significant fall in sales. There will only be a small substitution effect because consumers have been led to believe that there are no close substitutes.

? 1. Think of some advertisements that deliberately seek to make demand less elastic.
2. Imagine that 'Sunshine' sunflower margarine, a well-known brand, is advertised with the slogan, 'It helps you live longer'. What do you think would happen to the demand curve for a supermarket's own brand of sunflower margarine? Consider both the direction of shift and the effect on elasticity. Will the elasticity differ markedly at different prices? How will this affect the pricing policy and sales of the supermarket's own brand?

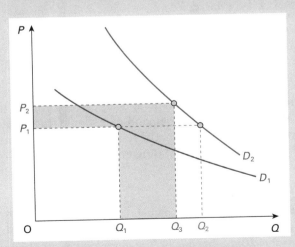

Effect of advertising on the demand curve

The determinants of price elasticity of supply

The amount that costs rise as output rises.   The less the additional costs of producing additional output, the more will firms be encouraged to produce for a given price rise: the more elastic will supply be.

Supply is thus likely to be elastic if firms have plenty of spare capacity, if they can readily get extra supplies of raw materials, if they can easily switch away from producing alternative products, and if they can avoid having to introduce overtime working (at higher rates of pay). If all these conditions hold, costs will be little affected by a rise in output and supply will be relatively elastic. The less these conditions apply, the less elastic will supply be.

Time period

- Immediate time period. Firms are unlikely to be able to increase supply by much immediately. Supply is virtually fixed, or can vary only according to available stocks. Supply is highly inelastic.
- Short run. If a slightly longer time period is allowed to elapse, some inputs can be increased (e.g. raw materials) while others will remain fixed (e.g. heavy machinery). Supply can increase somewhat.
- Long run. In the long run, there will be sufficient time for all inputs to be increased and for new firms to enter the industry. Supply, therefore, is likely to be highly elastic. In some circumstances the long-run supply curve may even slope downwards (see Section 3.2).

Recap

1. Price elasticity of supply measures the responsiveness of supply to a change in price. It has a positive value.

2. Supply will be more elastic the less costs per unit rise as output rises and the longer the time period.

2.4   OTHER ELASTICITIES

How does demand respond to changes in income and to changes in the price of other goods?

Income elasticity of demand

So far we have looked at the responsiveness of demand and supply to a change in price. But price is just one of the determinants of demand and supply. In theory, we could look at the responsiveness of demand or supply to a change in *any* one of their determinants. We could have a whole range of different types of elasticity of demand and supply.

> **Elasticity.** The responsiveness of one variable (e.g. demand) to a change in another (e.g. price). This concept is fundamental to understanding how markets work and is thus one of our **Threshold Concepts** (no. 8). The more elastic variables are, the more responsive is the market to changing circumstances.
>
>
> Key Idea 11
> TC 8

In practice there are just two other elasticities that are particularly useful to us, and both are demand elasticities.

The first is the **income elasticity of demand** ($Y\varepsilon_D$). This measures the responsiveness of demand to a change in consumer incomes (Y).[1] It enables us to predict how much the demand curve will shift for a given change in income. The **formula for income elasticity of demand** is: the percentage (or proportionate) change in demand divided by the percentage (or proportionate) change in income. Putting this in symbols gives:

$$Y\varepsilon_D = \frac{\%\Delta Q_D}{\%\Delta Y}$$

In other words, the formula is identical to that for the price elasticity of demand, except that we are dividing the change in demand by the change in *income* that caused it rather than by a change in price. Thus if a 2 per cent rise in income caused an 8 per cent rise in a product's demand, then its income elasticity of demand would be:

$$8\%/2\% = 4$$

The major determinant of income elasticity of demand is the degree of 'necessity' of the good. In a developed country, the demand for luxury goods expands rapidly as people's incomes rise, whereas the demand for basic goods, such as bread, rises only a little. Thus items such as cars and holidays abroad have a high income elasticity of demand, whereas items such as potatoes and bus journeys have a low income elasticity of demand (see Table 2.2).

The demand for some goods actually decreases as income rises. These are *inferior goods* such as cheap margarine. As people earn more, so they switch to butter or better-quality margarine. Unlike **normal goods**, which have a positive income elasticity of demand, **inferior goods** have a negative income elasticity of demand.

> **Pause for thought**
>
> *Assume that you decide to spend a quarter of your income on clothes. What is (a) your income elasticity of demand; (b) your price elasticity of demand?*

> **Definitions**
>
> **Income elasticity of demand ($Y\varepsilon_D$)**
> The responsiveness of demand to a change in consumer incomes.
>
> **Formula for income elasticity of demand**
> The percentage (or proportionate) change in demand divided by the percentage (or proportionate) change in income: $\%\Delta Q_D \div \%\Delta Y$
>
> **Normal goods**
> Goods whose demand increases as consumer incomes increase. They have a positive income elasticity of demand. Luxury goods will have a higher income elasticity of demand than more basic goods.
>
> **Inferior goods**
> Goods whose demand *decreases* as consumer incomes increase. Such goods have a negative income elasticity of demand.

Table 2.2	Estimates of income elasticity of demand for the USA
Product	**Income elasticity of demand**
Food	+0.28
Medical services	+0.22
Housing	
Rental	+1.00
Owner occupied	+1.20
Electricity	+0.61
Cars	+3.00
Beer	+0.38
Wine	+0.97
Cigarettes	−0.50
Transatlantic air travel	+1.40
Imports	+2.73

Source: W. Nicholson, *Intermediate Microeconomics*, 9th edition (South-Western, 2004)

---

[1] Note that we use the letter Y rather than the letter I to stand for 'income'. This is normal practice in economics. The reason is that the letter I is used for 'investment'.

Income elasticity of demand is an important concept to firms considering the future size of the market for their product. If the product has a high income elasticity of demand, sales are likely to expand rapidly as national income rises, but may also fall significantly if the economy moves into recession. (See Case 2.5, *Income elasticity of demand and the balance of payments*, on MyEconLab. This shows how the concept of income elasticity of demand can help us understand why so many developing countries suffer from chronic balance of trade problems.)

TC8 p64

Cross-price elasticity of demand

This is often known by its less cumbersome title of **cross elasticity of demand**. It is a measure of the responsiveness of demand for one product to a change in the price of another (either a substitute or a complement). It enables us to predict how much the demand curve for the first product will shift when the price of the second product changes. For example, knowledge of the cross elasticity of demand for Coca-Cola to the price of Pepsi would allow Coca-Cola to predict the effect on its own sales if the price of Pepsi were to change.

The **formula for the cross-price elasticity of demand ($C\varepsilon_{D_{ab}}$)** is: the percentage (or proportionate) change in demand for good a divided by the percentage (or proportionate) change in price of good b. Putting this in symbols gives:

$$C\varepsilon_{Dab} = \frac{\%\Delta Q_{D_a}}{\%\Delta P_b}$$

If good b is a *substitute* for good a, a's demand will *rise* as b's price rises. In this case, cross elasticity will be a positive figure. For example, if the demand for butter rose by 2 per cent when the price of margarine (a substitute) rose by 8 per cent, then the cross elasticity of demand for butter with respect to margarine would be:

2%/8% = 0.25

If good b is *complementary* to good a, however, a's demand will *fall* as b's price rises and thus as the quantity of b demanded falls. In this case, cross elasticity of demand will be a negative figure. For example, if a 4 per cent rise in the price of bread led to a 3 per cent fall in demand for butter, the cross elasticity of demand for butter with respect to bread would be:

−3%/4% = −0.75

The major determinant of cross elasticity of demand is the closeness of the substitute or complement. The closer it is, the bigger will be the effect on the first good of a change in the price of the substitute or complement, and hence the greater the cross elasticity – either positive or negative.

Firms will wish to know the cross elasticity of demand for their product when considering the effect on the demand for their product of a change in the price of a rival's product or of a complementary product. These are vital pieces of information for firms when making their production plans.

Another example of the usefulness of the concept of cross elasticity of demand is in the field of international trade and the balance of payments. A government will wish to know how a change in domestic prices will affect the demand for imports. If there is a high cross elasticity of demand for imports (because they are close substitutes for home-produced goods), and if prices at home rise due to inflation, the demand for imports will rise substantially, thus worsening the balance of trade.

TC8 p64

Recap

1. Income elasticity of demand measures the responsiveness of demand to a change in income. For normal goods it has a positive value; for inferior goods it has a negative value.
2. Demand will be more income elastic the more luxurious the good and the less rapidly demand is satisfied as consumption increases.
3. Cross-price elasticity of demand measures the responsiveness of demand for one good to a change in the price of another. For substitute goods the value will be positive; for complements it will be negative.
4. The cross-price elasticity will be more elastic the closer the two goods are as substitutes or complements.

MARKETS AND ADJUSTMENT OVER TIME 2.5

How do markets respond over the longer term to a change in demand or supply?

The full adjustment of price, demand and supply to a situation of disequilibrium will not be instantaneous. It is necessary, therefore, to analyse the time path which supply takes in responding to changes in demand, and which demand takes in responding to changes in supply.

Short-run and long-run adjustment

As we have already seen, the price elasticities of demand and supply vary with the time period under consideration. The reason is that producers and consumers take time to respond to a change in price. The longer the time period, the bigger the response, and thus the greater the elasticity of demand and supply.

This is illustrated in Figures 2.5 and 2.6. In both cases, as equilibrium moves from points a to b to c, there is a large short-run price change (P_1 to P_2) and a small short-run quantity change (Q_1 to Q_2), but a small long-run price change (P_1 to P_3) and a large long-run quantity change (Q_1 to Q_3).

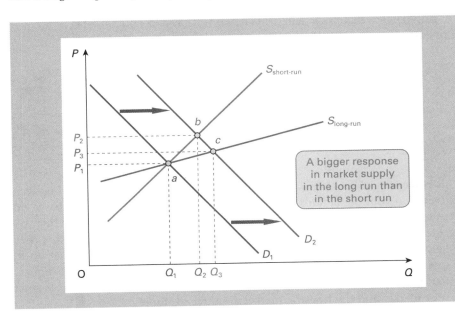

Figure 2.5
Response of supply to an increase in demand

Figure 2.6
Response of demand
to an increase in
supply

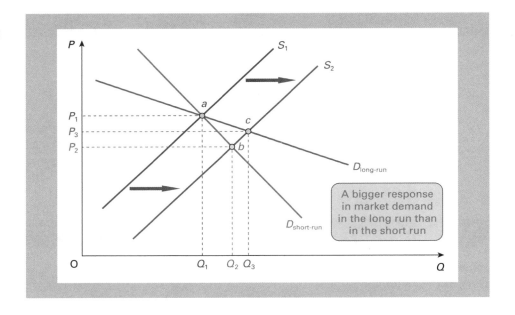

Price expectations and speculation

In a world of shifting demand and supply curves, prices do not stay the same.
Sometimes they go up; sometimes they come down. If prices are likely to change in
the foreseeable future, this will affect the behaviour of buyers and sellers *now*. If, for
example, it is now December and you are thinking of buying a new winter coat, you
might decide to wait until the January sales, and in the meantime make do with your
old coat. If, on the other hand, when January comes you see a new summer jacket
in the sales, you might well buy it now and not wait until the summer for fear that
the price will have gone up by then. Thus a belief that prices will go up will cause
people to buy now; a belief that prices will come down will cause them to wait.

The reverse applies to sellers. If you are thinking of selling your house and prices
are falling, you will want to sell it as quickly as possible. If, on the other hand,
prices are rising sharply, you will wait as long as possible so as to get the highest
price. Thus a belief that prices will come down will cause people to sell now; a belief
that prices will go up will cause them to wait.

People's actions are influenced by their expectations. People respond not
just to what is happening now (such as a change in price), but to what they
anticipate will happen in the future. Understanding the crucial role that expectations play in determining economic behaviour makes this a **Threshold Concept**
– the ninth of our fifteen.

This behaviour of looking into the future and making buying and selling decisions based on your predictions is called **speculation**. Speculation is often based on
current trends in price behaviour. If prices are currently rising, people may then try
to decide whether they are about to peak and go back down again, or whether they
are likely to go on rising. Having made their prediction, they will then act on it.
This speculation will thus affect demand and supply, which in turn will affect price.
Speculation is commonplace in many markets: the stock exchange, the foreign
exchange market and the housing market are three examples.

Speculation tends to be **self-fulfilling**. In other words, the actions of speculators tend to bring about the very effect on prices that speculators had anticipated. For example, if speculators believe that the price of British Airways shares is about to rise, they will buy more BA shares. But by doing this they will ensure that the price will rise. The prophecy has become self-fulfilling.

Speculation can either help to reduce price fluctuations or aggravate them: it can be stabilising or destabilising.

Stabilising speculation

Speculation will tend to have a **stabilising** effect on price fluctuations when suppliers and/or demanders believe that a change in price is only *temporary*.

Assume, for example, that there has recently been a rise in price, caused, say, by an increase in demand. In Figure 2.7(a) demand has shifted from D_1 to D_2. Equilibrium has moved from point a to point b, and price has risen from P_1 to P_2. How do people react to this rise in price?

Given that they believe this rise in price to be only temporary, suppliers bring their goods to market now, before price falls again. Supply shifts from S_1 to S_2. Demanders, however, hold back until price does fall. Demand shifts from D_2 to D_3. The equilibrium moves to point c, with price falling back towards P_1.

A good example of stabilising speculation occurs in agricultural commodity markets. Take the case of wheat. When it is harvested in the autumn there will be a plentiful supply. If all this wheat were to be put on the market, the price would fall to a very low level. Later in the year, when most of the wheat would have been sold, the price would then rise to a very high level. This is all easily predictable.

So what do farmers do? The answer is that they speculate. When the wheat is harvested they know the price will tend to fall, and so instead of bringing it all to market they put a lot of it into store. The more the price falls, the more they will put into store *anticipating that the price will later rise*. But this holding back of supplies prevents prices from falling. In other words, it stabilises prices.

Later in the year, when the price begins to rise, they will gradually release grain on to the market from the stores. The more the price rises, the more they will release on to the market *anticipating that the price will fall again by the time of the next harvest*. But this releasing of supplies will again stabilise prices by preventing them rising so much.

Figure 2.7
Speculation (initial rise in price)

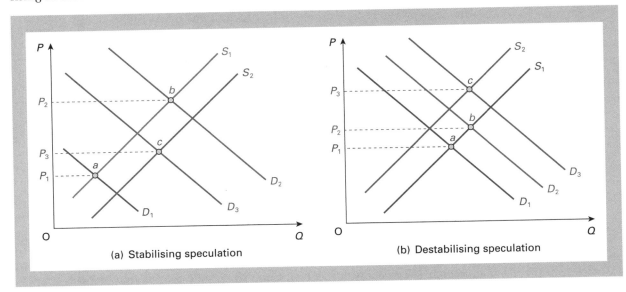

(a) Stabilising speculation

(b) Destabilising speculation

Rather than the farmers doing the speculation, it could be done by grain merchants. When there is a glut of wheat in the autumn, and prices are relatively low, they buy wheat on the grain market and put it into store. When there is a shortage in the spring and summer they sell wheat from their stores. In this way they stabilise prices just as the farmers did when they were the ones that operated the stores.

Destabilising speculation

Speculation will tend to have a **destabilising** effect on price fluctuations when suppliers and/or buyers believe that a change in price heralds similar changes to come.

Assume again that there has recently been a rise in price, caused by an increase in demand. In Figure 2.7(b), demand has shifted from D_1 to D_2 and price has risen from P_1 to P_2. This time, believing that the rise in price heralds further rises to come, suppliers wait until the price rises further. Supply shifts from S_1 to S_2. Demanders buy now before any further rise in price. Demand shifts from D_2 to D_3. As a result, the price continues to rise: to P_3.

Box 1.3 examined the housing market. In this market, speculation is frequently destabilising. Assume that people see house prices beginning to move upwards. This might be the result of increased demand brought about by a cut in mortgage interest rates or by growth in the economy. People may well believe that the rise in house prices signals a boom in the housing market: that prices will go on rising. Potential buyers will thus try to buy as soon as possible before prices rise any further. This increased demand (as in Figure 2.7(b)) will thus lead to even bigger price rises. This is precisely what happened in the UK housing market in 1999–2003.

Conclusion

In some circumstances, then, the action of speculators can help keep price fluctuations to a minimum (stabilising speculation). This is most likely when markets are relatively stable in the first place, with only moderate underlying shifts in demand and supply.

In other circumstances, however, speculation can make price fluctuations much worse. This is most likely in times of uncertainty, when there are significant changes in the determinants of demand and supply. Given this uncertainty, people may see price changes as signifying some trend. They then 'jump on the bandwagon' and do what the rest are doing, further fuelling the rise or fall in price.

Dealing with uncertainty and risk

When price changes are likely to occur, buyers and sellers will try to anticipate them. Unfortunately on many occasions no one can be certain just what these price changes will be. Take the case of stocks and shares. If you anticipate that the price of, say, Toyota shares is likely to go up substantially in the near future, you may well decide to buy some now and then sell them later after the price has risen. But you cannot be certain that they will go up in price; they may fall instead. If you buy the shares, therefore, you will be taking a gamble.

Now gambles can be of two types. The first is where you know the odds. Let us take the simplest case of a gamble on the toss of a coin. Heads you win; tails you lose. You know that the odds of winning are precisely 50 per cent. If you bet on the toss of a coin, you are said to be operating under conditions of **risk**. *Risk is when the probability of an outcome is known.* Risk itself is a measure of the *variability* of an outcome. For example, if you bet £1 on the toss of a coin, such that heads you win £1 and tails you lose £1, then the variability is –£1 to +£1.

The second form of gamble is the more usual. This is where the odds are not known or are known only roughly. Gambling on the stock exchange is like this. You may have a good idea that a share will go up in price, but is it a 90 per cent chance, an 80 per cent chance or what? You are not certain. Gambling under these sort of conditions is known as operating under uncertainty. *This is when the probability of an outcome is not known.*

You may well disapprove of gambling and want to dismiss people who engage in it as foolish or morally wrong. But 'gambling' is not just confined to horses, cards, roulette and the like. Risk and uncertainty pervade the whole of economic life and decisions are constantly having to be made whose outcome cannot be known for certain. Even the most morally upright person will still have to decide which career to go into, whether and when to buy a house, or even something as trivial as whether or not to take an umbrella when going out. Each of these decisions and thousands of others are made under conditions of uncertainty (or occasionally risk).

> **Definition**
>
> **Uncertainty**
> When an outcome may or may not occur and its probability of occurring is not known.

> *People's actions are influenced by their attitudes towards risk.* Many decisions are taken under conditions of risk or uncertainty. Generally, the lower the probability of (or the more uncertain) the desired outcome of an action, the less likely will people be to undertake the action.
>
> **Key Idea 13**

Stock holding as a way of reducing the problem of uncertainty

A simple way that suppliers can reduce the problem of uncertainty is by holding stocks. Take the case of the wheat farmers we saw in the previous section. At the time when they are planting the wheat in the spring, they are uncertain as to what the price of wheat will be when they bring it to market. If they keep no stores of wheat, they will just have to accept whatever the market price happens to be at harvest time. If, however, they have storage facilities, they can put the wheat into store if the price is low and then wait until it goes up. Alternatively, if the price of wheat is high at harvest time, they can sell it straight away. In other words, they can wait until the price is right.

> **Pause for thought**
>
> *The demand for pears is more price elastic than the demand for bread and yet the price of pears fluctuates more than that of bread. Why should this be so? If pears could be stored as long and as cheaply as flour, would this affect the relative price fluctuations? If so, how?*

Web Appendix 2.2 gives fuller analysis of risk and uncertainty. It also examines the role of insurance as a way of reducing or eliminating risk.

Recap

1. A complete understanding of markets must take into account the time dimension.

2. Given that producers and consumers take a time to respond fully to price changes, we can identify different equilibria after the elapse of different lengths of time. Generally, short-run supply and demand tend to be less price elastic than long-run supply and demand. As a result, any shifts in *D* or *S* curves tend to have a relatively bigger effect on price in the short run and a relatively bigger effect on quantity in the long run.

3. People often anticipate price changes, and this will affect the amount they demand or supply. This speculation will tend to stabilise price fluctuations if people believe that the price changes are only temporary. However, speculation will tend to destabilise these fluctuations (i.e. make them more severe) if people believe that prices are likely to continue to move in the same direction as at present (at least for some time).

4. Many economic decisions are taken under conditions of risk or uncertainty. Uncertainty over future prices can be tackled by holding stocks. When prices are low, the stocks can be built up. When they are high, stocks can be sold.

2.6   MARKETS WHERE PRICES ARE CONTROLLED

What happens if the government fixes prices?

At the equilibrium price, there will be no shortage or surplus. The equilibrium price, however, may not be the most *desirable* price. The government, therefore, may prefer to keep prices above or below the equilibrium price.

TC 7
p47

Setting a minimum (high) price

TC 8
p64

If the government sets a **minimum price** above the equilibrium (a price floor), there will be a surplus: $Q_s - Q_d$ in Figure 2.8. Price will not be allowed to fall to eliminate this surplus. The government may do this for various reasons:

- To protect producers' incomes. If the industry is subject to supply fluctuations (e.g. crops, due to fluctuations in weather) and if industry demand is price inelastic, prices are likely to fluctuate severely. Minimum prices will prevent the fall in producers' incomes that would accompany periods of low prices.
- To create a surplus (e.g. of grains), particularly in periods of plenty, which can be stored in preparation for possible future shortages.
- In the case of wages (the price of labour), minimum wages legislation can be used to prevent workers' wage rates from falling below a certain level (see Box 5.4).

There are various methods the government can use to deal with the surpluses associated with minimum prices.

- The government could buy the surplus and store it, destroy it or sell it abroad in other markets.
- Supply could be artificially lowered by restricting producers to particular quotas. In Figure 2.8, supply could therefore be reduced to Q_d.
- Demand could be raised by advertising, by finding alternative uses for the good, or by reducing consumption of substitute goods (e.g. by imposing taxes or quotas on substitutes, such as imports).

Figure 2.8
Minimum price: price floor

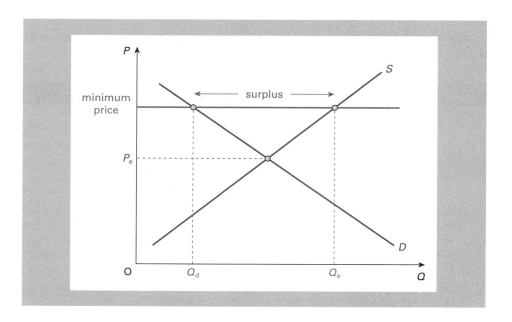

One of the problems with minimum prices is that firms with surplus on their hands may try to evade the price control and cut their prices.

Another problem is that high prices may cushion inefficiency. Firms may feel less need to find more efficient methods of production and cut their costs if their profits are being protected by the high price. Also the high price may discourage firms from producing alternative goods which they could produce more efficiently or which are in higher demand, but which nevertheless have a lower (free-market) price.

One of the best-known examples of governments fixing high minimum prices is the Common Agricultural Policy (CAP) of the European Union. This is examined in Box 2.4.

> ### *Pause for thought*
>
> *Draw a supply and demand diagram with the price of labour (the wage rate) on the vertical axis and the quantity of labour (the number of workers) on the horizontal axis. What will happen to employment if the government raises wages from the equilibrium to some minimum wage above the equilibrium?*

Setting a maximum (low) price

If the government sets a **maximum price** below the equilibrium (a price ceiling), there will be a shortage: $Q_d - Q_s$ in Figure 2.9. Price will not be allowed to rise to eliminate this shortage. The government may set maximum prices to prevent them rising above a certain level. This will normally be done for reasons of fairness. In wartime, or times of famine, the government may set maximum prices for basic goods so that poor people can afford to buy them.

The resulting shortages, however, create further problems. If the government merely sets prices and does not intervene further, the shortages will lead to the following:

■ Allocation on a 'first come, first served' basis. This is likely to lead to queues developing, or firms adopting waiting lists. Queues were a common feature of life in the former communist eastern European countries where governments kept prices below the level necessary to equate demand and supply. In recent years, as part of their economic reforms, they have allowed prices to rise. This has had the obvious benefit of reducing or eliminating queues, but at the same time it has made life very hard for those on low incomes.

> ### Definition
>
> **Maximum price**
> A price ceiling set by the government or some other agency. The price is not allowed to rise above this level (although it is allowed to fall below it).

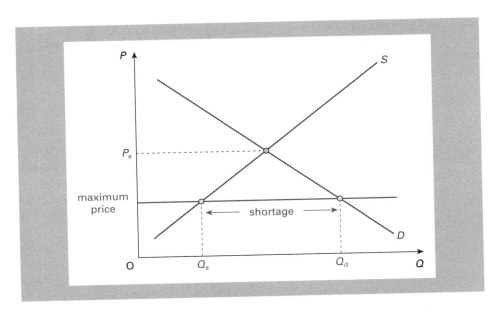

Figure 2.9
Maximum price: price ceiling

Box 2.4

Agriculture and minimum prices

A problem of surpluses

TC7
p47

Governments in many countries intervene in agricultural markets. The problems of fluctuating prices, dependency on foreign food imports, and the maintenance of farmers' and farm workers' incomes are but a few of the reasons for such intervention. The form that government intervention takes varies, from a series of subsidies or tax reliefs for farmers, to the more formal fixing of high minimum prices.

Until recently, the fixing of high minimum prices was the main policy used by the European Union in its Common Agricultural Policy (CAP). Here the Intervention Boards of the EU buy up any surpluses that result at a given 'intervention' price, usually set above the equilibrium.

The effects of this system are illustrated in the diagram, which shows the demand and supply of a particular agricultural product. Assume that the EU demand is D_{EU} and that EU supply is S_{EU}. Assume also that the world price is P_w. This will be the equilibrium price, since any shortage at P_w (i.e. $b - a$) will be imported at that price. Thus before intervention, EU demand is Q_{d_1} and EU supply is Q_{s_1} and imports are $Q_{d_1} - Q_{s_1}$.

Now assume that the EU sets an intervention price of P_i. At this high price, there will now be a surplus of $d - e$ (i.e. $Q_{s_2} - Q_{d_2}$). This will be bought by the appropriate Intervention Board. The cost to the EU of buying this surplus is shown by the total shaded area ($edQ_{s_2}Q_{d_2}$: i.e. the surplus multiplied by the intervention price). Unless the food is thrown away or otherwise disposed of, there will obviously then be the additional costs of storing this food: costs that

have been very high in some years as wine 'lakes' and grain and dairy 'mountains' have built up.

An alternative to storing the food is for the Board to sell the surpluses on the world market at the world price (P_w). In this case, the net cost to the Intervention Board would only be the area $edcf$: in other words, the amount purchased by the Board ($d - e$) multiplied by the difference in price paid by the Board and the price it receives on the world market ($P_i - P_w$). Alternatively, export subsidies could be paid to farmers who sell on world markets to bring the amount they receive up to the intervention price.

The justifications for such a policy are that: it assures food supplies (i.e. it encourages countries to be self-sufficient in food); it stabilises prices; and, by

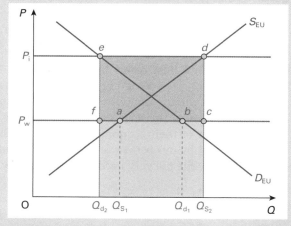

The system of high minimum prices in agricultural products

- Firms deciding which customers should be allowed to buy: for example, giving preference to regular customers.

Neither of the above may be considered to be fair. Certain needy people may be forced to go without. Therefore, the government may adopt a system of **rationing**. People could be issued with a set number of coupons for each item rationed.

A major problem with maximum prices is likely to be the emergence of **black markets**, where customers, unable to buy enough in legal markets, may well be prepared to pay very high prices: prices above P_e in Figure 2.9.

Another problem is that the maximum prices reduce the quantity produced of an already scarce commodity. For example, artificially low prices in a famine are likely to reduce food supplies: if not immediately, then at the next harvest, because of less being sown. In many developing countries, governments control the price

Definition

Rationing
Where the government restricts the amount of a good that people are allowed to buy.

increasing farmers' incomes, it encourages them to invest in agriculture, which, in turn, results in a growth in agricultural productivity.

The system of high minimum prices has been criticised on a number of counts:

- Food surpluses have been a costly waste of scarce resources.
- Although food prices were kept high generally, some were kept much higher above free-market prices than others. The effect was to give a very uneven amount of protection.
- The system increased inequalities within agriculture. The bigger the farm, the bigger its output, and therefore the bigger the benefit the farmer received from high prices. Similarly, richer agricultural regions of the EU received more support than poorer ones.
- Higher food prices penalise the poor, who spend a larger proportion of their income on food than do the rich.
- The system had harmful effects on the environment. By encouraging increased output, the CAP encouraged the destruction of hedgerows and wildlife, and the increased use of chemical fertilisers and pesticides. Many of these chemicals have caused pollution.
- EU food surpluses 'dumped' on to world markets have had a doubly damaging effect on agriculture in developing countries: (a) exporters of foodstuffs find it very difficult to compete with subsidised EU exports; (b) farmers in developing countries who are producing for their domestic market find that they cannot compete with cheap imports of food from the EU.

Agriculture in the developing world thus declines. Farmers' incomes are too low to invest in the land. Many migrate to the overcrowded cities and become slum dwellers in shanty towns, with little or no paid employment. The neglect of agriculture can then lead to famines if there is poor rainfall in any year. Calls are then made for European (and North American) food surpluses to be used for emergency aid: the same food surpluses that contributed to the problem in the first place!

As a result of these problems, various reforms to the CAP have been or are in the process of being implemented. These include: reducing supply by requiring farmers to 'set aside' (i.e. take out of use) a certain percentage of their land; cutting the level of intervention prices; providing grants or other incentives for farmers to farm less intensively or to diversify into alternative rural industries (such as tourism and forestry). The main reform, however, has been to 'decouple' support to farmers from the level of production. Farmers are given 'direct aid' related to the size of the farm and past output, not to current levels of production.

? *What is the effect on output of replacing high minimum prices with grants to farmers unrelated to current production?*

of basic foodstuffs in order to help the urban poor. The effect, however, is to reduce incomes for farmers, who are then encouraged to leave the land and flock into the ever-growing towns and cities.

To minimise these types of problem the government may attempt to reduce the shortage by encouraging supply: by drawing on stores, by direct government production, or by giving subsidies or tax relief to firms. Alternatively, it may attempt to reduce demand: by the production of more alternative goods (e.g. home-grown vegetables in times of war) or by controlling people's incomes.

One example of a maximum price is considered in Box 2.5. The 'price' in this case is the rent paid by tenants for private rented accommodation. Should the government set a rent ceiling in order to guarantee affordable accommodation? Would there be any problems with such a policy?

Box 2.5   Case Studies and Applications

Rent control

Cheap housing for all?

The purpose of rent control is to protect tenants from paying high rent, as well as to provide cheap housing for the very poor. However, many economists argue that in practice such rent controls only succeed in making a larger part of the population worse off. How is this so?

Referring to the diagram, assume that the rent for a particular type of accommodation is initially at the equilibrium level, R_0, where $D = S$. Now assume that legislation is passed that sets a rent ceiling of R_1. Despite this reduction in rent, the supply of rental accommodation will fall only slightly in the short run, as landlords cannot quickly transfer their accommodation to other uses. In the diagram this is shown by a movement from point a to point b on the relatively inelastic supply curve S.

With the rent set below equilibrium, there will be a shortage of rented property. In the short run, however, this will be relatively small (i.e. $Q_2 - Q_1$), and hence only a relatively small number of people will be unable to find accommodation. The remainder will benefit from the lower rents.

In the long run, however, many landlords will respond to the lower rent by putting their accommodation to other uses. The supply curve will become more elastic (curve S') and the supply of rented property will fall to Q_3 (point c). Shortages now increase (to $Q_2 - Q_3$) as less rental housing is available. More people become homeless – more, perhaps, than in an unregulated market.

Rent controls may have further adverse effects. First, on equity grounds it is somewhat arbitrary as to who gets and who does not get housing at the lower rent. Second, in the long run, those landlords who still keep their property available for rent may cut maintenance costs and let their property fall into disrepair.

Those in favour of rent controls counter these arguments by claiming that the demand and supply curves of rented accommodation are very inelastic. Take the case of the demand curve. People have got to live somewhere. If rent control is abolished, people will just have to pay the higher rent, or become homeless; and given that people will only sacrifice their home as a last resort, demand remains inelastic, and rents could rise to a very high level.

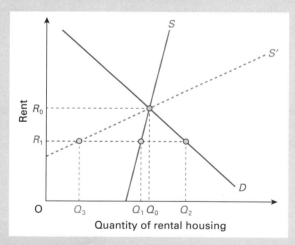

Effect of rent control

1. How could housing supplied by the public sector be made to rectify some of the problems we have identified above? (What would it do to the supply curve?)
2. If the government gives poor people rent allowances (i.e. grants), how will this affect the level of rents in an uncontrolled market? What determines the size of the effect?
3. The case for and against rent controls depends to a large extent on the long-run elasticity of supply. Do you think it will be relatively elastic or inelastic? Give reasons.

Box 2.6 **Case Studies and Applications**

The effect of imposing taxes on goods

Who ends up paying?

Another example of government intervention in markets is the imposition of taxes on goods. These indirect taxes, as they are called, include taxes such as value added tax (VAT) and excise duties on cigarettes, petrol and alcoholic drinks.

These taxes can be a fixed amount per unit sold – a specific tax. An example is the tax on petrol, which is set at so much per litre. Alternatively, they can be a percentage of the price, or value added, at each stage of production – an *ad valorem* tax. An example is VAT.

When a tax is levied on a good or service, this has the effect of shifting the supply curve upwards by the amount of the tax (see diagram (a)). In the case of a specific tax, it will be a parallel shift, since the amount of the tax is the same at all prices.

But why does the supply curve shift upwards by the amount of the tax? In diagram (a), the supply curve (S) shows that to supply Q_1, producers need to receive a price of P_1. Now a tax is levied of an amount shown by the arrow. For producers to continue receiving P_1 and hence producing Q_1, the price charged to consumers has to be P_{1+tax}. Thus the new supply curve is shown by the red line S_T.

The incidence of the tax

What will be the effect of the tax on the price and the quantity sold? This is illustrated in diagram (b). Before the tax is imposed, Q_1 units are sold at a price of P_1. The effect of the tax is to shift the supply curve to S_T. Price rises to P_2 and quantity falls to Q_2.

Notice, however, that price does not rise by the full amount of the tax, because the demand curve is downward sloping. The amount of the tax is $P_2 - C$, whereas the price increase is only $P_2 - P_1$. Thus the burden or incidence of such taxes is distributed between consumers and producers. Consumers pay to the extent that price rises. Producers pay to the extent that this rise in price is not sufficient to cover the tax.

We can also show in diagram (b) the revenue the government receives from the tax. The tax per unit is $P_2 - C$ and the quantity sold is Q_2 (shown by the distance CB). Thus the revenue raised is the total area of the shaded rectangle, P_2ABC.

The rise in price from P_1 to P_2 multiplied by the number of goods sold (Q_2) (the green area) is the amount of the tax passed on to consumers and thus represents the consumers' share of the tax. The remainder (the lilac area) is the producers' share. This is the amount by which the producers' net price is below the original price (i.e. $P_1 - C$) multiplied by Q_2.

Elasticity and the incidence of taxation

It is easy to see that the less elastic is demand:

- the less quantity sold falls and hence the greater the revenue the government raises from the tax;
- the more price rises and hence the greater the proportion of the tax paid by consumers.

Thus in most countries, cigarettes, petrol and alcohol have been major targets for indirect taxes. In many cases the tax accounts for well over half of the market price! Demand for each of them is high and relatively inelastic. Thus the tax raises a lot of revenue and does not curb demand greatly.

> **?** *Demand tends to be more elastic in the long run than in the short run. Assume that a tax is imposed on a good that was previously untaxed. How will the incidence of this tax change as time passes?*

TC 8 p64

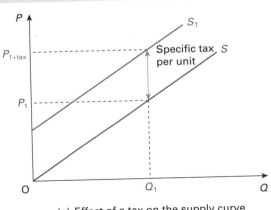

(a) Effect of a tax on the supply curve

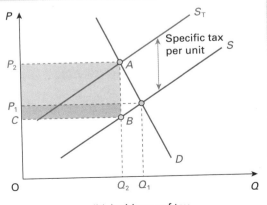

(b) Incidence of tax

Recap

1. The government may fix minimum or maximum prices. If a minimum price is set above the equilibrium price, a surplus will result. If a maximum price is set below the equilibrium price, a shortage will result.

2. Minimum prices are set as a means of protecting the incomes of suppliers or of creating a surplus for storage in case of future reductions in supply. If the government is not deliberately trying to create a surplus, it must decide what to do with it.

3. Maximum prices are set as a means of keeping prices down for the consumer. The resulting shortage will cause queues, waiting lists or the restriction of sales by firms to favoured customers. Alternatively, the government could introduce a system of rationing. If it does, then black markets are likely to arise. This is where goods are sold illegally above the maximum price.

Questions

1. Draw a diagram with two supply curves, one steeply sloping and one gently sloping. Ensure that the two curves cross. Draw a demand curve through the point where they cross and mark the equilibrium price and quantity. Now assume that the demand curve shifts to the right. Show how the shape of the supply curve will determine just what happens to price and quantity.

2. Which of the following will have positive signs and which will have negative ones? (a) price elasticity of demand; (b) income elasticity of demand (normal good); (c) income elasticity of demand (inferior good); (d) cross elasticity of demand (with respect to changes in price of a substitute good); (e) cross elasticity of demand (with respect to changes in price of a complementary good); (f) price elasticity of supply.

3. Demand for oil might be relatively elastic over the longer term, and yet it could still be observed that over time people consume more oil (or only very slightly less) despite rising oil prices. How can this apparent contradiction be explained?

4. How might a firm set about making the demand for its brand less elastic?

5. Assuming that a firm faces an inelastic demand and wants to increase its total revenue, in what direction should it change its price? Is there any limit to how far it should go in changing its price in this direction?

6. Why are both the price elasticity of demand and the price elasticity of supply likely to be greater in the long run?

7. Which are likely to have the highest cross elasticity of demand: two brands of coffee, or coffee and tea? Explain.

8. Redraw both diagrams in Figure 2.7, only this time assume that it was an initial shift in supply that caused price to change in the first place.

9. What are the advantages and disadvantages of speculation from the point of view of (a) the consumer; (b) firms?

10. Give some examples of decisions you have taken recently that were made under conditions of uncertainty. With hindsight do you think you made the right decisions?

11. Assume that the (weekly) market demand and supply of tomatoes are given by the figures shown below:

Price (£ per kilo)	4.00	3.50	3.00	2.50	2.00	1.50	1.00
Q_d (000 kilos)		30	35	40	45	50	55	60
Q_s (000 kilos)		80	68	62	55	50	45	38

(a) What are the equilibrium price and quantity?
(b) What will be the effect of the government fixing a minimum price of (i) £3.00 per kilo; (ii) £1.50 per kilo?
(c) Suppose that the government paid tomato producers a subsidy of £1.00 per kilo. (i) Give the new supply schedule. (ii) What will be the new equilibrium price? (iii) How much will this cost the government?
(d) Alternatively, suppose that the government guaranteed tomato producers a price of £2.50 per kilo. (i) How many tomatoes would it have to buy in order to ensure that all the tomatoes produced were sold? (ii) How much would this cost the government?
(e) Alternatively, suppose it bought all the tomatoes produced at £2.50. (i) At what single price would it have to sell them in order to dispose of the lot? (ii) What would be the net cost of this course of action?

12. Think of two things that are provided free. In each case, identify when and in what form a shortage might occur. In what ways are/could these shortages be dealt with? Are they the best solution to the shortages?

13. Think of some examples where the price of a good or service is kept below the equilibrium. In each case consider the advantages and disadvantages of the policy.

Additional case studies on the *Essentials of Economics* MyEconLab (www.pearsoned.co.uk/sloman)

2.1 **Rationing.** A case study in the use of rationing as an alternative to the price mechanism. In particular, it looks at the use of rationing in the UK during the Second World War.

2.2 **Adjusting to oil price shocks.** A case study showing how demand and supply analysis can be used to examine the price changes in the oil market since 1973.

2.3 **Advertising and its effects on the demand curve.** How advertising a product can both shift the demand curve and change its elasticity.

2.4 **Any more fares?** Pricing on the buses: an illustration of the relationship between price and total revenue.

2.5 **Income elasticity of demand and the balance of payments.** This examines how a low income elasticity of demand for the exports of many developing countries can help to explain their chronic balance of payments problems.

2.6 **Black markets.** How black markets can develop when prices are fixed below the equilibrium.

2.7 **Elasticities of demand for various foodstuffs.** An examination of the evidence about price and income elasticities of demand for food in the UK.

2.8 **The role of the speculator.** This assesses whether the activities of speculators are beneficial or harmful to the rest of society.

2.9 **The CAP and the environment.** This case shows how the system of high intervention prices had damaging environmental effects. It also examines the more recent measures that the EU has adopted to reverse the effects.

2.10 **The fallacy of composition.** An illustration of how something that applies to an individual may not apply to a larger group. The example is taken from agriculture.

2.11 **The Cobweb model.** An outline of the theory that explains price fluctuations in terms of time lags in supply.

2.12 **Dealing in futures markets.** How buying and selling in futures markets can reduce uncertainty.

Sections of chapter covered in *WinEcon* – Sloman, *Essentials of Economics*

Essentials of Economics section	*WinEcon* section
2.1	2.1
2.2	2.2
2.3	2.3
2.4	2.4
2.5	2.5
2.6	2.6

Websites relevant to this chapter

Numbers and sections refer to websites listed in the Web Appendix and hotlinked from MyEconLab. Visit:

www.pearsoned.co.uk/sloman

- For news articles relevant to this chapter, see the *Economics News Articles* link from MyEconLab.
- For general news on markets and market intervention, see websites in section A, and particularly A1–5, 7–9, 18, 24, 25, 26, 33, 36. See also A38, 43 and 44 for links to newspapers worldwide; and A42 for links to economics news video and audio.
- For information on advertising (Box 2.3), see site E37.
- For information on agriculture and the Common Agricultural Policy (Box 2.4), see sites E14 and G9.
- For student resources relevant to this chapter, see sites C1–7, 9, 10, 19; D3.
- For sites favouring the free market, see C17 and E34.

Web Appendices

2.1 **Point elasticity.** An alternative way of measuring elasticity.

2.2 **Risk and uncertainty.** An analysis of consumer decision making when knowledge is imperfect. The appendix also looks at the role of insurance in reducing or eliminating uncertainty.

PART SIX
Costs and Revenues

Chapter 14

The Supply Decision

The supply decision

So far we have assumed that supply curves are generally upward sloping: that a higher price will encourage firms to supply more. But just how much will firms choose to supply at each price? It depends largely on the amount of profit they will make. If a firm can increase its profits by producing more, it will normally do so.

Profit is made by firms earning more from the sale of goods than they cost to produce. A firm's total profit is thus the difference between its total sales revenue (TR) and its total costs of production (TC). In order then to discover how a firm can maximise its profit or even get a sufficient level of profit, we must first consider what determines costs and revenue.

In Sections 3.1 and 3.2 we examine short-run and long-run costs respectively. Over the short run a firm will be limited in what inputs it can expand. For example, a manufacturing company might be able to use more raw materials, or possibly more labour, but it will not have time to open up another factory. Over the long run, however, a firm will have much more flexibility. It can, if it chooses, expand the whole scale of its operations.

In Section 3.3 we turn to the revenue side and see how a firm's revenue varies with output. Finally, Section 3.4 puts revenue and cost together to see how profit is determined. In particular, we shall see how profit varies with output and how the point of maximum profit is found.

After studying this chapter, you should be able to answer the following questions:

- What is the relationship between inputs and outputs in both the short and long run?
- How do costs vary with output and just what do we mean by 'costs'?
- What are meant by 'economies of scale' and what are the reasons for such economies?
- How does a firm's sales revenue vary with output?
- How do we measure profits?
- At what output will a firm maximise its profits? How much profit will it make at this output?

3.1   SHORT-RUN COSTS

How do a firm's costs vary with output over the short term?

The cost of producing any level of output will depend on the amount of inputs used and the price the firm must pay for them. Let us first focus on the quantity of inputs used.

> *Output depends on the amount of resources and how they are used.* Different amounts and combinations of inputs will lead to different amounts of output. If output is to be produced efficiently, inputs should be combined in the optimum proportions.
>
> **Key Idea 14**

Short-run and long-run changes in production

If a firm wants to increase production, it will take time to acquire a greater quantity of certain inputs. For example, a manufacturer can use more electricity by turning on switches, but it might take a long time to obtain and install more machines, and longer still to build a second or third factory.

If, then, the firm wants to increase output in a hurry, it will only be able to increase the quantity of certain inputs. It can use more raw materials, more fuel, more tools and possibly more labour (by hiring extra workers or offering overtime to its existing workforce). But it will have to make do with its existing buildings and most of its machinery.

The distinction we are making here is between **fixed factors** and **variable factors**. A *fixed* factor is an input that cannot be increased within a given time period (e.g. buildings). A *variable* factor is one that can.

The distinction between fixed and variable factors allows us to distinguish between the short run and the long run.

The short run.   The **short run** is a time period during which at least one factor of production is fixed. In the short run, then, output can be increased only by using more variable factors. For example, if a shipping line wanted to carry more passengers in response to a rise in demand, it could possibly accommodate more passengers on existing sailings if there were space. It could possibly increase the number of sailings with its existing fleet, by hiring more crew and using more fuel. But in the short run it could not buy more ships: there would not be time for them to be built.

The long run.   The **long run** is a time period long enough for all inputs to be varied. Given long enough, a firm can build a second factory and install new machines.

The actual length of the short run will differ from firm to firm. It is not a fixed period of time. Thus if it takes a farmer a year to obtain new land, buildings and equipment, the short run is any time period up to a year and the long run is any time period longer than a year. On the other hand, if it takes a shipping company three years to obtain an extra ship, the short run is any period up to three years and the long run is any period longer than three years.

For the remainder of this section we will concentrate on *short-run* production and costs. We will look at the long run in Section 3.2.

Production in the short run: the law of diminishing returns

Production in the short run is subject to *diminishing returns*. You may well have heard of 'the law of diminishing returns': it is one of the most famous of all 'laws' of economics. To illustrate how this law underlies short-run production let us take the simplest possible case where there are just two factors: one fixed and one variable.

Take the case of a farm. Assume that the fixed factor is land and the variable factor is labour. Since the land is fixed in supply, output per period of time can be increased only by increasing the amount of workers employed. But imagine what would happen as more and more workers crowd on to a fixed area of land. The land cannot go on yielding more and more output indefinitely. After a point the additions to output from each extra worker will begin to diminish.

We can now state the law of diminishing (marginal) returns.

> *The law of diminishing marginal returns.* When increasing amounts of a variable factor are used with a given amount of a fixed factor, there will come a point when each extra unit of the variable factor will produce less extra output than the previous unit.
>
> **Key Idea 15**

Box 3.1 is a case study illustrating the law of diminishing returns. Another good example is given in Web Case 3.3, which looks at diminishing returns to the application of nitrogen fertiliser on farmland. Box 3.2 shows that the law has potentially dire implications for us and the future inhabitants of our planet.

The relationship between inputs and output is explained in more detail in Web Appendix 3.1, which looks at the short-run 'production function'.

Box 3.1   **Case Studies and Applications**

Diminishing returns in the bread shop

Is the baker using his loaf?

KI 15
p83

Just up the road from where I live is a bread shop. Like many others, I buy my bread there on a Saturday morning. Not surprisingly, Saturday morning is the busiest time of the week for the shop and as a result it takes on extra assistants.

During the week only one assistant serves the customers, but on a Saturday morning there used to be five serving. But could they serve five times as many customers? No, they could not. There were diminishing returns to labour.

The trouble is that certain factors of production in the shop are fixed:

- The shop is a fixed size. It gets very crowded on Saturday morning. Assistants sometimes have to wait while customers squeeze past each other to get to the counter, and with five serving, the assistants themselves used to get in each other's way.

- There is only one cash till. Assistants frequently had to wait while other assistants used it.
- There is only one pile of tissue paper for wrapping the bread. Again the assistants often had to wait.

The fifth and maybe even the fourth assistant ended up serving very few extra customers.

I am still going to the same bread shop and they still have only one till and one pile of tissue paper. But now only three assistants are employed on a Saturday! The shop, however, is just as busy.

How would you advise the baker as to whether he should (a) employ four assistants on a Saturday; (b) extend his shop, thereby allowing more customers to be served on a Saturday morning?

Box 3.2

Malthus and the dismal science of economics

Population growth + diminishing returns = starvation

KI 15
p83

The law of diminishing returns has potentially cataclysmic implications for the future populations of the world.

If the population of the world grows rapidly, then food output may not keep pace with it. There will be diminishing returns to labour as more and more people crowd on to the limited amount of land available.

This is already a problem in some of the poorest countries of the world, especially in sub-Saharan Africa. The land is barely able to support current population levels. Only one or two bad harvests are needed to cause mass starvation – witness the appalling famines in recent years in Ethiopia and the Sudan.

The relationship between population and food output was analysed as long ago as 1798 by the Reverend Thomas Robert Malthus (1766–1834) in his *Essay on the Principle of Population*. This book was a bestseller and made Robert Malthus perhaps the best known of all social scientists of his day.

Malthus argued as follows:

I say that the power of population is indefinitely greater than the power in the earth to produce subsistence for man.

Population when unchecked, increases in a geometrical ratio. Subsistence increases only in an arithmetical ratio. A slight acquaintance with numbers will show the immensity of the first power in comparison with the second.[1]

What Malthus was saying is that world population tends to double about every 25 years or so if unchecked. It grows geometrically, like the series: 1, 2, 4, 8, 16, 32, 64, etc. But food output, because of diminishing returns, cannot keep pace with this. It is likely to grow at only an arithmetical rate, like the series: 1, 2, 3, 4, 5, 6, 7, etc. It is clear that population, if unchecked, will soon outstrip food supply.

So what is the check on population growth? According to Malthus, it is starvation. As population grows, so food output per head will fall until, with more and more people starving, the death rate will rise. Only then will population growth stabilise at the rate of growth of food output.

Have Malthus' gloomy predictions been borne out by events? Two factors have mitigated the forces that Malthus described:

- The rate of population growth tends to slow down as countries become more developed. Although improved health prolongs life, this tends to be more than offset by a decline in the birth rate as people choose to have smaller families.
- Technological improvements in farming have greatly increased food output per hectare.

[1] T. R. Malthus, *First Essay on Population* (Macmillan, 1926), pp. 13–14.

Measuring costs of production

We are now ready to look at short-run costs. First of all, we will need to define just what we mean by costs. The term is used differently by economists and accountants.

When measuring costs, economists always use the concept of **opportunity cost**. Remember from the Introduction how we defined opportunity cost. It is the cost of any activity measured in terms of the *sacrifice* made in doing it: in other words, the cost measured in terms of the opportunities forgone.

TC 1
p7

How do we apply this principle of opportunity cost to a firm? First we must discover what factors of production it is using. Then we must measure the sacrifice involved. To do this it is necessary to put factors into two categories.

Definition

Opportunity cost
Cost measured in terms of the best alternative forgone.

World population levels and growth: actual and projected

Year	World population (billions)	Average annual rate of increase (%)		
		World	More developed regions	Less developed regions
1950	2.6			
		1.7	1.2	2.1
1960	3.0			
		2.0	1.0	2.4
1970	3.7			
		1.8	0.7	2.2
1980	4.5			
		1.7	0.6	2.1
1990	5.3			
		1.4	0.3	1.8
2000	6.1			
		1.2	0.2	1.5
2010	6.8			
		1.0	0.2	1.2
2020	7.6			
		0.8	0.1	1.1
2030	8.2			

Source: Various

The growth in food output has thus exceeded the rate of population growth in advanced countries.

The picture is much more gloomy, however, in developing countries. There *have* been advances in agriculture. The 'green revolution', whereby new high-yielding crop varieties have been developed (especially in the cases of wheat and rice), has led to food output growth outstripping population growth in many developing countries. India, for example, now exports grain.

Nevertheless, the Malthusian spectre is very real for some of the poorest developing countries, which are simply unable to feed their populations satisfactorily. It is these poorest countries of the world which have some of the highest rates of population growth. Many African countries have population growth rates of around 3 per cent per annum.

? *The figures in the table above are based on the assumption that birth rates will fall faster than death rates. Under what circumstances might these forecasts underestimate the rate of growth of world population?*

Factors not owned by the firm: explicit costs

The opportunity cost of those factors not already owned by the firm is simply the price that the firm has to pay for them. Thus if the firm uses £100 worth of electricity, the opportunity cost is £100. The firm has sacrificed £100 that could have been spent on something else.

These costs are called **explicit costs** because they involve direct payment of money by firms.

Factors already owned by the firm: implicit costs

When the firm already owns factors (e.g. machinery), it does not as a rule have to pay out money to use them. Their opportunity costs are thus **implicit costs**. They are equal to what the factors could earn for the firm in some alternative use, either within the firm or hired out to some other firm.

Definitions

Explicit costs
The payments to outside suppliers of inputs.

Implicit costs
Costs that do not involve a direct payment of money to a third party, but which nevertheless involve a sacrifice of some alternative.

Here are some examples of implicit costs:

- A firm owns some buildings. The opportunity cost of using them is the rent it could have received by letting them out to another firm.
- A firm draws £100 000 from the bank out of its savings in order to invest in new plant and equipment. The opportunity cost of this investment is not just the £100 000 (an explicit cost), but also the interest it thereby forgoes (an implicit cost).
- The owner of the firm could have earned £15 000 per annum by working for someone else. This £15 000, then, is the opportunity cost of the owner's time.

If there is no alternative use for a factor of production, as in the case of a machine designed to make a specific product, and if it has no scrap value, the opportunity cost of using it is *zero*. In such a case, if the output from the machine is worth more than the cost of all the *other* inputs involved, the firm might as well use the machine rather than let it stand idle.

What the firm paid for the machine – its **historic cost** – is irrelevant. Not using the machine will not bring that money back. It has been spent. These are sometimes referred to as 'sunk costs'.

Costs and output

A firm's costs of production depend on its output. The reason is simple. The more it produces, the greater the quantity of factors of production it must use. The more factors it uses, the greater its costs will be. More precisely, this relationship depends on two elements:

- The productivity of the factors. The greater their productivity, the smaller will be the quantity of them that is needed to produce a given level of output, and hence the lower will be the cost of that output.
- The price of the factors. The higher their price, the higher will be the costs of production.

In the short run, some factors used by the firm are fixed in supply. Their total costs, therefore, are fixed, in the sense that they do not vary with output. Rent on land is a **fixed cost**. It is the same whether the firm produces a lot or a little.

The total cost of variable factors, however, does vary with output. The cost of raw materials is a **variable cost**. The more that is produced, the more raw materials are used and therefore the higher is their total cost.

Total cost (TC) is thus total fixed cost (TFC) plus total variable cost (TVC).

Average and marginal cost

In addition to total costs (fixed and variable), there are two other categories of costs that are particularly important for our analysis of profit. These are average cost and marginal cost.

Average cost (AC) is cost per unit of production.

$$AC = TC/Q$$

Thus if it costs a firm £2000 to produce 100 units of a product, the average cost would be £20 for each unit (£2000/100).

Like total cost, average cost can be divided into the two components, fixed and variable. In other words, average cost equals **average fixed cost** ($AFC = TFC/Q$) plus **average variable cost** ($AVC = TVC/Q$).

$$AC = AFC + AVC$$

Marginal cost (*MC*) is the *extra* cost of producing *one more unit*: that is, the rise in total cost per one unit rise in output.

$$MC = \frac{\Delta TC}{\Delta Q}$$

where Δ means 'a rise in'.

For example, assume that a firm is currently producing 1 000 000 boxes of matches a month. It now increases output by 1000 boxes (another batch): ΔQ = 1000. Assume that, as a result, total costs rise by £40: ΔTC = £40. What is the cost of producing one more box of matches? It is:

$$MC = \frac{\Delta TC}{\Delta Q} = \frac{£40}{1000} = 4p$$

(Note that all marginal costs are variable, since, by definition, there can be no extra fixed costs as output rises.)

Table 3.1 shows costs for an imaginary firm, firm X, over a given period of time (e.g. a week). The table shows how average and marginal costs can be derived from total costs. It is assumed that total fixed costs are £12 000 (column 2) and that total variable costs are as shown in column 3.

The figures for *TVC* have been chosen to illustrate the law of diminishing returns. Initially, *before* diminishing returns set in, *TVC* rises less and less rapidly as more variable factors are added. For example, in the case of a factory with a fixed supply of machinery, initially as more workers are taken on the workers can do increasingly specialist tasks and make a fuller use of the capital equipment. Above a certain output (3 units in Table 3.1), diminishing returns set in. Given that extra workers (the extra variable factors) are producing less and less extra output, the extra units of output they do produce will be costing more and more in terms of wage costs. Thus *TVC* rises more and more rapidly. You can see this by examining column 3.

The figures in the remaining columns in Table 3.1 are derived from columns 1 to 3. Look at the figures in each of the columns and check how the figures are derived. Note that the figures for marginal cost are plotted between the lines to illustrate that marginal cost represents the increase in costs as output increases from one unit to the next. We can use the figures in Table 3.1 to draw *MC*, *AFC*, *AVC* and *AC* curves.

Definitions

Marginal cost
The cost of producing one more unit of output: $MC = \Delta TC/\Delta Q$

Table 3.1	Costs for firm X						
Output (Q) (1)	TFC (£000) (2)	TVC (£000) (3)	TC (TFC+TVC) (£000) (4)	AFC (TFC/Q) (£000) (5)	AVC (TVC/Q) (£000) (6)	AC (TC/Q) (£000) (7)	MC (ΔTC/ΔQ) (£000) (8)
0	12	0	12	–	–	–	10
1	12	10	22	12	10	22	6
2	12	16	28	6	8	14	5
3	12	21	33	4	7	11	7
4	12	28	40	3	7	10	12
5	12	40	52	2.4	8	10.4	20
6	12	60	72	2	10	12	31
7	12	91	103	1.7	13	14.7	

Figure 3.1
Average and
marginal costs

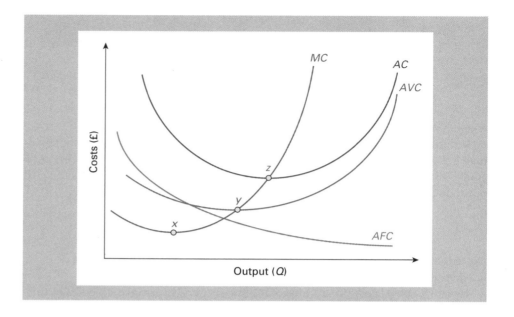

KI 15
p83

Pause for thought

Before you read on, can you explain why the marginal cost curve will always cut the average cost curve at its lowest point?

Marginal cost (MC). The shape of the *MC* curve follows directly from the law of diminishing returns. Initially, in Figure 3.1, as more of the variable factor is used, extra units of output cost less than previous units. *MC* falls.

Beyond a certain level of output, diminishing returns set in. This is shown as point *x*. Thereafter *MC* rises. Additional units of output cost more and more to produce, since they require ever-increasing amounts of the variable factor.

Box 3.3   **Exploring Economics**

The relationship between averages and marginals

In this chapter we have just examined the concepts of *average* and *marginal* cost. We shall be coming across several other average and marginal concepts later on. It is useful at this stage to examine the general relationship between averages and marginals. In all cases there are three simple rules that relate them.

To illustrate these rules, consider the following example.

Imagine a room with ten people in it. Assume that the *average* age of those present is 20.

Now if a 20-year-old enters the room (the *marginal* age), this will not affect the average age. It will remain at 20. If a 56-year-old now comes in, the average age will rise: not to 56, of course, but to 23. This is found by dividing the sum of everyone's ages (276) by the number of people (12). If then a child of 10 were to enter the room, this would pull the average age down.

From this example we can derive the three universal rules about averages and marginals:

- If the marginal equals the average, the average will not change.
- If the marginal is above the average, the average will rise.
- If the marginal is below the average, the average will fall.

? *A cricketer scores the following number of runs in five successive innings:*

Innings:	1	2	3	4	5
Runs:	20	20	50	10	0

These can be seen as the marginal number of runs from each innings. Calculate the total and average number of runs after each innings. Show how the average and marginal scores illustrate the three rules above.

Average fixed cost (AFC). This falls continuously as output rises, since total fixed costs are being spread over a greater and greater output.

Average (total) cost (AC). The shape of the AC curve depends on the shape of the MC curve. As long as new units of output cost less than the average, their production must pull the average cost down. That is, if MC is less than AC, AC must be falling. Likewise, if new units cost more than the average, their production must drive the average up. That is, if MC is greater than AC, AC must be rising. Therefore, the MC curve crosses the AC curve at its minimum point (point z in Figure 3.1). This relationship between averages and marginals is explored in Box 3.3.

Average variable cost (AVC). Since AVC = AC − AFC, the AVC curve is simply the vertical difference between the AC and the AFC curves. Note that as AFC gets less, the gap between AVC and AC narrows. Since all marginal costs are variable (by definition, there are no marginal fixed costs), the same relationship holds between MC and AVC as it did between MC and AC. That is, if MC is less than AVC, AVC must be falling, and if MC is greater than AVC, AVC must be rising. Therefore, as with the AC curve, the MC curve crosses the AVC curve at its minimum point (point y in Figure 3.1).

Pause for thought

Why is the minimum point of the AVC curve at a lower level of output than the minimum point of the AC curve?

Recap

1. Production in the short run is subject to diminishing returns. As greater quantities of the variable factor(s) are used, so each additional unit of the variable factor will add less to output than previous units: i.e. output will rise less and less rapidly.

2. When measuring costs of production, we should be careful to use the concept of opportunity cost. In the case of inputs not owned by the firm, the opportunity cost is simply the explicit cost of purchasing or hiring them. It is the price paid for them. In the case of inputs already owned by the firm, it is the implicit cost of what the factor could have earned for the firm in its best alternative use.

3. As some factors are fixed in supply in the short run, their total costs are fixed with respect to output. In the case of variable factors, their total cost increases as more output is produced and hence as more of them are used. Total cost can be divided into total fixed and total variable cost.

4. Marginal cost is the cost of producing one more unit of output. It will probably fall at first but will start to rise as soon as diminishing returns set in.

5. Average cost, like total cost, can be divided into fixed and variable costs. Average fixed cost will decline as more output is produced. The reason is that the total fixed cost is being spread over a greater and greater number of units of output. Average variable cost will tend to decline at first, but once the marginal cost has risen above it, it must then rise. The same applies to average cost.

LONG-RUN COSTS
3.2

How do a firm's costs vary with output over the longer term?

 In the long run, *all* factors of production are variable. There is time for the firm to build a new factory (maybe in a different part of the country), to install new machines, to use different techniques of production, and in general to combine its inputs in whatever proportion and in whatever quantities it chooses.

In the long run, then, a firm will have to make a number of decisions: about the scale of its operations and the techniques of production it will use. These decisions will affect the costs of production. It is important, therefore, to get them right.

Table 3.2	Short-run and long-run increases in output				
Short run			**Long run**		
Input 1	Input 2	Output	Input 1	Input 2	Output
3	1	25	1	1	15
3	2	45	2	2	35
3	3	60	3	3	60
3	4	70	4	4	90
3	5	75	5	5	125

The scale of production

If a firm were to double all of its inputs – something it could do in the long run – would it double its output? Or would output more than double or less than double? We can distinguish three possible situations:

Constant returns to scale.   This is where a given percentage increase in inputs will lead to the same percentage increase in output.

Increasing returns to scale.   This is where a given percentage increase in inputs will lead to a *larger* percentage increase in output.

Decreasing returns to scale.   This is where a given percentage increase in inputs will lead to a *smaller* percentage increase in output.

Notice the terminology here. The words 'to scale' mean that *all* inputs increase by the same proportion. Decreasing returns to *scale* are therefore quite different from diminishing *marginal* returns (where only the *variable* factor increases). The differences between marginal returns to a variable factor and returns to scale are illustrated in Table 3.2.

In the short run, input 1 is assumed to be fixed in supply (at 3 units). Output can be increased only by using more of the variable factor (input 2). In the long run, however, both input 1 and input 2 are variable.

In the short-run situation, diminishing returns can be seen from the fact that output increases at a decreasing rate (25 to 45 to 60 to 70 to 75) as input 2 is increased. In the long-run situation, the table illustrates increasing returns to scale. Output increases at an *increasing* rate (15 to 35 to 60 to 90 to 125) as both inputs are increased.

Economies of scale

The concept of increasing returns to scale is closely linked to that of **economies of scale**. A firm experiences economies of scale if costs per unit of output fall as the scale of production increases. Clearly, if a firm is getting increasing returns to scale from its factors of production, then as it produces more it will be using smaller and smaller amounts of factors per unit of output. Other things being equal, this means that it will be producing at a lower average cost.

There are a number of reasons why firms are likely to experience economies of scale. Some are due to increasing returns to scale; some are not.

Specialisation and division of labour.   In large-scale plants, workers can do more simple, repetitive jobs. With this **specialisation and division of labour** less training is needed; workers can become highly efficient in their particular job, especially

Definitions

Economies of scale
Where increasing the scale of production leads to a lower cost per unit of output.

Specialisation and division of labour
Where production is broken down into a number of simpler, more specialised tasks, thus allowing workers to acquire a high degree of efficiency.

with long production runs; there is less time lost by workers switching from one operation to another; and supervision is easier. Workers and managers can be employed who have specific skills in specific areas.

Indivisibilities.   Some inputs are of a minimum size: they are indivisible. The most obvious example is machinery. Take the case of a combine harvester. A small-scale farmer could not make full use of one. They only become economical to use, therefore, on farms above a certain size. The problem of indivisibilities is made worse when different machines, each of which is part of the production process, are of a different size. For example, if there are two types of machine, one producing 6 units a day, the other packaging 4 units a day, a minimum of 12 units per day will have to be produced, involving two production machines and three packaging machines, if all machines are to be fully utilised.

The 'container principle'.   Any capital equipment that contains things (e.g. blast furnaces, oil tankers, pipes, vats) tends to cost less per unit of output the larger its size. The reason has to do with the relationship between a container's volume and its surface area. A container's cost depends largely on the materials used to build it and hence roughly on its *surface area*. Its output depends largely on its *volume*. Large containers have a bigger volume relative to surface area than do small containers. For example, a container with a bottom, top and four sides, with each side measuring 1 metre, has a volume of 1 cubic metre and a surface area of 6 square metres (6 surfaces of 1 square metre each). If each side was doubled in length to 2 metres, the volume would be 8 cubic metres and the surface area 24 square metres (6 surfaces of 4 square metres each). Thus an eightfold increase in capacity has been gained at only a fourfold increase in the container's surface area, and hence an approximate fourfold increase in cost.

Greater efficiency of large machines.   Large machines may be more efficient in the sense that more output can be gained for a given amount of inputs. For example, only one worker may be required to operate a machine, whether it be large or small. Also, a large machine may make more efficient use of raw materials.

By-products.   With production on a large scale, there may be sufficient waste products to make some by-product.

Multi-stage production.   A large factory may be able to take a product through several stages in its manufacture. This saves time and cost moving the semi-finished product from one firm or factory to another. For example, a large cardboard-manufacturing firm may be able to convert trees or waste paper into cardboard and then into cardboard boxes in a continuous sequence.

All the above are examples of plant economies of scale. They are due to an individual factory or workplace or machine being large. There are other economies of scale that are associated with the *firm* being large – perhaps with many factories.

Organisational economies.   With a large firm, individual plants can specialise in particular functions. There can also be centralised administration of the firms. Often, after a merger between two firms, savings can be made by rationalising their activities in this way.

Spreading overheads.   There are some expenditures that are only economic when the *firm* is large, such as research and development: only a large firm can afford to set up a research laboratory. This is another example of indivisibilities, only this time at the level of the firm rather than the plant. The greater the firm's output, the more these overhead costs are spread.

Financial economies. Large firms may be able to obtain finance at lower interest rates than small firms. They may be able to obtain certain inputs cheaper by buying in bulk. (These are examples of economies of scale which are not the result of increasing returns to scale.)

Economies of scope. Often a firm is large because it produces a range of products. This can result in each individual product being produced more cheaply than if it was produced in a single-product firm. The reason for these economies of scope is that various overhead costs and financial and organisational economies can be shared among the products. For example, a firm that produces a whole range of CD players, DVD players and recorders, amplifiers, PlayStations, TVs and so on can benefit from shared marketing and distribution costs and the bulk purchase of electronic components.

Diseconomies of scale

When firms get beyond a certain size, costs per unit of output may start to increase. There are several reasons for such diseconomies of scale:

- Management problems of co-ordination may increase as the firm becomes larger and more complex, and as lines of communication get longer. There may be a lack of personal involvement by management.
- Workers may feel 'alienated' if their jobs are boring and repetitive, and if they feel an insignificantly small part of a large organisation. Poor motivation may lead to shoddy work.
- Industrial relations may deteriorate as a result of these factors and also as a result of the more complex interrelationships between different categories of worker.
- Production-line processes and the complex interdependencies of mass production can lead to great disruption if there are hold-ups in any one part of the firm.

Whether firms experience economies or diseconomies of scale depends on the conditions applying in each individual firm.

The size of the whole industry

As an *industry* grows in size, this can lead to external economies of scale for its member firms. This is where a firm, whatever its own individual size, benefits from the *whole industry* being large. For example, the firm may benefit from having access to specialist raw material or component suppliers, labour with specific skills, firms that specialise in marketing the finished product, and banks and other financial institutions with experience of the industry's requirements. What we are referring to here is the industry's infrastructure: the facilities, support services, skills and experience that can be shared by its members.

The member firms of a particular industry might, however, experience external diseconomies of scale. For example, as an industry grows larger, this may create a growing shortage of specific raw materials or skilled labour. This will push up their prices, and hence the firms' costs.

The relationship between inputs and outputs in the long run is examined in Web Appendices 3.2 and 3.3. These look at ways of combining inputs so as to minimise costs for a given output or maximise output for a given cost.

Long-run average cost

We turn now to *long-run* cost curves. Since there are no fixed factors in the long run, there are no long-run fixed costs. For example, the firm may rent more land in order

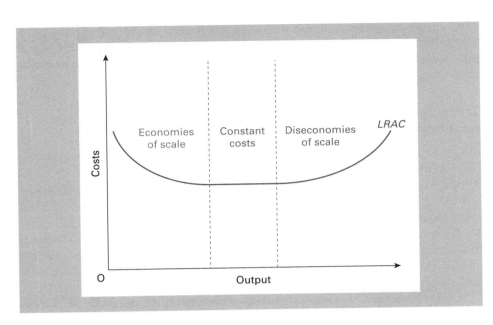

Figure 3.2
A typical long-run average cost curve

to expand its operations. Its rent bill therefore goes up as it expands its output. All costs, then, in the long run are variable costs.

Although it is possible to draw long-run total, marginal and average cost curves, we will concentrate on **long-run average cost (*LRAC*) curves**. These can take various shapes, but a typical one is shown in Figure 3.2.

It is often assumed that, as a firm expands, it will initially experience economies of scale and thus face a downward-sloping *LRAC* curve. After a point, however, all such economies will have been achieved and thus the curve will flatten out. Then, possibly after a period of constant *LRAC*, the firm will get so large that it will start experiencing diseconomies of scale and thus a rising *LRAC*. At this stage, production and financial economies begin to be offset by the managerial problems of running a giant organisation.

The effect of this is to give a saucer-shaped curve, as in Figure 3.2.

Assumptions behind the long-run average cost curve

There are three key assumptions that we make when constructing long-run average cost curves:

Factor prices are given. At each level of output it is assumed that a firm will be faced with a given set of factor prices. If factor prices *change*, therefore, both short- and long-run cost curves will shift. Thus an increase in nationally negotiated wage rates would shift the curves upwards.

However, factor prices might be different at *different* levels of output. For example, one of the economies of scale that many firms enjoy is the ability to obtain bulk discount on raw materials and other supplies. In such cases the curve does *not* shift. The different factor prices are merely experienced at different points along the curve, and are reflected in the shape of the curve. Factor prices are still given for any particular level of output.

The state of technology and factor quality are given. These are assumed to change only in the *very* long run (see page 95). If a firm gains economies of scale, it is because it is being able to exploit *existing* technologies and make better use of the existing availability of factors of production.

Definition

Long-run average cost curve
A curve that shows how average cost varies with output on the assumption that *all* factors are variable. (It is assumed that the least-cost method of production will be chosen for each output.)

Firms choose the least-cost combination of factors for each output. The assumption here is that firms operate efficiently: that they choose the cheapest possible way of producing any level of output. If the firm did not operate efficiently, it would be producing at a point *above* the LRAC curve.

The relationship between long-run and short-run average cost curves

Take the case of a firm that has just one factory and faces a short-run average cost curve illustrated by $SRAC_1$ in Figure 3.3.

In the long run, it can build more factories. If it thereby experiences economies of scale (due, say, to savings on administration), each successive factory will allow it to produce with a new lower *SRAC* curve. Thus with two factories it will face curve $SRAC_2$; with three factories curve $SRAC_3$, and so on. Each *SRAC* curve corresponds to a particular amount of the factor that is fixed in the short run: in this case, the factory. (Many more *SRAC* curves could be drawn between the ones shown, since factories of different sizes could be built or existing ones could be expanded.)

From this succession of short-run average cost curves we can construct a long-run average cost curve. This is shown in Figure 3.3. This is known as the **envelope curve**, since it envelops the short-run curves.

Long-run cost curves in practice

Firms do experience economies of scale. Some experience continuously falling *LRAC* curves. Others experience economies of scale up to a certain output and thereafter constant returns to scale.

Evidence is inconclusive on the question of diseconomies of scale. There is little evidence to suggest the existence of *technical* diseconomies, but the possibility of diseconomies due to managerial and industrial relations problems cannot be ruled out.

Some evidence on economies of scale in the UK is considered in Box 3.4.

Figure 3.3
Constructing a long-run average cost curve from short-run average cost curves

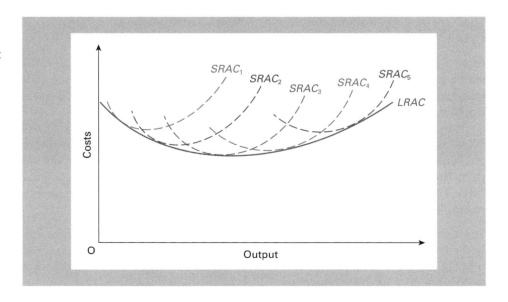

Postscript: Decision making in different time periods

We have distinguished between the short run and the long run. Let us introduce two more time periods to complete the picture. The complete list then reads as follows.

Very short run (immediate run).   All factors are fixed. Output is fixed. The supply curve is vertical. On a day-to-day basis a firm may not be able to vary output at all. For example, a flower seller, once the day's flowers have been purchased from the wholesaler, cannot alter the amount of flowers available for sale on that day. In the very short run, all that may remain for a producer to do is to sell an already produced good.

Short run.   At least one factor is fixed in supply. More can be produced, but the firm will come up against the law of diminishing returns as it tries to do so.

Long run.   All factors are variable. The firm may experience constant, increasing or decreasing returns to scale. But although all factors can be increased or decreased, they are of a fixed *quality*.

Very long run.   All factors are variable, *and* their quality and hence productivity can change. Labour productivity can increase as a result of education, training, experience and social factors. The productivity of capital can increase as a result of new inventions (new discoveries) and innovation (putting inventions into practice).

Improvements in factor quality will reduce costs and thus shift the short- and long-run cost curves downwards.

Just how long the 'very long run' is will vary from firm to firm. It will depend on how long it takes to develop new techniques, new skills or new work practices.

It is important to realise that decisions *for* all four time periods can be made *at* the same time. Firms do not make short-run decisions *in* the short run and long-run decisions *in* the long run. They can make both short-run and long-run decisions today. For example, assume that a firm experiences an increase in consumer demand and anticipates that it will continue into the foreseeable future. It thus wants to increase output. Consequently, it makes the following four decisions *today*.

- (*Very short run*) It accepts that for a few days it will not be able to increase output. It informs its customers that they will have to wait. It may temporarily raise prices to choke off some of the demand.
- (*Short run*) It negotiates with labour to introduce overtime working as soon as possible, to tide it over the next few weeks. It orders extra raw materials from its suppliers. It launches a recruitment drive for new labour so as to avoid paying overtime longer than is necessary.
- (*Long run*) It starts proceedings to build a new factory. The first step may be to discuss requirements with a firm of consultants.
- (*Very long run*) It institutes a programme of research and development and/or training in an attempt to increase productivity.

> **Pause for thought**
>
> *Why are Christmas trees and fresh foods often sold cheaply on Christmas Eve? Why do shops find it most profitable to lower the price of these items to the point where the price elasticity of demand equals −1?*

Although we distinguish these four time periods, it is the middle two we are primarily concerned with. The reason for this is that there is very little the firm can do in the *very* short run. And in the *very* long run, although the firm will obviously want to increase the productivity of its inputs, it will not be in a position to make precise calculations of how to do it. It will not know precisely what inventions will be made, or just what will be the results of its own research and development.

Box 3.4

Minimum efficient scale

The extent of economies of scale in practice

Two of the most important studies of economies of scale have been those made by C. F. Pratten[1] in the late 1980s and by a group advising the European Commission[2] in 1997. Both studies found strong evidence that many firms, especially in manufacturing, experienced substantial economies of scale.

In a few cases long-run average costs fell continuously as output increased. For most firms, however, they fell up to a certain level of output and then remained constant.

The extent of economies of scale can be measured by looking at a firm's *minimum efficient scale* (*MES*). The *MES* is the size beyond which no significant additional economies of scale can be achieved: in other words, the point where the *LRAC* curve flattens off. In Pratten's studies he defined this level as the minimum scale above which any possible doubling in scale would reduce average costs by less than 5 per cent (i.e. virtually the bottom of the *LRAC* curve). In the diagram *MES* is shown at point *a*.

The *MES* can be expressed in terms either of an individual factory or of the whole firm. Where it refers to the minimum efficient scale of an individual factory, the *MES* is known as the *minimum efficient plant size* (*MEPS*).

The *MES* can then be expressed as a percentage of the total size of the market or of total domestic production. Table (a), based on the Pratten study, shows *MES* for plants and firms in various industries. The first column shows *MES* as a percentage of total UK production. The second column shows *MES* as a percentage of total EU production. Table (b), based on the 1997 study, shows *MES* for various plants as a percentage of total EU production.

Expressing *MES* as a percentage of total output gives an indication of how competitive the industry could be. In some industries (such as footwear and tufted carpets), economies of scale were exhausted

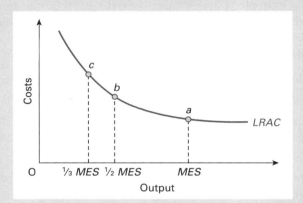

(i.e. *MES* was reached) with plants or firms that were still small relative to total UK production and even smaller relative to total EU production. In such industries there would be room for many firms and thus scope for considerable competition.

In other industries, however, even if a single plant or firm were large enough to produce the whole output of the industry in the UK, it would still not be large enough to experience the full potential economies of scale: the *MES* is greater than 100 per cent. Examples from Table (a) include factories producing cellulose fibres, and car manufacturers. In such industries there is no possibility of competition. In fact, as long as the *MES* exceeds 50 per cent there will not be room for more than one firm large enough to gain full economies of scale. In this case the industry is said to be a *natural monopoly*. As we shall see in Chapters 4 and 6, when competition is lacking, consumers may suffer by firms charging prices considerably above costs.

A second way of measuring the extent of economies of scale is to see how much costs would increase if production were reduced to a certain fraction of *MES*. The normal fractions used are ½ or ⅓ *MES*. This is illustrated in the diagram. Point *b* corresponds to ½ *MES*; point *c* to ⅓ *MES*. The greater the percentage by which *LRAC* at point *b* or *c* is higher than at point *a*, the greater will be the economies of scale to be gained by producing at *MES* rather than at ½ *MES* or ⅓ *MES*. For example, the table shows that greater economies of scale can be gained by moving from ½ *MES* to *MES* in the production of electric motors than of cigarettes.

[1] C. F. Pratten, 'A survey of the economies of scale', in *Research on the 'Costs of Non-Europe'*, vol. 2 (Office for Official Publications of the European Communities, 1988).

[2] European Commission/Economists Advisory Group Ltd, 'Economies of Scale', *The Single Market Review, Sub-series V, Volume 4*. Office for Official Publications of the European Communities, Luxembourg, 1997.

Table (a)

Product	MES as % of production		% additional cost at $^1/_2$ MES
	UK	EU	
Individual plants			
Cellulose fibres	125	16	3
Rolled aluminium semi-manufactures	114	15	15
Refrigerators	85	11	4
Steel	72	10	6
Electric motors	60	6	15
TV sets	40	9	9
Cigarettes	24	6	1.4
Ball-bearings	20	2	6
Beer	12	3	7
Nylon	4	1	12
Bricks	1	0.2	25
Tufted carpets	0.3	0.04	10
Shoes	0.3	0.03	1
Firms			
Cars	200	20	9
Lorries	104	21	7.5
Mainframe computers	>100	n.a.	5
Aircraft	100	n.a.	5
Tractors	98	19	6

Source: See footnote 1 opposite

Table (b)

Plants	MES as % of total EU production
Aerospace	12.19
Tractors and agricultural machinery	6.57
Electric lighting	3.76
Steel tubes	2.42
Shipbuilding	1.63
Rubber	1.06
Radio and TV	0.69
Footwear	0.08
Carpets	0.03

Source: See footnote 2 opposite

The main purpose of the studies was to determine whether a single EU market is big enough to allow both economies of scale and competition. The tables suggest that in all cases, other things being equal, the EU market is large enough for firms to gain the full economies of scale *and* for there to be enough firms for the market to be competitive.

The second study also found that 47 of the 53 manufacturing sectors analysed had scope for further exploitation of economies of scale.

? 1. Why might a firm operating with one plant achieve MEPS and yet not be large enough to achieve MES? (Clue: are all economies of scale achieved at plant level?)

2. Why might a firm producing bricks have an MES that is only 0.2 per cent of total EU production and yet face little effective competition from other EU countries?

Recap

1. In the long run, a firm is able to vary the quantity it uses of all factors of production. There are no fixed factors and hence no long-run fixed costs.

2. If it increases all factors by the same proportion, it may experience constant, increasing or decreasing returns to scale.

3. Economies of scale occur when costs per unit of output fall as the scale of production increases. This can be the result of a number of factors, some of which are directly due to increasing (physical) returns to scale. These include the benefits of specialisation and division of labour, the use of larger and more efficient machines, and the ability to have a more integrated system of production. Other economies of scale arise from the financial and administrative benefits of large-scale organisations.

4. When constructing long-run cost curves it is assumed that factor prices are given, that the state of technology is given, and that firms will choose the least-cost method of production for each given output.

5. The *LRAC* curve can be downward sloping, upward sloping or horizontal, depending in turn on whether there are economies of scale, diseconomies of scale or neither. Typically *LRAC* curves are drawn as saucer-shaped. As output expands, initially there are economies of scale. When these are exhausted the curve will become flat. When the firm becomes very large it may begin to experience diseconomies of scale. If this happens, the *LRAC* curve will begin to slope upwards again.

6. An envelope curve can be drawn which shows the relationship between short-run and long-run average cost curves. The *LRAC* curve envelops the short-run *AC* curves: it is 'tangential' to them (i.e. just touches them).

7. Four distinct time periods can be distinguished. In addition to the short- and long-run periods, we can also distinguish the very-short- and very-long-run periods. The very short run is when all factors are fixed. The very long run is where not only the quantity of factors but also their quality is variable (as a result of changing technology, etc.).

3.3 REVENUE

How does a firm's revenue vary with its level of sales?

Remember that we defined a firm's total profit as its total revenue minus its total costs of production. In the last two sections we looked at costs. We now turn to revenue.

As with costs, we distinguish between three revenue concepts: total revenue (*TR*), average revenue (*AR*) and marginal revenue (*MR*).

Total, average and marginal revenue

Total revenue (TR)

Total revenue is the firm's total earnings per period of time from the sale of a particular amount of output (*Q*).

For example, if a firm sells 1000 units (*Q*) per month at a price of £5 each (*P*), then its monthly total revenue will be £5000: in other words, £5 × 1000 (*P* × *Q*). Thus:

$$TR = P \times Q$$

Average revenue (AR)

Average revenue is the amount that the firm earns per unit sold. Thus:

$$AR = TR/Q$$

So if the firm earns £5000 (*TR*) from selling 1000 units (*Q*), it will earn £5 per unit. But this is simply the price! Thus:

$$AR = P$$

(The only exception to this is when the firm is selling its products at different prices to different consumers. In this case *AR* is simply the (weighted) average price.)

Marginal revenue (MR)

Marginal revenue is the extra total revenue gained by selling one more unit (per time period). So if a firm sells an extra 20 units this month compared with what it expected to sell, and in the process earns an extra £100, then it is getting an extra £5 for each extra unit sold: *MR* = £5. Thus:

$$MR = \Delta TR/\Delta Q$$

We now need to see how each of these three revenue concepts (*TR*, *AR* and *MR*) varies with output. We can show this relationship graphically in the same way as we did with costs.

The relationship will depend on the market conditions under which a firm operates. A firm that is too small to be able to affect market price will have different-looking revenue curves from a firm that is able to choose the price it charges. Let us examine each of these two situations in turn.

Average and marginal revenue curves when price is not affected by the firm's output

Average revenue

If a firm is very small relative to the whole market, it is likely to be a **price taker**. That is, it has to accept the price given by the intersection of demand and supply in the whole market. But, being so small, it can sell as much as it is capable of producing at that price. This is illustrated in Figure 3.4.

Definitions

Average revenue
Total revenue per unit of output. When all output is sold at the same price, average revenue will be the same as price:
$AR = TR/Q = P$

Marginal revenue
The extra revenue gained by selling one more unit per period of time:
$MR = \Delta TR/\Delta Q$

Price taker
A firm that is too small to be able to influence the market price.

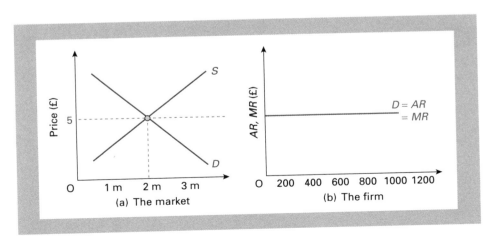

Figure 3.4
Deriving a firm's *AR* and *MR*: price-taking firm

Diagram (a) shows market demand and supply. Equilibrium price is £5. Diagram (b) looks at the demand for an individual firm that is tiny relative to the whole market. (Look at the difference in the scale of the horizontal axes in the two diagrams.)

Being so small, any change in its output will be too insignificant to affect the market price. It thus faces a horizontal demand 'curve' at this price. It can sell 200 units, 600 units, 1200 units or whatever without affecting this £5 price.

Average revenue is thus constant at £5. The firm's average revenue curve must therefore lie along exactly the same line as its demand curve.

Marginal revenue

In the case of a horizontal demand curve, the marginal revenue curve will be the same as the average revenue curve, since selling one more unit at a constant price (AR) merely adds that amount to total revenue. If an extra unit is sold at a constant price of £5, an extra £5 is earned.

Average and marginal revenue curves when price varies with output

The curves (AR and MR) will look quite different when price does vary with the firm's output.

If a firm has a relatively large share of the market, it will face a downward-sloping demand curve. This means that if it is to sell more, it must lower the price. But it could also choose to raise its price. If it does so, however, it will have to accept a fall in sales.

Average revenue

Remember that average revenue equals price. If, therefore, the price has to be reduced to sell more output, average revenue will fall as output increases.

Table 3.3 gives an example of a firm facing a downward-sloping demand curve. The demand curve (which shows how much is sold at each price) is given by the first two columns.

Note that, as in the case of a price-taking firm, the demand curve and the AR curve lie along exactly the same line (see Figure 3.5). The reason for this is simple: $AR = P$, and thus the curve relating price to quantity (the demand curve) must be the same as that relating average revenue to quantity (the AR curve).

Table 3.3	Revenues for a firm facing a downward-sloping demand curve		
Q (units)	*P = AR* (£)	*TR* (£)	*MR* (£)
1	8	8	
2	7	14	6
3	6	18	4
4	5	20	2
5	4	20	0
6	3	18	−2
7	2	14	−4
.	.	.	.

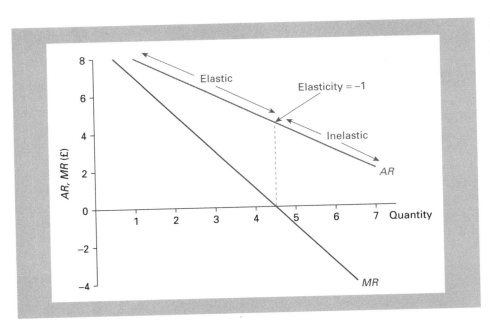

Figure 3.5
AR and *MR* curves for a firm facing a downward-sloping *D* curve

Marginal revenue

When a firm faces a downward-sloping demand curve, marginal revenue will be less than average revenue, and may even be negative. But why?

If a firm is to sell more per time period, it must lower its price (assuming it does not advertise). This will mean lowering the price not just for the extra units it hopes to sell, but also for those units it would have sold had it not lowered the price.

Thus the marginal revenue is the price at which it sells the last unit, *minus* the loss in revenue it has incurred by reducing the price on those units it could otherwise have sold at the higher price. This can be illustrated with Table 3.3.

Assume that price is currently £7. Two units are thus sold. The firm now wishes to sell an extra unit. It lowers the price to £6. It thus gains £6 from the sale of the third unit, but loses £2 by having to reduce the price by £1 on the two units it could otherwise have sold at £7. Its net gain is therefore £6 − £2 = £4. This is the marginal revenue: it is the extra revenue gained by the firm from selling one more unit. Try using this method to check out the remaining figures for *MR* in Table 3.3. (Note that in the table the figures for *MR* are entered in the spaces between the figures for the other three columns.)

There is a simple relationship between marginal revenue and *price elasticity of demand*. Remember from Chapter 2 (page 58) that if demand is price elastic, a *decrease* in price will lead to a proportionately larger increase in the quantity demanded and hence to an *increase* in revenue. Marginal revenue will thus be positive. If, however, demand is inelastic, a decrease in price will lead to a proportionately smaller increase in sales. In this case the price reduction will more than offset the increase in sales and as a result revenue will fall. Marginal revenue will be negative.

If, then, marginal revenue is a positive figure (i.e. if sales per time period are 4 units or less in Figure 3.5), the demand curve will be elastic at that quantity, since a rise in quantity sold (as a result of a reduction in price) would lead to a rise in total revenue. If, on the other hand, marginal revenue is negative (i.e. at a level of sales of 5 or more units in Figure 3.5), the demand curve will be inelastic at that quantity, since a rise in quantity sold would lead to a *fall* in total revenue.

Thus the demand (*AR*) curve of Figure 3.5 is elastic to the left of point *r* and inelastic to the right.

Shifts in revenue curves

We saw in Chapter 1 that a change in *price* will cause a movement along a demand curve. It is similar with revenue curves, except that here the causal connection is in the other direction. Here we ask what happens to revenue when there is a change in the firm's *output*. Again the effect is shown by a movement along the curves.

A change in any *other* determinant of demand, such as tastes, income or the price of other goods, will shift the demand curve. As this change affects the price at which each level of output can be sold, there will be a shift in all three revenue curves. An increase in revenue is shown by a vertical shift upwards; a decrease by a shift downwards.

Recap

1. Total revenue (*TR*) is the total amount a firm earns from its sales in a given time period. It is simply price times quantity: $TR = P \times Q$.
2. Average revenue (*AR*) is total revenue per unit: $AR = TR/Q$. In other words, $AR = P$.
3. Marginal revenue is the extra revenue earned from the sale of one more unit per time period: $MR = \Delta TR/\Delta Q$.
4. The *AR* curve will be the same as the demand curve for the firm's product. In the case of a price taker, the demand curve and hence the *AR* curve will be a horizontal straight line and will also be the same as the *MR* curve.
5. A firm that faces a downward-sloping demand curve must obviously also face the same downward-sloping *AR* curve. The *MR* curve will also slope downwards, but will be below the *AR* curve and steeper than it.
6. When demand is price elastic, marginal revenue will be positive. When demand is price inelastic, marginal revenue will be negative.
7. A change in output is represented by a movement along the revenue curves. A change in any other determinant of revenue will shift the curves up or down.

3.4   PROFIT MAXIMISATION

How much output should a firm produce if it wants to maximise its profit?

We are now in a position to put costs and revenue together to find the output at which total profit *TΠ* is maximised, and also to find out how much that profit will be. We take the case of a firm facing a downward-sloping demand curve whose revenue, cost and profit are shown in Table 3.4.

Finding the maximum profit that the firm can make is a two-stage process. The first stage is to find the profit-maximising output. To do this we use the *MC* and *MR* curves. The second stage is to find out just how much profit is at this output. To do this we use the *AR* and *AC* curves.

Table 3.4 Revenue, cost and profit

Q (units)	P = AR (£)	TR (£)	MR (£)	TC (£)	AC (£)	MC (£)	TΠ (£)	AΠ (£)
0	9	0		6	–		−6	–
			8			4		
1	8	8		10	10		−2	−2
			6			2		
2	7	14		12	6		2	1
			4			2		
3	6	18		14	4⅔		4	1⅓
			2			4		
4	5	20		18	4½		2	½
			0			7		
5	4	20		25	5		−5	−1
			−2			11		
6	3	18		36	6		−18	−3
			−4			20		
7	2	14		56	8		−42	−6
.	.	.	.	.	.	.	.	.

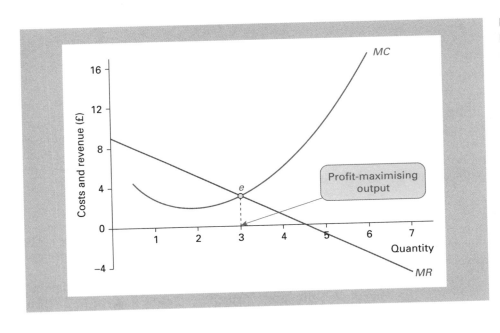

Figure 3.6
Finding the profit-maximising output using marginal curves

Stage 1: Using marginal curves to arrive at the profit-maximising output

There is a very simple profit-maximising rule: if profits are to be maximised, *MR must equal MC*. From Table 3.4 it can be seen that $MR = MC$ at an output of 3. This is shown as point *e* in Figure 3.6.

But why are profits maximised when $MR = MC$? The simplest way of answering this is to see what the position would be if MR did not equal MC.

Referring to Figure 3.6, at a level of output below 3, MR exceeds MC. This means that by producing more units there will be a bigger addition to revenue (MR) than to cost (MC). Total profit will *increase*. As long as MR exceeds MC, profit can be increased by increasing production.

At a level of output above 3, MC exceeds MR. All levels of output above 3 thus add more to cost than to revenue and hence *reduce* profit. As long as MC exceeds MR, profit can be increased by cutting back on production.

Profits are thus maximised where $MC = MR$: at an output of 3. This can be confirmed by reference to the $T\Pi$ column in Table 3.4.

Definition

Profit-maximising rule
Profit is maximised where marginal revenue equals marginal cost.

Figure 3.7
Measuring the
maximum profit using
average curves

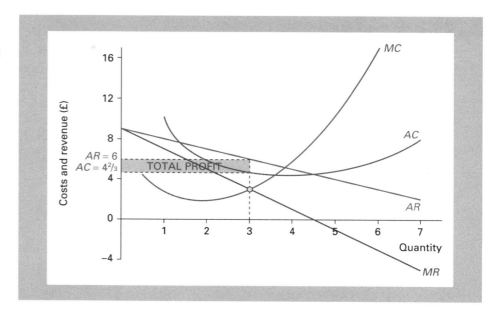

Students worry sometimes about the argument that profits are maximised when $MR = MC$. Surely, they say, if the last unit is making no profit, how can profit be at a *maximum*? The answer is very simple. If you cannot add anything more to a total, the total must be at the maximum. Take the simple analogy of going up a hill. When you cannot go any higher, you must be at the top.

Stage 2: Using average curves to measure the size of the profit

Once the profit-maximising output has been discovered, we now use the average curves to measure the *amount* of profit at the maximum. Both marginal and average curves corresponding to the data in Table 3.4 are plotted in Figure 3.7.

First, average profit ($A\Pi$) is found. This is simply $AR - AC$. At the profit-maximising output of 3, this gives a figure for $A\Pi$ of £6 − £$4^2/_3$ = £$1^1/_3$. Then total profit is obtained by multiplying average profit by output:

$$T\Pi = A\Pi \times Q$$

This is shown as the shaded area. It equals £$1^1/_3 \times 3$ = £4. This can again be confirmed by reference to the $T\Pi$ column in Table 3.4.

> **Pause for thought**
>
> What will be the effect on a firm's profit-maximising output of a rise in fixed costs?

Some qualifications

Long-run profit maximisation

Assuming that the AR and MR curves are the same in the long run as in the short run, long-run profits will be maximised at the output where MR equals the *long-run MC*. The reasoning is the same as with the short-run case.

The meaning of 'profit'

One element of cost is the opportunity cost to the owners of the firm incurred by being in business. This is the minimum return that the owners must make on their capital in order to prevent them from eventually deciding to close down and perhaps move into some alternative business. It is a *cost* since, just as with wages, rent,

TC 1
p7

etc., it has to be covered if the firm is to continue producing. This opportunity cost to the owners is sometimes known as **normal profit**, and is *included in the cost curves*.

What determines this normal rate of profit? It has two components. First, someone setting up in business invests capital in it. There is thus an opportunity cost. This is the interest that could have been earned by lending it in some riskless form (e.g. by putting it in a savings account in a bank). Nobody would set up a business unless they expected to earn at least this rate of profit. Running a business is far from riskless, however, and hence a second element is a return to compensate for risk. Thus:

Normal profit (%) = Rate of interest on a riskless loan + A risk premium

The risk premium varies according to the line of business. In those businesses with fairly predictable patterns, such as food retailing, it is relatively low. Where outcomes are very uncertain, as in mineral exploration or the manufacture of fashion garments, it is relatively high.

Thus if owners of a business earn normal profit, they will (just) be content to remain in that industry. If they earn more than normal profit, they will also (obviously) prefer to stay in this business. If they earn less than normal profit, then after a time they will consider leaving and using their capital for some other purpose.

Given that normal profits are included in costs, any profit that is shown diagrammatically (e.g. the shaded area in Figure 3.7) must therefore be over and above normal profit. It is known by several alternative names: **supernormal profit**, pure profit, economic profit, abnormal profit, producer's surplus (or sometimes simply profit). They all mean the same thing: the excess of total profit over normal profit.

Loss minimising

Sometimes there is no output at which the firm can make a profit. Such a situation is illustrated in Figure 3.8: the *AC* curve is above the *AR* curve at all levels of output.

In this case, the output where *MR* = *MC* will be the loss-minimising output. The amount of loss at the point where *MR* = *MC* is shown by the shaded area in Figure 3.8.

> ### Definitions
>
> **Normal profit**
> The opportunity cost of being in business. It consists of the interest that could be earned on a riskless asset, plus a return for risk taking. It is counted as a cost of production.
>
> **Supernormal profit**
> (also known as pure profit, economic profit, abnormal profit, producer's surplus or simply profit). The excess of total profit above normal profit.

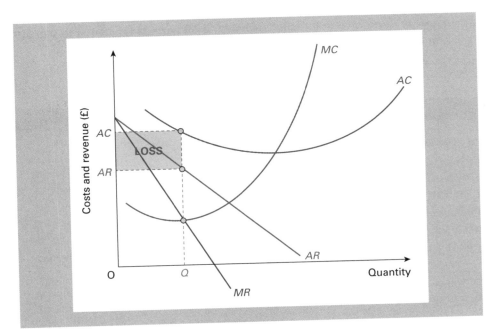

Figure 3.8
Loss-minimising output

Figure 3.9
The short-run
shut-down point

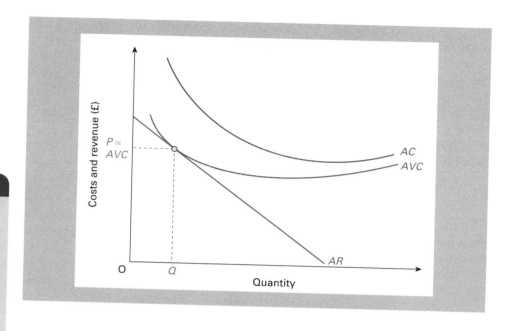

Definitions

Short-run shut-down point
Where the *AR* curve is tangential to the *AVC* curve. The firm can only just cover its variable costs. Any fall in revenue below this level will cause a profit-maximising firm to shut down immediately.

Long-run shut-down point
Where the *AR* curve is tangential to the *LRAC* curve. The firm can just make normal profits. Any fall in revenue below this level will cause a profit-maximising firm to shut down once all costs have become variable.

Whether or not to produce at all

The short run.   Fixed costs have to be paid even if the firm is producing nothing at all. Rent has to be paid, business rates have to be paid, and so forth. Provided, therefore, that the firm is more than covering its *variable* costs, it can go some way to paying off these fixed costs and therefore will continue to produce.

It will shut down if it cannot cover its variable costs: that is, if the *AVC* curve is above, or the *AR* curve is below, that illustrated in Figure 3.9. This situation is known as the **short-run shut-down point**.

The long run.   All costs are variable in the long run. If, therefore, the firm cannot cover its long-run average costs (which include normal profit), it will close down. The **long-run shut-down point** will be where the *AR* curve is tangential to (i.e. just touches) the *LRAC* curve.

Recap

1. Total profit equals total revenue minus total cost.
2. Graphically, profits are maximised at the output where marginal revenue equals marginal cost. Having found this output, the level of maximum profit can be found by finding the average profit (*AR* – *AC*) and then multiplying it by the level of output.
3. Normal profit is the minimum profit that must be made to persuade a firm to stay in business in the long run. It is counted as part of the firm's costs. Supernormal profit is any profit over and above normal profit.
4. For a firm that cannot make a profit at any level of output, the point where *MR* = *MC* represents the loss-minimising output.
5. In the short run, a firm will close down if it cannot cover its variable costs. In the long run, it will close down if it cannot make normal profits.

The logic of logistics

Driving up profits

One key to a company's success is the logistics of its operations. 'Logistics' refers to the management of the inflow of resources to a company and the outflow of goods from it: in other words, to 'supply-chain management'. It includes the purchasing of supplies, transporting them, production sequencing, stock control, delivery to customers, and so on.

Modern developments in logistics have transformed the operation of many industries.

Driving down costs

With the widespread use of containerisation and the development of giant distribution companies, such as FedEx, UPS and DHL, transporting materials and goods around the world has become much faster and much cheaper. Instead of having to make parts and materials in-house, companies can now use the logistics industry to obtain them at lower cost elsewhere, often from the other side of the world.

With deliveries becoming more and more reliable, firms no longer need to keep large stocks of parts. They simply buy them as they need them.

The globalisation of logistics, with increasing use of the Internet, has resulted in a hugely complex logistics industry. Companies that were once solely concerned with delivery, are now being employed to manage companies' supply chains and achieve large cost savings for them.

Driving up revenue

Efficient logistics has not just resulted in lower costs. The flexibility it gives firms has allowed many to increase their sales.

Carrying small stocks and switching from supplier to supplier, with the process often being managed by a logistics company, can allow companies to change their products more rapidly. They can be more responsive to consumer demand.

Fashion goods can get to the shops ahead of the competition. Perishable goods can arrive fresher.

What dangers are there in keeping stocks to a minimum and relying on complex supply chains?

Questions

1. Up to roughly how long is the short run in the following cases?
   (a) A mobile disco firm.
   (b) Electricity power generation.
   (c) A small grocery retailing business.
   (d) 'Superstore Hypermarkets plc'.
   In each case specify your assumptions.

2. Given that there is a fixed supply of land in the world, what implications can you draw from the law of diminishing returns about the effects of an increase in world population on food output per head?

3. The following are some costs incurred by a shoe manufacturer. Decide whether each one is a fixed cost or a variable cost or has some element of both.
   (a) The cost of leather.
   (b) The fee paid to an advertising agency.
   (c) Wear and tear on machinery.

   (d) Business rates on the factory.
   (e) Electricity for heating and lighting.
   (f) Electricity for running the machines.
   (g) Basic minimum wages agreed with the union.
   (h) Overtime pay.
   (i) Depreciation of machines as a result purely of their age (irrespective of their condition).

4. What economies of scale is a large department store likely to experience?

5. Why are many firms likely to experience economies of scale up to a certain size and then diseconomies of scale after some point beyond that?

6. Name some industries where external economies of scale are gained. What are the specific external economies in each case?

7. Examine Figure 3.2 (on page 93). What would (i) the firm's long-run total cost curve, and (ii) its long-run marginal cost curve look like?

8. Under what circumstances is a firm likely to experience a flat-bottomed *LRAC* curve?

9. Draw a downward-sloping demand curve. Now choose scales for both axes. Read off various points on the demand curve and use them to construct a table showing price and quantity. Use this table to work out the figures for a marginal revenue column. Now use these figures to draw an *MR* curve.

10. Copy Figure 3.5 (which is based on Table 3.3). Now assume that incomes have risen and that, as a result, two more units per time period can be sold at each price. Construct a new table and plot the resulting new *AR* and *MR* curves on your diagram. Are the new curves parallel to the old ones? Explain.

11. Using the data in Table 3.3 (on page 100), construct a *total revenue* curve and mark the parts of the curve where the price elasticity of demand is (a) elastic; (b) unit elastic; (c) inelastic.

12. From the information given in the following table, construct a table like Table 3.4.

Q	0	1	2	3	4	5	6	7
P	12	11	10	9	8	7	6	5
TC	2	6	9	12	16	21	28	38

Use your table to draw a diagram like Figure 3.7. Use this diagram to show the profit-maximising output and the level of maximum profit. Confirm your findings by reference to the table you have constructed.

13. Normal profits are regarded as a cost (and are included in the cost curves). Explain why.

14. What determines the size of normal profit? Will it vary with the general state of the economy?

15. A firm will continue producing in the short run even if it is making a loss, provided it can cover its variable costs. Explain why. Just how long will it be willing to continue making such a loss?

16. The price of pocket calculators and digital watches fell significantly in the years after they were first introduced, and at the same time demand for them increased substantially. Use cost and revenue diagrams to illustrate these events. Explain the reasoning behind the diagram(s) you have drawn.

17. The table below shows the average cost and average revenue (price) for a firm at each level of output.

(a) Construct a table to show *TC*, *MC*, *TR* and *MR* at each level of output (put the figures for *MC* and *MR* midway between the output figures).
(b) Using *MC* and *MR* figures, find the profit-maximising output.
(c) Using *TC* and *TR* figures, check your answer to (b).
(d) Plot the *AC*, *MC*, *AR* and *MR* figures on a graph.
(e) Mark the profit-maximising output and the *AR* and *AC* at this output.
(f) Shade in an area to represent the level of profits at this output.

18. In February 2000, Unilever, the giant consumer products company, announced that it was to cut 25 000 jobs, close 100 plants and rely more on the Internet to purchase its supplies. It would use part of the money saved to increase promotion of its leading brands, such as Dove skin-care products, Lipton tea, Omo detergents and Calvin Klein cosmetics. The hope was to boost sales and increase profits. What was the likely effect of meeting these targets on its total costs, total revenue, average costs and average revenue? Give reasons for your answer.

Output	1	2	3	4	5	6	7	8	9	10
AC (£)	7.00	5.00	4.00	3.30	3.00	3.10	3.50	4.20	5.00	6.00
AR (£)	10.00	9.50	9.00	8.50	8.00	7.50	7.00	6.50	6.00	5.50

Additional case studies on the *Essentials of Economics* MyEconLab (www.pearsoned.co.uk/sloman)

3.1 **The legal and organisational structure of firms.** This case looks at the distinction between sole proprietorships, partnerships, private limited companies and public limited companies. It also distinguishes between U-form, M-form and H-form organisations.

3.2 **Division of labour in a pin factory.** This is the famous example of division of labour given by Adam Smith in his *Wealth of Nations* (1776).

3.3 **Diminishing returns to nitrogen fertiliser.** This case study provides a good illustration of diminishing returns in practice by showing the effects on grass yields of the application of increasing amounts of nitrogen fertiliser.

3.4 **The fallacy of using historic costs.** This looks at the example of the pricing of Christmas trees.

3.5 **Followers of fashion.** This case study examines the effects of costs on prices of fashion-sensitive goods.

3.6 **Cost curves in practice.** What do cost curves look like when fixed factors are divisible?

Sections of chapter covered in *WinEcon* – Sloman, *Essentials of Economics*

Essentials of Economics section	*WinEcon* section
3.1	3.1
3.2	3.2
3.3	Covered in 3.4
3.4	3.4

Websites relevant to this chapter

Numbers and sections refer to websites listed in the Web Appendix and hotlinked from MyEconLab. Visit:

www.pearsoned.co.uk/sloman

■ For news articles relevant to this chapter, see the *Economics News Articles* link from MyEconLab.
■ For student resources relevant to this chapter, see sites C1–7, 9, 10, 14, 19, 20.
■ For a case study examining costs, see site D2.
■ For sites that look at companies, their scale of operation and market share, see B2 (third link); E4, 10; G7, 8.
■ For links to sites on various aspects of production and costs, see section *Microeconomics* > *Production* in sites I7 and 11.

Web Appendices

3.1 **The short-run production function.** An analysis of how output varies with increases in the quantity of the variable factor used. The appendix looks at the concepts of total, average and marginal product.

3.2 **The optimum combination of factors.** This appendix examines how factors can be combined so as to minimise costs for any given output. It uses the concept of marginal product and develops the 'equi-marginal principle' developed in Web Appendix 1.1.

3.3 **Isoquant analysis.** This develops a model to show the optimum combination of factors to minimise costs for any given output or maximise output for any given cost. The analysis is similar to indifference analysis, developed in Web Appendix 1.2.

PART SEVEN

Balance of Payments, Exchange Rates and EMU

Chapter 15
International Markets
and Trade

International markets and trade

Chris Britton

The importance of international markets will vary between firms and industries but most businesses do not operate solely within national boundaries. Businesses which operate in the export market will obviously need an understanding of international markets but even the sole proprietor producing for a small local market may well use imported raw materials in the production process and so will be affected by changes that take place internationally.

Learning outcomes

Having read this chapter you should be able to:

● explain why international trade takes place

● examine the international organisations which serve to promote free trade

● outline the balance of payments position in the United Kingdom

● describe the working of the foreign exchange markets

Key terms

Balance of payments
Balance of trade
Capital account
Common agricultural policy (CAP)
Common external tariff (CET)
Common market
Current account
Current balance
Customs union
Deficit
Devaluation

European Economic Area (EEA)
European Monetary System
Exchange control
Exchange rate
Exchange Rate Mechanism (ERM)
Financial account
Fixed exchange rate
Floating exchange rate
Foreign direct investment
Free trade
Import control

Import penetration
Invisible trade
J-curve effect
Multinational enterprises
Qualitative control
Quota
Single market
Specialisation
Speculation
Subsidy
Surplus
Tariff
Visible trade

Introduction

International markets are important to most firms; even if they do not produce for the export market they may well be dependent upon raw materials which are imported and they will almost definitely be affected by movements in the exchange rate. Britain, like all other advanced industrial countries, is highly dependent upon international markets and that dependence has grown over the years. What makes international trade different from trade within a country is that the trade is taking place across national borders. Thus a system for international payments is needed. It is essential for students of business to have an understanding of international markets, exchange rates and the balance of payments.

International trade – why it takes place

Trade between countries takes place because resources are unevenly distributed through the world and the mobility of the factors of production is limited, consequently some countries are better at producing certain goods than others. Some countries could not actually produce a particular good: for example, Britain cannot produce minerals that are not indigenous or fruit that can only be grown in tropical weather conditions. If there is a demand for these goods in Britain, there are a number of possibilities: either the British could do without these goods; or an attempt could be made to grow them (in the case of the fruit) despite the climatic conditions; or Britain could buy the goods from other countries that can produce them. In other words it can trade for them.

It is easy to see that if country A can produce video cameras more cheaply than country B and B can produce wheat more cheaply than A, **specialisation** should occur and A should produce video cameras and B should produce wheat and they should trade with one another. Complete specialisation is, however, unlikely, for strategic reasons. It is also true that even if country A can produce both goods more cheaply than country B there is scope for benefits from trade. As this may not be so easy to imagine, Table 16.1 gives a numerical example. Country A can produce 100 video cameras or 100 units of wheat using 100 workers. Country B can produce 20 video cameras or 40 units of wheat with the same number of workers. Country A can therefore produce both goods at lower cost than country B. To show that even in this situation trade will benefit the world, assume that both countries produce both goods and that they each devote half of their workforce to each good.

Table 16.1 Production of video cameras and wheat

	Number of units that 100 workers can produce	
	Video cameras	Wheat
Country A	100	100
Country B	20	40

The total output of video cameras is 60 units and of wheat is 70 units. Country A is 5 times more efficient at producing video cameras than country B, but only 2.5 times more efficient than B in producing wheat (see Table 16.2). It would therefore benefit both countries if production was rearranged. If B specialised completely in wheat and A produced 35 units of wheat and 65 video cameras, world output would be as indicated in Table 16.3.

Table 16.2 Production of video cameras and wheat

	Video cameras	Wheat
Country A	50	50
Country B	10	20
	60	70

Table 16.3 Production of video cameras and wheat

	Video cameras	Wheat
Country A	65	35
Country B	0	40
	65	75

In short, world output has been increased and everyone is better off provided that trade takes place. This simplified example illustrates the basic argument for **free trade**. Free trade brings the advantages of higher world output and higher standards of living. Countries will produce the goods in which they have a cost advantage and trade with other countries for other goods. So countries can buy goods at lower prices than they could be produced for at home. Where economies of scale are present, the savings as a result of specialisation can be immense.

Theoretically, free trade brings most benefit; however, there are often restrictions to such trade and it is unlikely that complete specialisation will take place. Most countries would regard being totally dependent on another country for a particular good as a risky proposition.

Restrictions to international trade

There are a number of things that governments do to restrict international trade. These restrictions include:

- **Quotas** A physical limitation on the import of certain goods into a country, sometimes by mutual agreement (e.g. voluntary export restraints).
- **Tariffs** A tax placed on imported goods.
- **Exchange controls** A limit to the amount of a currency that can be bought, which will limit the import of goods.
- **Subsidies** Payments made to domestic producers to reduce their costs and therefore make them more competitive on world markets.

● **Qualitative controls** Controls on the quality of goods rather than on quantity or price.

All of these serve to restrict international trade, and therefore reduce specialisation on a world level. They invite retaliation and could lead to inefficiencies. **Import controls** have a wide effect on industry. The 200 per cent tariffs that the Americans threatened to impose on French cheeses and wines at the end of 1992 if the GATT talks were not successful, would have impacted on many other industries like the bottle-making industry or the insurance industry. But there are powerful arguments used in support of import controls. For example, they can be used to protect industries, whether these industries are 'infant' industries or strategic industries. In the 1999 debate within the EU on bananas, it was argued by the African, Caribbean and Pacific countries which receive preferential treatment in the EU for their bananas that the relaxation of these preferential terms might lead to the complete devastation of their economies. Import controls can also be used to improve the balance of payments position in the case where a deficit exists.

The United Kingdom is a member of a number of international organisations that serve to promote free trade and control the restrictions to free trade, like the World Trade Organisation (see Chapter 5 and the Mini case below).

mini case The World Trade talks

The 'Doha round' of trade talks was aimed at reducing world trade barriers with the specific aim of helping the developing countries. The talks started in 2001 and were due to end in 2004 but collapsed in 2003 as poorer countries refused to continue until concessions had been promised by the richer countries. Talks restarted in 2004 but stalled again in 2006 and then restarted in July 2008. This time the talks only lasted nine days before they collapsed. There are 149 countries involved in the WTO talks, which makes agreement difficult to achieve. However, there are calls for negotiations to start again as the issues are important. The World Bank estimates that the abolition of agricultural subsidies would increase global trade by $300 billion per year by 2015. Agricultural tariffs and subsidies have disastrous effects on developing countries which are highly dependent on agriculture – in Africa, for example, 70 per cent of the population is involved in agricultural production.

The WTO wants the EU to open up its markets more readily to foreign producers. For example, the EU produces sugar at three times the world price but keeps imports of sugar out of the EU with high tariffs. The EU has offered to cut tariffs on some goods (in exchange for concessions) but wants to maintain them on 'sensitive' food products. The WTO also wants the USA to reduce the subsidies it pays to its farmers. The US has offered to reduce agricultural subsidies by up to 50 per cent, again in return for concessions. Both the EU and US want increased access to non-agricultural markets in newly developing countries like India and Brazil. These countries are reluctant to do this as the reduction of trade barriers may lead to an influx of cheap manufactured goods from China.

Complete failure of the Doha talks could see the end of multilateral trade agreements and an increased reliance on bilateral trade agreements negotiated between countries. This is problematic for businesses where bilateral agreements overlap, causing difficult regulatory requirements. The real losers in this will be the developing nations; anti-poverty groups argue very strongly that increased trade is better for these countries than increased aid. If developing countries do not become self-sufficient in trade they will continue to need aid in the future.

web link   For information on the work of the World Trade Organisation see *www.wto.org*

The European Union (EU)

The EU was established in 1958 by the Treaty of Rome. The six original members, France, West Germany, Italy, Holland, Belgium and Luxembourg, were joined in 1972 by the United Kingdom, Ireland and Denmark. Greece joined in 1981, followed by Spain and Portugal in 1986 and Austria, Finland and Sweden on 1 January 1995. In 2004 ten further countries joined the EU, mainly from eastern Europe: Czech Republic, Cyprus, Estonia, Hungary, Latvia, Lithuania, Malta, Poland, Slovakia and Slovenia. In January 2007 Romania and Bulgaria were admitted. These countries, along with the former East Germany, currently constitute the 27 member states of the Union, a number which is likely to grow further by the end of the decade. Other countries which are waiting to join are Croatia and Turkey.

As a result of the enlargement of the EU, a new constitution was put forward which included changes in voting rights, the size of the EU commission and maintaining national sovereignty. The new constitution had to be ratified by all member states of the EU. The new constitution was shelved in 2005 after 'no' votes in referenda held in France and the Netherlands. In 2007 a new reform treaty was agreed by EU leaders – the Lisbon Treaty – again needing to be ratified by all 27 members of the EU. Many members ratified it through their parliaments but in Ireland, the only country to hold a public vote, the vote was against ratification of the treaty. This has caused turmoil within the EU. Some have argued that the treaty is dead (Poland has decided not to put the treaty forward for ratification because of the Irish 'no' vote) while some argue that the treaty should never have been put to a public vote at all so that the 'no' vote can be ignored. The President of the EU has vowed to solve this problem by the end of 2008 so that the treaty can be put in place in 2009.

> **web link**
>
> For information on the European commission see *http://europa.eu.int/comm/index_en.htm*
> For European statistics see *http://europa.eu.int/comm/eurostat*

The primary aim of the Treaty of Rome was to create a '**common market**' in which member states were encouraged to trade freely and to bring their economies closer together, ultimately culminating in the creation of a '**single market**' within the Union. To bring this about, a protected free trade area or '**customs union**' was established, which involved the removal of tariff barriers between member states and the institution of a **common external tariff (CET)** on goods from outside the Union. Institutional structures (see Chapter 4) and Union policies – most notably the **common agricultural policy (CAP)** – also contributed to this end and to the creation of a trading bloc of immense proportions. Within this bloc, member states were expected to gain numerous advantages, including increased trade and investment, huge economies of scale and improvements in productivity and cost reductions. To support the goal of increased trade and co-operation between community members, a **European monetary system** was established in 1979 in which a majority of member states undertook to fix their exchange rates within agreed limits (see below).

A significant step towards the creation of a single market – capable of competing effectively with the United States and Japan – was taken in 1986 when the then 12 community members signed the Single European Act. This Act established 31 December 1992 as the target date for the creation of a Single European market: an area (comprising the 12 EU countries) without internal frontiers, in which the free movement of goods, services, people and capital was to be ensured within the provisions contained in the Treaty. Among the measures for making the single market a reality were agreements on the following issues:

- the removal or reduction in obstacles to cross-border travel and trade (e.g. customs checks);
- the harmonisation or approximation of technical and safety standards on a large number of products;
- closer approximation of excise duties and other fiscal barriers (e.g. VAT);
- the removal of legal obstacles to trade (e.g. discriminatory purchasing policies);
- the mutual recognition of qualifications.

Further steps in the development of the EU came with the decision to establish a **European Economic Area (EEA)** – which permits members of the European Free Trade Area (EFTA) to benefit from many of the single market measures – and, in particular, from the Treaty on European Union, agreed by the 12 member states in December 1991 at Maastricht. Apart from the institutional changes mentioned in Chapter 4, the Maastricht Treaty contained provisions for:

- increased economic and monetary union between member states;
- a single currency;
- a social charter to protect workers' rights;
- a common foreign and security policy;
- community citizenship.

These various measures were scheduled to be introduced over a number of years, although in some cases – most notably the United Kingdom – specially negotiated 'opt-out' clauses meant that some provisions were not implemented simultaneously by all member states (e.g. the single currency; the social charter).

European monetary union was finally achieved on 1 January 1999 with the creation of the Eurozone. Eleven members of the EU were included – the UK, Denmark and Sweden chose not to participate, while Greece failed the convergence criteria for membership but has since joined in 2001. In 2007, Slovenia joined the Eurozone and in 2008 Malta and Cyprus joined, taking the total up to 15 (EU-15). The Eurozone is effectively a single economic zone since it operates with a single currency – the euro (see the text later in this chapter) and members have given up sovereignty over monetary policy, which is now determined by the European Central Bank. National sovereignty over fiscal policy has been retained, so there can be some differences in tax rates and government spending, but this is to operate in a framework of 'harmonisation'. The creation of the Eurozone enables increased specialisation across the whole of Europe and bigger economies of scale. It embraces more than 300 million people and is responsible for one-fifth of the world's output and as such comes a close second to the USA as an economic superpower.

The UK has chosen not to join the Eurozone and the single currency until a referendum has been held. In 1997 the Chancellor of the Exchequer set out five economic tests of whether the UK should join or not. These were:

1 Are business cycles and economic structures of the UK and the Eurozone compatible and *sustainable*?
2 If problems emerge, is there sufficient flexibility to deal with them?
3 Would joining EMU encourage long-term investment in the UK?
4 What impact would it have on the competitive position of the UK's financial services industry?
5 Will joining EMU promote higher growth, stability and employment?

By 2008, the debate over membership of the euro in the UK has receded from the political agenda (at least for the time being) in view of the more pressing problems encountered by the EU during the year over the new constitution and the global financial crisis.

The balance of payments

The **balance of payments** is a record of a country's international trade with other countries over a period of time, usually a year. It records the flows of money rather than goods, so that an import will be recorded as a negative amount since the money is flowing out of the country to pay for the good, and an export is recorded as a positive amount. Money flows into and out of a country for two basic reasons: first, in exchange for goods and services (current transactions), and second, for investment purposes (capital transactions). In the UK these two flows are recorded separately in the UK balance of payments accounts which are produced by the government. Since 1992, when customs posts were abolished, balance of payment figures have been collected through Intrastat and are based on VAT returns.

For information on the balance of payments in the UK see *www.statistics.gov.uk*
For information on international trade see *www.oecd.org* and *www.wto.org*

Current transactions

In the UK the **current account** records the flows of money received and paid out in exchange for goods and services. It is subdivided into **visible trade** (the import and export of goods) and **invisible trade** (the import and export of services). Invisible trade includes:

1 Services like banking, insurance, tourism.
2 Interest, profits and dividends.
3 Transfers, which include grants to developing countries, payments to international bodies like the EU and private transfers such as gifts.

The balance of these flows on visible trade is called the **balance of trade** and the balance on the current account overall is called the **current balance**. It is to one of these balances that journalists and politicians are usually referring when they talk about the balance of payments. Table 16.4 shows the balance of payments for the United Kingdom in 2007. It can be seen that the balance of trade was –£89 515 million, the invisible balance was +£29 840 million and the current balance was –£59 675 million. More will be said later about the history of the balance of payments in the United Kingdom.

Table 16.4 UK balance of payments, 2007 (£m)

Visible balance		–89 515
Invisible trade		
Services	38 331	
Current income	5 302	
Current transfers	–13 793	
Invisible trade balance		29 840
Current account balance		–59 675
Capital account balance		2 528
Financial account		
Direct investment	–20 903	
Equity capital		
Reinvested earnings		
Other capital transactions		
Portfolio investment	79 925	
Equity securities		
Debt securities		
Financial derivatives	–17 871	
Other investments	18 361	
Reserve assets	–1 191	
Net transactions on financial account		58 321
Balancing item		–1 174

Source: Adapted from *www.statistics.gov.uk/statbase/tsdataset/asp?vlink=209&more=Y.*

Capital transactions

As well as these current transactions there are flows of money for investment purposes. These include funds from both the public and private sectors and long-term and short-term monetary movements.

Long-term capital transactions include:

● Overseas investment in the United Kingdom (e.g. purchase of shares, acquisition of real assets, purchase of government securities by non-residents).
● UK private investment overseas, where UK residents buy shares, acquire real assets, and so on, in overseas countries. The capital account does not include interest, dividends or profits but only flows of money for investment purposes. A capital transaction can give rise to a current flow in the future. If a non-resident bought shares in a UK company the initial amount would appear on the capital account. The resulting flow of dividends paid in the future would be recorded as a flow on the invisible account.
● Official long-term capital (i.e. loans from the UK government to other governments).

Short-term transactions include:

- Trade credit – as goods are often not paid for as they are received the physical export and import of goods is not matched with an inflow or outflow of money. In order that the balance of payments balances, these amounts would be included here as trade credit.
- Foreign currency borrowing and lending abroad by UK banks.
- Exchange reserves held by other countries and other organisations in sterling.
- Other external banking and money market liabilities in sterling.

These capital transactions are recorded in the UK balance of payments as changes from the previous year; they are not a record of all the transactions that have taken place over time. If money is flowing into the United Kingdom for investment purposes there is an increase in the UK liabilities and these are shown as positive amounts on the balance of payments. If money is flowing out of the country there is an increase in the UK assets and these are shown as negative amounts in the balance of payments.

Until 1986, capital flows to/from the private sector and capital flows to/from the public sector were shown in two separate accounts. In 1986 the format of the balance of payments was changed to show all capital transactions in one account under the heading of 'UK transactions in external assets and liabilities'. In 1998 the format of the balance of payments was changed once more to bring it into line with the standards published in the fifth edition of the *IMF Balance of Payments Manual*. The UK balance of payments now comprises three sections:

- the current account, as before;
- the **capital account**, which records capital transfers and transfers of non-financial assets into and out of the UK. As Table 16.4 shows, the balance on this account was £2528 million in 2007;
- the **financial account**, which gives the balance of trade in financial assets. This section of the balance of payments is itself subdivided between direct investment, portfolio investment, other investments and reserve assets. The balance on the financial account for 2007 was +£58 321 million.

Speculative flows of currencies would appear in the financial account of the balance of payments. Portfolio investment is the purchasing of shares in companies while direct investment is the setting up of subsidiaries. Reserve assets shows the change in official reserves – an increase in official reserves is shown as a negative amount and a decrease is shown as a positive amount.

The balance of payments overall should balance as negative flows will be balanced by positive flows. As this is often hard to understand two examples will be given.

Example 1

If a UK resident buys foreign goods there will be a negative entry in the current account equal to the value of those goods. That individual has to pay for those goods in foreign currency and could do this by using money from a foreign currency bank account if he or she has one, or by borrowing the foreign currency from a bank in that country. Either way there is an increase in the amount of liabilities and the same amount would be shown as a positive amount in the capital account.

Example 2

If a foreign investor purchased shares in a UK company, there would be a positive amount recorded in the capital account. The investor might pay for these shares by using sterling from a sterling bank account and so there would be an equal negative amount shown in the capital account.

The balance of payments should therefore always balance but invariably fails to do so, owing to errors and omissions in the recording process, and so a balancing item is included to ensure that it does. As can be seen from Tables 16.4 and 16.5, the balancing item can be very large, and this calls into question the accuracy of the figures.

Table 16.5 UK balance of payments, 1994–2007 (£m)

	1994	1996	1998	2000	2001	2002	2003	2004	2005	2006	2007
Visible balance	−11126	−13722	−21813	−32976	−40648	−46675	−47665	−57944	−68789	−77555	−89515
Invisible balance	4358	6721	17841	8882	18257	29060	28926	32262	32804	26830	29840
Current account	−6768	−7001	−3972	−24094	−22391	−17615	−18739	−25682	−30985	−50725	−59675
Capital account	33	1260	516	1527	1206	868	1296	2073	1491	853	2528
Financial account	2126	3961	2219	24944	23816	10272	15961	27028	33954	44800	58321
Balancing item	4609	1780	1237	−2377	−2631	6475	1482	−3419	−4460	5072	−1174
Drawings on (+) or additions to (−) official reserves	−1045	510	164	−3915	3085	459	1559	−193	−656	426	−1191

Source: Adapted from *www.statistics.gov.uk/statbase/tsdataset.asp?vlink=209&more=Y.*

Equilibrium in the balance of payments

If the balance of payments always balances how can there be a deficit on the balance of payments? The answer is that the media and politicians are referring to the current balance or the balance of trade rather than the overall balance of payments position. A balance of payments surplus on the current account is where the value of exports exceeds the value of imports. A deficit is where the value of imports exceeds the value of exports. As explained above, if there is a surplus on the current account, this will be matched by an outflow in the capital account, for example a reduction in the size of sterling bank balances, or an increase in official reserves. The opposite is true for a deficit. This implies that there cannot be a balance of payments problem; however, persistent surpluses or deficits on the current account are considered to be problematic. A persistent deficit has to be financed in some way, either through borrowing, to increase the external liabilities, or by selling more of its assets. A deficit will also lead to pressure on the exchange rate, as will be shown later. A continued surplus is also a problem, since one country's surplus must mean that other countries are experiencing a deficit, and they will be faced with the problem of financing the deficit. Political pressure will be brought to bear, and there is the possibility of the introduction of tariffs or other import controls in order to reduce a deficit.

Methods of correcting balance of payments deficits

Since **surpluses** are not regarded as being such a problem as **deficits**, this section will concentrate on action needed to overcome a deficit, although the actions would be reversed for a surplus. When there is a current account deficit, the out-flow of funds is greater than the inflow of funds from international trade. The authorities need to increase exports and/or reduce imports. Thus:

1 A fall in the exchange rate will have the double effect of making exports cheaper abroad and imports dearer at home, thus encouraging exports and discouraging imports. This will be explained fully later.
2 To increase exports British companies that produce for the export market could be subsidised. This would have the effect of reducing the price of UK goods abroad, making them more competitive.
3 Import controls could be imposed to restrict the level of imports coming in to the country.
4 A rise in the rate of interest would make Britain more attractive to investors and therefore increase capital flows into Britain and help offset the current account deficit.

The history of the balance of payments in the United Kingdom

Table 16.5 gives a summary of the balance of payments in the United Kingdom between 1994 and 2007. The table shows that the current account was in deficit for the whole period. The weaknesses on the current account pre-date this and are somewhat hidden in the overall figures. The current account deficits started in 1987, the visible balance has been in deficit since 1983 (and still is) and within this the non-oil balance has been in deficit since 1982. This did not show in the overall current account figures until 1987 because of the offsetting effect of invisibles and oil. The United Kingdom's underlying weaknesses on the current account come from several sources:

1 Exports have risen but imports have risen faster. In the United Kingdom there is a high propensity to import goods.
2 The collapse of oil prices during the 1990s reduced the value of the United Kingdom's oil exports.
3 The recession of the early 1980s left the UK manufacturing base in an extremely weak position. This meant that it was difficult to produce enough goods for export or even to meet domestic demand, so the balance of payments was hit from both directions. The changes in the structure of industry in the United Kingdom described in Chapter 12 have implications for the balance of payments, as services are less exportable than goods.
4 The consumer booms that occurred in the late 1980s and in the late 1990s led to increases in the level of imports.

5 The impact of oil has been twofold. First, as the United Kingdom is now an oil-exporting country it brings in revenue which helps to improve the balance of payments. Second, it has tended to keep the exchange rate higher than it would have been, as will be shown in the next section, which makes UK goods less competitive in world markets and will therefore lead to a worsening of the balance of payments.

6 The high value of the pound in the late 1990s hit the UK's export market.

7 The most recent deterioration is due to a fall in the level of non-European exports, especially to Asia and Russia.

Figure 16.1 shows the breakdown of the current account between visibles and invisibles and it is clear that good performance on invisibles has partly offset poor performance in visibles.

Figure 16.1 Components of the current account, UK, 1991–2007

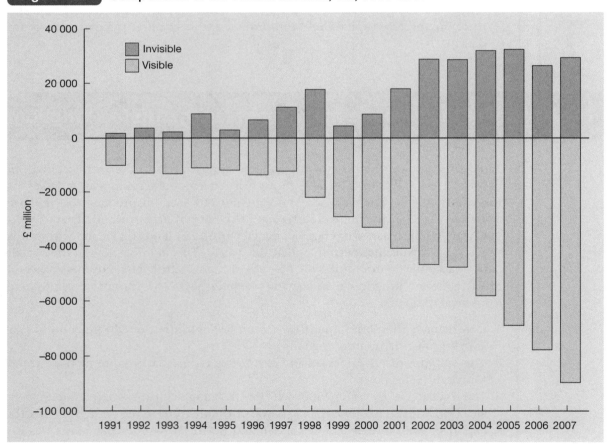

Source: Adapted from *www.statistics.gov.uk/statbase/tsdataset.asp?vlink=209&more=Y.*

mini case   The current account of the balance of payments

Figures on the balance of payments are produced every month by the government in the UK and are often seized upon by commentators as indications of either an improvement in the UK's economic performance or a deterioration, depending upon the details of the figures. There are a number of reasons why their observation is incorrect. First, balance of payments figures are notoriously unreliable, and are often revised by very large amounts. In June 1996, for example, the estimated deficit on the balance of payments for 1995 was revised from £6.7 billion to £2.9 billion because of the discovery of large investment flows. Second – and this applies to all short-term economic indicators – there are very short-term changes in economic variables which are not translated into long-term trends. So the balance of payments can vary quite dramatically each month due to short-term factors which are evened out over the course of the year. In addition, the balance of payments, like other indicators, often does not behave as expected.

Figure 16.2 shows the UK current balance for the period 1970 to 2007. Two points can immediately be made about the behaviour of the balance of payments. First, the data move in a cyclical way and are therefore affected by the trade cycle. Second, the balance of payments generally improves in times of recession (e.g. the early 1980s and early 1990s) and worsens in times of boom. The reasons for this are twofold – in a recession the level of imports falls as income falls and the level of exports is unlikely to fall unless other countries are experiencing the same level of economic downturn. The balance of payments therefore improves. Usually the balance of payments improves enough in a recession to push it into surplus, although this did not happen in the early 1990s when the UK's current account remained in the red.

The unpredictability of the balance of payments is very evident in the figures for the 1990s. In 1994 the balance of payments improved, despite the recovery in economic conditions which would have

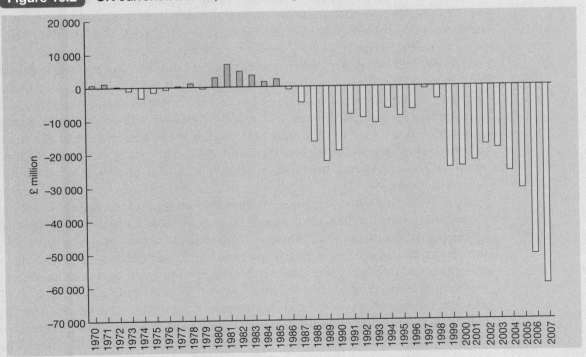

Figure 16.2   UK current balance, 1970–2007 (£ million)

Source: Adapted from *www.statistics.gov.uk/statbase/tsdataset.asp?vlink=209&more=Y.*

been expected to worsen the balance of payments. This improvement continued in the late 1990s despite economic conditions which implied the opposite. The balance of payments should have suffered as a result of the high value of the pound and the economic turmoil in Asia and Russia. One possible explanation for the apparently contrary behaviour of the balance of payments is the J-curve effect (see Figure 16.7). It could be that the improvement in the balance of payments in the mid-1990s was caused by the fall in the value of the pound after the UK left the ERM, even though that happened in 1992, because of the time lags involved. Similarly, the effects of the high value of the pound were not evident until 1999 onwards.

The deficit on the balance of payments in the UK in the last quarter of 2001 was the worst ever, mainly due to the global economic downturn after September 11. The two main contributors were the collapse in investment income abroad and the increase in direct payments to the EU. Commentators were surprised at the speed with which the balance of payments had been affected, although the UK was not as badly affected as other countries. The balance of payments did recover in 2002–2003 but the deficit deepened in 2004–2007. There are two main reasons for the high deficits seen in this period: UK banks are paying higher interest to foreign banks and UK consumers are borrowing heavily to buy imported products.

The multitude of factors which impact upon the balance of payments and the difficulties involved in accurate data collection make the balance of payments figures unreliable and very difficult to predict. The use of one month's figures by commentators to prove either that recovery is under way or that a recession is imminent is unsound.

Patterns of trade

Over time, patterns of trade change, for many reasons, Table 16.6 shows UK patterns of trade by destination/source and Table 16.7 shows UK trade by type of good. From these tables it is possible to look at how the country's patterns of trade have changed.

The most obvious change, as can be seen in Table 16.6, is that trade with the EU has become more important over the last 30 years while trade with the rest of western Europe has declined. In 2007 55 per cent of Britain's imports came from the EU and 60 per cent of exports went to the EU. Despite this, the USA remains important to Britain. There has been a decline in Britain's trade with other OECD countries over the whole period, although the importance of Japan within that group has increased, particularly with respect to imports. Britain's trade with the oil-exporting countries has declined in importance, as too has trade with the rest of the world, although this increased between 1990 and 2007. The rest of the world includes many of the old Commonwealth countries, which at one time were Britain's biggest markets.

Since 1970 the United Kingdom has been importing less food and fewer animals for consumption. The impact of oil can be seen in Table 16.7, as the quantities of oil-related products imported into the United Kingdom have generally fallen over the period. Manufacturing is clearly the most important category of good as far as the balance of payments is concerned. Manufacturing has retained its importance for exports, accounting for 76 per cent of exports in 1970 and 62 per cent in 2007. As far as imports are concerned, the percentage has increased a great deal over the last 30 years. The United Kingdom is now a net importer of manufactured goods. In 2007 the value of imported manufactured goods was £203 836 million, whereas the value of exported manufactured goods was £138 716 million. One reason for this is

Table 16.6 UK's imports and exports of goods by destination/source (%)

	1970		1980		1990		2003		2007	
	Exports	Imports	Exports	Imports	Exports	Imports	Exports	Imports	Exports	Imports
European Union	32	32	46	44	53	52	59	58	60	55
Other W. Europe	13	12	12	12	9	13	4	6	4	8
United States	12	11	10	12	13	11	18	12	15	8
Other OECD countries, of which Japan	11	10	6	7	5	7	4	6	6	7
which Japan	2	2	1	4	2	6	2	3	2	3
Oil-exporting countries	6	11	10	9	6	2	4	2	4	2
Rest of the world	18	14	12	11	10	10	12	18	13	21

Source: Adapted from Tables 19.5, 19.6, *Annual Abstract of Statistics*, various, ONS, UK.

Table 16.7 Pattern of trade by type of good (%)

	1970		1990		2003		2007	
	Exports	Imports	Exports	Imports	Exports	Imports	Exports	Imports
Food and animals	3	20	4	8	3	7	4	7
Beverages and tobacco	3	2	3	1	2	2	2	2
Crude materials except fuels	3	12	2	5	2	2	2	3
Minerals, fuels	3	14	8	7	9	5	11	10
Chemicals and related products	9	6	13	9	17	11	18	11
Manufactured goods	24	20	15	17	12	13	13	13
Machinery	43	19	41	38	42	43	37	38
Miscellaneous manufacturing	9	7	13	15	12	16	12	16
Total manufacturing	76	46	69	70	67	72	62	67
Others	3	2	2	1	1	1	1	1

Source: Adapted from Tables 19.4, 19.3, *Annual Abstract of Statistics*, various, ONS, UK.

the increased import penetration in the United Kingdom. Table 16.8 shows import penetration in UK manufacturing for 1970, 1980, 1990, 1994, 1996, 2003 and 2005 from which it can be seen that the penetration has increased over this time period.

Table 16.8 Import penetration[a] in manufacturing in UK (%)

1970	1980	1990	1994	1996	2003	2005
16.6	26.2	36.7	50[b]	56	60	62

Notes: [a]Measured as $\frac{\text{import value}}{\text{home demand}} \times 100$

[b]New SIC definition.

Source: *Annual Abstract of Statistics*, 1972, 1982, 1992, 1996, 1999, 2005, 2008.
Crown copyright. Reproduced by permission of the Controller of HMSO and of the Office for National Statistics, UK.

In 2007, the percentage of Britain's trade with the rest of the world stood at a similar level to that in 1970 but the percentages were reversed, with the country exporting less to the rest of the world and importing more. For 2007, China accounted for 6 per cent of the rest of the world total imports.

Exchange rates

The **exchange rate** of a currency is the price of that currency in terms of other currencies. If each country has its own currency and international trade is to take place an exchange of currencies needs to occur. When a UK resident buys goods from France, these must be paid for in euros. The individual will probably purchase euros from a bank in exchange for sterling in order to carry out the transaction. There must therefore be an exchange rate between sterling and euros. Likewise there will be exchange rates between sterling and all other currencies.

Basically, there are two types of exchange rate: the **floating exchange rate**; and the **fixed exchange rate**. There are also hybrid exchange rate systems which combine the characteristics of the two main types.

The floating exchange rate

A floating exchange rate is one that is determined within a free market, where there is no government intervention, and the exchange rate is free to fluctuate according to market conditions. The exchange rate is determined by the demand for and the supply of the currency in question.

As far as sterling is concerned, the demand for the currency comes from exports – that is, overseas residents buying pounds either to buy British goods and services or for investment purposes. The supply of pounds comes from imports – that is, UK residents who are buying foreign currencies to purchase goods and services or for investment purposes and who are therefore at the same time supplying pounds to the market.

The market for sterling can then be drawn using simple demand and supply diagrams. In Figure 16.3, the price axis shows the price of £1 in terms of US dollars and the quantity axis shows the quantity of pounds being bought and sold. The equilibrium exchange rate is determined by the intersection of demand and supply at £1 = $2. As this is a totally free market, if any of the conditions in the market change the exchange rate will also change.

Figure 16.3   The determination of the exchange rate of £ for $

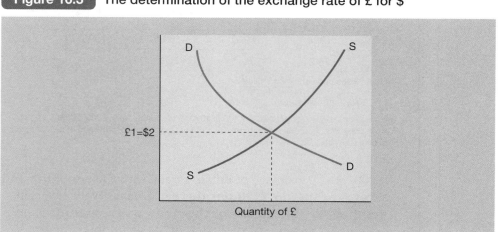

The demand for and supply of sterling, and therefore the exchange rate, is affected by:

1 Changes in the balance of payments.
2 Changes in investment flows.
3 Speculation in the foreign exchange markets.

Changes in the balance of payments

Figure 16.4 shows the effect on the exchange rate of changes in the balance of payments. The original demand curve is DD and the original supply curve is SS. At the equilibrium exchange rate of £1 = $2 the demand for pounds is equal to the supply of pounds. In other words, if the demand for pounds comes from exports and the supply of pounds comes from imports, imports and exports are equal and the balance of payments is in equilibrium. Now it is assumed that a balance of payments deficit appears, caused by the level of imports rising while the level of exports stays the same. If exports remain the same there will be no change in the demand curve for pounds. As imports rise there will be a rise in the supply of pounds to the market; the supply curve moves to the right to S^1S^1. At the old exchange rate of £1 = $2, there is now excess supply of pounds, and as this is a free market there will be downward pressure on the value of the pound until equilibrium is re-established at the new lower exchange rate of £1 = $1. At this exchange rate the demand for pounds is again equal to the increased supply of pounds and the balance between imports and exports is re-established.

How does this happen? When the value of the pound falls two things happen: the price of imports rises and the price of exports falls. Thus the level of imports falls and the level of exports rises and the deficit is eradicated. A simple numerical example illustrates this point:

At old exchange rate £1 = $2:

An American car which costs $20000 in USA costs £10000 in UK.
A British car which costs £10000 in UK costs $20000 in USA.

Figure 16.4   The effect of changes in the balance of payments on the exchange rate

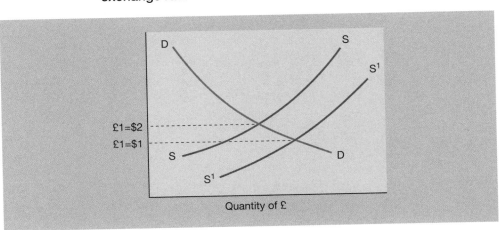

If the exchange rate falls to £1 = $1:

> The American car still costs $20 000 in USA but now costs £20 000 in UK.
> The British car still costs £10 000 in UK but now costs $10 000 in USA.

Therefore a depreciation in the exchange rate has made imports dearer (the American car) and exports cheaper (the British car). Thus a fall in the value of the pound helps to re-establish equilibrium in the balance of payments.

In the case of a surplus on the balance of payments, the exchange rate will rise, making exports more expensive and imports cheaper and thereby re-establishing equilibrium in the balance of payments. You should test your understanding of the working of the foreign exchange markets by working through what happens if a surplus develops.

A fall in the value of the pound in a free market is called a 'depreciation' in the value of the pound, a rise in its value is called an 'appreciation'.

Changes in investment flows

In Figure 16.5, the original equilibrium exchange rate is £1 = $2. If there is an increase in the level of investment in the UK from overseas, there will be an increase in the demand for pounds. The demand curve moves to the right (to D^1D^1), and the exchange rate rises to £1 = $2.5.

The effect of speculation

If the exchange rate of sterling is expected to rise, **speculators** will buy sterling in order to make a capital gain by selling the currency later at a higher exchange rate. There will be an increase in the demand for pounds and the exchange rate will rise. If the exchange rate is expected to fall, speculators will sell sterling in order to avoid a capital loss, there will be an increase in the supply of sterling and therefore a fall in the exchange rate. Illustrate these changes yourself using demand and supply diagrams.

Figure 16.5 The effect of changes in the investment flows on the exchange rate

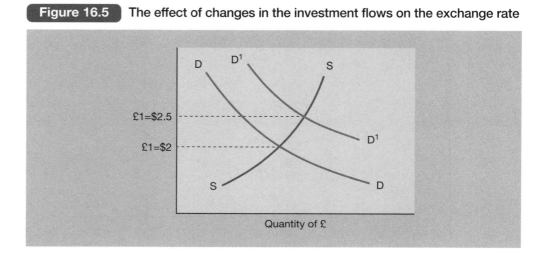

The important thing about speculation is that it tends to be self-fulfilling. If enough people believe that the exchange rate is going to rise and act accordingly, the exchange rate will rise.

The main advantage of the floating exchange rate is the automatic mechanism it provides to overcome a balance of payments deficit or surplus. Theoretically, if a deficit develops, the exchange rate will fall and the balance of payments is brought back into equilibrium. The opposite occurs in the case of a surplus. Of course in reality it does not work as smoothly or as quickly as the theory suggests. A depreciation is supposed to work as demonstrated in Figure 16.6.

There are, however, a number of problems which may occur to prevent this self-correcting mechanism working properly. First, if in the United Kingdom the goods which are imported are necessities that cannot be produced at home, then even if their price goes up as a result of a depreciation, they will continue to be demanded. Thus, not only will the balance of payments deficit not be automatically rectified, another economic problem will result, that of inflation. The United Kingdom will continue to buy the imported goods at the new higher price. A second problem occurs on the other side of the equation. It is assumed above that, as the price of exports falls, more exports are sold. This presupposes that in the United Kingdom the capacity is there to meet this increased demand, but this may not be the case, especially if the economy is fully employed already or if the export-producing industries are not in a healthy enough state to produce more.

These problems give rise to what is called the '**J-curve effect**'. A fall in the exchange rate may well lead to a deterioration in the balance of payments in the short term, until domestic production can be increased to meet the extra demand for exports and as substitutes for imported goods. Once this can be done there will be an improvement in the balance of payments, hence the J-curve effect pictured in

Figure 16.6   The effect of depreciation

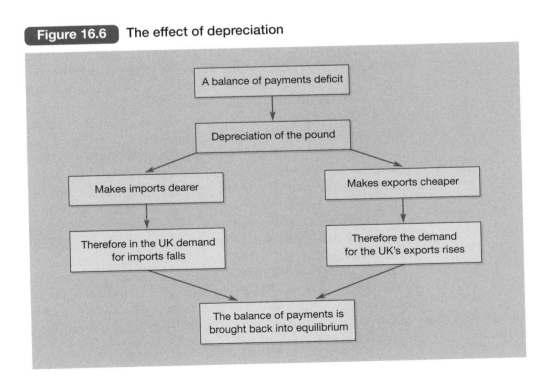

Figure 16.7. The effect of a fall in the exchange rate is limited and the curve levels off after a certain time period. The depreciation in the value of the pound seen when Britain left the ERM did not have an immediate effect on the balance of payments and many argued that this was due to the J-curve effect.

One big disadvantage of the floating exchange rate is that it introduces uncertainty into the market, and for firms that operate internationally, this is another variable which needs to be considered when planning. Moreover, since the possibility of speculation exists with the floating exchange rate, this can be destabilising and unsettling to markets, something which businesses do not welcome.

Figure 16.7   J-curve

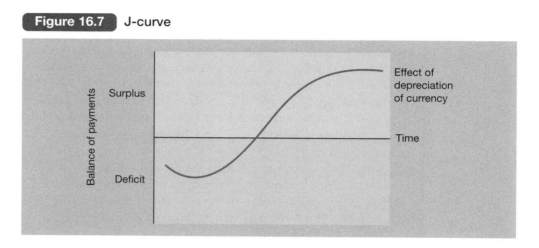

The fixed exchange rate

The fixed exchange rate is one that is fixed and maintained by the government. An exchange rate can be fixed in terms of other currencies, gold or a basket of other currencies. In order to maintain a fixed exchange rate the government has actively to intervene in the market, either buying or selling currencies.

Figure 16.8 shows the action needed by the UK authorities in the case of downward pressure on the value of the pound. The exchange rate is fixed at £1 = $2, and the government wants to maintain that rate. If a balance of payments deficit develops, brought about by an increase in imports, exports remaining the same, there will be excess supply of pounds at the fixed exchange rate. In a free market the value of the pound would fall until the excess supply had disappeared. However, this is not a free market, and the government must buy up the excess supply of pounds in order to maintain the exchange rate at £1 = $2. Thus the demand curve moves to the right and the exchange rate has been maintained at the same level. Alternatively if there is excess demand for pounds, the government has to supply pounds to the market in order to maintain the fixed exchange rate.

A prime advantage of a fixed exchange rate is that there is less uncertainty in the market; everyone knows what the exchange rate will be in a year's time, and long-term planning is made easier. It also reduces the likelihood of speculation in the foreign exchange markets. One serious disadvantage, however, is that there is no longer an automatic mechanism for rectifying any balance of payments problems

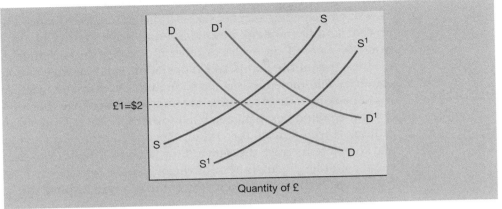

Figure 16.8 The effect of changes in the balance of payments on a fixed exchange rate

as there is in the case of the floating exchange rate and this means that government intervention is necessary not just to support the exchange rate, but also to overcome any balance of payments problems. Added to this, a fixed exchange rate is not sustainable in the case of persistent deficits or surpluses. In the event of a surplus, the government must supply pounds to the market and if the surplus persists then eventually the government will exhaust its reserves and might well have to revalue the pound (i.e. increase the exchange rate of the pound). In the case of a persistent deficit, the size of the government's reserves will be increasing over time and the government may have to **devalue** the pound to correct the problem.

There are, then, advantages and disadvantages to both types of exchange rate and there have been hybrid exchange rate systems which serve to combine the advantages of both systems. In such an exchange rate system the exchange rate is basically fixed but is allowed to fluctuate by a small amount either side of the central value. The **Exchange Rate Mechanism (ERM)** of the European Union was an example of this. When the United Kingdom entered the ERM the exchange rate was fixed against other member currencies but allowed to vary by 6 per cent either side of the central value before action was needed.

Over the years the United Kingdom has had a variety of different types of exchange rate. Before the First World War and for some time between the wars, the exchange rate was fixed in terms of gold – the gold standard. From the Second World War until 1972, the United Kingdom was part of the Bretton Woods system of fixed exchange rates, where the pound was fixed in terms of dollars. Then from 1972 to 1990, there was a floating exchange rate. In 1990, however, Britain joined the Exchange Rate Mechanism of the European Union, which was again a fixed exchange rate. In September 1992, the pound left the ERM and was allowed to float once more.

The Exchange Rate Mechanism

In October 1990, the United Kingdom joined the ERM, which was a system of fixed exchange rates. The currencies within the ERM were fixed against the European currency unit (ECU) and were therefore fixed against one another. Exchange rates were allowed to fluctuate by a small percentage around their par values. The ECU was a weighted basket of EU currencies, designed to act as a unit of account and eventually as an international currency.

The essence of the ERM was that it provided a means of stabilising the exchange rates of participating member states. If the pound, for instance, strayed too far from its central rate the Bank of England and other central banks of ERM members would buy or sell currencies in order to stabilise the exchange rate. Each member held reserves in the European Co-operation Fund in order to settle debts between countries, and these funds could be used to stabilise currencies. Another thing that could be done to help an ailing currency was to change the domestic rate of interest. If the pound's exchange rate fell towards its lower limit, an increase in the rate of interest would make the United Kingdom a more attractive place for investors and therefore increase the demand for pounds. If both of these approaches failed, there could be a realignment of the currencies within the ERM. This happened from time to time, but such realignments were against the spirit of the fixed exchange rate, and countries were expected to avoid this if possible.

Britain's reasons for entering the ERM in 1990 were as follows:

● To enjoy the benefits of fixed exchange rates and, in particular, less uncertainty and reduced speculation.
● As part of the government's anti-inflationary stance, since the discipline of the ERM would force the United Kingdom's rate of inflation towards the lower European average.
● As part of Britain's commitment to Europe, the Maastricht Treaty and the Delors plan called for economic and monetary union between the countries of the EU.

Figure 16.9 shows the fluctuations in sterling's exchange rate after joining the ERM. The exchange rate of the pound was much more stable while the UK was a member

Figure 16.9   **Exchange rate of sterling with the Deutschmark**

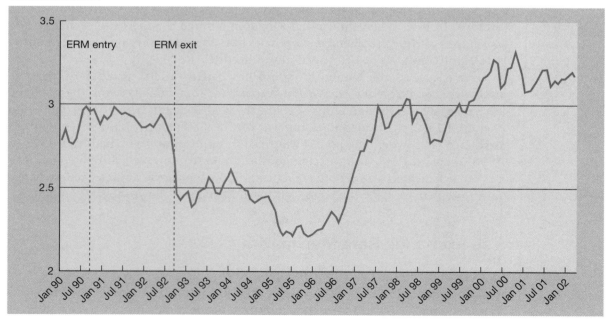

Source: Adapted from *www.statistics.gov.uk/statbase/tsdataset.asp?vlink=210&more=Y.*

of the ERM, but sterling ran into problems in mid-1992, mainly as a result of speculation against the pound. The Bank of England intervened in the market but was unable to stop the fall in the value of the currency. An increase in interest rates was announced but then withdrawn very quickly because of political pressures and the effect such a move would have on UK industry in the midst of recession. In the end the pound was suspended from the ERM and allowed to float, and subsequently fell in value sharply.

 For information on exchange rates see *www.bankofengland.co.uk*

The single European currency

On 1 January 1999 the single European currency – the euro – was introduced. In order to qualify for membership of the single currency, EU members had to fulfil strict convergence criteria with respect to inflation rates, budget deficits and the rates of interest.[1] In the end all countries qualified except Greece, where there were problems with high inflation rates. The UK, Denmark and Sweden decided not to join the single currency while Greece, Slovenia, Malta and Cyprus have since joined. Each of the currencies of these 15 members is fixed to the euro at a specified rate, but each is a sub-unit of the euro rather than a separate currency.

Even though the UK has not joined the single currency, many businesses in the UK have already adapted to its existence. Many large companies use the euro for accounting purposes – Marks & Spencer stores are fully equipped to accept the euro. Even without entry, preparation is necessary for practical reasons, since many large companies have started to invoice and pay bills in euros – computer systems will have to be adapted to allow for this. There will also be a cost involved in the UK as banks are charging fairly high commission for converting euros, particularly for small users. Preparation is also a strategic issue for business. First, EMU will result in greater competition, as price differences will be more obvious to consumers. The cost of converting currencies serves to increase the costs of UK businesses and make them less competitive. Second, EMU will probably result in more mergers and acquisitions across Europe and this will have dramatic effects on the structures of industries.

In the UK the debate over the single European currency continues, although as previously noted this issue has been pushed into the background by other problems. The pro single currency camp claims that the UK will be further marginalised in Europe if it does not join in the single currency. It also argues that there are great benefits to membership – a reduction in transaction costs like the cost of currency exchange, a reduction in the uncertainty caused by changing exchange rates, lower interest rates and the continuance of London as a financial centre in currencies. The anti camp argues just as vociferously that all of this would be at the expense of the loss of sovereignty – the UK would be unable to change its exchange rate in order to boost the competitiveness of UK goods. The performance of the euro since its birth has been variable. Figure 16.10 shows the value of the euro against sterling since January 1999 when €1 was worth 70p. In June 2008 one euro was worth 79p in the UK.

Figure 16.10 Exchange rate of the euro with sterling

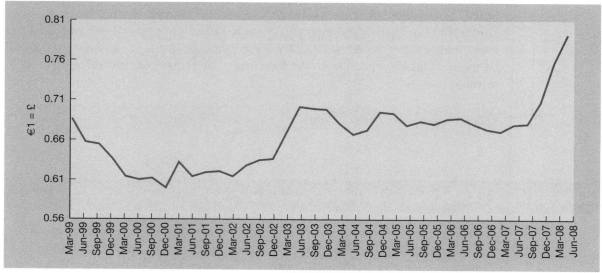

Source: Adapted from *www.bankofengland.co.uk*.

There are a number of problems brewing in Europe. First, there are the problems associated with the lack of agreement on the new constitution which have already been discussed. Second, it seems that the imposition of a single interest rate across Europe has caused problems as some countries are growing and could bear a higher rate of interest while others are in recession and therefore could not. Third, member countries have to act to reduce the size of their budget deficit if it exceeds 3 per cent of GDP. Again this might be acceptable in a booming economy but not in an economy heading for recession. At the end of 2008 there is not much evidence of economic convergence and there is a strong anti-euro feeling in parts of the EU.

Exchange rates and business

Reference has already been made to the fact that changes in exchange rates can affect businesses in several ways. These would include:

● making it easier or harder to export (as prices change);
● making it easier or harder for foreign competitors to penetrate the domestic market (again through the price effect);
● causing uncertainty in both trading and investment terms;
● adding to or reducing the cost of imported raw materials and component parts.

In addition, if a falling exchange rate causes inflationary pressures within the economy, this could add to a firm's production costs (e.g. through higher wage bills) and could encourage the government to introduce counter-inflationary policies which might subsequently depress demand in the home market.

For businesses regularly involved in currency dealing and/or multinational activities, changing currency values can also bring other gains or losses. Shell and Allied Lyons, for example, lost over £100 million each on currency gambles in the early 1990s by entering into deals when the exchange rate between currencies was not fixed in advance. In contrast, Unilever's record profits for the financial year 1992/93 included substantial overseas earnings, some of which were the direct result of a weaker pound, which in turn meant that remitted profits increased when converted back into sterling. Clearly the introduction of a single European currency will impact upon such gains or losses.

Synopsis

This chapter has looked at the international marketplace and, in particular, the benefits that derive from international trade. Consideration has also been given to some of the restrictions that exist to free trade and the organisations that are active in promoting it. Patterns of trade in the United Kingdom have been examined, as well as a recent history of the balance of payments position. Exchange rates were covered, including an analysis of how businesses are affected by changes in the value of currencies.

Summary of key points

- International trade takes place because it increases the output of the whole world.

- Despite this there are restrictions to international trade which include tariffs and quotas, but there are international organisations which seek to limit these and promote free trade.

- The balance of payments is a record of one country's trade with other countries.

- A balance of payments deficit is a situation where imports are greater than exports, a balance of payments surplus is the opposite, where exports are greater than imports.

- The exchange rate is the price of one currency in terms of another.

- A floating exchange rate is determined by the free market, a fixed exchange rate is determined by the government or some other authority.

- The euro is a single currency introduced into circulation in January 2002 by the members of the Eurozone.

case study   Enlargement of the European Union

The European Union has gone through five enlargements, increasing its initial membership of 6 countries in 1957 to 27 members in 2008. The reasons for the establishment of the EU are well documented in this chapter and they provide the rationale for the enlargement of the EU. EU-27 covers an area of 4 million km² and a population of 493 million people. In population size it is the third largest after China and India. Its trade with the rest of the world accounts for 20 per cent of global trade and trade between members accounts for two-thirds of all EU trade. Figure 16.11 shows current membership of the EU and candidates for membership.

Figure 16.11   A map of Europe

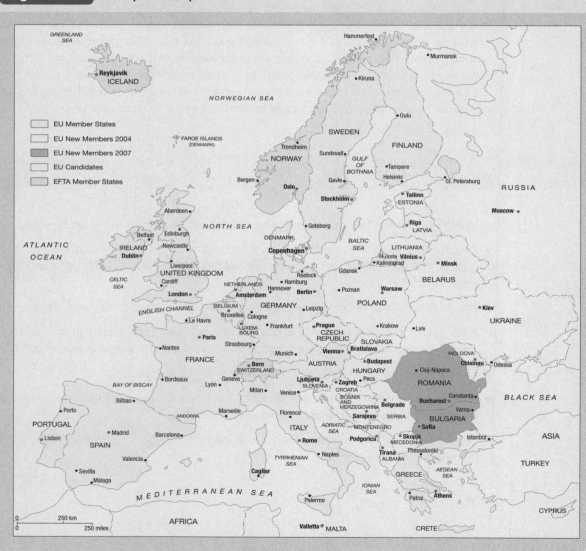

The benefits arising from the enlargement of the EU include:

1 *Political stability* – expansion of the EU gives European leaders the chance to bring political stability to Europe and end the divisions which twice last century ended in war. Membership of the EU should help to entrench the new-found democracies of the former communist countries in eastern Europe. In addition, the size of the EU makes possible a concerted and joint response to the severe financial problems currently facing the world.

2 *Economic benefits* – the fifth enlargement of the EU increased the size of the population of the EU by about 30 per cent. This enhanced the EU position as a major trading bloc in the world. At the time of the last two enlargements, the new members had growing economies which extended the market size for existing members and the potential growth of the EU.

EU candidates

In 2008 there were three candidate countries – Turkey, Croatia and the Former Yugoslav Republic of Macedonia. The first two of these are in accession negotiations to join the EU while the last has not yet reached that stage. Other Balkan countries – Albania, Bosnia and Herzegovina, Montenegro, Serbia and Kosovo – are potential candidates countries. Table 16.9 gives some basic information on the three candidates.

The accession of these countries will expand the population of the EU by a further 16 per cent. The GDPs are all significantly lower than the EU-27 average but this was also true for the two newest members of the EU – Bulgaria and Romania. This should not then be an impediment to accession but there are other factors which need to be taken into account. There is the impact on the EU budget as the accession of poorer countries with large agricultural sectors has implications for both regional aid and the Common Agricultural Policy budget which together account for around 80 per cent of the EU's budget. The feeling among existing members (particularly the older members) is not as positive as it was at the time of the last two accessions, largely because of the effects of the credit crunch and the perceived loss of jobs to the poorer members of the EU. In addition to this there is the problem of relations with Russia (especially important to the Baltic states) and in the case of the Former Yugoslav Republic of Macedonia, Greek objection to the country's name. Most commentators expect further expansion to happen more slowly in the future, not least because EU treaties need to be amended to accommodate additional members.

Case study questions

1 What are the main economic benefits to *existing* members of enlarging the EU?

2 What are the main economic benefits to the *applicants* of joining the EU?

Table 16.9 Population and GDP per capita for EU candidate countries

Country	Population size (million)	GDP per capita as a % of EU-27 average
Turkey	72.5	29
Croatia	4.4	27
Former Yugoslav Republic of Macedonia	2	50

Source: Eurostat, 2008.

Review and discussion questions

1 For a business considering expansion into Europe, what methods of expansion are available?

2 Using demand and supply diagrams, show the effect on the market for foreign exchange of the following:
(a) a decreased level of imports;
(b) a fall in the rate of interest; and
(c) the development of a balance of payments surplus.

3 What is the likely effect on a system of fixed exchange rates of continued speculation in one of the member currencies?

4 Explain why businesses generally prefer fixed rather than floating rates of exchange.

5 How might the US government help its ailing steel industry without resorting to trade sanctions?

Assignments

1 You work in a local chamber of commerce and have been asked to make a presentation to its members on the arguments for and against UK membership of the single European currency. The audience is likely to be mixed in its attitude to the single European currency. Prepare the presentation, anticipating and answering any possible questions the audience might have.

2 You work for a trade union in the hosiery industry which strongly supports the use of import restrictions to protect its workers from competition from countries where wage rates are much lower. You have been asked to take part in a debate on the issue by the local Conservative MP, who is a champion of the free market. Present a set of arguments that will counter any points that your opponent is likely to make.

Notes and references

1   See the 2nd edition of this book, Chapter 13.

Further reading

Ellis, J. and Williams, D., *International Business Strategy*, Pitman Publishing, 1995.

Griffiths, A. and Wall, S., *Applied Economics,* 10th edition, Financial Times/Prentice Hall, 2004.

Worthington, I., Britton, C. and Rees, A., *Business Economics: Blending Theory and Practice*, 2nd edition, Financial Times/Prentice Hall, 2005.

Web links and further questions are available on the website at:

www.pearsoned.co.uk/worthington

Chapter 16

Balance of Payments and Exchange Rates

Balance of payments and exchange rates

In this chapter we will first explain what is meant by the balance of payments. In doing so we will see just how the various monetary transactions between the domestic economy and the rest of the world are recorded.

Then (in Sections 12.2 and 12.3) we will examine how rates of exchange are determined, and how they are related to the balance of payments. We will see what causes exchange rate fluctuations, and how the government can attempt to prevent these fluctuations.

A government could decide to leave its country's exchange rates entirely to market forces (a free-floating exchange rate). Alternatively, it could attempt to fix its currency's exchange rate to some other currency (e.g. the US dollar). Or it could simply try to reduce the degree to which its currency fluctuates. In Section 12.4, we look at the relative merits of different degrees of government intervention in the foreign exchange market: of different 'exchange rate regimes'.

We then turn to look at attempts to achieve greater currency stability between the members of the EU. Section 12.5 looks at the European exchange rate mechanism, which sought in the 1980s and 1990s to limit the amount that member currencies were allowed to fluctuate against each other. Then Section 12.6 examines the euro. Has the adoption of a single currency by twelve EU countries been of benefit to them? Would it benefit the UK to join?

We then take a global perspective. We ask whether an expansion of global trade and a closer integration of the economies of the world has led to greater or less stability. Finally, as with Chapter 11, we look at the position of developing countries, and in particular focus on the issue of debt. Why are so many developing countries facing severe debt problems and what can be done about it?

After studying this chapter, you should be able to answer the following questions:

- What is meant by 'the balance of payments' and how do trade and financial movements affect it?
- How are exchange rates determined and what effects do changes in the exchange rate have on the economy?
- How do governments and/or central banks seek to influence the exchange rate and what are the advantages and disadvantages of such intervention?
- How do the major economies of the world seek to co-ordinate their policies and what difficulties arise in the process?
- What are the advantages and disadvantages of the euro for member countries?
- What are the origins of the severe debt problem faced by many developing countries? What can be done about the problem?

12.1   THE BALANCE OF PAYMENTS ACCOUNT

What is meant by a balance of payments deficit or surplus?

In Chapter 7 we identified balance of payments deficits as one of the main macro-economic problems that governments face. But what precisely do we mean by 'balance of payments deficits' (or surpluses), and what is their significance?

A country's balance of payments account records all the flows of money between residents of that country and the rest of the world. *Receipts* of money from abroad are regarded as credits and are entered in the accounts with a positive sign. *Outflows* of money from the country are regarded as debits and are entered with a negative sign.

There are three main parts of the balance of payments account: the *current account*, the *capital account* and the *financial account*. Each part is then subdivided. We shall look at each part in turn, and take the UK as an example. Table 12.1 gives a summary of the UK balance of payments for 2005.

The current account

The **current account** records payments for imports and exports of goods and services, plus incomes flowing into and out of the country, plus net transfers of money into and out of the country. It is normally divided into four subdivisions.

The trade in goods account.   This records imports and exports of physical goods (previously known as 'visibles'). Exports result in an inflow of money and are therefore a credit item. Imports result in an outflow of money and are therefore a debit item. The balance of these is called the **balance on trade in goods or balance of visible trade or merchandise balance**. A *surplus* is when exports exceed imports. A deficit is when imports exceed exports.

The trade in services account.   This records imports and exports of services (such as transport, tourism and insurance). Thus the purchase of a foreign holiday would be a debit, since it represents an outflow of money, whereas the purchase by an overseas resident of a UK insurance policy would be a credit to the UK services account. The balance of these is called the **services balance**.

The balance of both the goods and services accounts together is known as the **balance on trade in goods and services** or simply the **balance of trade**.

Income flows.   These consist of wages, interest and profits flowing into and out of the country. For example, dividends earned by a foreign resident from shares in a UK company would be an outflow of money (a debit item).

Current transfers of money.   These include government contributions to and receipts from the EU and international organisations, and international transfers of money by private individuals and firms. Transfers out of the country are debits. Transfers into the country (e.g. money sent from Greece to a Greek student studying in the UK) would be a credit item.

The **current account balance** is the overall balance of all the above four subdivisions. A *current account surplus* is where credits exceed debits. A *current account deficit* is where debits exceed credits. Figure 12.1 shows the current account balances of the UK, the USA and Japan as a proportion of their GDP (national output).

The capital account

The **capital account** records the flows of funds, into the country (credits) and out of the country (debits), associated with the acquisition or disposal of fixed assets (e.g.

KI 29
p239

Table 12.1 UK balance of payments: 2005	£ million	
Current account		
1. Trade in goods	+210 182	
(a) Exports of goods	−275 813	
(b) Imports of goods	−65 631	
Balance on trade in goods		
2. Trade in services	+105 732	
(a) Exports of services	−86 998	
(b) Imports of services	+18 734	
Balance on trade in services		−46 897
Balance on trade in goods and services		+27 408
3. Net income flows (wages and investment income)		−12 401
4. Net current transfers (government and private)		**−31 890**
Current account balance		
Capital account		+2 301
5. Net capital transfers, etc:		**+2 301**
Capital account balance		
Financial account		
6. Investment (direct and portfolio)	+221 626	
(a) Net investment in UK from abroad	−219 293	
(b) Net UK investment abroad		+2 333
Balance of direct and portfolio investment		
7. Other financial flows (mainly short-term)	+523 673	
(a) Net deposits in UK from abroad and borrowing from abroad by UK residents	−500 539	
(b) Net deposits abroad by UK residents and UK lending to overseas residents		−23 134
Balance of other financial flows		+656
8. Reserves (drawing on + adding to −)		**+24 811**
Financial account balance		
Total of all three accounts		−4 788
9. Net errors and omissions		+4 788
		0

Source: data in various tables in *UK Economic Accounts* (National Statistics).

land), the transfer of funds by migrants, and the payment of grants by the government for overseas projects and the receipt of EU money for capital projects (e.g. from the Agricultural Guidance Fund).

The financial account[1]

The financial account of the balance of payments records cross-border changes in the holding of shares, property, bank deposits and loans, government securities, etc. In other words, unlike the current account, which is concerned with money incomes, the financial account is concerned with the purchase and sale of assets.

[1] Prior to October 1998, this account was called the 'capital account'. The account that is *now* called the capital account used to be included in the transfers section of the current account. This potentially confusing change of names was adopted in order to bring the UK accounts in line with the system used by the International Monetary Fund (IMF), the EU and most individual countries.

Figure 12.1
Current account
balance as a
percentage of GDP in
selected countries:
1970–2006

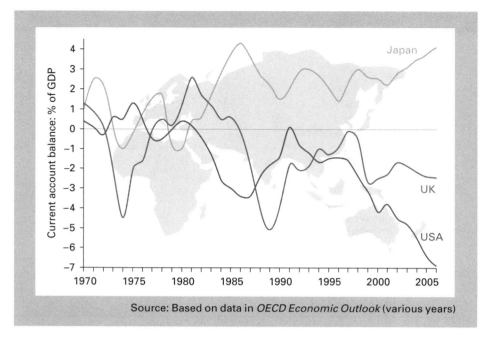

Source: Based on data in *OECD Economic Outlook* (various years)

Investment (direct and portfolio).   This account covers primarily long-term investment.

■ Direct investment. If a foreign company invests money from abroad in one of its
branches or associated companies in the UK, this represents an inflow of money
when the investment is made and is thus a credit item. (Any subsequent profit
from this investment that flows abroad will be recorded as an *investment income
outflow* on the current account.) Investment abroad by UK companies represents
an outflow of money when the investment is made. It is thus a debit item.

Note that what we are talking about here is the acquisition or sale of assets:
e.g. a factory or farm, or the takeover of a whole firm, not the imports or exports
of equipment.

■ Portfolio investment. This is changes in the holding of paper assets, such as company shares. Thus if a UK resident buys shares in an overseas company, this is
an outflow of funds and is hence a debit item.

Other financial flows.   These consist primarily of various types of short-term monetary movement between the UK and the rest of the world. Deposits by overseas residents in banks in the UK and loans to the UK from abroad are credit items, since they
represent an inflow of money. Deposits by UK residents in over-
seas banks and loans by UK banks to overseas residents are debit
items. They represent an outflow of money.

Short-term monetary flows are common between international financial centres to take advantage of differences in
countries' interest rates and changes in exchange rates.

> **Pause for thought**
>
> *Where would interest payments on short-
> term foreign deposits in UK banks be
> entered on the balance of payments
> account?*

Flows to and from the reserves.   The UK, like all other countries, holds reserves of
gold and foreign currencies. From time to time the Bank of England (acting as the
government's agent) will sell some of these reserves to purchase sterling on the
foreign exchange market. It does this normally as a means of supporting the rate of
exchange (as we shall see below). Drawing on reserves represents a *credit* item in the
balance of payments accounts: money drawn from the reserves represents an *inflow*
to the balance of payments (albeit an outflow from the reserves account). The
reserves can thus be used to support a deficit elsewhere in the balance of payments.

Conversely, if there is a surplus elsewhere in the balance of payments, the Bank of England can use it to build up the reserves. Building up the reserves counts as a debit item in the balance of payments, since it represents an outflow from it (to the reserves).

When all the components of the balance of payments account are taken together, the balance of payments should exactly balance: credits should equal debits. As we shall see below, if they were not equal, the rate of exchange would have to adjust until they were, or the government would have to intervene to make them equal.

When the statistics are compiled, however, a number of errors are likely to occur. As a result there will not be a balance. To 'correct' for this, a **net errors and omissions item** is included in the accounts. This ensures that there will be an exact balance. The main reason for the errors is that the statistics are obtained from a number of sources, and there are often delays before items are recorded and sometimes omissions too.

> **Definition**
>
> **Net errors and omissions item**
> A statistical adjustment to ensure that the two sides of the balance of payments account balance. It is necessary because of errors in compiling the statistics.

Recap

1. The balance of payments account records all payments to and receipts from foreign countries.
2. The current account records payments for the imports and exports of goods and services, plus incomes and transfers of money to and from abroad.
3. The capital account records all transfers of capital to and from abroad.
4. The financial account records inflows and outflows of money for investment and as deposits in banks and other financial institutions. It also includes dealings in the country's foreign exchange reserves.
5. The whole account must balance, but surpluses or deficits can be recorded on any specific part of the account. Thus the current account could be in deficit, but it would have to be matched by an equal and opposite capital plus financial account surplus.

EXCHANGE RATES   12.2

What causes exchange rates to change?

An exchange rate is the rate at which one currency trades for another on the foreign exchange market.

If you want to go abroad, you will need to exchange your pounds into euros, dollars, Swiss francs or whatever. To do this you will go to a bank. The bank will quote you that day's exchange rates: for example, €1.45 to the pound, or $1.50 to the pound. It is similar for firms. If an importer wants to buy, say, some machinery from Japan, it will require yen to pay the Japanese supplier. It will thus ask the foreign exchange section of a bank to quote it a rate of exchange of the pound into yen. Similarly, if you want to buy some foreign stocks and shares, or if companies based in the UK want to invest abroad, sterling will have to be exchanged into the appropriate foreign currency.

Likewise, if Americans want to come on holiday to the UK or to buy UK assets, or American firms want to import UK goods or to invest in the UK, they will require sterling. They will be quoted an exchange rate for the pound in the USA: say, £1 = $1.54. This means that they will have to pay $1.54 to obtain £1 worth of UK goods or assets.

Exchange rates are quoted between each of the major currencies of the world. These exchange rates are constantly changing. Minute by minute, dealers in the foreign exchange dealing rooms of the banks are adjusting the rates of exchange. They charge commission when they exchange currencies. It is important for them, therefore, to ensure that they are not left with a large amount of any currency unsold. What they need to do is to balance the supply and demand of each currency: to balance the amount they purchase to the amount they sell. To do this they will need to adjust the price of each currency – namely, the exchange rate – in line with changes in supply and demand.

Not only are there day-to-day fluctuations in exchange rates, but also there are long-term changes in them. Table 12.2 shows the average exchange rate between the pound and various currencies for selected years from 1960 to 2006.

One of the problems in assessing what is happening to a particular currency is that its rate of exchange may rise against some currencies (weak currencies) and fall against others (strong currencies). In order to gain an overall picture of its fluctuations, therefore, it is best to look at a weighted average exchange rate against all other currencies. This is known as the **exchange rate index**. The weight given to each currency in the index depends on the proportion of trade done with that country. The last column in Table 12.2 shows the sterling exchange rate index based on 1 January 2000 = 100. Table 12.3 gives the current weights of the various currencies that make up the sterling index. Since 2005, these weights change every year to reflect changing patterns of trade.

Definition

Exchange rate index
A weighted average exchange rate expressed as an index, where the value of the index is 100 in a given base year. The weights of the different currencies in the index add up to 1.

Pause for thought

How did the pound 'fare' compared with the dollar, the (former) lira and the yen from 1960 to 2006? What conclusions can be drawn about the relative movements of these three currencies?

Table 12.2	Sterling exchange rates: 1960–2006 (annual averages)						
	US dollar	Japanese yen	French franc	German mark	Italian lira	Euro[a]	Sterling exchange rate index (1/1/00 = 100)
1960	2.80	1008	13.82	11.76	1747	–	–
1970	2.40	858	13.33	8.78	1500	–	–
1975	2.22	658	9.50	5.45	1447	(1.70)	119.9
1980	2.33	526	9.83	4.23	1992	(1.62)	115.1
1985	1.30	307	11.55	3.78	2463	(1.71)	99.8
1990	1.79	257	9.69	2.88	2133	(1.37)	96.2
1992	1.77	224	9.32	2.75	2163	(1.33)	93.8
1994	1.53	156	8.49	2.48	2467	(1.27)	85.9
1996	1.56	170	7.99	2.35	2408	(1.21)	83.6
1998	1.66	217	9.77	2.91	2876	(1.49)	99.7
1999	1.62	184	(9.96)	(2.97)	(2941)	1.52	99.1
2000	1.52	163	(10.77)	(3.21)	(3180)	1.64	100.9
2001	1.44	175	(10.55)	(3.15)	(3115)	1.61	99.2
2002	1.50	188	–	–	–	1.59	100.4
2003	1.64	189	–	–	–	1.45	96.9
2004	1.83	198	–	–	–	1.47	101.6
2005	1.82	200	–	–	–	1.46	100.5
2006 (Q2)	1.83	209	–	–	–	1.45	100.2

[a] The euro was introduced in 1999, with notes and coins circulating from 2001. The 'dummy' euro exchange rate figures prior to 1999 are projections backwards in time based on the weighted average exchange rates of the currencies that made up the euro.

Source: *Monetary and Financial Statistics Interactive Database* (Bank of England)

Country	Weight	Country	Weight
Eurozone	0.552	South Korea	0.014
USA	0.188	Singapore	0.014
Japan	0.049	Australia	0.014
China	0.035	Denmark	0.013
Switzerland	0.028	South Africa	0.012
Sweden	0.022	Turkey	0.012
Canada	0.019	Norway	0.011
Hong Kong	0.018	Total	1.000

Table 12.3 The weights of currencies of various countries in the sterling exchange rate index (2006)

Determination of the rate of exchange in a free market

In a free foreign exchange market, the rate of exchange is determined by demand and supply. This is known as a **floating exchange rate**, and is illustrated in Figure 12.2. For simplicity, assume that there are just two countries: the UK and the USA. When UK importers wish to buy goods from the USA, or when UK residents wish to invest in the USA, they *supply* pounds on the foreign exchange market in order to obtain dollars. In other words, they go to banks or other foreign exchange dealers to buy dollars in exchange for pounds. The higher the exchange rate, the more dollars they obtain for their pounds. This effectively makes American goods cheaper to buy, and investment more profitable. Thus the *higher* the exchange rate, the *more* pounds are supplied. The supply curve of pounds therefore typically slopes upwards.

When US residents wish to purchase UK goods or to invest in the UK, they require pounds. They *demand* pounds by selling dollars on the foreign exchange market. In other words, they go to banks or other foreign exchange dealers to buy pounds in exchange for dollars. The lower the dollar price of the pound (the exchange rate), the cheaper it is for them to obtain UK goods and assets, and hence

Definition

Floating exchange rate When the government does not intervene in the foreign exchange markets, but simply allows the exchange rate to be freely determined by demand and supply.

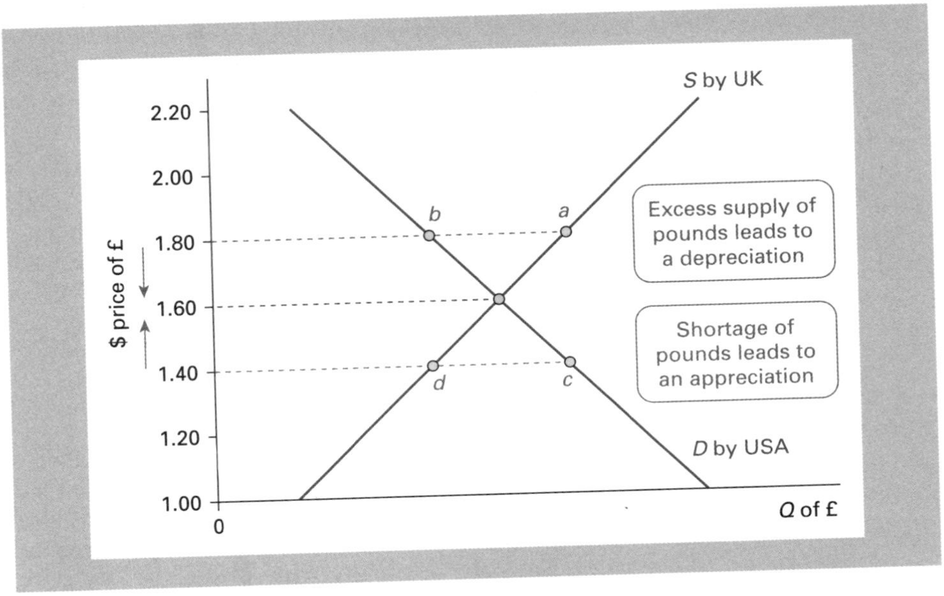

Figure 12.2 Determination of the rate of exchange

the more pounds they are likely to demand. The demand curve for pounds, therefore, typically slopes downwards.

The equilibrium exchange rate is where the demand for pounds equals the supply. In Figure 12.2 this is at an exchange rate of £1 = $1.60. But what is the mechanism that equates demand and supply?

If the current exchange rate were above the equilibrium, the supply of pounds being offered to the banks would exceed the demand. For example, in Figure 12.2 if the exchange rate were $1.80, there would be an excess supply of pounds of $a - b$. Banks would not have enough dollars to exchange for all these pounds. But the banks make money by *exchanging* currency, not by holding on to it. They would thus lower the exchange rate in order to encourage a greater demand for pounds and reduce the excessive supply. They would continue lowering the rate until demand equalled supply.

Similarly, if the rate were below the equilibrium, say at $1.40, there would be a shortage of pounds of $c - d$. The banks would find themselves with too few pounds to meet all the demand. At the same time they would have an excess supply of dollars. The banks would thus raise the exchange rate until demand equalled supply.

In practice, the process of reaching equilibrium is extremely rapid. The foreign exchange dealers in the banks are continually adjusting the rate as new customers make new demands for currencies. What is more, the banks have to watch closely what each other is doing. They are constantly in competition with each other and thus have to keep their rates in line. The dealers receive minute-by-minute updates on their computer screens of the rates being offered round the world.

Shifts in the currency demand and supply curves

Any shift in the demand or supply curves will cause the exchange rate to change. This is illustrated in Figure 12.3, which this time shows the euro/sterling exchange rate. If the demand and supply curves shift from D_1 and S_1 to D_2 and S_2 respectively, the exchange rate will fall from €1.40 to €1.20. A fall in the exchange rate is called a **depreciation**. A rise in the exchange rate is called an **appreciation**.

But why should the demand and supply curves shift? The following are the major possible causes of a depreciation:

KI 6
p27

TC5
p39

Definitions

Depreciation
A fall in the free-market exchange rate of the domestic currency with foreign currencies.

Appreciation
A rise in the free-market exchange rate of the domestic currency with foreign currencies.

Figure 12.3
Floating exchange rates: movement to a new equilibrium

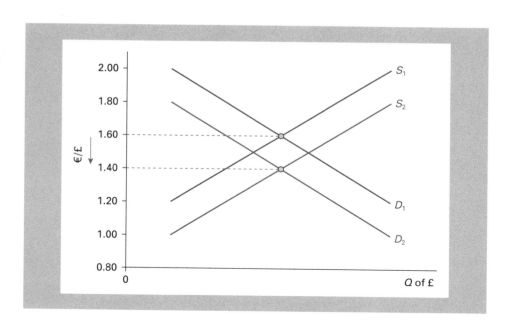

- *A fall in domestic interest rates.* UK rates would now be less competitive for savers and other depositors. More UK residents would be likely to deposit their money abroad (the supply of sterling would rise), and fewer people abroad would deposit their money in the UK (the demand for sterling would fall).

- *Higher inflation in the domestic economy than abroad.* UK exports will become less competitive. The demand for sterling will fall. At the same time, imports will become relatively cheaper for UK consumers. The supply of sterling will rise.

- *A rise in domestic incomes relative to incomes abroad.* If UK incomes rise, the demand for imports, and hence the supply of sterling, will rise. If incomes in other countries fall, the demand for UK exports, and hence the demand for sterling will fall.

- *Relative investment prospects improving abroad.* If investment prospects become brighter abroad than in the UK, perhaps because of better incentives abroad, or because of worries about an impending recession in the UK, again the demand for sterling will fall and the supply of sterling will rise.

- *Speculation that the exchange rate will fall.* If businesses involved in importing and exporting, and also banks and other foreign exchange dealers, think that the exchange rate is about to fall, they will sell pounds now before the rate does fall. The supply of sterling will thus rise.

> **Pause for thought**
>
> Go through each of the above reasons for shifts in the demand for and supply of sterling and consider what would cause an appreciation of the pound.

Recap

1. The rate of exchange is the rate at which one currency exchanges for another. Rates of exchange are determined by demand and supply in the foreign exchange market. Demand for the domestic currency consists of all the credit items in the balance of payments account. Supply consists of all the debit items.

2. The exchange rate will depreciate (fall) if the demand for the domestic currency falls or the supply increases. These shifts can be caused by a fall in the domestic interest rates, higher inflation in the domestic economy than abroad, a rise in domestic incomes relative to incomes abroad, relative investment prospects improving abroad or the belief by speculators that the exchange rate will fall.

3. The opposite in each case would cause an appreciation (rise).

EXCHANGE RATES AND THE BALANCE OF PAYMENTS   12.3

How does the balance of payments affect the exchange rate?

Exchange rates and the balance of payments: no government or central bank intervention

In a free foreign exchange market, the balance of payments will *automatically* balance. But why?

The credit side of the balance of payments constitutes the demand for sterling. For example, when people abroad buy UK exports or assets they demand sterling in order to pay for them. The debit side constitutes the supply of sterling. For example, when UK residents buy foreign goods or assets, the importers of them require foreign currency to pay for them. They thus supply pounds. A floating exchange rate ensures that the demand for pounds is equal to the supply. It thus also ensures that the credits on the balance of payments are equal to the debits: that the balance of payments balances.

Box 12.1

Dealing in foreign currencies

A daily juggling act

Imagine that a large car importer in the UK wants to import 5000 cars from Japan costing ¥15 billion. What does it do?

It will probably contact a number of banks' foreign exchange dealing rooms in London and ask them for exchange rate quotes. It thus puts all the banks in competition with each other. Each bank will want to get the business and thereby obtain the commission on the deal. To do this it must offer a higher rate than the other banks, since the higher the ¥/£ exchange rate, the more yen the firm will get for its money. (For an importer a rate of, say, ¥200 to £1 is better than a rate of, say, ¥180.)

Now it is highly unlikely that any of the banks will have a spare ¥15 billion. But a bank cannot say to the importer 'Sorry, you will have to wait before we can agree to sell them to you.' Instead the bank will offer a deal and then, if the firm agrees, the bank will have to set about obtaining the ¥15 billion. To do this it must offer Japanese who are supplying yen to

obtain pounds at a sufficiently *low* ¥/£ exchange rate. (The lower the ¥/£ exchange rate, the fewer yen the Japanese will have to pay to obtain pounds.)

The banks' dealers thus find themselves in the delicate position of wanting to offer a *high* enough exchange rate to the car importer in order to gain its business, but a *low* enough exchange rate in order to obtain the required amount of yen. The dealers are thus constantly having to adjust the rates of exchange in order to balance the demand and supply of each currency.

In general, the more of any foreign currency that dealers are asked to supply (by being offered sterling), the lower will be the exchange rate they will offer. In other words, a higher supply of sterling pushes down the foreign currency price of sterling.

? *Assume that an American firm wants to import Scotch whisky from the UK. Describe how foreign exchange dealers will respond.*

This does not mean that each part of the balance of payments account separately balances, but simply that any current account deficit must be matched by a capital plus financial account surplus and vice versa.

For example, suppose initially that each part of the balance of payments *did* separately balance. Then let us assume that interest rates rise. This encourages larger short-term financial inflows as people abroad are attracted to deposit money in the UK: the demand for sterling would shift to the right (e.g. from D_2 to D_1 in Figure 12.3). It will also cause smaller short-term financial outflows as UK residents keep more of their money in the country: the supply of sterling shifts to the left (e.g. from S_2 to S_1 in Figure 12.3). The financial account will go into surplus. The exchange rate will appreciate.

As the exchange rate rises, this will cause imports to be cheaper and exports to be more expensive. The current account will move into deficit. There is a movement up along the new demand and supply curves until a new equilibrium is reached. At this point, any financial account surplus is matched by an equal current (plus capital) account deficit.

Exchange rates and the balance of payments: with government or central bank intervention

The government or central bank may be unwilling to let the country's currency float freely. Frequent shifts in the demand and supply curves would cause frequent changes in the exchange rate. This, in turn, might cause uncertainty for businesses, which might curtail their trade and investment.

The central bank may thus intervene in the foreign exchange market. But what can it do? The answer to this depends on its objectives. It may simply want to reduce the day-to-day fluctuations in the exchange rate, or it may want to prevent longer-term, more fundamental shifts in the rate.

Reducing short-term fluctuations

Assume that the UK government believes that an exchange rate of €1.40 to the pound is approximately the long-term equilibrium rate. Short-term leftward shifts in the demand for sterling and rightward shifts in the supply, however, are causing the exchange rate to fall below this level (see Figure 12.3). What can the government do to keep the rate at €1.40?

Using reserves. The Bank of England can sell gold and foreign currencies from the reserves to buy pounds. This will shift the demand for sterling back to the right.

Borrowing from abroad. The government can negotiate a foreign currency loan from other countries or from an international agency such as the International Monetary Fund. The Bank of England can then use these moneys to buy pounds on the foreign exchange market, thus again shifting the demand for sterling back to the right.

Raising interest rates. If the Bank of England raises interest rates, it will encourage people to deposit money in the UK and encourage UK residents to keep their money in the country. The demand for sterling will increase and the supply of sterling will decrease.

Maintaining a fixed rate of exchange over the longer term

Governments may choose to maintain a fixed rate over a number of months or even years. The following are possible methods it can use to achieve this (we are assuming that there are downward pressures on the exchange rate: e.g. as a result of higher aggregate demand and higher inflation).

Contractionary policies. This is where the government deliberately curtails aggregate demand by either *fiscal policy or monetary policy* or both.

Contractionary fiscal policy involves raising taxes and/or reducing government expenditure. Contractionary monetary policy involves reducing the supply of money and raising interest rates. Note that in this case we are talking about not just the temporary raising of interest rates to prevent a short-term outflow of money from the country, but the use of higher interest rates to reduce borrowing and hence dampen aggregate demand.

A reduction in aggregate demand works in two ways:

- It reduces the level of consumer spending. This directly cuts imports, since there will be reduced spending on Japanese videos, German cars, Spanish holidays and so on. The supply of sterling coming on to the foreign exchange market thus decreases.
- It reduces the rate of inflation. This makes UK goods more competitive abroad, thus increasing the demand for sterling. It will also cut back on imports as UK consumers switch to the now more competitive home-produced goods. The supply of sterling falls.

Supply-side policies. This is where the government attempts to increase the long-term competitiveness of UK goods by encouraging reductions in the costs of production and/or improvements in the quality of UK goods. For example, the government may attempt to improve the quantity and quality of training and research and development (see Section 10.4).

Controls on imports and/or foreign exchange dealing. This is where the government restricts the outflow of money, either by restricting people's access to foreign exchange, or by the use of tariffs (customs duties) and quotas.

Recap

1. In a free foreign exchange market, the balance of payments will automatically balance, since changes in the exchange rate will balance the demand for the currency (credits on the balance of payments) with the supply (debits on the balance of payments).

2. There is no guarantee, however, that there will be a balance on each of the separate parts of the balance of payments account.

3. The government can attempt to prevent the rate of exchange falling by central bank purchases of the domestic currency in the foreign exchange market, either by selling foreign currency reserves or by using foreign loans. Alternatively, the government can raise interest rates. The reverse actions can be taken if it wants to prevent the rate from rising.

4. In the longer term, it can attempt to prevent the rate from falling by pursuing contractionary policies, protectionist policies or supply-side policies to increase the competitiveness of the country's exports.

12.4 FIXED VERSUS FLOATING EXCHANGE RATES

Should exchange rates be 'left to the market'?

Are exchange rates best left free to fluctuate and be determined purely by market forces, or should the government or central bank intervene to fix exchange rates, either rigidly or within bands? Unfortunately, the answer is not clear cut. Both floating and fixed exchange rates have their advantages and disadvantages.

Advantages of fixed exchange rates

Surveys reveal that most business people prefer relatively rigid exchange rates: if not totally fixed, then at least pegged for periods of time. The following arguments are used to justify this preference.

Certainty. With fixed exchange rates, international trade and investment become much less risky, since profits are not affected by movements in the exchange rate.

Assume that a firm correctly forecasts that its product will sell in the USA for $1.50. It costs 80p to produce. If the rate of exchange is fixed at £1 = $1.50, each unit will earn £1 and hence make a 20p profit. If, however, the rate of exchange were not fixed, exchange fluctuations could wipe out this profit. If, say, the rate appreciated to £1 = $2, and if units continued to sell for $1.50, they would now earn only 75p each, and hence make a 5p loss.

Little or no speculation. Provided the rate is *absolutely* fixed – and people believe that it will remain so – there is no point in speculating. For example, between 1999 and 2001, when the old currencies of the eurozone countries were still used, but were totally fixed to the euro, there was no speculation that the German mark, say, would change in value against the French franc or the Dutch guilder.

Prevents governments pursuing 'irresponsible' macroeconomic policies.   If a government deliberately and excessively expands aggregate demand – perhaps in an attempt to gain short-term popularity with the electorate – the resulting balance of payments deficit will force it to constrain demand again (unless it resorts to import controls).

Governments cannot allow their economies to have a persistently higher inflation rate than competitor countries without running into balance of payments crises, and hence a depletion of reserves. Fixed rates thus force governments (in the absence of trade restrictions) to keep the rate of inflation roughly to world levels.

Disadvantages of fixed exchange rates

Exchange rate policy may conflict with the interests of domestic business and the economy as a whole.   A balance of payments deficit can occur even if the economy is not 'overheating'. For example, there can be a fall in the demand for the country's exports as a result of an external shock (such as a recession in other countries) or because of increased foreign competition. If protectionism is to be avoided, and if supply-side policies work only over the long run, the government will be forced to raise interest rates. This is likely to have two adverse effects on the domestic economy:

- Higher interest rates may discourage long-term business investment. This in turn will lower firms' profits in the long term and reduce the country's long-term rate of economic growth. The country's capacity to produce will be restricted and businesses are likely to fall behind in the competitive race with their international rivals to develop new products and improve existing ones.
- Higher interest rates will have a dampering effect on the economy by making borrowing more expensive and thereby cutting back on both consumer demand and investment. This can result in a recession with rising unemployment. It will, however, improve the balance of payments. There will be an improvement not only on the financial account, as money flows into the country to take advantage of the higher rates of interest, but also on the current account. The recession will lead to reduced demand for imports, and lower inflation is likely to make exports more competitive and imports relatively more expensive.

The problem is that, with fixed exchange rates, domestic policy is entirely constrained by the balance of payments. Any attempt to reflate and cure unemployment will simply lead to a balance of payments deficit and thus force governments to deflate again.

Competitive contractionary policies leading to world depression.   If deficit countries pursued contractionary policies, but surplus countries pursued expansionary policies, there would be no overall world contraction or expansion. Countries may be quite happy, however, to run a balance of payments surplus and build up reserves. Countries may thus competitively deflate – all trying to achieve a balance of payments surplus. But this is beggar-my-neighbour policy. Not all countries can have a surplus! Overall the world must be in balance. The result of these policies is to lead to general world recession and a restriction in growth.

Problems of international liquidity.   If trade is to expand, there must be an expansion in the supply of currencies acceptable for world trade (dollars, euros, pounds, gold, etc.): there must be adequate international liquidity. Countries' reserves of these currencies must grow if they are to be sufficient to maintain a fixed rate at times of balance of payments disequilibrium. Conversely, there must not be excessive international liquidity. Otherwise the extra demand that would result would lead to world inflation. It is important under fixed exchange rates, therefore, to avoid too much or too little international liquidity. The problem is whether there is adequate control of international liquidity. The supply of dollars, for example, depends largely on US policy, which may be dominated by its internal economic situation rather than by a concern for the wellbeing of the international community.

> ### Definition
>
> **Devaluation**
> Where the government refixes the exchange rate at a lower level.

Inability to adjust to shocks. With sticky prices and wage rates, there is no swift mechanism for dealing with sudden balance of payments crises – like that caused by a sudden increase in oil prices. In the short run, countries will need huge reserves or loan facilities to support their currencies. There may be insufficient international liquidity to permit this. In the longer run, countries may be forced into a depression by having to deflate. The alternative may be to resort to protectionism, or to abandon the fixed rate and devalue.

Speculation. If speculators believe that a fixed rate simply cannot be maintained, speculation is likely to be massive. If, for example, there is a large balance of payments deficit, speculative selling will worsen the deficit and may itself force a devaluation.

Advantages of a free-floating exchange rate

The advantages and disadvantages of free-floating rates are to a large extent the opposite of fixed rates.

Automatic correction. The government simply lets the exchange rate move freely to the equilibrium. In this way, balance of payments disequilibria are automatically and instantaneously corrected without the need for specific government policies.

No problem of international liquidity and reserves. Since there is no central bank intervention in the foreign exchange market, there is no need to hold reserves. A currency is automatically convertible at the current market exchange rate.

Insulation from external economic events. A country is not tied to a possibly unacceptably high world inflation rate, as it could be under a fixed exchange rate. It is also to some extent protected against world economic fluctuations and shocks.

Governments are free to choose their domestic policy. Under a floating rate the government can choose whatever level of domestic demand it considers appropriate, and simply leave exchange rate movements to take care of any balance of payments effect. Similarly, the central bank can choose whatever rate of interest is necessary to meet domestic objectives, such as achieving a target rate of inflation. The exchange rate will simply adjust to the new rate of interest – a rise in interest rates causing an appreciation, a fall causing a depreciation. This freedom for the government and central bank is a major advantage, especially when the effectiveness of contractionary policies under fixed exchange rates is reduced by downward wage and price rigidity, and when competitive contractionary policies between countries may end up causing a world recession.

Disadvantages of a free-floating exchange rate

Despite these advantages there are still a number of serious problems with free-floating exchange rates.

Unstable exchange rates. The less elastic are the demand and supply curves for the currency in Figure 12.3, the greater the change in exchange rate that will be necessary to restore equilibrium following a shift in either demand or supply. In the long run, in a competitive world with domestic substitutes for imports and foreign substitutes for exports, demand and supply curves are relatively elastic. Nevertheless, in the short run, given that many firms have contracts with specific overseas suppliers or distributors, the demands for imports and exports are less elastic.

 Speculation. In an uncertain world, where there are few restrictions on currency speculation, where the fortunes and policies of governments can change rapidly, and where large amounts of short-term deposits are internationally 'footloose', speculation can be highly destabilising in the short run. If people think that the exchange rate will fall, then they will sell the currency, and this will cause the exchange rate to fall even further, perhaps overshooting the eventual equilibrium. At times of international currency turmoil, such speculation can be enormous. Worldwide, over a trillion dollars on average passes daily across the foreign exchanges: greatly in excess of countries' foreign exchange reserves!

> **Pause for thought**
>
> *If speculators on average gain from their speculation, who loses?*

 Uncertainty for traders and investors. The uncertainty caused by currency fluctuations can discourage international trade and investment. To some extent the problem can be overcome by using the **forward exchange market**. Here traders agree with a bank *today* the rate of exchange for some point in the *future* (say, six months' time). This allows traders to plan future purchases of imports or sales of exports at a known rate of exchange. Of course, banks charge for this service, since they are taking on the risks themselves of adverse exchange rate fluctuations.

But dealing in the futures market only takes care of short-run uncertainty. Banks will not be prepared to take on the risks of offering forward contracts for several

> **Definition**
>
> **Forward exchange market**
> Where contracts are made today for the price at which a currency will be exchanged at some specified future date.

Box 12.2   **Exploring Economics**

The importance of international financial movements

How a current account deficit can coincide with an appreciating exchange rate

Since the early 1970s, most of the major economies of the world have operated with floating exchange rates. The opportunities that this gives for speculative gain have led to a huge increase in short-term international financial movements. Vast amounts of moneys transfer from country to country in search of higher interest rates or a currency that is likely to appreciate. This can have a bizarre effect on exchange rates.

If a country pursues an expansionary fiscal policy, the current account will tend to go into deficit as extra imports are 'sucked in'. What effect will this have on exchange rates? You might think that the answer is obvious: the higher demand for imports will create an extra supply of domestic currency on the foreign exchange market and hence drive down the exchange rate.

In fact the opposite is likely. The higher interest rates resulting from the higher domestic demand can lead to a massive inflow of short-term finance. The financial account can thus move sharply into surplus. This is likely to outweigh the current account deficit and cause an *appreciation* of the exchange rate.

Exchange rate movements, especially in the short term, are largely brought about by changes on the financial rather than the current account.

 Why do high international financial mobility and an absence of exchange controls severely limit a country's ability to choose its interest rate?

Box 12.3

The euro/dollar seesaw

Ups and downs in the currency market

For periods of time, world currency markets can be quite peaceful, with only modest changes in exchange rates. But with the ability to move vast sums of money very rapidly from one part of the world to another and from one currency to another, speculators can suddenly turn this relatively peaceful world into one of extreme turmoil.

In this box we examine the huge swings of the euro against the dollar since the euro's launch in 1999. In Web Case 12.5 we examine two other examples of currency turmoil: both from the 1990s.

First the down . . .

On 1 January 1999, the euro was launched and exchanged for $1.16. By October 2000 the euro had fallen to $0.85. What was the cause of this 27 per cent depreciation? The main cause was the growing fear that inflationary pressures were increasing in the USA and that, therefore, the Federal Reserve Bank would have to raise interest rates. At the same time, the eurozone economy was growing only slowly and inflation was well below the 2 per cent

ceiling set by the European Central Bank. There was thus pressure on the ECB to cut interest rates.

The speculators were not wrong. As the diagram shows, US interest rates rose, and ECB interest rates initially fell, and when eventually they did rise (in October 1999), the gap between US and ECB interest rates soon widened again.

In addition to the differences in interest rates, a lack of confidence in the recovery of the eurozone economy and a continuing confidence in the US economy encouraged investment to flow to the USA. This inflow of finance (and lack of inflow to the eurozone) further pushed up the dollar relative to the euro.

The low value of the euro meant a high value of the pound relative to the euro. This made it very difficult for UK companies exporting to eurozone countries and also for those competing with imports from the eurozone (which had been made cheaper by the fall in the euro).

In October 2000, with the euro trading at around 85¢, the ECB plus the US Federal Reserve Bank (America's central bank), the Bank of England and the Japanese central bank all intervened on the

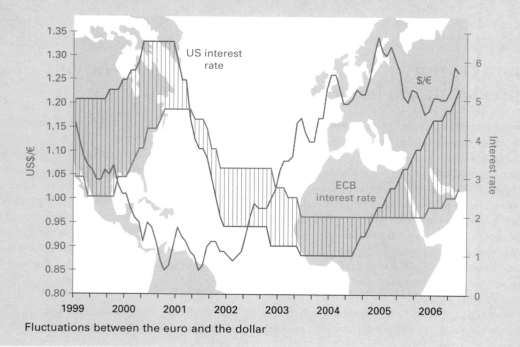

Fluctuations between the euro and the dollar

foreign exchange market to buy euros. This arrested the fall, and helped to restore confidence in the currency. People were more willing to hold euros, knowing that central banks would support it.

. . . Then the up

The position completely changed in 2001. With the US economy slowing rapidly and fears of an impending recession, the Federal Reserve Bank reduced interest rates 11 times during the year: from 6.5 per cent at the beginning of the year to 1.75 per cent at the end (see the chart). Although the ECB also cut interest rates, the cuts were relatively modest: from 4.75 at the beginning of the year to 3.25 at the end. With eurozone interest rates now considerably above US rates, the euro began to rise.

In addition, massive debts on the US current account, and a budget deficit nearing 4 per cent of GDP, made foreign investors reluctant to invest in the American economy. In fact, investors were pulling out of the USA. One estimate suggests that European investors alone sold $70 billion of US assets during 2002. The result of all this was a massive depreciation of the dollar and appreciation of the euro, so that by March 2005 the exchange rate had risen to $1.35: a 60 per cent appreciation since July 2001! By 2004, the US budget deficit had risen to 4.5 per cent of GDP – well above the budget deficits in France and Germany (see Boxes 10.1 and 10.2).

From 2004, the weakening dollar was becoming a cause of increasing concern for the USA, with fears that it would discourage inward investment. What is more, despite the resulting lower prices of US exports and the higher prices of imports to the USA, increasing competition from China and other low-cost countries caused the US current account deficit to deepen further (see Figure 12.1 on page 440).

There were also worries about the US economy overheating, with excessive growth in demand leading to a rise in inflation. In response, the Fed raised interest rates in a number of steps, from 1.25 per cent in mid–2004 to 5.25 per cent by mid–2006 (see chart). However, although this prevented a further

decline in the dollar, and even encouraged a modest strengthening in 2005, the dollar still remained weak and the euro strong.

The effects on business in the eurozone

So is a strong euro bad for European business? With over 20 per cent of the eurozone's GDP determined by export sales, and a large part of those exports going to America, the dollar/euro exchange rate will invariably be significant. The question is: how significant? The concern was that, with slow growth in the eurozone, the rise in the euro and the resulting fall in exports would slow growth rates even further. The investment bank Morgan Stanley estimated that for every 10 per cent rise in the value of the euro against the dollar, European corporate profits fall by 3 per cent.

However, the impact of the euro's rise on eurozone business was tempered by a number of other factors:

- Companies are increasingly using sophisticated management and operational systems, in which value creation is spread throughout a global value chain. Often procurement systems are priced in dollars.
- Firms hedge their currency risks. BMW, for example, uses forward exchange markets to agree to buy or sell currencies in the future at a price quoted today (this, of course, costs it a premium).
- Many European companies (again BMW is an example) have located some of their production facilities in the USA and use them to help meet demand in the American market. This helps to insulate them from the effects of the rise in the value of the euro.

Find out what has happened to the euro/ dollar exchange rate over the past 12 months. (You can find the data from the Bank of England's Statistical Interactive Database at www.bankofengland.co.uk/statistics.htm.) Explain why the exchange rate has moved the way it has.

Figure 12.4
Dollar/sterling
exchange rate and
sterling exchange rate
index: 1976–2006

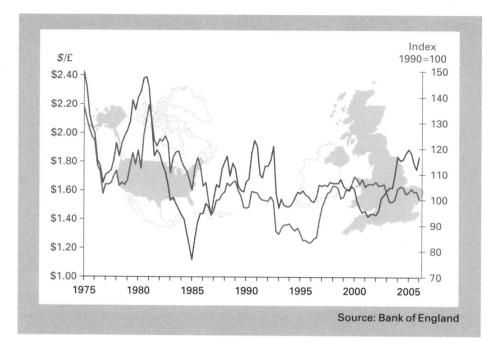

Source: Bank of England

years hence. Thus firms simply have to live with the uncertainty over exchange rates in future years. This will discourage long-term investment. For example, the possibility of exchange rate appreciation may well discourage firms from investing abroad, since a higher exchange rate means that foreign exchange earnings will be worth less in the domestic currency.

Figure 12.4 shows the fluctuations in the dollar/pound exchange rate and the exchange rate index from 1976 to 2006. As you can see, there have been large changes in exchange rates. Such changes do not only make it difficult for exporters. Importers too will be hesitant about making long-term deals. For example, a UK manufacturing firm signing a contract to buy US components in 1980, when $2.40 worth of components could be purchased for £1, would find a struggle to make a profit some four years later when only just over $1.00 worth of US components could be purchased for £1!

Lack of discipline on the domestic economy.   Governments may pursue irresponsibly inflationary policies (for short-term political gain, say). This will have adverse effects over the longer term as the government will at some point have to deflate the economy again, with a resulting fall in output and rise in unemployment.

Exchange rates in practice

Exchange rates have become extremely volatile. Currencies can gain or lose several percentage points in the space of a few days. These changes can then make all the difference between profit and loss for trading companies. There are a number of reasons for this volatility:

- Inflation or money supply targets. Central banks may have to make considerable changes to interest rates in order to keep to their targets. These in turn cause exchange rate fluctuations.
- A huge growth in international financial markets. This has encouraged the international transfer of money and capital.

- The abolition of exchange controls in most industrialised countries.
- The growth in information technology. The simple use of a computer can transfer capital and finance internationally in a matter of seconds.
- The preference for liquidity. With the danger of currency fluctuations, companies prefer to keep their financial capital as liquid as possible. They do not want to be locked into assets denominated in a declining currency.
- The growing speculative activities of trading companies. Many large companies have a team of dealers to help manage their liquid assets: to switch them from currency to currency in order to take advantage of market movements.
- The growing speculative activities of banks and other financial institutions.
- The growing belief that rumour and 'jumping on the bandwagon' are more important determinants of currency buying or selling than cool long-term appraisal. If people *believe* that speculation is likely to be destabilising, their actions will ensure that it is. Many companies involved in international trade and finance have developed a 'speculative mentality'.
- The growing belief that governments are powerless to prevent currency movements. As short-term capital (or 'hot money') grows relative to official reserves, it is increasingly difficult for central banks to stabilise currencies through exchange market intervention.

Recap

1. Completely fixed exchange rates bring the advantage of certainty for the business community, which encourages trade and foreign investment. They also help to prevent governments from pursuing irresponsible macroeconomic policies.

2. However, with fixed rates domestic policy is entirely constrained by the balance of payments. What is more, they can lead to competitive contractionary policies worldwide; there may be problems of excessive or insufficient international liquidity; there may be difficulty in adjusting to external shocks; and speculation could be very severe if people came to believe that a fixed rate was about to break down.

3. The advantages of free-floating exchange rates are that they automatically correct balance of payments disequilibria; they eliminate the need for reserves; and they give governments a greater independence to pursue their chosen domestic policy.

4. On the other hand, a completely free exchange rate can be highly unstable, especially when the elasticities of demand for imports and exports are low and there are shifts in currency demand and supply; in addition, speculation may be destabilising. This may discourage firms from trading and investing abroad. What is more, a flexible exchange rate, by removing the balance of payments constraint on domestic policy, may encourage governments to pursue irresponsible domestic policies for short-term political gain.

5. The volatility of exchange rates around the world has tended to grow. There are many reasons for this, including a growth in international financial markets and a liberalisation of international financial movements combined with easier computer transfer of funds, a growth in speculative activities and a growing belief in the impotence of governments acting on their own to stabilise rates.

12.5   THE ORIGINS OF THE EURO

How did the majority of the EU countries arrive at a single currency?

Adjustable peg
A system whereby exchange rates are fixed for a period of time, but may be devalued (or revalued) if a deficit (or surplus) becomes substantial.

Managed floating
A system of flexible exchange rates, but where the government intervenes to prevent excessive fluctuations or even to achieve an unofficial target exchange rate.

The exchange rate mechanism (ERM)
A semi-fixed system whereby participating EU countries allow fluctuations against each other's currencies only within agreed bands. Collectively they float freely against all other currencies.

There have been many attempts to regulate exchange rates since 1945. By far the most successful was the Bretton Woods system, which was adopted worldwide from the end of the Second World War until 1971. This was a form of adjustable peg exchange rate, where countries pegged (i.e. fixed) their exchange rate to the US dollar, but could re-peg it at a lower or higher level ('devalue' or 'revalue' their exchange rate) if there was a persistent and substantial balance of payments deficit or surplus.

With growing world inflation and instability from the mid-1960s, it became more and more difficult to maintain fixed exchange rates, and the growing likelihood of devaluations and revaluations fuelled speculation. The system was abandoned in the early 1970s. What followed was a period of exchange rate management known as managed floating. Under this system, exchange rates were not pegged but allowed to float. However, central banks intervened from time to time to prevent excessive exchange rate fluctuations. This system largely continues to this day.

However, on a regional basis, especially within Europe, there were attempts to create greater exchange rate stability. The European system involved establishing exchange rate bands: upper and lower limits within which exchange rates were allowed to fluctuate. The name given to the EU system was the exchange rate mechanism (ERM).

The ERM

The ERM came into existence in March 1979, and the majority of the EU countries were members. The UK, however, chose not to join. Spain joined in 1989, the UK in 1990 and Portugal in April 1992. Then in September 1992, the UK and Italy indefinitely suspended their membership of the ERM, but Italy rejoined in November 1996 as part of its bid to join the single European currency (see Section 12.6). Austria joined in 1995, Finland in 1996 and Greece in 1998. By the time the ERM was replaced by the single currency in 1999, only Sweden and the UK were outside the ERM.

Features of the ERM

Under the system, each currency was given a central exchange rate with each of the other ERM currencies in a grid. However, fluctuations were allowed from the central rate within specified bands. For most countries these bands were set at $\pm 2^1/_4$ per cent. The central rates could be adjusted from time to time by agreement, thus making the ERM an 'adjustable peg' system. All the currencies floated jointly with currencies outside the ERM.

If a currency approached the upper or lower limit against *any* other ERM currency, intervention would take place to maintain the currencies within the band. This would take the form of central banks in the ERM selling the strong currency and buying the weak one. It could also involve the weak-currency countries raising interest rates and the strong-currency countries lowering them.

The ERM in practice

In a system of pegged exchange rates, countries should harmonise their policies to avoid excessive currency misalignments and hence the need for large devaluations or revaluations. There should be a convergence of their economies: they should be at a similar point on the business cycle and have similar inflation rates and interest rates.

The ERM in the 1980s.   In the early 1980s, however, French and Italian inflation rates were persistently higher than German rates. This meant that there had to be several realignments (devaluations and revaluations). After 1983 realignments became less frequent, and then from 1987 to 1992 they ceased altogether. This was due to a growing convergence of members' internal policies.

By the time the UK joined the ERM in 1990, it was generally seen by its existing members as being a great success. It had created a zone of currency stability in a world of highly unstable exchange rates, and had provided the necessary environment for the establishment of a truly common market by the end of 1992.

Crisis in the ERM.   Shortly after the UK joined the ERM, strains began to show. The reunification of Germany involved considerable reconstruction in the eastern part of the country. Financing this reconstruction was causing a growing budget deficit. The Bundesbank (the German central bank) thus felt obliged to maintain high interest rates in order to keep inflation in check. At the same time, the UK was experiencing a massive current account deficit (partly the result of entering the ERM at what many commentators argued was too high an exchange rate). It was thus obliged to raise interest rates in order to protect the pound, despite the fact that the economy was sliding rapidly into recession. The French franc and Italian lira were also perceived to be overvalued, and there were the first signs of worries as to whether their exchange rates within the ERM could be retained.

At the same time, the US economy was moving into recession and, as a result, US interest rates were cut. This led to a large outflow of capital from the USA. With high German interest rates, much of this capital flowed to Germany. This pushed up the value of the German mark and with it the other ERM currencies. In September 1992, things reached crisis point. First the lira was devalued. Then two days later, on 'Black Wednesday' (16 September), the UK and Italy were forced to suspend their membership of the ERM: the pound and the lira were floated. At the same time, the Spanish peseta was devalued by 5 per cent.

> **Pause for thought**
>
> *Under what circumstances may a currency bloc like the ERM (a) help to prevent speculation; (b) aggravate the problem of speculation?*

Turmoil returned in the summer of 1993. The French economy was moving into recession and there were calls for cuts in French interest rates. But this was only possible if Germany was prepared to cut its rates too, and it was not. Speculators began to sell francs and it became obvious that the existing franc/mark parity could not be maintained. In an attempt to rescue the ERM, the EU finance ministers agreed to adopt very wide ±15 per cent bands. The result was that the franc and the Danish krone depreciated against the mark.

A return of calm.   The old ERM appeared to be at an end. The new ±15 per cent bands hardly seemed like a 'pegged' system at all. However, the ERM did not die. Within months, the members were again managing to keep fluctuations within a very narrow range (for most of the time, within ±2¼ per cent!). The scene was being set for the abandonment of separate currencies and the adoption of a single currency: the euro.

The Maastricht Treaty and the road to the single currency

The ERM was conceived as a stage on the road to complete economic and monetary union (EMU) of member states. Details of the path towards EMU were finalised in the Maastricht Treaty, which was signed in February 1992. The timetable for EMU involved the adoption of a single currency by 1999 at the latest.

One of the first moves was to establish a European Monetary Institute (EMI). Its role was to co-ordinate monetary policy and encourage greater co-operation between EU central banks. It also monitored the operation of the ERM and prepared the ground for the establishment of a European central bank in time for the launch of the single currency.

Before they could join the single currency, member states were obliged to achieve convergence of their economies. Each country had to meet five convergence criteria:

- Inflation: should be no more than $1\frac{1}{2}$ per cent above the average inflation rate of the three countries in the EU with the lowest inflation.
- Interest rates: the rate on long-term government bonds should be no more than 2 per cent above the average of the three countries with the lowest inflation.
- Budget deficit: should be no more than 3 per cent of GDP.
- National debt: should be no more than 60 per cent of GDP.
- Exchange rates: the currency should have been within the normal ERM bands for at least two years with no realignments or excessive intervention.

Before the launch of the single currency, the Council of Ministers had to decide which countries had met the convergence criteria and would thus be eligible to form a **currency union** by fixing their currencies permanently to the euro. Their national currencies would effectively disappear.

At the same time a European System of Central Banks (ESCB) would be created, consisting of a European Central Bank (ECB) and the central banks of the participating member states. The ECB would be independent, both from governments and from EU political institutions. It would operate the monetary policy on behalf of the countries that had adopted the single currency.

Definition

Currency union
A group of countries (or regions) using a common currency.

Recap

1. One means of achieving greater currency stability is for a group of countries to peg their internal exchange rates and yet float jointly with the rest of the world. The exchange rate mechanism of the EU (ERM) was an example. Members' currencies were allowed to fluctuate against other member currencies within a band. The band was $\pm2\frac{1}{4}$ per cent for the majority of the ERM countries until 1993.

2. The need for realignments seemed to have diminished in the late 1980s as greater convergence was achieved between the members' economies. However, growing strains in the system in the early 1990s led to a crisis in September 1992. The UK and Italy left the ERM. There was a further crisis in July 1993 and the bands were widened to ±15 per cent.

3. Thereafter, as convergence of the economies of ERM members increased, fluctuations decreased and remained largely within $\pm2\frac{1}{4}$ per cent.

4. The ERM was seen as an important first stage on the road to complete economic and monetary union (EMU) in the EU.

5. The Maastricht Treaty set out a timetable for achieving EMU. This would culminate in the creation of a currency union: a single European currency with a common monetary policy operated by an independent European Central Bank.

Do countries benefit from using the euro?

Birth of the euro

In March 1998, the European Commission ruled that 11 of the 15 member states were eligible to proceed to EMU in January 1999. The UK and Denmark were to exercise an opt-out negotiated at Maastricht, and Sweden and Greece failed to meet one or more of the convergence criteria. (Greece joined the euro in 2001.)

All 11 countries unambiguously met the interest rate and inflation criteria, but doubts were expressed by many 'Eurosceptics' as to whether they all genuinely met the other three criteria.

- Exchange rates. Neither Finland nor Italy had been in the ERM for two years (Finland had joined the ERM in October 1996 and Italy had rejoined in November 1996), and the Irish punt was revalued by 3 per cent on 16 March 1998. However, the Commission regarded these three countries as being sufficiently close to the reference value.
- Government deficits. All 11 countries met this criterion, but some countries only managed to achieve a deficit of 3 per cent or below by taking one-off measures, such as a special tax in Italy, and counting privatisation receipts in Germany. Yet, under the Stability and Growth Pact, eurozone countries would be required to keep their deficits within the 3 per cent limit (see Box 10.2). The concern was that countries that only just met this criterion at time of entry would find it difficult to keep within the limit in times of recession or low growth, when tax revenues were not keeping pace with government expenditure. This proved to be the case with Germany and France in 2002 to 2005.
- Government debt. Only four countries had debts that did not exceed 60 per cent (France, Finland, Luxembourg and the UK). However, the Maastricht Treaty allowed countries to exceed this value as long as the debt was 'sufficiently diminishing and approaching the reference value at a satisfactory pace'. Critics argued that this phrase was interpreted too loosely.

The euro came into being on 1 January 1999, but euro banknotes and coins were not introduced until 1 January 2002. In the meantime, national currencies continued to exist alongside the euro, but at irrevocably fixed rates. The old notes and coins were withdrawn a few weeks after the introduction of euro notes and coins.

In May 2004, ten new members joined the EU. They all stated their intention to join the euro, but to do so, they have to be members of an ERM version 2 for at least two years. Estonia, Lithuania and Slovenia were the first to join ERM2 in June 2004, with the wide band of ±15 per cent. Slovenia joined the eurozone on 1 January 2007, being the first of the new member states to meet the convergence criteria.

How desirable is EMU?

Advantages of the single currency

Elimination of the costs of converting currencies. With separate currencies in each of the EU countries, costs were incurred each time one currency was exchanged into another. The elimination of these costs, however, was probably the least important benefit from the single currency. The European Commission estimated that the effect was to increase the GDP of the countries concerned by an average of only

0.4 per cent. The gains to countries like the UK, which have well-developed financial markets, would be even smaller.

Increased competition and efficiency. Despite the advent of the single market, large price differences remained between member states. Not only has the single currency eliminated the need to convert one currency into another (a barrier to competition), but it has brought more transparency in pricing, and has put greater downward pressure on prices in high-cost firms and countries.

Elimination of exchange-rate uncertainty (between the members). Removal of exchange rate uncertainty has helped to encourage trade between the eurozone countries. Perhaps more importantly, it has encouraged investment by firms that trade between these countries, given the greater certainty in calculating costs and revenues from such trade.

Increased inward investment. Investment from the rest of the world is attracted to a eurozone of over 300 million inhabitants, where there is no fear of internal currency movements. By contrast, the UK, by not joining, has found that inward investment has been diverted away to countries within the eurozone. From 1990 to 1999, the UK's share of inward investment to the EU was nearly 40 per cent. From 1999 to 2004, it was 16 per cent.

Lower inflation and interest rates. A single monetary policy forces convergence in inflation rates (just as inflation rates are very similar between the different regions *within* a country). With the ECB being independent from short-term political manipulation, this has resulted in a lower average inflation rate in the eurozone countries. This, in turn, has helped to convince markets that the euro will be strong relative to other currencies. The result is lower long-term rates of interest. This, in turn, further encourages investment in the eurozone countries, both by member states and by the rest of the world.

Opposition to EMU

Monetary union has been bitterly opposed, however, by certain groups. Many Eurosceptics see within it a surrender of national political and economic sovereignty. The lack of an independent monetary and exchange rate policy is a serious problem, they argue, if an economy is at all out of harmony with the rest of the Union. For example, if countries such as Italy and Spain have higher endemic rates of inflation (due, say, to greater cost-push pressures), then how are they to make their goods competitive with the rest of the Union? With separate currencies these countries could allow their currencies to depreciate. With a single currency, however, they could become depressed 'regions' of Europe, with rising unemployment and all the other regional problems of depressed regions *within* a country. This may then require significant regional policies – policies that may not be in place or, if they were, would be seen as too interventionist by the political right.

> **Pause for thought**
>
> How might multiplier effects (the principle of cumulative causation) lead to prosperous regions becoming more prosperous and less prosperous regions falling even further behind?

The answer given by proponents of EMU is that it is better to tackle the problem of high inflation in such countries by the disciplines of competition from other EU countries, than merely to feed that inflation by keeping separate currencies and allowing repeated devaluations, with all the uncertainty that that brings. What is more, the high-inflation countries tend to be the poorer ones with lower wage levels (albeit faster wage *increases*). With the high mobility of labour and capital that will accompany the development of the single market, resources are likely to be attracted to such countries. This could help to narrow the gap between the richer and poorer member states.

The critics of EMU argue that labour is relatively immobile, given cultural and language barriers. Thus an unemployed worker in Wales could not easily move to a job in Turin or Helsinki. What the critics are arguing here is that the EU is not an optimal currency area (see Box 12.4).

Perhaps the most serious criticism is that the same rate of interest must apply to all eurozone countries: the 'one-size-fits-all' problem. The trouble is that while one country might require a lower rate of interest in order to ward off recession (such as Germany in 2003), another might require a higher one to prevent inflation. As convergence between the member economies increases, however, this problem is likely to lessen.

Another problem for members of a single currency occurs in adjusting to a shock when that shock affects members to different degrees. These are known as **asymmetric shocks**. For example, a sudden change in the price of oil would affect an oil-exporting country like the UK differently from oil-importing countries. This problem is more serious, the less the factor mobility between member countries and the less the price flexibility within member countries.

This problem, however, should not be overstated. The divergences between economies are often the result of a lack of harmony between countries in their demand-management policies: something that is impossible in the case of monetary policy, and more difficult in the case of fiscal policy, for countries in the eurozone. Also, many of the shocks that face economies today are global and have similar (albeit not identical) effects on all countries. Adjustment to such shocks would often be better with a single co-ordinated policy – something that would be much easier with a single currency and a single central bank.

Even when shocks are uniformly felt in the member states, however, there is still the problem that policies adopted centrally will have different impacts on each country. For example, in the UK, a large proportion of borrowing is at variable interest rates. In Germany, by contrast, much is at fixed rates. Thus if the ECB were to raise interest rates, the contractionary effects would be felt disproportionately in the UK. Of course, were this balance to change – and there is some evidence that types of borrowing are becoming more uniform across the EU – this problem would diminish.

The problem for economists is that the issue of monetary union is a very emotive one. 'Europhiles' often see monetary union as a vital element in their vision of a united Europe. Many Eurosceptics, however, see EMU as a surrender of sovereignty and a threat to nationhood. In such an environment, a calm assessment of the arguments and evidence is very difficult.

The UK Labour government specified five convergence criteria that must be met before it would put the question of UK adoption of the euro to the electorate in a referendum. These are examined in Web Case 12.12.

Definitions

Optimal currency area
The optimal size of a currency area is one that maximises the benefits from having a single currency relative to the costs. If the area were to be increased or decreased in size, the costs would rise relative to the benefits.

Asymmetric shocks
Shocks (such as an oil price increase or a recession in another part of the world) that have different-sized effects on different industries, regions or countries.

Recap

1. The euro was born on 1 January 1999. Twelve countries adopted it, having at least nominally met the Maastricht convergence criteria. Euro notes and coins were introduced on 1 January 2002, with the notes and coins of the old currencies withdrawn a few weeks later.

Box 12.4

Exploring Economics

Optimal currency areas

When it pays to pay in the same currency

Imagine that each town and village used a different currency. Think how inconvenient it would be having to keep exchanging one currency into another, and how difficult it would be working out the relative value of items in different parts of the country.

Clearly there are benefits of using a common currency, not only within a country but across different countries. The benefits include greater transparency in pricing, more open competition, greater certainty for investors and the avoidance of having to pay commission when you change one currency into another. There are also the benefits from having a single monetary policy if that is delivered in a more consistent and effective way than by individual countries.

So why not have a single currency for the whole world? The problem is that the bigger a single-currency area gets, the more likely the conditions are to diverge in the different parts of the area. Some parts may have high unemployment and require expansionary policies. Others may have low unemployment and suffer from inflationary pressures. They may require *contractionary* policies.

What is more, different members of the currency area may experience quite different shocks to their economies, whether from outside the union (e.g. a fall in the price of one of their major exports) or from inside (e.g. a prolonged strike). These 'asymmetric shocks' would imply that different parts of the currency area should adopt different policies. But with a common monetary policy and hence common interest rates, and with no possibility of devaluation/revaluation of the currency of individual members, the scope for separate economic policies is reduced.

The costs of asymmetric shocks (and hence the costs of a single-currency area) will be greater, the less the mobility of labour and capital, the less the flexibility of prices and wage rates, and the fewer

the alternative policies there are that can be turned to (such as fiscal and regional policies).

So is the eurozone an optimal currency area? Certainly strong doubts have been raised by many economists.

■ Labour is relatively immobile.
■ There are structural differences between the member states.
■ The transmission effects of interest rate changes are different between the member countries, given that countries have proportions of borrowing at variable interest rates and different proportions of consumer debt to GDP.
■ Exports to countries outside the eurozone account for different proportions of the members' GDP, and thus their economies are affected differently by a change in the rate of exchange of the euro against other currencies.
■ Wage rates are relatively inflexible.
■ Under the Stability and Growth Pact (see Box 10.2 on page 362), the scope for using discretionary fiscal policy is curtailed.

This does not necessarily mean, however, that the costs of having a single European currency outweigh the benefits. Also, the problems outlined above should decline over time as the single market develops. Finally, the problem of asymmetric shocks can be exaggerated. European economies are highly diversified; there are often more differences *within* economies than between them. Thus shocks are more likely to affect different industries or localities than whole countries. Changing the exchange rate, if that were still possible, would hardly be an appropriate policy in these circumstances.

? *Why is a single currency area likely to move towards becoming an optimal currency area over time?*

2. The advantages claimed for EMU are that it eliminates the costs of converting currencies and the uncertainties associated with possible changes in inter-EU exchange rates. This encourages more investment, both inward and by domestic firms. What is more, a common central bank, independent from domestic governments, provides the stable monetary environment necessary for a convergence of the EU economies and the encouragement of investment and inter-Union trade.

3. Critics claim, however, that it might make adjustment to domestic economic problems more difficult. The loss of independence in policy making is seen by such people to be a major issue, not only because of the loss of political sovereignty, but also because domestic economic concerns may be at variance with those of the Union as a whole. A single monetary policy is claimed to be inappropriate for dealing with asymmetric shocks. What is more, countries and regions at the periphery of the Union may become depressed unless there is an effective regional policy.

GLOBALISATION AND THE PROBLEM OF INSTABILITY 12.7

Can governments do anything to create greater harmony in the world economy?

We live in an interdependent world. Countries are affected by the economic health of other countries and by their governments' policies. Problems in one part of the world can spread like a contagion to other parts, with perhaps no country immune.

There are two major ways in which this process of 'globalisation' affects individual economies. The first is through trade. The second is through financial markets.

Interdependence through trade

So long as nations trade with one another, the domestic economic actions of one nation will have implications for those which trade with it. For example, if the US administration feels that the US economy is growing too fast, it might adopt various contractionary fiscal and monetary measures, such as higher tax rates or interest rates. US consumers will not only consume fewer domestically produced goods but also reduce their consumption of imported products. But US imports are other countries' exports. A fall in these other countries' exports will lead to a multiplier effect in these countries. Output and employment will fall.

Changes in aggregate demand in one country thus send ripples throughout the global economy. The process whereby changes in imports into (or exports from) one country affect national income in other countries is known as the international trade multiplier.

TC 15
p253

The more open an economy, the more vulnerable it will be to changes in the level of economic activity in the rest of the world. This problem will be particularly acute if a nation is heavily dependent on trade with one other nation (e.g. Canada on the USA) or one other region (e.g. Switzerland on the EU).

As we saw in Figure 11.1 (see page 396), international trade has been growing as a proportion of countries' national income for many years. With most nations committed to freer trade, and with the WTO overseeing the dismantling of trade barriers, so international trade is likely to continue growing as a proportion of world GDP. This will increase countries' interdependence and their vulnerability to world trade fluctuations.

> **Definition**
>
> **International trade multiplier**
> The effect on national income in country B of a change in exports (or imports) of country A.

Financial interdependence

International trade has grown rapidly over the past 30 years, but international financial flows have grown much more rapidly. The value of banks' holdings of liabilities to foreign residents (individuals and institutions) has been increasing by an average of some 15 per cent per year over the past 25 years. The value of cross-border transactions in bonds and equities has increased by nearly 30 per cent per year over the same period. Even after taking inflation into account, this is still a very large real rate of increase.

Each day, over $1.2 trillion of assets are traded across the foreign exchanges. Many of the transactions are short-term financial flows, moving to where interest rates are most favourable or to currencies where the exchange rate is likely to appreciate. This again makes countries interdependent.

Assume that the Federal Reserve Bank (the Fed) in the USA, worried about rising inflation, decides to raise interest rates. These higher interest rates will attract an inflow of funds from other countries. This will cause the dollar to appreciate. Knowing that this will happen, speculators will seek to buy dollars quickly before the exchange rate has finished appreciating. They may well buy dollars *before* the Fed raises interest rates, in anticipation that it will do so.

The inflow of funds to the USA represents an outflow from other countries and will thus have a knock-on effect on their interest rates (pushing them up). And just as the dollar has appreciated against other currencies, so these other currencies have depreciated against the dollar. The larger the financial flows, the more will interest rate changes in one country affect the economies of other countries: the greater will be the financial interdependence.

> **Pause for thought**
>
> What will be the effect on the UK economy if the European Central Bank cuts interest rates?

The need for international policy co-ordination

There is an old saying: 'If America sneezes, the rest of the world catches a cold.' Viruses of a similar nature regularly infect the world economy. A dramatic example was the 'Asian contagion' of 1997–8. Economic crises spread rapidly around southeast and east Asia and then to Russia and then to Brazil (see Web Case 12.6). World leaders were seriously worried that the whole world would plunge into recession. What was needed was a co-ordinated policy response.

For many years now the leaders of the eight major industrial countries – the USA, Japan, Germany, France, the UK, Italy, Canada and, more recently, Russia – have met once a year at an economic summit conference (and more frequently if felt necessary). Top of the agenda in most of these 'Group of Eight' (G8) meetings has been how to generate world economic growth without major currency fluctuations. But to achieve this it is important that there is a harmonisation of economic policies between nations. In other words, it is important that all the major countries are pursuing consistent policies aiming at common international goals.

But how can policy harmonisation be achieved? As long as there are significant domestic differences between the major economies, there is likely to be conflict not harmony. For example, if one country, say the USA, is worried about the size of its budget deficit, it may be unwilling to respond to world demands for a stimulus to aggregate demand to pull the world economy out of recession. What is more, speculators, seeing differences between countries, are likely to exaggerate them by their actions, causing large changes in exchange rates. The G8 countries have therefore sought to achieve greater convergence of their economies. However, although convergence may be a goal of policy, in practice it has proved elusive.

> **Definitions**
>
> **International harmonisation of economic policies**
> Where countries attempt to co-ordinate their macroeconomic policies so as to achieve common goals.
>
> **Convergence of economies**
> When countries achieve similar rates of growth, inflation, budget deficits as a percentage of GDP, balance of payments, etc. and when they are at a similar point in the business cycle.

Because of a lack of convergence, there are serious difficulties in achieving international policy harmonisation:

- Countries' budget deficits and national debt differ substantially as a proportion of their national income. This puts very different pressures on the interest rates necessary to service these debts.
- Harmonising rates of monetary growth or inflation targets would involve letting interest rates fluctuate with the demand for money. Without convergence in the demand for money, interest rate fluctuations could be severe.
- Harmonising interest rates would involve abandoning monetary, inflation and exchange rate targets (unless interest rate 'harmonisation' meant adjusting interest rates so as to maintain monetary or inflation targets or a fixed exchange rate).
- Countries have different internal structural relationships. A lack of convergence here means that countries with higher endemic *cost* inflation would require higher interest rates and higher unemployment if international inflation rates were to be harmonised, or higher inflation if interest rates were to be harmonised.
- Countries have different rates of productivity increase, product development, investment and market penetration. A lack of convergence here means that the growth in exports (relative to imports) will differ for any given level of inflation or growth.
- Countries may be very unwilling to change their domestic policies to fall in line with other countries. They may prefer the other countries to fall in line with them!

If any one of the four – interest rates, growth rates, inflation rates or current account balance of payments – could be harmonised across countries, it is likely that the other three would then not be harmonised.

Total convergence and thus total harmonisation may not be possible. Nevertheless most governments favour some movement in that direction: some is better than none.

Recap

1. Changes in aggregate demand in one country will affect the amount of imports purchased and thus the amount of exports sold by other countries and hence their national income. There is thus an international trade multiplier effect.

2. Changes in interest rates in one country will affect financial flows to and from other countries, and hence their exchange rates, interest rates and national income.

3. To prevent problems in one country spilling over to other countries and to stabilise the international business cycle will require co-ordinated policies between nations.

4. Leaders of the G8 countries meet regularly to discuss ways of harmonising their policies. Usually, however, domestic issues are more important to the leaders than international ones, and frequently they pursue policies that are not in the interests of the other countries.

DEBT AND DEVELOPING COUNTRIES   12.8

Can their debt burden be lifted?

Perhaps the most serious of all balance of payments problems in the world today is that faced by some of the poorest developing countries. Many of them experience

Table 12.4	Debt ratios: average of all developing countries, selected years										
	1974	**1980**	**1984**	**1986**	**1988**	**1990**	**1994**	**1998**	**2000**	**2002**	**2004**
Ratio of debt to GNY (%)	11	21	31	35	36	36	41	42	39	39	34
Ratio of debt to exports (%)	80	86	160	225	198	179	169	155	122	117	89
Ratio of debt service to exports (%)	12	14	21	27	25	20	17	19	20	18	14

Source: *Global Development Finance* (World Bank, 2006)

massive financial outflows year after year as a result of having to 'service' debts that they have incurred in their attempts to finance development (see Table 12.4). This debt problem has its origins back in the 1970s.

The oil shocks of the 1970s

In 1973–4, oil prices quadrupled and the world went into recession. Oil imports cost more and export demand was sluggish. The current account deficit of oil-importing developing countries rose from 1.1 per cent of GDP in 1973 to 4.3 per cent in 1975.

It was not difficult to finance these deficits, however. The oil surpluses deposited in commercial banks in the industrialised world provided an important additional source of finance. The banks, flush with money and faced with slack demand in the industrialised world, were very willing to lend to developing countries to help them finance continued expansion. The world recession was short lived, and with a recovery in the demand for their exports and with their debts being eroded by high world inflation, developing countries found it relatively easy to service these increased debts (i.e. pay interest and make the necessary capital repayments).

In 1979/80 world oil prices rose again (from $15 to $38 per barrel). This second oil shock, like the first one, caused a large increase in the import bills of developing countries. But the full effects on their economies this time were very much worse, given the debts that had been accumulated in the 1970s and given the policies adopted by the industrialised world after 1979. But why were things so much worse this time?

■ The world recession was deeper and lasted longer (1980–3) and, when recovery came, it came very slowly. Developing countries' current account balance of payments deteriorated sharply. This was due both to a marked slowing down in the growth of their exports and to a fall in their export prices.
■ The tight monetary policies pursued by the industrialised countries led to a sharp increase in interest rates. This greatly increased developing countries' costs of servicing their debts. It also led to a sharp fall in inflation, which meant that the debts were not being eroded so rapidly.
■ The problem was made worse by the growing proportion of debt that was at variable interest rates. This was largely due to the increasing proportion of debt that was in the form of loans from commercial banks.

After 1979, many developing countries found it increasingly difficult to service their debts. Then in 1982 Mexico, followed by several other countries such as Brazil, Bolivia, Zaire and Sudan, declared that it would have to suspend payments. There was now a debt crisis, which threatened not only the debtor countries, but also the world banking system.

Coping with debt: rescheduling

There are two dimensions to dealing with debt problems of developing countries. The first is to cope with difficulties in servicing their debt. This usually involves some form of rescheduling of the repayments. The second dimension is to deal with the underlying causes of the problem. Here we will focus on rescheduling.

Rescheduling official loans

Official loans are renegotiated through the 'Paris Club'. Industrialised countries are members of the club, which arranges terms for the rescheduling of their loans to developing countries. Agreements normally involve delaying the date for repayment of loans currently maturing, or spreading the repayments over a longer period of time. Paris Club agreements are often made in consultation with the International Monetary Fund (IMF), which works out a programme for the debtor country to tackle its underlying economic problems.

Several attempts have been made since the mid-1980s to make rescheduling terms more generous, with longer periods before repayments start, longer to repay when they do start, and lower interest rates. In return, the developing countries have had to undertake various 'structural adjustment programmes' supervised by the IMF (see below).

But despite apparent advances made by the Paris Club in making its terms more generous, the majority of low-income countries failed to meet the required IMF conditions, and thus failed to have their debts reduced. What is more, individual Paris Club members were often reluctant to reduce debts unless they were first convinced that other members were 'paying their share'. Nevertheless some creditor countries have unilaterally introduced more generous terms and even cancelled some debts.

Rescheduling commercial bank loans

After the declarations by Mexico and other countries of their inability to service their debts, there was fear of an imminent collapse of the world banking system. Banks realised that disaster could only be averted by collective action of the banks to reschedule debts. Banks were prepared to reschedule some of the debts and to provide some additional loans in return for debtor countries undertaking structural adjustment (as described below). Additional loans, however, fell well short of the amount that was needed. Banks were unwilling to supply extra money to deal with current debt-servicing problems when they saw the problem as a long-term one of countries' inability to pay. Nevertheless, banks were increasingly setting aside funds to cover bad debt, and thus the crisis for the banks began to recede.

As banks felt less exposed to default, so they became less worried about it and less concerned to negotiate deals with debtor countries. Many of the more severely indebted countries, however, found their position still deteriorating rapidly. What is more, many of them were finding that the IMF adjustment programmes were too painful (often involving deep cuts in government expenditure) and were therefore abandoning them. Thus in 1989 US Treasury Secretary Nicholas Brady proposed measures to *reduce* debt.

The *Brady Plan* involved the IMF and the World Bank lending funds to debtor countries to enable them to repay debts to banks. In return for this instant source of liquidity, the banks would have to be prepared to accept repayment of less than the full sum (i.e. they would sell the debt back to the country at a discount). To benefit from such deals, the debtor countries would have to agree to structural adjustment programmes.

> **Pause for thought**
>
> *What are the relative advantages and disadvantages to a developing country of rescheduling its debts compared with simply defaulting on them (either temporarily or permanently)?*

Dealing with the debt

Structural reforms

The severe structural adjustment programmes frequently demanded by the IMF before it is prepared to sanction the rescheduling of debts include:

- Tight fiscal and monetary policies to reduce government deficits and reduce inflation.
- Supply-side reforms to encourage greater use of the market mechanism and greater incentives for investment.
- A more open trade policy and devaluation of the currency in order to encourage more exports and more competition.

These policies, however, can bring extreme hardship as countries are forced to deflate. Unemployment and poverty increase and growth slows down or becomes negative. Even though in the long run developing countries may emerge as more efficient and better able to compete in international trade, in the short run the suffering may be too great to bear. Popular unrest and resentment against the IMF and the country's government may lead to riots and the breakdown of law and order, and even to the overthrow of the government.

A more 'complete' structural adjustment would extend beyond simple market liberalisation and tough monetary policies to much more open access to the markets of the rich countries, to more aid and debt relief being channelled into health and education, and to greater research and development in areas that will benefit the poor (e.g. into efficient labour-intensive technology and into new strains of crops that are suitable for countries' specific climate and soil conditions and which do not require large amounts of chemicals).

Debt forgiveness

By the end of the 1990s, the debt burden of many of the poorest countries had become intolerable. Despite portions of their debt being written off under Paris Club terms, the debts of many countries were still rising. Between 1980 and 2000, the debt of sub-Saharan Africa had quadrupled from $61 billion to nearly $250 billion. Some countries, such as Ethiopia and Mozambique, were spending nearly half their export earnings on merely servicing their debt.

Even with substantial debt rescheduling and some debt cancellation, highly indebted countries have been forced to make savage cuts in government expenditure, much of it on health, education and transport. The consequence has been a growth in poverty, hunger, disease and illiteracy. African countries on average were paying four times more to rich countries in debt servicing than they were spending on health and education: it was like a patient giving a blood transfusion to a doctor! The majority of these countries had no chance of 'growing their way out of debt'. The only solution for them was for a more substantial proportion of their debt to be written off.

The heavily indebted poor countries (HIPC) initiative. In 1996 the World Bank and the IMF launched the HIPC initiative. A total of 42 countries, mainly in Africa, were identified as being in need of substantial debt relief. The number of countries was subsequently reduced to 38. The object of the initiative was to reduce the debts of such countries to 'sustainable' levels by cancelling debts above 200–250 per cent of GDP (this was reduced to 150 per cent in 1999 and to a lower level for five countries).

The HIPC process involves countries passing through two stages. In the first stage, eligible countries must demonstrate a track record of 'good performance'.

This means that they must satisfy the IMF, World Bank and Paris Club that they are undertaking adjustment measures, such as cutting government expenditure and liberalising their markets. It also involves the countries preparing a Poverty Reduction Strategy Paper (PRSP) to show how they will use debt relief to tackle poverty, and especially how they will improve health and education. Once the IMF and World Bank are satisfied that the country is making sufficient progress, the 'decision point' is reached and the country enters the second stage.

During this second stage, some interim debt relief is provided. Meanwhile the country must establish a 'sound track record' by implementing policies established at the decision point and based on the PRSP. The length of this stage depends on how long it takes the country to implement the policies. At the end of the second stage, the country reaches the 'completion point' and debts are cancelled by the various creditors, on a pro rata basis, to bring the debt to the sustainable threshold.

Despite the initial welcome given to the HIPC initiative, it has been heavily criticised:

- The thresholds have been set too high, with the resulting reduction in debt servicing being quite modest, or in many cases zero. Although, when complete, it will reduce the qualifying countries' debt stock by about 50 per cent, much of this debt was not being serviced and thus the deal resulted in only a modest reduction (less than one-third) in the crippling interest payments that most of these countries were paying. These savings amount to only 1.2 per cent of the HIPCs' GDP.
- The qualifying period has been too long. Despite having a previous 'good track record' many countries still had to adhere to the full two-stage process, which, in many cases, has turned out to be very lengthy.
- Countries in arrears to multilateral agencies, such as the World Bank and the IMF, have first had to make the back payments due. For some of the poorest countries, particularly those which have suffered civil wars (such as the Republic of Congo), such a requirement has been virtually impossible to meet. Individual donor countries have sometimes agreed to partial forgiveness of arrears, but this has generally been insufficient to allow enough funds to be diverted to clear arrears with multilateral agencies.
- The IMF reform programmes have been too harsh. The required reductions in government expenditure lead to deep cuts in basic health and education, and contractionary policies lead to reductions in investment. What is more, past experience shows that two-thirds of IMF programmes in the poorest countries break down within three years. If such experience were repeated, most countries would never receive HIPC relief.

According to many charities, such as Oxfam, a much better approach would be to target debt relief directly at poverty reduction, with the resources released being used for investment in fields such as health, education, rural development and basic infrastructure.

Nevertheless, many commentators argue that the rich world could do much more to help developing countries, particularly those ravaged by war, drought or AIDS. The United Nations has for many years called on wealthy countries to give 0.7 per cent of their GDP in aid. In practice, they give only a little over 0.2 per cent.

> **Pause for thought**
>
> *Should rich countries cancel all debts owed to them by developing countries?*

At the Gleneagles summit in Scotland in 2005, G8 leaders agreed to cancel all remaining debts of 18 HIPC countries owed to the World Bank, the IMF and the African Development Bank. This followed just four days after the Live 8 concerts which called to 'make poverty history'. Most of this debt relief, however, had already been committed under the original HIPC programme and, as Gordon Brown admitted, debt relief was required by some 70 poor countries, not just 18.

Recap

1. After the 1973 oil crisis, many developing countries borrowed heavily in order to finance their balance of trade deficits and to maintain a programme of investment. After the 1979 oil price rises, the debt problem became much more serious. There was a world recession and real interest rates were much higher. Debt increased dramatically, and much of it at variable interest rates.

2. Rescheduling can help developing countries cope with increased debt in the short run and various schemes have been adopted by creditor countries and the banks.

3. If the problem of developing countries' debt is to be tackled then simple rescheduling is not enough. The IMF favours harsh structural adjustment programmes, involving tight fiscal and monetary policies and market-orientated supply-side policies. A more 'complete' structural adjustment, however, would involve more open access to the markets of the rich countries, more aid and debt relief being channelled into health and education, and greater research and development in areas that will benefit the poor.

4. In 1996 the World Bank and the IMF launched the HIPC initiative to help reduce the debts of heavily indebted poor countries to sustainable levels. HIPC relief has been criticised, however, for being made conditional on the debtor countries pursuing excessively tough IMF adjustment programmes, for being too modest in the amount of debts cancelled, for having an excessively long qualifying period and for delays in its implementation. A better approach might be to target debt relief directly at programmes to help the poor.

QUESTIONS

1. Which of the following items are credits on the UK balance of payments and which are debits?

   (a) The expenditure by UK tourists on holidays in Greece.
   (b) The payment of dividends by foreign companies to investors resident in the UK.
   (c) Foreign residents taking out insurance policies with UK companies.
   (d) Drawing on reserves.
   (e) Investment by UK companies overseas.

2. The table shows the items in the UK's 2004 balance of payments. Calculate the following: (a) the balance on trade in goods; (b) the balance on trade in goods and services; (c) the balance of payments on current account; (d) the financial account balance; (e) the total current plus capital plus financial account balance; (f) net errors and omissions.

	£ billions
Exports of goods	190.7
Imports of goods	248.6
Exports of services	95.9
Imports of services	76.8
Net income flows	+24.0
Net current transfers	−10.9
Net capital transfers	+2.1
Net investment in UK from abroad (direct and portfolio)	126.6
Net UK investment abroad (direct and portfolio)	183.1
Other financial inflows	407.5
Other financial outflows	323.8
Reserves	−0.2

3. Explain how the current account of the balance of payments is likely to vary with the course of the business cycle.

4. Is it a 'bad thing' to have a deficit on the direct and portfolio investment part of the financial account?

5. Why may credits on a country's short-term financial account create problems for its economy in the future?

6. List some factors that could cause an increase in the credit items of the balance of payments and a decrease in the debit items. What would be the effect on the exchange rate (assuming that it is freely floating)? What effect would these exchange rate movements have on the balance of payments?

7. What policy measures could the government adopt to prevent the exchange rate movements in question 6?

8. What are the major advantages and disadvantages of fixing the exchange rate with a major currency such as the US dollar?

9. What adverse effects on the domestic economy may follow from (a) a depreciation of the exchange rate and (b) an appreciation of the exchange rate?

10. What will be the effects on the domestic economy under free-floating exchange rates if there is a rapid expansion in world economic activity? What will determine the size of these effects?

11. Why would banks not be prepared to offer a forward exchange rate to a firm for, say, five years' time?

12. Under what circumstances would the demand for imports be likely to be inelastic? How would an inelastic demand for imports affect the magnitude of fluctuations in the exchange rate?

13. Why are the price elasticities of demand for imports and exports likely to be lower in the short run than in the long run?

14. Assume that the government pursued an expansionary fiscal policy and that the resulting budget deficit led to higher interest rates. What would happen to (a) the current account and (b) the financial account of the balance of payments? What would be the likely effect on the exchange rate, given a high degree of international financial mobility?

15. Consider the argument that in the modern world of large-scale short-term international financial movements, the ability of individual countries to affect their exchange rate is very limited.

16. Why do high international financial mobility and an absence of exchange controls severely limit a country's ability to choose its interest rate?

17. What practical problems are there in achieving a general harmonisation of economic policies between (a) EU countries; (b) the major industrialised countries?

18. What are the causes of exchange rate volatility? Have these problems become greater or lesser in the past ten years? Explain why.

19. Why did the ERM with narrow bands collapse in 1993? Could this have been avoided?

20. Did the exchange rate difficulties experienced by countries under the ERM strengthen or weaken the arguments for progressing to a single European currency?

21. Under what circumstances may a pegged exchange rate system like the ERM (a) help to prevent speculation; (b) aggravate the problem of speculation?

22. By what means would a depressed country in an Economic Union with a single currency be able to recover? Would the market provide a satisfactory solution or would (Union) government intervention be necessary, and if so, what form would the intervention take?

23. Assume that just some of the members of a common market like the EU adopt full economic and monetary union, including a common currency. What are the advantages and disadvantages to those members joining the full EMU and to those not joining?

24. Is the eurozone likely to be an optimal currency area? Is it more or less likely to be so over time? Explain your answer.

25. It is often argued that international convergence of economic indicators is a desirable objective. Does this mean that countries should seek to achieve the same rate of economic growth, monetary growth, interest rates, budget deficits as a percentage of their GDP, etc?

26. Why is it difficult to achieve international harmonisation of economic policies?

27. To what extent was the debt crisis of the early 1980s caused by inappropriate policies that had been pursued by the debtor countries?

28. Imagine that you are an ambassador of a developing country at an international confer- ence. What would you try to persuade the rich countries to do in order to help you and other poor countries overcome the debt problem? How would you set about persuading them that it was in their own interests to help you?

Additional case studies on the *Essentials of Economics* MyEconLab (www.pearsoned.co.uk/sloman)

12.1 **The UK's balance of payments deficit.** An examination of the UK's persistent trade and current account deficits.

12.2 **The Gold Standard.** A historical example of fixed exchange rates.

12.3 **A high exchange rate.** This case looks at whether a high exchange rate is necessarily bad news for exporters.

12.4 **The sterling crisis of early 1985.** When the pound fell almost to $1.00.

12.5 **Currency turmoil in the 1990s.** A crisis in Mexico; a rising yen and German mark; a falling US dollar – why did this all happen?

12.6 **The 1997/8 crisis in Asia.** The role played by the IMF.

12.7 **Argentina in crisis.** An examination of the collapse of the Argentinian economy in 2001/2.

12.8 **Attempts at harmonisation.** A look at the meetings of the G7 economies, where they attempt to come to agreement on means of achieving stable and sustained worldwide economic growth.

12.9 **The Tobin tax.** An examination of the possible use of small taxes on foreign exchange trans- actions. The purpose is to reduce currency fluctuations.

12.10 **The euro, the US dollar and world currency markets.** An analysis of the relationship between the euro and the dollar.

12.11 **Using interest rates to control both aggregate demand and the exchange rate.** A problem of one instrument and two targets.

12.12 **The UK Labour government's convergence criteria for euro membership.** An examination of the five tests set by the UK government that would have to be passed before the question of euro membership would be put to the electorate in a referendum.

12.13 **Debt and the environment.** How high levels of debt can encourage developing countries to damage their environment in an attempt to increase export earnings.

12.14 **The great escape.** This case examines the problem of capital flight from developing countries to rich countries.

12.15 **Swapping debt.** Schemes to convert a developing country's debt into other forms, such as shares in its industries.

12.16 **Economic aid.** Does aid provide a solution to the debt problem?

Sections of chapter covered in *WinEcon* – Sloman, *Essentials of Economics*

Essentials of Economics section	*WinEcon* section
12.1	12.1
12.2	12.2
12.3	12.3
12.4	–
12.5	–
12.6	–
12.7	–
12.8	12.8

See also, *WinEcon* Chapter 13 on Basic Maths for Economics.

Websites relevant to this chapter

Numbers and sections refer to websites listed in the Web Appendix and hotlinked from MyEconLab. Visit:

www.pearsoned.co.uk/sloman

- For news articles relevant to this chapter, see the *Economics News Articles* link from MyEconLab.
- For general news on countries' balance of payments and exchange rates, see websites in section A, and particularly A1–5, 7–9, 20–25, 31. For articles on various aspects of economic development, see A27, 28; I9. See also links to newspapers worldwide in A38, 43 and 44, and the news search feature in Google at A41. See also links to news video and audio in A42.
- For international data on balance of payments and exchange rates, see *World Economic Outlook* in H4 and *OECD Economic Outlook* in B21 (also in section 6 of B1). See also the trade topic in I14.
- For details of individual countries' balance of payments, see B32.
- For UK data on balance of payments, see B1, *1. National Statistics* > the fourth link > *Economy* > *United Kingdom Balance of Payments – the Pink Book*. See also B3, 34; F2. For EU data, see G1 > *The Statistical Annex* > *Foreign trade and current balance*.
- For exchange rates, see A3; B34; F2, 6, 8.
- For data on debt and development, see B24 (*Global Development Finance*), B31 and 40. Also see the debt section in I14.
- For discussion papers on the balance of payments and exchange rates, see H4 and 7.
- For information on debt and developing countries, see H4, 7, 9, 10, 12–14, 17–19. See also links to development sites in I9.
- Sites I7 and 11 contain links to *Balance of payments and exchange rates* in *International economics* and to *Capital flows and aid* in *Economic Development*.
- For student resources relevant to this chapter, see sites C1–7, 9, 10, 19. See also *Virtual Developing Country* in *Virtual Worlds* in site C2.

Web Appendix

12.1 The effectiveness of fiscal and monetary policies. A comparison of the effectiveness of fiscal and monetary policies under fixed and floating exchange rates.

PART EIGHT

Government Intervention
and Business

Chapter 17
Governments and Markets

Governments and markets

Ian Worthington

The central role played by government in the operation of the economy and its markets has been a recurrent theme of this book. Paradoxically, many of the government's interventionist policies have been designed to remove existing barriers to the operations of free markets and to promote greater competition and choice. In some cases, the government's strategy has been to disengage the state from some of its involvement in the economy – as in the case of 'privatisation'. In other cases, policy changes and legislation have been deemed the appropriate course of action – as in the government's approach to competition policy and to the operation of the labour market.

Learning outcomes

Having read this chapter you should be able to:

● outline the rationale underlying the government's approach to markets

● analyse and evaluate UK privatisation policy and give examples of privatisation in other countries

● explain the changing nature of UK competition policy, including the legislative and institutional framework within which it operates

● identify government initiatives in the labour market and, in particular, its approach to employment and trade union power

Key terms

Competition Act 1998
Competition Commission
Competition policy
Director General of Fair
  Trading
Economic efficiency

Keynesianism
Labour market
Labour market flexibility
Learning and Skills
  Council
Monetarism

New Deal
Office of Fair Trading
Privatisation
Third way
Training and Enterprise
  Councils

Introduction

A belief in the virtue of competition and in the need to develop competitive markets remains a central tenet of government economic policy in capitalist states. At the heart of this belief lies the widely accepted view that competition provides the best means of improving **economic efficiency** and of encouraging wealth creation. Proponents of this view argue that competition:

- ensures an efficient allocation of resources between competing uses, through the operation of the price system;
- puts pressure on firms to perform as efficiently as possible;
- provides a mechanism for flexible adjustment to change, whether in consumption or in the conditions of supply;
- protects consumers from potential exploitation by producers, by offering alternative sources of purchase.

It follows that an absence or lack of competition in either the factor or product markets is seen as detrimental to the well-being of the economy as a whole and that governments have a responsibility for ensuring wherever possible that markets operate freely, with a minimum of state interference.

Much of the philosophical basis for this perspective can be traced to the **monetarists** who tended to dominate official thinking in Britain and elsewhere for much of the last two decades of the twentieth century. Broadly speaking, monetarists argue that levels of output and employment in the economy are supply-determined, in contrast to the **Keynesian** view which emphasises the importance of demand in shaping economic activity. Accordingly, supply-side policies seek to improve the output responsiveness of the economy, by focusing on the workings of markets and in particular on removing the obstacles which prevent markets from functioning efficiently.

The influence of the supply-side approach to economic management can be seen in a number of key areas, and in particular, in the UK government's policy of privatisation and in the reforms in the labour market in the 1980s. Concerns over competition and potential abuses of market power also figure prominently in governmental approaches to monopolies and mergers. These three aspects of government intervention in markets – privatisation, competition policy and labour market reforms – are considered separately below and illustrate how state involvement can be a key influence in the environment of individual business organisations on both the input and output side.

Privatisation policy

On privatisation

In its broadest sense, **privatisation** involves the transfer of assets or different forms of economic activity from the public sector to the private sector. In the United Kingdom such transfers occurred throughout the 1980s and 1990s under different

Conservative administrations. Although the current Labour government has continued the process to some degree (e.g. with the partial privatisation of the National Air Traffic Services), the heyday of huge state sell-offs in Britain has probably passed. In government circles the talk is now of public/private partnerships as a mechanism for increasing private sector investment in the public services – part of what has become known as the **third way** in British politics.

In practice, the term privatisation has been applied to a range of activities that involve a measure of state disengagement from economic activity. Typically these have included:

- The sale of government-owned assets, especially nationalised industries (e.g. British Telecom, British Gas) or industries in which the government had a substantial shareholding (e.g. BP).
- The contracting out of services normally provided by the public sector (e.g. school meals, hospital cleaning).
- The deregulation or liberalisation of activities over which the state had previously placed some restriction (e.g. the deregulation of bus routes or postal services).
- The injection of private capital into areas traditionally financed by the public sector, including various Private Financing Initiatives aimed at large public sector projects such as building schools, hospitals and roads.
- The sale of local authority-owned property to private citizens or organisations (e.g. council houses, school playing fields).
- The privatisation of government agencies (e.g. Her Majesty's Inspectors for Education).

Of these, the sale of state assets – especially the public corporations and nationalised industries – has been the main plank of UK privatisation policy and the one which has captured the most public and media attention. For this reason, in the discussion below attention is focused on this aspect of the privatisation programme.

The scope of government asset sales in the period 1979–96 is indicated in Table 17.1. In the first phase, between 1979 and 1983, these tended to generate relatively small sums of money compared with what was realised in later years and generally involved the sale of government shares in companies such as British Aerospace, Britoil, BP, ICL and Ferranti. Between 1983 and 1988, the government disposed of a

Table 17.1 Major asset sales, 1979–1996

Amersham International	British Telecom	National Grid
Associated British Ports	Britoil	Railtrack
British Aerospace	Cable & Wireless	Rolls-Royce
British Airports Authority	Electricity industry	Rover Group
British Airways	Enterprise Oil	Royal Ordnance
British Coal	Fairey Aviation	Sealink (British Rail)
British Energy	Ferranti	Short Brothers
British Gas	Forestry Commission	Unipart (Rover)
British Petroleum	Istel (Rover)	Water authorities
British Rail Hotels	Jaguar (British Leyland)	Wytch Farm onshore oil (British Gas)
British Steel	National Bus Company	
British Sugar Corporation	National Enterprise Board Holding	

number of its largest industrial and commercial undertakings, including British Telecom, British Gas and British Airways, along with Rolls-Royce and Jaguar. These were followed by the sale of British Steel, the Rover Group, the National Bus Company and, more significantly, by the regional water authorities and the electricity industry in the late 1980s and early 1990s.[1] In the most recent phase, major sales have included British Coal, Railtrack, the flotation of the National Grid, the privatisation of the nuclear industry and the selling off of the National Air Traffic Services (NATS). It is worth noting that Railtrack, having gone through a period of administration, has subsequently been turned into a not-for-profit organisation called Network Rail.

In disposing of national assets governments have used a number of different methods, including selling shares to a single buyer, usually another company (e.g. the sale of Rover), selling shares to the company's management and workers (e.g. the management buyout of the National Freight Corporation), and selling shares on the open market for purchase by individuals and institutions (e.g. the stock market flotation of British Telecom). In some cases the process took place in several stages, as a proportion of shares was released on to the market over several years (e.g. BP); in other cases a one-off sale occurred, with investors invited to subscribe for the whole of the equity (e.g. British Steel). As Figure 17.1 indicates, proceeds from privatisation sales between 1979 and 1991 exceeded £34 billion, with the majority of the revenue being raised in the mid- to late 1980s. Estimates for the period 1991–4 suggest that privatisation yielded a further £25–£30 billion for the Exchequer. Over the whole period of privatisation it is thought that total revenues

Figure 17.1   Proceeds from privatisation

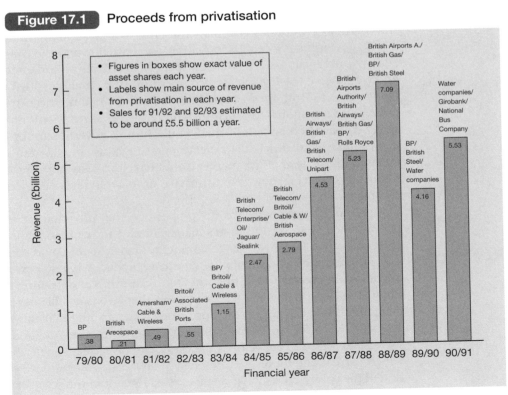

Source: Cook, G. C., *Privatisation in the 1980s and 1990s*, Hidcote Press, 1992.

from the sale of state-owned industries amounted to around £100 billion (at 2000 prices). This is equivalent to approximately 2 per cent of total government expenditure (or revenues) for that period. Interestingly, these amounts now seem rather modest when set against the significant sums invested by the UK Treasury in supporting Northern Rock during the 2008 credit crisis. As part of this support, the bank has been 'nationalised' in order to protect the taxpayers' interest.

Postscript

The global financial crisis (see 'International business in action', below) has resulted in a number of governments taking steps to protect their financial institutions. In some cases this has meant the nationalisation or part-nationalisation of those institutions. While this suggests a reversal of the privatisation process, in reality this should be seen as a particular response aimed at addressing a specific problem. It is not a general trend.

Rationale

The roots of privatisation policy lie in the attempt by the Conservative government, then under the leadership of Margaret Thatcher (1979–90), to tackle the perceived deficiencies in the supply side of the UK economy. Central to the government's philosophy was the belief that the free market was a superior method of allocating economic resources and that large-scale state involvement in business activity hampered economic progress. 'Rolling back the frontiers of the state' – by reducing the size of the public sector – was consequently seen as a key component in improving the country's economic performance at both national and international level.

The government's case for privatisation centred round the claim that the sale of state-owned businesses would improve their efficiency and general performance, and would give rise to increased competition that would broaden consumer choice. Under state control, it was argued that businesses had no incentive to strive for efficiency or to respond to consumer preferences, since many of them lacked any direct competition and all of them could turn to government for financial support, if revenue was insufficient to meet operating costs. In contrast, firms which were exposed to the 'test' of the market would have to satisfy both the consumer and the financial markets if they were to survive or to avoid takeover by more efficient and competitive organisations.[2]

Allied to this argument was the proposition that privatisation would improve the performance of an organisation's management and workers. Freed from the need to meet objectives laid down by government, management could concentrate on commercial goals such as profitability, improved productivity and cost reduction, and on encouraging greater flexibility and technical innovation within the organisation. Implicit in these claims was the acceptance that a considerable degree of restructuring would need to occur within each privatised company and that this was likely to act as an incentive to the workforce to improve its performance. Additional encouragement was also expected to derive from the use of employee share-ownership schemes, under which current employees within a newly privatised company were offered a proportion of the equity, thus giving them a vested interest in the organisation's fortunes.

The sale of shares to employees and to the public generally was also presented as a benefit of privatisation in that it helped to encourage wider share ownership and to create a 'share-owning democracy', with increased sympathies towards capitalist modes of production (and possibly the Conservative party). Concomitantly, the sale of state assets also served to reduce the size of the public sector borrowing requirement (PSBR) – since revenue from sales was counted as negative public expenditure – and this helped to reduce the government's debt burden and to take some of the pressure off interest rates, as well as releasing funds for use by the private sector.

Criticisms of privatisation

Opponents of privatisation have likened the process to 'selling the family silver' – disposing of important national assets for short-term financial gains. Under privatisation, these assets, once owned by the general public, have passed into the hands of those individuals and organisations able and willing to buy shares including overseas buyers who could ultimately gain control of important parts of British industry, unless prevented from doing so by government action (e.g. through a 'golden share'). To add to this criticism, some observers claimed that valuable assets, bought over many years by public funds, were sold off too cheaply to private investors who have reaped the benefit at the expense of the general public. Only industries which were not attractive to the stock market have tended to remain in public ownership and this has meant that the taxpayer has had to pay the bill to support their continued existence.

Further criticisms have included the loss of future government revenue from the sale of profitable state-owned businesses and the problem of ensuring that commercial goals are not allowed to displace completely the broader economic goals once pursued by nationalised industries (e.g. the possible closure of unprofitable rural telephone boxes or railway lines under privatisation). In essence, the fear has been that once freed from government regulation, privatised companies will tend to replace the loss-making 'public service' element of their former activities with products or services that offer the greatest levels of profit. While this will benefit some consumers, the cost is likely to be borne by other buyers who have limited market power and, in some cases, no alternative product to turn to.

This problem of lack of choice has been particularly acute where the privatisation of a state monopoly has given rise to a private monopoly, as initially was the case with many of the privatised utilities. Despite the establishment of 'regulators' to oversee the operations of some of the newly privatised concerns (see Table 17.2) and to act as a kind of proxy for true competition, some opponents still feel that the interest of consumers is not fully protected under the current arrangements. They also feel that exploitation through higher prices or other abuses of market power remains possible. Evidence from investigations by the former Monopolies and Mergers Commission (see below) and from the regulatory authorities suggests that this view is not without foundation. This evidence has also conveniently been used by the Treasury in recent years as a justification for levying windfall taxes on the profits of the privatised utilities as a means of boosting Exchequer revenues.

Table 17.2 Key regulatory bodies for selected privatised utilities

Name	Date established	Main activities
Office of Tele-communications (OFTEL)	1984	Regulated BT – especially line rentals, inland calls, overseas calls; provided conditions for new entrants and regulated the equipment market. Its duties have now passed to OFCOM (see below).
Office of Water Services (OFWAT)	1989	Regulates domestic and non-domestic supply by water and sewerage companies. Regulates price increases to customers.
Office of Gas and Electricity Markets (OFGEM)	2000	Regulates the gas and electricity industries in England, Scotland and Wales with the aim of enhancing customer choice and value by promoting competition and controlling monopolies. Replaced OFGAS and OFFER.
Office of Communications (OFCOM)	2003	Regulates the UK communications industries with responsibilities for television, radio, telecommunications and wireless communications services.

web link

Regulatory body websites include *www.ofcom.gov.uk*, *www.ofwat.gov.uk*, *www.ofgem.gov.uk*

Privatisation overseas

Before offering an assessment of privatisation in the United Kingdom, it is worth noting that most other states have embarked on similar experiments in economic liberalisation, irrespective of their size, ideology or level of economic development. At the end of the 1980s it was estimated that worldwide sales of state assets to the private sector exceeded $25 billion or about £14 000 million and this figure has continued to grow with the ongoing privatisation process in eastern Europe and elsewhere. For example, according to *The Economist* (23 November 1996), in the period 1985–95 the combined revenues from privatisation in France, Germany, Italy, the Netherlands and Spain alone were in excess of $70 billion, with France having the lion's share of $34 billion. For the same period the United Kingdom's receipts were estimated at $85 billion, making it the most significant privatisation programme within the OECD.

The following examples of overseas privatisation give some idea of the wide range of state assets from different sectors of the economy that have been sold by governments of different political complexions over the last two to three decades.

● In Portugal major privatisations between 1989 and 1997 included banks, insurance companies, public utilities and businesses producing cement, oil, paper products, tobacco and beer.
● In the Netherlands privatisations have included the national airline (KLM) and the water, gas and electricity utilities.
● In Brazil part of the country's rail network has been sold off; in Jamaica privatisation has included the National Commercial Bank and the Caribbean Cement Company.

- In France privatisations range from chemicals and oil to insurance, banking, public utilities, vehicles and parts of the motorway network.
- In India the government has divested a significant proportion of public sector enterprises with sales including businesses involved with steel, zinc and petro-chemicals.
- In China the government has proceeded cautiously with privatisation, starting with the sale of the smaller state-owned enterprises to private owners and more recently the partial privatisation of some larger listed companies.

Arguably the most dramatic and exciting experiments in privatisation have taken place in eastern Europe, particularly among the transition economies which have moved from a planned economic system towards private enterprise. In the newly unified Germany, for instance, the federal government decided to appoint a special privatisation agency (Treuhand) to oversee and assist in the large-scale privatisation of former East German state industries and firms, and other governments (including those in Hungary, the Czech Republic and Poland) have embarked on similar programmes of rolling privatisation and have undertaken legal and institutional changes to speed up the process. While progress has varied in the different states and has generally been influenced by questions of economic and political stability (e.g. in the Russian Federation), the large-scale sell-off of public assets by the former communist states will undoubtedly continue into the foreseeable future. Current evidence suggests that the transition in these countries is proving a significantly more painful experience than that encountered in states already possessing a market-based economic system (see e.g. the article by Nick Potts in the Further reading section at the end of the chapter).

mini case   Government to the rescue

While privatisation has gripped the imaginations of governments of all persuasions for the last two to three decades, there often comes a time in economic history when circumstances dictate that a particular economic orthodoxy has to be temporarily (if not permanently) abandoned. Arguably one of the best examples of this was the decision by the US government to take the two American mortgage giants Fanny Mae and Freddie Mac into temporary public ownership.

The two companies concerned account for about 50 per cent of all US home loans and play an active role in buying up mortgages from lenders, parcelling them up and then selling them on to financial institutions across the globe. With the onset of the credit crisis in 2007/8, Fanny Mae and Freddie Mac were faced with multi-billion-dollar losses as homeowners defaulted and house prices tumbled.

While the two US institutions were far from being the only businesses facing severe financial problems, their importance to the US housing market meant that their precarious position threatened not just the property market in America, but also the wider global financial system (see 'International business in action: The global financial crisis').

In an effort to reassure the financial markets, the US decided that the two government-sponsored enterprises should become government-owned businesses on a temporary basis, what in the US is known as 'conservatorship'. For the foreseeable future, Fanny Mae and Freddy Mac are to be run by the Federal Housing Finance Agency and underwritten by public money. This is similar to the arrangement in the UK, where Northern Rock Building Society – another victim of the credit crisis – has been temporarily nationalised by the UK government.

Assessment[3]

Measured against some of the UK government's stated objectives, privatisation appears to have been successful, and has involved a transfer of ownership of over 7 per cent of GDP from the public to the private sector. Apart from the fact that many other national governments have sought to emulate Britain's approach to asset sales, the privatisation programme has been cited as an important component of the improvement in the supply side of the economy after 1979. It has also been a critical element in promoting the free market approach which has come to dominate governmental thinking in Britain and elsewhere for over two decades. All of this has evidently been achieved with the support of the British public (although some opinion polls have indicated a decline in the popularity of privatisation). In 1979, for instance, only 7 per cent of adults owned shares in public companies. By the early 1990s this figure had risen to 25 per cent, or 11 million shareholders, many of whom had bought shares for the first time in the 1980s with the sale of the big public utilities.

This significant growth in the number of ordinary shareholders can be explained in a number of ways. For a start, most stock market flotations were accompanied by extensive and costly advertising campaigns which helped to raise public awareness and to attract investors (e.g. British Gas's 'Tell Sid' campaign). Added to this, investors in public utilities were often offered special incentives to buy shares in businesses they dealt with on a regular basis (e.g. cheaper telephone bills) or in which some of them worked and therefore had a vested interest. Perhaps most importantly, and with the benefit of hindsight, some privatisation stock appears to have been sold at substantially lower prices than the market would bear and this guaranteed quick profits for people who bought and then sold immediately as prices rose. In the circumstances it is not surprising that many flotations were hugely oversubscribed – a fact which led to criticism that some privatisation stock had been considerably undervalued.

Many shareholders who invested for longer-term capital gains also benefited from underpricing of share issues and in some cases received free additional shares and other benefits (including annual dividends) by holding on to their investment. An analysis by Gary Cook of the share performance of privatised companies shows that some of the earlier privatisations have produced spectacular long-term gains, though some privatised company shares performed less well.[4] Cable & Wireless shares, for example, were issued at an average price of 56p in the early 1980s and were trading at 588p by August 1991. Similarly, BT's initial issue price of 130p in 1984/5 had risen to 391p by the same date, a threefold increase despite the stock market crash in 1987.

Whatever the reason for the growth in share ownership, it is clear that privatisation, along with the sale of council houses, helped the Conservative government of the day to claim that it encouraged the growth of a 'property-owning democracy' in which an increasing number of citizens held a stake in the success of the economy and therefore in the performance of the private sector. That said, it is still the case that the majority of shares in public companies are held by individuals in better-paid professional and managerial occupations and that overall the percentage of *all* UK shares owned by individuals has fallen dramatically over the last 30 years. In contrast, the holdings of institutional investors (such as insurance companies and pension funds) have risen rapidly – a fact which not only gives them significant influence over the future of many public companies, but which also suggests that the claim of wider share ownership has to be treated with a degree of caution.[5]

Notwithstanding this latter point, the government's relative success in selling state assets also helped it initially to achieve another one of its objectives – that of reducing the size of the PSBR. From the early 1980s onwards, public expenditure as a percentage of GDP fell substantially – partly as a result of the revenues from the privatisation programme – and by the latter part of the decade the government had a budget surplus (or public sector debt repayment) as revenue exceeded spending. Once again, however, this apparent benefit needs to be seen in context. For a start, much of the improvement in public finances during this period was a result of the government's restraint on public spending, rather than the effects of privatisation, though the receipts clearly helped the government to balance its books. Added to this, by the early 1990s, as the recession took hold, public spending rapidly began to outstrip the amounts raised in revenue, causing a dramatic growth in the size of government borrowing, despite a decade of privatisation receipts. Understandably, some critics have asked whether the sale of valuable state assets was in vain and distracted the incumbent government from addressing some of the underlying structural weaknesses in the British economy.

With regard to privatisation as a spur to greater organisational efficiency and performance, this is an area in which assessment is particularly problematical. Part of the difficulty arises from the fact that direct comparisons between state and privatised companies are often impossible, since some goods and services have not normally been provided by both the public and private sectors simultaneously (e.g. railways). In addition, even where such provision occurs (e.g. the health service), the public sector usually has to pursue a number of non-commercial objectives laid down by politicians and this makes direct comparisons somewhat unfair, particularly if profitability alone is taken as a measure of performance.

One way of approaching some of these problems is to attempt a comparison between the performance of an organisation before privatisation and its performance after it has become part of the private sector – using measures such as relative profitability, productivity or levels of service. Yet, once again, significant methodological difficulties exist which call into question the validity of many of the conclusions. Industries such as British Gas and British Telecom, for instance, have always been profitable and profits have tended to grow since privatisation; but this could as easily reflect the benefits of monopoly price rises as improvements in efficiency resulting from a change in ownership. Conversely, the decline in the fortunes of the once publicly owned steel industry could be interpreted as a decline in efficiency and/or performance under privatisation, when in fact a combination of overcapacity in the world steel industry and the impact of the recession have clearly been the main culprits.

Comparisons of productivity can also be misleading and usually fail to take into account the substantial 'economic' costs of privatisation (e.g. large-scale redundancies). Many state industries were substantially restructured prior to flotation in order to attract investors, and the resulting job losses – invariably at the taxpayer's expense – helped many newly privatised businesses to claim substantial productivity gains in their first few years of trading. Perhaps ironically, the greatest improvements in productivity in the period 1984–91 often occurred within industries nationalised at the time – such as British Coal and British Rail – whose massive redundancy programmes helped them to outpace the productivity gains of manufacturing industry by anything up to three times, according to Treasury figures. In such circumstances, it would be easy – though probably unreasonable – to conclude that while being privatised was good for productivity, it was not as good as not being privatised!

Further complications arise when one compares the performance of privatised companies which have remained monopolies with the performance of those which have consistently operated under competitive market conditions. Writing in the heyday of privatisation (the *Guardian*, 3 March 1993), Victor Keegan argued that the fortunes of companies such as British Steel, Rolls-Royce and Rover had been seriously affected by the sort of violent cyclical disturbances which had previously driven them into the public sector and that this had significantly influenced their attractiveness to private investors. In comparison, businesses which had faced little effective competition in some areas of the market (e.g. Cable & Wireless, British Airways) and those facing none (e.g. the water companies, British Gas) had invariably performed well for their shareholders; though the price of this success had frequently been paid by customers (in the form of inflated charges) and workers (in the form of redundancy).

Keegan's conclusion, that it is competition rather than ownership which acts as a spur to increased efficiency, is one that is widely held and underlies some of the recent attempts by government and by the regulatory bodies to identify ways of reducing the monopoly power of the privatised public utilities. The proposition is that under a more competitive market structure the commercial pressures of the marketplace force management to seek ways of improving organisational efficiency and performance, for fear of the consequences if they fail to meet the needs of the consumer and the investor. If left to their own devices, the large utilities are unlikely to put themselves to such 'tests' voluntarily, and this approach would presumably find favour with shareholders who have a vested interest in maximising revenue. Paradoxically, in order to improve the position of the consumer, government may be forced to intervene more aggressively and imaginatively in the marketplace, in order to promote greater competition among producers and increased choice for the consumer. Such intervention could easily be justified under current competition policy.

Competition policy

Whereas privatisation has focused on the balance between public and private provision within the overall economy, UK government **competition policy** has largely been concerned with regulating market behaviour and in particular with controlling potential abuses of market power by firms acting singly or in concert in specific markets. To achieve these aims, successive British governments have relied mainly on legislation, as well as on a measure of self-regulation and persuasion, and have generally taken a more liberal view of market structures than that taken in the United States, where monopolies have been deemed illegal for over a century. This legislative framework to regulate market activity, and the institutional arrangements established to support it, are considered immediately below.

There are lots of useful websites relating to UK competition policy. A good starting point is the Office of Fair Trading (OFT) which is at *www.oft.gov.uk*
You could also try the Competition Commission at *www.competition-commission.org.uk* and the Deparment of Business, Enterprise and Regulatory Reform at *www.berr.gov.uk*

The evolving legislative framework

Official attempts to control market behaviour through statutory means date back to the late 1940s with the passage of the Monopolies and Restrictive Practices Act 1948. This Act, which established the Monopolies Commission (later the Monopolies and Mergers Commission), empowered it to investigate industries in which any single firm (a unitary monopoly), or a group of firms acting together, could restrict competition by controlling at least one-third of the market. Following such an investigation, the Commission would publish a report which was either factual or advisory and it was then the responsibility of the relevant government department to decide what course of action, if any, to take to remove practices regarded as contrary to the public interest. In the event, the majority of the Commission's recommendations tended to be ignored, though it did have some success in highlighting the extent of monopoly power in the United Kingdom in the early post-war period.

In 1956 investigations into unitary monopolies were separated from those into restrictive practices operated by a group of firms, with the enactment of the Restrictive Trade Practices Act. This Act, which outlawed the widespread custom of manufacturers jointly enforcing the retail prices at which their products could be sold, also required firms to register any form of restrictive agreement that they were operating (e.g. concerning prices, sales, production) with the Registrar of Restrictive Practices. It was the latter's responsibility to bring such agreements before the Restrictive Practices Court and they were automatically deemed 'against the public interest', unless they could be justified in one of a number of ways (e.g. benefiting consumers, employment, exports). Further extensions to the Act in 1968 (to cover 'information agreements') and in 1973 (to cover services) were ultimately consolidated in the Restrictive Trade Practices Act 1976. This new Act vested the responsibility for bringing restrictive practices before the court in the recently established Director General of Fair Trading (see below).

A further extension of legislative control came with the passage of the Monopolies and Mergers Act 1965. The Act allowed the Monopolies Commission to investigate actual or proposed mergers or acquisitions which looked likely to enhance monopoly power and which involved, at that time, the takeover of assets in excess of £5 million. The aim of this Act was to provide a means of regulating activities which threatened to be contrary to the public interest, by permitting government to decide which mergers and acquisitions should be prohibited and which should be allowed to proceed and, if necessary, under what terms. Additional steps in this direction were taken with the passage of the Fair Trading Act 1973 and the Competition Act 1980, the main provisions of which are summarised below:

1 A scale monopoly exists where at least 25 per cent of a market is controlled by a single buyer or seller; this can be applied to sales at local as well as national level and can include monopolies resulting from nationalisation.

2 Investigations can occur when two related companies (e.g. a parent and a subsidiary) control 25 per cent of a market or when separate companies operate to restrict competition even without a formal agreement (e.g. tacit collusion).

3 Mergers involving gross worldwide assets of over £70 million or a market share of over 25 per cent can be investigated.

4 Responsibility for overseeing consumer affairs, and competition policy generally, lies with the Director General of Fair Trading (DGFT), operating from the Office of Fair Trading (OFT). The DGFT has the power to make monopoly references to the renamed Monopolies and Mergers Commission (MMC) and to advise the relevant government minister on whether merger proposals should be investigated by the MMC.

In the latter context, it is worth noting that while there was no legal obligation on companies to inform the OFT of their merger plans, the Companies Act 1989 introduced a formal procedure enabling them to pre-notify the DGFT of merger proposals, in the expectation that such pre-notification would enhance the prospects for rapid clearance in cases which were deemed straightforward.

While the question of market share still remains an important influence on official attitudes to proposed mergers or takeovers, there is no doubt that in recent years increasing attention has focused on anti-competitive practices and under the Competition Act 1980 such practices by individuals or firms – as opposed to whole markets – could be referred to the MMC for investigation. In addition the Act allowed the Commission to scrutinise the work of certain public sector agencies and to consider the efficiency and costs of the service they provided and any possible abuses of monopoly power, and similar references could also be made in the case of public utilities which had been privatised (e.g. under the Telecommunication Act 1984, the Gas Act 1986, the Water Industry Act 1991).

Additional statutory control has also come in the form of EU legislation governing activities which have cross-border implications. Article 81 (formerly Article 85) of the Treaty of Rome prohibits agreements between enterprises which result in a restriction or distortion in competition within the Union (e.g. price fixing, market sharing). Article 82 (formerly Article 86) prohibits a dominant firm, or group of firms, from using their market power to exploit consumers, while further Articles prohibit the provision of government subsidies if they distort, or threaten to distort, competition between industries or individual firms.

Moreover, under Regulation 4064/89 which came into force in September 1990, concentrations or mergers which have a 'Community dimension' have become the subject of exclusive jurisdiction by the European Commission. Broadly speaking, this means that mergers involving firms with a combined worldwide turnover of more than €5 billion became subject to Commission control, provided that the EU turnover of each of at least two companies involved exceeded €250 million and the companies concerned did not have more than two-thirds of their EU turnover within one and the same member state. Mergers which do not qualify under the regulation remain, of course, subject to national competition law.

Since previous editions of this book were published the UK government has acted to bring UK competition policy into line with EU law. Under the **Competition Act 1998** – which came into force on 1 March 2000 – two basic prohibitions have been introduced:

1 A prohibition on anti-competitive agreements, based closely on Article 85 of the Treaty of Rome (now Article 81).

2 A prohibition of abuse of dominant position in a market, based on Article 86 (now Article 82).

These prohibitions, which replace a number of other pieces of legislation (e.g. the Restrictive Trade Practices Act 1976; the Resale Prices Act 1976; the majority of the Competition Act 1980), were designed to be enforced primarily by the DGFT, together with the utility regulators, who would have concurrent powers in their own sphere of operations. Companies breaching either or both of the prohibitions would be liable to fines and may be required to pay compensation to third parties affected by their anti-competitive behaviour.

mini case Accusations of price fixing

Governments in market-based economies normally argue that markets work best when there is competition between businesses and that this benefits consumers in a variety of ways, including increased choice and more competitive prices. For a market to work effectively and in the interests of consumers, firms involved in the supply side of the market (e.g. producers and retailers) need to work independently and should not collude or share information with their rivals in any way that could distort competition. Cartels, price fixing and other anti-competitive practices are usually outlawed by governments, but this does not guarantee that such practices do not exist in some markets.

To illustrate the 'problem' of anti-competitive behaviour, we can examine a number of recent cases in the UK where there have been allegations of 'price fixing' by suppliers/retailers:

- Major supermarkets were accused of price fixing of dairy products and were fined over £100 million after admitting they acted together on the pricing of milk, butter and cheese.
- British Airways and Virgin Atlantic admitted colluding to fix fuel surcharges for passengers on the transatlantic route and large fines were imposed.

- In 2008, the Office of Fair Trading accused the tobacco groups Imperial and Gallagher of collaborating with some major retailers (including major supermarkets) on the prices of cigarettes and rolling tobacco.
- OFT is also investigating over a hundred British construction companies that are alleged to have fixed bids when tendering for major contracts such as schools, hospitals and private sector developments.

A central feature of all these cases is the claim that the alleged collaboration between the companies involved worked to the disadvantage of consumers (whether individuals, other businesses or public sector bodies such as local authorities). In short, price fixing – whatever form it takes – tends to make products/services more expensive than they would be under truly competitive market conditions. Under UK law, firms that are found to engage in such practices can be fined up to 10 per cent of their UK turnover, although this rarely happens, particularly as some of the accused tend to admit a degree of liability in exchange for a reduced fine.

With the passage of the Enterprise Act in 2002, further significant changes have been introduced, including the addition of strong deterrents for individuals involved in breaches of competition law, the modernisation of the monopoly and merger rules, and the restructuring and extension of the powers of the competition authorities (see below). Whereas the Fair Trading Act emphasised the notion of the 'public interest' in examining anti-competitive practices, the new legislation applies the test of a 'substantial lessening of competition' when the competition authorities are called upon to assess an existing or planned merger. To be deemed a 'relevant merger situation', one of two thresholds has to be met: the value of UK turnover of the enterprise acquired/to be acquired exceeds £70 million (the turnover test); or the share of goods/services in the UK or a large part of the UK that is/will be held by the merged enterprise is at least 25 per cent (the share of supply test).

In a further development in 2004, the European Commission adopted a regulation which gives the national competition authorities and courts additional responsibilities for the application of Articles 81 and 82 (see above). In essence the Office of Fair Trading and the sectoral regulators now have the power to enforce EC competition rules and, as a consequence, the Competition Act 1998 has been amended to bring it in line with the new European system.

The institutional framework

The formulation and implementation of UK competition policy has traditionally involved a variety of agencies, including the former Department of Trade and Industry, the **Office of Fair Trading**, the Monopolies and Mergers Commission and the Mergers Panel. Of these, the MMC (now the Competition Commission) and the OFT deserve special attention.

From its foundation in 1948 until its replacement in 1999, the Monopolies and Mergers Commission remained a statutory body, independent of government both in the conduct of its inquiries and in its conclusions which were published in report form. Funded by the DTI, the Commission had a full-time chairperson, and around 35 other part-time members, three of whom were deputy chairpeople and all of whom were appointed by the Secretary of State for Trade and Industry. Such appointments normally lasted for three years at the outset and included individuals drawn from business, the professions, the trade unions and the universities. To support the work of the appointed members, the Commission had a staff of about 80 officials, two-thirds of whom it employed directly, with the remainder being on loan from government departments (especially the DTI) and increasingly from the private sector.

It is important to note that the Commission had no legal power to initiate its own investigations, instead, references – requests for it to carry out particular inquiries – came either from the Secretary of State for Trade and Industry or the Director General of Fair Trading, or from the appropriate regulator in the case of privatised industries and the broadcasting media. Where a possible merger reference was concerned, the initial evaluation of a proposal was made by a panel of civil servants (the Mergers Panel) who considered whether the merger should be referred to the MMC for further consideration. The decision then rested with the Secretary of State, who took advice from the Director General of Fair Trading before deciding whether the proposal should be investigated or should be allowed to proceed.

Under the legislation, references to the Commission could be made on a number of grounds. As indicated above, these included not only monopoly and merger references but also references concerned with the performance of public sector bodies and privatised industries and with anti-competitive practices by individual firms (i.e. competition references). In addition, the Commission was empowered to consider general references (involving practices in industry), restrictive labour practices and references under the Broadcasting Act 1990, as well as questions of proposed newspaper mergers, where special provisions apply.

On receipt of a reference, the Commission's chairperson appointed a small group of members to carry out the relevant inquiry and to report on whether the company (or companies) concerned was operating – or could be expected to operate – against the public interest. Supported by a team of officials, and in some cases including members appointed to specialist panels (e.g. newspaper, telecommunications, water and electricity), the investigating group gathered a wide range of written and oral evidence from both the party (parties) concerned and from others likely to have an interest in the outcome of the inquiry. In reaching its conclusions, which tended to take several months or more, the group had to take into account the 'public interest', as defined under section 84 of the Fair Trading Act 1973, which stressed the importance of competition, the protection of consumer interests and the need to consider issues related to employment, trade and the overall industrial structure. While in most references, issues relating to competition were the primary concern, the Commission was able to take wider public interest issues into account and could rule in favour of a proposal on these grounds, even if the measure appeared anti-competitive.

The culmination of the Commission's inquiry was its report which, in most cases, was submitted to the Secretary of State for consideration and was normally laid before Parliament, where it often formed the basis of a debate or parliamentary questions. In the case of monopoly references judged to be against the public interest, the Secretary of State – with the advice of the DGFT – decided on an appropriate course of action, which could involve an order to prevent or remedy the particular adverse effects identified by the Commission. In the case of merger references, a similar procedure occurred in the event of an adverse judgement by the Commission. The Secretary of State, however, was not bound to accept the Commission's recommendations, nor was he or she able to overrule the conclusion that a merger does not operate, or may be expected not to operate, against the public interest.

It is important to note that at all stages of this multi-stage process, a considerable degree of lobbying occurred by the various interested parties, in an attempt to influence either the outcome of the investigations or the subsequent course of action decided upon. Moreover, considerable pressure tended to occur, even before a decision was taken as to whether or not to make a reference to the MMC. As a number of recent cases have shown, lobbying *against* a reference can represent a key step in justifying a proposed merger. By the same token, lobbying *for* a reference has tended to become an important weapon used by companies wishing to resist an unwelcome takeover, particularly where matters of public interest appear paramount.

Following the passage of the Competition Act 1998, the MMC was replaced (on 1 April 1999) by the **Competition Commission**, an independent public body. The chairperson (full-time) and members (part-time) of the Commission are appointed by the government following an open competition and – as in the case of the MMC – are drawn from a variety of backgrounds and initially serve for a period of eight years. Organised into a series of panels, the Commission is supported by a staff of about 150, who include administrators, specialists and individuals engaged in support services. Most of these are direct employees; the remainder are seconded from government departments.

The role of the Commission is to examine mergers and market situations referred to it by another authority, usually the Office of Fair Trading. It has no powers to conduct enquiries on its own initiative. Under the Enterprise Act 2002, the Commission has been given the responsibility for making decisions on competition questions and for making and implementing decisions on appropriate remedies. It also investigates references on the regulated sectors of the economy, including the privatised public utilities, the broadcasting and media businesses and the financial services sector.

The **Office of Fair Trading** was initially a non-ministerial government department headed until recently by a **Director General**, who was appointed by the Secretary of State for Trade and Industry. Under the Fair Trading Act 1973, the DGFT was given the responsibility of overseeing consumer affairs as well as competition policy and this included administering various pieces of consumer legislation, such as the Consumer Credit Act 1974 and the Estate Agents Act 1979. In carrying out his or her responsibilities in both these areas, the Director General was supported by a team of administrative, legal, economic and accountancy staff and had a Mergers Secretariat to co-ordinate the Office's work in this field.

With regard to competition policy, the OFT's duties were originally governed primarily by the Fair Trading Act and the Competition Act 1980; in addition, under the Restrictive Trade Practices Act 1976 the Director General had responsibility for bringing cases of restrictive practices before the Restrictive Practices Court. With the passage of the Competition Act 1998, the new prohibition regime has been applied and enforced by the DGFT, and the OFT was given additional resources to root out cartels and restrictive behaviour. The legislation gave the Director General considerable powers to investigate if he/she had a reasonable suspicion that either of the prohibitions was being infringed. Under certain circumstances the DGFT could also grant exemptions from the scope of the two prohibitions and could be called upon to defend her/his decisions before the Competition Commission.

Following the Enterprise Act 2002, the OFT has become a corporate body headed by a board which has replaced the role of the DGFT. Under the legislation, the OFT has been given a leading role in promoting competition and consumer interests and is now the main source of reference for mergers referred to the Competition Commission. According to the OFT website, the organisation has three main operational areas of responsibility: competition enforcement, consumer regulation enforcement, and markets and policy initiatives. Its Annual Plan – required under the 2002 Act – is a useful source of reference on the work of the OFT and on its key objectives.

Some illustrative cases of competition policy

Since it was established in 1948, the MMC/Competition Commission has produced hundreds of reports, covering a wide range of issues and affecting firms of different sizes in a variety of markets. At the outset most of its inquiries concerned monopolies – reflecting its initial role as the Monopolies Commission. In more recent times, its work has embraced not only mergers, which have tended to be its major preoccupation, but also nationalised industries and, more recently, the work of the privatised large utilities.

The examples below provide a good insight into the Commission's role in competition policy and its relationship with the Office of Fair Trading. Students wishing to investigate a particular case in more detail should consult the appropriate report, a full list of which can be obtained from the Commission's library in London or via its website (*www.competition-commission.org.uk*).

Nestlé, 1991

This concerned the claim that the Swiss-based foods group was using its monopoly on the supply of instant coffee in the United Kingdom to keep prices high. Concerned that the company was being slow to pass on to consumers the benefits of a fall in the price of raw coffee beans, the DGFT asked the MMC to investigate the instant coffee market. Following a nine-month investigation, the Commission concluded that, while the company supplied more than 47 per cent (by volume) of the United Kingdom's instant coffee, there was still effective competition in the market and a wide degree of consumer choice, with more than 200 brands available (in 1989) and the leading supermarkets stocking on average 30 brands. Despite the facts that Nestlé had higher levels of profitability than its main competitors, and that there was a tendency for branded coffees generally to respond less quickly than own brands to reductions in input prices, the Commission concluded that Nestlé's monopoly did not operate against the public interest. The DGFT indicated, however, that the operation of the soluble coffee market should be kept under review to ensure that it remained competitive.

British Gas, 1992

This involved two parallel references to the Commission by both the President of the Board of Trade (under the terms of the Fair Trading Act) and the Director General of Gas Supply (under the Gas Act 1986). The first asked the Commission to investigate the supply of gas through pipes to both tariff and non-tariff customers; the second to investigate the supply of gas conveyance and gas storage facilities. According to the Office of Fair Trading, very little competition existed in the gas industry, since 17 million domestic household customers had no alternative source of supply and BG's control over storage and transmission facilities inhibited true competition in the industrial market where, theoretically, industrial customers could buy from other suppliers. In the Commission's report published in August 1993, the MMC called for British Gas to lose its monopoly of supply to domestic households by no later than 2002 and for the privatised utility to be split into two separately owned companies.

Midland Bank, 1992

This concerned two bids for the Midland Bank, made by Lloyds Bank and the Hong Kong and Shanghai Banking Corporation, and illustrates the question of split jurisdiction between the United Kingdom and the EU. Lloyds' bid fell within the United Kingdom's jurisdiction and was referred to the MMC as raising potential competition issues – a course of action which caused Lloyds to abandon its proposed merger. In contrast, the HSBC bid was deemed to be of wider concern and was referred to the competition authorities in Brussels. Following clearance by the EU, the HSBC proceeded with its bid and this was accepted by Midland's shareholders.

Video games, 1995

This investigation concerned the supply of video games to the UK market which was dominated by two Japanese companies, Nintendo and Sega. The Commission found the existence of a monopoly situation which affected pricing and entry by new firms. It recommended the abolition of licence controls which allowed the two suppliers to charge excessive prices and the removal of restrictions on rental of games.

UK car prices, 1999–2002

After persistent claims that UK car prices were higher on average than prices in other European countries, the OFT called for a full-scale monopolies investigation into the relationship between car makers and dealerships. In its most recent report the Competition Commission found that the existing system operated against the public interest, particularly with regard to prices, choice and innovation (see e.g. *www.competition-commission.org.uk/reports/439cars*). It highlighted, in particular, the adverse effects of the selective and exclusive distribution system permitted by the block exemption within the EU (see case study below).

Morrison's takeover of Safeway, 2003

In March 2003 the Competition Commission was asked to look at the proposed acquisition of the supermarket chain Safeway by four other rival supermarket groups: Asda, William Morrison, Sainsbury's and Tesco. The key concern was whether the proposed acquisition would lead to a lessening of competition that would adversely affect the consumer. After a lengthy investigation of the likely competitive impact, if any, of the proposed mergers went ahead, the Commission recommended that Asda, Sainsbury's and Tesco be prohibited from acquiring the whole or any part of Safeway, while Morrison's bid could go ahead subject to the company divesting some Safeway stores in certain localities.

Supermarkets enquiry, 2006–8

A two-year enquiry by the Competition Commission into the major UK supermarkets basically concluded that consumers were getting a 'good deal' from the Big 4 supermarket chains. The investigation found evidence that the major grocery retailers at times exercised considerable power in their relationship with suppliers, but this issue was beyond the Commission's responsibilities, which are essentially to protect the interest of consumers. The Commission did, however, propose an enhanced code of practice to govern retailer/supplier relationships which would be overseen by an independent ombudsman.

Government and the labour market

Government involvement in the **labour market** has taken a variety of forms and its influence on market conditions can be direct or indirect and can operate at different spatial levels. Many of the government initiatives mentioned in Chapter 13, for example, seek to affect employment prospects in the regions or in local economies and thus clearly have labour market implications. Similarly, in its general management of the economy through fiscal and monetary means (see Chapter 5), the government will influence the overall demand for labour, which is derived from the demand for the products that labour produces. Some of that demand, of course, will come from the government itself, as a central provider of goods and services and hence a key employer of labour, and its attitude to pay settlements will affect wage levels throughout the public sector. This, in turn, can spill over to the wage bargaining process in the private sector and on occasions may even involve the use of statutory or voluntary restrictions on wage rises that invariably interfere with the operations of the free market (e.g. incomes policies).

While all of these areas would need to be considered in any detailed analysis of labour market policies, in the brief discussion below attention is focused on government initiatives to improve employment prospects and training opportunities for the unemployed, and on the government's efforts to curb the power of the trade unions. Both of these approaches are particularly pertinent to the discussion on how government has sought to improve the efficiency of markets as part of its supply-side approach to economic management – using, in this case, a combination of policy and legislation to achieve its objectives.

Curbing trade union power

As a major force in the labour market, representing the interests of millions of workers, trade unions have been seen as an obstacle to the operation of market forces and as a cause of high wage costs and low labour productivity in the United Kingdom. For almost 20 years after 1979, Conservative governments sought to curb the influence of the trade unions through legislative means, in the belief that more **labour market flexibility** would develop and that this would benefit businesses seeking to respond to competition and change. To assist further in this direction, the government – with the general support of industry – abolished the Wages Councils (which were set up to protect the interests of the lower-paid) and originally refused to participate in the Social Chapter of the Maastricht Treaty (which included a provision for works' councils and the principle of equal pay for male and female workers for equal work).

The government's step-by-step approach to reducing the influence of trade unions is demonstrated by the following legislative measures, enacted in the period 1980–93.

The Employment Act 1980

This Act gave employers legal remedies against secondary picketing and most other types of secondary action. It also provided for all new 'closed shops' to be approved by four-fifths of the workforce and for public funds to be made available to encourage unions to hold postal ballots.

The Employment Act 1982

This Act further tightened the law on closed shops and outlawed union-labour-only contracts. Employers were given legal remedies against 'political' strikes and trade unions were made liable for damages, if they instigated unlawful industrial action (e.g. 'secondary' action).

The Trade Union Act 1984

This Act sought to strengthen internal union democracy. Unions were required to hold a secret ballot every ten years if they wished to keep a political fund and union executives had to submit themselves for re-election by secret ballot every five years. In addition, pre-strike ballots were required if unions wished to retain their immunity from civil action for damages in the event of a strike.

The Employment Act 1988

This Act strengthened the rights of individual union members. Unions were banned from disciplining members who refused to support strike action; all senior union officials had to be elected by secret ballot; workers were permitted to apply for court orders instructing unions to repudiate industrial action organised without a secret ballot. Moreover strikes in defence of the closed shop lost all legal protection.

The Employment Act 1990

This Act made unions legally liable for 'wildcat' strikes called by shop stewards without a proper ballot. Pre-entry closed shops were banned and so individuals could not be refused a job for not belonging to a trade union prior to appointment.

Trade Union and Labour Relations (Consolidation) Act 1992

This Act consolidated previous legislation in the field of labour relations.

The Trade Union Reform and Employment Rights Act 1993

This Act essentially had two main purposes: first, to impose further restrictions on trade unions and trade union activity; second, to enact certain employment rights as a consequence of EU directives and case law. Under section 13, for example, employers are permitted to provide inducements to employees to opt out of collective bargaining or to leave a union, while section 17 introduces a requirement for industrial action ballots to be conducted fully by postal voting.

While there is no doubt that such legislation has altered the balance of power between employee and employer and has significantly weakened the power of the trade unions, this has been only one influence, and arguably not the most important. Apart from the fact that union membership has fallen significantly over the last decade, weakening their financial position and making them less able to sustain union action, the unions have at times had to operate in a market that has been severely affected by changes in the economic cycle. Gone are the days when governments aspired to full employment and were willing to use fiscal and monetary means to achieve this objective. In the new climate of less than full employment, the influence of organised labour in the economy has inevitably been reduced and has been replaced, to some degree, by the pursuit of individual self-interest.

As a postscript it is worth noting that since the election of a Labour government in 1997 there has been a kind of rehabilitation of the trade unions and an attempt by government to enshrine certain employment rights in law. Following the Employment Rights Act of 1996, other significant pieces of legislation have included the Employment Rights (Dispute Reduction) Act 1998, the National Minimum Wage Act 1998, the Working Time Regulations 1998, the Human Rights Act 1998, the Employment Relations Act 1999, the Employment Act 2002, the Employment Relations Act 2004, Work and Families Act 2006, the Employment Equality (Age) Regulations 2006 and the Disability Discrimination Act 2005.

Employment policies

Employment policies are targeted specifically at the unemployed and over recent decades have included a wide range of measures aimed at assisting individuals to prepare themselves for employment and to gain a job. Many of the schemes have been designed to give a limited amount of work experience and/or to improve vocational training, with increasing emphasis being given to the problem of skills shortages in the economy and to matching the needs of labour with the requirements of firms. Additionally, as the following examples illustrate, governments have sought to promote the idea of 'self-help' among the unemployed and to encourage the growth of self-employment, in the hope that an expanding small firms sector will generate a large number of jobs, to replace those lost in medium- and larger-sized enterprises.

- *Restart* – introduced in 1986 and requiring anyone drawing unemployment benefit for over six months to see a specialist counsellor to try to identify possible routes back into employment.
- *Youth Training (YT)* – replaced the Youth Training Scheme in 1990. Under this scheme any person under 18 who was unemployed was guaranteed a YT place (with some exceptions, e.g. students). It has been used to combine training and education and to allow individuals to acquire nationally recognised qualifications (e.g. NVQs).
- *Employment Training (ET)* – introduced in 1988 for long-term unemployed people and others with specific needs, including those returning to the labour market. It aimed to provide training in order to help individuals to acquire the skills needed to get jobs and vocational qualifications (or credits towards them).
- *Employment Action (EA)* – introduced in 1991 and designed to help the unemployed to maintain their skills and find employment. It provided opportunities for individuals to undertake community work and offered structured jobsearch support.
- *Training for Work (TfW)* – started in 1993 to replace ET and EA, combining the characteristics of both programmes.
- *Work Trials* – designed to give long-term unemployed people a chance to prove themselves to employers by working on a trial basis while receiving benefit.

The change in government in 1997 saw the introduction of the **New Deal**, a flagship scheme designed to get individuals claiming unemployment benefits off welfare and into work. Targeted initially at 18-24-year-olds, the scheme has now been extended to other categories of person (e.g. those over 25 and those over 50, lone parents, the disabled and partners). Funded from the windfall tax levied on the privatised utility companies, the New Deal is an attempt to reduce reliance on state benefits and to make work more attractive to groups often excluded from the labour force. Like other measures, including working families' tax credits and efforts to increase the numbers going into further and higher education, it is part of an attempt by government to improve the supply side of the economy.

Local schemes

Historically, local schemes have taken a variety of forms, including interest-free loans for individuals wishing to set up a local business (e.g. Sir Thomas Whyte Charity in Leicester), local training awards to stimulate interest among local employers or individuals (e.g. Bedfordshire TEC), programmes for groups with specific training needs such as women returners (e.g. Calderdale and Kirklees TEC) and partnerships with local companies to part-fund new training initiatives (e.g. Birmingham TEC's Skills Investment Programme). As a final comment it is important to note that the government's national training programme was initially run by a system of local **Training and Enterprise Councils (TECs)** which were responsible for providing training schemes for the unemployed and school leavers and for administering various business enterprise schemes. Funded by central government and run by a board of directors drawn predominantly from industry, the TECs (known as Local Enterprise Councils in Scotland) had control of the training funds for existing training programmes and were given the wider role of encouraging training and enterprise in the economy, including supporting initiatives aimed at promoting local economic development. To this end the TECs were expected to work closely with local employers in both the public and private sector and to improve the quality and effectiveness of training in their locality, by identifying priorities and needs within the local community. TECs were replaced by the **Learning and Skills Council (LSC)** in April 2001 which became responsible for all post-16 education and training, excluding higher education. The LSC operates through a network of local LSCs which deliver national priorities at a local level (N.B. LECs in Scotland still exist). The Council is scheduled to be wound up in 2010 and replaced by two other bodies.

Synopsis

In market-based economies, governments exercise considerable influence over the structure and functioning of markets, not only through their own economic activities but also through their legislative and policy preferences. Privatisation policy seeks to reduce the role of the state in the workings of the economy through the sale of government-owned assets, in the belief that this will improve the operation of the free market. Competition policy tends to focus on the use of legal and institutional changes to curb the growth of monopoly power and to regulate market behaviour in a manner felt to be conducive to the public interest.

In both these areas the focus of government attention is essentially on the supply side of the economy and this parallels its approach to the operation of the labour market. Through a variety of legislative and administrative changes, the government has sought to create a more 'flexible' market for labour through the introduction of initiatives on training and employment and through its attempts to curb the power of the trade unions through statutory means.

Summary of key points

- Competitive markets are thought to provide major advantages, particularly with regard to enhancing wealth creation, economic efficiency and consumer choice.

- Governments, through policy and legislation, can promote increased competition within the economy and its markets.

- Privatisation has become a global phenomenon and reflects the belief in official circles that competitive, private markets are a superior method of allocating economic resources.

- Privatisation in practice has both advantages and disadvantages.

- Competition policy is basically concerned with regulating market behaviour and with controlling potential abuses of market power.

- Governments in the UK and elsewhere use legislation and regulation to promote competition and have established institutional arrangements to implement and oversee their chosen policies.

- Through its membership of the EU, the UK is influenced by competition laws that have been adopted at Community level.

- Other forms of government intervention in markets include steps taken to improve the workings of the labour market and, in particular, to promote greater labour market flexibility.

- Key approaches in this area in the UK have included legislation to curb the power of the trade unions and the use of targeted employment policies designed to boost employment opportunities and generally improve the supply side of the economy.

case study The end of the block exemption

As we have seen in the chapter, governments frequently use laws and regulations to promote competition within the marketplace in the belief that this has significant benefits for the consumer and for the economy generally. Such interventions occur not only at national level, but also in situations where governments work together to provide mutual benefits, as in the European Union's attempts to set up a 'Single Market' across the member states of the EU.

While few would deny that competitive markets have many benefits, the search for increased competition at national level and beyond can sometimes be restrained by the political realities of the situation, a point underlined by a previous decision of the EU authorities to allow a block exemption from the normal rules of competition in the EU car market. Under this system, motor manufacturers operating within the EU were permitted to create networks of selective and exclusive dealerships and to engage in certain other activities normally outlawed under the competition provisions of the single market. It was argued that the system of selective and exclusive distribution (SED) benefited consumers by providing them with a cradle-to-grave service, alongside what was said to be a highly competitive supply situation within the heavily branded global car market.

Introduced in 1995, and extended until the end of September 2002, the block exemption was highly criticised for its impact on the operation of the car market in Europe. Following a critical report by the UK competition authorities in April 2000, the EU published a review (in November 2000) of the workings of the existing arrangement for distributing and servicing cars, highlighting its adverse consequences for both consumers and retailers and signalling the need for change. Despite intensive lobbying by the major car manufacturers, and by some national governments, to maintain the current rules largely intact, the European Commission announced its intention of replacing the block exemption regulation when it expired in September, subject of course to consultation with interested parties.

In essence the Commission's proposals aimed to give dealers far more independence from suppliers by allowing them to solicit for business anywhere in the EU and to open showrooms wherever they want; they would also be able to sell cars supplied by different manufacturers under the same roof. The plan also sought to open up the aftersales market by breaking the tie which existed between sales and servicing. The proposal was that independent repairers would in future be able to get greater access to the necessary spare parts and technology, thereby encouraging new entrants to join the market with reduced initial investment costs.

While these proposals were broadly welcomed by groups representing consumers (e.g. the Consumer Association in the UK), some observers felt that the planned reforms did not go far enough to weaken the power of the suppliers over the market (see e.g. the editorial in the *Financial Times*, 11 January 2002). For instance it appeared to be the case that while manufacturers would be able to supply cars to supermarkets and other new retailers, they would not be required by law to do so, suggesting that a market free-for-all was highly unlikely to emerge in the foreseeable future. Equally the Commission's plans appeared to do little to protect dealers from threats to terminate their franchises should there be a dispute with the supplier.

In the event the old block exemption scheme expired at the end of September 2002 and the new rules began the next day. However, the majority of the provisions under the EC rules did not come into effect until the following October (2003) and the ban on 'location clauses' – which limit the geographical scope of dealer operations – only came into effect two years later. Since October 2005 dealers have been free to set up secondary sales outlets in other areas of the EU, as well as their own countries. This is expected to stengthen competition between dealers across the Single Market to the advantage of consumers (e.g. greater choice and reduced prices).

Current evidence suggests, however, that consumer decisions in future will be influenced more by considerations such as fuel efficiency and carbon impact than by the location of dealerships.

Case study questions

1 Can you suggest any reasons why the European Commission was willing to grant the block exemption in the first place, given that it ran counter to its proposals for a Single Market?

2 Why might the new reforms make cars cheaper for European consumers?

Review and discussion questions

1 Explain the paradox that government needs to intervene in the economy to allow markets to work more freely. What forms does this intervention take?

2 Why is privatisation felt to be a spur to greater efficiency in the major utilities? How would you measure such efficiency 'gains'?

3 In what ways might a government's policy on privatisation be related to its policy on competition?

4 Examine the basis of the previous government's attempts to reform the labour market. How far do you think its reforms have been successful?

Assignments

1 Draft a press release on behalf of the government explaining why it favoured turning Railtrack into a not-for-profit company. Indicate in your statement why the option to renationalise the company was rejected.

2 You are employed by a firm of professional lobbyists which has been commissioned by a group representing European consumer interests to lobby the European Commission over the labelling of food products (e.g. contents, origin, environmental aspects). Produce a report outlining the benefits of more informative labelling on food products within the EU.

Notes and references

1 Numerous books and articles exist on privatisation within the United Kingdom. An excellent starting-point for students wishing to study UK policy is G. C. Cook's *Privatisation in the 1980s and 1990s*, Hidcote Press, 1992.

2 The concept of 'market testing' has increasingly been applied to all parts of the public service, including the civil service, with some civil servants being required to compete with the private sector for their jobs.

3 For a more detailed assessment of the UK's privatisation experience, including a review of numerous studies over recent years, see the paper by Parker in the Further reading section below.

4 Cook, *op. cit.*, pp. 23–4.

5 In a sense, however, individuals invest indirectly in shares through their pension funds, insurance policies, unit trusts and bank accounts.

Further reading

Cook, G. C., *Privatisation in the 1980s and 1990s*, Hidcote Press, 1992.

Cook, M. and Farquharson, C., *Business Economics*, FT/Prentice Hall, 1998, esp. chs. 22 and 24.

Griffiths, A. and Wall, S. (eds), *Applied Economics*, 11th edition, Financial Times/Prentice Hall, 2007.

Guislain, P., *The Privatization Challenge: A Strategic, Legal and Institutional Analysis of International Experience*, The World Bank, 1997.

Livesey, F., 'Competition Policy' in Atkinson, B., Livesey, F. and Milward, B., *Applied Economics*, Macmillan, 1998.

Martin, S. and Parker, S., *The Impact of Privatisation: Ownership and Corporate Performance in the UK*, Routledge, 1997.

Parker, D., 'The UK's Privatisation Experiment: The passage of time permits a sober assessment', CESIFO Working Paper No 1126, 2004, available in electronic form from *www.cesifo.de*.

Potts, N., 'Privatisation: a false hope', *International Journal of Public Sector Management*, 12 (5), pp. 388–409, 1999.

Worthington, I., Britton, C. and Rees, A., *Economics for Business: Blending Theory and Practice*, 2nd edition, Financial Times/Prentice Hall, 2005.

Web links and further questions are available on the website at:
www.pearsoned.co.uk/worthington

International business in action

The global financial crisis

In economics the term 'market' basically means a situation where buyers and sellers come together to effect an exchange. Some markets have a physical manifestation (e.g. a local farmers' market), others do not (e.g. eBay). The essential point is that a market is an arrangement where a transaction takes place; this can occur at any spatial level from local to national through to international and global and under differing structural conditions (e.g. oligopoly, monopoly, monopsony etc.). Some markets can be relatively free from government control, while others may be heavily regulated and/or, in some cases, dominated by state intervention. How a market operates, and under what conditions, can, of course, vary both spatially and temporally and will differ in other terms including the degree of formality or complexity.

As we saw in Chapter 17, for much of the last 30 years political leaders across the globe have tended to favour an increased measure of state disengagement from economic activity and have embarked on programmes of privatisation and state deregulation in many sectors of their respective economies. In doing so governments have sought to improve economic efficiency (e.g. by making markets more competitive) and to encourage wealth creation for the benefit of individuals, businesses and governments alike. In this, as in other spheres, changes of this kind can bring benefits for the business community and can open up multiple opportunities for firms operating in the marketplace for their goods or services. By the same token, the process of change brings with it certain risks and threats, some of which may apply to the market as a whole and not just to the individual participants involved in buying and selling in a particular market.

An excellent contemporary example of the latter is the global financial crisis which gripped the world in 2008 and which resulted in action at both national and international levels (see below) in an attempt to stabilise the international financial system which was under serious threat of collapse. While it is very difficult to pinpoint any single cause for this crisis, many commentators are agreed that a contributory factor was the deregulation of financial markets in previous decades, which helped to encourage credit expansion and the emergence of new forms of complex and often highly risky financial instruments (e.g. collateralised debt obligations) that were traded globally between financial institutions. One area where this 'securitisation' of debt had a very significant impact was in the housing market in countries such as the United States and the UK, with lenders granting mortgages to some customers without necessarily confirming their ability to repay. Some of these loans (subsequently known as sub-prime mortgages) proved to be highly risky and when the US housing market declined in 2007, the problem and reach of the so-called 'toxic' debt rapidly became apparent.

A noteable feature of this situation is how quickly the financial contagion spread, impacting on a wide range of financial institutions across the globe and on stock markets, currency markets and on the 'real' economies in many countries. Some of the key events are worth repeating here:

- October 2007 – Citigroup announced a multi-billion-dollar write-off of sub-prime mortgage losses.
- February 2008 – a run on Northern Rock in the UK ultimately resulted in part-nationalisation by the UK government.
- March 2008 – the collapse of the US investment bank Bear Stearns resulted in its takeover by its competitor JPMorgan which was underwritten by the US government.
- September 2008 – US mortgage giants Fanny Mae and Freddy Mac were taken into temporary public ownership (see Mini case, Chapter 17, 'Government to the rescue').
- September 2008 – Lehman Brothers (US) was declared bankrupt and allowed to collapse by the US government.
- September 2008 – Merrill Lynch was taken over by the Bank of America.
- September 2008 – Washington Mutual went into receivership following a bank run.

- September 2008 – Goldman Sachs and Morgan Stanley were pressured by the US government into changing their status from investment to deposit banks.
- September 2008 – plans were unveiled for the takeover of HBOS by Lloyds.
- September 2008 – Bradford and Bingley in the UK was nationalised.
- September 2008 – nationalisation of the Fortis Bank by the Luxembourg, Belgian and Dutch governments.
- September/October 2008 – the Icelandic government nationalises the country's three main banks: Giltnir, Landsbanki, Kaupthing.
- October 2008 – the commercial property loan giant Hypo Real Estate was bailed out by the German government.

In seeking to address the various problems that were both causes and effects of the global financial crisis, governments have intervened both unilaterally and collectively in a variety of ways. Among the key instruments used have been the following:

- Nationalisation or partial nationalisation of some financial institutions to guarantee their continued existence.
- Injections of hundreds of billions of dollars by central banks to recapitalise the international financial system.
- Temporary bans on short-selling of bank shares in order to prevent speculative pressures that could cause institutional collapse.
- Temporary suspension of competition rules to allow bank mergers/takeovers.
- Financial support from the International Monetary Fund for countries in severe difficulties, including Iceland, Hungary and the Ukraine.
- Government underwriting of bank assets (e.g. loans) and provision of short-term loans to increase inter-bank lending.
- Cuts in interest rates (e.g. in the US, UK, China, Sweden, Canada) to try to stimulate borrowing in order to offset recessionary pressures in the global economy.

What is particularly significant about the global financial crisis is the recognition that action by any one government alone is insufficient to address the problems that have emerged in this and related markets (e.g. the stock market; the foreign exchange market). Moreover, while it seems unlikely that national governments will wish to retain control of key financial institutions in the future, it seems equally unlikely that they will be prepared to allow largely unfettered market capitalism to shape the global financial system in the coming decades. Indeed, it may be that the lasting legacy of this crisis is not so much the gradual restructuring of financial institutions and markets, but the demise of the mystical belief in the ability of markets to deliver optimum outcomes that has dominated political and economic thinking and discourse for much of the last 30 years.

Chapter 18
Market Failures and
Government Policy

Market failures and government policy

In recent years, governments throughout the world have tended to put more reliance on markets as the means of allocating resources. Policies of privatisation, deregulation, cutting government expenditure and taxes, and generally 'leaving things to the market' have been widely adopted, not only by conservative governments, but also by those of the centre and centre left.

But despite this increased reliance on markets, markets often fail. Despite our growing wealth and prosperity, our rivers are polluted, our streets are congested and often strewn with litter, our lives are dominated by the interests of big business, and the quality of many of the goods we buy is very poor.

Governments are thus still expected to play a major role in the economy: from the construction and maintenance of roads, to the provision of key services such as education, health care and law and order, to social protection in the form of pensions and social security, to the regulation of businesses, to the passing of laws to protect the individual.

In this chapter we identify the various ways in which the market fails to look after society's interests (Sections 6.1–6.4). Then we look at how the government can set about putting right these failings (Sections 6.5–6.7). Then we look at some of the shortcomings of governments, and ask: should we have more or less intervention? In the final section we turn to problems of the environment as a case study in market failure and government intervention.

After studying this chapter, you should be able to answer the following questions:

- What is the meaning of a 'socially-efficient' allocation of resources, and to what extent will a perfectly competitive market achieve social efficiency?
- For what reasons do real-world markets fail to achieve social efficiency?
- How can governments put right the failings of the market?
- How successful are they likely to be?
- How can economists explain environmental degradation?
- What policies can be pursued to achieve environmental sustainability?

6.1 SOCIAL EFFICIENCY

Is this something that the free market will achieve?

In order to decide the optimum amount of government intervention, it is first necessary to identify the various social goals that intervention is designed to meet. Two of the major objectives of government intervention identified by economists are social efficiency and equity.

Equity

Most people would argue that the free market fails to lead to a *fair* distribution of resources, if it results in some people living in great affluence whilst others live in dire poverty. Clearly what constitutes 'fairness' is a highly contentious issue: those on the political right generally have a quite different view from those on the political left. Nevertheless, most people would argue that the government does have some duty to redistribute incomes from the rich to the poor through the tax and benefit system, and perhaps to provide various forms of legal protection for the poor (such as a minimum wage rate). We looked at the causes of inequality and policies of redistribution in Chapter 5. In this chapter, therefore, we focus on the second issue: that of social efficiency.

Social efficiency

If the marginal benefits to society – or 'marginal social benefits' (MSB) – of producing (or consuming) any given good or service exceed the marginal costs to society – or 'marginal social costs' (MSC) – then it is said to be socially efficient to produce (or consume) more. For example, if people's gains from having additional motorways exceed *all* the additional costs to society (both financial and non-financial), then it is socially efficient to construct more motorways.

If, however, the marginal social costs of producing (or consuming) any good or service exceed the marginal social benefits, then it is socially efficient to produce (or consume) less.

It follows that if the marginal social benefits of any activity are equal to the marginal social costs, then the current level is the optimum. To summarise: to achieve social efficiency in the production of any good or service, the following should occur:

$$MSB > MSC \rightarrow \text{produce more}$$

$$MSC > MSB \rightarrow \text{produce less}$$

$$MSB = MSC \rightarrow \text{keep production at its current level}$$

Similar rules apply to consumption. For example, if the marginal social benefits of consuming more of any good or service exceed the marginal social cost, then society would benefit from more of the good being consumed.

Social efficiency is an example of 'allocative efficiency': in other words, the best allocation of resources between alternative uses.

The concept of allocative efficiency is another of our *Threshold Concepts* (no. 10). It is a threshold concept, because to understand it is to understand how to make the most of scarce resources: and scarcity is the core problem of economics for all of us.

In the real world, however, the market rarely leads to social efficiency: the marginal social benefits of most goods and services do not equal the marginal social costs. Part of the problem is that many of our actions have spillover effects on other people (these are known as 'externalities'), part is a lack of competition, part is a lack of knowledge by both producers and consumers, and part is the fact that markets may take a long time to adjust to any disequilibrium, given the often considerable short-run immobility of factors of production.

> *Markets generally fail to achieve social efficiency.* There are various types of market failure. Market failures provide one of the major justifications for government intervention in the economy.
> **Key Idea 21**

In this chapter we examine these various 'failings' of the free market and what the government can do to rectify the situation. We also examine why the government itself may fail to achieve social efficiency.

General equilibrium

Markets are in a constant state of flux. Demand changes as consumer tastes change and as income changes; supply changes as technology, the availability of natural resources and costs change. These changes in demand and supply cause markets to adjust to a new equilibrium.

At any one time, it is useful to look at the overall equilibrium towards which markets are heading: the **general equilibrium** of all markets. The concept of general equilibrium is a *Threshold Concept* because it gives us an insight into how market forces apply to a whole economy, and not just to its individual parts. It is about seeing how the whole jigsaw fits together and how changes ripple throughout the economy.

> *General equilibrium.* The situation where all individual markets in the economy are in equilibrium: in other words, where demand equals supply in all markets. If demand or supply changes in any market, there are likely to be ripple effects into other markets (i.e. for substitute or complementary goods, in both demand and supply), until a new general equilibrium is reached. This is **Threshold Concept 11**.
> **Key Idea 22**
> **TC 11**

We can then ask whether this general equilibrium is socially efficient, or whether a reallocation of resources in the economy would lead to greater social efficiency.

An economy where all markets are perfectly competitive and where there are no externalities *will* be socially efficient when there is a state of general equilibrium. Why will this be so?

Take the case of goods markets. In any given goods markets, the consumer will achieve private efficiency where marginal utility (i.e. marginal benefit) equals price (see Box 1.2 on page 33); and the producer where marginal cost equals price (see Section 4.2, page 117). Given that all producers and consumers face the same market price, in equilibrium marginal utility will equal marginal cost.

Definitions

Externalities
Costs or benefits of production or consumption experienced by society but not by the producers or consumers themselves. Sometimes referred to as 'spillover' or 'third-party' costs or benefits.

General equilibrium
Where all the millions of markets throughout the economy are in a simultaneous state of equilibrium.

But will this be socially efficient? In the absence of externalities, benefits from consumption are confined to the consumers themselves. In other words, as members of society, their benefit is the whole social benefit. Thus $P = MU = MSB$. Likewise, the costs of production are confined to the producers; there are no costs imposed on *other* members of society. Thus $P = MC = MSC$.

To summarise:

$$MU = MSB = P = MC = MSC$$

and hence:

$$MSB = MSC$$

Thus equilibrium in any market under perfect competition with no externalities is socially efficient. When this applies to all markets, then general equilibrium is socially efficient.

Web Appendix 6.1 looks at social efficiency in more detail. It uses 'general equilibrium analysis' – which involves the use of indifference curves (see Web Appendix 1.2) and production possibility curves – to show how a perfect market economy in the absence of externalities will lead to a socially optimal allocation of resources.

6.2   MARKET FAILURES: EXTERNALITIES AND PUBLIC GOODS

What will happen if certain markets are 'missing'?

Externalities

The market will not lead to social efficiency if the actions of producers or consumers affect people *other than themselves*. These effects on other people are known as externalities: they are the side-effects, or 'third-party' effects, of production or consumption. Externalities can be either desirable or undesirable. Whenever other people are affected beneficially, there are said to be **external benefits**. Whenever other people are affected adversely, there are said to be **external costs**.

> ***Externalities are spillover costs or benefits.*** Where these exist, even an otherwise perfect market will fail to achieve social efficiency.
>
>
> **Key Idea 23**

Thus the full cost to society (the **social cost**) of the production of any good or service is the private cost faced by firms plus any externalities of production (positive or negative). Likewise the full benefit to society (the **social benefit**) from the consumption of any good is the private benefit enjoyed by consumers plus any externalities of consumption (positive or negative).

There are four major types of externality.

External costs of production (MSC > MC)

When a chemical firm dumps waste into a river or pollutes the air, the community bears costs additional to those borne by the firm. The marginal *social* cost (MSC) of chemical production exceeds the marginal private cost (MC). Diagrammatically, the MSC curve is above the MC curve. This is shown in Figure 6.1(a), which assumes

---

Definitions

External benefits
Benefits from production (or consumption) experienced by people *other* than the producer (or consumer).

External costs
Costs of production (or consumption) borne by people *other* than the producer (or consumer).

Social cost
Private cost plus externalities in production.

Social benefit
Private benefit plus externalities in consumption.

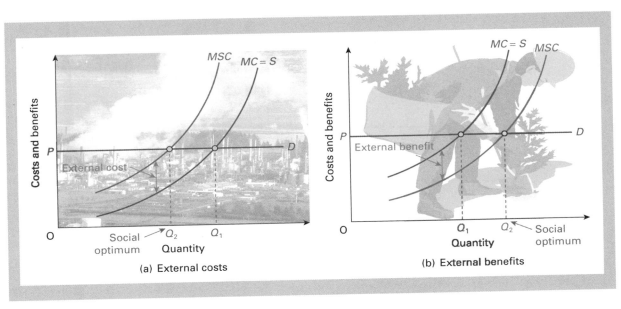

(a) External costs

(b) External benefits

Figure 6.1
Externalities in
production

that the firm in other respects is operating in a perfect market, and is therefore a price taker (i.e. faces a horizontal demand curve).

The firm maximises profits at Q_1: the output where marginal cost equals price (see Section 4.2). The price is what people buying the good are prepared to pay for one more unit (if it wasn't, they wouldn't buy it) and therefore reflects their marginal benefit. We assume no externalities from consumption, and therefore the marginal benefit to consumers is the same as the marginal *social* benefit (*MSB*). The *socially* optimum output would be Q_2, where P (i.e. MSB) = MSC. The firm, however, produces Q_1, which is more than the optimum. Thus external costs lead to over-production from society's point of view.

The problem of external costs arises in a free-market economy because no one has legal ownership of the air or rivers and no one, therefore, can prevent or charge for their use as a dump for waste. Such a 'market' is missing. Control must, therefore, be left to the government or local authorities.

Other examples include extensive farming that destroys hedgerows and wildlife, and global warming caused by CO_2 emissions from power stations.

External benefits of production (MSC < MC)

If a forestry company plants new woodlands, there is a benefit not only to the company itself, but also to the world through a reduction of CO_2 in the atmosphere (forests are a carbon sink). The marginal *social* cost of providing timber, therefore, is less than the marginal *private* cost to the company.

In Figure 6.1(b), the *MSC* curve is *below* the *MC* curve. The level of output provided by the forestry company is Q_1, where $P = MC$, a *lower* level than the social optimum, Q_2, where $P = MSC$.

Another example of external benefits in production is that of research and development. If other firms have access to the results of the research, then clearly the benefits extend beyond the firm that finances it. Since the firm only receives the private benefits, it will conduct a less than optimal amount of research.

External costs of consumption (MSB < MB)

Figure 6.2(a) shows the marginal benefit and price to a motorist (i.e. the consumer) of using a car. It is assumed that the marginal benefit declines as the motorist

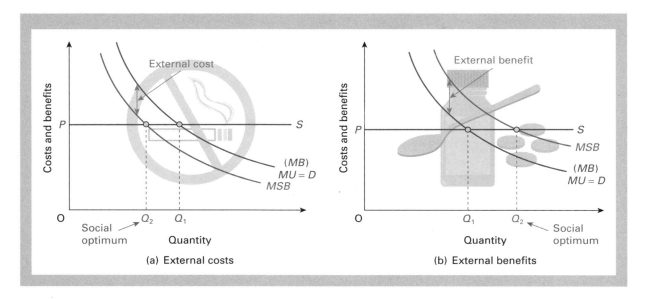

Figure 6.2
Externalities in
consumption

travels more miles.[1] The optimal distance travelled for this motorist will be Q_1 miles: i.e. where marginal benefit (MB) = price (P) (where price is the cost of petrol, oil, wear and tear, etc. per mile). The reasoning is as follows: if the marginal benefit from the consumption of any good or service, measured in terms of what you are prepared to pay for it, exceeds its price (i.e. the marginal cost to the consumer), the consumer will gain by consuming more of it. If, however, the marginal benefit is less than the price, the consumer will gain by consuming less. The optimum level of consumption from the motorist's point of view, therefore, will be where $MB = P$: i.e. Q_1 miles.

When people use their cars, however, other people suffer from their exhaust, the added congestion, the noise, etc. These 'negative externalities' make the marginal social benefit of using cars less than the marginal private benefit of the motorist. Thus the MSB curve is below the MB curve. Assuming that there are no externalities in *production*, and therefore that marginal social cost is given by the price, the *social* optimum will be where $MSB = P$: i.e. at Q_2. But this is less than the actual level of consumption, Q_1. Thus, when there are negative externalities in consumption, the actual level of consumption will be too great from society's point of view.

Other examples of negative externalities of consumption include the effects on other people of noisy radios in public places, the smoke from cigarettes, and litter.

External benefits of consumption ($MSB > MB$)

When people travel by train rather than by car, other people benefit by there being less congestion and exhaust and fewer accidents on the

Definition

Principle of diminishing marginal utility
As more units of a good are consumed, additional units will provide less additional satisfaction than previous units.

[1] To understand this, consider your own position (assuming you have a car). If you had only a little money available for motoring, or if the price of petrol were very high, then you would only use your car for essential journeys: journeys with a high marginal private benefit (or 'marginal utility' as it is often referred to by economists). If your income increased, or if the price of petrol came down, you would use your car more (i.e. travel additional miles), but these additional journeys would be yielding you less additional benefit per mile than previous journeys, since they would be less essential to you. The more miles you travel, the less essential each *additional* mile: i.e. the marginal benefit diminishes. This is an example of the **principle of diminishing marginal utility**, which we saw in Box 1.2.

KI 7
p33

roads. Thus the marginal social benefit of rail travel is *greater* than the marginal private benefit to the rail passenger. There are external benefits from rail travel. In Figure 6.2(b), the *MSB* curve is *above* the private *MB* curve. The actual level of consumption (Q_1) is thus below the socially optimal level of consumption (Q_2).

Other examples include the beneficial effects for other people of deodorants, vaccinations and attractive clothing.

To summarise: whenever there are external benefits, there will be too little produced or consumed. Whenever there are external costs, there will be too much produced or consumed. The market will not equate *MSB* and *MSC*.

The above arguments have been developed in the context of perfect competition, with prices given to the producer or consumer by the market. Externalities also occur in all other types of market.

Public goods

There is a category of goods where the positive externalities are so great that the free market, whether perfect or imperfect, may not produce at all. They are called **public goods**. Examples include lighthouses, pavements, flood-control dams, public drainage, public services such as the police and even government itself.

Public goods have two important characteristics: *non-rivalry* and *non-excludability*.

- If I consume a bar of chocolate, it cannot then be consumed by someone else. If, however, I enjoy the benefits of street lighting, it does not prevent you or anyone else doing the same. There is thus what we call **non-rivalry** in the consumption of such goods. These goods tend to have large external benefits relative to private benefits. This makes them socially desirable, but privately unprofitable. No single individual would pay to have a pavement built along his or her street. The private benefit would be too small relative to the cost. And yet the social benefit to all the other people using the pavement may far outweigh the cost.
- If I spend money erecting a flood-control dam to protect my house, my neighbours will also be protected by the dam. I cannot prevent them enjoying the benefits of my expenditure. This feature of **non-excludability** means that they would get the benefits free, and would therefore have no incentive to pay themselves. This is known as the **free-rider problem**.

Definitions

Public good
A good or service that has the features of non-rivalry and non-excludability and as a result would not be provided by the free market.

Non-rivalry
Where the consumption of a good or service by one person will not prevent others from enjoying it.

Non-excludability
Where it is not possible to provide a good or service to one person without it thereby being available to others to enjoy.

Free-rider problem
Where it is not possible to exclude other people from consuming a good that someone has bought.

> *Pause for thought*
>
> *Which of the following have the property of non-rivalry: (a) a can of drink; (b) public transport; (c) a commercial radio broadcast; (d) the sight of flowers in a public park?*

> ***The free-rider problem.*** People are often unwilling to pay for things if they can make use of things other people have bought. This problem can lead to people not purchasing things that would be to the benefit of themselves and other members of society.
>
> **Key Idea 24**

When goods have these two features, the free market will simply not provide them. Thus these public goods can only be provided by the government or by the government subsidising private firms. (Note that not all goods and services produced by the public sector come into the category of 'public goods and services': thus education and health are publicly provided, but they *can* be, and indeed are, privately provided as well.)

1. Social efficiency will be achieved where $MSC = MSB$ for each good and service. In practice, however, markets fail to achieve social efficiency. One reason for this is the existence of externalities.

2. Externalities are spillover costs or benefits. Whenever there are external costs, the market will (other things being equal) lead to a level of production and consumption *above* the socially efficient level. Whenever there are external benefits, the market will (other things being equal) lead to a level of production and consumption *below* the socially efficient level.

3. Public goods will not be provided by a free market. The problem is that they have large external benefits relative to private benefits, and without government intervention it would not be possible to prevent people having a 'free ride' and thereby escaping contributing to their cost of production.

6.3 MARKET FAILURES: MONOPOLY POWER

What problems arise from big business?

Whenever markets are imperfect, whether as pure monopoly or monopsony, or whether as some form of imperfect competition, the market will fail to equate MSB and MSC, even if there are no externalities.

    Take the case of monopoly. A monopoly will produce less than the socially efficient output. This is illustrated in Figure 6.3. A monopoly faces a downward-sloping demand curve, and therefore marginal revenue is below average revenue ($= P = MSB$). Profits are maximised at an output of Q_1, where marginal revenue equals marginal cost (see Figure 4.5 on page 122). If there are no externalities, the socially efficient output will be at the higher level of Q_2, where $MSB = MSC$.

KI 21
p191

Figure 6.3
A monopolist producing less than the social optimum

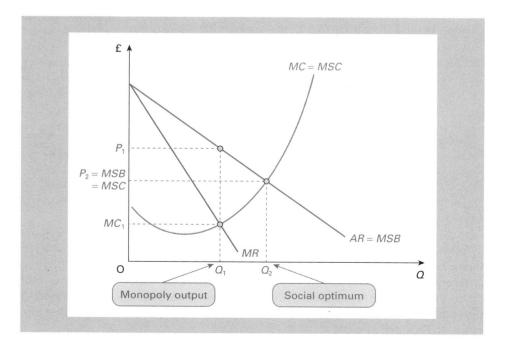

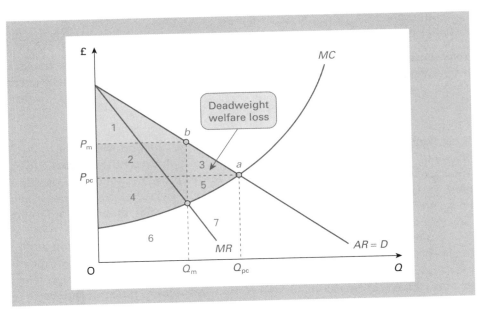

Figure 6.4
Deadweight loss
under monopoly

Deadweight loss under monopoly

Consumer and producer surplus

One way of analysing the welfare loss that occurs under monopoly is to use the concepts of *consumer* and *producer surplus*. Consumer surplus is the excess of consumers' total benefit (or 'utility') from consuming a good over their total expenditure on it. Producer surplus is just another name for profit. The two concepts are illustrated in Figure 6.4. The diagram shows an industry that is initially under perfect competition and then becomes a monopoly (but faces the same revenue and cost curves).

Let us start by examining consumer and producer surplus under *perfect competition*.

Consumer surplus. Under perfect competition the industry will produce an output of Q_{pc} at a price of P_{pc}, where $MC = P$ (= AR): i.e. at point *a* (see pages 122–3).

Consumers' total benefit is given by the area under the demand curve (the sum of all the areas 1–7). The reason for this is that each point on the demand curve shows how much the last consumer is prepared to pay (i.e. the benefit to the marginal consumer). The area under the demand curve thus shows the total of all these marginal benefits from zero consumption to the current level: i.e. it gives total benefit.

Consumers' total expenditure is $P_{pc} \times Q_{pc}$ (areas 4 + 5 + 6 + 7).

Consumer surplus is the difference between total benefit and total expenditure: in other words, the area between the price and the demand curve (areas 1 + 2 + 3).

Producer surplus. Producer surplus (profit) is the difference between total revenue and total cost.

Total cost is the area under the *MC* curve (areas 6 + 7). The reason for this is that each point on the marginal cost curve shows what the last unit costs to produce. The area under the *MC* curve thus gives all the marginal costs starting from an output of zero to the current output: i.e. it gives total costs.[2]

[2] Strictly speaking, the sum of all marginal costs gives total *variable* costs. Producers' surplus is therefore total revenue minus total variable costs: i.e. total profit plus total fixed costs.

Total revenue is $P_{pc} \times Q_{pc}$ (areas 4 + 5 + 6 + 7).

Producer surplus is thus the area between the price and the *MC* curve (areas 4 + 5).

Total (private) surplus. Total consumer plus producer surplus is therefore the area between the demand and *MC* curves. This is shown by the total shaded area (areas 1 + 2 + 3 + 4 + 5).

The effect of monopoly on total surplus

What happens when the industry is under *monopoly*? The firm will produce where $MC = MR$, at an output of Q_m and a price of P_m (at point *b* on the demand curve). Total revenue is $P_m \times Q_m$ (areas 2 + 4 + 6). Total cost is the area under the *MC* curve (area 6). Thus producer surplus is areas 2 + 4. This is clearly a *larger* surplus than under perfect competition (since area 2 is larger than area 5): monopoly profits are larger than profits under perfect competition.

KI 16
p112

Consumer surplus, however, will be much smaller. With consumption at Q_m, total benefit to consumers is given by areas 1 + 2 + 4 + 6, whereas consumer expenditure is given by areas 2 + 4 + 6. Consumer surplus, then, is simply area 1. (Note that area 2 has been transformed from consumer surplus to producer surplus.)

Total surplus under monopoly is therefore areas 1 + 2 + 4: a smaller surplus than under perfect competition. 'Monopolisation' of the industry has resulted in a loss of total surplus of areas 3 + 5. The producer's gain is less than consumers' loss. This net loss of total surplus is known as the **deadweight welfare loss** of monopoly.

KI 21
p191

Definition

Deadweight welfare loss

The loss of consumer plus producer surplus in imperfect markets (when compared with perfect competition).

Conclusions

Pause for thought

Assume that a monopoly existed in an industry where there were negative externalities. Could the socially efficient output be Q_m in Figure 6.4? If so, would this make monopoly socially efficient?

As was shown in Section 4.3, there are possible social *advantages* from powerful firms: advantages such as economies of scale and more research and development. These advantages may outweigh deadweight loss from monopoly power. It can be argued that an ideal situation would be where firms are large enough to gain economies of scale and yet were somehow persuaded or compelled to produce where $P = MC$ (assuming no externalities).

Recap

1. Monopoly power will (other things being equal) lead to a level of output below the socially efficient level.

2. This will result in deadweight welfare loss, which is the loss in total producer and consumer surplus.

3. Consumer surplus is the excess of what consumers are prepared to pay (which is how we measure the benefit to consumers) over what they actually pay. Producer surplus is the excess of total revenue over total cost (i.e. total profit).

4. The effect of monopoly will be to give a higher producer surplus than under perfect competition, but a much lower consumer surplus. Thus total surplus is lower.

5. There are potential gains from monopoly, such as economies of scale and higher investment. Such gains have to be offset against the deadweight loss.

OTHER MARKET FAILURES   6.4

In what other ways may a market fail to make the best use of scarce resources?

Ignorance and uncertainty

Perfect competition assumes that consumers, firms and factor suppliers have perfect knowledge of costs and benefits. In the real world there is often a great deal of ignorance and uncertainty. Thus people are unable to equate marginal benefit with marginal cost.

Consumers purchase many goods only once or a few times in a lifetime. Cars, washing machines, televisions and other consumer durables fall into this category. Consumers may not be aware of the quality of such goods until they have purchased them, by which time it is too late. Advertising may contribute to people's ignorance by misleading them as to the benefits of a good.

Firms are often ignorant of market opportunities, prices, costs, the productivity of labour (especially white-collar workers), the activity of rivals, etc.

Many economic decisions are based on expected future conditions. Since the future can never be known for certain, many decisions may turn out to be wrong.

In some cases it may be possible to obtain the information through the market. There may be an agency that will sell you the information, or a newspaper, magazine or website that contains the information. In such cases you will have to decide whether the cost to you of obtaining the information is worth the benefit it will provide you. A problem here is that you may not have sufficient information to judge how reliable the information is that you are obtaining!

The principal–agent problem

The problem of dependants is an example of a wider issue, known as the **principal–agent problem**. One of the features of a complex modern economy is that people (principals) have to employ others (agents) to carry out their wishes. If you want to go on holiday, it is easier to go to a travel agent to sort out the arrangements than to do it all yourself. Likewise, if you want to buy a house, it is more convenient to go to an estate agent. The point is that these agents have specialist knowledge and can save you, the principal, a great deal of time and effort. This is merely an example of the benefits of specialisation and the division of labour.

It is the same with firms. They employ people with specialist knowledge and skills to carry out specific tasks. Companies frequently employ consultants to give them advice, or engage the services of specialist firms such as an advertising agency. It is the same with the employees of the company. They can be seen as 'agents' of their employer. In the case of workers, they can be seen as the agents of management. Junior managers are the agents of senior management. Senior managers are the agents of the directors, who are themselves agents of the shareholders. Thus in large firms there is often a complex chain of principal–agent relationships. Indeed, it is often claimed that in large companies there tends to be a 'divorce' between the owners of the firm (the shareholders), who are the principals, and the controllers of the firm (the managers), who are the shareholders' agents.

These relationships have an inherent danger for the principal: there is **asymmetric information** between the two sides. The agent knows more about the situation than the principal – in fact, this is part of the reason why the principal employs the agent in the first place. The danger is that the agent may well not act in the

Definitions

Principal–agent problem
Where people (principals), as a result of lack of knowledge, cannot ensure that their best interests are served by their agents.

Asymmetric information
Where one party in an economic relationship (e.g. an agent) has more information than another (e.g. the principal).

principal's best interests, and may be able to get away with it because of the principal's imperfect knowledge. The estate agent trying to sell you a house may not tell you about the noisy neighbours or that the vendor is prepared to accept a much lower price. A second-hand car dealer may 'neglect' to tell you about the rust on the underside of the car or that it has a history of unreliability.

> ***The principal–agent problem.*** Where people (principals), as a result of a lack of knowledge, cannot ensure that their best interests are served by their agents. Agents may take advantage of this situation to the disadvantage of the principals.
>
> Key Idea 25

So how can principals tackle the problem? There are two elements in the solution:

- The principals must have some way of *monitoring* the performance of their agents. Thus a company might employ efficiency experts to examine the operation of its management.
- There must be *incentives* for agents to behave in the principals' interests. Thus managers' salaries could be more closely linked to the firm's profitability.

TC 4
p26

In a competitive market, managers' and shareholders' interests are more likely to coincide. Managers have to ensure that the company remains efficient or it may not survive the competition and they might lose their jobs. In monopolies and oligopolies, however, where supernormal profits can often be relatively easily earned, the interests of shareholders and managers are likely to diverge. Here it will be in shareholders' interests to institute incentive mechanisms that ensure that their agents, the managers, are motivated to strive for profitability.

Immobility of factors and time lags in response

Even under conditions of perfect competition, factors may be very slow to respond to changes in demand or supply. Labour, for example, may be highly immobile both occupationally and geographically. This can lead to large price changes and hence to large supernormal profits and high wages for those in the sectors of rising demand or falling costs. The long run may be a very long time coming!

In the meantime, there will be further changes in the conditions of demand and supply. Thus the economy is in a constant state of disequilibrium and the long run never comes. As firms and consumers respond to market signals and move towards equilibrium, so the equilibrium position moves and the social optimum is never achieved.

> ***The problem of time lags.*** Many economic actions can take a long time to take effect. This can cause problems of instability and an inability of the economy to achieve social efficiency.
>
> Key Idea 26

Whenever monopoly/monopsony power exists, the problem is made worse as firms or unions put up barriers to the entry of new firms or factors of production.

Protecting people's interests

Dependants

People do not always make their own economic decisions. They are often dependent on decisions made by others. Parents make decisions on behalf of their children;

partners on each other's behalf; younger adults on behalf of old people; managers on behalf of shareholders, etc.

A free market will respond to these decisions, however good or bad they may be; whether they be in the interest of the dependant or not. Thus the government may feel it necessary to protect dependants.

Poor economic decision making by individuals on their own behalf

The government may feel that people need protecting from poor economic decisions that they make on their *own* behalf. It may feel that in a free market people will consume too many harmful things. Thus if the government wants to discourage smoking and drinking, it can put taxes on tobacco and alcohol. In more extreme cases it could make various activities illegal: activities such as prostitution, certain types of gambling, and the sale and consumption of drugs.

On the other hand, the government may feel that people consume too little of things that are good for them: things such as education, health care and sports facilities. Such goods are known as **merit goods**. The government could either provide them free or subsidise their production.

Pause for thought

How do merit goods differ from public goods?

Macroeconomic goals

The free market is unlikely to achieve simultaneously the *macroeconomic* objectives of rapid economic growth, full employment, stable prices and a balance of international payments. These problems and the methods of government intervention to deal with them are examined in the second part of this book.

How far can economists go in advising governments?

It is not within the scope of economics to make judgements as to the relative importance of social goals. Economics can only consider means to achieving stated goals. First, therefore, the goals have to be clearly stated by the policy makers. Second, they have to be quantifiable so that different policies can be compared as to their relative effectiveness in achieving the particular goal. Certain goals, such as growth in national income, changes in the distribution of income and greater efficiency, are relatively easy to quantify. Others, such as enlightenment or the sense of community wellbeing, are virtually impossible to quantify. For this reason, economics tends to concentrate on the means of achieving a relatively narrow range of goals. The danger is that by economists concentrating on a limited number of goals, they may well influence the policy makers – the government, local authorities, various pressure groups, etc. – into doing the same, and thus into neglecting other perhaps important social goals.

Different objectives are likely to conflict. For example, economic growth may conflict with greater equality. In the case of such 'trade-offs', all the economist can do is to demonstrate the effects of a given policy, and leave the policy makers to decide whether the benefits in terms of one goal outweigh the costs in terms of another goal.

Definition

Merit goods
Goods which the government feels that people should consume but tend to underconsume and which therefore ought to be subsidised or provided free.

TC 1
p7

Societies face trade-offs between economic objectives. For example, the goal of faster growth may conflict with that of greater equality; the goal of lower unemployment may conflict with that of lower inflation (at least in the short run). This is an example of opportunity cost: the cost of achieving more of one objective may be achieving less of another. The existence of trade-offs means that policy makers must make choices.

Key Idea 27

Box 6.1

Should health-care provision be left to the market?

A case of multiple market failures

When you go shopping you may well pay a visit to the chemist and buy some paracetamol tablets, some sticking plasters or a tube of ointment. These health-care products are being sold through the market system in much the same way as other everyday goods and services such as food, household items and petrol.

But many health-care services and products are not allocated through the market in this way. In the UK, the National Health Service provides free hospital treatment, a free general practitioner service and free prescriptions for certain categories of people (such as pensioners and children). Their marginal cost to the patient is thus zero. Of course, these services use resources and they thus have to be paid for out of taxes. In this sense they are not free. (Have you heard the famous saying, 'There's no such thing as a free lunch'?)

But why are these services not sold directly to the patient, thereby saving the taxpayer money? There are, in fact, a number of reasons why the market would fail to provide the optimum amount of health care.

People may not be able to afford treatment

This is a problem connected with the distribution of income. Because income is unequally distributed, some people will be able to afford better treatment than others, and the poorest people may not be able to afford treatment at all. On grounds of equity, therefore, it is argued that health care should be provided free – at least for poor people.

The concept of equity that is usually applied to health care is that of treatment according to medical need rather than according to the ability to pay.

1. Does this argument also apply to food and other basic goods?

Difficulty for people in predicting their future medical needs

If you were suddenly taken ill and required a major operation, or maybe even several, it could be very expensive indeed for you if you had to pay. On the other hand, you may go through life requiring very little if any medical treatment. In other words, there is great uncertainty about your future medical needs. As a result it would be very difficult to plan your finances and budget for possible future medical expenses if you had to pay for treatment. Medical insurance is a possible solution to this problem, but there is still a problem of equity. Would the chronically sick or very old be able to obtain cover, and if so, would they be able to afford the premiums?

Externalities

Health care generates a number of benefits external to the patient. If you are cured of an infectious disease, for example, it is not just you who benefits but also others, since you will not infect them. In addition, your family and friends benefit from seeing you well; and if you have a job you will be able to get back to work, thus reducing the disruption there. These external benefits of health care could be quite large.

If the sick have to pay the cost of their treatment, they may decide not to be treated – especially if they are poor. They may not take into account the effect that their illness has on other people. The market, by equating *private* benefits and costs, would produce too little health care.

Recap

1. Ignorance and uncertainty may prevent people from consuming or producing the levels they would otherwise choose. Information may sometimes be provided (at a price) by the market, but it may be imperfect and in some cases not available at all.

2. Markets may respond sluggishly to changes in demand and supply. The time lags in adjustment can lead to a permanent state of disequilibrium and to problems of instability.

Patient ignorance

Markets only function well to serve consumer wishes if the consumer has the information to make informed decisions. For many products that we buy, we have a pretty good idea how much we will like them. In the case of health care, however, 'consumers' (i.e. patients) may have very poor knowledge. If you have a pain in your chest, it may be simple muscular strain, or it may be a symptom of heart disease. You rely on the doctor (the *supplier* of the treatment) to give you the information: to diagnose your condition. Two problems could arise here with a market system of allocating health care.

The first is that unscrupulous doctors might advise more expensive treatment than is necessary, or drugs companies might try to persuade you to buy a more expensive branded product rather than an identical cheaper version. This is an example of the principal–agent problem and the problem of asymmetric information (see pages 199–200).

The second is that patients suffering from the early stages of a serious disease might not consult their doctor until the symptoms become acute, by which time it might be too late to treat the disease, or very expensive to do so. With a free health service, however, a person is likely to receive an earlier diagnosis of serious conditions. On the other hand, some patients may consult their doctors over trivial complaints.

Oligopoly

If doctors and hospitals operated in the free market as profit maximisers, it is unlikely that competition would drive down their prices. Instead it is possible that they would collude to fix standard prices for treatment, so as to protect their incomes.

Even if doctors did compete openly, it is unlikely that consumers would have the information to enable them to 'shop around' for the best value. Doctor A may charge less than doctor B, but is the quality of service the same? Simple bedside manner – the thing that may most influence a patient's choice – may be a poor indicator of the doctor's skill and judgement.

To argue that the market system will fail to provide an optimal allocation of health-care resources does not in itself prove that free provision is the best alternative. In the USA there is much more reliance on *private medical insurance*. Only the very poor get free treatment. Alternatively, the government may simply *subsidise* the provision of health care, so as to make it cheaper rather than free. This is the case with prescriptions and dental treatment in the UK, where many people have to pay part of the cost of treatment. Also the government can *regulate* the behaviour of the providers of health care, so as to prevent exploitation of the patient. Thus only people with certain qualifications are allowed to operate as doctors, nurses, pharmacists, etc.

? 2. If health care is provided free, the demand is likely to be high. How is this high demand dealt with? Is this a good way of dealing with it?

3. Go through each of the market failings identified in this box. In each case consider what alternative policies are open to a government to tackle them. What are the advantages and disadvantages of these alternatives?

3. In a free market there may be inadequate provision for dependants and an inadequate output of merit goods. Also, because of asymmetric information, agents may not always act in the best interests of their principals.

4. Although economists cannot make ultimate pronouncements on the rights and wrongs of the market – that involves making moral judgements (and economists here are no different from any other person) – they can point out the consequences of the market and of various government policies, and also the trade-offs that exist between different objectives.

6.5   GOVERNMENT INTERVENTION: TAXES AND SUBSIDIES

Will taxing the bad and subsidising the good solve the problem of externalities?

Faced with all the problems of the free market, what is a government to do?

There are several policy instruments that the government can use. At one extreme it can totally replace the market by providing goods and services itself. At the other extreme it can merely seek to persuade producers, consumers or workers to act differently. Between the two extremes the government has a number of instruments it can use to change the way markets operate. These include taxes, subsidies, laws and regulatory bodies. In this and the next two sections we examine these different forms of government intervention.

TC 7
p47

The use of taxes and subsidies

A policy instrument particularly favoured by many economists is that of taxes and subsidies. They can be used for two main purposes: (a) to promote greater social efficiency by altering the composition of production and consumption, and (b) to redistribute incomes. We examined their use for the second purpose in the last chapter. Here we examine their use to achieve greater social efficiency.

When there are imperfections in the market, social efficiency will not be achieved. Marginal social benefit (*MSB*) will not equal marginal social cost (*MSC*). A different level of output would be more desirable. Taxes and subsidies can be used to correct these imperfections. Essentially the approach is to tax those goods or activities where the market produces too much, and subsidise those where the market produces too little.

Taxes and subsidies to correct externalities

The rule here is simple: the government should impose a tax equal to the marginal external cost (or grant a subsidy equal to the marginal external benefit).

KI 23
p192

Assume, for example, that a chemical works emits smoke from a chimney and thus pollutes the atmosphere. This creates external costs for the people who breathe in the smoke. The marginal social cost of producing the chemicals thus exceeds the marginal private cost to the firm: $MSC > MC$.

This is illustrated in Figure 6.5. The marginal pollution cost (the externality) is shown by the vertical distance between the MC and MSC curves. For simplicity, it is assumed that the firm is a price taker. It produces Q_1 where $P = MC$ (its profit-maximising output), but in doing so takes no account of the external pollution costs it imposes on society.

If the government now imposes a tax on production equal to the marginal pollution cost, it will effectively 'internalise' the externality. The firm will have to pay an amount in tax equal to the external cost it creates. It will therefore now maximise profits at Q_2, where $P = MC + tax$. But this is the socially optimum output where $MSB = MSC$.

TC 10
p190

Taxes and subsidies to correct for monopoly

If the problem of monopoly that the government wishes to tackle is that of *excessive profits*, it can impose a lump-sum tax on the monopolist: that is, a tax of a fixed absolute amount irrespective of how much the monopolist produces, or the price it charges. Since a lump-sum tax is an additional *fixed* cost to the firm, and hence will

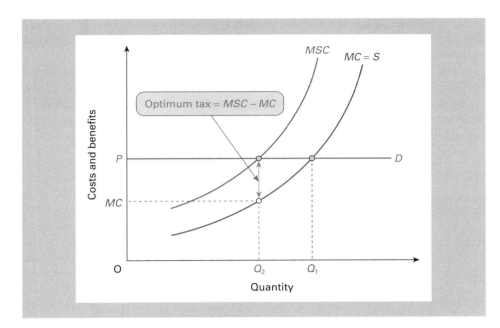

Figure 6.5
Using taxes to correct
a market distortion

not affect the firm's marginal cost, it will not reduce the amount that the monopolist produces (which *would* be the case with a per-unit tax). Two examples of such taxes are the 'windfall tax' imposed in 1997 by the UK Labour government on the profits of various privatised utilities, and in 2005 on the profits of oil companies operating in the North Sea, following large increases in world oil prices.

If the government is concerned that the monopolist produces less than the socially efficient output, it could give the monopolist a *per-unit subsidy* (which would encourage the monopolist to produce more). But would this not *increase* the monopolist's profit? The answer to this is to impose a harsh lump-sum tax in addition to the subsidy. The tax would not undo the subsidy's benefit of encouraging the monopolist to produce more, but it could be used to reduce the monopolist's profits below the original (i.e. pre-subsidy) level.

Advantages of taxes and subsidies

Many economists favour the tax/subsidy solution to market imperfections (especially the problem of externalities) because it still allows the market to operate. It forces firms to take on board the full social costs and benefits of their actions. It is also adjustable according to the magnitude of the problem.

Moreover, if firms are taxed for polluting, they are encouraged to find cleaner ways of producing. The tax acts as an incentive over the longer run to reduce pollution. Likewise, by subsidising *good* practices, firms are given the incentive to adopt more good practices.

Disadvantages of taxes and subsidies

Infeasible to use different tax and subsidy rates.   Each firm produces different levels and types of externalities and operates under different degrees of imperfect competition. It would be administratively very difficult and expensive, if not impossible, to charge every offending firm its own particular tax rate (or grant every relevant firm its own particular rate of subsidy). Even in the case of pollution where it is possible to measure a firm's emissions, there would still have to be a different tax rate for each pollutant and even for each environment, depending on its ability to absorb the pollutant and the number of people affected.

Using combinations of lump-sum taxes and per-unit subsidies to correct monopoly distortions to price, output and profit would also probably be impractical. Given that cost and revenue curves differ substantially from one firm to another, separate tax and subsidy rates would be needed for each firm. An army of tax inspectors would be necessary to administer the system!

Lack of knowledge.   Even if a government did decide to charge a tax equal to each offending firm's marginal external costs, it would still have the problem of measuring those costs and apportioning blame. The damage to lakes and forests from acid rain has been a major concern since the beginning of the 1980s. But just how serious is that damage? What is its current monetary cost? How long lasting is the damage? Just what and who are to blame? These are questions that cannot be answered precisely. It is thus impossible to fix the 'correct' pollution tax on, say, a particular coal-fired power station.

> **Pause for thought**
>
> *Why is it easier to use taxes and subsidies to tackle the problem of car exhaust pollution than to tackle the problem of peak-time traffic congestion in cities?*

Despite these problems, it is nevertheless possible to charge firms by the amount of a particular emission. For example, firms could be charged for chimney smoke by so many parts per million of a given pollutant. Although it is difficult to 'fine-tune' such a system so that the charge reflects the precise number of people affected by the pollutant and by how much, it does go some way to internalising the externality. As Box 6.4 on pages 222–3 shows, many countries in recent years have introduced 'green' taxes, seeing them as an effective means of protecting the environment.

Recap

1. Taxes and subsidies are one means of correcting market distortions.
2. Externalities can be corrected by imposing tax rates equal to the size of marginal external costs, and granting rates of subsidy equal to marginal external benefits.
3. Taxes and subsidies can also be used to affect monopoly price, output and profit. Subsidies can be used to persuade a monopolist to increase output (and reduce price) to the competitive level. Lump-sum taxes can then be used to reduce monopoly profits without affecting the new price or output.
4. Taxes and subsidies have the advantages of 'internalising' externalities and of providing incentives to reduce external costs. On the other hand, they may be impractical to use when different rates are required for each case, or when it is impossible to know the full effects of the activities that the taxes or subsidies are being used to correct.

6.6   GOVERNMENT INTERVENTION: LAWS AND REGULATION

Should the government try to stop 'bad behaviour' by big business?

Laws prohibiting or regulating undesirable structures or behaviour

Laws are frequently used to correct market imperfections. Laws can be of three main types: those that prohibit or regulate behaviour that imposes external costs, those that prevent firms providing false or misleading information, and those that prevent or regulate monopolies and oligopolies. For example, in the UK, under the

2002 Enterprise Act, it is a criminal offence for two or more firms to engage in cartel agreements, such as price fixing, market sharing or supply restrictions (see pages 133 and 136). Convicted offenders may receive a prison sentence of up to five years and/or an unlimited fine.

Advantages of legal restrictions

- They are usually simple and clear to understand and are often relatively easy to administer. For example, various polluting activities could be banned or restricted.
- When the danger is very great, or when the extent of the danger is not as yet known, it might be much safer to ban various practices altogether (e.g. the use of various toxic chemicals) rather than to rely on taxes.
- When a decision needs to be taken quickly, it might be possible to invoke emergency action. For example, in a city like Athens it has been found to be simpler to ban or restrict the use of private cars during a chemical smog emergency than to tax their use.
- Because consumers suffer from imperfect information, consumer protection laws can make it illegal for firms to sell shoddy or unsafe goods, or to make false or misleading claims about their products.

Disadvantages of legal restrictions

The main problem is that legal restrictions tend to be a rather blunt weapon. If, for example, a firm were required to reduce the effluent of a toxic chemical to 20 tonnes per week, there would be no incentive for the firm to reduce it further. With a tax on the effluent, however, the more the firm reduced the effluent, the less tax it would pay. Thus with a system of taxes there is a *continuing* incentive to cut pollution, to improve safety, or whatever.

Regulatory bodies

Rather than using the blunt weapon of general legislation to ban or restrict various activities, a more 'subtle' approach can be adopted. This involves the use of various regulatory bodies. Having identified possible cases where action might be required (e.g. potential cases of pollution or misleading information), the regulatory body would probably conduct an investigation and then prepare a report containing its findings and recommendations. It might also have the power to enforce its decisions.

In most industrial countries, governments have in place a 'competition policy', which attempts to control the worst abuses of market power. In the EU, the European Commission can order an investigation of firms operating in two or more EU countries if it is suspected that they are engaging in anti-competitive practices. These include such things as price fixing by oligopolists (see Web Case 4.12), the refusal by a manufacturer to supply retailers that discount its products, or a firm conducting 'predatory pricing' – deliberately selling at a loss in part of the market in order to undercut the price of a new entrant. Practices that are found, after investigation, to be detrimental to competition are prohibited, and heavy fines can be imposed, even for a first offence.

In the UK, the Office of Fair Trading (OFT) is the official body that investigates and reports on suspected cases of anti-competitive practices. The OFT can order such firms to cease or modify these practices. If they do not, the OFT can impose fines of up to 10 per cent of the firm's annual revenue. Alternatively the OFT can refer such firms to the Competition Commission. The Commission then conducts an investigation, and makes a ruling.

In the UK there are also regulatory bodies for each of the major privatised utilities (see Box 6.2).

Box 6.2

Regulating privatised industries

Is it the best way of dealing with their monopoly power?

From the early 1980s, the Thatcher and Major governments engaged in extensive programmes of 'privatisation', returning most of the nationalised industries to the private sector. Nationalised industries, they claimed, were bureaucratic, inefficient, unresponsive to consumer wishes, and often a burden on the taxpayer.

Other countries have followed similar programmes of privatisation in what has become a worldwide phenomenon. Privatisation has been seen by many governments as a means of revitalising ailing industries and raising revenues to ease budgetary problems.

However, privatisation has brought its own problems. Consumers have complained of poor service and high prices. The result is that governments have been increasingly concerned to *regulate* the behaviour of these industries, many of which have considerable market power.

The system of regulation in the UK

In each of the major privatised industries – gas and electricity, telecommunications, water and railways – there is a separate regulatory office. Their legal authority is contained in the Act of privatisation, but their real power lies in the terms of their licences and price-setting formulae.

The price-setting formulae are essentially of the '*RPI* minus *X*' variety. What this means is that the industries can raise their prices by the rate of increase in the retail price index (RPI) (i.e. by the rate of inflation) *minus* a certain percentage (*X*) to take account of expected increases in efficiency. The idea is that this will force the industry to pass such cost savings on to the consumer.

The licence also permits the regulator to monitor other aspects of the behaviour of the industry and to require it to take various measures. For example, the Strategic Rail Authority sets minimum standards for the punctuality and frequency of trains. Generally, however, the approach has been one of negotiation with the industry.

Assessing the system of regulation in the UK

The system that has evolved in the UK has various advantages.

■ It is a *discretionary* system, with the regulator able to judge individual examples of the behaviour of the industry on their own merits. The regulator has a detailed knowledge of the industry, which would not be available to government ministers or other bodies such as the Office of Fair Trading. The regulator could thus be argued to be the best person to decide on whether the industry is acting in the public interest.

■ The system is *flexible*, since it allows for the licence and price formula to be changed as circumstances change.

■ The '*RPI* minus *X*' formula provides an *incentive* for the privatised firms to be as efficient as possible. If they can lower their costs by more than *X*, they will, in theory, be able to make larger profits and keep them. If, on the other hand, they do not succeed in reducing costs sufficiently, they will make a loss. There is thus a continuing pressure on them to cut costs.

There are, however, some inherent problems with the way in which regulation operates in the UK.

■ The '*RPI* minus *X*' formula was designed to provide an incentive for the firms to cut costs. But if *X* is too low, the firm might make excessive profits. Frequently regulators have underestimated the scope for cost reductions resulting from new technology and reorganisation, and have thus initially set *X* too low. As a result, instead of *X* remaining constant for a number of years, as intended, new higher values for *X* have been set after only one or two years. Alternatively, one-off price cuts have been ordered, as happened when the water companies were required by OFWAT to cut prices by an average of 10 per cent in 2000. In either case the incentive for the industry to cut costs is reduced. What is the point of being more efficient if the regulator is merely going to take away the extra profits?

■ Regulation is becoming increasingly complex. This makes it difficult for the industries to plan, and may lead to a growth of 'short-termism'. One of the claimed advantages of privatisation was to give greater independence to the industries from short-term government interference, and allow them to plan for the longer term. In practice, one type of interference may have been replaced by another.

- There may also be the danger of regulatory capture. As regulators become more and more involved in their industry and get to know the senior managers at a personal level, so they are increasingly likely to see the managers' point of view and become less and less tough. Commentators do not believe that this has happened yet; the regulators are generally independently minded. But it is a danger for the future.
- Alternatively, regulators could be captured by government. Instead of being totally independent, there to serve the interests of the consumer, they might bend to pressures from the government to do things which might help the government win the next election.

Increasing competition in the privatised industries

Where natural monopoly exists (see page 120), competition is impossible in a free market. Of course, the industry *could* be broken up by the government, with firms prohibited from owning more than a certain percentage of the industry. But this would lead to higher costs of production. Firms would be operating further back up a downward-sloping long-run average cost curve.

But many parts of the privatised industries are not natural monopolies. Generally it is only the *grid* that is a natural monopoly. In the case of gas and water, it is the pipelines. It would be wasteful to duplicate these. In the case of electricity it is the power lines: the national grid and the local power lines. In the case of the railways it is the track. *Other* parts of these industries, however, have generally been opened up to competition (with the exception of water). Thus there are now many producers and

sellers of electricity and gas. This is possible because they are given access, by law, to the national and local electricity grids and gas pipelines.

Even for the parts where there is a natural monopoly, they could be made contestable monopolies. One way of doing this is by granting operators a licence for a specific period of time. This is known as franchising, which has been the approach used for the railways. Once a company has been granted a franchise, it has the monopoly of passenger rail services over specific routes. But the awarding of the franchise can be highly competitive, with rival companies putting in competitive bids, in terms of both price (or, in the case of railways, the level of government subsidy required) and the quality of service.

Despite attempts to introduce competition into the privatised industries, they are still dominated by giant companies. Even if they are no longer strictly monopolies, they still have considerable market power. Competition is far from being perfect! The scope for price leadership or other forms of oligopolistic collusion is great. Thus although regulation through the price formula has been progressively abandoned as elements of competition have been introduced, the regulators have retained a role similar to that of the OFT: they can intervene to prevent cases of collusion and the abuse of monopoly power. The companies, however, do have the right of appeal to the Competition Commission.

1. *Should regulators of utilities that have been privatised into several separate companies allow (a) mergers between these companies or similar companies from abroad; (b) mergers with firms in other industries?*
2. *If an industry regulator adopts an RPI − X formula for price regulation, is it desirable that the value of X should be adjusted as soon as cost conditions change?*

Definitions

Regulatory capture
Where the regulator is persuaded to operate in the industry's interests rather than those of the consumer.

Franchising
Where a firm is granted the licence to operate a given part of an industry for a specified length of time.

Pause for thought

What other forms of intervention are likely to be necessary to back up the work of regulatory bodies?

The advantage of such bodies is that a case-by-case approach can be adopted and, as a result, the most appropriate solution adopted. However, investigations may be expensive and time-consuming, only a few cases may be examined, and offending firms may make various promises of good behaviour which, owing to a lack of follow-up by the regulatory body, may not in fact be carried out.

Recap

1. Laws can be used to regulate activities that impose external costs, to regulate monopolies and oligopolies, and to provide consumer protection. Legal controls are often simpler and easier to operate than taxes, and are safer when the danger is potentially great. Nevertheless, legal controls tend to be rather a blunt weapon, although discretion can sometimes be allowed in the administration of the law.

2. Regulatory bodies can be set up to monitor and control activities that might be against the public interest (e.g. anti-competitive behaviour of oligopolists). They can conduct investigations of specific cases and can be very thorough. The investigations, however, may be expensive and time consuming, and may not be acted on by the authorities.

6.7 OTHER FORMS OF GOVERNMENT INTERVENTION

What other means does the government have to correct market failures?

Changes in property rights

One cause of market failure is the limited nature of property rights. If someone dumps a load of rubble in your garden, the law should protect you. It is *your* property, and you can thus insist that it is removed. If, however, someone dumps a load of rubble in his or her *own* garden, but which is next door to yours, what can you do? You can still see it from your window. It is still an eyesore. But you have no property rights over the next-door garden.

Property rights define who owns property, to what uses it can be put, the rights other people have over it and how it may be transferred. By *extending* these rights, individuals may be able to prevent other people imposing costs on them, or charge them for doing so.

The socially efficient level of charge would be one that was equal to the marginal external cost (and would have the same effect as the government's charging a tax on the firm of that amount: see Figure 6.5 on page 205). The **Coase theorem**[3] states that in an otherwise perfectly competitive market, the socially efficient charge *will* be levied. But why?

Let us take the case of river pollution by a chemical works that imposes a cost on people fishing in the river. If property rights to the river were now given to the fishing community they could impose a charge on the chemical works per unit of output. If they charged *less* than the marginal external cost, they would suffer more

Definition

The Coase theorem
By sufferers from externalities doing deals with perpetrators (by levying charges or offering bribes), the externality will be 'internalised' and the socially efficient level of output will be achieved.

---
[3] Named after Ronald Coase, who developed the theory. See his 'The problem of social cost', *Journal of Law and Economics* (1960).

from the last unit (in terms of lost fish) than they were being compensated. If they charged *more*, and thereby caused the firm to cut back its output below the socially efficient level, they would be sacrificing receiving charges that would be greater than the marginal suffering. It will be in the sufferers' best interests, therefore, to charge an amount *equal* to the marginal externality.

In most instances, however, this type of solution is totally impractical. It is impractical when *many* people are *slightly* inconvenienced, especially if there are many culprits imposing the costs. For example, if I were disturbed by noisy lorries outside my home, it would not be practical to negotiate with every haulage company involved. What if I wanted to ban the lorries from the street but my next-door neighbour wanted to charge them 10p per journey? Who gets their way?

Where the extension of private property rights becomes a more practical solution is when the culprits are few in number, are easily identifiable and impose clearly defined costs. Thus a noise abatement Act could be passed which allowed me to prevent my neighbours playing noisy radios, having noisy parties or otherwise disturbing the peace in my home. The onus would be on me to report them. Or if I chose, I could agree not to report them if they paid me adequate compensation.

But even in cases where only a few people are involved, there may still be the problem of litigation. Justice may not be free, and there is thus a conflict with equity. The rich can afford 'better' justice. They can employ top lawyers. Thus even if I have a right to sue a large company for dumping toxic waste near me, I may not have the legal muscle to win.

KI 19
p177

Finally there is the broader question of *equity*. The extension of private property rights may favour the rich (who tend to have more property) at the expense of the poor. Ramblers may get great pleasure from strolling across a great country estate, along public rights of way. This may annoy the owner. If the owner's property rights are now extended to exclude the ramblers, is this a social gain?

Of course, equity considerations can also be dealt with by altering property rights, but in a different way. *Public* property like parks, open spaces, libraries and historic buildings could be extended. Also the property of the rich could be redistributed to the poor. Here it is less a question of the rights that ownership confers, and more a question of altering the ownership itself.

Provision of information

When ignorance is a reason for market failure, the direct provision of information by the government or one of its agencies may help to correct that failure. An example is the information on jobs provided by job centres to those looking for work. They thus help the labour market to work better and increase the elasticity of supply of labour. Another example is the provision of consumer information – for example, on the effects of smoking, or of eating certain foodstuffs. Another is the provision of government statistics on prices, costs, employment, sales trends, etc. This enables firms to plan with greater certainty.

The direct provision of goods and services

In the case of public goods and services, such as streets, pavements, seaside illumination and national defence, the market may completely fail to provide. In this case the government must take over the role of provision. Central government, local government or some other public agency could provide these goods and services directly. Alternatively, they could pay private firms to do so. The public would pay through central and local taxation.

But just what quantity of the public good should be provided? How can the level of public demand or public 'need' be identified? Should any charge at all be made to consumers for each unit consumed?

With a pure public good, once it is provided the marginal cost of supplying one more consumer is zero. Take the case of a lighthouse. Once it is constructed and in operation, there is no extra cost of providing the service to additional passing ships. Even if it were *possible* to charge ships each time they make use of it, it would not be socially desirable. Assuming no external costs, MSC is zero. Thus $MSB = MSC$ at a price of zero. Zero is thus the socially efficient price.

But what about the construction of a new public good, like a new road or a new lighthouse? How can a rational decision be made by the government as to whether it should go ahead? This time the marginal cost is not zero; extra roads and lighthouses cost money to build. The solution is to identify all the costs and benefits to society from the project (private and external) and to weigh them up. This is known as **cost–benefit analysis** (see Web Appendix 6.2 for details of how cost–benefit analysis is conducted). If the social benefits of the project exceed the social costs, then it would be socially efficient to go ahead with it. Many proposed public projects are subjected to cost–benefit analysis in order to assess their desirability.

The government could also provide goods and services directly which are *not* public goods. Examples include health and education. There are four reasons why such things are provided free or at well below cost.

Social justice. Society may feel that these things should not be provided according to ability to pay. Rather they should be provided as of right: an equal right based on need.

Large positive externalities. People other than the consumer may benefit substantially. If a person decides to get treatment for an infectious disease, other people benefit by not being infected. A free health service thus helps to combat the spread of disease.

Dependants. If education were not free, and if the quality of education depended on the amount spent, and if parents could choose how much or little to buy, then the quality of children's education would depend not just on their parents' income, but also on how much they cared. A government may choose to provide such things free in order to protect children from 'bad' parents. A similar argument is used for providing free prescriptions and dental treatment for all children.

Ignorance. Consumers may not realise how much they will benefit. If they had to pay, they might choose (unwisely) to go without. Providing health care free may persuade people to consult their doctors before a complaint becomes serious.

Definition

Cost–benefit analysis
The identification, measurement and weighing-up of the costs and benefits of a project in order to decide whether or not it should go ahead.

Recap

1. An extension of property rights may allow individuals to prevent others imposing costs on them, or to charge them for so doing. This is not practical, however, when many people are affected to a small degree, or where several people are affected but differ in their attitudes towards what they want doing about the 'problem'.

2. The government may provide information in cases where the private sector fails to provide an adequate level.

3. The government may also provide goods and services directly. These could be in the category of public goods or other goods where the government feels that provision by the market is inadequate.

MORE OR LESS INTERVENTION?   6.8

Can the government always put things right?

Government intervention in the market can itself lead to problems.

Drawbacks of government intervention

Shortages and surpluses. If the government intervenes by fixing prices at levels other than the equilibrium, this will create either shortages or surpluses (see Section 2.6).

If the price is fixed *below* the equilibrium, there will be a shortage. For example, if the rent of council houses is fixed below the equilibrium in order to provide cheap housing for poor people, demand will exceed supply. In the case of such shortages the government will have to adopt a system of waiting lists, or rationing, or giving certain people preferential treatment. Alternatively it will have to allow allocation to be on a first-come, first-served basis or allow queues to develop. Black markets are likely to occur.

If the price is fixed *above* the equilibrium price, there will be a surplus. Such surpluses are obviously wasteful. (The problem of food surpluses in the European Union was examined in Box 2.4.)

Poor information. The government may not know the full costs and benefits of its policies. It may genuinely wish to pursue the interests of consumers or any other group and yet may be unaware of people's wishes or misinterpret their behaviour.

Bureaucracy and inefficiency. Government intervention involves administrative costs. The more wide reaching and detailed the intervention, the greater the number of people and material resources that will be involved. These resources may be used wastefully.

Lack of market incentives. If government intervention removes market forces or cushions their effect (by the use of subsidies, welfare provisions, guaranteed prices or wages, etc.), it may remove certain useful incentives. Subsidies may allow inefficient firms to survive. Welfare payments may discourage effort. The market may be imperfect, but it does tend to encourage efficiency by allowing the efficient to receive greater rewards.

Shifts in government policy. The economic efficiency of industry may suffer if government intervention changes too frequently. It makes it difficult for firms to plan if they cannot predict tax rates, subsidies, price and wage controls, etc.

Lack of freedom for the individual. Government intervention involves a loss of freedom for individuals to make economic choices. The argument is not just that the pursuit of individual gain is seen to lead to the social good, but that it is desirable in itself that individuals should be as free as possible to pursue their own interests with the minimum of government interference: that minimum being largely confined to the maintenance of laws consistent with the protection of life, liberty and property.

The case for non-intervention (*laissez-faire*), or very limited intervention, is not that the market is the *perfect* means of achieving given social goals, but that the above problems created by intervention are greater than the problems it overcomes.

Advantages of the free market

Although markets in the real world are not perfect, even imperfect markets can be argued to have positive advantages over government provision or even government regulation. These might include the following:

Automatic adjustments. Government intervention requires administration. A free-market economy, on the other hand, leads to automatic, albeit imperfect, adjustment to demand and supply changes.

Dynamic advantages of capitalism. The chances of making high monopoly/oligopoly profits will encourage businesspeople to invest in new products and new techniques. Prices may be high initially, but consumers will gain from the extra choice of products. Furthermore, if profits are high, new firms will sooner or later break into the market and competition will ensue.

> **Pause for thought**
>
> *Are there any features of free-market capitalism that would discourage innovation?*

A high degree of competition even under monopoly/oligopoly. Even though an industry at first sight may seem to be highly monopolistic, competitive forces may still work as a result of the following:

- A fear that excessively high profits might encourage firms to attempt to break into the industry (assuming that the market is contestable).
- Competition from closely related industries (e.g. coach services for rail services, or electricity for gas).
- The threat of foreign competition.
- Countervailing powers (see page 147). Large powerful producers often sell to large powerful buyers. For example, the power of detergent manufacturers to drive up the price of washing powder is countered by the power of supermarket chains to drive down the price at which they purchase it. Thus power is to some extent neutralised.
- The competition for corporate control (see page 123).

Should there be more or less intervention in the market?

No firm conclusions can be drawn in the debate between those who favour more and those who favour less government intervention, for the following reasons:

- Many moral, social and political issues are involved which cannot be settled by economic analysis. For example, it could be argued that freedom to set up in business and freedom from government regulation are desirable *for their own sake*. As a fundamental ethical point of view this can be disputed, but not disproved.
- In principle, the issue of whether a government ought to intervene in any situation could be settled by weighing up the costs and benefits of that intervention. However, such costs and benefits, even if they could be identified, are extremely difficult if not impossible to measure, especially when the costs are borne by different people from those who receive the benefits and when externalities are involved.
- Often the effect of more or less intervention simply cannot be predicted; there are too many uncertainties.

Nevertheless, economists can make a considerable contribution to analysing problems of the market and the effects of government intervention.

Recap

1. Government intervention in the market may lead to shortages or surpluses; it may be based on poor information; it may be costly in terms of administration; it may stifle incentives; it may be disruptive if government policies change too frequently; it may remove certain liberties.

2. By contrast, a free market leads to automatic adjustments to changes in economic conditions; the prospect of monopoly/oligopoly profits may stimulate risk taking and hence research and development and innovation; there may still be a high degree of actual or potential competition under monopoly and oligopoly.

3. It is impossible to draw firm conclusions about the 'optimum' level of government intervention. This is partly due to the moral/political nature of the question, partly due to the difficulties of measuring costs and benefits of intervention/non-intervention, and partly due to the difficulties of predicting the effects of government policies, especially over the longer term.

THE ENVIRONMENT: A CASE STUDY IN MARKET FAILURE 6.9

How can economists contribute to the environmental debate?

The environmental problem

Global warming, pollution of the land, rivers and seas, the depletion of fish stocks, the chopping down of rainforests, the reduction in biodiversity, the dirty and rubbish-strewn nature of many cities and the despoiling of the countryside have become major concerns around the world in recent years. And yet, in many cases the degradation of the environment is getting worse.

There are some grounds for optimism, however. Many newer industrial processes are cleaner and make a more efficient use of resources. This leads to less waste and a slowdown in the rate of extraction of various minerals and fossil fuels.

In addition, as resources become scarcer, so their prices rise. This encourages people to use less of them, either by using more efficient technology or by switching to renewable alternatives. Thus as fossil fuels gradually run out, so a rise in their price will encourage the switch to solar, wave and wind power.

Finally, public opinion can put important pressure on governments and firms. Many firms have found it to be in their commercial interests to have a 'green image'. Likewise, governments see electoral advantage in policies to create a cleaner, greener environment.

Despite these developments, however, many aspects of environmental degradation continue to worsen. Many natural species continue to be destroyed; fish stocks in many parts of the world are dangerously low; tropical forests are being cut down at an alarming rate; toxic chemicals are widespread in the environment; fossil fuel usage grows apace as large developing countries, such as China and India, continue on a path of rapid industrialisation, and as road and air travel throughout the world seem inexorably to grow; global warming is set to accelerate, with consequent rises in sea levels and dramatically changing rainfall patterns.

Part of the problem is the growing pressure on the environment of a rapidly expanding world population (see Box 3.2 on page 84). But a major cause of the problem is the failure of the market system.

Market failures

The market system will fail to provide an adequate protection for the environment for a number of reasons.

The environment as a common resource. The air, the seas and many other parts of the environment are not privately owned. They are a global 'commons', and thus have the characteristic of 'non-excludability' (see page 195). Many of the 'services' provided by the environment do not have a price, so there is no economic incentive to economise on their use.

Yet most environmental resources are *scarce*: there is 'rivalry' in their use. This is where common resources differ from public goods. One person's use of a common resource diminishes the amount or quality available for others. At a zero price, these resources will be overused. This is why fish stocks in many parts of the world are severely depleted, why virgin forests are disappearing (cut down for timber or firewood), why many roads are so congested, and why the atmosphere is becoming so polluted (being used as a common 'dump' for emissions). In each case, a resource that is freely available is overused. This is known as the 'tragedy of the commons'. Web Appendix 6.3 examines the economics of common resources.

Externalities. One of the major problems of the environment being a public good is that of externalities. When people pollute the environment, the costs are borne mainly by others. The greater these external costs, the lower will be the socially efficient level of output (Q_2 in Figure 6.1(a) on page 193). Because no one owns the environment, there is no one to enforce property rights over it. If a company pollutes the air that I breathe, I cannot stop it because the air does not belong to me.

Ignorance. There have been many cases of people causing environmental damage without realising it, especially when the effects build up over a long time. Take the case of aerosols. It was not until the 1980s that scientists connected their use to ozone depletion. Even when the problems are known to scientists, consumers may not appreciate the full environmental costs of their actions. So even if people would like to be more 'environmentally friendly' in their activities, they might not have the knowledge to be so.

Inter-generational problems. The environmentally harmful effects of many activities are long term, whereas the benefits are immediate. Thus consumers and firms are frequently prepared to continue with various practices and leave future generations to worry about their environmental consequences. The problem, then, is a reflection of the importance that people attach to the present relative to the future.

KI 2
p191
KI 2
p195
KI 1
p5
KI 2
p192
KI 2
p200

> **Pause for thought**
>
> Look through the categories of possible market failings in Sections 6.2 to 6.4. Are there any others, in addition to the four we have just identified, that will result in a socially inefficient use of the environment?

Policy alternatives

Charging for use of the environment (as a resource or a dump)

One way of 'pricing the environment' is for the government to impose **environmental charges** on consumers or firms. Thus *emissions charges* could be levied on firms discharging waste. Another example is the use of *user charges* to households for sewage disposal or rubbish collection. The socially efficient level of environmental use would be where the marginal social benefits and costs of that use were equal. This is illustrated in Figure 6.6, which shows the emission of toxic waste into a river by a chemical plant.

> **Definition**
>
> **Environmental charges**
> Charges for using natural resources (e.g. water or national parks), or for using the environment as a dump for waste (e.g. factory emissions or sewage).

TC 7
p47

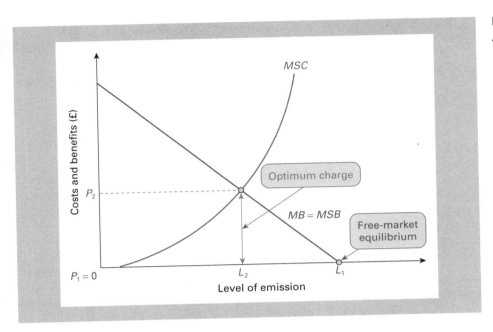

Figure 6.6
An emissions charge

It is assumed that all the benefits from emitting the waste into the river accrue to the firm (i.e. there is no external benefit). Marginal private and marginal social benefits are thus the same ($MB = MSB$). The curve slopes downwards because, with a downward-sloping demand curve for the *good*, higher output will have a lower marginal benefit, and so too will the waste associated with it.

KI 23
p192

But what about the marginal costs? Without charges, the marginal private cost of using the river for emitting the waste is zero. The pollution of the river, however, imposes an external cost on those living by the river or using it for fishing or water supply. The marginal external cost rises as the river becomes less and less able to cope with increased levels of emission. As there is no private cost, the marginal social cost is the same as the marginal external cost.

TC 10
p190

Without a charge, the firm will emit L_1, since this is where its private marginal cost (= 0) equals its private marginal benefit. The socially efficient level of emission is L_2 and the socially efficient level of emission charge, therefore, is P_2.

Environmental ('green') taxes and subsidies

Rather than charging for environmental use, a tax could be imposed on the output (or consumption) of a *good*, wherever external environmental costs are generated. These are known as **green taxes**. In this case, the good already has a price: the tax has the effect of increasing the price. To achieve a socially efficient output, the rate of tax should be equal to the marginal external cost (see Figure 6.5 on page 205). The alternative is to subsidise activities that reduce pollution (such as the installation of loft insulation). Here the rate of subsidy should be equal to the marginal external benefit.

Although green taxes and subsidies are theoretically a means of achieving social efficiency, they do have serious limitations (see Box 6.4).

Laws and regulations

The traditional way of tackling pollution has been to set maximum permitted levels of emission or resource use, or minimum acceptable levels of environmental quality, and then to fine firms contravening these limits. Clearly, there have to be

Definition

Green tax
A tax on output designed to charge for the adverse effects of production on the environment. The socially efficient level of a green tax is equal to the marginal environmental cost of production.

Box 6.3

A deeper shade of green

How should we treat the environment?

How green are you? Do you see the environment as there for you to use as you choose, or do we all have responsibilities for looking after the environment – responsibilities towards each other, or to future generations, or to the animals and plants that share the planet with us, or even to the planet itself? In this box we examine some of the different approaches to looking after the environment, and ask what implications they have for sustainability.

The free-market approach. At one extreme, we could regard the world as there purely for ourselves: a resource that belongs to individual property owners to do with as they choose; or a 'common asset', such as the air and seas, for individuals to use for their own benefit. In this view of the world, we are entitled simply to weigh up the marginal costs and benefits to ourselves of any activity. Sustainability is only achieved in this free-market world to the extent that resource prices rise as they become scarce and to the extent that environmentally friendly technologies are in firms' (or consumers') private interests.

In terms of Figure 6.1(a) on page 193, assuming that there were external environmental costs (shown by the vertical difference between the *MSC* and *MC* curves), no account would be taken of these, and

production would remain at the free-market level of Q_1.

The social efficiency approach. A somewhat less extreme version of this view is one that takes the social costs and benefits of using the environment into account: i.e. not just the costs and benefits to the direct producer or consumer, but to people in general. Here we would apply the standard rules for social efficiency: that if marginal social benefit exceeds marginal social cost we should do more of the activity, and if marginal social cost exceeds marginal social benefit we should do less. In Figure 6.1(a), the social efficiency approach would give an optimum output of Q_2.

Even though this approach does take into account environmental externalities (such as pollution) these environmental costs are only costs to the extent that they adversely affect *human beings*.

Within this general approach, however, more explicit account can be taken of sustainability, by including in the external costs the costs of our use of the environment today to *future* generations. For example, we could take into account the effects of global warming not just on ourselves, but on our children and their descendants.

inspectors to monitor the amount of pollution, and the fines have to be large enough to deter firms from exceeding the limit.

Virtually all countries have environmental regulations of one sort or another. For example, the EU has over 200 items of legislation covering areas such as air and water pollution, noise, the marketing and use of dangerous chemicals, waste management, the environmental impacts of new projects (such as power stations, roads and quarries), recycling, depletion of the ozone layer and global warming.

Given the uncertainty over the environmental impacts of pollutants, especially in the longer term, it is often better to play safe and set tough emissions or ambient standards. These could always be relaxed at a later stage if the effects turn out not to be so damaging, but it might be too late to reverse damage if the effects turn out to be more serious. Taxes may be a more sophisticated means of reaching a socially efficient output, but regulations are usually more straightforward to devise, easier to understand by firms and easier to implement.

Education

People's attitudes are very important in determining the environmental consequences of their actions. Fortunately for the environment, people are not always

The conservationist approach. Many environment-alists argue that our responsibilities should not be limited to each other, or even to future generations, but should include the environment for its own sake. Such a view would involve downplaying the relative importance of material consumption and economic growth and putting greater emphasis on the mainten-ance of ecosystems. Growth in consumption would be ethically acceptable only if it led to no (or only very minor) environmental degradation. Maintenance of the environment is thus seen as an ethical con-straint on human activity. In Figure 6.1(a) the optimum production would be below Q_2 as long as the *MSC* curve only included costs to *society* and not the broader costs to the environment for its own sake.

The Gaia approach. The strongest approach to sus-tainability involves a fundamentally different ethical standpoint. Here the Earth itself, and its various nat-ural species of animals and plants have moral rights. According to this 'Gaia philosophy', people are seen as mere custodians of the planet: the planet does not belong to us, any more than a dog belongs to the fleas on its back! This view of the environment is similar to that held by indigenous peoples living in marginal areas, such as the Aborigines in Australia

and the Bushmen of the Kalahari, and to various other 'hunter-gatherer' peoples in developing coun-tries. Their ethic is that the land they leave their descendants should be as good as, if not better, than the land they inherited from their ancestors. Conservation is the 'prime directive'. This approach to the environment has been dubbed the 'deep green' approach.

In this approach, Figure 6.1(a) is irrelevant. The question is not whether environmental degradation is a price worth paying for the benefits of consump-tion. Production should be avoided that involves *any* environmental degradation.

1. If, according to the deep green approach, we should not do anything that involves environ-mental degradation, does this imply that the cost of environmental damage is infinite?
2. If the adverse effects on the environment of a person's actions were confined to that person's own property (e.g. a farmer cutting down hedgerows on his or her own land), would this matter if we took a social efficiency approach towards sustainability? Would there be any external costs?

out simply to maximise their own self-interest. If they were, then why would people often buy more expensive 'green' products, such as environmentally friendly deter-gents? The answer is that many people like to do their own little bit, however small, towards protecting the environment.

This is where education can come in. If children, and adults for that matter, were made more aware of environmental issues and the consequences of their actions, then people's consumption habits could change and more pressure would be put on firms to improve their 'green credentials'.

Tradable permits

A policy measure that has grown in popularity in recent years is that of **tradable permits**. This is a combination of regulations and market-based systems. A max-imum permitted level of emission is set for a given pollutant for a given factory, and the firm is given a permit to emit up to this amount. If it emits less than this amount, it is given a credit for the difference, which it can then use in another of its factories, or sell to other firms. These other firms are then allowed to emit that amount *over* their permitted level. Thus the overall level of emissions is given by regulations, whereas their distribution is determined by the market.

Definition

Tradable permits
Each firm is given a permit to produce a given level of pollution. If less than the permitted amount is produced, the firm is given a credit. This can then be sold to another firm, allowing it to exceed its original limit.

Take the example of firms A and B, which are currently producing 12 units of a pollutant each. Now assume that a standard is set permitting them to produce only 10 units each. If firm A managed to reduce the pollutant to 8 units, it would be given a credit for 2 units. It could then sell this to firm B, enabling B to continue emitting 12 units. The effect would still be a total reduction of 4 units between the two firms. However, the trade in pollution permits allows pollution reduction to be concentrated where it can be achieved at lowest cost. In our example, if it cost firm B more to reduce its pollution than firm A, the permits could be sold from A to B at a price that was profitable to both (i.e. at a price above the cost of emission reduction to A, but below the cost of emission reduction to B). Given the resulting reduced cost of pollution control, it might be politically easier to impose tougher standards (i.e. impose lower permitted levels of emission).

The principle of tradable permits can be used as the basis of international agreements on pollution reduction. Each country could be required to achieve a certain percentage reduction in a pollutant (e.g. carbon dioxide – CO_2 – or sulphur dioxide – SO_2), but any country exceeding its reduction could sell its right to these emissions to other (presumably richer) countries.

A similar principle can be adopted for using natural resources. Thus fish quotas could be assigned to fishing boats or fleets or countries. Any parts of these quotas not used could then be sold.

The EU carbon trading system.   In the EU, a carbon Emissions Trading Scheme (ETS) has been in place since January 2005 as part of the EU's approach to meeting its targets under the Kyoto Treaty (see Web Case 6.7). Under the scheme, some 12 000 industrial plants have been allocated CO_2 emissions allowances, or credits, by their respective governments. Companies that exceed their limits must purchase credits to cover the difference, while those that reduce their emissions can sell their surplus credits for a profit. Companies can trade directly with each other or through brokers operating throughout Europe.

Assessing the system of tradable permits.   The main advantage of tradable permits is that they combine the simplicity of regulations with the benefits of achieving pollution reduction in the most efficient way. There is also the advantage that firms have a financial incentive to cut pollution. This might then make it easier for governments to impose tougher standards (i.e. impose lower permitted levels of emission).

There are, however, various problems with tradable permits. One is how to distribute the permissions in a way that all firms regard as fair. Another is the possibility that trade will lead to pollution being concentrated in certain geographical areas. Another is that it may reduce the pressure on dirtier factories (or countries) to cut their emissions.

> **Pause for thought**
>
> To what extent will the introduction of tradable permits lead to a lower level of total pollution (as opposed to its redistribution)?

Finally, the system will only lead to significant cuts in pollution if the permitted levels are low. Once the system is in place, the government might then feel the pressure is off to *reduce* the permitted levels. This has been a major criticism of the EU Emissions Trading Scheme. Quotas have been relatively generous. As a result many firms have found it easy to produce surplus credits, which has pushed their price to a low level. This, in turn, makes it cheap for 'dirty' firms to buy credits and thus reduces the pressure on them to cut pollution.

How much can we rely on governments?

If governments are to be relied upon to set the optimum green taxes or regulations, several conditions must be met.

First, they must have the will to protect the environment. But governments are accountable to their electorates and must often appease various pressure groups, such as representatives of big business. In the USA, for example, there has been great resistance to cuts in greenhouse gases from the automobile, power and various other industries, many of which have powerful representation in Congress. One of the problems is that many of the environmental effects of our actions today will be on future generations, but governments represent today's generation, and today's generation may not be prepared to make the necessary sacrifices. This brings us back to the importance of education.

Second, it must be possible to identify just what the optimum is. This requires a knowledge of just what the environmental effects are of various activities, such as the emission of CO_2 into the atmosphere, and that is something on which scientists disagree.

Finally, there is the problem that many environmental issues are global and not just local or national. Many require concerted action by governments around the world. The history of international agreements on environmental issues, however, is plagued with difficulties between countries, which seem concerned mainly with their own national interests.

Recap

1. The effects of population pressures and market failures have led to growing environmental degradation.

2. The market fails to achieve a socially efficient use of the environment because large parts of the environment are a common resource, because production or consumption often generates environmental externalities, because of ignorance of the environmental effects of our actions, and because of a lack of concern for future generations.

3. One approach to protecting the environment is to impose charges for using the environment or taxes per unit of output. The problem with these methods is in identifying the appropriate charges or tax rates, since these will vary according to the environmental impact.

4. Another approach is to use laws and regulations, such as making certain practices illegal or putting limits on discharges. This is a less sophisticated alternative to taxes or charges, but it is safer when the environmental costs of certain actions are unknown.

5. Education can help to change attitudes towards the environment and the behaviour of consumers and firms.

6. Tradable permits are a mix of regulations and market-based systems. Firms are given permits to emit a certain level of pollution, and these can then be traded. A firm that can reduce its pollution relatively cheaply below its permitted level can sell this credit to another firm that finds it more costly to do so. The system is an efficient and administratively cheap way of limiting pollution to a designated level. It can, however, lead to pollution being concentrated in certain areas and can reduce the pressure on firms to find cleaner methods of production.

7. Although governments can make a major contribution to reducing pollution, government action is unlikely to lead to the optimum outcome (however defined). Governments may be more concerned with short-run political considerations and will not have perfect information.

Box 6.4

Green taxes

Their growing popularity in the industrialised world

Increasingly, countries are introducing 'green' taxes in order to discourage pollution as goods are produced, consumed or disposed of. The table below shows the range of green taxes used around the world and the chart shows green tax revenues as a percentage of GDP in various countries. As you can see, they are higher than average in Scandinavian countries, reflecting the strength of their environmental concerns. They are lowest in the USA. By far the largest green tax revenues come from fuel taxes. Fuel taxes are relatively high in the UK and so, therefore, are green tax revenues.

There are various problems, however, with using the tax weapon in the fight against pollution.

Identifying the socially efficient tax rate

It will be difficult to identify the appropriate amount of tax for each firm, given that each one is likely to produce different amounts of pollutants for any given level of output. Even if two firms produce exactly the same amount of pollutants, the environmental damage might be quite different because

the ability of the environment to cope with it will differ between the two locations. Also the number of people suffering will differ (a factor that is very important when considering the *human* impact of pollution). What is more, the harmful effects are likely to build up over time, and predicting these effects is fraught with difficulty.

Problems of demand inelasticity

The less elastic the demand for the product, the less effective will be a tax in cutting production and hence in cutting pollution. Thus taxes on petrol would have to be very high indeed to make significant reductions in the consumption of petrol and hence significant reductions in the exhaust gases that contribute to global warming and acid rain.

Problems with international trade

If a country imposes pollution taxes on its industries, its products will become less competitive in world trade. To compensate for this, it may be necessary to

Types of environmental taxes and charges

Motor fuels	**Other goods**	**Air transport**
Leaded/unleaded	Batteries	Noise charges
Diesel (quality differential)	Plastic carrier bags	Aviation fuels
Carbon/energy taxation	Glass containers	
Sulphur tax	Drink cans	**Water**
	Tyres	Water charges
Other energy products	CFCs/halons	Sewage charges
Carbon/energy tax	Disposable razors/cameras	Water effluent charges
Sulphur tax or charge	Lubricant oil charge	Manure charges
NO_2 charge	Oil pollutant charge	
Methane charge	Solvents	**Direct tax provisions**
		Tax relief on green investment
Agricultural inputs	**Waste disposal**	Taxation on free company cars
Fertilisers	Municipal waste charges	Employer-paid commuting expenses taxable
Pesticides	Waste-disposal charges	Employer-paid parking expenses taxable
Manure	Hazardous waste charges	Commuter use of public transport tax deductible
	Landfill tax or charges	
Vehicle-related taxation	Duties on waste water	
Sales tax depends on car size		
Road tax depends on car size		

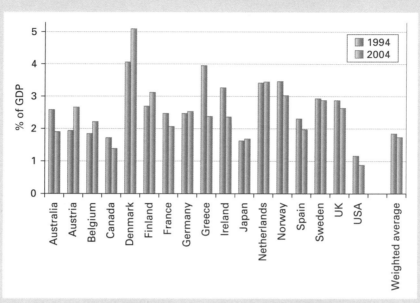

Source: *Environmentally Related Taxes Database* (OECD, 2006)

Green tax revenues as a percentage of GDP

give the industries tax rebates for exports. Also, taxes would have to be imposed on imports of competitors' products from countries where there is no equivalent green tax.

Effects on employment

Reduced output in the industries affected by green taxes will lead to a reduction in employment. If, however, the effect were to encourage investment in new cleaner technology, employment might not fall. Furthermore, employment opportunities could be generated elsewhere, if the extra revenues from the green taxes were spent on alternative products (e.g. buses and trains rather than cars).

Redistributive effects

The poor spend a higher proportion of their income on domestic fuel than the rich. A 'carbon tax' on such fuel will, therefore, have the effect of redistributing incomes away from the poor. The poor also spend a larger proportion of their income on food than do the rich. Taxes on agriculture, designed to reduce intensive use of fertilisers and pesticides, will again tend to hit the poor proportionately more than the rich.

Not all green taxes, however, are regressive. The rich spend a higher proportion of their income on motoring than the poor. Thus petrol and other motoring taxes could have a progressive effect.

Despite these problems, such taxes can still move output closer to the socially efficient level. What is more, they have the major advantage of providing a continuing incentive to firms to find cleaner methods of production and thereby save more on their tax bills.

? *Is it a good idea to use the revenues from green taxes to subsidise green alternatives (e.g. using petrol taxes for subsidising rail transport)?*

Box 6.5

The problem of urban traffic congestion

Does Singapore have the answer?

It takes only one hour to drive from one end of Singapore to the other. Yet the average Singaporean driver travels an estimated 18 600 km per year, more than the average US driver, and over 50 per cent more than the average Japanese driver. In Singapore in 2003 there were a little over 400 000 cars, giving a vehicle density of 225 motor vehicles per km of road. This compares with a vehicle density in the USA of only 27 motor vehicles per km. It is hardly surprising that traffic congestion has become a major focus of public debate, particularly as the demand for cars is set to increase as consumer affluence grows.

The problem of traffic congestion

KI 23
p192

Traffic congestion is a classic example of the problem of externalities. When people use their cars, not only do they incur private costs (petrol, wear and tear on the vehicle, tolls, the time taken to travel, etc.), but also they impose costs on other people. These external costs include the following:

Congestion costs: time. When a person uses a car on a congested road, it will add to the congestion. This will therefore slow down the traffic even more and increase the journey time of other car users.

Congestion costs: monetary. Congestion increases fuel consumption, and the stopping and starting increases the costs of wear and tear. When a motorist adds to congestion, therefore, there will be additional monetary costs imposed on other motorists.

Environmental costs. When motorists use a road they reduce the quality of the environment for others. Cars emit fumes and create noise. This is bad enough for pedestrians and other car users, but can be particularly distressing for people living along the road. Driving can cause accidents – a problem that increases as drivers become more impatient as a result of delays.

Exhaust gases cause long-term environmental damage and are one of the main causes of the greenhouse effect and of the increased acidity of lakes and rivers and the poisoning of forests. They can also cause long-term health problems (e.g. for asthma sufferers).

The socially efficient level of road usage

These externalities mean that road usage will be above the social optimum. This is illustrated in the diagram. Costs and benefits are shown on the vertical axis and are measured in money terms. Thus any non-monetary costs or benefits (such as time costs) must be given a monetary value. The horizontal axis measures road usage in terms of cars per minute passing a specified point on the road.

For simplicity it is assumed that there are no external benefits from car use and that therefore marginal private and marginal social benefits are the same. The *MSB* curve is shown as downward sloping. The reason for this is that different road users put a different value on any given journey. If the marginal (private) cost of making the journey were high, only those for whom the journey had a high marginal benefit would travel along the road. If the marginal cost of making the journey fell, more people would make the journey: people choosing to make the journey as long as the marginal cost of the journey was less than the marginal benefit. Thus the greater the number of cars, the lower the marginal benefit.

The marginal (private) cost curve (*MC*) is likely to be constant up to the level of traffic flow at which congestion begins to occur. This is shown as point *a* in the diagram. Beyond this point, marginal cost is likely to rise as time costs increase (i.e. journey times lengthen) and as fuel consumption rises.

The marginal *social* cost curve (*MSC*) is drawn above the marginal private cost curve. The vertical difference between the two represents the external costs. Up to point *b*, external costs are simply the environmental costs. Beyond point *b*, there are also external congestion costs, since additional road users slow down the journey of *other* road users. These external costs get progressively greater as traffic grinds to a halt.

The actual level of traffic flow will be at Q_1, where marginal private costs and benefits are equal (point *e*). The socially efficient level of traffic flow, however, will be at the lower level of Q_2 where marginal social costs and benefits are equal (point *d*). In other words, there will be an excessive level of road usage.

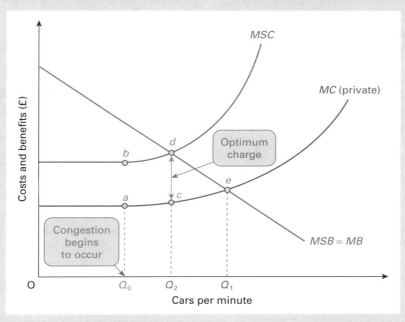

Actual and optimum road usage

So what can governments do to 'internalise' these externalities?

The Singapore solution

In contrast to its neighbours, many of which are suffering more acute urban traffic congestion problems, Singapore has an integrated transport policy. This includes the following:

- Restricting the number of new car licences, and allowing their price to rise to the corresponding equilibrium. This makes car licences in Singapore among the most expensive in the world.
- A 111-kilometre-long mass rail transit (MRT) system with subsidised fares. Trains are comfortable, clean and frequent. Stations are air-conditioned.
- A programme of building new estates near MRT stations.
- Cheap, frequent buses, serving all parts of the island.

But it is in respect of road usage that the Singaporean authorities have been most innovative.

The first innovation came in 1975. The city centre was made a restricted zone. Motorists who wished to enter this zone had to buy a ticket (an 'area licence') at any one of 33 entry points. Police were stationed at these entry points to check that cars had paid and displayed.

Then in 1990 a quota system for new cars was established. The government decides the total number of cars the country should have, and issues just enough licences each month to maintain that total. These licences (or 'Certificates of Entitlement') are for ten years and are offered at auction. Their market price varies from around £10 000 to £30 000.

A problem with the licences is that they are a once-and-for-all payment, which does not vary with the amount people use their car. In other words, their marginal cost (for additional miles driven) is zero. Many people feel that, having paid such a high price for their licence, they ought to use their car as much as possible in order to get value for money!

With traffic congestion steadily worsening, it was recognised that something more had to be done.

Either the area licensing scheme had to be widened, or some other form of charging had to be adopted. The decision was taken to introduce electronic road pricing (ERP). This alternative would not only save on police labour costs, but also enable charge rates to be varied according to levels of congestion, times of the day, and locality. What, then, would be the optimum charge? If the objective is to reduce traffic from Q_1 to Q_2 in the diagram, then a charge of $d - c$ should be levied.

Since 1998 all vehicles in Singapore have been fitted with an in-vehicle unit (IU). Every journey made requires the driver to insert a smart card into the IU. On specified roads, overhead gantries read the IU and deduct the appropriate charge from the card. If a car does not have sufficient funds on its smart card, the car's details are relayed to a control centre and a fine is imposed. The system has the benefit of operating on three-lane highways and does not require traffic to slow down.

The ERP system operates on Mondays to Fridays from 7.30 a.m. to 7.00 p.m. in the central area and from 7.30 a.m. to 9.30 a.m. on the expressways and outer ring roads, with charges varying every 5, 20 or 30 minutes within these times. Rates are published in advance but are reviewed every three months. The system is thus very flexible to allow traffic to be kept at the desired level.

The system was expensive to set up, however. Cheaper schemes have been adopted elsewhere, such as Norway and parts of the USA. These operate by funnelling traffic into a single lane in order to register the car, but this has the disadvantage of slowing the traffic down.

One message is clear from the Singapore solution. Road pricing alone is not enough. Unless there are fast, comfortable and affordable public transport alternatives, the demand for cars will be highly price inelastic. People have to get to work!

1. Referring to a town or city with which you are familiar, consider what would be the most appropriate mix of policies to deal with its traffic congestion problems.
2. Explain how, by varying the charge debited from the smart card according to the time of day or level of congestion, a socially optimal level of road use can be achieved.

Questions

1. The table at the top of the next page gives the costs and benefits of an imaginary firm operating under perfect competition whose activities create a certain amount of pollution. (It is assumed that the costs of this pollution to society can be accurately measured.)

   (a) What is the profit-maximising level of output for this firm?
   (b) What is the socially efficient level of output?
   (c) Why might the marginal pollution costs increase in the way illustrated in this example?

2. In Figure 6.1 (page 193) the *MSC* curve is drawn parallel to the *MC* curve. Under what circumstances would it have a steeper slope than the MC curve?

3. Give additional examples of each of the four types of externality to those given on pages 192–5.

4. Give some examples of public goods (other than those given on page 195). Does the provider of these goods or services (the government or local authority) charge for their use? If so, is the method of charging based on the amount of the good people use? Is it a good method of charging? Could you suggest a better method?

5. Distinguish between publicly provided goods, public goods and merit goods.

6. Name some goods or services provided by the government or local authorities that are not public goods.

7. Some roads could be regarded as a public good, but some could be provided by the market. Which types of road could be provided by the market? Why? Would it be a good idea?

8. Assume that you have decided to buy a new video recorder. How do you set about ensuring that you make the right choice between the available makes?

9. Assume that you wanted the information given in (a)–(h) below. In which cases could you (i) buy perfect information; (ii) buy imperfect information; (iii) obtain information without paying for it; (iv) not obtain information?

Output (units)	Price per unit (MSB) (£)	Marginal (private) costs to the firm (MC)(£)	Marginal external (pollution) costs (MEC) (£)	Marginal social costs (MSC=MC+MEC) (£)
1	100	30	20	50
2	100	30	22	52
3	100	35	25	60
4	100	45	30	75
5	100	60	40	100
6	100	78	55	133
7	100	100	77	177
8	100	130	110	240

(a) Which washing machine is the more reliable?

(b) Which of two jobs that are vacant is the more satisfying?

(c) Which builder will repair my roof most cheaply?

(d) Which builder will make the best job of repairing my roof?

(e) Which builder is best value for money?

(f) How big a mortgage would it be wise for me to take out?

(g) What course of higher education should I follow?

(h) What brand of washing powder washes whiter?

In which cases are there non-monetary costs to you of finding out the information? How can you know whether the information you acquire is accurate or not?

10. Make a list of pieces of information a firm might want to know and consider whether it could buy the information and how reliable that information might be.

11. Assume that a country had no state education at all. For what reasons might the private education system not provide the optimal allocation of resources to and within education?

12. Assume that a firm discharges waste into a river. As a result, the marginal social costs (MSC) are greater than the firm's marginal (private) costs (MC). The table at the bottom of this page shows how MC, MSC, AR and MR vary with output. Assume that the marginal private benefit (MB) is given by the price (AR). Assume also that there are no externalities on the consumption side, and that therefore MSB = MB.

(a) How much will the firm produce if it seeks to maximise profits?

(b) What is the socially efficient level of output (assuming no externalities on the demand side)?

(c) How much is the marginal external cost at this level of output?

(d) What size of tax would be necessary for the firm to reduce its output to the socially efficient level?

(e) Why is the tax less than the marginal externality?

(f) Why might it be equitable to impose a lump-sum tax on this firm?

(g) Why will a lump-sum tax not affect the firm's output (assuming that in the long run the firm can still make at least normal profit)?

13. On a diagram similar to Figure 6.5 (on page 205), demonstrate how a subsidy can correct for an external benefit.

14. Why might it be better to ban certain activities that cause environmental damage rather than to tax them?

15. To what extent could property rights (either public or private) be successfully extended and invoked to curb the problem of industrial pollution (a) of the atmosphere, (b) of rivers, (c) by the dumping of toxic waste, (d) by the erection of ugly buildings and (e) by the creation of high levels of noise?

16. What protection do private property rights in the real world give to sufferers of noise (a) from neighbours, (b) from traffic, (c) from transistor radios at the seaside?

17. How suitable are legal restrictions in the following cases?

Output	1	2	3	4	5	6	7	8
MC	23	21	23	25	27	30	35	42
MSC	35	34	38	42	46	52	60	72
TR	60	102	138	168	195	219	238	252
AR	60	51	46	42	39	36.5	34	31.5
MR	60	42	36	30	27	24	19	14

(a) Ensuring adequate vehicle safety (e.g. that tyres have sufficient tread or that the vehicle is roadworthy).
(b) Reducing traffic congestion.
(c) Preventing the abuse of monopoly power.
(d) Ensuring that mergers are in the public interest.
(e) Ensuring that firms charge a price equal to marginal cost.

18. How would you evaluate the following?

    (a) The external effects of building a reservoir in an area of outstanding natural beauty.
    (b) The external effects of acid rain pollution from a power station.

19. Many economists have argued that a form of 'congestion tax' ought to be imposed on motorists who use their cars on busy roads, to take account of the external costs they impose on other road users and pedestrians. Compare the relative advantages and disadvantages of the following measures:

    (a) Increasing the rate of duty on petrol.
    (b) Increasing the annual road fund licence.

(c) Using a system such as that in Singapore (see Box 6.5), where charges are deducted from a pre-paid smart card inserted into a device in the car. Charges vary according to the time of day and/or the level of congestion.
(d) Installing cameras that record number plates of cars in a designated zone, and then fining their owners if a daily fixed fee for driving in the zone has not been paid (this system is used in London).
(e) Setting up toll booths to charge motorists for using certain stretches of road.
(f) The use of bus and cycle lanes at peak times.
(g) Subsidising public transport.

20. Give examples of how the government intervenes to protect the interests of dependants from bad economic decisions taken on their behalf.

21. What are the possible arguments in favour of fixing prices (a) below and (b) above the equilibrium? Are there any means of achieving the same social goals without fixing prices?

22. Make out a case for (a) increasing and (b) decreasing the role of the government in the allocation of resources.

Additional case studies on the *Essentials of Economics* MyEconLab (www.pearsoned.co.uk/sloman)

6.1 Corporate social responsibility. An examination of social responsibility as a goal of firms and its effect on business performance.

6.2 The police as a public service. The extent to which policing can be classified as a public good.

6.3 Deadweight loss from taxes on goods and services. This shows the welfare loss from the imposition of a tax, which must be weighed against the redistributive and other gains from the tax.

6.4 Libertarianism. The views of the 'neo Austrian' right that market capitalism has dynamic advantages in creating incentives to innovate and take risks.

6.5 Public choice theory. This examines how economists have attempted to extend their analysis of markets to the field of political decision making.

6.6 Perverse subsidies. An examination of the use of subsidies around the world that are harmful to the environment.

6.7 Selling the environment. This looks at the proposals made at international climate conferences to use market-based solutions to global warming.

6.8 Restricting car access to Athens. A case study that examines how the Greeks have attempted to reduce local atmospheric pollution from road traffic.

6.9 The right track for reform? How successful has rail privatisation been in the UK?

6.10 Can the market provide adequate protection for the environment? This explains why markets generally fail to take into account environmental externalities.

6.11 Environmental auditing. Are businesses becoming greener? A growing number of firms are subjecting themselves to an 'environmental audit' to judge just how 'green' they are.

Sections of chapter covered in *WinEcon* – Sloman, *Essentials of Economics*

Essentials of Economics section	*WinEcon* section
6.1	6.1
6.2	6.2
6.3	6.3
6.4	6.4
6.5	6.5
6.6	–
6.7	–
6.8	Covered in 6.1

Websites relevant to this chapter

Numbers and sections refer to websites listed in the Web Appendix and hotlinked from MyEconLab. Visit:

www.pearsoned.co.uk/sloman

- For news articles relevant to this chapter, see the *Economics News Articles* link from MyEconLab.
- For general news on market failures and government intervention, see websites in section A, and particularly A1–5, 18, 19, 24, 31. See also links to newspapers in A38, 43 and 44; and see A42 for links to economics news video and audio.
- Sites I7 and 11 contain links to *Competition and monopoly*, *Policy and regulation* and *Transport* in the *Microeconomics* section; they also have an *Industry and commerce* section. Site I4 has links to *Environmental* and *Environmental Economics* in the *EconDirectory* section. Site I17 has several sections of links in the *Issues in Society* section.
- UK and EU departments relevant to competition policy can be found at sites E10; G7, 8.
- UK regulatory bodies can be found at sites E4, 11, 16, 18, 19, 21, 22, 25, 29.
- For information on taxes and subsidies, see E30, 36; G13. For use of green taxes (Box 6.4), see H5; G11; E2, 14, 30.
- For information on health and the economics of health care (Box 6.1), see E8; H9. See also links in I8 and 17.
- For sites favouring the free market, see C17; D34. See also C18 for the development of ideas on the market and government intervention.
- For the economics of the environment, see links in I4, 7, 11, 17. For policy on the environment and transport, see E2, 7, 11, 14, 29; G10, 11. See also H11.
- For student resources relevant to this chapter, see sites C1–7, 9, 10, 19.

Web Appendices

6.1 **Private and social efficiency.** This appendix uses general equilibrium analysis to show how a perfect market economy in the absence of externalities will lead to a socially optimal allocation of resources.

6.2 **Cost–benefit analysis.** A technique to help decide whether or not a project should go ahead.

6.3 **The economics of common resources.** Why commonly owned resources tend to be overused.

PART NINE

Corporate Responsibility and the Environment

Chapter 19

The Ethical and Ecological Environment

The ethical and ecological environment

Ian Worthington and Dean Patton

There is a growing body of opinion that businesses have a duty to fulfil objectives that stretch beyond the simple well-being of the organisation to the promotion of greater corporate social responsibility, particularly with regard to the natural environment. This chapter looks at the reasons which lie behind this perspective and speculates on how businesses can be encouraged to accommodate environmental policies into their strategic management techniques.

Learning outcomes

Having read this chapter you should be able to:

- demonstrate the involvement that business has with other elements of society
- identify a corporation's primary and secondary stakeholders and their respective interests
- define the meaning of corporate social responsibility and determine the actions business needs to undertake in order to be considered socially responsible
- analyse the benefits that are available to business from following a strategy of corporate social responsibility

Key terms

Business culture
Business ethics
Competitive advantage
Corporate social
  responsibility (CSR)
Eco-label
Eco-Management and
  Audit Scheme (EMAS)

Environmental
  management systems
  (EMS)
Genetically modified
  (GM) foods
Learning curve effect
Life-cycle analysis
Market niche

Polluter pays principle
Resource-based view
Self-regulation
Stakeholders
Sustainable development
Top-down approaches

Introduction

In May 1999 the largest ever survey of global public opinion took place into the changing expectations of businesses in the twenty-first century. Twenty-five thousand people in 23 countries on 6 continents were interviewed about their perceptions of the roles and responsibilities of business organisations in the social and environmental as well as the economic spheres. This worldwide survey – known as the Millennium Poll on Corporate Social Responsibility (CSR) – confirmed what many business researchers and corporate leaders had come to recognise over the course of the previous decade or so. Namely, that a firm's social and environmental performance was no less important to the general public (and, therefore, customers) than its traditional roles of making profits, paying taxes and complying with the law. While there were differences in the strengths of opinions expressed in the different countries surveyed, the overall message of the poll was clear: consumers believe that business organisations should behave in a socially and environmentally responsible way and should be held accountable for their actions across a range of areas from protecting the health and safety of their employees, through avoiding unethical business practices, to protecting the natural environment.

In the analysis below, the focus is on ethical and ecological issues in business which have become an increasingly important aspect of the macroenvironmental context within which firms exist and operate. This development can be illustrated in a number of ways. For example, many larger organisations now publish annual social and environmental reports which are designed to highlight improvements in the firm's performance on a range of indicators (e.g. employee training; charitable donations; reduction in carbon emissions) to a variety of stakeholder groups including customers, shareholders, creditors, employees, suppliers, NGOs and government (see below). To achieve these claimed improvements, a growing number of firms in recent years have appointed senior executives and managers with responsibility for directing, monitoring and auditing the social and environmental performance of the business and for communicating this both internally and externally to the various interested parties. In the lexicon of business, concepts such as corporate social responsibility, social responsiveness, corporate social performance, corporate citizenship and corporate sustainability have become relatively commonplace, as have notions such as supply chain ethics, green marketing and triple bottom line accounting. Parallel developments have also taken place in the academic world as a growing number of business and management programmes now incorporate the study of business ethics, CSR and sustainable development into the curriculum, supported by a burgeoning literature in these fields and an expanding group of international journals on the ethical and environmental aspects of business (e.g. the *Journal of Business Ethics*; *Journal of Environmental Management*; *Business Strategy and the Environment*).

To provide an insight into how businesses can be affected by ethical and ecological pressures, the chapter begins with a general discussion of the notions of business ethics and corporate social responsibility before moving on to a more detailed examination of the very topical issue of environmental management in business. For students wishing to investigate these issues in more detail, we have recommended some useful sources in the 'Further reading' section at the end of the chapter. You could also consult the websites of leading multinational corporations and bodies such as business representative organisations (e.g. Confederation of British Industry; Institute of

Directors; Chambers of Commerce), environmental NGOs (e.g. Greenpeace; Friends of the Earth; Forum for the Future), advocacy groups (e.g. Business in the Community) and the various international groups/agencies whose work includes consideration of ethical and environmental issues in business (e.g. UN, World Bank).

Ethics and business

As we saw in the previous chapter, business organisations exist and function within a framework of law emanating from various sources including government. In many areas of life laws essentially direct what individuals and/or organisations can or cannot do and set minimum standards of behaviour based on underlying ethical principles. Not all ethical aspects of business, however, are covered by government legislation or the common law, as in the case of selling weapons to overseas governments or paying low wages to workers producing a product in other countries. By the same token, not all laws governing individual or organisational behaviour raise what would be regarded as important ethical issues.

As Crane and Matten (2004) suggest, **business ethics** is basically concerned with those issues in business that are not covered by law or where there is no definite consensus on what is 'right' or 'wrong' behaviour. Accordingly they define business ethics as 'the study of business situations, activities and decisions where issues of right and wrong are addressed', stressing quite rightly that in terms of organisational behaviour right and wrong should be seen in a moral sense, not from a financial or strategic point of view. It might make financial sense, for instance, for an organisation to exploit cheap labour or flush its waste products into a river at no cost to the business, and it might not be illegal, but is it ethical? As the Millenium Poll and other surveys have illustrated, a firm's stance on ethical issues in business are an important aspect of its external environment and one that applies to enterprises of all kinds and in all sectors of the economy.

While it is beyond the scope of this chapter to discuss all the potential ethical dilemmas faced by modern business organisations, it is worth noting that these have tended to intensify and broaden as business activity has become more globalised and as technological transformation has given rise to the globalisation of communications and the 24-hour instant news culture. Multinational corporations in particular are facing much closer scrutiny by different groups of stakeholders that are increasingly willing to pressurise larger businesses to behave in a more ethically and ecologically sustainable way. Allegations that some high-profile western companies are (sometimes unwittingly) exploiting child labour in the developing world or are involved in ethically questionable commercial practices (e.g. bribery; price fixing) or in environmentally damaging activities (e.g. illegal logging; oil exploration in unspoiled natural environments) inevitably attract media attention and can result in significant damage to a firm's reputation and, potentially, its bottom line. By the same token, firms recognised for having a good ethical stance may find favour with the different stakeholder interests and this could bring organisational benefits of various kinds, including increased sales, access to new customers/markets, improvements in labour recruitment and retention, lower insurance premiums and less scrutiny by governments and/or NGOs.

Whether 'good ethics' and 'good business' are always complementary has been the subject of considerable debate in both practitioner and academic circles and is one which is far from resolved.[1] That said, what is clear is that the question of ethics in business and the related concept of corporate social responsibility are no longer peripheral issues and have been rapidly moving up the corporate agenda in most large business organisations in recent years. If firms are to avoid the potential risks posed by a poor ethical performance (e.g. Enron) and/or exploit the anticipated opportunities offered by a positive ethical stance (e.g. the Co-operative Bank), they need to put in place appropriate mechanisms for managing the ethical issues they face (e.g. values statements; codes of ethics; accredited auditing and reporting systems). They also need to think more broadly about society's expectations or corporate behaviour and of their obligations and responsibilities beyond those to the immediate owners of the business. This notion of a firm's social responsibilities is the issue to which we now turn.

Corporate social responsibility (CSR)

As indicated above, the idea of CSR essentially means that business organisations have responsibilities that go beyond mere profit making and encompass voluntary activities and actions that affect people, their communities and the natural environment. The question of whether, and how far, a firm should engage in such activities if they might adversely affect profitability remains a contested arena. A central theme in this debate has been the issue of the central purpose of the business organisation and the knowledge, abilities and responsibilities of those that run profit-seeking enterprises. Under the neo-classical view of the firm, private sector businesses exist to make profits for the owners (e.g. shareholders) and the responsibility of the firm's managers is to act in a way which enhances the position of the providers of capital, for example by maximising profits and/or shareholder value. Writing in *The New York Times* in 1970, the economist Milton Friedman basically echoed this perspective when he argued that the social responsibility of a business was to increase its profits so long as it obeyed the law and operated ethically.[2] In Friedman's opinion a firm's directors were not only ill-equipped to make decisions on social and environmental matters but, as agents for the firm's owners (the principals), they also had a fiduciary responsibility to the shareholders, not to some broader conception of the social good. Under this interpretation, allocating some of the firm's resources to the pursuit of socially responsible objectives could effectively be construed as unethical since it involves spending money that belongs to other individuals.

This conventional view of the role of business in society has been challenged on a number of grounds and, to many observers of the business scene, now seems very outdated, narrow and arguably naïve. As Chapter 1 has indicated, businesses exist within and draw their resources from the broader society and therefore could be said to have a moral obligation to take account of their social and environmental performance. Added to this, shareholders are only one of the groups with which the firm interacts and consequently there are other stakeholder interests to whom a business has responsibilities and obligations when carrying out its activities (see e.g.

Chapter 20). Such **stakeholders** are both internal (e.g. employees) and external (e.g. customers) to the organisation and under the stakeholder view of the firm (see e.g. Freeman, 1984) businesses have a social responsibility to take into account the interests of all parties affected by their actions and decisions, not just the owners of the business. In contrast to the neo-classical view of the firm, the stakeholder approach stresses the necessity for managers to try to operate the business to the benefit of all stakeholder groups and to seek to gain an effective balance between the different interested parties. Using some of the firm's profits to achieve such an outcome is not necessarily detrimental to the firm's owners and indeed may ultimately help to enhance shareholder value, particularly over the longer term.

More recent discussions of why businesses should take account of their social and environmental responsibilities have tended to focus on the strategic benefits of CSR; in essence how acting 'responsibly' can leverage advantage for the business on both the demand and the supply side (see e.g. McWilliams *et al.*, 2006). Writers such as Porter and Kramer (2002), for example, have argued that a firm can gain a **competitive advantage** by investing in CSR, particularly if its actions in this area become an intrinsic part of its business and corporate differentiation strategies. One important element in this debate has been the application of a **resource-based view (RBV)** of the firm in which social and environmental responsibility are portrayed as an organisational resource/capability that can lead to sustained competitive advantage.[3] Under this perspective, engaging in CSR has the potential to enhance a firm's reputation with key stakeholder groups and this could give it an advantage over its rivals that is both valuable and potentially difficult to imitate. One arena where this might be particularly important is with regard to an organisation's environmental performance, given the growing international concerns over the impact of business activity on the natural environment. This is an issue to which we now turn in more detail.

Environmental management: an issue of corporate responsibility

Organisations accepting responsibility for the impacts they have on air, land and water is just one of the issues to be addressed within the debate on business attitudes towards corporate responsibility. It is, however, the one area where governments, communities and business have worked most closely to improve their understanding of the issues and resolve the identified problems; in particular, to reconcile the perceived need for economic growth with the demand for greater environmental protection and reduced levels of ecological degradation.

Historically, economic development and growth through business activity have been portrayed as beneficial to the well-being of a society and as an important influence on the quality of life of its citizens. Accordingly, organisational practices and processes designed to increase production and consumption have generally been encouraged and welcomed, even though their detrimental effects on the natural environment have been recognised for some time.[4]

While growth invariably remains an objective of governments, its environmental impact has become part of the political agenda at both national and international level, where particular concern has been expressed about the extent of ecological degradation, the rate at which limited resources are being depleted, the frequency and scale of accidents caused as a result of business practice and the global threat of climate change with its attendant problems. Pessimists have argued that in the pursuit of growth many countries may have already surpassed levels of usage of essential resources and sustainable levels of pollution, and have blighted future generations for the sake of present consumption. The more optimistic view is that individual and collective action can give rise to sustainable development which allows for present requirements to be met without compromising the ability of successive generations to meet their own needs. The concept of scarcity and choice is not new, but the way in which human needs are to be met while seeking not to compromise the future is the practical challenge that will face society and therefore all business organisations.

It is the philosophy of **sustainable development** that many argue is the only way forward for the world economy. The problem of environmental degradation is closely related to the issue of economic growth, and both industry and society need to balance environmental protection with economic development. The difficulties in finding an appropriate balance lie not just in the need to reconcile a range of conflicting interests but also in the relative lack of information on the relationship between economic development and its long-term impact on the natural environment.

The seriousness of the situation and its potentially disastrous consequences suggest that an environmental revolution is needed which may require a dramatic change in the behaviour of society and industry as both consumers and producers. Much attention has, of course, been focused on political initiatives which are testimony to the widely accepted view that environmental policy needs to be formalised and co-ordinated at international level if it is to be effective in tackling the salient issues. **Top-down approaches**, however, can only be part of the overall solution and much depends on the actions of firms and individuals in the marketplace and on their willingness to accept responsibility for their own behaviour and its consequences. In short, concern for the environment needs to be expressed through the actions of a myriad of actors, and for a revolution in environmental responsibility to be successful it must permeate all levels of society, including members of the business community.

Business response to environmental concerns

Corporately responsible actions and/or expenditures have a trade-off cost: the alternatives that the money, resources, time and effort could have been used for if they had not been devoted to more socially oriented goals. As indicated previously, this is generally known as the 'opportunity cost', the notion that in a world of finite resources, whatever a business chooses to do, it does at the expense of something else, the opportunity forgone. As a result, the timing of returns is a critical factor in the decision-making process. The returns to investment in greater environmental responsibility are, however, likely to be of a long-term nature, a situation which may offer little comfort to firms, particularly small businesses that are fighting for survival and need short-term returns. Thus while businesses, in general, may want to provide a more environmentally responsible policy – particularly if their stakeholders are forcing them to look to the wider concerns of business practice and process – the implementation of such a policy may only occur if it is deemed to be in the best interests of the business: that is, where the resources are used in an optimum way to provide sufficient reward for the hierarchy of stakeholders.

Business culture at present is still largely driven by short-term profit and the stakeholders that generally hold the most influence are the providers of financial capital, the shareholders or owners of the business. In order to develop greater environmental awareness in business it is necessary to review the way objectives are prioritised to take account of the viewpoints of indirect stakeholders, thus ensuring that the issue of sustainable development is brought on to the corporate agenda. The willingness and/or ability of a firm to be corporately responsible for its own sake has little, if any, precedent in current business practice; organisational policy is far more dependent upon the business environment in which the organisation works. All business activity, by definition, involves some environmental damage and the best a business can achieve is to clear up its own mess while searching hard for ways to reduce its impact on the environment.

It is, therefore, impossible to expect the type of business environment not to influence the level of corporate responsibility, and the degree of change, the intensity of competition and the scale of complexity will all be factors in the creation of policy, whether this be to increase market share or to reduce the levels of air emissions.

If firms are to provide a greater level of corporate responsibility, does society have to resort to the use of laws and government regulation, or will business perceive the change in societal expectations and decide voluntarily to act more responsibly towards the general environment? The answer probably lies somewhere between the two, but there is obviously a close association between the level of legislative impact upon a firm and the degree of perceived impact the organisation would expect to have upon the environment that may lead to the implementation of environmental management systems. Sethi puts forward a threefold typology:[5]

1 *Social obligation.* A situation where the organisation uses legal and economic criteria to control corporate behaviour. The strategy is, therefore, reactive and dependent upon change instigated by the market or through legislation. The organisation exhibits an exploitative strategy, giving in to environmental concerns only when it can obtain direct benefit. The principal stakeholder in this type of organisation is the shareholder and the pursuit of profit the primary objective.

2 *Social responsibility.* This type of organisation tries to go beyond the requirements prescribed by law and instead seeks to conform to the current values and norms of society. The organisation will, therefore, accept responsibility for solving current environmental problems and will attempt to maintain current standards of both the social and physical environment. In order to achieve this the organisation must be accountable to a range of stakeholders and this assumes that profit, although the dominant motive, is not the only one.

3 *Social responsiveness*. This organisation exhibits a proactive strategy, actively seeking future social change. The policies of the organisation are followed with a fervent zeal, the business seeks to lead the field in terms of promoting a corporately responsible attitude. It accepts public evaluation of its policies and procedures and is prepared to impinge upon profit to maintain the high profile it has established through its corporately responsible actions.

As Seth's typology indicates, business responses to CSR can vary and some firms will tend to take a reactive and/or defensive approach in which their response to environmental concerns tends to be minimal and compliance driven. In contrast, other businesses may actually follow a socially responsible approach as a result of the possible advantages it might afford the organisation. In general the hypothesis can be supported that a better society produces a better environment for business. Further, environmental proactivity often makes sound investment sense, leading to increases in market share, a lowering of costs through energy and material savings and finally an improvement in the 'corporate image'. Provision for responsible behaviour is therefore financially good for the business. A further possible impetus for implementing environmental management systems could come from political rather than economic sources. In simple terms, organisations that instigate their own environmental policies and/or regulations tend to face a reduced threat from external regulatory bodies and this improves company image while reducing possible checks upon corporate practices and processes.

 web link   The Body Shop's website address is *www.thebodyshop.com*

In essence, the conclusions reached highlight the fact that organisations will not necessarily pursue a proactive role in the development of environmentally responsible policies. The initial short-run costs are prohibitive when the payback is generally assumed to be over the long term. What might be required is a re-education of those involved in the decision-making process so that they understand the benefit of a longer-term view and can identify policies that offer a sustainable competitive advantage over time. This is true for all strategy and is therefore applicable to the implementation of environmental policies.

mini case   Environmental performance in the small firms sector

Numerically, small firms dominate the global economy. In the UK, for example, approximately 97 per cent of firms have fewer than 50 employees. These firms account for 50 per cent of the total working population and around one-third of the country's GDP. The economic importance of the sector has grown since 1979 and as a consequence the environmental impact of the sector has also become more significant.

The small-firm sector has not, however, kept pace with the general environmental awareness of business. Small firms have continually underperformed in the use of environmental audits, knowledge of environmental legislation and the publication of environmental reports.

A number of reasons have been put forward for the perceived failure of small firms to become environmentally aware. These include:

1 *Cost*. Small firms have limited resources and in general do not perceive an economic gain from implementing environmental policies.

2 *Lack of expertise*. Small firms simply do not have the human or physical resources for developing improved environmental practices. In addition they are very sceptical of inviting expensive outside consultants to investigate their existing practices.

3 *Ignorance of legislation*. The plethora of small firms limits the ability of any agency to monitor the whole sector. As a consequence many small firms rely upon the fact that 'what they do not know cannot hurt them'. Small firms are notoriously 'ignorant' about their environmental responsibilities and rely to some extent upon the problems of scale that monitoring agencies face.

4 *Scale advantages*. Small firms cannot spread the cost of any environmental initiatives over a large product range. Nor can they benefit significantly from the improved public relations often generated by environmental good practice.

These factors may have led to a market imperfection in the development of environmental responsibility within business. As a result, new and imaginative initiatives are needed to create greater interest within the small-firm sector and to improve its environmental practices.

Methods of encouraging environmental concern within business

The quality of the existing environment and improvements in it would be regarded by economists as a form of public good. This is a good for which the principle of exclusion does not apply; it can be jointly consumed by many individuals simultaneously, at no additional cost and with no reduction in the quality or quantity of the public good consumed by any citizen.

The fact that the principle of exclusion does not apply creates the 'free-rider' problem because some groups will believe that others will take on the burden of paying for the public good, in this case the extra cost incurred to improve the quality of the environment. Historically, the government has taken charge of public goods (e.g. the fire and police services or the provision of street lighting) in order to ensure that they are provided and not left to the vagaries of the market. Recent events suggest, however, that state intervention in the future cannot be taken for granted, particularly in areas where market solutions appear possible.

Government intervention

Direct action by government within the business sector has not led to improved environmental responsibility. Nationalised industries have not been the bastions of the ecological environment and in some instances in the United Kingdom (e.g. the 'tall stacks' policy) have appeared to disregard the environmental degradation that they created. Indirect action through regulation or legislation may be more effective, but this is not in keeping with the general policy of *laissez-faire* which operated in the United Kingdom under the Conservative government throughout the 1980s and in the 1990s and has been largely followed by the Labour government post-1997.

Furthermore, there are a number of dangers associated with a reliance solely upon a regulatory system as a means of control. Laws tend to be reactive and there may be significant differences between the letter and the spirit of the law. Industry may hold a monopoly of expertise, making government regulation ineffective. Finally, transnational issues (e.g. leaks from nuclear power stations, global warming, acid rain) are far too multifarious and intricate to resolve through regulation. This is not to say that the legal system is always ineffectual, but simply that it is not a precise means of control, often providing the unscrupulous with scope to act as they please.

Indeed, regulation has become an increasingly complex tool to control business practice.[6] The globalisation of business means that organisations are having to deal with different legislative controls and requirements in different countries. In some instances, company policies change from country to country to meet the lowest standards possible. The tragedy at Bhopal, in India, illustrated how the multinational organisation Union Carbide was willing to accept lower standards of safety in a Third World plant than would have been deemed appropriate for a domestic plant in the United States. It pursued a policy of satisfying the law or regulatory frameworks of the individual host country. Similar arguments can be made for the many shipping organisations registering under flags of convenience which allow cost reductions.

Alternatively, to sell in all markets may require working to the highest common denominator. Not all countries operate the same environmental standards and, although the EU has attempted to standardise some legislation there are still differences in what environmental requirements organisations must fulfil in different countries. Conforming to the stringent requirements of certain markets may improve the competitive position of firms in other markets.

Proposed or possible regulation may also persuade organisations to consider the impact of their activities, particularly if in future more stringent legislation looks likely as governments accept the principle of the **polluter paying** for any environmental damage caused. To judge by American experience, it is possible that retrospective action may be taken, with companies being penalised for decisions taken years previously.[7]

For some organisations legal compliance is an end in itself, for others regulations form a minimum standard of behaviour. The culture of the organisation, within obvious cost constraints, will determine the level of behaviour above the law. For the organisation that sees its responsibilities over and above the law, there may be some additional benefits. Those organisations that develop environmentally sensitive processes and systems first will have greater experience than those slower to react, who may find themselves overtaken by the quickening rate of new legislation. It may also be the case that those firms that undertake environmental initiatives first are able to develop a competitive advantage over other businesses in the same sector because they are able to take advantage of benefits associated with experience and **learning curve effects**. There is, however, a danger that organisations view the use of environmental management tools as a one-off measure. Like any business plan, such a process must be regularly reviewed in order to take account of our increasing knowledge of this subject and the changing needs of the organisation.

To summarise, legislation and regulation do have an important role to play in improving the environmental performance of business overall; this is most evident when governments have the relevant information concerning business practice and process. Frequently, however, business possesses the necessary information and the government has to incur a significant resource cost to acquire the relevant knowledge; suggesting that other tools of control are necessary to instil within business the required corporate responsibility. A strong argument can be made for providing greater information concerning products to the consumer, thereby offering the opportunity to individuals to make more informed decisions about which products to consume. Such a policy would reduce the level of government involvement and help to educate individuals as to the part they play in creating environmental hazards and damage.

Market mechanisms

The increased level of environmental awareness among the population – owing to the easier availability of information – has already led to more informed choices being made by various stakeholder groups that interact with business.[8] Customers, suppliers, employees and investors are all more aware of their responsibilities to the environment, and there are various ways in which their considered decisions can influence the overall objectives of business and ensure that the organisation is corporately responsible for its actions. Increasingly, discerning consumers offer a powerful inducement to firms and despite the lack of perfect information some product switching is already occurring. Firms seeking to maintain current market share, or looking for new opportunities, must be aware of these changes. There has been a number of eco-labelling schemes that have been developed which have assisted consumers in identifying products which are thought to have the least impact upon the environment in their particular class.

An EU **eco-label** was launched in 1993, but take-up has been slow across EU members and only around 200 products have been successfully introduced and certified under the scheme. In the UK the former Department of the Environment, Transport and the Regions (DETR) decided in 1998 no longer to continue with the scheme and called upon the EU member states to push for an 'integrated product policy'.

Well-labelled eco-friendly products are far more prevalent in Europe, where there is a much broader view of nature rather than a focus upon particular issues, such as animal rights or certified forestry schemes. This has led to better-regulated and publicised initiatives on encouraging and labelling eco-friendly products. For example, nine national eco-labels are currently operated in seven EU member states (the Netherlands and Spain each have two) and eco-label schemes in Europe are generally well respected, with certification controlled by independent bodies.

The forerunner of these various labels was established in Germany in 1978 and was colloquially known as the 'Blue Angel'. The label has been adopted by more than 4300 products and 90 product groups, and it is claimed that the majority of households look out for the Blue Angel when choosing environmentally friendly products. Other labels include, in the Netherlands, Stichting Milieukeur; in France, NF Environnement; in Finland, Norway and Sweden, the Nordic White Swan. Most importantly, businesses that wish to apply for these labels will have to provide proof of environmental performance from their suppliers to qualify. In this way products will be evaluated using **life-cycle analysis**, a cradle-to-grave assessment of a product's impact upon the environment.

Further emphasis upon the environment has been created with the introduction of a number of **environmental management systems (EMS)** standards. The UK developed the first EMS (British Standard 7750) but this has subsequently been replaced by ISO 14001 to allow the introduction of a common international EMS standard. There is, however, a European Union EMS standard known as the **Eco-Management and Audit Scheme (EMAS)** which is generally regarded as the most demanding EMS standard. EMS standards have followed the same basic approach as the quality standards and it is hoped that these EMS standards will be able to enjoy the same level of success as the quality standards (BS 5750/ISO 9001). This theme is highlighted by the actions of the Body Shop which demanded that Peter Lane, the organisation chosen to distribute its stock, had satisfactorily to pass an environmental audit before being given the contract. The point is further supported by the actions of B&Q, a UK chain of hardware stores, which has audited not only its own products but those of its suppliers. These audits were the precursor of implemented environmental policies, including the delisting of a large peat supplier who refused to desist from sourcing from Sites of Special Scientific Interest. It seems safe to argue that business will in future face greater pressures to meet new demands from the more discerning customer, be they individuals or other businesses.

It is interesting to note that premiums paid to insurance companies have increased in line with losses incurred for environmental damage caused by normal business activity. In the same way that householders who can demonstrate increased security measures in their homes are rewarded with lower premiums, companies which demonstrate evidence of environmental safeguards may also reap such rewards. More critically, failure to demonstrate extensive environmental management systems may lead to a refusal to offer insurance cover. Moreover, lending institutions may not wish to be associated with poorly safeguarded organisations. In the United States, a further development in legislation means that lending institutions may be held liable for environmental damage caused by plant held as collateral for loans. As a result there has been a significant tightening in the flow of funds to polluting industries such as scrap merchants, businesses dealing with hazardous waste, pulp and paper mills and petrol filling stations. Similar trends are evident in the United Kingdom, where banks have become increasingly careful about loans made to small businesses that have any conceivable environmental risk potential. Therefore, finance that is already limited is being further reduced not because of the viability of the business but because of the environmental liability hanging over them. Thus, while the United Kingdom is yet to see this type of legislation, banks and other lending institutions are already very aware of their environmental responsibilities and this is increasingly encapsulated in their lending policies.

External pressure

There has been a considerable amount of pressure from external groups upon business; these have ranged from *ad hoc* groups formed in local communities to large transnational organisations like Greenpeace. The size and scale of the groups may differ but their objectives are similar: to use whatever power they have at their disposal to influence the decision-making process, and there have been a number of notable successes. For many groups, however, this does not go far enough and accordingly the calls for increased democratisation of the decision-making process to include wider stakeholder groups are becoming more frequent and vociferous.

Effective democratisation assumes greater stakeholder access, with attendant changes in structure and culture; the depth of access and the magnitude of change depends upon the degree to which democratisation is embraced. Participatory democracy may be the most effective form, if yet a largely untested philosophy; however, the success of such an approach will require not only involvement in the decision-making processes, but also access to information and expert knowledge which provide the basis for effective power and influence. Significantly, this approach has still to be culturally accepted by the majority of businesses in the United Kingdom.

Finally, there are the dangers of companies burying their heads in the sand in the hope that the 'new environmentalism' is the latest management fad. The costs, however, of a late response and the possible threat of legal action as well as punitive fines could be critical for those that are slow to develop environmentally sensitive policies. Organisations must realise that the stakes are high and that the costs of getting it wrong (e.g. a serious incident causing environmental damage) are significant in terms of company image, fines, lost production, lost sales, insurance premiums and customer loyalty.

Self-regulation

As noted previously, industry is frequently the holder of the information and expertise required for the effective and efficient implementation of regulation. To regulate, the government has to acquire that information and this can be an expensive process. However, if industry were to **self-regulate** and adopt environmental controls without waiting for the government, then this process of information gathering could be avoided. There are obvious drawbacks to this type of approach. Mintzberg has pointed out that often the implementation of self-regulation is a response by business to attempt to offset on-coming regulation. This has two very positive outcomes for the business sector. First, it offers credibility with society that as a sector it has the interests of the environment in mind when conducting business. Second, it provides a convenient smokescreen for practices which may be regarded as dubious by an external body. It is, therefore, inherent in the idea of self-regulation that the organisation can be trusted to fulfil the environmental requirements of the rest of society.

Growing public awareness of environmental issues and the subsequent regulation of business activities have demonstrated that society is not prepared to allow business to be conducted without restriction or without consideration of its impact upon the environment. The assumption that organisations will abide by the rules and norms of their society has been seen to be misplaced. If society is to trust managers of businesses, it must ask by whose social norms they are controlling their organisations. The growing trend for annual environmental reports is a positive step in this direction; many FTSE 100 companies now publish a separate 'green' report which recognises the impact that business has on the environment. The Body Shop has gone one stage further with the publication of a 'values' report, a wide-ranging, independently verified audit of the company's track record on the issues of the environment, animal protection and human relationships within the business. Most reports, however, provide little in the way of substantive statements and disclosures of what remains very sensitive information and, not being covered by any regulation or standard, they tend to lack consistency. Governments are, therefore, likely to be forced to continue to monitor self-regulatory systems and to retain the power to enforce environmental objectives.

mini case   Carbon footprinting

Walkers Snackfoods (UK) is a subsidiary of Pepsico (US) and produces a range of snack products including Walkers Crisps, Doritos, Wotsits and Quavers. In 2005, the company agreed to participate in a pilot study with the Carbon Trust (a government-sponsored body) aimed at helping businesses to cut their carbon emissions across the supply chain, thereby reducing the carbon footprints of their products. Working with the Trust, and with the different organisations involved in its supply chain, Walkers collected data on carbon emissions at each stage of the life cycle of one of its leading products, from the raw materials stage (i.e. potato production, vegetable oil manufacture etc.) to the ultimate disposal of the package after consumption. These data provided the company with an insight into the carbon impact of its activities on the environment and pointed to areas in which that impact could be reduced to the advantage of both the company and the natural environment (e.g. by saving on energy usage). On certain packets of Walkers Crisps consumers will now find a logo identifying the carbon footprint associated with the product throughout its life cycle (i.e. grams of CO_2 emitted per packet). How far this will influence consumers in their choice of brands remains to be seen, but it is noteworthy that a number of other leading brand names (e.g. Tesco) have indicated their intention of carbon footprinting their products in the future.

Note: Several other companies have been involved in similar initiatives with the Carbon Trust, including Boots, Cadbury Schweppes, and Marks & Spencer.

 web link   For further details see the Carbon Trust website at *www.carbontrust.co.uk*

The benefits to business from the implementation of environmental policies

The previous section has indicated that industry is being driven to develop more environmentally friendly policies; the implication is that organisations would revert to previous policies if the forces driving environmentalism were negated. This assumption, however, fails to take account of the benefits that the implementation of corporately responsible policies has brought some organisations. The drive for greater corporate responsibility has emanated from North America where companies are increasingly expected to draw up their own plans for meeting environmental obligations, putting a premium on having accurate knowledge about their own performance. Business strategists within North America have suggested that in the coming years environmentalism will be at the cutting edge of social reform and therefore one of the most important areas that business must consider. The commitment of industry, however, lags behind the rhetoric and this is particularly true within business in the UK. In order to improve environmental performance there needs to be an increase in information and training, not simply about the environmental consequences, but also concerning the benefits that are being obtained by organisations that are adopting greater corporate responsibility.

Efficiency of factor inputs

Business strategists as well as organisations have already generated a considerable amount of pro-environmental jargon; PPP (Pollution Prevention Pays), WOW (Wipe Out Waste) and WRAP (Waste Reduction Always Pays) are some of the better-known acronyms. The obvious message is that more efficient use of materials and energy will reduce cost, provide a positive effect on the company's accounts and improve the bottom line. In essence, the argument is that by reducing pollution and resource utilisation firms can become more 'eco-efficient' and this can save money as well as protecting the environment. The message that businesses are beginning to receive is that too much attention has been extended to labour and capital costs at the expense of material and energy costs and the new environmental management systems are highlighting this issue.

Improved market image

The image that organisations portray to the rest of society is increasingly important, owing to the development of rapid information flows. Creating this image can be expensive and resources may be wasted as a result of a careless action or remark. A good example of this would be the aggressive marketing campaign used by Monsanto to introduce **genetically modified (GM) foods** into the European market. This campaign had not taken account of the specific market conditions in Europe and the acute concerns of the consumer towards food products. As a result the campaign backfired. In a similar vein a chance remark by a BP representative concerning the oil spillage from the tanker *Braer* in the Shetlands (see case study) was used in an advertising campaign by Greenpeace to illustrate the lack of responsibility shown by large corporations. BP spent an undisclosed sum promoting and implementing a green strategy in order to project the image of an organisation that cares. It can be assumed that the Greenpeace advertisement will have at the very least reduced the effectiveness of this campaign.

Given the current climate of public opinion, organisations which are seen to be improving their levels of corporate responsibility and are able to communicate this to the consumer are likely to improve their market share and to develop customer loyalty (e.g. Varta's development of technology which reduced the heavy metal content of its consumer batteries). The image that a company portrays could also affect the quality of human resources available. Increasingly employees are taking into account an organisation's record on corporate responsibility when deciding upon future employment. The claims of companies must, however, be supported by actions that can be readily communicated and understood by the consumer. Initiatives such as the eco-label and ISO 14001/EMAS will assist in providing clear statements of intent that provide better information for a more informed purchase.

Providing new market niches

The clear message from the market is that there is a growing number of consumers who are prepared to be more discerning about the type of goods they buy, thereby taking into account the impact their purchases have upon the environment. As a result, a number of **market niches** has developed and this has proved attractive to business, given that consumers are prepared to pay extra for a product that is less harmful to the environment. In many cases this means that margins can be increased, a factor which is sometimes contrary to market trends.

In addition to this, there are other market opportunities that result from the need to take action to improve the degree of environmental responsibility. Levels of environmental expenditure are increasing, and this extra expenditure must be generating revenue for those organisations providing the right type of product or service. There are significant market opportunities available, for example, in pollution reduction, energy saving and waste control technologies, and if it is assumed that the push towards more sustainable development will continue, then there will be further opportunities for firms in the field of product and process design.

Proactive legislative compliance

The legislative framework within which businesses operate involves a growing number of regulatory bodies. As indicated in various chapters, legislation from the UK government is supported and often surpassed by EU directives, and organisations seeking to operate successfully in the Single Market must demonstrate compliance if they wish to compete. Regulations which were once confined to product and process now often extend to the way in which decisions are made within organisations and it seems more likely that the Cadbury Report on corporate governance has started a process of increased democratisation of the decision-making process which businesses will have difficulty in preventing. Past organisational performance on environmental issues has not instilled confidence and trust, and it is unlikely that mere rhetoric will calm the calls for more accountability. In future it seems more likely that the demand will be for a socially responsive organisation that accepts full public evaluation of its activities and makes itself accountable to all interested parties; in short, an organisation which is proactive in developing greater corporate responsibility and which is committed in practice as well as in principle to the concept of sustainable development.

Corporate responsibility without intervention?

Many businesses at present appear to be taking up the challenge of corporate responsibility if only out of the slow realisation that it is in their own interest – that is, to avoid regulation, to increase market share and/or to reduce costs. In its purest form, corporate responsibility could be supported for its own sake as representing a noble way for corporations to behave and such a stance can be closely associated with a business attitude of social responsiveness. Since this approach can conflict with a key objective of business – namely, profit maximisation – the question is whether the two are mutually exclusive or if a way can be found to combine profitability and corporate responsibility. Many observers believe that a business environment which is allowed to operate without government intervention seems unlikely to engender corporately responsible organisations. By the same token, legislation on its own cannot be expected to oversee all aspects of business, including the impact that firms have on the natural environment.

Arguably what is required is that a tone is set, through both legislation and societal norms and values, that provides clear signals to businesses; it will then be up to organisations to interpret these signals and to transmit them into policies which provide for the wants of society and at the same time satisfy the requirements of legislation. In this way corporate responsibility will tend to be seen as essential to competitive advantage and will become an integral part of the strategic management process. In short, the pursuit of a philosophy of sustainable development can be instilled into business practice without the excessive use of intervention that so often impinges upon the entrepreneurial flair of organisations. Businesses, however, need to play their part.

Synopsis

The ethical and ecological context of business operations and decisions has become increasingly important as individuals, groups and governments show a greater inclination to look beyond the commercial impact of the business community. Concepts such as business ethics, corporate social responsibility and environmental management have become mainstream issues in the world of business and firms face growing pressures to consider and improve upon their social and environmental performance. While the relative costs and benefits of a proactive response remain open to dispute, many observers believe that 'doing good' can pay, not least by reducing organisational 'threats' and enhancing business 'opportunities'.

Summary of key points

- Business ethics is concerned with issues of 'right' and 'wrong' behaviour in a business context.

- Corporate social responsibility (CSR) is the idea that organisations should be held accountable for the effects of their actions on people, their communities and the environment.

- CSR has become an important consideration for modern businesses, alongside traditional concerns with profitability and growth.

- Being socially responsible as a business does not preclude being profitable.

- Increasingly, business organisations have to take account of the views of their stake-holders on questions of social responsibility.

- One area where this has become particularly significant is with regard to the impact of business operations and decisions on the natural environment.

- Different businesses respond in different ways, ranging from reactive stances through to more proactive environmental approaches which go beyond compliance with regulatory demands.

- The key 'drivers' of corporate environmental responsiveness include government intervention, market forces, external pressures and self-regulation by organisations.

- Firms which implement environmental policies can find they benefit from improved resource efficiency, enhanced market image, new market opportunities, increased competitive advantage and anticipatory reaction.

case study

The *Braer* oil tanker disaster

Introduction

The *Braer* was built by Oshima Shipbuilding in Nagasaki in 1975; it was a single-engined vessel, 241.5 m long, with a dead weight of 89 730 tons. It was registered with the Norwegian classification society Det Norske Veritas (DNV) in 1985 and according to that particular institution had an exceptional record. The ship was required to undergo rigorous surveys every five years and an annual inspection; the last periodic survey was carried out in July 1989 while the last annual inspection occurred in May 1992. Records show that neither of these inspections found anything that could improve seaworthiness and DNV regarded the *Braer* as a very good ship. The vessel itself had not previously been involved in a shipping casualty and Skuld Protection and Indemnity, the insurers of the ship, stated that in their opinion it was a sound ship managed by a sound and responsible company.

The emergency began at about 5.30 a.m. on 5 January 1993 when the tanker, carrying 85 000 tons of light crude oil from Norway to Quebec was passing through the 22-mile gap between Shetland and Fair Isle. The storm force seas had somehow managed to drive seawater into the fuel tank and by 6 a.m. the *Braer* was

without power and drifting sideways towards Shetland. The first tug was dispatched from Lerwick harbour, 30 miles from the incident, at approximately 7.30 a.m., a crucial delay of at least 90 minutes from the time the engines failed. Despite the efforts of the salvage crews, the tanker hit the rocks at 11.30 a.m.; by 3 p.m. there were already reports of large oil slicks, with their subsequent effects on wildlife in the area.

Consequences of the oil spillage

The environmental impact of the wrecked *Braer* oil tanker near Sumburgh Head in Shetland was described by the World Wide Fund for Nature as 'potentially catastrophic'. The site of the disaster is a region of high cliffs and sheltered coves teeming with wildlife all year round. At the time Sumburgh Head was due to be designated a special protection area under the European Community birds directive. The oil coating the rocks settled on plants and fish in the intertidal zone and moved through the food chain, poisoning the feeding sea birds and threatening both the otter and seal population which had a stronghold in the area. A spokesperson for the Wildfowl and Wetlands Trust stated that they were particularly worried about the spillage, in light of a previous incident in 1979 when the ▶

Esso Bernicia spilled 1174 tonnes of fuel oil at Sullem Voe. This spillage had been fatal for all the ducks in the immediate area and the general population declined by 25 to 30 per cent.

While many Shetlanders were dismayed by the threat to the birds and sea life caused by the pollution, their main concern was the economic threat to the fishing and fish farming industries. In spite of oil wealth, Shetland still earned much of its living from fish. Almost a third of the islands' 10 000-strong labour force worked in the fish industry, including fishermen, fish processors and salmon farmers. A spokesperson for the Shetlands Fishermen Association stated that 'the Shetlands were more dependent on fish than any other part of the EC'. Without fishing, the future of the community appeared doubtful. The Shetland salmon industry alone was worth approximately £35 million of the £80 million turnover of the islands' fishing industry. Although the ship's cargo was largely harmless to fish because the oil floats upon the surface, the chemical dispersants employed against oil slicks produce an oily emulsion that can kill fish as it sinks to the sea bed. The combination of dispersant and oil was known to be more toxic than oil alone.

Historical precedent

The *Braer* disaster was yet another example of oil tankers which have come to grief on the seas. In 1967 the *Torrey Canyon* disaster released 30 000 tons of oil in a 35-mile-long slick off Cornwall. It was the first and remains the largest oil disaster in the United Kingdom. At the time one senior government official claimed that it had created 'an oil pollution problem of unparalleled magnitude'. There has been a regular stream of similar occurrences since this date, including:

1970	*Pacific Glory*, 3500 tons of oil
1978	*Eleni V*, 5000 tons of oil
	Amoco Cadiz, 223 000 tons of oil
1979	*Atlantic Empress* and *Aegean Captain*, 1.2 million barrels of oil
1987	*Exxon Valdez*, 240 000 barrels of oil
1990	*American Trader*, 7600 barrels of oil
1992	*Aegean Sea*, 24 million gallons of oil

From July 1993, under anti-pollution rules negotiated by the International Maritime Organisation (IMO), all new tankers had to be constructed with a double-skinned hull. Since 1995 existing vessels also have to meet more stringent standards. In practice, this has

sometimes meant sending many older ships to the scrapyard because they are not worth the cost of rebuilding to meet these standards. However, as a spokesperson for the IMO indicated at the time, ships built in the 1970s were regarded as technically out of date but needed to be retained to meet the demand for oil. With 136 governments involved during that period and a world tanker fleet of 2900 ships, it was accepted that change could not happen overnight.

The issues of corporate responsibility

The ship's course

Environmental experts initially found it difficult to understand why the captain of the *Braer* had followed a course that took it so close to the Shetland coastline. The waters around the Shetland Isles are classified as 'an area to be avoided' and this was confirmed by the IMO. Furthermore, International Collision Regulations say a ten-mile protection zone is necessary to avoid the risk of oil pollution and severe damage to the environment and the economy of Shetland. The regulations stipulated that all shipping of more than 5000 gross tons should avoid the area. The main reason offered for the presence of the *Braer* in the area was the extreme bad weather, which may have led the captain to put the safety of the crew before any risk to the environment. Weather forecasts can, however, be brought into the equation, since the vast majority of crews usually relied on three-day forecasts rather than the longer ten-day forecasts that were available. In effect the dependence on the shorter prediction means that the crew was committed to a route as soon as a vessel left port. Paul Roberts, a representative of Oceanroutes, which advised the shipping industry on weather conditions along prime trading routes, stated that oil tankers did not have standard routes: 'From Norway it is fairly natural for tankers to go around the top of Britain. If conditions are horrendous we might recommend the Channel, but extra miles means extra days means lots of bucks.'

Safety standards and flags of convenience

There has been a gradual increase over the years in the number of owners cutting costs by registering ships under overseas 'flags of convenience'. At times of worldwide recession, some owners burdened by ageing fleets have adopted the lower safety standards of countries such as Cyprus, Panama and Liberia, whose flag was carried by the *Braer*. The

Merchant Navy Officers' union, NUMAST, said it had warned the government about the dangers of allowing so-called coffin ships to carry dangerous goods around Britain's coast. More than 60 per cent of foreign ships checked in British ports in 1991 were found to have defects. The union's then general secretary, John Newman, said a disaster was inevitable given the increasing amounts of hazardous cargoes being carried by vessels with 'safety records up to 100 times worse than British vessels'.

The structure of the ship's hull

US legislation, in response to the *Exxon Valdez* disaster, had concentrated on the gradual introduction of double-hulled tankers and the phasing out of the older oil carriers with a single-skinned hull. This stance was subsequently incorporated into new international law which required all new tankers to be constructed using the double-hull technique. This belated response hides a number of issues. First, the legislation does not indicate what should happen to the vessels built before 1993 but which were still very much in use. Second, it has been cogently argued by Joe Nichols, technical manager at the International Tanker Owners' Pollution Federation, that the double hull would not necessarily have prevented either the *Braer* or the *Exxon Valdez* disaster. Moreover the double-hull design itself can cause problems through the build-up of gases and new so-called mid-deck designs may yet prove superior. Legislation, in other words, may not be sufficiently flexible to accommodate all the necessary safety requirements.

The level and quality of training offered to the crew

The concentration upon the technical and safety requirements of the tanker could have meant that an important issue had been overlooked. Approximately 80 per cent of oil spills are caused by human error, which indicates an urgent need to harmonise training procedures throughout the seafaring world. Although tanker crew members must have internationally recognised certificates of training, it is notoriously difficult to obtain uniformity within the awarding bodies. Possibly of more concern is the incidence of such certificates being purchased from markets in the Far East. According to a director of the International Shipping Federation 'there are indications that the overall world training standards have diminished'.

The depressed costs of chartering vessels

Training problems may be a symptom of the very low charter rates for oil tankers caused by over-capacity in the industry. A company which during that period invested in an up-to-date tanker with the necessary pollution control measures needed to make approximately $60 000 a day on charter rates, compared to the $15 000 a day offered by the hard-bargaining oil companies. In effect charterers were not prepared to pay for quality shipping and could be said to have indirectly sponsored the continuation of substandard shipping.

The delayed request for assistance

Comparison has been made between the *Braer* and the *Amoco Cadiz* (1978) disasters, given the critical delay by the *Braer*'s captain in acknowledging the fact that the tanker was in extreme danger and in need of salvage under Lloyd's 'open form'. The *Braer*'s captain may have felt in no imminent danger as the ship was lying roughly midway between the islands when the power failed, and he may have assumed that the tanker had a good chance of making it through the channel to relative safety. With the benefit of hindsight, it is difficult to understand how someone in such a position could make a rational decision based upon some form of cost-benefit analysis, given that the intangible costs of ecological and environmental damage and the secondary effects of lost income and quality of life would at the time be unquantifiable.

Conclusion

The *Braer*, built in 1975, was owned by B & H Ship Management of New York. The pollution protection held by the company was in keeping with that of other businesses with interests in shipping: B & H had contributed to a 'protection and indemnity' club under the management of Skuld in Oslo. These clubs are groups of like-minded shipowners which were formed at the turn of the twentieth century to provide for areas not covered by conventional policies. The cover they offer is compulsory for ships carrying 2000 tonnes or more of crude oil to or from UK ports. If this was not enough, the state-supported International Oil Pollution Compensation Fund, administered by the IMO, came into force, providing a ceiling of £662 per tonne of ship. In the case of the *Braer* this would be £54.63 million. Both schemes come under UK law. In effect, shipowners become liable for damage caused by the spillage itself, for the clean-up costs, and any damage caused by the clean-up measures. Skuld provided a standard $500 million-worth of coverage which in this case was never going to be enough once the full scale of the disaster was known, and this has led to renewed calls for raising minimum levels of compensation paid on oil spills. These calls have been consistently thwarted by tanker owners who face rising premiums and other costs. It is widely accepted that the compensation levels are set too low now and that delays in paying out compensation are far too long.

Case study questions

1 In the *Braer* case who are the stakeholders, what are their interests and how might they influence future decisions to avoid further environmental incidents such as the tanker disaster?

2 What part do you think that environmental organisations can play in reducing the likelihood of future environmental disasters of this kind?

Review and discussion questions

1 To what extent are governments responsible for establishing the parameters by which organisations conduct business? Should a business be free to decide its own level of corporate responsibility?

2 Consider the case for greater democracy in the decision process of firms. To what extent is it feasible for businesses to implement the recommendations of the Cadbury Report?

3 Writers have argued that the only objective of business is to make profit, within the boundaries established by government. Do you agree?

Assignments

1 As a group, select an environmental issue (e.g. business or natural feature) and write a report to the leader of a local pressure group which details an environmental impact assessment of the issue. The report should make clear reference to:
   (a) a cost-benefit analysis, carried out by the group, of the salient factors;
   (b) any legislation/regulation that concerns the case; and
   (c) the provision of a stakeholder map that illustrates who the stakeholders are, their importance to the case and their ability to affect future decisions.

2 As a newly appointed trainee manager you have been asked to look afresh at the business, with particular reference to the implementation of an environmental management system. Your immediate superior has asked you to write a report. Accordingly, you are required to:
   (a) consult the available literature and identify what you consider to be the necessary processes and procedures that would comprise an environmental management system;
   (b) indicate the areas within the organisation that need to be addressed; and
   (c) explain how such a policy should be implemented within the organisation.

Notes and references

1 For a discussion see, for example, Vogel, D. (2005).

2 Friedman, M., 'The social responsibility of business is to increase its profits', *New York Times Magazine*, 13 September 1970, pp. 7–13.

3 See e.g. Hart, S., 'A natural resource-based view of the firm', *Academy of Management Review*, 20, pp. 986–1014, 1995.

4 For a fuller discussion of the issues involved see Worthington, I., Britton, C. and Rees, A., *Business Economics: Blending Theory and Practice*, 2nd edition, Financial Times/Prentice Hall, 2005, Chapter 14.

5 Sethi, S. P., 'Dimensions of corporate social performance: an analytical framework', *California Management Review*, Spring 1975.

6 The complexity associated with implementing environmental policy is illustrated by the setting up of the Environment Agency in the UK. This is a 'quango' which has taken over the functions of the National Rivers Authority, Her Majesty's Inspectorate of Pollution and the local authority waste regulators, and has the task of regulating the water, air and land environment in an integrated way.

7 Simon, B., 'Sharks in the water', *Financial Times*, 27 November 1991.

8 Peattie, K., *Green Marketing*, Pitman Publishing, 1992.

Further reading

Bansal, P. and Roth, K., 'Why companies go green: a model of ecological responsiveness', *Academy of Management Journal*, 43 (4), 2000, pp. 717–36.

Cairncross, F., *Green Inc: A Guide to Business and the Environment*, Earthscan Publications, 1995.

Cannon, T., *Corporate Responsibility: A Textbook on Business Ethics, Governance, Environment*, Pitman, 1994.

Crane, A. and Matten, D., *Business Ethics*, Oxford University Press, 2004. A second edition was published in 2006.

Esty, D. C. and Winston, A. S., *Green to Gold: How Smart Companies Use Environmental Strategy to Innovate, Create Valve and Build Competitive Advantage*, Yale University Press, 2006.

Frederick, W. C., Post, J. E. and Davis, K., Business and Society: *Corporate Strategy, Public Policy, Ethics*, 8th edition, McGraw-Hill, 1996.

Freeman, R. E., *Strategic Management: A Stakeholder Perspective*, Prentice Hall, 1984.

Kolk, A., *Economics of Environmental Management*, Financial Times/Prentice Hall, 2000.

McWilliams, A., Siegel, D.S. and Wright, P.M., 'Corporate Social Responsibility: Strategic Implications', *Journal of Management Studies*, 43(1), 2006, pp. 1–18.

Mercado, S., Welford, R. and Prescott, K., *European Business*, 4th edition, Financial Times/ Prentice Hall, 2001, Chapter 11.

Pearce, D. and Barbier, E., *Blueprint for a Sustainable Economy*, Earthscan Publications, 2000.

Pearce, D. W. and Turner, R. K., *Economics of Natural Resources and the Environment*, Harvester Wheatsheaf, 1990.

Porter, M. E. and Kramer, M. R., 'The Competitive Advantage of Corporate Philanthropy', *Harvard Business Review*, 80(12), 2002, pp. 56–69.

Roberts, P., *Environmentally Sustainable Business: A Local and Regional Perspective*, Paul Chapman Publishing, 1995.

Vogel, D., *The Market for Virtue: The Potential and Limits of Corporate Social Responsibility*, Brookings Institution, 2005.

Welford, R., *Corporate Environmental Management: Systems and Strategies*, Earthscan Publications, 1996.

Welford, R. and Gouldson, A., *Environmental Management and Business Strategy*, Pitman Publishing, 1993.

Welford, R. and Starkey, R. (eds), *Business and the Environment*, Earthscan Publications, 1996.

Worthington, I., Britton, C. and Rees, A., *Economics for Business: Blending Theory and Practice*, 2nd edition, Financial Times/Prentice Hall, 2005, Chapter 14.

Web links and further questions are available on the website at:
www.pearsoned.co.uk/worthington

Chapter 20
Legal Structures

Legal structures

Ian Worthington

Market-based economies comprise a rich diversity of business organisations, ranging from the very simple enterprise owned and operated by one person, to the huge multinational corporation with production and distribution facilities spread across the globe. Whatever the nature of these organisations or their scale of operation, their existence is invariably subject to legal definition and this will have consequences for the functioning of the organisation. Viewing the business as a legal structure provides an insight into some of the important influences on business operations in both the private and public sectors.

Learning outcomes

Having read this chapter you should be able to:

● discuss the legal structure of UK business organisations in both the private and public sectors

● compare UK business organisations with those in other parts of Europe

● illustrate the implications of a firm's legal structure for its operations

● explain franchising, licensing and joint ventures

Key terms

Articles of Association	Joint venture	Public limited company
'Black economy'	Licensing	(PLC)
Company	Managing director	Public sector
Company directors	Memorandum of	organisations
Consortium	Association	Shareholders
Consumer societies	Nationalised industry	Sole trader
Executive directors	Non-executive directors	Stakeholders
Franchising	Partnership	Unlimited personal liability
Gearing	Private limited company	Workers' co-operatives
Golden share	Public corporation	

Introduction

Business organisations can be classified in a variety of ways, including:

- size (e.g. small, medium, large);
- type of industry (e.g. primary, secondary, tertiary);
- sector (e.g. private sector, public sector); and
- legal status (e.g. sole trader, partnership, and so on).

These classifications help to distinguish one type of organisation from another and to focus attention on the implications of such differences for an individual enterprise. In the discussion below, business organisations are examined as legal structures and the consequences of variations in legal status are discussed in some detail. Subsequent chapters in this section investigate alternative structural perspectives in order to highlight how these too have an important bearing on the environment in which businesses operate.

Private sector organisations in the UK

The sole trader

Many individuals aspire to owning and running their own business – being their own boss, making their own decisions. For those who decide to turn their dream into a reality, becoming a sole trader (or sole proprietor) offers the simplest and easiest method of trading.

As the name suggests, a **sole trader** is a business owned by one individual who is self-employed and who may, in some cases, employ other people on either a full-time or a part-time basis. Normally using personal funds to start the business, the sole trader decides on the type of goods or services to be produced, where the business is to be located, what capital is required, what staff (if any) to employ, what the target market should be and a host of other aspects concerned with the establishment and running of the enterprise. Where the business proves a success, all profits accrue to the owner and it is common for sole traders to reinvest a considerable proportion of these in the business and/or use them to reduce past borrowings. Should losses occur, these too are the responsibility of the sole trader, who has **unlimited personal liability** for the debts of the business.

Despite this substantial disadvantage, sole proprietorship tends to be the most popular form of business organisation numerically. In the United Kingdom, for example, it is estimated that about 80 per cent of all businesses are sole traders and in some sectors – notably personal services, retailing, building – they tend to be the dominant form of business enterprise. Part of the reason for this numerical dominance is the relative ease with which an individual can establish a business of this type. Apart from minor restrictions concerning the use of a business name – if the name of the proprietor is not used – few other legal formalities are required to set up the enterprise, other than the need to register for Value Added Tax if turnover exceeds a certain sum (e.g. £67 000 in 2008) and/or to fulfil any special requirements laid down by the local authority prior to trading (e.g. some businesses require licences). Once established, of course, the sole trader, like other forms of business, will be subject to a variety of legal requirements (e.g. contract law, consumer law, employment law) – though not the requirement to file information about the business in a public place. For some, this ability to keep the affairs of the enterprise away from public scrutiny provides a further incentive to establishing this form of business organisation – some of which may operate wholly or partly in the **black economy** (i.e. beyond the gaze of the tax authorities).

A further impetus towards sole ownership comes from the ability of the individual to exercise a considerable degree of control over her/his own destiny. Business decisions – including the day-to-day operations of the enterprise as well as long-term plans – are in the hands of the owner and many individuals evidently relish the risks and potential rewards associated with entrepreneurial activity, preferring these to the relative safety of employment in another organisation. For others less fortunate, the 'push' of unemployment rather than the 'pull' of the marketplace tends to be more of a deciding factor and one which clearly accounts for some of the growth in the number of small businesses in the United Kingdom in the later part of the twentieth century.

Ambitions and commitment alone, however, are not necessarily sufficient to guarantee the survival and success of the enterprise and the high mortality rate among businesses of this kind, particularly during a recession, is well known and well documented. Part of the problem may stem from developments largely outside the control of the enterprise – including bad debts, increased competition, higher interest rates, falling demand – and factors such as these affect businesses of all types and all sizes, not just sole traders. Other difficulties, such as lack of funds for expansion, poor marketing, lack of research of the marketplace and insufficient management skills are to some extent self-induced and emanate, at least in part, from the decision to become a sole proprietor rather than some other form of business organisation. Where such constraints exist, the sole trader may be tempted to look to others to share the burdens and the risks by establishing a partnership or co-operative or limited company or by seeking a different approach to the business venture, such as through franchising. These alternative forms of business organisation are discussed in detail below.

The partnership

The Partnership Act 1890 defines a **partnership** as 'the relation which subsists between persons carrying on a business in common with a view to profit'. Like the sole trader, this form of business organisation does not have its own distinct legal personality and hence the owners – the partners – have unlimited personal liability both jointly and severally. This means that in the case of debts or bankruptcy of the partnership, each partner is liable in full for the whole debt and each in turn may be sued or their assets seized until the debt is satisfied. Alternatively, all the partners may be joined into the action to recover debts, unless by dint of the Limited Partnership Act 1907, a partner (or partners) has limited liability. Since it tends to be much easier to achieve the same ends by establishing a limited company, limited partnerships are not common, nor can all partners in a partnership have limited liability. Hence in the discussion below, attention is focused on the partnership as an unincorporated association, operating in a market where its liability is effectively unlimited.

In essence, a partnership comes into being when two or more people establish a business which they own, finance and run jointly for personal gain, irrespective of the degree of formality involved in the relationship. Such a business can range from a husband and wife running a local shop as joint owners, to a very large firm of accountants or solicitors, with in excess of a hundred partners in offices in various locations. Under the law, most partnerships are limited to 20 or less, but some types of business, particularly in the professions, may have a dispensation from this rule (Companies Act 1985, s 716). This same Act requires businesses which are not exempt from the rule and which have more than 20 partners to register as a company.

While it is not necessary for a partnership to have a formal written agreement, most partnerships tend to be formally enacted in a Deed of Partnership or Articles, since this makes it much easier to reduce uncertainty and to ascertain intentions when there is a written document to consult. Where this is not done, the Partnership Act 1890 lays down a minimum code which governs the relationship between partners and which provides, amongst other things, for all partners to share equally in the capital and profits of the business and to contribute equally towards its losses.

In practice, of course, where a Deed or Articles exist, these will invariably reflect differences in the relative status and contribution of individual partners. Senior partners, for example, will often have contributed more financially to the partnership and not unnaturally will expect to receive a higher proportion of the profits. Other arrangements – including membership, action on dissolution of the partnership, management responsibilities and rights, and the basis for allocating salaries – will be outlined in the partnership agreement and as such will provide the legal framework within which the enterprise exists and its co-owners operate.

Unlike the sole trader, where management responsibilities devolve on a single individual, partnerships permit the sharing of responsibilities and tasks and it is common in a partnership for individuals to specialise to some degree in particular aspects of the organisation's work – as in the case of a legal or medical or veterinary practice. Added to this, the fact that more than one person is involved in the ownership of the business tends to increase the amount of finance available to the organisation, thus permitting expansion to take place without the owners losing control of the enterprise. These two factors alone tend to make a partnership an attractive proposition for some would-be entrepreneurs, while for others the rules of their professional body – which often prohibits its members from forming a company – effectively provide for the establishment of this type of organisation.

On the downside, the sharing of decisions and responsibilities may represent a problem, particularly where partners are unable to agree over the direction the partnership should take or the amount to be reinvested in the business, unless such matters are clearly specified in a formal agreement. A more intractable problem is the existence of unlimited personal liability – a factor which may inhibit some individuals from considering this form of organisation, particularly given that the actions of any one partner are invariably binding on the other members of the business. To overcome this problem, many individuals, especially in manufacturing and trading, look to the limited company as the type of organisation which can combine the benefits of joint ownership and limited personal liability – a situation not necessarily always borne out in practice. It is to this type of business organisation that the discussion now turns.

Limited companies

In law a **company** is a corporate association having a legal identity in its own right (i.e. it is distinct from the people who own it, unlike in the case of a sole trader or partnership). This means that all property and other assets owned by the company belong to the company and not to its members (owners). By the same token, the personal assets of its members (the **shareholders**) do not normally belong to the business. In the event of insolvency, therefore, an individual's liability is limited to the amount invested in the business, including any amount remaining unpaid on the shares for which they have subscribed.[1] One exception to this would be where a company's owners have given a personal guarantee to cover any loans they have obtained from a bank or other institution – a requirement for many small, private limited companies. Another occurs where a company is limited by guarantee rather than by shares, with its members' liability being limited to the amount they have undertaken to contribute to the assets in the event of the company being wound up. Companies of this type are normally non-profit-making organisations – such as professional, research or trade associations – and are much less common than companies limited by shares. Hence in the discussion below, attention is focused on the latter as the dominant form of business organisation in the corporate sector of business.[2]

Companies are essentially business organisations consisting of two or more individuals who have agreed to embark on a business venture and who have decided to seek corporate status rather than to form a partnership.[3] Such status could derive from an Act of Parliament or a Royal Charter, but is almost always nowadays achieved through 'registration', the terms of which are laid down in the various Companies Acts. Under legislation, enacted in 1985, 1989 and 2006 individuals seeking to form a company are required to file numerous documents, including a **Memorandum of Association** and **Articles of Association**, with the Registrar of Companies. If satisfied, the Registrar will issue a Certificate of Incorporation, bringing the company into existence as a legal entity. As an alternative, the participants could buy a ready-formed company 'off the shelf', by approaching a company registration agent who specialises in company formations. In the United Kingdom, advertisements for ready-made companies appear regularly in magazines such as *Exchange and Mart* and *Dalton's Weekly*.

Companies' House can be accessed at *www.companieshouse.gov.uk*

Information on how companies are created, run and wound up is contained in the 2006 Companies Act which essentially consolidates all previous legislation and case law into one Act of Parliament. As this Act shows, under British law a distinction is made between public and private companies. **Public limited companies** (PLCs) – not to be confused with public corporations, which in the UK are state-owned businesses (see below) – are those limited companies which satisfy the conditions for being a 'PLC'. These conditions require the company to have:

- a minimum of two shareholders;
- at least two directors;
- a minimum (at present) of £50 000 of authorised and allotted share capital;
- the right to offer its shares (and debentures) for sale to the general public;
- a certificate from the Registrar of Companies verifying that the share capital requirements have been met; and
- a memorandum which states it to be a public company.

A company which meets these conditions must include the title 'public limited company' or 'PLC' in its name and is required to make full accounts available for public inspection. Any company unable or unwilling to meet these conditions is therefore, in the eyes of the law, a 'private limited company', normally signified by the term 'Limited' or 'Ltd'.

Like the public limited company, the **private limited company** must have a minimum of two shareholders, but its shares cannot be offered to the public at large, although it can offer them to individuals through its business contacts. This restriction on the sale of shares, and hence on their ability to raise considerable sums of money on the open market, normally ensures that most private companies are either small or medium sized, and are often family businesses operating in a relatively restricted market; there are, however, some notable exceptions to this general rule (e.g. Virgin). In contrast, public companies – many of which began life as private companies prior to 'going public' – often have many thousands, even millions, of owners (shareholders) and normally operate on a national or international scale, producing products as diverse as computers, petro-chemicals, cars and banking services. Despite being outnumbered by their private counterparts, public companies dwarf private companies in terms of their capital and other assets, and their collective influence on output, investment, employment and consumption in the economy is immense.

Both public and private companies act through their **directors**. These are individuals chosen by a company's shareholders to manage its affairs and to make the important decisions concerning the direction the company should take (e.g. investment, market development, mergers and so on). The appointment and powers of directors are outlined in the Articles of Association (the 'internal rules' of the organisation) and so long as the directors do not exceed their powers, the shareholders do not normally have the right to intervene in the day-to-day management of the company. Where a director exceeds his or her authority or fails to indicate clearly that they are acting as an agent for the company, they become personally liable for any contracts they make. Equally, directors become personally liable if they continue to trade when the company is insolvent and they may be dismissed by a court if it considers that an individual is unfit to be a director in view of their past record (Company Directors Disqualification Act 1985).

The 2006 Act sets out in detail the duties of company directors, including the duty to promote the success of the organisation, to exercise reasonable care, skill and diligence and to give appropriate consideration to issues that go beyond the balance sheet. For example, directors of UK companies now have a duty to consider the impacts of their business operations on the environment and the community generally and quoted public companies must report on issues of social and environmental responsibility as part of an expanded review of the business (see Chapter 9).

In practice it is usual for a board of directors to have both a chairperson and a managing director, although some companies choose to appoint one person to both roles. The chairperson, who is elected by the other members of the board, is usually chosen because of their knowledge and experience of the business and their skill both internally in chairing board meetings and externally in representing the best interest of the organisation. As the public face of the company, the chairperson has an important role to play in establishing and maintaining a good public image and hence many large public companies like to appoint well-known public figures to this important position (e.g. ex-Cabinet ministers). In this case knowledge of the business is less important than the other attributes the individual might possess, most notably public visibility and familiarity, together with a network of contacts in government and in the business world.

The **managing director**, or chief executive, fulfils a pivotal role in the organisation, by forming the link between the board and the management team of senior executives. Central to this role is the need not only to interpret board decisions but to ensure that they are put into effect by establishing an appropriate structure of delegated responsibility and effective systems of reporting and control. This close contact with the day-to-day operations of the company places the appointed individual in a position of considerable authority and he/she will invariably be able to make important decisions without reference to the full board. This authority is enhanced where the managing director is also the person chairing the board of directors and/or is responsible for recommending individuals to serve as executive directors (i.e. those with functional responsibilities such as production, marketing, finance).

Like the managing director, most, if not all, **executive directors** will be full-time executives of the company, responsible for running a division or functional area within the framework laid down at board level. In contrast, other directors will have a **non-executive** role and are usually part-time appointees, chosen for a variety of reasons, including their knowledge, skills, contacts, influence, independence or previous experience. Sometimes, a company might be required to appoint such a director at the wishes of a third party, such as a merchant bank which has agreed to fund a large capital injection and wishes to have representation on the board. In this case, the individual tends to act in an advisory capacity – particularly on matters of finance – and helps to provide the financing institution with a means of ensuring that any board decisions are in its interests.

In Britain the role of company directors and senior executives in recent years has come under a certain amount of public scrutiny and has culminated in a number of enquiries into issues of power and pay. In the Cadbury Report (1992), a committee, with Sir Adrian Cadbury as chairperson, called for a non-statutory code of practice which it wanted applied to all listed public companies. Under this code the committee recommended:

- a clear division of responsibilities at the head of a company to ensure that no individual had unfettered powers of decision;
- a greater role for non-executive directors;
- regular board meetings;
- restrictions on the contracts of executive directors;
- full disclosure of directors' total enrolments;
- an audit committee dominated by non-executives.

The committee's stress on the important role of non-executive directors was a theme taken up in the Greenbury Report (1995) which investigated the controversial topic of executive salaries in the wake of a number of highly publicised pay rises for senior company directors. Greenbury's recommendations included:

- full disclosure of directors' pay packages, including pensions;
- shareholder approval for any long-term bonus scheme;
- remuneration committees consisting entirely of non-executive directors;
- greater detail in the annual report on directors' pay, pensions and perks;
- an end to payments for failure.

Greenbury was followed by a further investigation into corporate governance by a committee under the chairmanship of ICI chairman Ronald Hampel. The Hampel Report (1998) advocated company self-regulation and called for greater shareholder responsibility by companies and increased standards of disclosure of information; it supported Cadbury's recommendation that the role of chairperson and chief executive should normally be separated. A year later, the Turnbull Report (1999) considered the issue of corporate governance and information disclosure from the perspective of risk management, arguing that companies need to take steps to manage and disclose corporate risks formally.

As far as the issue of non-executive directors was concerned, this was investigated further by the Higgs Committee which was set up in 2002 and which reported the following year. In essence the Higgs Report set down a code of non-binding corporate guidelines regarding the role of non-executive directors on company boards. Like the Cadbury Report, Higgs recommended that the role of chairperson and chief executive should be kept separate and that the former should be independent, though not necessarily non-executive. As for non-executive directors, Higgs recommended that at least half the board should be independent and that non-executives should play key roles in areas such as strategy, performance, risk and the appointment and remuneration of executive directors. The latter issue, in particular, has been an area of considerable controversy in the UK in recent years and seems destined to remain so for some time.

mini case   Companies under pressure

Public companies have to satisfy the conflicting demands of a range of stakeholder groups (see below), not least their shareholders who expect the organisation to operate in their interest. On the whole, individual shareholders are usually relatively quiescent, leaving the strategic and day-to-day decisions to the organisation's directors and senior executives. As an increasing number of public companies have found, however, many shareholders are becoming more actively involved in corporate decisions which they believe affect their investments and have been willing to voice their feelings at shareholders' meetings and to the media. This is particularly true of large corporate investors.

In the 5th edition of this book we reported on the rise of shareholder militancy at Daimler-Benz, with shareholders expressing dissatisfaction over the company's poor performance and its effect on shareholder value. This is only one issue that has been exercising company shareholders in recent years, however. At the large UK retail chain Marks & Spencer, for example, investors are unhappy at the decision to combine the position of executive chairman annd chief executive in contravention of City corporate governance rules; at Exxon Mobil shareholder concerns have focused on the company's environmental record, particularly with regard to its impact on climate change. At other companies, executives' pay and rewards have been the central issues that have provoked shareholder anger.

From a company's point of view, challenges such as these are not especially welcome and the board of directors may be forced to spend time and resources to justify its actions to the protestors. Apart from the negative publicity that shareholder revolts can evoke, large corporations are particularly concerned when the protests come from very large corporate investors such as pension funds, since their reactions can affect not only the current but also the future position of the organisation.

Co-operatives

Consumer co-operative societies

Consumer societies are basically 'self-help' organisations which have their roots in the anti-capitalist sentiment which arose in mid-nineteenth-century Britain and which gave rise to a consumer co-operative movement dedicated to the provision of cheap, unadulterated food for its members and a share in its profits. Today this movement boasts a multibillion-pound turnover, a membership numbered in millions and an empire which includes thousands of food stores (including the Alldays convenience chain purchased in 2002), numerous factories and farms, dairies, travel agencies, opticians, funeral parlours, a bank and an insurance company, and property and development business. Taken together, these activities ensure that the Co-operative Group remains a powerful force in British retailing into the early twenty-first century. Indeed, it is the world's largest consumer co-operative employing around 85 000 people (in 2007) following the merger of the Co-operative Group and United Co-operatives. Survey evidence indicates that in retailing it is the UK's most trusted and ethical brand name.

 The Co-operative Group's website address is *www.co-operative.coop*

Although the co-operative societies, like companies, are registered and incorporated bodies – in this case under the Industrial and Provident Societies Act – they are quite distinct trading organisations. These societies belong to their members (i.e. invariably customers who have purchased a share in the society) who elect Area Committees to oversee trading areas. These committees have annual elections and meetings for all members and these in turn appoint members on to regional boards and elect individual member directors to the Group Board. The Group Board also includes directors of corporate members who are representatives of other societies. Individual stores may also have member forums. Any profits from the Group's activities are supposed to benefit the members. Originally this took the form of a cash dividend paid to members in relation to their purchases, but this was subsequently replaced either by trading stamps or by investment in areas felt to benefit the consumer (e.g. lower prices, higher-quality products, modern shops, and so on) and/or the local community (e.g. charitable donations, sponsorship). The twice-yearly cash dividend was, however, reintroduced in 2006, a move which saw a significant increase in the membership of the organisation.

The societies differ in other ways from standard companies. For a start, shares are not quoted on the Stock Exchange and members are restricted in the number of shares they can purchase and in the method of disposal. Not having access to cheap sources of capital on the stock market, co-operatives rely heavily on retained surpluses and on loan finance, and the latter places a heavy burden on the societies when interest rates are high. The movement's democratic principles also impinge on its operations and this has often been a bone of contention as members have complained about their increasing remoteness from decision-making centres. Some societies have responded by encouraging the development of locally elected committees to act in an advisory or consultative capacity to the society's board of directors and it looks likely that others will be forced to consider similar means of increasing member participation, which still remains very limited.

web link

The Co-operative Commission has put forward numerous proposals for changes which are designed to improve the performance of societies. See *www.co-opcommission.org.uk*

The movement's historical links with the British Labour Party are also worth noting and a number of parliamentary candidates are normally sponsored at general elections. These links, however, have tended to become slightly looser in recent years, although the movement still contributes to Labour Party funds and continues to lobby politicians at both national and local level. It is also active in seeking to influence public opinion and, in this, claims to be responding to customer demands for greater social and corporate responsibility. Among its initiatives are the establishment of a customer's charter (by the Co-operative Bank) and the decision to review both its investments and the individuals and organisations it does business with, to ascertain that they are acceptable from an ethical point of view.

Workers' co-operatives

In Britain, **workers' co-operatives** are found in a wide range of industries, including manufacturing, building and construction, engineering, catering and retailing. They are particularly prevalent in printing, clothing and wholefoods, and some have been in existence for over a century. The majority, however, are of fairly recent origin, having been part of the growth in the number of small firms which occurred in the 1980s.

As the name suggests, a workers' co-operative is a business in which the ownership and control of the assets are in the hands of the people working in it, having agreed to establish the enterprise and to share the risk for mutual benefit. Rather than form a standard partnership, the individuals involved normally register the business as a friendly society under the Industrial and Provident Societies Acts 1965–78, or seek incorporation as a private limited company under the Companies Act 1985. In the case of the former, seven members are required to form a co-operative, while the latter only requires two. In practice, a minimum of three or four members tends to be the norm and some co-operatives may have several hundred participants, frequently people who have been made redundant by their employers and who are keen to keep the business going.

The central principles of the movement – democracy, open membership, social responsibility, mutual co-operation and trust – help to differentiate the co-operative from other forms of business organisation and govern both the formation and operation of this type of enterprise. Every employee may be a member of the organisation and every member owns one share in the business, with every share carrying an equal voting right. Any surpluses are shared by democratic agreement and this is normally done on an equitable basis, reflecting, for example, the amount of time and effort an individual puts into the business. Other decisions, too, are taken jointly by the members and the emphasis tends to be on the quality of goods or services provided and on creating a favourable working environment, rather than on the pursuit of profits – although the latter cannot be ignored if the organisation is to survive. In short, the co-operative tends to focus on people and on the relationship between them, stressing the co-operative and communal traditions associated with its origins, rather than the more conflictual and competitive aspects inherent in other forms of industrial organisation.

Despite these apparent attractions, workers' co-operatives have never been as popular in Britain as in other parts of the world (e.g. France, Italy, Israel), although a substantial increase occurred in the number of co-operatives in the 1980s, largely as a result of growing unemployment, overt support across the political spectrum and the establishment of a system to encourage and promote the co-operative ideal (e.g. Co-operative Development Agencies).[4] More recently, however, their fortunes have tended to decline, as employee shareholding and profit schemes (ESOPs) have grown in popularity. It seems unlikely that workers' co-operatives will ever form the basis of a strong third sector in the British economy, between the profit-oriented firms in the private sector and the nationalised and municipal undertakings in the public sector.

Public sector business organisations in the UK

Public sector organisations come in a variety of forms. These include:

- central government departments (e.g. Department of Innovation, Universities and Skills);
- local authorities (e.g. Lancashire County Council);
- regional bodies (e.g. Regional Development Agencies);
- non-departmental public bodies or quangos (e.g. the Arts Council);
- central government trading organisations (e.g. The Stationery Office); and
- public corporations and nationalised industries (e.g. the BBC).

Some of these were discussed in Chapter 4, which examined the political environment, and numerous other references to the influence of government on business activity can be found throughout the book. In the discussion below, attention is focused on those public sector organisations which most closely approximate businesses in the private sector, namely, public corporations and municipal enterprises. An examination of the transfer of many of these public sector bodies to the private sector – usually termed 'privatisation' – is contained in Chapter 17.

Public corporations

Private sector business organisations are owned by private individuals and groups who have chosen to invest in some form of business enterprise, usually with a view to personal gain. In contrast, in the public sector the state owns assets in various forms, which it uses to provide a range of goods and services felt to be of benefit to its citizens, even if this provision involves the state in a loss. Many of these services are provided directly through government departments (e.g. social security benefits) or through bodies operating under delegated authority from central government (e.g. local authorities, health authorities). Others are the responsibility of state-owned industrial and commercial undertakings, specially created for a variety of reasons and often taking the form of a **public corporation**. These state corporations are an important part of the public sector of the economy and have contributed significantly to national output, employment and investment. Their numbers, however, have declined substantially following the wide-scale privatisation of state industries which occurred in the 1980s and this process has continued through the 1990s and beyond with the sale of corporations such as British Coal, British Rail and British Energy (see Chapter 17).

Public corporations are statutory bodies, incorporated (predominantly) by special Act of Parliament and, like companies, they have a separate legal identity from the individuals who own them and run them. Under the statute setting up the corporation, reference is made to the powers, duties and responsibilities of the organisation and to its relationship with the government department which oversees its operations. In the past these operations have ranged from providing a variety of national and international postal services (the Post Office), to the provision of entertainment (the BBC), an energy source (British Coal) and a national rail network (British Rail). Where such provision involves the organisation in a considerable degree of direct contact with its customers, from whom it derives most of its revenue, the corporation tends to be called a **nationalised industry**. In reality, of course, the public corporation is the legal form through which the industry is both owned and run and every corporation is to some degree unique in structure as well as in functions.

As organisations largely financed as well as owned by the state, public corporations are required to be publicly accountable and hence they invariably operate under the purview of a 'sponsoring' government department, the head of which (the Secretary of State) appoints a board of management to run the organisation. This board tends to exercise a considerable degree of autonomy in day-to-day decisions and operates largely free from political interference on most matters of a routine nature. The organisation's strategic objectives, however, and important questions concerning reorganisation or investment, would have to be agreed with the sponsoring department, as would the corporation's performance targets and its external financing limits.

The link between the corporation and its supervising ministry provides the means through which Parliament can oversee the work of the organisation and permits ordinary Members of Parliament to seek information and explanation through question time, through debates and through the select committee system. Additionally, under the Competition Act 1980, nationalised industries can be subject to investigation by the Competition Commission (see Chapter 17), and this too presents opportunities for further parliamentary discussion and debate, as well as for government action.

A further opportunity for public scrutiny comes from the establishment of industry-specific Consumers' or Consultative Councils, which consider complaints from customers and advise both the board and the department concerned of public attitudes to the organisation's performance and to other aspects of its operations (e.g. pricing). In a number of cases, including British Rail before privatisation, pressure on government from consumers and from other sources has resulted in the establishment of a 'Customers' Charter', under which the organisation agrees to provide a predetermined level of service or to give information and/or compensation where standards are not achieved. Developments of this kind are already spreading to other parts of the public sector and in future may be used as a means by which governments decide on the allocation of funds to public bodies, as well as providing a vehicle for monitoring organisational achievement.

It is interesting to note that mechanisms for public accountability and state regulation have been retained to some degree even where public utilities have been privatised (i.e. turned into public limited companies). Industries such as gas, electricity, water and telecommunications are watched over by newly created regulatory bodies which are designed to protect the interests of consumers, particularly with regard to pricing and the standard of service provided. Ofgas, for example, which used to regulate British Gas, monitored gas supply charges to ensure that they reasonably reflected input costs and these charges could be altered by the regulator if they were seen to be excessive. Similarly, in the case of non-gas services, such as maintenance, the legislation privatising the industry only allowed prices to be raised to a prescribed maximum, to ensure that the organisation was not able to take full advantage of its monopoly power. The regulator of the gas market is now Ofgem – see Chapter 17.

An additional source of government influence has come through its ownership of a **golden share** in a privatised state industry which effectively gives the government a veto in certain vital areas of decision making. This notional shareholding – which is written into the privatisation legislation – tends to last for a number of years and can be used to protect a newly privatised business from a hostile takeover, particularly by foreign companies or individuals. Ultimately, however, the expectation is that this veto power will be relinquished and the organisation concerned will become subject to the full effects of the market – a point exemplified by the government's decision to allow Ford to take over Jaguar in 1990, having originally blocked a number of previous takeover bids (see also Chapter 4 Mini case: The demise of the VW law).

The existence of a golden share should not be equated with the decision by government to retain (or purchase) a significant proportion of issued shares in a privatised (or already private) business organisation, whether as an investment and/or future source of revenue, or as a means of exerting influence in a particular industry or sector. Nor should it be confused with government schemes to attract private funds into existing state enterprises, by allowing them to achieve notional company status in order to overcome Treasury restrictions on borrowing imposed on public bodies. In the latter case, which often involves a limited share issue, government still retains full control of the organisation by owning all (or the vast majority) of the shares – as in the case of Consignia (formerly known as the Post Office). In March 2001 Consignia was incorporated as a government-owned public company. This change in legal status allowed the company more freedom to borrow and invest in the business, to make acquisitions and to enter into joint ventures and to expand internationally. The name Consignia was subsequently dropped in favour of the brand name Royal Mail.

Municipal enterprises

UK local authorities have a long history of involvement in business activity. In part this is a function of their role as central providers of public services (e.g. education, housing, roads, social services) and of their increasing involvement in supporting local economic development initiatives (see Chapter 13). But their activities have also traditionally involved the provision of a range of marketable goods and services, not required by law but provided voluntarily by a local authority and often in direct competition with the private sector (e.g. theatres, leisure services, museums). Usually such provision has taken place under the aegis of a local authority department which appoints staff who are answerable to the council and to its committees through the department's chief officer and its elected head. Increasingly, though, local authorities are turning to other organisational arrangements – including the establishment of companies and trusts – in order to separate some of these activities from the rest of their responsibilities and to create a means through which private investment in the enterprise can occur.

One example of such a development can be seen in the case of local authority controlled airports which are normally the responsibility of a number of local authorities who run them through a joint board, representing the interests of the participating district councils (e.g. Manchester International Airport). Since the Airports Act 1986, local authorities with airports have been required to create a limited company in which their joint assets are vested and which appoints a board of directors to run the enterprise. Like other limited companies, the organisation can, if appropriate, seek private capital and must publish annual accounts, including a profit and loss statement. It can also be privatised relatively easily if the local authorities involved decide to relinquish ownership (e.g. East Midlands Airport is part of the Manchester Airports Group).

Such developments, which have parallels in other parts of the public sector, can be seen to have had at least four benefits:

1 They have provided a degree of autonomy from local authority control that is seen to be beneficial in a competitive trading environment.
2 They have given access to market funds by the establishment of a legal structure that is not fully subject to central government restrictions on local authority borrowing.
3 They helped local authority organisations to compete more effectively under the now defunct system of compulsory competitive tendering (CCT), by removing or reducing charges for departmental overheads that are applied under the normal arrangements.
4 They have provided a vehicle for further private investment and for ultimate privatisation of the service.

Given these benefits and the current fashion for privatisation, there is little doubt that they will become an increasing feature of municipal enterprise in the foreseeable future. That said, local authorities are restricted in their degree of ownership of companies following the passage of the 1990 Local Government and Housing Act.

Business organisations in mainland Europe

Sole traders, partnerships, co-operatives and limited companies are to be found throughout Europe and beyond, and in many cases their legal structure is similar to that of their British counterparts. Where differences occur, these are often a reflection of historical and cultural factors which find expression in custom and practice as well as in law. Examples of some of these differences are contained in the discussion below, which focuses on France, Germany, Denmark and Portugal.

France

Numerically, the French economy is dominated by very small businesses (i.e. fewer than ten employees), the majority of which are sole traders. As in Britain, these are owner-managed-and-operated enterprises, with a husband and wife often assuming joint responsibility for the business. Formal requirements in this type of organisation tend to be few, although individuals as well as companies engaging in a commercial business are required to register before trading officially begins. Since this process is relatively simple and there are no minimum capital requirements nor significant reporting obligations, sole traderships tend to be preferred by the vast majority of individuals seeking to start a business and they are particularly prevalent in the service sector. They carry, however, unlimited personal liability for the owner, whose personal assets are at risk in the event of business failure.

Most of the remaining French business organisations are limited companies, many of which are Petites et Moyennes Entreprises (PMEs) – small and medium enterprises – employing between 10 and 500 employees. These companies come in a variety of legal forms, but two in particular predominate: the Société à Responsabilité Limitée (SARL) and the Société Anonyme (SA). A new company form, the Société Anonyme Simplifée was created by statute in 1994 and combines the legal status of a corporation with the flexibility of a partnership.

The SARL tends to be the form preferred by smaller companies, whose owners wish to retain close control of the organisation; hence many of them are family businesses – an important feature of the private sector in France. This type of enterprise can be established (currently) with a minimum capital of €7500, cannot issue shares to the general public, has restrictions on the transfer of shares and is run by individuals appointed by the shareholders – usually the shareholders themselves and/or relatives. In practice, these various restrictions help to ensure that the owner-managers remain dominant in the organisation and the appointed head of the company will invariably be the most important decision maker. Concomitantly, they help to provide the organisation with a defence against hostile takeover, particularly by overseas companies looking for a French subsidiary in order to avoid the special rules which apply to branches and agencies (e.g. a foreign parent company has unlimited liability for the debts of its branch or agency, since these do not have a separate legal identity).

The SA is the legal form normally chosen by larger companies seeking access to substantial amounts of capital. In the case of a privately owned company, the minimum capital requirement is currently €37 000; if publicly owned the minimum is €225 000 million. Where capital assets are substantial, this tends to ensure that financial institutions are large shareholders in SAs and many of them have interests in a wide range of enterprises which they often manage through a holding company (see below). One advantage of this arrangement is that it provides the financial institution with a means of managing its investments and of exerting influence over companies in which it has a large minority stake. Another is that it provides a means of defending French companies from hostile takeovers and hence small and medium enterprises often seek backing from holding companies to help fend off foreign predators.

As in Britain, the legal basis of the SA provides for a clear distinction between the roles of the owners (the shareholders) and the salaried employees, and it is the former who appoint the company's board of directors. In smaller companies, the chairperson and managing director is often the same person and many smaller French companies continue to have extremely strong central control, often by the head of the owning family. In larger companies, the two roles are normally separated, with the managing director assuming responsibility for the day-to-day operations of the enterprise and forming the link between the board and the company's senior executives and managers, some of whom may have considerable delegated authority.

It is worth noting that in companies with more than 50 employees, there is a legal requirement to have elected work councils, and workers' delegates have the right to attend board meetings as observers and to be consulted on matters affecting working conditions. In companies with more than ten employees, workers have the right to elect representatives to look after their interests and regular meetings have to take place between management and workers, over and above the obligation of employers to negotiate annually on pay and conditions. Despite these arrangements and the legal right for unions to organise on a company's premises, trade union membership – outside state-run companies – remains low and hence union influence tends to be limited. Recent steps to encourage local agreements on pay and conditions seem destined to reduce this influence even further – a situation which has parallels in Britain.

Germany

All major forms of business organisation are to be found in Germany, but it is the limited company which is of particular interest. Some of these are of relatively recent origin, having formerly been East German state-owned enterprises which have undergone privatisation following the reunification of the country.

In numerical terms it is the private limited company (*Gesellschaft mit beschränkter Haftung* – GmbH) which predominates and which is the form chosen by most foreign companies seeking to establish an enterprise in Germany. As in Britain, this type of organisation has to be registered with the authorities and its founding members must prepare Articles of Association for signature by a public notary. The Articles include information on the purpose of the business, the amount of capital subscribed, the members' subscriptions and obligations and the company's name and registered address. Once the registration process is complete – usually a matter of a few days – the personal liability of the members becomes limited to the amount invested in the business. Currently, the minimum amount of subscribed share capital required for registration is €10 000, half of which must be paid up by the company itself.

Large numbers of GmbHs are owned and run by German families, with the banks often playing an influential role as guarantors of part of the initial capital and as primary sources of loan finance. As in France, this pattern of ownership makes hostile takeovers less likely, as well as ensuring that the management of the enterprise remains in the hands of the owners. Significantly, the management of a proposed GmbH is subject to quality control, being required to prove that they are qualified for the task prior to trading. This requirement stands in stark contrast to arrangements in Britain, where no such guarantees are needed, other than those implicit in a bank's decisions to help finance a proposed venture on the basis of a business plan.

The procedures for establishing other types of business organisation are similar to those of the GmbH, although in the case of the public limited company (*Aktiengesellschaft* – AG), the current minimum amount of capital required at start-up is €50 000 in negotiable share certificates. Unlike British companies, the AG usually consists of two boards of directors, one of which (the supervisory board) decides on longer-term strategy, while the other (the managing board) concentrates on more immediate policy issues, often of an operational kind. Normally half the members of the supervisory board (*Aufsichtrat*) are elected by shareholders, while the other half are employees elected by the workforce, and it is the responsibility of the board to protect the interests of employees as well as shareholders.

Such worker representation at senior levels is an important element of the German system of business organisation and even in smaller enterprises workers have the right to establish works councils and to be consulted on social and personnel issues and on strategic decisions. Equally, all employees have a constitutional right to belong to a trade union – most of which are organised by industry rather than by craft or occupation, as is largely the case in the United Kingdom. Consequently, German companies typically negotiate with only one union, usually in an atmosphere which stresses consensus and an identity of social and economic interests, rather than conflict and confrontation.

Corporate finance is another area in which German experience differs from that in the United Kingdom, although the situation has changed to some degree in recent years. Historically, in Britain a substantial amount of company finance has been raised through the stock market and this is also the case in the United States and Japan. In Germany (and for that matter in France, Italy and Spain), the banks and a number of other special credit institutions play a dominant role, with bank loans far outstripping joint-stock financing as a source of long-term capital. Traditionally, German banks have been willing to take a longer-term view of their investment, even at the expense of short-term profits and dividends, and this has benefited German companies seeking to expand their operations. In return, the banks have tended to exert a considerable amount of influence in the boardrooms of many German companies, usually by providing a substantial number of members of a company's supervisory board, including the chairperson.

Denmark

Denmark, like France, is a country whose economy is dominated by small businesses, many of which are sole traders. As in other countries, there are very few regulations governing the establishment of this type of enterprise, other than the need to register for VAT if turnover exceeds a predetermined limit and to meet taxation and social security requirements. In keeping with practice throughout Europe and beyond, sole traders have unlimited personal liability and this imposes a considerable burden on the organisation's owner and family, who often run the business jointly. The same conditions also apply in the case of Danish partnerships – whether formal or informal – with the joint owners having full and unlimited liability for all debts accruing to the organisation.

Limited companies in Denmark also reflect practice elsewhere, being required to register under the Companies Act and having a legal existence separate from the owners and employees. Three main types of limited liability company can be distinguished:

1 The *Anpartselskaber* (ApS), which is a private joint-stock company, often run by a family and owned and controlled by a handful of individuals, one of whom may simultaneously occupy the roles of main owner, chairperson and managing director. Many of these companies began life as sole traders, but for reasons of taxation and liability have registered as an ApS.

2 The *Aktieselskaber* (A/S), which is a quoted or (more regularly) unquoted public limited company, subject essentially to the same regulations as the ApS, but having a much larger minimum capital requirement on registration. A large number of A/S companies are still small businesses, run by family members who wish to retain control of the enterprise as an increase in assets occurs.

3 The AMBA is a special kind of limited company – in essence a tax-free co-operative with its own regulations. Many of these companies have grown over the years through merger and acquisition and some of them belong to larger Danish companies and employ a substantial number of workers. They tend to be concentrated in farm-related products, but can also be found in the service sector, especially wholesaling and retailing.

Portugal

A brief look at Portuguese business organisations reveals a range of legal structures which includes sole traders, joint ventures, complementary groups, unlimited companies, limited partnerships and public and private limited companies. In the case of the latter, capital requirements tend to be an important distinguishing feature with the Public Limited Company or Corporation (*Sociedade Anonima* – SA) having a much larger minimum capital requirement than the private company (*Sociedade Por Quotas or Limitada* – LDA) as in other countries.

The public sector in mainland Europe

Given the number of countries involved, it is impossible to survey the whole of the public sector in the rest of Europe. Students with an interest in this area are encouraged to read further and to consult the various specialist sources of information covering the countries they wish to investigate. A number of general points, however, are worthy of note:

1 Public sector business organisations can be found in all countries and invariably exist because of the decision by the state to establish a particular organisation under state ownership and control, or to nationalise an existing private business (or industry).

2 In some countries (e.g. France, Greece, Portugal) the state has traditionally played an important role in business and still controls some key sectors of the economy.

3 State involvement in business often includes significant shareholdings in a number of large enterprises, not only by the national government but also by regional and/or local government (e.g. in Germany).

4 State intervention often occurs in organisations or industries which can be deemed 'problematic' (e.g. in Greece).

5 Privatisation of state-owned enterprises has occurred throughout Europe and in other parts of the world. In the former East Germany, for example, most of the state-owned companies have been transferred to private ownership, by turning them initially into trusts which became the vehicle for privatisation and/or joint ventures. Similarly in Portugal, the wholesale nationalisation of the economy after the 1974 Revolution has been reversed and the government is committed to a phased programme of privatisation, involving employees and small investors as well as large national and international organisations (see also Chapter 17 for a further discussion).

This latter point serves to re-emphasise that the business environment is subject to change over time and the fashions of today may tomorrow become things of the past. This fluctuating environment is as applicable to the public sector as it is to the private sector of the economy.

Legal structure: some implications

For businesses in the private sector, the choice of legal structure has important implications. Among the factors which the aspiring entrepreneur has to take into account when deciding what form of business enterprise to establish are:

- the degree of personal liability;
- the willingness to share decision-making powers and risks;
- the costs of establishing the business;
- the legal requirements concerning the provision of public information;
- the taxation position;
- commercial needs, including access to capital; and
- business continuity.

For some, retaining personal control will be the main requirement, even at the risk of facing unlimited personal liability and reducing the opportunities for expansion. For others, the desire to limit personal liability and to provide increased capital for growth will dictate that the owner seeks corporate status, even if this necessitates sharing decision-making powers and may ultimately result in a loss of ownership and/or control of the enterprise.

This link between an organisation's legal structure and its subsequent operations can be illustrated by examining three important facets of organisational life: the organisation's objectives, its sources of finance and its stakeholders. As the analysis below illustrates, in each of these areas, significant differences occur between alternative forms of business organisation, both *within* the private sector and *between* the state and non-state sectors of the economy. In some cases, these differences can be attributed directly to the restraints (or opportunities) faced by an organisation as a result of its legal status, suggesting that the legal basis of the enterprise conditions its operations. In other cases operational considerations tend to dictate the organisation's legal form, indicating that these are as much a cause of its legal status as a result of it – a point well illustrated by the workers' co-operative and the public corporation.

Organisational objectives

All business organisations pursue a range of objectives and these may vary to some degree over time. New private sector businesses, for example, are likely to be concerned initially with survival and with establishing a position in the marketplace, with profitability and growth seen as less important in the short term. In contrast, most well-established businesses will tend to regard profits and growth as key objectives and may see them as a means towards further ends, including market domination, maximising sales revenue and/or minimising operating costs.

Organisational objectives are also conditioned by the firm's legal structure. In sole traders, partnerships and some limited companies, control of the enterprise rests in the hands of the entrepreneur(s) and hence organisational goals will tend to coincide with the personal goals of the owner(s), whatever the point in the organisation's life cycle. In public companies, however – where ownership tends to be separated from control – the goals of the owners (shareholders) may not always correspond with those of the directors and senior managers who run the organisation, particularly when the latter are pursuing personal goals to enhance their own organisational position, status and/or rewards.

It is worth noting that the possibility of goal conflict also occurs where an individual company becomes a subsidiary of another organisation, whether by agreement or as a result of a takeover battle. This parent–subsidiary relationship may take the form of a holding company which is specially created to purchase a majority (sometimes all) of the shares in other companies, some of which may operate as holding companies themselves. Thus, while the individual subsidiaries may retain their legal and commercial identities and may operate as individual units, they will tend to be controlled by a central organisation which may exercise a considerable degree of influence over the objectives to be pursued by each of its subsidiaries. It is not inconceivable, for example, that some parts of the group may be required to make a loss on paper, particularly when there are tax advantages to be gained by the group as a whole from doing so.

Workers' co-operatives and public corporations provide further evidence of the relationship between an organisation's legal status and its primary objectives. In the case of the former, the establishment of the enterprise invariably reflects a desire on the part of its members to create an organisation which emphasises social goals (e.g. democracy, co-operation, job creation, mutual trust) rather than the pursuit of profits – hence the choice of the 'co-operative' form. Similarly in the case of the public corporation, a decision by government to establish an entity which operates in the interests of the public at large (or 'national interest') favours the creation of a state-owned-and-controlled organisation, with goals laid down by politicians and generally couched in social and financial terms (e.g. return on assets, reinvestment, job creation) rather than in terms of profit maximisation.

This apparent dichotomy between the profit motive of the private sector and the broader socio-economic goals of public bodies has, however, become less clear-cut over the last decade, as an increasing number of state-owned organisations have been 'prepared' for privatisation and successive governments have sought to bring private money into public projects by creating public/private partnerships. Equally, in other parts of the public sector – including the health service and local government – increasing stress is being laid on 'best value' and on operating within budgets – concepts which are familiar to businesses in the private sector. While it is not inconceivable that a change in government could reverse this trend, current evidence suggests that a shift in cultural attitudes has occurred and public bodies can no longer rely on unconditional government support for their activities. If this is the case, further convergence is likely to occur between state and privately owned bodies, with the former moving towards the latter rather than vice versa.

Finance

Business organisations finance their activities in a variety of ways and from a range of sources. Methods include reinvesting profits, borrowing, trade credit and issuing shares and debentures. Sources include the banks and other financial institutions, individual investors and governments, as well as contributions from the organisation's original owners.

In the context of this chapter it is appropriate to make a number of observations about the topic as it relates generally to the business environment:

1 All organisations tend to fund their activities from both internal (e.g. owner's capital, reinvested profits) and external sources (e.g. bank borrowing, sale of shares).

2 Financing may be short term, medium term or longer term, and the methods and sources of funding chosen will reflect the time period concerned (e.g. bank borrowing on overdraft tends to be short term and generally needed for immediate use).

3 Funds raised from external sources inevitably involve the organisation in certain obligations (e.g. repayment of loans with interest, personal guarantees, paying dividends) and these will act as a constraint on the organisation at some future date.

4 The relationship between owner's capital and borrowed funds – usually described as an organisation's **gearing** – can influence a firm's activities and prospects in a variety of ways (e.g. high-geared firms with a large element of borrowed funds will be adversely affected if interest rates are high).

5 Generally speaking, as organisations become larger many more external sources and methods of funding become available and utilising these can have implications for the structure, ownership and conduct of the organisation.

This latter point is perhaps best illustrated by comparing sole traders and partnerships with limited companies. In the case of the former, as unincorporated entities neither the sole trader nor the partnership can issue shares (or debentures) and hence their access to large amounts of external capital is restricted by law. Companies have no such restrictions – other than those which help to differentiate a private company from a public one – and consequently they are able to raise larger amounts by inviting individuals (and organisations) to subscribe for shares. Where a company is publicly quoted on the stock market, the amounts raised in this way can be very large indeed and the resultant organisation may have millions of owners who change on a regular basis as shares are traded on the second-hand market.

Organisations which decide to acquire corporate status in order to raise funds for expansion (or for some other purposes) become owned by their shareholders, who may be the original owners or may be individual and institutional investors holding equity predominantly as an investment and with little, if any, long-term commitment to the organisation they own. As indicated above, in the latter case, a separation tends to occur between the roles of owner (shareholder) and controller (director) and this can lead to the possibility of conflicting aims and objectives or differences in opinion over priorities within the enterprise – a problem discussed in more detail below under 'Stakeholders'.

A further illustration of the relationship between an organisation's legal structure and its ability to raise finance is provided by the public corporation. In this case, as a public body accountable to Parliament and the public via government, the public corporation is normally required to operate within a financial context largely controlled by government and this will be conditioned by the government's overall fiscal policy, including its attitude to the size of the Public Sector Borrowing Requirement (PSBR). One aspect of this context in Britain has been the establishment of external financing limits (EFLs) for each nationalised industry, arrived at by negotiation between government and the board running the public corporation, and used as a means of restraining monetary growth and hence the size of the PSBR. Unfortunately this has also tended to prevent the more financially sound corporations, such as British Telecom before privatisation, from borrowing externally on a scale necessary to develop their business – a restriction which tends to disappear when the corporation becomes a fully fledged public company, either through privatisation or by some other means.

Stakeholders

All organisations have **stakeholders**; these are individuals and/or groups who are affected by or affect the performance of the organisation in which they have an interest. Typically they would include employees, managers, creditors, suppliers, shareholders (if appropriate) and society at large. As Table 10.1 illustrates, an organisation's stakeholders have a variety of interests which range from the pursuit of private gain to the more nebulous idea of achieving public benefit. Sometimes these interests will clash as, for example, when managers seek to improve the organisation's cash flow by refusing to pay suppliers' bills on time. On other occasions, the interests of different stakeholders may coincide, as when managers plan for growth in the organisation and in doing so provide greater job security for employees and enhanced dividends for investors.

Table 10.1 Organisational stakeholders and their interests

Types of stakeholder	Possible principal interests
Employees	Wage levels; working conditions; job security; personal development
Managers	Job security; status; personal power; organisational profitability; growth of the organisation
Shareholders	Market value of the investment; dividends; security of investment; liquidity of investment
Creditors	Security of loan; interest on loan; liquidity of investment
Suppliers	Security of contract; regular payment; growth of organisation; market development
Society	Safe products; environmental sensitivity; equal opportunities; avoidance of discrimination

The legal structure of an organisation has an impact not only on the type of stakeholders involved but also to a large degree on how their interests are represented. In sole traders, partnerships and smaller private companies, the coincidence of ownership and control limits the number of potential clashes of interest, given that objectives are set by and decisions taken by the firm's owner-manager(s). In larger companies, and, in particular, public limited companies, the division between ownership and control means that the controllers have the responsibility of representing the interests of the organisation's shareholders and creditors and, as suggested above, their priorities and goals may not always correspond.

A similar situation occurs in public sector organisations, where the interest of taxpayers (or ratepayers) is represented both by government and by those individuals chosen by government to run the organisation. In this case, it is worth recalling that the broader strategic objectives of the enterprise and the big decisions concerning policy, finance and investment tend to be taken by politicians, operating with advice from their officials (e.g. civil servants, local government officers) and within the context of the government's overall economic and social policies. The organisation's board of management and its senior executives and managers are mainly responsible for the day-to-day operations of the business, although the board and the person chairing it would normally play a key role in shaping overall objectives and decisions, through regular discussions with government and its officials.

One important way in which public sector organisations differ from their private sector counterparts is in the sanctions available to particular groups of stakeholders who feel that the organisation is not representing their best interests. Shareholders in a company, for example, could withdraw financial support for a firm whose directors consistently disregard their interests or take decisions which threaten the security and/or value of their investment, and the possibility of such a reaction normally guarantees that the board pays due attention to the needs of this important group of stakeholders. The taxpayer and ratepayer have no equivalent sanction and in the short term must rely heavily on government and its agencies or, if possible, their power as consumers to represent their interest *vis-à-vis* the organisation. Longer term, of course, the public has the sanction of the ballot box, although it seems highly unlikely that the performance of state enterprises would be a key factor in determining the outcome of general or local elections.

The relative absence of market sanctions facing state-owned organisations has meant that the public has had to rely on a range of formal institutions (e.g. parliamentary scrutiny committees, consumer consultative bodies, the audit authorities) and on the media to protect its interest in areas such as funding, pricing and quality of service provided. As these organisations are returned to the private sector, the expectation is that the sanctions imposed by the free market will once again operate and shareholders in privatised utilities will be protected like any other group of shareholders in a privately owned enterprise. To what extent this will occur in practice, of course, is open to question, while the newly privatised public corporations face little, if any, competition. Government, it seems, prefers to hedge its bets on this question, at least in the short term – hence the establishment of regulators with powers of investigation into performance and some degree of control over pricing.

mini case | Big Mac gets bigger and more selective

Growth through franchising has become a preferred option for many organisations, typified by McDonald's, which is the world's biggest fast food chain. Established in 1955 when Raymond Croc opened his first burger restaurant, McDonald's was estimated to have had in excess of 20 000 outlets spread across the globe by the end of 1996. Contrary to popular predictions, the organisation continued to expand at a significant rate and benefited from the opening of new markets in eastern Europe and the Far East. In the mid-1990s, for example, it was estimated that at its current rate of growth, a new McDonald's was opening somewhere in the world every three hours.

When considering applicants for a coveted McDonald's franchise the company has always been concerned to ensure that its reputation for quality and service is maintained. Potential franchisees have to demonstrate not only a successful track record in a previous occupation, but also that they have the necessary financial resources and a willingness to commit themselves to the organisation. Individuals making the grade have traditionally been offered two kinds of franchise scheme. The conventional franchise involves a 20-year agreement between the franchisee and the company under which the latter buys and develops the site which the former takes over and operates for an agreed price, as well as paying McDonald's a royalty fee based on a pre-agreed percentage of turnover. Under the other option – the business facilities lease – the individual leases the restaurant normally for a three-year period, prior to being offered the opportunity to convert to a conventional franchise if funds permit.

Like any business, McDonald's fortunes have fluctuated over time. In late October 2002 McDonald's announced its intention of sharply cutting back on its expansion plans and redirecting its efforts towards supporting its existing chain of restaurants (see the *Guardian,* 23 October 2002). By 2005, McDonald's claimed to have over 30 000 local restaurants serving nearly 50 million people each day in more than 119 countries. Adverse publicity, following the documentary *Super Size Me* appears to have led to a consumer backlash in recent years and the company has closed some stores, while opening new ones. McDonald's strategy is to undertake a programme of worldwide restructuring coupled with more careful targetting of the market. This includes getting the 'right restaurants' in the 'right places' and responding to local requirements (e.g. Kosher outlets in some Israeli branches of McDonald's).

web link The website for McDonald's is *www.mcdonalds.com*

Franchising, licensing and joint ventures

To complete this review of the legal structure of business organisations, it is useful to consider three developments which have a legal aspect: franchising, licensing and joint ventures. All three may be seen as a means of carrying out a business venture in a way that reduces some of the risks normally faced by the entrepreneur.

Franchising

Franchising, which has grown significantly in recent years, is an arrangement where one party (the franchiser) sells the right to another party (the franchisee) to market its product or service. In terms of their legal status the parties involved could be any of the forms described above, but in practice it is usually the case that the franchiser is a company while the franchisee tends to be a sole trader or partnership. Both parties in law have a separate legal identity, but the nature of the contract between them makes their relationship interdependent and this has important implications for the operation of the franchise.

Franchise arrangements come in a variety of forms. Probably the best known is the 'business format franchise' (or 'trade name franchise') under which the franchiser agrees to allow the franchisee to sell the product or service with the help of a franchise package which contains all the elements needed to set up and run a business at a profit. These would typically include the brand name, any associated supplies, promotional material and other forms of support and assistance. In return the franchisee usually pays an initial sum or fee for the use of the service and its various elements, remits royalties based on sales and/or profits, agrees to make a contribution for consultancy, training and promotion, and undertakes to maintain standards. Wimpy, Kentucky Fried Chicken, Burger King, Prontaprint and Dynarod are examples of this type of franchise.

Other forms include manufacturer/retailer franchises (e.g. car dealers), manufacturer/wholesaler franchises (e.g. Coca-Cola, Pepsi) and wholesaler/retailer franchises (e.g. Spar and Mace) and it is estimated by the industry's trade body – the British Franchise Association – that in retailing alone franchising accounts for over 20 per cent of sales in the United Kingdom. One indication of its growing significance is the spread of franchising into further and higher education, with universities and other colleges of higher education franchising some of their courses to local further education colleges, which in turn may franchise some of their courses to schools and/or sixth-form colleges. Another indicator is the decision by many clearing banks and firms of accountants to establish franchise sections to help and advise individuals who want to open a franchise or who have already done so and are seeking further guidance.

 The British Franchise Association's main website is *www.thebfa.org*

Undoubtedly the mutual benefits to be derived from a franchise arrangement help to explain its popularity as a way of doing business in both domestic and external markets and it has proved an attractive vehicle for some companies seeking rapid overseas expansion, without undertaking substantial direct investments – although this is sometimes necessary to support the operation (e.g. McDonald's had to invest in a plant to make hamburger buns in the United Kingdom). Equally, many would-be entrepreneurs find the security of a franchise more attractive than other methods of starting a business, especially as there is some evidence to suggest that franchises have better survival rates than the more conventional forms of independent enterprise (e.g. sole traders).

Current indications are that this popularity is likely to continue into the foreseeable future, although it is more likely that greater selectivity of potential franchisees will occur as the franchise industry becomes more mature and attempts to gain an increased degree of public respectability. Franchisees, too, are likely to become more particular about the businesses they agree to deal with, as they endeavour to join the enterprise culture. It is, after all, the franchisee who has to bear the financial risk of the business in return for a share in the profits; the franchiser has a reputation to think about.

Licensing

Licensing is another form of non-equity agreement under which a firm in one country (the licensor) authorises a firm in another country (the licensee) to use its intellectual property (e.g. patents, copyrights, trade names, know-how) in return for certain considerations, usually royalty payments. Licences may be granted to individuals, independent companies, subsidiaries of a multinational company or to government agencies and the rights granted may be exclusive or non-exclusive.

Companies invariably enter into licensing agreements to gain certain advantages. These might include:

- Reducing competition by sharing technology.
- Seeking overseas profits without direct foreign investment.
- Protecting an asset from potential 'pirates'.
- Avoiding restrictions on foreign investment or imports imposed by other countries.
- Recouping some research and development costs.
- Gaining a share of an overseas market.

Needless to say, most organisations granting licences tend to be based in the advanced industrial economies and are frequently multinationals which regard their trade marks and technologies as an integral part of their asset base. One problem of transferring the use of such assets to another firm is that the owner loses a degree of control over the asset, including the quality of production, and this may affect the product's image and sales elsewhere. Another is the possibility of the licensee dominating the market after the agreement ends, even to the extent of excluding the licensor from the marketplace by aggressive competition or the development of an alternative product.

Joint ventures

The term **joint venture** tends to be used in two ways: to describe a contractual agreement involving two or more parties, or to describe a jointly owned and independently incorporated business venture involving more than one organisation. It is the latter usage which is mainly applied here.

Joint ventures – which are popular with international companies – can take a variety of legal forms and almost every conceivable type of partnership may exist, ranging from two companies joining together in the same domestic market (e.g. Sainsbury's and British Home Stores set up the Savacentre chain), to joint private/public sector ventures between participants from different countries. Sometimes numerous organisations may be involved and these may be based in one country or in several. Where this occurs the term **consortium** is often used, as in the case of TransManche Link (TML), the international joint venture which built the Channel Tunnel.

As with licensing and franchising, joint ventures have increased in popularity in the last 25–30 years and have been one of the ways in which international companies have sought to develop an overseas market, particularly in the face of import restrictions, or heavy research and development costs. Multinational car companies have been active in this field – as evidenced by past links between General Motors and Toyota, Ford and Mazda – and these arrangements look likely to continue as markets become more global. For western companies wishing to exploit the gradual privatisation of the former planned economies of eastern Europe, joint ventures with indigenous producers are likely to prove a safer bet than direct inward investment, particularly given the degree of economic and political uncertainty. They are also likely to prove more politically acceptable in states seeking to establish their own economic independence and identity after almost 50 years of regional domination.

Synopsis

Market-based economies throughout Europe and beyond have a range of business organisations with broadly similar legal structures. These legal structures help to determine not only the ownership and control of the enterprise, but also other aspects of its operations, including its objectives, its access to finance and its external relationships and obligations. Viewing businesses as legal entities provides a useful insight into a number of the external influences which impinge upon their daily existence and highlights some of the consequences faced by organisations which transfer from public (i.e. state) to private ownership. It also sheds light on other important developments in entrepreneurial activity, including franchising, licensing and joint ventures.

Summary of key points

- Business organisations have a legal structure.

- The three commonest forms of business in the private sector are sole traders, partnerships and limited companies.

- Whereas the owners of the first two types of business organisation face unlimited personal liability, in companies the legal separation of the firm from its owners affords the latter limited personal liability.

- Companies are normally run by directors who are appointed to represent the interest of the owners (the shareholders). In public companies this separation of ownership and control is a key distinguishing feature.

- Other forms of business organisation exist in the public sector (e.g. the public corporation) and the 'third sector' (e.g. the co-operative).

- Government-owned businesses are increasingly adopting private sector forms of organisation to provide for greater flexibility and freedom of action.

- The legal status of the organisation has implications for the objectives of the enterprise, how it is financed and for its stakeholder relationships.

case study The entrepreneurial spirit

Business studies textbooks teach us that new businesses invariably come into existence to satisfy the needs and ambitions of their owners. Once established, it is assumed that an enterprise will begin to grow and that the owner(s) will sanction this and take steps to bring it about. As the two case studies below illustrate, these assumptions may be correct or not, according to specific circumstances. Arguing from the particular to the general needs to be approached with caution in business, as in any other field of study.

T & S Stores PLC

Like many medium- to large-sized businesses, T & S Stores started from relatively modest origins and was the brainchild of one individual, Kevin Threlfall, a Wolverhampton entrepreneur.

A barrow boy by background, Threlfall received his early business training working from the age of 12 on his parents' pitch in West Midlands markets.

Despatched to public school, Threlfall soon found this market background was treated contemptuously by his fellow pupils and this made him determined to prove his worth in the business world. On leaving school he began providing pet-foods in bulk, before selling out his business and founding the Lo Cost food chain in 1972. This was subsequently bought for £1.5 million by Oriel Foods, later owned by the Argyll Group.

Threlfall's T & S Stores grew from the Wolverhampton market stalls and quickly expanded into retail outlets, with their emphasis on discount tobacco and convenience shopping. Using day-glo starbursts offering low-priced cigarettes, Threlfall cleverly attracted customers into his stores where they were tempted by the use of colourful confectionery gondolas and other techniques into impulse purchases of products carrying high margins. By keeping costs to a minimum, Threlfall was able to turn his company into a highly profitable enterprise with a stock market capitalisation of almost £140 million by 1991 and a chain of almost 600 stores.

In 1989, T & S acquired the Dillons and Preedy chains from Next for £54 million and subsequently purchased 22 stores from Johnson News Group for £4.25 million in February 1991, thus helping to increase the organisation's interest in convenience stores, which Threlfall believed would be the company's main area of future growth. Trading from outlets larger than most of the T & S shops and offering an extended range of grocery and frozen-food lines, Threlfall's One Stop convenience stores generally achieved higher gross margins than the core tobacco shops and helped to contribute to the company's strong net cash position in the early 1990s. Despite these developments, Threlfall maintained close contacts with what was happening on the ground and attempted to maintain a degree of individual customer attention in a field of retailing which is rapidly changing.

Threlfall's entrepreneurial skills, coupled with the gains from introducing National Lottery and other facilities in many of the group's outlets, continued to strengthen the organisation's financial and trading position. With hundreds of stores and increasing turnover and pre-tax profits, T & S attracted outside investment from reputable fund managers who expressed confidence in the management's strategy of refocusing the business towards the growing convenience store market. Turnover by 2001 was recorded at £933 million; in 1995 it had been £445 million.

T & S was subsequently acquired by Tesco in January 2003 and now trades under the One Stop brand, with some stores being converted to the Tesco Express format. An Office of Fair Trading investigation into the acquisition concluded that the purchase of T&S by Tesco did not lead to any significant lessening of competition.

Dave Noble (Windsurfing)

Unlike Kevin Threlfall, Dave Noble came from a non-business background and had no ambitions as a child to seek a career in industry or commerce. Following A-levels at the local grammar school in Woking, Noble went to Aberystwyth University where he obtained a degree in philosophy, before continuing his studies at postgraduate level. After a brief spell doing research, he left university and worked on building sites, subsequently returning to study for a postgraduate certificate of education, a move which was to take him into teaching in Loughborough.

With the start of a family, Noble gave up his full-time teaching post to look after the children, continuing as a supply teacher as and when circumstances allowed. As a keen windsurfer, with an established reputation in the sport, he decided to use some of his time at home to make his own boards, buying the necessary fittings from suppliers to the trade. As requests from friends for similar equipment began to grow, Noble found himself dealing with suppliers on a larger scale and spending an increasing amount of his time making and equipping windsurfing boards. Before he had fully realised what was happening, Noble found himself in business as a sole trader, operating in the leisure industry, a growing sector in the UK economy.

With an initial injection of his own capital, supported by a weekly income from the government's Enterprise Allowance Scheme, Noble established his own venture in late 1986/early 1987, operating from home in Shepshed in Leicestershire. Despite only limited expenditure on advertising, the business began to grow quickly, allowing the venture to become totally self-financing. Before long, it became obvious that new premises would be needed and so in 1989 the Noble family (now five in total) moved to a Georgian house in the village of Wymeswold on the Leicestershire/Nottinghamshire border. Apart from providing adequate space for a growing family, the new house had numerous outbuildings suitable for making and selling equipment and for storing supplies and material. It was also sufficiently close to Shepshed to allow Noble to keep his existing customer and supplier bases which were fundamental to the success of the business.

Noble's initial enthusiasm at working from his village home – in a manner reminiscent of a traditional cottage industry – was soon to be dampened following complaints from neighbours who objected to the traffic from customers seeking boards and other equipment. Consequently, the business was forced to relocate to the nearby Wymeswold Airfield Industrial Estate, where Noble acquired two units from which to operate. Like other units on the estate, Noble's premises were relatively basic, but provided sufficient space for production, storage and sales and had more than adequate parking for customers and suppliers. Being in a rural location, with no houses in the immediate vicinity, complaints concerning disturbance ceased to be a problem for the business.

▶

Despite the successive moves, Noble's business continued to grow, even in the recession years in the early 1990s. Part of this growth was manifestly attributable to the increased demand for leisure products, and the decision to add mountain bikes and ski equipment to the range of items on offer was clearly beneficial, although by no means part of a deliberate strategy of diversification. The most significant factor in the firm's success, however, and one which resulted in the need to hire additional staff to meet the increased demand, appears to have been Noble's deliberate policy of keeping customers and suppliers happy. By paying all his bills on time, Noble was able to strike good bargains with suppliers and to pass savings on to the customer in the form of highly competitive prices which other traders could not meet. In addition, Noble and his staff did their best to meet their customers' needs individually, even if it meant working extra hours and incurring some additional expense.

By the mid-1990s Dave Noble (Windsurfing) had become a formidable operator in the marketplace, with a dominant share of the market in the East Midlands and a loyal and extensive customer base. As the firm continued to prosper, Noble eventually planned to sell his business to the staff and to go into semi-retirement. He has, however, maintained an interest in the leisure industry, importing snowboards which he sells to the trade via mail order. He has recently taken back control of parts of the main business as the anticipated sale did not materialise and this is now being run by two of his sons.

Case study questions

1 What characteristics have Threlfall and Noble in common which might help to explain their success as entrepreneurs?

2 Can you identify any changes in the external environment of either of the businesses in the case study which proved beneficial to their development?

 web link You can find information on this and other companies at *www.hoovers.com*

Review and discussion questions

1 Numerically, the sole proprietorship is the most popular form of business organisation throughout Europe. How would you account for this?

2 To what extent is corporate status an asset to a business organisation? Does it have any disadvantages?

3 Examine the implications of privatising a public sector business organisation.

4 Discuss how the legal status of a business affects its objectives, its methods of finance and its stakeholders.

5 How would you explain the rise in the popularity of franchising in recent years?

Assignments

1 You have recently been made redundant and decide to set up your own small business, possibly with a friend. Assuming that you have £25 000 to invest in your new venture, draft a business plan which is to be presented to your bank manager in the hope of gaining financial support. Your plan should include a clear rationale for the legal form you wish your business to take, your chosen product(s) or service(s), evidence of market research, an indication of anticipated competition and supporting financial information.

2 You work in a local authority business advice centre. One of your clients wishes to start a business in some aspect of catering. Advise your client on the advantages and disadvantages of the various legal forms the proposed enterprise could take.

Notes and references

1 Liability may be extended where a company continues trading after insolvency.

2 It is also possible to have unlimited companies.

3 Under regulations issued in 1992 it is possible to have single member private companies with limited liability status, but these are the exception rather than the general rule.

4 A similar growth occurred in the number of 'community businesses' in Scotland during this period. Though not strictly 'co-operatives', they are also part of the so-called third sector of business.

Further reading

Campbell, D. J. and Craig, T., *Organizations and the Business Environment*, Butterworth-Heinemann, 2005.

Morrison, J., *The International Business Environment*, 2nd edition, Macmillan, 2006.

Palmer, A. J. and Hartley, R., *The Business Environment*, 5th edition, McGraw-Hill, 2005.

Worthington, I., Britton, C. and Rees, A., *Economics for Business: Blending Theory and Practice*, 2nd edition, Financial Times/Prentice Hall, 2005.

Web links and further questions are available on the website at:
www.pearsoned.co.uk/worthington

PART TEN

The Technological Environment: E-Business

Chapter 21

The Technological Environment: E-Business

The technological environment: e-business

Martyn Kendrick

Thus far the development of Internet technology and the emergence of electronic marketplaces and electronic networks have complemented rather than simply replaced existing industry value systems and market structures. That said, technology is starting to revolutionise the way that some businesses operate, and we are seeing new business models emerge. Undoubtedly the emergence of e-business will have a significant global economic impact over the next 10–20 years.

Learning outcomes

Having read this chapter you should be able to:

- identify, describe and define e-business and its sub-categories
- explain emerging business models, such as business-to-business (B2B) and business-to-consumer (B2C)
- highlight the key theoretical benefits, opportunities and limitations of e-business with respect to businesses, consumers and society
- illustrate the impact of technology on industry value systems and market structures

Key terms

Business-to-business (B2B) commerce
Business-to-consumer (B2C) commerce
Buy-side marketplace
Demand chain management (DCM)
Electronic business (e-business)
Electronic commerce (e-commerce)
Electronic customer relationship management (eCRM)

Electronic data interchange (EDI)
Electronic fund transfer (EFT)
Electronic markets (e-markets)
Electronic point-of-sale (EPOS)
Extranet
First-mover advantage
Internet
Intranet
Knowledge management system

Mass customisation
One-to-one database marketing
Sell-side marketplace
Smart cards
Supply chain management (SCM)
Value system

Introduction

We are on the verge of a revolution that is just as profound as the change in the economy that came with the industrial revolution. Soon electronic networks will allow people to transcend the barriers of time and distance and take advantage of global markets and business opportunities not even imaginable today, opening up a new world of economic possibility and progress. (US Vice-President, Al Gore Jnr, July 1998)

This is undoubtedly an exciting time to be considering developments in the technological environment, with the emergence of new business terms and concepts such as electronic markets (e-markets), electronic business (e-business) and electronic commerce (e-commerce). In the so-called 'new economy' digital networking and communication infrastructures provide a global platform through which enterprises and people interact, collaborate, communicate and search for information.

The potential growth for electronic business worldwide is impressive. A wealth of complementary digital technologies, including digital communications networks (Internet, intranets, extranets), computer hardware and software, and other related networks, databases and information systems, distribution and supply chains, knowledge management and procurement are being merged into a powerful combination for business change using the World Wide Web (WWW) as the driving force. Starting more or less from zero in 1995, e-commerce has recently celebrated its tenth anniversary, and for many of us it is difficult to remember the pre-Internet business environment. In the US, it is estimated that the 200 million Americans with access to the web will soon be spending more than $145 billion annually online, equivalent to 7 per cent of all US retail sales. Similarly, in western Europe, a quarter of all Europeans do some shopping via the Internet. Globally, e-business has grown from $26 billion in 1997 to an estimated $1 trillion by 2005.[1] Predicting the future growth of e-business is fraught with difficulty, but given that it has the potential to deliver a low-cost, universal, interactive and global medium that provides a simple and secure method for exchanging information instantaneously, the business case appears compelling.

In addition, we might speculate that an Internet-based society will also notice a dramatic change to other aspects of people's lives, outside of the workplace. For instance, changes such as new distance-learning methods and material are starting to emerge in education and many other areas of daily life are increasingly being affected by technological developments.

However, we should also remember that while terms such as e-business and e-commerce are relatively new, they are part of an evolutionary technology process dating back over 30 years. The concept of e-business has actually emerged from a fusion of various separate technologies, such as **electronic data interchange (EDI)**, **electronic fund transfer (EFT)**, **electronic point-of-sale (EPOS)** and **smart cards** that had previously struggled in isolation to achieve mass acceptance.

Indeed, the terms 'electronic business' and 'electronic commerce' have no universally accepted definitions, and confusingly are often used interchangeably. However, for our purposes there is a significant difference between the two terms.

Broadly, **e-business** means doing any element of business over the Internet, and embraces activities such as servicing customers and collaborating with partners, in addition to buying goods, services and information. E-business can be formally defined

Figure 16.1   The value system

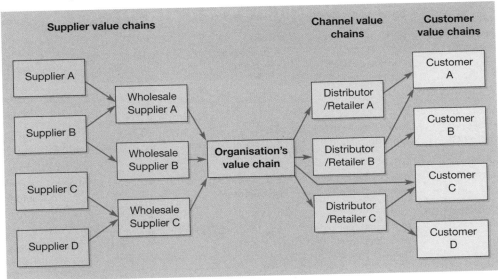

as the exchange of products, services or information, whether paid or unpaid, across electronic networks, at any stage within the **value system**, including the supply chain, the value chain and the distribution chain (see Figure 16.1). There are a number of potential sub-sets within the general term 'e-business'.

E-commerce covers a narrower sphere of activities than e-business, and refers in particular to the process of electronic transactions involved in the exchange of products, services and information between buyer and seller. The activities of e-retailers such as Amazon would fall under this category.

 You can access Amazon at *www.amazon.com*

Within an organisation, there are several activities (for example, information and knowledge management, resource co-ordination etc.) that might be more effectively achieved through use of an intranet. Table 16.1 provides a common classification of e-business by nature of transaction. For the purposes of analysis, business organisations have been sub-divided into private sector (B), public sector (G) and third sector (T) organisations. There is also a column for consumers (C).

It can be seen from Table 16.1 that e-business encompasses a wide spectrum of potential external commercial and information exchanges and applications. However, the classifications business-to-business (B2B) and business-to-consumer (B2C) represent the core of electronic commerce and these are the areas that have received the most interest and development to date. These classifications are now considered below in some detail.

	Business sector (B)	Public sector (G)	Third sector (T)	Consumers (C)
Business sector (B)	(B2B) e.g. electronic commerce (Dell), business marketplaces	(B2G) e.g. procurement partnering	(B2T) e.g. procurement partnering	(B2C) e.g. electronic commerce (Dell, Amazon), consumer marketplaces (Shopsmart.com)
Public sector (G)	(G2B) e.g. information	(G2G) e.g. co-ordination	(G2T) e.g. information	(G2C) e.g. information
Third sector (T)	(T2B) e.g. partnering procurement	(T2G) e.g. partnering procurement	(T2T) e.g. co-ordination	(T2C) e.g. services information
Consumers (C)	(C2B) e.g. consumer bids (Priceline.com)	(C2G) e.g. tax compliance	(C2T) e.g. Information	(C2C) e.g. auction models (eBay, QXL), consumer reviews (Deja.com)

Table 16.1   Broad spectrum of e-business applications

Source: Adapted from OECD, 2000

Business applications 1: business-to-business (B2B) commerce

Features of B2B

Business-to-business (B2B) transactions account for, in terms of value, about 80 per cent of all Internet transactions. Both the buyer and seller are business organisations. The technological and legal aspects of B2B commerce tend to be more complex than business-to-consumer (B2C) commerce, and it often requires sophisticated software. It can be arranged through either inter-organisational systems (IOS) or electronic markets.

B2B commerce is characterised by a number of key features, many of which differentiate it from B2C commerce. Turban and colleagues[2] suggest that the following are some of its salient aspects:

- an automated trading process;
- high volumes of goods traded;
- high net value of goods traded;
- multiple forms of electronic payment and funds transfer are permitted, unlike B2C commerce, which tends to be restricted to credit cards and smart cards;
- high level of information exchange, including shared databases, between the different trading partners. This often involves the use of extranets;
- prior agreements or contracts between the business partners requiring a higher level of documentation;
- different types of legal and taxation regimes depending on where the two parties are based, and what type of goods or services are the subject of the transaction;

- multiple levels of authorisation of purchases, each level having its own limits on expenditure or types of goods.

Benefits of B2B

On examination there appear to be a number of potential benefits and drivers of B2B commerce. The first of these is that it encourages the adoption of an Internet electronic data interchange (EDI) system to improve the efficiency of business processes. The DTI describes EDI as 'the computer-to-computer exchange of structured data, sent in a form that allows for automatic processing with no manual intervention. This is usually carried out over specialist EDI networks'.[3]

Using EDI to streamline business processes has a number of discernible benefits. These would include the following:

- A safe, secure and verifiable electronic environment that allows manufacturers or retailers to link their stock databases directly to suppliers. This reduces lead times by reducing the time taken in placing and receiving orders.
- Lower costs in creating, processing, distributing, storing, retrieving and destroying paper-based information; fewer errors in data entry; improved inventory control, and reduced staff time involved in the process.
- Improved warehouse logistics, and improved co-ordination for moving goods to the appropriate place, at the defined time and in the correct quantities.
- Better and more efficient integration of support functions such as human resources, inventory control, order processing, accounting and payment processing.
- More efficient strategic alliances and partnering with suppliers, customers and competitors. For instance, in the motor industry, leading firms such as General Motors, Ford and Chrysler have set up a joint extranet with suppliers.

It should be recognised that EDI has been around since the 1960s, but before the development of an integrated Internet EDI system, it was seen to have some serious shortcomings that undermined the potential benefits. Two in particular are worth noting:

- It required an expensive private dedicated network connection between two established trading partners. According to Forrester Research (*www.forrester.research.com*) only 100 000 of the 2 million companies in the USA employing 10 or more employees chose to deploy traditional EDI. The rest felt that it was too expensive, was not interactive enough, and did not enable them to access or negotiate with their suppliers and other partners.
- The lack of agreed international standards for document formats meant that early EDI was based on proprietary technologies such as value added networks (VANs). Each EDI tended to be set up specifically for a single buyer and supplier, and consequently became heavily embedded deep within the organisation's IT systems. This served to inhibit change within the organisation, making it difficult and expensive to change suppliers because of the difficulties of switching the existing system to a new supplier. It also meant that where a firm was multisourcing, a separate EDI might be needed for each supplier.

However, Internet-based EDI overcomes most of these shortcomings. Rather than using proprietary technology (VANs) it makes use of the public **Internet**. Therefore, Internet EDI, unlike traditional EDI, is ubiquitous, global, cheap, easy to use, and readily available and accessible both within (**intranet**) and outside (**extranet**) the company.

In addition, Internet EDI standards are becoming increasingly compatible with eXtensible Mark-up Language (XML). XML is already the key international standard for transferring structured data, and has wide acceptance, having been championed by organisations such as Microsoft, Netscape and Sun Microsystems, as well as by the WorldWideWeb consortium. The widespread adoption of XML means that most companies are now able to use Internet-based EDI to exchange documents cheaply and quickly. The International Data Corporation (IDC) reported that Internet EDI's share of EDI revenues has risen from 12 per cent to 41 per cent over the period 1999–2003, with this trend likely to continue into the future.[4]

A further potential benefit and driver of B2B commerce is that it provides for expansion from a local or national market to a global **electronic market (e-market)**. For a relatively minimal capital outlay, a business can access a wider range of (better and/or cheaper) suppliers, and contact a larger potential customer base.

B2B activities vary from firm to firm, and industry to industry, but as well as global electronic markets, where many buyers and sellers meet for the purposes of trading electronically together, other common types of markets include a **sell-side marketplace** (where one company does all the selling), and a **buy-side marketplace** (where one company does all the buying).

Other benefits and drivers of B2B commerce include the following:

● That it provides an opportunity to market, sell and distribute goods and services to other businesses for 24 hours a day, 365 days a year, the so-called 'martini effect'.
● That it can sometimes significantly reduce fixed costs, perhaps through savings on premises, where a website has effectively become the organisation's showroom.
● That it also has the potential to improve pull-type supply chain management, such as JIT manufacture and delivery, based on integrated and fully-automatic **supply chain management (SCM)** and **demand chain management (DCM)** systems.
● That it can encourage organisations to adopt a more customer-centric approach, in which the business tracks consumers' preferences and re-engineers itself quickly to meet consumer needs. This might involve developing a **mass customisation** business model such as that adopted by Dell Computers, and discussed in the case study below.
● That it can facilitate the development of an integrated **electronic customer relationship management (eCRM)** system, based on customer information gathering, data warehousing and other market intelligence.
● That it may improve **knowledge management systems** within the organisation as employees use the company intranet system to access organisation-wide know-how.

Many of these potential advantages of B2B can be illustrated by looking at the following case study, based on Dell Computers. To facilitate your understanding of the issues discussed in the text an extended case study has been used in this chapter rather than two mini cases and there are additional questions at the end of the case study which you might like to attempt.

web link   The web address for Dell computers is *www.dell.com*

Dell Computers

Dell Computers was developed in the early 1980s by Michael Dell; by 1990 Dell was assembling its own brand personal computers and sales were over $500 million, with an established reputation for both laptops and desktop computers. Sales efforts were focused on selling directly to business customers, including educational and government agencies.

In the early 1990s Michael Dell developed a small team to explore using the Internet as a way of communicating with customers, and selling products on-line. This team increasingly became convinced that the Internet was an ideal channel for Dell products. There were a number of reasons for this:

- The number of Internet users was 20 million in 1996, and this was expected to double every year.
- Dell's major customers – business users – were already involved in the Internet, both in their use of the Internet, and the development of intranets.

Dell Computer launched its on-line website in July 1996, selling computers direct to customers. Company sales at this point had reached $7.8 billion, with an operating income in excess of $710 million. After six months Internet sales had reached about $1 million per day, and by autumn 1999, Internet sales accounted for 27 per cent of total revenue, at $15 million per day.

Dell is now the world's number one PC maker, having overtaken Compaq in July 2001, with a 13 per cent share of the market, and in the near future expects to see 50 per cent of its revenue come from Internet selling. So what are the critical success factors behind Dell's use of the Internet to grow its business, and why have rivals struggled to copy its business model?

First, Dell now sells all the items it produces via the Internet: desktops, workstations, notebooks, network servers and storage devices, software, and add-ons (e.g., zip drive, printer, etc.). These items are also sold by telephone, fax and mail, with an additional call centre service that can complement the Internet home page. Service, support and an introduction to the company are also presented on the home page.

Second, Dell has achieved high price competitiveness, because its business model centres on having the lowest costs in the industry. For instance, its sales representatives need fewer calls to close a sale generated from an Internet lead, and achieve higher sales than the industry average. Furthermore, order processing via the Internet is more efficient. Each quarter Dell receives 200 000 visits to its website to check order status, 500 000 technical service visits and 400 000 library downloads. Each of these transactions would have cost between $5 and $15 in time if handled over the telephone. In addition, technical manuals are available on-line, instead of Dell having to print these out and mail them.

Third, Dell was the first Web-based computer seller, and already had significant experience in direct marketing. Some commentators suggest that this has given it a significant **first-mover advantage** over its rivals.

Fourth, Dell is a relatively young company, which was built on a business model based on direct telemarketing, so there was no need for Dell to change its business strategy to adopt Internet commerce. The Internet is simply another medium for contacting distant customers interactively. However, for other rival companies this was not the case. For them, changing business strategy fundamentally was difficult, expensive and time-consuming. Dell is also predominantly a one-product company, unlike many others in the electronics and computer industry.

Fifth, Dell has readily invested in the most advanced technology available, to provide a fully integrated value network, linking end consumers all the way back through the supply chain. In 1999, Dell invested in i2 Technologies software. The software enables it to monitor practically every part, every day. Dell also uses the Web thoroughly and creatively. Dell allows business buyers to download Premier Pages, enabling customers to configure what information their employees can see, and even which employees can see it.

Sixth, Dell has pioneered the concept of **mass customisation**, with its adaptive build-to-order fashion manufacturing system. To keep the price competitive without longer delivery time, efficient procurement of small numbers of parts from vendors, flexible manufacturing systems, and economical distribution to customers are essential. Dell computers can be assembled to order in about four minutes, with a further 90 minutes needed to load the software. They are delivered, on average, within three days of order.

Seventh, Dell uses the Internet effectively to manage and enhance its relationships with its suppliers, as well as with its customers. It has a fully integrated supply chain management system, and consequently Dell has relatively few suppliers, fewer than 200 in total. Many of its main rivals have at least 2000 suppliers.

Eighth, Dell's direct relationship with all of its customers makes **one-to-one database marketing** more effective. Dell learns about its customers by monitoring how they use the website, and is able to identify new market trends through analysing changes it notes in new build-to-order specifications over time.

Ninth, Dell provides global reach and value-added services as a single contact point. It currently sells computers in more than 170 countries. Dell has more than 10 000 service providers around the world who provide technology planning and acquisition, system deployment, network and product maintenance. The Internet can provide an efficient single point of contact for these services backed by corporate-level accountability for their products and services. The Internet makes it easier and reduces costs for customers to do business with Dell. Because the customers spend their own time to obtain service from the Internet, which previously required human agents in the call centre, the Internet has also reduced Dell's cost.

Finally, Dell has worked hard to establish a high reputation for quality and reliability. For instance, Dell products such as OptiPlex and Dell Dimension Desktop computer have picked up over 174 industry awards for performance, reliability and service. Internet customers in particular will hesitate to order expensive and complicated items without a trial, unless they are satisfied by the prior reputation of the company concerned.

Case study questions

1 Identify all the key elements of Dell's successful business model. Using a rating scale of 1–5 for each element identified (where 1 denotes the most important factor), summarise these into a single table.

2 Critically examine the four most important (highest rated) elements that you believe explain Dell's success. Explain your rationale for selecting those particular factors.

3 In your opinion, to what extent are other businesses (not just in the computer industry, but in any sector of the economy) able to successfully replicate Dell's business model? Illustrate your answer with appropriate examples.

4 Draw up a list of potential 'opportunities' and 'threats' facing Dell over the next 5 years.

Potential problems and limitations of B2B

As we have illustrated, there are a number of significant advantages to the widespread adoption of B2B commerce. However, it should be noted that there are also some potential limitations or barriers that may serve to delay or hamper the growth in B2B commerce. These include:

- Internet technology is continually developing, encouraging some organisations to postpone investment in the short term;
- technical limitations such as lack of system security, reliability and protocols – there are also currently some problems with telecommunications bandwidth and speed;
- the cost and difficulty of integrating existing (legacy) IT applications and databases with Internet and related software;
- the slow progress made in achieving universal international standards for the electronic transfer of information documentation;
- many legal, taxation and regulatory issues remain unresolved.

Even successful companies such as Dell face challenges as the e-business market matures. In August 2005, Dell announced a slowdown on quarterly sales to 14.7 per cent, and saw its share price immediately fall by nearly 10 per cent as investors worried that it was running out of opportunities for further growth and was starting to face increasing competition from low-cost rivals such as the Asian company Lenovo, the Chinese manufacturer that recently acquired IBM.

Nevertheless, on balance the clear benefits of B2B commerce are likely to outweigh the disadvantages, and we should expect to see continued dynamic growth in this area for some years to come.

Business applications 2: business-to-consumer (B2C) commerce

Key features

The **business-to-consumer (B2C)** model was the first to mature on the Internet, and has generated the most publicity. It involves a simple, singular retailing transaction between a business and a consumer. About one-fifth of e-business is between businesses and consumers. One example of the successful development and use of a B2C business model is by the e-retailer Amazon.com, which we will look at in more detail later.

It has been estimated that retail sales over the Internet in the UK totalled £39.5 billion in 2004, while wider forms of IT sales, such as email, electronic data exchange and automated phone sales, accounted for £195.6 billion, which is equivalent to one-fifth of the UK economy.

B2C commerce can be characterised by a number of key features, including:

- Goods or services are offered for sale and purchased over the Internet; these may include both *digitised* products, such as music, airline tickets or computer software that can be delivered *virtually* direct on the Internet, or physical products such as books, flowers and groceries that are delivered by post or courier. Currently in the UK, two-thirds of Internet sales are in physical products rather than digitised products.
- Transactions are typically quick and interactive.
- There are no pre-established business agreements.
- Security is primarily an issue for the buyer, rather than the seller.
- Low volume between each individual purchaser and supplier, often for relatively inexpensive items and/or frequently purchased items such as groceries.
- Well known packaged items, which have standard specifications.
- Items backed by a security guarantee and/or high brand recognition. The remoteness from the customer means that a strong reputation may be required to establish consumer confidence.
- Items whose operating procedures can be most effectively demonstrated by animation or video.
- Well designed websites, which are attractive and easy to use, are essential.

Emerging B2C and e-retailing business models

There are a number of ways of classifying the various B2C business models that are emerging:

- Direct marketing product websites – where manufacturers advertise and distribute their own products to customers via Internet-based stores, bypassing the use of intermediaries. Examples include Dell Computers, Nike, Cisco, The Gap and Sony.
- Pure electronic retailers (e-retailers) that have no physical stores, being purely cyber-based, such as Amazon.com.
- Traditional retailers with websites – sometimes called brick-and-click organisations – where the Internet provides an additional distribution channel for an existing business. Examples include Wal-Mart, Tesco and Barnes & Noble.
- Best price searching agents – intermediaries, such as BestBuyBooks.com and Buy.com, that use software to search for the lowest prices available on the Net.
- Buyer sets the price – the customer nominates a price which they are willing to pay for certain goods or services, and the intermediary then tries to find a seller willing to sell at that price or lower. An example is Priceline.com.
- Electronic (on-line) auctions – host sites, such as eBay, act like brokers, offering website services where sellers post their goods for sale, thereby allowing buyers to bid on those items.

Data suggests that the main users of e-commerce are across the manufacturing, retail and travel sectors.

Benefits of B2C commerce

There are a number of potential benefits and drivers of B2C commerce. Some of the more important are as follows:

1 For existing business organisations, many of the benefits are similar to B2B commerce, in that B2C commerce can expand the marketplace, lower costs, and improve management support systems, internal communications and knowledge sharing. It can also allow firms to focus more effectively on customer relationships. However, it might also promote more competition.
2 For new businesses, the Internet can reduce barriers to entry, and thus make it easier to enter new markets. One example would be Amazon.com, which did not need to incur the expense of opening up high street shops in order to successfully enter the retail book industry.
3 For customers, B2C on average provides faster and more complete information, a wider choice, and cheaper products and services. It also allows greater interaction with other customers.
4 For the wider community, an increase in B2C commerce may well have an impact in employment patterns, perhaps with an increase in home-working.

Possible limitations

While B2C commerce has some obvious benefits for the parties involved in transactions of this kind, as one might anticipate there are a number of potential limitations to its future growth and development. These include:

- lack of trust and consumer resistance;
- unresolved security, legal and privacy issues;
- insufficient buyers and sellers on-line;
- technical issues such as poor reliability, insufficient bandwidth, and speed;
- hardware and software tools are rapidly evolving and changing;
- the very expensive off-line marketing costs involved in building brand recognition for new on-line companies;
- lower barriers to entry will increase competition, and potentially increase rather than decrease consumer search and selection costs, as well as possible reduced industry profits overall;
- there are still significant distribution and storage costs involved for the sale of physical goods;
- existing bricks-and-mortar companies will not go away, and will continue to compete hard to maintain existing market share.

Many of the potential advantages and disadvantages of B2C can be illustrated by looking at the case study below, based on Amazon.com. As with the previous case study, you are encouraged to attempt at least some of the questions at the end of the text.

Synopsis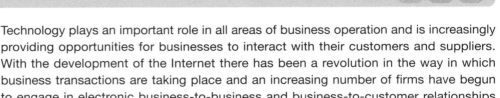

Technology plays an important role in all areas of business operation and is increasingly providing opportunities for businesses to interact with their customers and suppliers. With the development of the Internet there has been a revolution in the way in which business transactions are taking place and an increasing number of firms have begun to engage in electronic business-to-business and business-to-customer relationships alongside their traditional methods of doing business. We have even seen the emergence of some new businesses which have only an electronic existence. While such electronic relationships can have their problems and limitations, this is an area of the business environment in which there is likely to be significant developments in the coming years.

Summary of key points

- Technological developments have revolutionised the global marketplace and have spawned a whole new business vocabulary including the notion of e-business.

- The concept of e-business relates to the different aspects of doing business over the Internet and embraces a whole range of activities concerned with the exchange of products, services or information across electronic networks.

- E-commerce denotes a narrower range of activities related to the process of electronic transactions between buyer and seller.

- B2B and B2C represent the core of the notion of electronic commerce and provide a number of potential benefits for the parties involved in the transaction process.

- Both B2B and B2C, however, have their limitations which may hamper the growth of these two types of commerce.

- In the field of retailing a number of B2C business models have begun to emerge.

- Developments in this field have implications for both the demand side and supply side of markets.

- Technological advancement is a never-ending process that continues to shape the business environment.

CASE STUDY	Amazon.com

Bookselling over the Internet is one of the most sophisticated and successful B2C e-business sectors to have developed. The global cyber book market is expected to have grown beyond $1.1 billion by 2002.

Amazon is one of the most famous websites on the Internet, with 50 per cent of the cyber book market share. Amazon officially opened in July 1995, and had a turnover of $600 million by 1998, with an average monthly growth rate of 34 per cent.

As a pioneer, Amazon enjoyed considerable first-mover advantage, generating enormous publicity, which created awareness and established its brand name among the book buying public. Jeff Bezos, Amazon's founder, was convinced that consumers would enjoy the experience of browsing books electronically, reading reviews and excerpts from a particular book, and having it delivered a few days later. Bezos also felt that Amazon should be more profitable than traditional retailers in the longer term, on the basis that: 'We're short on real estate and long on technology. Technology gets cheaper every year and real estate more expensive.'

After initially gaining a reputation as a cyber bookstore, Amazon has gradually expanded its range of offerings into areas such as music, video, gifts and auctions. However, while Amazon has an impressive customer base, with over $1 billion in cash, and expanding sales, it has only just begun to make a profit (around £500 000 in 2004).

In fact, Amazon has found that it faces many of the problems of traditional retailers. For instance it has had to build a vast infrastructure of warehouse and distribution centres to house its burgeoning inventories of product lines, and has needed to spend heavily on off-line marketing to attract new customers.

Competition in the cyber book industry is also now very fierce with new competitors entering the market all the time. Barnes & Noble started to counterattack in 1997, and it quickly reached 15 per cent of the cyber book market share. Amazon also faces competition from software agents, such as BestBuyBooks.com and Buy.com, which offer to find the lowest prices available anywhere on the Net.

Nevertheless, Amazon still has many supporters. These argue that the lack of profits so far have arisen simply because the company has striven to build up a dominant position in e-commerce, and that triple-digit growth rates and expansion into new product lines will produce the increased sales needed to cross over into profitability. Also its rival on-line retailers lack scale. For instance, Barnes & Noble, Amazon's nearest rival, only attracts a third of Amazon's 14 million unique visitors a month.

Amazon has always shown an incredible ability to innovate and to diversify its product range. It has introduced ideas such as allowing customers to review books on its website, and publish rankings that assign a chart position to every book in print based on its sales. These ideas are now commonplace on other sites.

Amazon has also successfully patented its Associates programme that allows an on-line merchant to sell products through other websites by paying commissions for customer referrals. For instance, if you run a website selling rare coins, you can publish a website listing the best books available on rare coins. When visitors click on these titles they are transported (one-click) to the Amazon website, which will pay the referring website a commission, if the visitor buys a book. It is estimated that about $1 billion of Amazon's future sales (out of a total of $3.4 billion) per year could arise through this affiliate system.

To attract customers Amazon is also increasingly making special offers, such as free shipping, or further discounted prices, although critics claim this is financially unsound given the current lack of profitability.

Amazon though does have a number of opportunities to diversify and expand further. For instance, it has created partnerships with companies such as Toy 'R' Us, and Borders Groups Inc., which have found it difficult to operate their own on-line operations. What these companies are seeking is to share and benefit from Amazon's expertise in delivery. Bezos has made the point that while the distribution centres of traditional retailers are good at shipping containers of products to stores, they are not designed to deliver single items direct to customers, something which requires very different capabilities, and in which Amazon specialises.

Second, there are a number of economic opportunities to expand the selling of additional higher-priced (if lower-margin) items on-line. Amazon is currently able to offer a selection of 25 000 electronic items on its site, compared with say 5000 in a big electronic store. Although gross margins in electronics are smaller than books, at only 10–15 per cent, the costs of storage, packing and shipping are roughly the same for a £300 digital camera as for a book. So overall the net profit per unit for these goods is actually higher.

Third, there are emerging makets such as China, which has an 86 per cent literacy rate and five times the population of the USA. Local companies, such as Dangdang.com, China's biggest online bookseller, are already becoming established but have less than 0.25 per cent of the Chinese book market. The problem with the Chinese market at the moment is not price but a lack of Web access, consumer trust and online banking services. So far, only 6 million of the 50 million Internet users in China have shopped online.

Fourth, Amazon continues to innovate. It has recently entered the DVD rental market. It delivers DVDs by first-class post with pre-paid envelopes provided for returns. As technology develops it will undoubtedly be able to supply DVDs virtually in future, while it is able to use its current personalisation tools to recommend films to customers. In terms of technological improvements, by using sophisticated software tools to improve its internal operations management, it has managed to reduce distribution costs from 155 per cent of revenues in 1999 to 7 per cent today. Amazon was able to ship 1.4 million copies of *Harry Potter and the Order of the Phoenix* without a hitch on the day of its release in June 2003.

Postscript

Amazon's current sales were around $1.8 billion per quarter (October 2005), with 28 per cent of goods sold actually from third party sellers through its Associates Scheme.

Case study questions

1 Have a look at the websites of Amazon (*www.amazon.com* or *www.amazon.co.uk*) and its biggest American rival Barnes & Noble (*www.bn.com*) and compare what they do, and how their websites are structured.

2 Carry out a SWOT analysis of Amazon.com Inc. Using a rating scale of 1–5 for each factor identified (where 1 represents the most salient factor), summarise these into a single table.

3 Identify, in your opinion, the most important (highest-rated) factor for each category (strength, weakness, opportunity and threat), and explain your rationale for selecting those particular factors.

4 Try searching the WWW, using a search engine such as Google or Yahoo, for 'booksellers'. How many hits do you get? What do these results suggest?

5 In the light of question 4, and using Porter's five-forces model as a framework, consider the impact that Amazon.com Inc. has had on the book selling industry.

6 Consider whether the strategy pursued by Amazon (cyber-based only) or that of Barnes & Noble (traditional bricks and mortar plus cyber space) will be the more successful in the longer term. Explain your reasons.

Review and discussion questions

1 Do you expect to see faster growth in B2C or B2B commerce in future? Explain your answer.

2 Which items (goods and services) are likely to be sold successfully on-line? Which type of items would you never consider buying on-line? Why?

3 What is eCRM? Why is it important for on-line businesses?

4 What is EDI? In relative terms, large companies have adopted EDI in greater numbers than smaller companies. Why do you think this is?

5 What is a brick-and-click business? Do these businesses have advantages or disadvantages compared with bricks-and-mortar businesses? If so, what are they? Do these businesses have advantages or disadvantages over cyber-only based businesses? If so, what are they?

Assignments

1 You have been commissioned to identify a new B2B business model. Write a report explaining how your proposed business model will generate income.

2 Many Web-based businesses have failed. Search the Web, and identify such a business. Prepare a 10-minute PowerPoint presentation explaining what happened, and why you believe the business failed. In your conclusion, consider whether the same business concept might work in future, once the e-business environment has developed further.

Notes and references

1 *Business Week*, 20 December 2004.

2 Turban, E., Lee, J., King, D. and Chung, M. H., *Information Technology for Management*, 3rd edition, John Wiley, 2000.

3 DTI, *Business in the Information Age – International Benchmarking Study 2000*, UK Department of Trade and Industry, 2000. Available on-line at *www.ukonlineforbusiness.gov.uk*

4 IDC, *Reinventing EDI: Electronic Data Interchange Services Market Review and Forecast*, 1998–2003, International Data Corporation, 1999.

Further reading

Chaffey, D., *E-Business and E-Commerce Management*, Prentice Hall, 2nd edition, 2004.

Chen, S., *Strategic Management of e-Business*, 2nd edition, John Wiley, 2005.

IDC, *Reinventing EDI: Electronic Data Interchange Services Market Review and Forecast*, 1998–2003, International Data Corporation, 1999.

Jalassi, T. and Enders, A., *Strategies for e-business*, Financial Times/Prentice Hall, 2005.

McKay, J. and Marshall, P., *Strategic Management of E-Business*, John Wiley, 2004.

Rayport, J. and Jaworski, B., *Introduction to E-commerce*, 2nd edition, McGraw Hill, 2004.

Shapiro, C. and Varian, H., *Information Rules*, Harvard Business School Press, 1999.

Turban, E., King, D. Viehland, D. and Lee, J., *Electronic Commerce 2006: A Managerial Perspective*, Prentice Hall, 2006.

web link

Web links and further questions are available on the website at:
www.pearsoned.co.uk/worthington

APPENDICES

Answers to odd-numbered end-of-chapter questions

Chapter 1

1. (a) See Figure A1.1(a).
   (b) See Figure A1.1(b).

3. You would try to reduce the price of each item as little as was necessary to get rid of the remaining stock. The problem for shop owners is that they do not have enough information about consumer demand to make precise calculations here. Many shops try a fairly cautious approach first, and then, if that is not enough to sell all the stock, they make further 'end of sale' reductions later.

5. The reduction in supply will cause a shortage of oil at current prices. This will cause the price of oil to rise. This will then have a twin effect: it will reduce demand and it will also make it profitable to use more expensive extraction methods, thereby increasing supply. The effect of the higher price, therefore, will be to eliminate the shortage.

7. (a) Equilibrium is where quantity demanded equals quantity supplied: $P = £5$; $Q = 12$ million.
   (b) The schedules are shown in the following table:

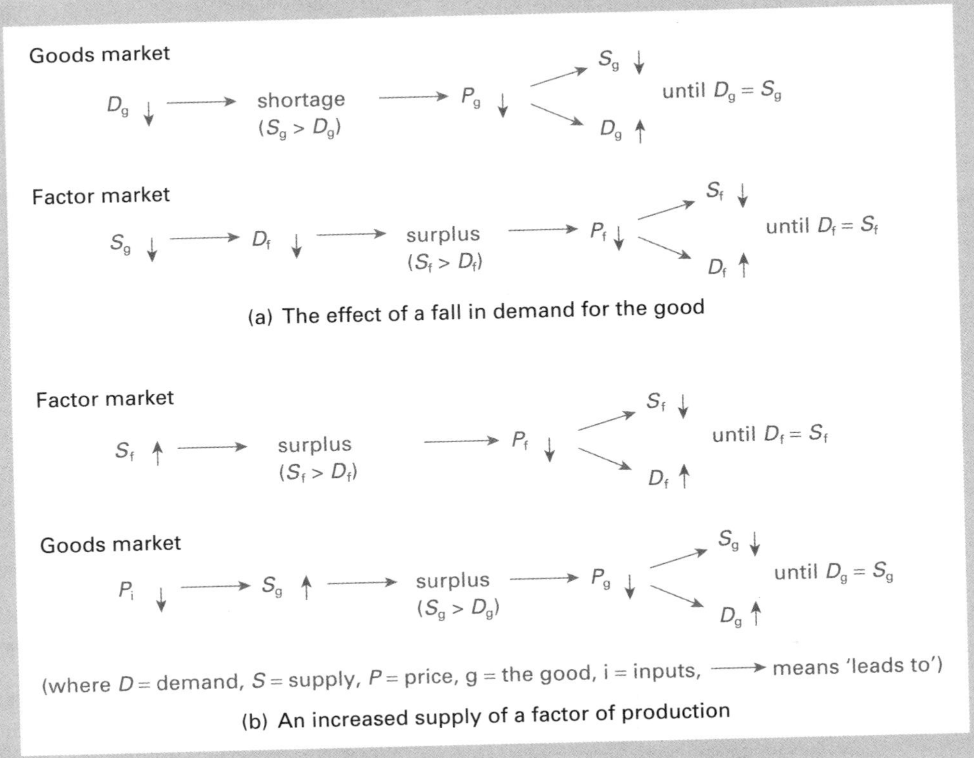

Goods market

$D_g \downarrow$ ⟶ shortage $(S_g > D_g)$ ⟶ $P_g \downarrow$ ⟶ $S_g \downarrow$ / $D_g \uparrow$ until $D_g = S_g$

Factor market

$S_g \downarrow$ ⟶ $D_f \downarrow$ ⟶ surplus $(S_f > D_f)$ ⟶ $P_f \downarrow$ ⟶ $S_f \downarrow$ / $D_f \uparrow$ until $D_f = S_f$

(a) The effect of a fall in demand for the good

Factor market

$S_f \uparrow$ ⟶ surplus $(S_f > D_f)$ ⟶ $P_f \downarrow$ ⟶ $S_f \downarrow$ / $D_f \uparrow$ until $D_f = S_f$

Goods market

$P_i \downarrow$ ⟶ $S_g \uparrow$ ⟶ surplus $(S_g > D_g)$ ⟶ $P_g \downarrow$ ⟶ $S_g \downarrow$ / $D_g \uparrow$ until $D_g = S_g$

(where D = demand, S = supply, P = price, g = the good, i = inputs, ⟶ means 'leads to')

(b) An increased supply of a factor of production

Figure A1.1
The price mechanism

Price (£)	8	7	6	5	4	3	2	1
Quantity demanded	10	12	14	16	18	20	22	24
Quantity supplied	18	16	14	12	10	8	6	4

Equilibrium price and quantity are now as follows: $P = £6$; $Q = 14$ million.

Demand has risen by 4 million but equilibrium quantity has only risen by 2 million (from 12 million to 14 million). The reason why quantity sold has risen by less than demand is that price has risen. This has choked off some of the extra demand (i.e. 2 of the 4 million).

(c) See Figure A1.2.

9. ■ A rise in the price of air travel (supply).
   ■ A fall in the exchange rate, giving less foreign currency for the pound (supply – tour operators' costs abroad rise when measured in pounds).
   ■ The economy booms (demand – more people can afford to go on holiday; supply – inflation raises tour operators' costs).
   ■ The price of domestic holidays increases (demand – a rise in the price of a substitute).
   ■ Certain tour operators go out of business or cut down on the number of holidays on offer (supply).
   ■ Poor weather at home (demand – more people decide to take their holidays abroad).

11. (a) Price rises, quantity rises (demand shifts to the right: butter and margarine are substitutes).
    (b) Price falls, quantity rises (supply shifts to the right: butter and yoghurt are in joint supply).
    (c) Price falls, quantity falls (demand shifts to the left: bread and butter are complementary goods).
    (d) Price rises, quantity rises (demand shifts to the right: bread and butter are complementary goods).
    (e) Price rises, quantity rises or falls depending on relative sizes of the shifts in demand and supply (demand shifts to the right as people buy now before the price rises; supply shifts to the left as producers hold back stocks until the price does rise).

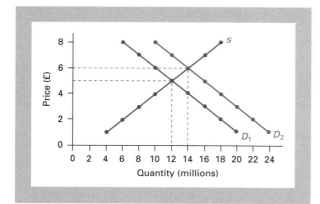

Figure A1.2 Market for t-shirts (weekly)

(f) Price rises, quantity falls (supply shifts to the left).
(g) Price rises, quantity rises or falls depending on the relative size of the shifts in demand and supply (demand shifts to the right as more health-conscious people start buying butter; supply shifts to the left as a result of the increased cost of production).

Chapter 2

1. With the flatter of the two supply curves, the price will rise less and the quantity rise more than in the case of the steeper supply curve.

3. Because there has been a *rightward shift* in the demand curve for oil. This is likely to be the result of rising incomes. Car ownership and use increase as incomes increase. Also tastes may have changed so that people want to drive more. There may also have been a decline in substitute modes of transport, such as rail transport and buses. Finally, people may travel longer distances to work as a result of a general move to the suburbs.

5. As long as demand remains inelastic, the firm should go on raising its price if it wants to increase revenue. Eventually consumers will stop buying the good: even if there is no close substitute, the income effect will become large – people will simply not be able to afford to buy the good. This illustrates the fact that a demand curve is likely to have different elasticities along its length.

7. Two brands of coffee, because they are closer substitutes than coffee and tea.

9. Generally, stabilising speculation will benefit both consumers and firms, as it will create a more stable market environment in which it is easier to plan purchases, production or investment. Generally people prefer certainty to uncertainty. Destabilising speculation, on the other hand, by exaggerating the upswings and downswings in markets, will make it more difficult to plan – something that will be unpopular with consumers and producers alike.

   Of course, to the extent that the consumers or producers are themselves taking part in the speculation, they will gain from it, whether it is stabilising or destabilising, provided that they predict correctly. For example, if you are thinking of buying a house and, correctly, predict that house prices will rise in the near future, then you will gain by buying now before they do.

11. (a) Equilibrium is where quantity demanded equals quantity supplied: where $P = £2.00$ per kilo; $Q = 50\ 000$ kilos.
    (b) (i) There will be a surplus of 22 000 kilos (i.e. 62 000 – 40 000).
       (ii) No effect. The equilibrium price of £2.00 is above the minimum.
    (c) (i) With the £1.00 subsidy, producers will supply at each price the amount that they were previously willing to supply for £1.00 more.

The schedules will now be as follows:

Price (£ per kilo)	4.00	3.50	3.00	2.50	2.00	1.50	1.00	0.50	0.00
Q_d (000 kilos)	30	35	40	45	50	55	60		
Q_s (000 kilos)			80	68	62	55	50	45	38

(ii) The new equilibrium price will be £1.50 (where quantity demanded and the new quantity supplied are equal).

(iii) The cost will be £1 × 55 000 = £55 000.

(d) (i) At a price of £2.50, (original) supply exceeds demand by 10 000 kilos. The government would therefore have to buy this amount in order to ensure that all the tomatoes produced were sold.

(ii) £2.50 × 10 000 = £25 000

(e) (i) It would have purchased 55 000. To dispose of all these, price would have to fall to £1.50.

(ii) The cost of this course of action would be (£2.50 − £1.50) × 55 000 = £55 000.

13. Two examples are:

- Rent controls. Advantages: makes cheap housing available to those who would otherwise have difficulty in affording reasonable accommodation. Disadvantages: causes a reduction in the supply of private rented accommodation; causes demand to exceed supply and thus some people will be unable to find accommodation.

- Tickets for a concert. Advantages: allows the price to be advertised in advance and guarantees a full house; makes seats available to those who could not afford the free-market price. Disadvantages: causes queuing or seats being available only to those booking well in advance.

Chapter 3

1. (a) Two or three days: the time necessary to acquire new equipment or DJs.

(b) Two or more years: the time taken to plan and build a new power station.

(c) Several weeks: the time taken to acquire additional premises.

(d) One or two years: the time taken to plan and build a new store.

3. (a) Variable.

(b) Fixed (unless the fee negotiated depends on the success of the campaign).

(c) Variable (the more that is produced, the more the wear and tear).

(d) Fixed.

(e) Fixed if the factory will be heated and lit to the same extent irrespective of output, but variable if the amount of heating and lighting depends on the amount of the factory in operation, which in turn depends on output.

(f) Variable.

(g) Variable (although the basic wage is fixed per worker, the cost will still be variable because the total cost will increase with output if the number of workers is increased).

(h) Variable.

(i) Fixed (because it does not depend on output).

5. Because economies of scale, given that most arise from increasing returns to scale, will be fully realised after a certain level of output (see Box 3.4 on page 100), whereas diseconomies of scale, given that they largely arise from the managerial problems of running large organisations, are only likely to set in beyond a certain level of output.

7. Diagram (a): The long-run marginal cost curve would be falling (and below the *LRAC* curve) and thus the long-run total cost would be rising less and less steeply.

Diagram (b): The long-run marginal cost curve would be rising (and above the *LRAC* curve) and thus the long-run total cost curve would be rising more and more steeply.

Diagram (c): The long-run marginal cost curve would be horizontal and (equal to the *LRAC* curve) and thus the long-run total cost curve would be rising at a constant rate: i.e. it would be a straight line up from the origin.

9. The diagram should look something like Figure 3.5. The table should be set out like Table 3.3. Total revenue (*TR*) is simply $P \times Q$ and marginal revenue (*MR*) is the rise in *TR* per 1 unit rise in *Q*. (The *MR* figures are plotted between the values for *Q*: i.e. between 1 and 2, 2 and 3, 3 and 4, etc.) The figures for *MR* should then be simply read off the table and plotted on your diagram.

11. See Figure A3.1.

13. Normal profit is the opportunity cost of capital for owners. It is the return they could have earned on

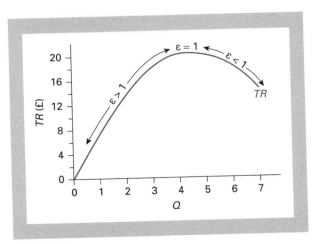

Figure A3.1 Total revenue for a firm facing a downward-sloping demand curve

their capital elsewhere, and is thus the minimum profit they must make to persuade them to continue producing in the long run and not to close down and move into some alternative business.

15. Its fixed costs have already been incurred. Provided, therefore, that it can cover its variable costs, any-

thing over can be used to help pay off these fixed costs. Once the fixed costs come up for renewal, however (and thus cease to be fixed costs), the firm will close down if it cannot cover these also. It will thus be willing to make a loss only as long as the fixed costs have been paid (or committed).

17. (a) See the following table:

Output	1	2	3	4	5	6	7	8	9	10
AC (£)	7.00	5.00	4.00	3.30	3.00	3.10	3.50	4.20	5.00	6.00
TC (£)	7.00	10.00	12.00	13.20	15.00	18.60	24.50	33.60	45.00	60.00
MC (£)		3.00	2.00	1.20	1.80	3.60	5.90	9.10	11.40	15.00
AR (£)	10.00	9.50	9.00	8.50	8.00	7.50	7.00	6.50	6.00	5.50
TR (£)	10.00	19.00	27.00	34.00	40.00	45.00	49.00	52.00	54.00	55.00
MR (£)		9.00	8.00	7.00	6.00	5.00	4.00	3.00	2.00	1.00

(b) Profit is maximised where $MC = MR$: at an output of 6.

(c) Total profit equals $TR - TC$.
At an output of 5, total profit is £40.00 − £15.00 = £25.00.
At an output of 6, total profit is £45.00 − £18.60 = £26.40.
At an output of 7, total profit is £49.00 − £24.50 = £24.50.
Profit rises up to 6 units of output and then falls. Profit is thus maximised at 6 units: it is £26.40 per period of time.

(d) See Figure A3.2.

(e) See Figure A3.2. Profit is maximised where $MC = MR$, at an output of 6. At this output, $AR = £7.50$ (point a); $AC = £3.10$ (point d).

(f) This area is shown by the rectangle $abcd$ in Figure A3.2.

Chapter 4

1. (a)

Output	0	1	2	3	4	5	6	7	8
TC (£)	10	18	24	30	38	50	66	91	120
AC (£)	–	18	12	10	9½	10	11	13	15
MC (£)		8	6	6	8	12	16	25	29

(b) See Figure A4.1.

(c) Profit is maximised where $MC = MR$ (point b): i.e. at an output of 5.

(d) £20
Profit per unit is given by $AR - AC$.
$AR (= MR)$ is constant at £14; AC at an output of 5 units is £10.
Thus profit per unit = 14 − 10 = 4.
Total profit is then found by multiplying this by the number of units sold:

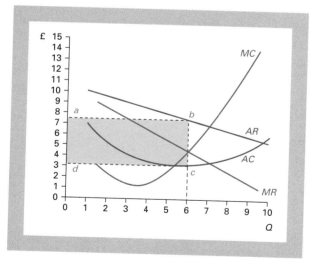

Figure A3.2   Profit maximisation for a firm facing a downward-sloping demand curve

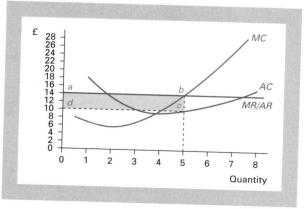

Figure A4.1   Profit maximisation under perfect competition

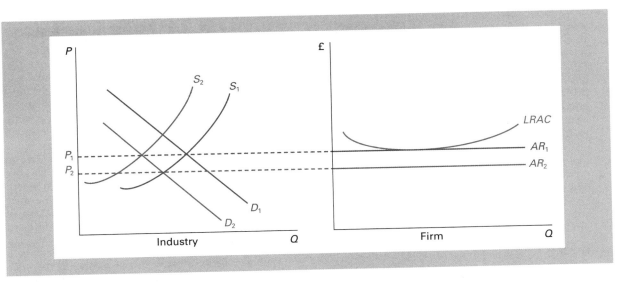

Figure A4.2   Long run under perfect competition

i.e. £4 × 5 = £20.

This is shown by the area *abcd*.

(e) Supernormal profit would encourage new firms to enter the industry. This would cause price to fall until it was equal to the minimum point of the *long-run* average cost curve (at that point, there would be no supernormal profit remaining and hence firms would stop entering and the price would stop falling).

3. This is illustrated in Figure A4.2. The long-run equilibrium is shown where the *AR* curve is tangential to the *LRAC* curve (and where, therefore, there is no supernormal profit). If the demand curve now shifts from D_1 to D_2, the equilibrium price will fall to P_2. Less than normal profit will now be made. Firms will therefore leave the industry. As they do, so the industry supply curve will shift to the left, causing the price to rise again. Once the supply curve has reached S_2 and price has risen back to P_1, long-run equilibrium will have been restored, with the remaining firms making normal profit again.

5. The criticism should really be directed at the market system as a whole: that where significant economies of scale exist, markets are bound to be imperfect. Of course, there may be significant benefits to consumers and society generally from such imperfect markets (see pages 122–3): there are advantages as well as disadvantages of imperfect markets. What is more, if the market is highly contestable, many of the advantages of perfect competition may be achieved even though the industry is actually a monopoly (or oligopoly).

7. Demand is elastic at the point where $MR = MC$. The reason is that MC must be positive and therefore MR must also be positive. But if MR is positive, demand must be elastic. Nevertheless, at any given price a monopoly will face a less elastic demand curve than a firm producing the same good under monopolistic

competition or oligopoly. This enables it to raise price further before demand becomes elastic (and before the point is reached where $MR = MC$).

9. (a) High. The plant cannot be used for other purposes.

(b) Relatively low. The industry is not very capital intensive, and the various tools and equipment could be sold or transferred to producing other crops.

(c) Very high. The plant cannot be used for other purposes and decommissioning costs are very high.

(d) Low. The capital costs are low and offices can be sold.

(e) Relatively low. The plant and machinery can probably be adapted to producing other toys.

(f) Low to moderate. It is likely that a pharmaceutical company can relatively easily switch to producing alternative drugs. Substantial exit costs are only likely to arise if the company is committed to a long-term research and development programme or if equipment is not transferable to producing alternative drugs.

(g) Low to moderate. Exit costs from one particular client are likely to be low if the firm can easily transfer to supplying alternative clients. Costs will be higher if there are penalties for breaking contracts, or if the firm wishes to exit from catering altogether. In this latter case the costs will depend on the second-hand value of its equipment.

(h) Low to moderate. The exit costs again will depend on the second-hand value of the equipment.

(i) Relatively low if the ships can be transferred to other routes. Much higher if the company wishes to move out of shipping entirely and if the market for second-hand ships is depressed.

11. You will see when you think about this question that it is often difficult to identify the boundaries of a market. Take a product like chocolate. If the product is defined as bars of chocolate, then there are probably about three or four different makes available, but maybe only one or two in any one shop. If, however, the product is defined to include filled chocolate bars, then there are many more varieties available, but, of course, several made by each individual company (such as Cadbury's, Mars, Nestlé, etc). You will also notice for many products that there are one or two large producers, and many small producers, making the market a hybrid form of oligopoly if the large producers dominate the market.

    The sorts of competition to look out for are: price competition, advertising, product specification, product availability, after-sales service, etc.

13. The first type of customer will have a lower price elasticity of demand, since they will not have the time to shop around, and will thus be prepared to pay a higher price than at the supermarket. It is this type of customer that the small shop relies on. The other type of customer will probably simply wait until they next visit the supermarket. For such customers, the supermarket provides a substitute service.

15. No. Demand would become less elastic and the lack of competition may enable remaining petrol stations to make supernormal profits in the long run as well as the short run. If, with a reduced number of firms, there was still sufficient competition to allow profits to be kept at a normal level, cost conditions would have to change so that the *LRAC* would now continue sloping downward for longer (so that the point of tangency is at a higher output): this would require changes in technology such as new computerised systems that allow one cashier to handle a larger number of customers.

17. In all cases collusion is quite likely: check out the factors favouring collusion on page 139. In some cases it is more likely than others: for example, in the case of cement, where there is little product differentiation and a limited number of producers, collusion is more likely than in the case of carpets, where there is much more product differentiation.

19. (a) and (c) are examples of effective countervailing power, because the individual purchasing firms are large relative to the total market for the product.

21. Examples include: a firm charging different prices for the same product in different countries; a supermarket chain charging higher prices in more affluent areas; airlines charging different prices for the same flight with the same booking conditions through different tour operators; cheaper travel for particular categories of person (children, students, elderly people).

    Generally consumers gain if they buy in the low-price market and lose if they buy in the high-price market. If the discrimination were first degree, however, no one would gain, since everyone would be charged the highest price they were prepared to pay. The use of price discrimination, by enabling the firm to make higher profits, may also enable it to compete more effectively with its rivals. This could help consumers if competition thereby increased (e.g. if a firm used price discrimination to enable it to compete more effectively against a powerful rival), but could be against consumers' interests if firms used it to drive rivals out of business.

    In order to form a judgement, it is necessary to know the extent of the gains and losses to consumers. It is also important to know to what extent differences in prices are the result of genuine price discrimination, rather than merely a reflection of the different costs that firms incur in different markets, or a reflection of a *different* service. For example, it is not price discrimination to charge a higher price for a better seat at a concert: the price difference is, at least in part, a reflection of the *quality* of the seat.

Chapter 6

1. (a) 7 units (where marginal revenue (= *P*) equals marginal cost).
   (b) 5 units (where marginal social benefit (= *P*) equals marginal social cost.
   (c) Because the environment becomes ever less able to cope with additional amounts of pollution.

3. (a) External costs of production (*MSC* > *MC*)
   The pollution of rivers and streams by slurry and nitrate run-off from farms; road congestion near a factory.
   (b) External benefits of production (*MSC* < *MC*)
   Beneficial spin-offs from the development of new products (for example, the various space programmes in the USA, the former Soviet Union and Europe have contributed to advances in medicine, materials technology, etc.); where the opening of a new environmentally friendly factory results in less output from factories that pollute.
   (c) External costs of consumption (*MSB* < *MB*)
   The effect of CFC aerosols on the ozone layer; the unpleasant sight of satellite dishes.
   (d) External benefits of consumption (*MSB* > *MB*)
   People decorating the outside of their houses or making their gardens look attractive benefits neighbours and passers-by; people insulating their houses reduces fuel consumption and the pollution associated with it.

5. *Publicly provided goods* are merely goods that the government or some other public agency provides, whether or not they could be provided by the market.

   Public goods are the much narrower category of goods that the market would fail to provide because of their characteristics of non-rivalry and non-excludability. Thus a local government might provide both street lighting and public libraries: they are both publicly provided goods, but only street lighting is a public good.

A *merit good* is either publicly provided or subsidised. It is one that the government feels that people would otherwise underconsume (e.g. health care). It is not normally a public good, however, because it *would* be provided by the market: it is just that people would consume too little of it.

7. Roads where there are relatively few access points and where therefore it would be practical to charge tolls. Charges could be regarded as a useful means of restricting use of the roads in question, or, by charging more at peak times, of encouraging people to travel at off-peak times. Such a system, however, could be regarded as unfair by those using the toll roads, and might merely divert congestion on to the non-toll roads.

9. (a) (i) or (ii) (e.g. *Which?* magazine);
   (b) (iii) (by asking people currently doing the job) or (iv);
   (c) (iii) (by obtaining estimates);
   (d) (iii) (albeit imperfect, by inspecting other work that the different builders have done) or (iv);
   (e) as (d);
   (f) (iii);
   (g) (iii);
   (h) (i) or (ii) (as in (a)) or (iii) by experimenting.
   All could involve the non-monetary costs of the time involved in finding out.

   If the information is purely factual (as in (c) above), and you can trust the source of your information, there is no problem. If you cannot trust the source, or if the information is subjective (such as other people's experiences in (b) above), then you will only have imperfect information of the costs and/or benefits until you actually experience them.

11. Virtually all the categories of market failure (except public goods) apply to a free-market system of educational provision.
   ■ In any given area there may be oligopolistic collusion to keep fees high.
   ■ There are positive externalities from education: for example, the benefits to other members of society from a well-educated workforce. Thus too few resources would be allocated to education.
   ■ Education can be seen as a merit good: something that the government feels that people are entitled to and should not depend on ability to pay.
   ■ Access to education would depend on parents' income: this could be argued to be unfair.
   ■ Children would also be dependent on their parents' *willingness* to pay. Parents differ in the amount that they care for their children's welfare.
   ■ Parents and potential students may be ignorant of the precise benefits of particular courses – something that an unscrupulous educational

establishment might exploit, by pushing the 'merits' of their establishment.

13. Assuming that the external benefit was in production, the *MSC* curve in Figure 6.5 would be *below* the *MC* curve. The optimum subsidy would be equal to the gap between *MSC* and *MC* at the point where the *MSC* curve crossed the *D = MSB* line.

15. (a) This would be very difficult given that large numbers of people are affected by the pollution. One possible answer would be to legislate such that if specific health problems could be traced to atmospheric pollution, then those affected would have rights to sue.
   (b) If tracts of the river were privately owned, then as relatively few owners would be involved, it would be relatively easy to pursue polluters through the courts, provided they could be clearly identified (i.e. it would be easier to pursue factories for specific toxic emissions than individuals for dumping litter).
   (c) Again if the dumpers could be identified and the dumping were on private ground, then the owners could use the courts to prevent it. The problem here is that the owners may be quite happy to charge the company for dumping, not caring about the effects on other people of polluting, say, the water table.
   (d) This is more difficult, given that the ugly buildings are on land owned by owners of the buildings! The law would have to give people the right to sue for *visual* pollution. This could be difficult to prove, as it involves aesthetic judgments.
   (e) There would have to be laws prohibiting noise above a certain level within the hearing of residents. Then it would be a relatively simple case of the affected residents demonstrating to the satisfaction of the courts that a noise offence had been committed. It would be easier if the summons could be brought by an environmental inspectorate.

   It should be clear from these answers that the boundaries between legal controls and exercising property rights are rather blurred. The ability of people to exercise property rights depends on the laws of property.

17. (a) Very suitable, provided that periodic tests and possibly spot checks are carried out.
   (b) Good in certain cases: e.g. one-way systems, banning lorries of a certain size from city centres during certain parts of the day, bus lanes.
   (c) Not very, given that the main problem is excessive profits, which would be difficult to define legally and relatively easy to evade even if they were defined. Various types of unsafe or shoddy goods (which are possibly more likely to be produced by firms not facing competition) could be made illegal, however.
   (d) Good. The law could give the government or some other body the right to ban any merger it

considered not to be in the public interest. (See Section 6.6.)

(e) Not. It would require an army of inspectors to identify marginal costs, or to check that a firm's reported marginal costs were what it claimed. The scope for evasion and ambiguity would be immense.

19. (a) This increases the marginal cost of motoring and thus does discourage people from using their cars. But it affects everyone, including those driving their cars on uncongested roads.

(b) This is not very effective at all, since it is not a marginal charge related to congestion. You do not pay more, the more you use your car: the marginal cost is zero. In fact it may even have the perverse effect of encouraging people to use their cars more. After all, if they are paying a large annual fee, they may feel that they want to get 'full value for money' by using their cars as much as possible. The only positive effect is that it may discourage people from owning a car or a second car, and for that reason may encourage the increased use of public transport.

(c) This is a version of 'road pricing' and is an example of a system most favoured by economists, since the charge is directly related to the level of congestion. It is quite expensive, however, to install and operate the system.

(d) This is a somewhat less sophisticated system of road pricing than that in (c), since the charge is fixed during the designated hours irrespective of the amount of congestion. It can also lead to a build-up of congestion outside the zone. It is generally cheaper to install, however, than that in (c).

(e) This is quite effective, especially if the tolls can vary according to the amount of congestion. They have the disadvantage, however, of causing possible tailbacks from the booths. There is also the problem that traffic may simply be diverted on to other roads where there are no tolls, thus worsening the problem of congestion elsewhere.

(f) These may encourage the use of bicycles and buses, but they can increase the level of congestion for cars, as they are forced into one lane.

(g) This can be effective, provided that public transport is fast, efficient, frequent and clean. They are especially useful when applied to city centre transport, or transport from park-and-ride car parks to city centres.

21. Fixing prices

(a) (i) to enable those on low incomes to be able to afford the good.
(ii) to prevent firms with market power from exploiting their position.
(iii) to help in the fight against inflation.

(b) (i) to protect the incomes of producers (e.g. farmers).
(ii) to increase profits and thereby encourage investment.

(iii) (in the case of wages) to protect workers' incomes.
(iv) to create a surplus in times of glut which can be stored in preparation for possible future shortages.

Alternatives to fixing prices

(a) (i) cash benefits and benefits in kind; subsidising the good.
(ii) anti-monopoly legislation; lump-sum taxes.
(iii) fiscal, monetary and supply-side policies (see Part B).

(b) (i) subsidies and tax relief.
(ii) subsidies and tax relief.
(iii) benefits and progressive taxation.
(iv) state acting as purchaser or seller on the open market.

Chapter 7

1. (a) See Table A7.1.
In each case the growth rate (G) is found by using the following formula:
$$G = (Y_t - Y_{t-1})/Y_{t-1} \times 100$$

Table A7.1

	2001	2002	2003	2004	2005
USA	0.80	1.88	3.02	4.44	3.26
Japan	0.40	−0.30	2.50	4.00	2.06
Germany	1.00	0.10	−0.10	1.19	1.37
France	2.10	1.08	0.48	1.16	1.98
UK	2.30	1.76	2.21	3.20	2.64

(b) See Figure A7.1.
The USA the UK and generally had a higher growth rate than France and Germany. Japan had negative growth in 2002. All five countries experienced relatively high growth in 2004 and 2005 and relatively low growth in 2002.

3. (a) Neither, there is merely a redistribution of factor payments on the left-hand side of the inner flow. (The only exception to this would be if a smaller proportion of wages were saved than of profits. In this case there would be a net reduction in withdrawals.)

(b) Increase in injections (investment).
(c) Decrease in withdrawals (taxes).
(d) Increase in withdrawals (saving). Note that 'investing' in building societies is really *saving* not investment.
(e) Fall in withdrawals (a reduction in net outflow abroad from the household sector).
(f) Neither. The inner flow is unaffected. If, however, this were financed from higher taxes, it would result in an increase in withdrawals.
(g) Neither. The inner flow is unaffected. The consumption of domestically produced goods and services remains the same.

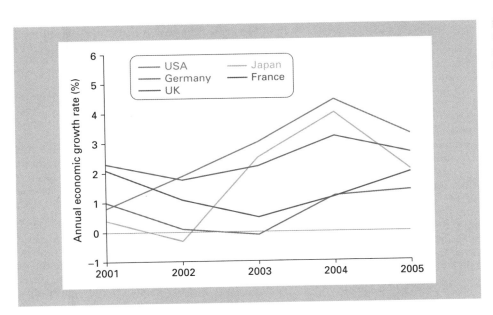

Figure A7.1
Growth rates of selected industrial countries 2001–5

(h) Decrease in withdrawals (saving).

(i) Neither. An increase in government expenditure is offset by an increase in saving (i.e. people buying government securities).

(j) Increase in injections. An increase in government expenditure is not offset by changes elsewhere. Extra money is printed to finance the net injection.

5. The curve would still slope upwards during phase 4, but its slope would be less than in the other phases. Its slope would also be less than that of the potential output curve, with the result that the gap between actual and potential output would widen.

7. Look back over the last few years and see what pattern emerges. What predictions are currently being made for output growth over the next two years in the press by various forecasting organisations and commentators?

9. (a) In equilibrium, income (Y) = expenditure (E)
$$\begin{aligned} E &= C + I + G + X - M \\ &= £60bn + £5bn + £8bn + £7bn - £10bn \\ &= £70bn \end{aligned}$$

(b) $$\begin{aligned} J &= I + G + X \\ &= £5bn + £8bn + £7bn \\ &= £20bn \end{aligned}$$

(c) In equilibrium, $W = J$. As this economy is in equilibrium, withdrawals will equal current injections.
$$W = £20bn$$

(d) $$\begin{aligned} W &= S + T + M \\ &= S + £7bn + £10bn \\ \therefore S &= £20bn - £7bn - £10bn \\ &= £3bn \end{aligned}$$

(e) $$\begin{aligned} C_d &= C - M = £50bn \\ mpc_d &= \Delta C_d / \Delta Y \\ &= (£58bn - £50bn)/(£80bn - £70bn) \\ &= £8bn/£10bn \\ &= 0.8 \text{ or } 4/5 \end{aligned}$$

(f) $$\begin{aligned} \text{Multiplier} &= 1/(1 - mpc_d) \\ &= 1/^1/_5 \\ &= 5 \end{aligned}$$

(g) Injections have risen by £4bn + £1bn − £2bn
$$= £3bn$$
∴ national income will rise by 5 times this amount
$$= \text{increase of } £15bn$$

11. Injections rise by £100m + (£200m − £50m) = £250m. Therefore, with a multiplier of 3, national income will rise by £750m.

13. The E line is parallel with the C_d line (assuming that the J 'curve' is a horizontal straight line). Thus the slope of the E line is the same as the slope of the C_d line, which is given by the mpc_d ($\Delta C_d/\Delta Y$).

15. ■ The lower a country's national income, the higher will tend to be its mpc and thus the higher will be its multiplier.
   ■ In some countries there is much more of a 'savings culture' and thus the mps is higher. Those with less of a savings culture will tend to have a lower mps and hence a higher multiplier.
   ■ In some countries, especially large ones, trade accounts for a relatively small proportion of national income. In such countries the mpm will be lower and hence the multiplier will be higher than in countries with a higher proportion of trade relative to national income.
   ■ The marginal tax rate, the mpt, differs from one country to another. The lower the mpt, the higher the multiplier.

17. The aggregate supply curve would be horizontal or virtually so. An increase in aggregate demand could lead to an increase in output with virtually no increase in prices as firms would have the spare capacity to produce more at little or no extra cost per unit.

Chapter 10

1. (a) Assuming that the government does not alter tax or benefit rates, the budget deficit is likely to increase as the economy moves into recession. Tax revenues will fall because people are earning and spending less. The payment of benefits, on the other hand, is likely to increase as more people claim unemployment benefit. In a boom, the budget deficit is likely to decrease and there may even be a budget surplus.

   (b) Since the budget deficit tends to increase in a recession, the size of the general government debt will increase more rapidly, as government debts are built up more rapidly. In a boom, the national debt will rise more slowly as the budget deficit falls. If there is a budget surplus, the general government debt will fall.

3. A rise in income tax has an income and a substitution effect. Higher taxes reduce people's incomes: this is the income effect. Being poorer, they have to work more to make up for some of their lost income. The income effect, therefore, makes income tax increases an incentive to work more. Higher taxes, however, also mean that work is worth less than before, and therefore people might well substitute leisure for work: there is no point in working so much if you bring home less. This is the substitution effect, and makes income tax increases a disincentive.

   (i) If the substitution effect is bigger than the income effect, then a rise in income tax will act as a net disincentive to work. As is shown on page 179, this is likely for those people with few commitments and for second income-earners in families where the second income is not relied on for 'essential consumption'. It is also likely for those who are only currently paying a small amount of tax, and for whom, therefore, the income effect is likely to be small; and also for those just in a higher tax bracket when that higher tax rate is raised.

   (ii) If the income effect is bigger than the substitution effect, a rise in tax will act as a net incentive. This is most likely for those currently paying a large amount of tax and who would suddenly be faced with a substantial increase in their tax bill. It is also likely if the tax increase takes the form of a cut in tax allowances. Except for those having to pay tax for the first time, or those pushed into a higher tax band, cutting allowances has no substitution effect since it does not alter the marginal rate.

5. ■ A rise in government expenditure on research and development or training may make firms feel less need to invest in these areas themselves.
   ■ A rise in taxes may make people feel less able to save such a large proportion of their income.
   ■ A rise in exports may stimulate firms to invest more in the export sector.

7. It will increase. The reason is that the overall level of liquidity has increased: Treasury bills and money market loans are regarded as liquid assets by banks, and can be used as the basis for credit creation.

9. It would drive them up. In order to sell the extra bills, the government would have to accept a lower discount price (a higher rate of discount). In order to sell the extra bonds, governments would have to offer them at a higher rate of interest, or at a lower price for a given interest payment (which amounts to a rise in the interest rate). These higher rates of interest on government securities would have a knock-on effect on other rates of interest.

11. Targeting the money supply could involve large changes in interest rates, given the unstable and interest-inelastic nature of the demand for money. This, in turn, could be very damaging to investment and reduce long-term growth. It is therefore better to avoid targeting the money supply. Instead, a discretionary approach should be adopted, with policies changed according to the changing nature of the real economy.

13. Yes. Targets could be set, but reassessed periodically in the light of the evidence of the success of policy and of changing circumstances. Alternatively, loose targets for a number of different objectives could be set, and then the government could seek to achieve the best compromise between them if there were any apparent conflict.

15. Tax cuts to increase incentives, other things being equal, will lead to a rise in aggregate demand. Unless the supply-side policy is able to cause a matching rightward shift in the aggregate supply curve, or unless the economy is currently operating below capacity, the effect will be inflationary. Cuts in government expenditure, if applied during a recession, will tend to make the recession worse.

17. Cuts in income tax will tend to encourage people to work more and/or harder, because they increase the opportunity cost of leisure. This is the substitution effect: an incentive. However, by increasing after-tax incomes, they will also tend to make people feel that they can afford to work less. This is the income effect: a disincentive. Cutting marginal rates of tax, especially for those just into a given tax bracket, will have a substitution effect, but very little income effect, and therefore have a net incentive effect. Increasing allowances, however, will have an income effect, but no substitution effect, since the marginal rate of tax is not altered. Cutting the marginal rate for those already paying a considerable amount of the tax, will have a large income effect relative to the substitution effect. In both these cases there is a net disincentive effect.

    Tax cuts for business will tend to have more of an incentive effect, the more that the benefits of the tax cuts are conditional upon increasing investment or cutting costs. Simple cuts in corporation tax (tax on profits), like cuts in income tax, will have both an income and a substitution effect. When the cut is first made, the windfall rise in profits may have a net disincentive effect. However, a country with relatively low corporation taxes is likely to encourage more investment over the longer term, both domestic and inward.

Chapter 12

1. (a) debit; (b) credit; (c) credit; (d) credit; (e) debit.

3. During the boom, the current account will tend to deteriorate. There are two reasons. The first is the direct result of higher incomes. Part of the extra incomes will be spent on imports. The second is the result of higher inflation. Higher prices of domestic goods and services relative to foreign ones will lead to both an increase in imports and a decrease in exports.

   The opposite effects are likely to occur during a recession. Lower incomes and relative prices of domestic goods and services will cause a fall in imports and a rise in exports: the current account will improve.

   In both cases we are assuming that other countries are not at the same time experiencing similar effects. If other countries were at the same phase of their business cycle, the above effects could be neutralised. For example, any fall in demand for imports by country A from country B could be offset by a fall in demand for imports by country B from country A. Imports and exports of both countries would fall (but not necessarily by the same amount).

5. Inward investment in the country (a credit on the financial account when it is made) will yield profits for the overseas investors in the future. This will enter as a *debit* on the investment income part of the current account.

7. Reduction in interest rates; the central bank buying in foreign currencies into the reserves by selling domestic currency on the foreign exchange market; lending abroad or paying back loans from abroad by the government/central bank; reflationary fiscal and monetary policy; lifting or reducing controls on imports or access to foreign exchange.

9. (a) It may fuel inflation by increasing the price of imported goods and reducing the need for export industries to restrain cost increases.
   (b) It may damage export industries and domestic import-competing industries, which would now find it more difficult to remain competitive.

11. It would involve too much risk. The longer the time period, the greater the scope for movements in the exchange rate and the more unpredictable they become. (Look at Figure 12.4 on page 454 of the text and see what happened to the exchange rate over the five-year period from 1980 to 1985!)

13. Both consumers and firms (when buying inputs) may take a time to change their consumption patterns. Thus the shorter the time period, the less will be the response to a change in the prices of imports

and exports, and therefore the less price elastic will be their demand.

15. It depends on the effect of government policy on the views of speculators. The point is that the power of speculation to influence the exchange rate is likely to exceed the power of governments. The exchange rate is dependent on the demand for and supply of the domestic currency on the foreign exchange market. If there are very large-scale short-term international financial movements, these will be the major short-term determinant of the rate of exchange – far more important than central bank intervention from the reserves. If speculators believe that the government is not going to be able to maintain the current exchange rate at such a high level, no matter how much it intervenes on the foreign exchange market or raises interest rates, then their actions will virtually ensure that the government will fail. This is why the UK was forced out of the ERM in September 1992.

17. In both cases the following problems are likely to arise:
   - Countries' budget deficits and national debt differ substantially as a proportion of their national income. This puts very different pressures on the interest rates necessary to service these debts.
   - Harmonising rates of monetary growth would involve letting interest rates fluctuate with the demand for money. Such fluctuations could be severe.
   - Harmonising interest rates would involve abandoning both monetary targets and exchange rate targets (unless interest rate 'harmonisation' meant adjusting interest rates so as to maintain monetary targets or a fixed exchange rate).
   - Countries have different internal structural relationships. A lack of convergence here means that countries with higher endemic *cost* inflation would require higher interest rates and higher unemployment if international inflation rates were to be harmonised, or higher inflation if interest rates were to be harmonised.
   - Countries have different rates of productivity increase, product development, investment and market penetration. A lack of convergence here means that the growth in exports (relative to imports) will differ for any given level of inflation or growth.
   - Countries may be very unwilling to change their domestic policies to fall in line with other countries.

19. Because there was too much divergence in the economic conditions of the member countries. Greater convergence would clearly have helped. Achieving such convergence, however, would have been difficult at the time, given the pressures arising from German reunification.

21. (a) By its persuading speculators that the combined strength of the countries' reserves and their combined monetary policies would guarantee

that rate of exchange could be maintained within their bands. Under these circumstances, speculation would be pointless.

(b) If exchange rates were being maintained at clearly disequilibrium levels. The longer devaluation/revaluation were put off, and the more inevitable speculators believed the devaluation to be, the more would speculation take place.

23. Trade is likely to be attracted to those countries that have joined, and they may have greater influence in determining future EU policy. Those that did not join are in principle able to take advantage of exchange rate movements to deal with any economic shocks that have a different effect on them from other members. They are vulnerable, however, to speculative international financial movements between their currency and others, including the euro: movements that are not merely a reflection of their *trade* account divergences. In the UK, however, exchange rate movements have *not* been used as a means of dealing with shocks and maintaining competitiveness. Instead, interest rates have been used as a means of keeping to the inflation target of 2 per cent. This has generally meant that the pound has been kept high relative to the euro, much to the consternation of UK exporters.

25. Given the differences between countries, it is unlikely that the same *levels* of these indicators could all be achieved simultaneously: achieving the same level of one indicator may mean divergence of another. What is more important is that countries' economies should be progressing together with the *minimum* degree of divergence of the various indicators. This will normally mean that countries need to be at the same phase of their business cycles and should be pursuing complementary policies.

27. Several of the causes of the crisis were outside the control of developing countries and could not therefore be blamed on them: for example, the world recession of the early 1980s and the much higher real interest rates that accompanied it. Nevertheless, it is easy with hindsight to put some of the blame on the policies of import-substituting industrialisation that many developing countries were pursuing: policies that involved large-scale borrowing to finance investment, with much of the borrowing at variable rates of interest. Although real rates of interest were low in the 1970s, there was still the *risk* that they might subsequently rise, making it difficult for the developing countries to service their debts.

Web appendix

All the following websites can be accessed from MyEconLab (www.pearsoned.co.uk/sloman) at **Hot Links**. You will find all the following sites listed. Click on the one you want and the 'hot link' will take you straight to it.

The sections and numbers below refer to the ones used in the Web references at the end of each chapter of the text. Thus if the reference were to number A21, this would refer to the Money World site.

GENERAL NEWS SOURCES   A

As the title of this section implies, the websites here can be used for finding material on current news issues or tapping into news archives. Most archives are offered free of charge. However, some do require you to register. As well as key UK and American sources, you will also notice some slightly different places from where you can get your news, such as the St Petersburg Times and Kyodo News (from Japan). Check out sites number 38 My Virtual Newspaper, 43 Guardian World News Guide and 44 Online Newspapers for links to newspapers across the world. Try searching for an article on a particular topic by using site number 41 Google News Search.

1. BBC news
2. The Economist
3. The Financial Times
4. The Guardian
5. The Independent
6. ITN
7. The Observer
8. The Telegraph
9. The Times, Sunday Times
10. The New York Times
11. Fortune
12. Time Magazine
13. The Washington Post
14. Moscow Times (English)
15. St Petersburg Times (English)
16. Straits Times
17. New Straits Times
18. The Scotsman
19. The Herald
20. Euromoney
21. Money World
22. Market News International
23. BusinessWeek online
24. Ananova
25. CNN Money
26. Wall Street Journal
27. Asia related news
28. allAfrica.com
29. Greek News Sources (English)
30. Kyodo News: Japan (English)
31. RFE/RL NewsLine
32. The Australian
33. Sydney Morning Herald
34. Japan Times
35. Reuters
36. Bloomberg
37. David Smith's Economics UK.com
38. My Virtual Newspaper (links to a whole range of news sources)
39. Newspapers on World Wide Web

40. Economics in the News from Gametheory.net
41. Google News Search
42. Blinkx (for video and audio)
43. Guardian World News Guide
44. Online Newspapers

B SOURCES OF ECONOMIC AND BUSINESS DATA

Using websites to find up-to-date data is of immense value to the economist. The data sources below offer you a range of specialist and non-specialist data information. Universities have free access to the MIMAS and ESDS sites, which are huge databases of statistics. Site 34, the Treasury Pocket Data Bank, is a very useful source of key UK and world statistics, and is updated monthly. It downloads as an Excel file.

1. Economics Network gateway to economic data
2. Biz/ed Gateway to economic and company data
3. National Statistics
4. Data Archive (Essex)
5. Econ Links
6. Economic Resources (About)
7. Nationwide House Prices
8. House Web (data on housing market)
9. Incomes Data Services
10. Keynote Publications Ltd.
11. Land Registry (house prices, etc.)
12. Manchester Information and Associated Services (MIMAS)
13. Global Financial Data
14. PACIFIC International trade and business reference page
15. Economagic
16. Groningen Growth and Development Centre
17. Resources for economists on the Internet
18. Joseph Rowntree Foundation
19. Social Science Information Gateway (SOSIG)
20. Slavic and East European Resources
21. OECD statistics
22. CIA world statistics site
23. UN Millennium Country Profiles
24. World Bank statistics
25. Japanese Economic Foundation
26. Ministry of International Trade and Industry (Japan)
27. Nomura Research Institute (Japan)
28. Nanyang Technological University, Singapore: Statistical Data Locators
29. Davidson Data Center and Network (DDCN)
30. Oanda Currency Converter
31. World Economic Outlook Database (IMF)
32. Economist Country Briefings
33. OFFSTATS links to data sets
34. Treasury Pocket Data Bank (source of UK and world economic data)
35. Economic and Social Data Service (ESDS)
36. The official yearbook of the UK
37. NationMaster
38. European Economy Statistical Annex
39. Business and Comsumer Surveys (all EU countries)
40. Gapminder (via Google)

C SITES FOR STUDENTS AND TEACHERS OF ECONOMICS

The following websites offer useful ideas and resources to those who are studying or teaching economics. It is worth browsing through some just to see what is on offer. Try out the first four sites, for starters. The Internet Economist is a very helpful tutorial for economics students on using the Internet.

1. Economics Network of the UK's Higher Education Academy
2. Biz/ed
3. Ecedweb
4. Econ Links: student resources
5. Economics and Business Education Association
6. Tutor2U
7. Economics America
8. The Internet Economist (tutorial on using the Web)
9. Oxford School of Learning
10. Teaching resources for economists
11. Resources for University Teachers of Economics (University of Melbourne)
12. Federal Reserve Bank of San Francisco: Economics Education
13. Federal Reserve Bank of Minneapolis Economic Education
14. WebEc resources
15. BibEc papers
16. Online Opinion (Economics)
17. The Idea Channel
18. History of Economic Thought
19. Resources For Economists on the Internet (RFE)
20. Classroom Expernomics
21. VCE Economics (Economics teaching resources – Australian)
22. Paul Krugman Website
23. Economics jokes!
24. Veconlab: Charles Holt's classroom experiments

ECONOMIC MODELS AND SIMULATIONS　D

Economic modelling is an important aspect of economic analysis. There are a number of sites that offer access to a model for you to use, e.g. Virtual economy (where you can play being Chancellor of the Exchequer). Using such models can be a useful way of finding out how economic theory works within an environment that claims to reflect reality.

1. Virtual economy
2. Virtual factory
3. Virtual Learning Arcade
4. About.com Economics
5. Estima (statistical analysis)
6. SPSS (statistical analysis)
7. National Institute of Economic and Social Research
8. Software available on Economics LTSN site
9. RFE Software
10. Virtual Chancellor
11. Virtual Bank of Biz/ed
12. Virtual Farm

UK GOVERNMENT AND UK ORGANISATIONS' SITES　E

If you want to see what a government department is up to, then look no further than the list below. Government departments' websites are an excellent source of information and data. They are particularly good at offering information on current legislation and policy initiatives.

1. Gateway site (DirectGov)
2. Department for Communities and Local Government
3. Central Office of Information
4. Competition Commission
5. Department for Education and Skills
6. Department for International Development
7. Department for Transport
8. Department of Health
9. Department for Work and Pensions
10. Department of Trade and Industry (DTI)

11. Environment Agency
12. UK euro information site
13. Low Pay Commission
14. Department for Environment, Food and Rural Affairs (DEFRA)
15. Office of Communications (Ofcom)
16. Office of Gas and Electricity Markets (Ofgem)
17. Official Documents OnLine
18. Office of Fair Trading (OFT)
19. Office of Rail Regulation (ORR)
20. The Takeover Panel
21. Sustainable Development Commission
22. OFWAT
23. National Statistics (NS)
24. National Statistics Time Series Data
25. Strategic Rail Authority (SRA)
26. Patent Office
27. Parliament website
28. Scottish Executive
29. Scottish Environment Protection Agency
30. Treasury
31. Equal Opportunities Commission
32. Trades Union Congress (TUC)
33. Confederation of British Industry
34. Adam Smith Institute
35. Royal Institute of International Affairs
36. Institute for Fiscal Studies
37. Advertising Standards Authority
38. Small Business Service

F SOURCES OF MONETARY AND FINANCIAL DATA

As the title suggests, here are listed useful websites for finding information on financial matters. You will see that the list comprises mainly central banks, both within Europe and further afield.

1. Bank of England
2. Bank of England Monetary and Financial Statistics
3. Banque de France
4. Bundesbank (German central bank)
5. Central Bank of Ireland
6. European Central Bank
7. Eurostat
8. US Federal Reserve Bank
9. Netherlands Central Bank
10. Bank of Japan
11. Reserve Bank of Austalia
12. Bank Negara Malaysia (English)
13. Monetary Authority of Singapore
14. National Bank of Canada
15. National Bank of Denmark (English)
16. Reserve Bank of India
17. Links to central bank websites from the Bank for International Settlements
18. The London Stock Exchange

G EUROPEAN UNION AND RELATED SOURCES

For information on European issues, the following is a wide range of useful sites. The sites maintained by the European Union are an excellent source of information and are provided free of charge.

1. Economic and Financial Affairs: (EC DG)
2. European Central Bank
3. EU official website
4. Eurostat
5. Employment and Social Affairs (EC DG)
6. Site for information on the euro and EMU
7. Enterprise: (EC DG)
8. Competition: (EC DG)
9. Agriculture: (EC DG)
10. Energy and Transport: (EC DG)
11. Environment: (EC DG)

12. Regional Policy: (EC DG)
13. Taxation and Customs Union: (EC DG)
14. Education and training: (EC DG)
15. European Patent Office
16. European Commission
17. European Parliament
18. European Council

INTERNATIONAL ORGANISATIONS H

This section casts its net beyond Europe and lists the Web addresses of the main international organisations in the global economy. You will notice that some sites are run by pressure groups, such as Jubilee Research, while others represent organisations set up to manage international affairs, such as the International Monetary Fund and the United Nations.

1. Food and Agriculture Organisation
2. International Air Transport Association (IATA)
3. International Labour Organisation (ILO)
4. International Monetary Fund (IMF)
5. Organisation for Economic Co-operation and Development (OECD)
6. OPEC
7. World Bank
8. World Health Organisation
9. United Nations
10. United Nations Industrial Development Organisation
11. Friends of the Earth
12. Jubilee Research
13. Oxfam
14. Christian Aid (reports on development issues)
15. European Bank for Reconstruction and Development (EBRD)
16. World Trade Organization (WTO)
17. United Nations Development Program
18. UNICEF
19. EURODAD – European Network on Debt and Development
20. NAFTA
21. South American free trade areas
22. ASEAN
23. APEC

ECONOMICS SEARCH AND LINK SITES I

If you are having difficulty finding what you want from the list of sites above, the following sites offer links to other sites and are a very useful resource when you are looking for something a little bit more specialist. Once again, it is worth having a look at what these sites have to offer in order to judge their usefulness.

1. Gateway for UK official sites
2. Alta Plana
3. Data Archive Search
4. Inomics (search engine for economics information)
5. International Digital Electronic Access Library
6. Links to economics resources sites
7. Social Science Information Gateway (SOSIG)
8. WebEc
9. One World (link to economic development sites)
10. Economic development sites (list) from OneWorld.net
11. Biz/ed Internet catalogue
12. Web links for economists from the Economics Network
13. Yahoo's links to economic data
14. OFFSTATS links to data sets
15. Excite Economics links
16. Internet Resources for Economists
17. Google Web Directory: Economics
18. Resources for Economists on the Internet

J   INTERNET SEARCH ENGINES

The following search engines have been found to be useful.

1. Google
2. Altavista
3. Overture
4. Excite
5. Infoseek
6. Search.com

7. MSN
8. UK Plus
9. Yahoo!
10. Teoma
11. Kartoo

Glossary and key ideas

KEY IDEAS AND THRESHOLD CONCEPTS

1. **Scarcity** is the excess of human wants over what can actually be produced. Because of scarcity, various choices have to be made between alternatives (page 5).

2. **Opportunity cost.** The cost of something measured in terms of what you give up to get it/do it. The best alternative forgone (page 7). (Threshold Concept 1)

3. **Rational decision making** involves weighing up the marginal benefit and marginal cost of any activity. If the marginal benefit exceeds the marginal cost, it is rational to do the activity (or to do more of it). If the marginal cost exceeds the marginal benefit, it is rational not to do it (or to do less of it) (page 10). (Threshold Concept 2)

4. **Modelling in economics** involves specifying how one variable (the 'dependent variable') depends on one or more other variables ('independent variables'). It involves 'holding constant' all other variables that might influence the outcome (the *ceteris paribus* assumption). A model can be expressed in words, as a graph, or mathematically in terms of one or more equations. In this book we use mainly verbal descriptions and graphs (page 11). (Threshold Concept 3)

5. **People respond to incentives.** It is important, therefore, that incentives are appropriate and have the desired effect (page 26). (Threshold Concept 4)

6. **Changes in demand or supply cause markets to adjust.** Whenever such changes occur, the resulting 'disequilibrium' will bring an automatic change in prices, thereby restoring equilibrium (i.e. a balance of demand and supply) (page 27).

7. **The principle of diminishing marginal utility.** The more of a product a person consumes over a given period of time, the less will be the additional utility gained from one more unit (page 33).

8. **Equilibrium is the point where conflicting interests are balanced.** Only at this point is the amount that demanders are willing to purchase the same as the amount that suppliers are willing to supply. It is a point that will be automatically reached in a free market through the operation of the price mechanism (page 39). (Threshold Concept 5)

9. **People gain from voluntary interaction.** When people buy from or sell to other people, or when they are employed by or employ other people, both parties will gain from the interaction (page 46). (Threshold Concept 6)

10. **Government intervention may be able to rectify various failings of the market.** Government intervention in the market can be used to achieve various economic objectives which may not be best achieved by the market. Governments, however, are not perfect and their actions may bring adverse as well as beneficial consequences (page 47). (Threshold Concept 7)

11. **Elasticity.** The responsiveness of one variable (e.g. demand) to a change in another (e.g. price). This concept is fundamental to understanding how markets work. The more elastic variables are, the more responsive is the market to changing circumstances (page 64). (Threshold Concept 8)

12. **People's actions are influenced by their expectations.** People respond not just to what is happening now (such as a change in price), but to what they anticipate will happen in the future (page 68). (Threshold Concept 9)

13. **People's actions are influenced by their attitudes towards risk.** Many decisions are taken under conditions of risk or uncertainty. Generally, the lower the probability of (or the more uncertain) the desired outcome of an action, the less likely it is that people will undertake the action (page 71).

14. **Output depends on the amount of resources and how they are used.** Different amounts and combinations of inputs will lead to different amounts of output. If output is to be produced efficiently, then inputs should be combined in the optimum proportions (page 82).

15. **The law of diminishing marginal returns.** When increasing amounts of a variable factor are used with a given amount of a fixed factor, there will come a point when each extra unit of the variable factor will produce less extra output than the previous unit (page 83).

16. **Market power benefits the powerful at the expense of others.** When firms have market power over prices, they can use this to raise prices and profits above the perfectly competitive level. Other things being equal, the firm will gain at the expense of the consumer. Similarly, if consumers or workers have market power, they can use this to their own benefit (page 112).

17. **Economic efficiency** is achieved when each good is produced at the minimum cost and where consumers get maximum benefit from their income (page 117).

18. **People often think and behave strategically.** How you think others will respond to your actions is likely to influence your own behaviour. Firms, for example, when considering a price or product change will often take into account the likely reactions of their rivals (page 133).

19. **Equity** is where income is distributed in a way that is considered to be fair or just. Note that an equitable distribution is not the same as a totally equal distribution and that different people have different views on what is equitable (page 177).

20. **Allocative efficiency in any activity is achieved where any reallocation would lead to a decline in net benefit.** It is achieved where marginal benefit equals marginal cost. Private efficiency is achieved where marginal private benefit equals marginal private cost ($MB = MC$). Social efficiency is achieved where marginal social benefit equals marginal social cost ($MSB = MSC$) (page 190). (Threshold Concept 10)

21. **Markets generally fail to achieve social efficiency.** There are various types of market failure. Market failures provide one of the major justifications for government intervention in the economy (page 191).

22. **General equilibrium.** A situation where all markets are in equilibrium. This situation can be assessed as to whether or not allocative efficiency is achieved. This will depend on whether or not markets are perfect (page 191). (Threshold Concept 11)

23. **Externalities are spillover costs or benefits.** Where these exist, even an otherwise perfect market will fail to achieve social efficiency (page 192).

24. **The free-rider problem.** People are often unwilling to pay for things if they can make use of things other people have bought. This problem can lead to people not purchasing things which would be to the benefit of themselves and other members of society to have (page 195).

25. **The principal–agent problem.** Where people (principals), as a result of a lack of knowledge, cannot ensure that their best interests are served by their agents. Agents may take advantage of this situation to the disadvantage of the principals (page 200).

26. **The problem of time lags.** Many economic actions can take a long time to take effect. This can cause problems of instability and an inability of the economy to achieve social efficiency (page 200).

27. **Societies face trade-offs between economic objectives.** For example, the goal of faster growth may conflict with that of greater equality; the goal of lower unemployment may conflict with that of lower inflation (at least in the short run). This is an example of opportunity cost: the cost of achieving more of one objective may be achieving less of another. The existence of trade-offs means that policy-makers must make choices (page 201).

28. **Economies suffer from inherent instability.** As a result, economic growth and other macroeconomic indicators tend to fluctuate (page 234). (Threshold Concept 12)

29. **Stocks and flows.** A stock is a quantity of something at a given point in time. A flow is an increase or decrease in something over a specified period of time. This is an important distinction and a common cause of confusion (page 239).

30. **The distinction between nominal and real figures.** Nominal figures are those using current prices, interest rates, etc. Real figures are figures corrected for inflation (page 242). (Threshold Concept 13)

31. **Long-term growth in a country's output depends on a growth in the quantity and/or productivity of its resources.** Potential economic growth depends on the country's resources, technology and productivity (page 243). (Threshold Concept 14)

32. **The principle of cumulative causation.** An initial event can cause an ultimate effect that is much larger (page 253). (Threshold Concept 15)

33. **Goodhart's Law.** Controlling a symptom (i.e. an indicator) of a problem will not cure the problem. Instead, the indicator will merely cease to be a good indicator of the problem (page 376).

34. **The law of comparative advantage.** Provided opportunity costs of various goods differ in two countries, both of them can gain from mutual trade if they specialise in producing (and exporting) those goods that have relatively low opportunity costs compared with the other country (page 399).

Absolute advantage A country has an absolute advantage over another in the production of a good if it can produce it with less resources than the other country can.

Accelerationist theory The theory that unemployment can only be reduced below the natural level at the cost of accelerating inflation.

Accelerator theory The *level* of investment depends on the *rate of change* of national income, and as a result tends to be subject to substantial fluctuations.

Active balances Money held for transactions and precautionary purposes.

Actual growth The percentage annual increase in national output actually produced.

Ad valorem tariffs Tariffs levied as a percentage of the price of the import.

Ad valorem tax A tax on a good levied as a percentage of its value. It can be a single-stage tax or a multi-stage tax (such as VAT).

Adaptive expectations hypothesis The theory that people base their expectations of inflation on past inflation rates.

Adjustable peg A system whereby exchange rates are fixed for a period of time, but may be devalued (or revalued) if a deficit (or surplus) becomes substantial.

Aggregate demand Total spending on goods and services made in the economy. It consists of four elements, consumer spending (C), investment (I), government spending (G) and the expenditure on exports (X), less any expenditure on imports of goods and services (M): $AD = C + I + G + X - M$.

Aggregate demand for labour curve A curve showing the total demand for labour in the economy at different levels of real wage rates.

Aggregate supply The total amount of output in the economy.

Aggregate supply of labour curve A curve showing the total number of people willing and able to work at different average real wage rates.

Allocative efficiency A situation where the current combination of goods produced and sold gives the maximum satisfaction for each consumer at their current levels of income. Note that a redistribution of income would lead to a different combination of goods that was allocatively efficient.

Appreciation A rise in the free-market exchange rate of the domestic currency with foreign currencies.

Arc elasticity The measurement of elasticity between two points on a curve.

Assets Possessions, or claims held on others.

Asymmetric information Where one party in an economic relationship (e.g. an agent) has more information than another (e.g. the principal).

Asymmetric shocks Shocks (such as an oil price increase or a recession in another part of the world) that have different-sized effects on different industries, regions or countries.

Automatic fiscal stabilisers Tax revenues that rise and government expenditure that falls as national income rises. The more they change with income, the bigger the stabilising effect on national income.

Average cost Total cost (fixed plus variable) per unit of output: $AC = TC/Q = AFC + AVC$.

Average cost pricing or **mark-up pricing** Where firms set the price by adding a profit mark-up to average cost.

Average fixed cost Total fixed cost per unit of output: $AFC = TFC/Q$.

Average (or 'mid-point') formula for price elasticity of demand ΔQ_D/average $Q_D \div \Delta P$/average P.

Average physical product Total output (TPP) per unit of the variable factor in question: $APP = TPP/Q_v$.

Average rate of income tax Income taxes as a proportion of a person's total (gross) income: T/Y.

Average revenue Total revenue per unit of output. When all output is sold at the same price, average revenue will be the same as price: $AR = TR/Q = P$.

Average variable cost Total variable cost per unit of output: $AVC = TVC/Q$.

Balance of payments account A record of the country's transactions with the rest of the world. It shows the country's payments to or deposits in other countries (debits) and its receipts or deposits from other countries (credits). It also shows the balance between these debits and credits under various headings.

Balance of payments on current account The balance on trade in goods and services plus net investment income and current transfers.

Balance on trade in goods Exports of goods minus imports of goods.

Balance on trade in goods and services (or balance of trade) Exports of goods and services minus imports of goods and services.

Balance on trade in services Exports of services minus imports of services.

Balancing item (in the balance of payments) A statistical adjustment to ensure that the two sides of the balance of payments account balance. It is necessary because of errors in compiling the statistics.

Bank bills Bills that have been accepted by another institution and hence insured against default.

Bank (or deposits) multiplier The number of times greater the expansion of bank deposits is than the additional liquidity in banks that causes it: $1/L$ (the inverse of the liquidity ratio).

Barometric firm price leadership Where the price leader is the one whose prices are believed to reflect market conditions in the most satisfactory way.

Barriers to entry Anything that prevents or impedes the entry of firms into an industry and thereby limits the amount of competition faced by existing firms.

Barter economy An economy where people exchange goods and services directly with one another without any payment of money. Workers would be paid with bundles of goods.

Base year (for index numbers) The year whose index number is set at 100.

Basic rate of tax The main marginal rate of tax, applying to most people's incomes.

Benefits in kind Goods or services which the state provides directly to the recipient at no charge or at a subsidised price. Alternatively, the state can subsidise the private sector to provide them.

Bilateral monopoly Where a monopsony buyer faces a monopoly seller.

Bill of exchange A certificate promising to repay a stated amount on a certain date, typically three months from the issue of the bill. Bills pay no interest as such, but are sold at a discount and redeemed at face value, thereby earning a rate of discount for the purchaser.

Bretton Woods system An adjustable peg system whereby currencies were pegged to the US dollar. The USA maintained convertibility of the dollar into gold at the rate of $35 to an ounce.

Broad definitions of money Items in narrow definitions plus other items that can be readily converted into cash.

Broad money in UK (M4) Cash in circulation plus retail and wholesale bank and building society deposits.

Budget deficit The excess of central government's spending over its tax receipts.

Budget surplus The excess of central government's tax receipts over its spending.

Business cycle or trade cycle The periodic fluctuations of national output round its long-term trend.

Capital All inputs into production that have themselves been produced: e.g. factories, machines and tools.

Capital account of the balance of payments The record of the transfers of capital to and from abroad.

Cartel A formal collusive agreement.

Central bank Banker to the banks and the government.

Centrally planned or command economy An economy where all economic decisions are taken by the central authorities.

Certificates of deposit (CDs) Certificates issued by banks for fixed-term interest-bearing deposits. They can be resold by the owner to another party.

Ceteris paribus Latin for 'other things being equal'. This assumption has to be made when making deductions from theories.

Change in demand This is the term used for a shift in the demand curve. It occurs when a determinant of demand *other* than price changes.

Change in supply The term used for a shift in the supply curve. It occurs when a determinant *other* than price changes.

Change in the quantity demanded The term used for a movement along the demand curve to a new point. It occurs when there is a change in price.

Change in the quantity supplied The term used for a movement along the supply curve to a new point. It occurs when there is a change in price.

Claimant unemployment Those in receipt of unemployment-related benefits.

Clearing system A system whereby inter-bank debts are settled.

Closed shop Where a firm agrees to employ only union members.

Coase theorem By sufferers from externalities doing deals with perpetrators (by levying charges or offering bribes), the externality will be 'internalised' and the socially efficient level of output will be achieved.

Collusive oligopoly Where oligopolists agree (formally or informally) to limit competition between themselves. They may set output quotas, fix prices, limit product promotion or development, or agree not to 'poach' each other's markets.

Collusive tendering Where two or more firms secretly agree on the prices they will tender for a contract. These prices will be above those which would be put in under a genuinely competitive tendering process.

Command-and-control (CAC) systems The use of laws or regulations backed up by inspections and penalties (such as fines) for non-compliance.

Commercial bills Bills of exchange issued by firms.

Common market A customs union where the member countries act as a single market with free movement of labour and capital, common taxes and common trade laws.

Comparative advantage A country has a comparative advantage over another in the production of a good if it can produce it at a lower opportunity cost: i.e. if it has to forgo less of other goods in order to produce it.

Competition for corporate control The competition for the control of companies through takeovers.

Complementary goods A pair of goods consumed together. As the price of one goes up, the demand for both goods will fall.

Compounding The process of adding interest each year to an initial capital sum.

Compromise strategy One whose worst outcome is better than the maximax strategy and whose best outcome is better than the maximin strategy.

Conglomerate merger When two firms in different industries merge.

Consumer durable A consumer good that lasts a period of time, during which the consumer can continue gaining utility from it.

Consumer sovereignty A situation where firms respond to changes in consumer demand without being in a position in the long run to charge a price above average cost.

Consumer surplus The excess of what a person would have been prepared to pay for a good (i.e. the utility) over what that person actually pays.

Consumption The act of using goods and services to satisfy wants. This will normally involve purchasing the goods and services.

Consumption function The relationship between consumption and national income. It can be expressed algebraically or graphically.

Consumption of domestically produced goods and services (C_d) The direct flow of money payments from households to firms.

Convergence of economies When countries achieve similar levels of growth, inflation, budget deficits as a percentage of GDP, balance of payments, etc.

Core workers Workers, normally with specific skills, who are employed on a permanent or long-term basis.

Cost–benefit analysis The identification, measurement and weighing up of the costs and benefits of a project in order to decide whether or not it should go ahead.

Cost-plus pricing (full-cost pricing) When firms price their product by adding a certain profit 'mark-up' to average cost.

Cost-push inflation Inflation caused by persistent rises in costs of production (independently of demand).

Countervailing power When the power of a monopolistic/oligopolistic seller is offset by powerful buyers who can prevent the price from being pushed up.

Cournot model A model of duopoly where each firm makes its price and output decisions on the assumption that its rival will produce a particular quantity.

Credible threat (or promise) One that is believable to rivals because it is in the threatener's interests to carry it out.

Cross-price elasticity of demand The percentage (or proportionate) change in quantity demanded of one good divided by the percentage (or proportionate) change in the price of another.

Cross-price elasticity of demand (arc formula) ΔQ_{Da}/average $Q_{Da} \div \Delta P_b$/average P_b.

Cross-subsidise To use profits in one market to subsidise prices in another.

Crowding out Where increased public expenditure diverts money or resources away from the private sector.

Currency union A group of countries (or regions) using a common currency.

Current account balance of payments Exports of goods and services minus imports of goods and services plus net incomes and current transfers from abroad. If inflows of money (from the sale of exports, etc.) exceed outflows of money (from the purchase of imports, etc.), there is a 'current account surplus' (a positive figure). If outflows exceed inflows, there is a 'current account deficit' (a negative figure).

Customs union A free trade area with common external tariffs and quotas.

Cyclical or demand-deficient unemployment Disequilibrium unemployment caused by a fall in aggregate demand with no corresponding fall in the real wage rate.

Deadweight loss of an indirect tax The loss of consumer plus producer surplus from the imposition of an indirect tax.

Deadweight welfare loss The loss of consumer plus producer surplus in imperfect markets (when compared with perfect competition).

Debit card A card that has the same use as a cheque. Its use directly debits the person's current account.

Debt servicing Paying the interest and capital repayments on debt.

Decision tree (or game tree) A diagram showing the sequence of possible decisions by competitor firms and the outcome of each combination of decisions.

Deflationary gap The shortfall of national expenditure below national income (and injections below withdrawals) at the full-employment level of national income.

Deflationary policy Fiscal or monetary policy designed to reduce the rate of growth of aggregate demand.

Demand curve A graph showing the relationship between the price of a good and the quantity of the good demanded over a given time period. Price is measured on the vertical axis; quantity demanded is measured on the horizontal axis. A demand curve can be for an individual consumer or group of consumers, or more usually for the whole market.

Demand management policies Demand-side policies (fiscal and/or monetary) designed to smooth out the fluctuations in the business cycle.

Demand schedule for an individual A table showing the different quantities of a good that a person is willing and able to buy at various prices over a given period of time.

Demand schedule (market) A table showing the different total quantities of a good that consumers are willing and able to buy at various prices over a given period of time.

Demand-deficient or cyclical unemployment Disequilibrium unemployment caused by a fall in aggregate demand with no corresponding fall in the real wage rate.

Demand-pull inflation Inflation caused by persistent rises in aggregate demand.

Demand-side policies Policies designed to affect aggregate demand: fiscal policy and monetary policy.

Dependency Where the development of a developing country is hampered by its relationships with the industrialised world.

Depreciation (of capital) The decline in value of capital equipment due to age, or wear and tear.

Depreciation (of a currency) A fall in the free-market exchange rate of the domestic currency with foreign currencies.

Deregulation Where the government removes official barriers to competition (e.g. licences and minimum quality standards).

Derived demand The demand for a factor of production depends on the demand for the good that uses it.

Destabilising speculation Where the actions of speculators tend to make price movements larger.

Devaluation Where the government re-pegs the exchange rate at a lower level.

Diminishing marginal utility As more units of a good are consumed, additional units will provide less additional satisfaction than previous units.

Diminishing marginal utility of income Where each additional pound earned yields less additional utility.

Direct taxes Taxes on income and wealth. Paid directly to the tax authorities on that income or wealth.

Discounting The process of reducing the value of future flows to give them a present valuation.

Discretionary fiscal policy Deliberate changes in tax rates or the level of government expenditure in order to influence the level of aggregate demand.

Diseconomies of scale Where costs per unit of output increase as the scale of production increases.

Disequilibrium unemployment Unemployment resulting from real wage rates in the economy being above the equilibrium level.

Disguised unemployment Where the same work could be done by fewer people.

Disposable income Household income after the deduction of taxes and the addition of benefits.

Diversification Where a firm expands into new types of business.

Dominant firm price leadership When firms (the followers) choose the same price as that set by a dominant firm in the industry (the leader).

Dominant strategy game Where the *same* policy is suggested by different strategies.

Dumping When exports are sold at prices below marginal cost – often as a result of government subsidy.

Duopoly An oligopoly where there are just two firms in the market.

Economic efficiency A situation where each good is produced at the minimum cost and where individual people and firms get the maximum benefit from their resources.

Economic model The representation, graphically, mathematically or in words, of the relationship between two or more variables. A model is a simplification of reality designed to explain just part of a complex process of economic relationships. It is thus based on various simplifying assumptions.

Economies of scale When increasing the scale of production leads to a lower cost per unit of output.

Economies of scope When increasing the range of products produced by a firm reduces the cost of producing each one.

ECU (European Currency Unit) The predecessor to the euro: a weighted average of EU currencies. It was used as a reserve currency and for the operation of the exchange rate mechanism (ERM).

Efficiency wage rate The profit-maximising wage rate for the firm after taking into account the effects of wage rates on worker motivation, turnover and recruitment.

Elastic demand (with respect to price) Where quantity demanded changes by a larger percentage than price. Ignoring the negative sign, it will have a value greater than 1.

Elasticity A measure of the responsiveness of a variable (e.g. quantity demanded or quantity supplied) to a change in one of its determinants (e.g. price or income).

Endogenous money supply Money supply that is determined (at least in part) by the demand for money.

Entrepreneurship The initiating and organising of the production of new goods, or the introduction of new techniques, and the risk taking associated with it.

Envelope curve A long-run average cost curve drawn as the tangency points of a series of short-run average cost curves.

Environmental charges Charges for using natural resources (e.g. water or national parks), or for using the environment as a dump for waste (e.g. factory emissions or sewage).

Equation of exchange $MV = PQ$. The total level of spending on GDP (MV) equals the total value of goods and services produced (PQ) that go to make up GDP.

Equilibrium A position of balance. A position from which there is no inherent tendency to move away.

Equilibrium price The price where the quantity demanded equals the quantity supplied: the price where there is no shortage or surplus.

Equilibrium unemployment ('natural') unemployment The difference between those who would like employment at the current wage rate and those willing and able to take a job.

Equities Company shares. Holders of equities are owners of the company and share in its profits by receiving dividends.

Equity A distribution of income that is considered to be fair or just. Note that an equitable distribution is not the same as an equal distribution, and that different people have different views on what is equitable.

ERM (the exchange rate mechanism) A system of semi-fixed exchange rates used by most of the EU countries prior to adoption of the euro. Members' currencies were allowed to fluctuate against each other only within agreed bands. Collectively they floated against all other currencies.

Excess capacity (under monopolistic competition) In the long run, firms under monopolistic competition will produce at an output below their minimum-cost point.

Exchange equalisation account The gold and foreign exchange reserves account in the Bank of England.

Exchange rate The rate at which one national currency exchanges for another. The rate is expressed as the amount of one currency that is necessary to purchase *one unit* of another currency (e.g. $1.60 = £1).

Exchange rate band Where a currency is allowed to float between an upper and lower exchange rate, but is not allowed to move outside this band.

Exchange rate index A weighted average exchange rate expressed as an index where the value of the index is 100 in a given base year. The weights of the different currencies in the index add up to 1.

Exchange rate overshooting Where a fall (or rise) in the long-run equilibrium exchange rate causes the actual exchange rate to fall (or rise) by a greater amount before eventually moving back to the new long-run equilibrium level.

Exchange rate regime The system under which the government allows the exchange rate to be determined.

Exogenous money supply Money supply that does not depend on the demand for money but is set by the authorities.

Exogenous variable A variable whose value is determined independently of the model of which it is part.

Expectations-augmented Phillips curve A (short-run) Phillips curve whose position depends on the expected rate of inflation.

Explicit costs The payments to outside suppliers of inputs.

External benefits Benefits from production (or consumption) experienced by people *other* than the producer (or consumer).

External costs Costs of production (or consumption) borne by people *other* than the producer (or consumer).

External diseconomies of scale Where a firm's costs per unit of output increase as the size of the whole industry increases.

External economies of scale Where a firm's costs per unit of output decrease as the size of the whole *industry* grows.

Externalities Costs or benefits of production or consumption experienced by society but not by the producers or consumers themselves. Sometimes referred to as 'spillover' or 'third-party' costs or benefits.

Factors of production (or resources) The inputs into the production of goods and services: labour, land and raw materials, and capital.

Financial account of the balance of payments The record of the flows of money into and out of the country for the purposes of investment or as deposits in banks and other financial institutions.

Financial crowding out When an increase in government borrowing diverts money away from the private sector.

Financial deregulation The removal of or reduction in legal rules and regulations governing the activities of financial institutions.

Financial flexibility Where employers can vary their wage costs by changing the composition of their workforce or the terms on which workers are employed.

Financial intermediaries The general name for financial institutions (banks, building societies, etc.) which act as a means of channelling funds from depositors to borrowers.

Fine tuning The use of demand management policy (fiscal or monetary) to smooth out cyclical fluctuations in the economy.

First-mover advantage When a firm gains from being the first one to take action.

Fiscal drag The tendency of automatic fiscal stabilisers to reduce the recovery of an economy from recession.

Fiscal policy Policy to affect aggregate demand by altering the balance between government expenditure and taxation.

Fiscal stance How expansionary or contractionary the Budget is.

Fixed costs Total costs that do not vary with the amount of output produced.

Fixed exchange rate (totally) Where the government takes whatever measures are necessary to maintain the exchange rate at some stated level.

Fixed factor An input that cannot be increased in supply within a given time period.

Flexible firm A firm that has the flexibility to respond to changing market conditions by changing the composition of its workforce.

Floating exchange rate When the government does not intervene in the foreign exchange markets, but simply allows the exchange rate to be freely determined by demand and supply.

Forward exchange market Where contracts are made today for the price at which currency will be exchanged at some specified future date.

Franchising Where a firm is given the licence to operate a given part of an industry for a specified length of time.

Free trade area A group of countries with no trade barriers between them.

Freely floating exchange rate Where the exchange rate is determined entirely by the forces of demand and supply in the foreign exchange market with no government intervention whatsoever.

Free-market economy An economy where all economic decisions are taken by individual households and firms and with no government intervention.

Free-rider problem When it is not possible to exclude other people from consuming a good that someone has bought.

Frictional (search) unemployment Unemployment that occurs as a result of imperfect information in the labour market. It often takes time for workers to find jobs (even though there are vacancies) and in the meantime they are unemployed.

Full-employment level of national income The level of national income at which there is no deficiency of demand.

Functional flexibility Where employers can switch workers from job to job as requirements change.

Funding Where the authorities alter the balance of bills and bonds for any given level of government borrowing.

Future price A price agreed today at which an item (e.g. commodities) will be exchanged at some set date in the future.

Futures or forward market A market in which contracts are made to buy or sell at some future date at a price agreed today.

Gaia philosophy The respect for the rights of the environment to remain unharmed by human activity. Humans should live in harmony with the planet and other species. We have a duty to be stewards of the natural environment, so that it can continue to be a self-maintaining and self-regulating system.

Game theory (or the theory of games) The study of alternative strategies oligopolists may choose to adopt, depending on their assumptions about their rivals' behaviour.

GDP (gross domestic product at market prices) The value of output (or income or expenditure) in terms of the prices actually paid. GDP = GVA + taxes on products – subsidies on products.

General equilibrium A situation where all the millions of markets throughout the economy are in a simultaneous state of equilibrium.

General government debt The combined accumulated debt of central and local government.

General government deficit (or surplus) The combined deficit (or surplus) of central and local government.

Geographical immobility The lack of ability or willingness of people to move to jobs in other parts of the country.

GNY (gross national income) GDP plus net income from abroad.

Goodhart's Law Controlling a symptom of a problem, or only part of the problem, will not cure the problem: it will simply mean that the part that is being controlled now becomes a poor indicator of the problem.

Government bonds or 'gilt-edged securities' A government security paying a fixed sum of money each year. It is redeemed by the government on its maturity date at its face value.

Government surplus (from a tax on a good) The total tax revenue earned by the government from sales of a good.

Green tax A tax on output designed to charge for the adverse effects of production on the environment. The socially efficient level of a green tax is equal to the marginal environmental cost of production.

Gross domestic product (GDP) The value of output produced within the country over a 12-month period.

Gross national income (GNY) GDP plus net income from abroad.

Gross value added at basic prices (GVA) The sum of all the values added by all industries in the economy over a year. The figures exclude taxes on products (such as VAT) and include subsidies on products.

Historic costs The original amount a firm paid for factors it now owns.

Hit-and-run competition When a firm enters an industry to take advantage of temporarily high profits and then leaves again as soon as the high profits have been exhausted.

Horizontal merger When two firms in the same industry at the same stage in the production process merge.

Households' disposable income The income available for households to spend: i.e. personal incomes after deducting taxes on incomes and adding benefits.

Human capital The qualifications, skills and expertise that contribute to a worker's productivity.

Human Development Index (HDI) A composite index made up of three elements: an index for life expectancy, an index for school enrolment and adult literacy, and an index for GDP per capita (in PPP$).

Hysteresis The persistence of an effect even when the initial cause has ceased to operate. In economics, it refers to the persistence of unemployment even when the demand deficiency that caused it no longer exists.

Idle balances Money held for speculative purposes: money held in anticipation of a fall in asset prices.

Imperfect competition The collective name for monopolistic competition and oligopoly.

Implicit costs Costs which do not involve a direct payment of money to a third party, but which nevertheless involve a sacrifice of some alternative.

Import-substituting industrialisation (ISI) A strategy of restricting imports of manufactured goods and using the foreign exchange saved to build up domestic substitute industries.

Income effect (of a price change) The effect of a change in price on quantity demanded arising from the consumer becoming better or worse off as a result of the price change.

Income effect of a rise in wage rates Workers get a higher income for a given number of hours worked and may thus feel they need to work *fewer* hours as wage rates rise.

Income effect of a tax rise Tax increases reduce people's incomes and thus encourage people to work more.

Income elasticity of demand The percentage (or proportionate) change in quantity demanded divided by the percentage (or proportionate) change in income.

Income elasticity of demand (arc formula) $\Delta Q_D /$ average $Q_D \div \Delta Y/$average Y.

Increasing opportunity costs of production When additional production of one good involves ever-increasing sacrifices of another.

Independence (of firms in a market) Where the decisions of one firm in a market will not have any significant effect on the demand curves of its rivals.

Independent risks Where two risky events are unconnected. The occurrence of one will not affect the likelihood of the occurrence of the other.

Index number The value of a variable expressed as 100 plus or minus its percentage deviation from a base year.

Indirect taxes Taxes on expenditure (e.g. VAT). Paid to the tax authorities, not by the consumer, but indirectly by the suppliers of the goods or services.

Indivisibilities The impossibility of dividing a factor into smaller units.

Induced investment Investment that firms make to enable them to meet extra consumer demand.

Industrial policies Policies to encourage industrial investment and greater industrial efficiency.

Inelastic demand Where quantity demanded changes by a smaller percentage than price. Ignoring the negative sign, it will have a value less than 1.

Infant industry An industry that has a potential comparative advantage, but which is as yet too underdeveloped to be able to realise this potential.

Inferior goods Goods whose demand *decreases* as consumer incomes increase. Such goods have a negative income elasticity of demand.

Inflationary gap The excess of national expenditure over income (and injections over withdrawals) at the full-employment level of national income.

Infrastructure (industry's) The network of supply agents, communications, skills, training facilities, distribution channels, specialised financial services, etc. that supports a particular industry.

Injections (J) Expenditure on the production of domestic firms coming from outside the inner flow of the circular flow of income. Injections equal investment (I) plus government expenditure (G) plus expenditure on exports (X).

Input–output analysis This involves dividing the economy into sectors where each sector is a user of inputs from and a supplier of outputs to other sectors. The technique examines how these inputs and outputs can be matched to the total resources available in the economy.

Insiders Those in employment who can use their privileged position (either as members of unions or because of specific skills) to secure pay rises despite an excess supply of labour (unemployment).

Interdependence (under oligopoly) One of the two key features of oligopoly. Each firm will be affected by its rivals' decisions. Likewise its decisions will affect its rivals. Firms recognise this interdependence. This recognition will affect their decisions.

International harmonisation of economic policies Where countries attempt to co-ordinate their macroeconomic policies so as to achieve common goals.

International liquidity The supply of currencies in the world acceptable for financing international trade and investment.

International trade multiplier The effect on national income in country B of a change in exports (or imports) of country A.

Intervention price (in the CAP) The price at which the EU is prepared to buy a foodstuff if the market price were to be below it.

Interventionist supply-side policies Policies to increase aggregate supply by government intervention to counteract the deficiencies of the market.

Investment The production of items that are not for immediate consumption.

Joint float Where a group of currencies pegged to each other jointly float against other currencies.

Joint supply Where the production of more of one good leads to the production of more of another.

Kinked demand theory The theory that oligopolists face a demand curve that is kinked at the current price, demand being significantly more elastic above the current price than below. The effect of this is to create a situation of price stability.

Labour All forms of human input, both physical and mental, into current production.

Labour force The number employed plus the number unemployed.

Land (and raw materials) Inputs into production that are provided by nature: e.g. unimproved land and mineral deposits in the ground.

Law of comparative advantage Trade can benefit all countries if they specialise in the goods in which they have a comparative advantage.

Law of demand The quantity of a good demanded per period of time will fall as price rises and will rise as price falls, other things being equal (*ceteris paribus*).

Law of diminishing (marginal) returns When one or more factors are held fixed, there will come a point beyond which the extra output from additional units of the variable factor will diminish.

Lender of last resort The role of the Bank of England as the guarantor of sufficient liquidity in the monetary system.

Liabilities All legal claims for payment that outsiders have on an institution.

Liquidity The ease with which an asset can be converted into cash without loss.

Liquidity preference The demand for holding assets in the form of money.

Liquidity ratio The proportion of a bank's total assets held in liquid form.

Lock-outs Union members are temporarily laid off until they are prepared to agree to the firm's conditions.

Long run The period of time long enough for *all* factors to be varied.

Long run under perfect competition The period of time that is long enough for new firms to enter the industry.

Long-run average cost curve A curve that shows how average cost varies with output on the assumption that *all* factors are variable. (It is assumed that the least-cost method of production will be chosen for each output.)

Long-run marginal cost The extra cost of producing one more unit of output assuming that all factors are variable. (It is assumed that the least-cost method of production will be chosen for this extra output.)

Long-run profit maximisation An alternative theory of the firm which assumes that managers aim to shift cost and revenue curves so as to maximise profits over some longer time period.

Long-run shut-down point This is where the *AR* curve is tangential to the *LRAC* curve. The firm can just make normal profits. Any fall in revenue below this level will cause a profit-maximising firm to shut down once all costs have become variable.

Lorenz curve A curve showing the proportion of national income earned by any given percentage of the population (measured from the poorest upwards).

Macroeconomics The branch of economics that studies economic aggregates (grand totals): e.g. the overall level of prices, output and employment in the economy.

Managed floating A system of flexible exchange rates but where the government intervenes to prevent excessive fluctuations or even to achieve an unofficial target exchange rate.

Marginal benefit The additional benefit of doing a little bit more (or 1 unit more if a unit can be measured) of an activity.

Marginal consumer surplus The excess of utility from the consumption of one more unit of a good (MU) over the price paid: $MCS = MU - P$.

Marginal cost (of an activity) The additional cost of doing a little bit more (or 1 unit more if a unit can be measured) of an activity.

Marginal cost (of production) The cost of producing one more unit of output: $MC = \Delta TC/\Delta Q$.

Marginal disutility of work The extra sacrifice/hardship to a worker of working an extra unit of time in any given time period (e.g. an extra hour per day).

Marginal physical product The extra output gained by the employment of one more unit of the variable factor: $MPP = \Delta TPP/\Delta Q_v$.

Marginal productivity theory The theory that the demand for a factor depends on its marginal revenue product.

Marginal propensity to consume The proportion of a rise in national income that goes on consumption: $mpc = \Delta C/\Delta Y$.

Marginal propensity to import The proportion of an increase in national income that is spent on imports: $mpm = \Delta M/\Delta Y$.

Marginal propensity to save The proportion of an increase in national income saved: $mps = \Delta S/\Delta Y$.

Marginal propensity to withdraw The proportion of an increase in national income that is withdrawn from the circular flow: $mpw = \Delta W/\Delta Y$, where $mpw = mps + mpt + mpm$.

Marginal rate of income tax The income tax rate. The rate paid on each *additional* pound earned: $\Delta T/\Delta Y$.

Marginal revenue The extra revenue gained by selling one more unit per time period: $MR = \Delta TR/\Delta Q$.

Marginal revenue product (of a factor) The extra revenue a firm earns from employing one more unit of a variable factor: $MRP_{factor} = MPP_{factor} \times MR_{good}$.

Marginal tax propensity The proportion of an increase in national income paid in tax: $mpt = \Delta T/\Delta Y$.

Marginal utility The extra satisfaction gained from consuming one extra unit of a good within a given time period.

Market The interaction between buyers and sellers.

Market clearing A market clears when supply matches demand, leaving no shortage or surplus.

Market for loanable funds The market for loans from and deposits into the banking system.

Market loans Short-term loans (e.g. money at call and short notice).

Market-orientated supply-side policies Policies to increase aggregate supply by freeing up the market.

Mark-up A profit margin added to average cost to arrive at price.

Maximax The strategy of choosing the policy that has the best possible outcome.

Maximin The strategy of choosing the policy whose worst possible outcome is the least bad.

Maximum price A price ceiling set by the government or some other agency. The price is not allowed to rise above this level (although it is allowed to fall below it).

Mean (or arithmetic mean) The sum of the values of each of the members of the sample divided by the total number in the sample.

Means-tested benefits Benefits whose amount depends on the recipient's income or assets.

Median The value of the middle member of the sample.

Medium of exchange Something that is acceptable in exchange for goods and services.

Menu costs of inflation The costs associated with having to adjust price lists or labels.

Merit goods Goods which the government feels that people will underconsume and which therefore ought to be subsidised or provided free.

Microeconomics The branch of economics that studies individual units: e.g. households, firms and industries. It studies the interrelationships between these units in determining the pattern of production and distribution of goods and services.

Minimum price A price floor set by the government or some other agency. The price is not allowed to fall below this level (although it is allowed to rise above it).

Minimum reserve ratio A minimum ratio of cash (or other specified liquid assets) to deposits (either total or selected) that the central bank requires banks to hold.

Mixed economy An economy where economic decisions are made partly by the government and partly through the market.

Mixed market economy A market economy where there is some government intervention.

Model in economics (see Economic model)

Monetarists Those who attribute inflation solely to rises in money supply.

Monetary base Notes and coin outside the central bank.

Monetary policy Policy to affect aggregate demand by altering the supply or cost of money (rate of interest).

Money illusion When people believe that a money wage or price increase represents a *real* increase: in other words, they ignore or underestimate inflation.

Money market The market for short-term loans and deposits.

Money multiplier The number of times greater the expansion of money supply is than the expansion of the monetary base that caused it: $\Delta Ms/\Delta Mb$.

Monopolistic competition A market structure where, like perfect competition, there are many firms and freedom of entry into the industry, but where each firm produces a differentiated product and thus has some control over its price.

Monopoly A market structure where there is only one firm in the industry.

Monopsony A market with a single buyer or employer.

Multiplier (injections multiplier) The number of times a rise in income exceeds the rise in injections that caused it: $k = \Delta Y/\Delta J$.

Multiplier effect An initial increase in aggregate demand of £xm leads to an eventual rise in national income that is greater than £xm.

Multiplier formula (injections multiplier) The formula for the multiplier is $k = 1/mpw$ or $1/(1 - mpc_d)$.

Narrow definitions of money Items of money that can be spent directly (cash and money in cheque-book/debit-card accounts).

Nash equilibrium The position resulting from everyone making their optimal decision based on their assumptions about their rivals' decisions. Without collusion, there is no incentive for any firm to move from this position.

National debt The accumulated budget deficits (less surpluses) over the years: the total amount of government borrowing.

National expenditure on domestic product (E) Aggregate demand in the Keynesian model: i.e. $C_d + J$.

Nationalised industries State-owned industries that produce goods or services that are sold in the market.

Natural level of output The level of output in monetarist analysis where the vertical long-run aggregate supply curve cuts the horizontal axis.

Natural level of unemployment The level of equilibrium unemployment in monetarist analysis measured as the difference between the (vertical) long-run gross labour supply curve (N) and the (vertical) long-run effective labour supply curve (AS_L).

Natural monopoly A situation where long-run average costs would be lower if an industry were under monopoly than if it were shared between two or more competitors.

Natural rate of unemployment The rate of unemployment at which there is no excess or deficiency of demand for labour.

Natural wastage When a firm wishing to reduce its workforce does so by not replacing those who leave or retire.

Near money Highly liquid assets (other than cash).

Negative income tax A combined system of tax and benefits. As people earn more, they gradually lose their benefits until beyond a certain level they begin paying taxes.

Net errors and omissions A statistical adjustment to ensure that the two sides of the balance of payments account balance. It is necessary because of errors in compiling the statistics.

Net investment Total investment minus depreciation.

Net national product (NNY) GNY minus depreciation.

New classical school The school of economists which believes that markets clear virtually instantaneously and that expectations are formed 'rationally'.

New Keynesians Economists who seek to explain the downward stickiness of real wages and the resulting persistence of unemployment.

Nominal national income National income measured at current prices.

Nominal values Money values measured at *current* prices.

Non-accelerating-inflation rate of unemployment (NAIRU) The rate of unemployment consistent with a constant rate of inflation. (In monetarist analysis, this is the same as the natural rate of unemployment: the rate of unemployment at which the vertical long-run Phillips curve cuts the horizontal axis.)

Non-collusive oligopoly Where oligopolists have no agreement between themselves, either formal, informal or tacit.

Non-excludability Where it is not possible to provide a good or service to one person without it thereby being available for others to enjoy.

Non-price competition Competition in terms of product promotion (advertising, packaging, etc.) or product development.

Non-rivalry Where the consumption of a good or service by one person will not prevent others from enjoying it.

Normal goods Goods whose demand increases as consumer incomes increase. They have a positive income elasticity of demand. Luxury goods will have a higher income elasticity of demand than more basic goods.

Normal profit The opportunity cost of being in business: the profit that could have been earned in the next best alternative business. It is counted as a cost of production.

Normal rate of return The rate of return (after taking risks into account) that could be earned elsewhere.

Normative statement A value judgement.

Numerical flexibility Where employers can change the size of their workforce as their labour requirements change.

Occupational immobility The lack of ability or willingness of people to move to other jobs irrespective of location.

Oligopoly A market structure where there are few enough firms to enable barriers to be erected against the entry of new firms.

Oligopsony A market with just a few buyers or employers.

Open economy One that trades with and has financial dealings with other countries.

Open-market operations The sale (or purchase) by the authorities of government securities in the open market in order to reduce (or increase) money supply or influence interest rates.

Opportunity cost Cost measured in terms of the best alternative forgone.

Optimal currency area The optimal size of a currency area is the one that maximises the benefits from having a single currency relative to the costs. If the area were increased or decreased in size, the costs would rise relative to the benefits.

Outsiders Those out of work or employed on a casual, part-time or short-term basis, who have little or no power to influence wages or employment.

Overheads Costs arising from the general running of an organisation, and only indirectly related to the level of output.

Participation rate The percentage of the working-age population that is part of the workforce.

Perfect competition A market structure where there are many firms; where there is freedom of entry into the industry; where all firms produce an identical product; and where all firms are price takers.

Perfectly contestable market A market where there is free and costless entry and exit.

Phillips curve A curve showing the relationship between (price) inflation and unemployment. The original Phillips curve plotted *wage* inflation against unemployment for the years 1861–1957.

Picketing When people on strike gather at the entrance to the firm and attempt to persuade workers or delivery vehicles from entering.

Plant economies of scale Economies of scale that arise because of the large size of the factory.

Poll tax A lump-sum tax per head of the population. Since it is a fixed *amount*, it has a marginal rate of zero with respect to both income and wealth.

Portfolio balance The balance of assets, according to their liquidity, that people choose to hold in their portfolios.

Positive statement A value-free statement that can be tested by an appeal to the facts.

Potential growth The percentage annual increase in the capacity of the economy to produce.

Potential output The output that could be produced in the economy if there were a full employment of resources (including labour).

Poverty trap Where poor people are discouraged from working or getting a better job because any extra income they earn will be largely taken away in taxes and lost benefits.

Predatory pricing Where a firm sets its prices below average cost in order to drive competitors out of business.

Preferential trading arrangements A trade agreement whereby trade between the signatories is freer than trade with the rest of the world.

Price benchmark A price that is typically used. Firms, when raising prices, will usually raise them from one benchmark to another.

Price discrimination Where a firm sells the same product at different prices in different markets or different parts of the market or to different customers.

Price elasticity of demand ($P\varepsilon_D$) The percentage (or proportionate) change in quantity demanded divided by the percentage (or proportionate) change in price: $\%\Delta Q_D \div \%\Delta P$.

Price elasticity of demand (arc formula) $\Delta Q/$ average $Q \div \Delta P/$average P. The average in each case is the average between the two points being measured.

Price elasticity of supply The percentage (or proportionate) change in quantity supplied divided by the percentage (or proportionate) change in price: $\%\Delta Q_S \div \%\Delta P$.

Price elasticity of supply (arc formula) $\Delta Q_S/$ average $Q_S \div \Delta P/$average P.

Price mechanism The system in a market economy whereby changes in price in response to changes in demand and supply have the effect of making demand equal to supply.

Price taker A person or firm with no power to be able to influence the market price.

Primary labour market The market for permanent full-time core workers.

Principal–agent problem Where people (principals), as a result of lack of knowledge, cannot ensure that their best interests are served by their agents.

Prisoners' dilemma Where two or more firms (or people), by attempting independently to choose the best strategy for whatever the other(s) are likely to do, end up in a worse position than if they had co-operated in the first place.

Private efficiency Where a person's marginal benefit from a given activity equals the marginal cost.

Private limited company A company owned by its shareholders. Shareholders' liability is limited to the value of their shares. Shares can only be bought and sold privately.

Product differentiation When one firm's product is sufficiently different from its rivals' to allow it to raise the price of the product without customers all switching to the rivals' products. A situation where a firm faces a downward-sloping demand curve.

Production The transformation of inputs into outputs by firms in order to earn profit (or meet some other objective).

Production possibility curve A curve showing all the possible combinations of two goods that a country can produce within a specified time period with all its resources fully and efficiently employed.

Productive efficiency A situation where firms are producing the maximum output for a given amount of inputs, or producing a given output at the least cost.

Productivity deal When, in return for a wage increase, a union agrees to changes in working practices that will increase output per worker.

Profit (rate of) Total profit ($T\Pi$) as a proportion of the total capital employed (K): $r = T\Pi/K$.

Profit-maximising rule Profit is maximised where marginal revenue equals marginal cost.

Progressive tax A tax whose average rate with respect to income rises as income rises.

Proportional tax A tax whose average rate with respect to income stays the same as income rises.

Public good A good or service that has the features of non-rivalry and non-excludability and as a result would not be provided by the free market.

Public limited company A company owned by its shareholders. Shareholders' liability is limited to the value of their shares. Shares may be bought and sold publicly – on the Stock Exchange.

Public-sector borrowing requirement The old name for the public-sector net cash requirement.

Public-sector debt repayment (PSDR) or **Public-sector surplus** The old name for a negative public-sector net cash requirement. The (annual) surplus of the public sector, and thus the amount of debt that can be repaid.

Public-sector net cash requirement The (annual) deficit of the public sector (central government, local government and public corporations), and thus the amount that the public sector must borrow.

Purchasing-power parity exchange rate The rate of exchange of a country's currency into the US dollar that would allow a given amount of that currency to buy the same amount of goods in the USA as within the country concerned.

Pure fiscal policy Fiscal policy that does not involve any change in money supply.

Quantity demanded The amount of a good a consumer is willing and able to buy at a given price over a given period of time.

Quantity theory of money The price level (P) is directly related to the quantity of money in the economy (M).

Quota (set by a cartel) The output that a given member of a cartel is allowed to produce (production quota) or sell (sales quota).

Rate of economic growth The percentage increase in output over a 12-month period.

Rate of inflation The percentage increase in the level of prices over a 12-month period.

Rate of profit Total profit ($T\Pi$) as a proportion of the capital employed (K): $r = T\Pi/K$.

Rational choices Choices that involve weighing up the benefit of any activity against its opportunity cost.

Rational consumer A person who weighs up the costs and benefits to him or her of each additional unit of a good purchased.

Rational consumer behaviour The attempt to maximise total consumer surplus.

Rational economic behaviour Doing more of activities whose marginal benefit exceeds their marginal cost and doing less of those activities whose marginal cost exceeds their marginal benefit.

Rational expectations Expectations based on the *current* situation. These expectations are based on the information people have to hand. Whilst this information may be imperfect and therefore people will make errors, these errors will be random.

Rational producer behaviour When a firm weighs up the costs and benefits of alternative courses of action and then seeks to maximise its net benefit.

Rationalisation The reorganising of production (often after a merger) so as to cut out waste and duplication and generally to reduce costs.

Rationing Where the government restricts the amount of a good that people are allowed to buy.

Real business cycle theory The new classical theory that explains cyclical fluctuations in terms of shifts in aggregate supply, rather than aggregate demand.

Real growth values Values of the rate of growth of GDP or any other variable after taking inflation into account. The real value of the growth in a variable equals its growth in money (or 'nominal') value minus the rate of inflation.

Real income Income measured in terms of how much it can buy. If your *money* income rises by 10 per cent, but prices rise by 8 per cent, you can only buy 2 per cent more goods than before. Your *real* income has risen by 2 per cent.

Real national income National income after allowing for inflation: i.e. national income measured in constant prices: i.e. in terms of the prices ruling in some base year.

Real values Money values corrected for inflation.

Real-wage unemployment Disequilibrium unemployment caused by real wages being driven up above the market-clearing level.

Recession A period where national output falls for six months or more.

Recognised banks Banks licensed by the Bank of England. All financial institutions using the word 'bank' in their title have to be recognised by the Bank of England. This requires them to have paid-up capital of at least £5 million and to meet other requirements about their asset structure and range of services.

Rediscounting bills of exchange Buying bills before they reach maturity.

Reflationary policy Fiscal or monetary policy designed to increase the rate of growth of aggregate demand.

Regional multiplier effects When a change in injections into or withdrawals from a particular region causes a multiplied change in income in that region.

Regional unemployment Structural unemployment occurring in specific regions of the country.

Regressive tax A tax whose average rate with respect to income falls as income rises.

Relative price The price of one good compared with another (e.g. good X is twice the price of good Y).

Repos Sale and repurchase agreements. An agreement between two financial institutions whereby one in effect borrows from another by selling it assets, agreeing to buy them back (repurchase them) at a fixed price and on a fixed date.

Restrictive practice Where two or more firms agree to adopt common practices to restrict competition.

Retail banks 'High street banks'. Banks operating extensive branch networks and dealing directly with the general public, with published interest rates and charges.

Retail deposits and loans Deposits and loans made through bank/building society branches at published interest rates.

Retail price index (RPI) An index of the prices of goods bought by a typical household.

Revaluation Where the government re-pegs the exchange rate at a higher level.

Reverse repos When gilts or other assets are *purchased* under a sale and repurchase agreement. They become an asset to the purchaser.

Risk When an outcome may or may not occur, but its probability of occurring is known.

Sale and repurchase agreement (repos) An agreement between two financial institutions whereby one in effect borrows from another by selling it assets, agreeing to buy them back (repurchase them) at a fixed price and on a fixed date.

Scarcity The excess of human wants over what can actually be produced to fulfil these wants.

Search theory This examines people's behaviour under conditions of ignorance where it takes time to search for information.

Seasonal unemployment Unemployment associated with industries or regions where the demand for labour is lower at certain times of the year.

Secondary action Industrial action taken against a company not directly involved in a dispute (e.g. a supplier of raw materials to a firm whose employees are on strike).

Secondary labour market The market for peripheral workers, usually employed on a temporary or part-time basis, or a less secure 'permanent' basis.

Self-fulfilling speculation The actions of speculators tend to cause the very effect that they had anticipated.

Set-aside A system in the EU of paying farmers not to use a certain proportion of their land.

Short run (in production) The period of time over which at least one factor is fixed.

Short-run shut-down point This is where the AR curve is tangential to the AVC curve. The firm can only just cover its variable costs. Any fall in revenue below this level will cause a profit-maximising firm to shut down immediately.

Short run under perfect competition The period during which there is too little time for new firms to enter the industry.

Sight deposits Deposits that can be withdrawn on demand without penalty.

Social benefit Private benefit plus externalities in consumption.

Social cost Private cost plus externalities in production.

Social efficiency Production and consumption at the point where marginal social benefit equals marginal social cost ($MSB = MSC$).

Special deposits A system used up to 1980. Deposits that the banks could be required to make in the Bank of England. They remained frozen there until the Bank of England chose to release them.

Specialisation and division of labour Where production is broken down into a number of simpler, more specialised tasks, thus allowing workers to acquire a high degree of efficiency.

Specific tax A tax on a good levied at a fixed amount per unit of the good, irrespective of the price of that unit.

Speculation Where people make buying or selling decisions based on their anticipations of future prices.

Speculators People who buy (or sell) commodities or financial assets with the intention of profiting by selling them (or buying them back) at a later date at a higher (lower) price.

Spot price The current market price.

Stabilising speculation Where the actions of speculators tend to reduce price fluctuations.

Stakeholders (in a company) People who are affected by a company's activities and/or performance (customers, employees, owners, creditors, people living in the neighbourhood, etc.). They may or may not be in a position to take decisions, or influence decision taking, in the firm.

Standardised unemployment rate The measure of the unemployment rate used by the ILO and OECD. The unemployed are defined as persons of working age who are without work, available to start work within two weeks and either have actively looked for work in the last four weeks or are waiting to take up an appointment.

Structural unemployment Unemployment that arises from changes in the pattern of demand or supply in the economy. People made redundant in one part of the economy cannot immediately take up jobs in other parts (even though there are vacancies).

Substitute goods A pair of goods that are considered by consumers to be alternatives to each other. As the price of one goes up, the demand for the other rises.

Substitutes in supply These are two goods where an increased production of one means diverting resources away from producing the other.

Substitution effect of a price change The effect of a change in price on quantity demanded arising from the consumer switching to or from alternative (substitute) products.

Substitution effect of a rise in wage rates Workers will tend to substitute income for leisure as leisure now has a higher opportunity cost. This effect leads to *more* hours being worked as wage rates rise.

Substitution effect of a tax rise Tax increases reduce the opportunity cost of leisure and thus encourage people to work less.

Sunk costs Costs that cannot be recouped (e.g. by transferring assets to other uses).

Supernormal profit (also known as **pure profit, economic profit, abnormal profit**, or simply **profit**) The excess of total profit above normal profit.

Supply curve A graph showing the relationship between the price of a good and the quantity of the good supplied over a given period of time.

Supply schedule A table showing the different quantities of a good that producers are willing and able to supply at various prices over a given time period. A supply schedule can be for an individual producer or group of producers, or for all producers (the market supply schedule).

Supply-side economics An approach that focuses directly on aggregate supply and how to shift the aggregate supply curve outwards.

Supply-side policy Government policy that attempts to alter the level of aggregate supply directly (rather than through changes in aggregate demand).

Sustainability (environmental) The ability of the environment to survive its use for economic activity.

Sustainable output The level of national output corresponding to no excess or deficiency of aggregate demand.

Tacit collusion Where oligopolists take care not to engage in price cutting, excessive advertising or other forms of competition. There may be unwritten 'rules' of collusive behaviour such as price leadership.

Takeover bid Where one firm attempts to purchase another by offering to buy the shares of that company from its shareholders.

Tariff escalation The system whereby tariff rates increase the closer a product is to the finished stage of production.

Tariffs (or import levies) Taxes on imported products: i.e. customs duties.

Tax allowance An amount of income that can be earned tax-free. Tax allowances vary according to a person's circumstances.

Taylor rule A rule adopted by a central bank for setting the rate of interest. It will raise the interest rate if (a) inflation is above target or (b) real national income is above the sustainable level (or unemployment is below the equilibrium rate). The rule states how much interest rates will be changed in each case.

Technological unemployment Structural unemployment that occurs as a result of the introduction of labour-saving technology.

Terms of trade The price index of exports divided by the price index of imports and then expressed as a percentage. This means that the terms of trade will be 100 in the base year.

Third-degree price discrimination When a firm divides consumers into different groups and charges a different price to consumers in different groups, but the same price to all the consumers within a group.

Time deposits Deposits that require notice of withdrawal or where a penalty is charged for withdrawals on demand.

Total consumer expenditure on a product (TE) (per period of time) The price of the product multiplied by the quantity purchased: $TE = P \times Q$.

Total consumer surplus The excess of a person's total utility from the consumption of a good (TU) over the amount that person spends on it (TE): $TCS = TU - TE$.

Total cost The sum of total fixed costs and total variable costs: $TC = TFC + TVC$.

Total physical product The total output of a product per period of time that is obtained from a given amount of inputs.

Total (private) surplus Total consumer surplus ($TU - TE$) plus total producer surplus ($TR - TVC$).

Total producer surplus (TPS) Total revenue minus total variable cost ($TR - TVC$): in other words, total profit plus total fixed cost ($T\Pi + TFC$).

Total revenue (TR) (per period of time) The total amount received by firms from the sale of a product, before the deduction of taxes or any other costs. The price multiplied by the quantity sold: $TR = P \times Q$.

Total social surplus Total benefits to society from consuming a good minus total costs to society from producing it. In the absence of externalities, total social surplus is the same as total (private) surplus.

Total utility The total satisfaction a consumer gets from the consumption of all the units of a good consumed within a given time period.

Tradable permits Each firm is given a permit to produce a given level of pollution. If less than the permitted amount is produced, the firm is given a credit. This can then be sold to another firm, allowing it to exceed its original limit.

Trade creation Where a customs union leads to greater specialisation according to comparative advantage and thus a shift in production from higher-cost to lower-cost sources.

Trade cycle or business cycle The periodic fluctuations of national output round its long-term trend.

Trade diversion Where a customs union diverts consumption from goods produced at a lower cost outside the union to goods produced at a higher cost (but tariff free) within the union.

Traditional theory of the firm The analysis of pricing and output decisions of the firm under various market conditions, assuming that the firm wishes to maximise profit.

Transfer payments Moneys transferred from one person or group to another (e.g. from the government to individuals) without production taking place.

Treasury bills Bills of exchange issued by the Bank of England on behalf of the government. They are a means whereby the government raises short-term finance.

Uncertainty When an outcome may or may not occur and its probability of occurring is not known.

Underemployment Where people who want full-time work are only able to find part-time work.

Unemployment The number of people who are actively looking for work but are currently without a job. (Note that there is much debate as to who should officially be counted as unemployed.)

Unemployment rate The number unemployed expressed as a percentage of the labour force.

Unit elastic demand Where quantity demanded changes by the same percentage as price. Ignoring the negative sign, it will have a value equal to 1.

Universal benefits Benefits paid to everyone in a certain category irrespective of their income or assets.

Value added tax (VAT) A tax on goods and services, charged at each stage of production as a percentage of the value added at that stage.

Variable costs Total costs that vary with the amount of output produced.

Variable factor An input that can be increased in supply within a given time period.

Velocity of circulation The number of times annually that money on average is spent on goods and services that make up GDP.

Vent for surplus When international trade enables a country to exploit resources that would otherwise be unused.

Wage–price spiral Wages and prices chasing each other as the aggregate demand curve continually shifts to the right and the aggregate supply curve continually shifts upwards.

Weighted average The average of several items, where each item is ascribed a weight according to its importance. The weights must add up to 1.

Wholesale banks Banks specialising in large-scale deposits and loans and dealing mainly with companies.

Wholesale deposits and loans Large-scale deposits and loans made by and to firms at negotiated interest rates.

Wide monetary base (M0) Notes and coin outside the central bank plus banks' operational deposits with the central bank.

Withdrawals (*W*) (or leakages) Incomes of households or firms that are not passed on round the inner flow. Withdrawals equal net saving (*S*) plus net taxes (*T*) plus expenditure on imports (*M*): $W = S + T + M$.

Working to rule Workers do the bare minimum they have to, as set out in their job descriptions.

Index